SEVENTH EDITION

Teaching Strategies for Ethnic Studies

James A. Banks

University of Washington, Seattle

Boston   New York   San Francisco
Mexico City   Montreal   Toronto   London   Madrid   Munich   Paris
Hong Kong   Singapore   Tokyo   Cape Town   Sydney

Vice President, Publisher: *Paul A. Smith*
Series Editor: *Traci Mueller*
Editorial Assistant: *Erica Tromblay*
Marketing Manager: *Amy Cronin*
Editorial Production Service: *Chestnut Hill Enterprises, Inc.*
Manufacturing Buyer: *Chris Marson*
Cover Administrator: *Linda Knowles*
Electronic Composition: *Omegatype Typography, Inc.*

For related titles and support materials, visit our online catalog at www.ablongman.com

Between the time Website information is gathered and published, some sites may have closed. Also, the transcription of URLs can result in typographical errors. The publisher would appreciate notification where these occur so that they may be corrected in subsequent editions.

Library of Congress Cataloging-in-Publication Data

Banks, James A.
    Teaching strategies for ethnic studies / James A. Banks.—7th ed.
      p. cm.
    Includes bibliographical references and index.
    ISBN 0-205-33720-1
      1. Minorities—United States—Study and teaching.   2. Ethnicity—Study and teaching—United States.   3. Pluralism (Social sciences)—Study and teaching—United States.   4. Multiculturalism—Study and teaching—United States.   5. United States—Ethnic relations—Study and teaching.   I. Title.

E184.A1 B24 2002
305.8'0071'073–dc21

                                 2002018412

Printed in the United States of America

10   9   8   7   6   5   4   3   2   1   RRD-VA   07   06   05   04   03   02

To the memory of
Robert L. Banks (July 10, 1931–November 26, 1981)
my brother, who
shared my dream for a better world
and to Cherry, Angela, and Patricia,
my family

BRIEF CONTENTS

CONTENTS

3   Key Concepts for the Multicultural Curriculum   55

**14   Arab Americans: Concepts, Strategies,
and Materials   461**

APPENDIXES

PREFACE

The tragic events of September 11, 2001 reminded educators how important it is for students throughout the world to develop cultural understandings and to acquire the values and skills needed to get along with people from different cultural, racial, religious, and nationality groups. Helping students to deepen their cultural understandings and to interact effectively with people from diverse cultures and groups are major goals of multicultural education. Another important goal of multicultural teaching is to help students acquire the knowledge and skills needed to become effective citizens in pluralistic societies that are striving for ways to balance unity and diversity.

Because of the growing ethnic, cultural, racial, language, and religious diversity throughout the world, citizenship education needs to be changed in substantial ways to prepare students to function effectively in the twenty-first century. Today's citizens need the knowledge, attitudes, and skills required to function successfully in their ethnic and cultural communities as well as beyond their cultural borders. They should also be able and willing to participate in the construction of a moral and just national civic culture that embodies democratic ideals and values, such as those embodied in the Declaration of Independence, the Constitution, and the Bill of Rights. Students also need to become effective citizens in the global community.

Citizenship education in the past, in the United States as well as in many other nations, embraced an assimilationist ideology and rarely honored the home and community cultures of students in marginalized cultures. Citizens in a diverse democratic society should be able to maintain attachments to their cultural communities as well as participate effectively in the shared national culture. *Unity without diversity results in cultural repression and hegemony. Diversity without unity leads to Balkanization and the fracturing of the nation-state.* Diversity and unity should co-exist in a delicate balance in a democratic multicultural nation-state.

This seventh edition of *Teaching Strategies for Ethnic Studies* is designed to help teachers conceptualize, design, and implement a democratic, multicultural curriculum that respects and honors diversity as well as promotes national unity. A guiding principle of this text is that a multicultural curriculum should enable students to acquire the knowledge needed to become effective citizens of the United States and the world.

This edition reflects current and emerging concepts, perspectives, and issues in multicultural education. I have been able to incorporate information from the 2000 U.S. Census into this edition. The bibliographies have also been extensively revised, reflecting the large number of high-quality materials and resources that have been published since the last edition was prepared. The rich resources and publications that now exist in ethnic studies, women's studies, and multicultural education are evidence of the growth and maturity of the field.

Most of the books annotated in this seventh edition were not included in the previous one. Readers of this edition can refer to previous editions for older but nonetheless important titles. Each of the chapters on the ethnic groups has been updated with new information and census data. Appendix B is new to this edition and includes descriptions of Web sites for teaching about ethnic and cultural diversity. Appendix C, which describes videotapes and CD-ROMs, has been revised to include new and exciting audiovisual resources for teaching about U.S. ethnic groups.

Teaching Strategies for Ethnic Studies is divided into five parts. Part I presents a rationale, goals, and key concepts for incorporating ethnic content into the mainstream curriculum. The main goal of the multicultural curriculum should be to help students develop the ability to make reflective decisions so that they can, through thoughtful action, influence their personal, social, and civic worlds and help make them more democratic and just.

Parts II through V contain chapters on the major ethnic groups in the United States. These chapters contain: (1) chronologies of key events, (2) historical overviews of groups, (3) illustrative key concepts and teaching strategies, (4) annotated bibliographies for teachers, and (5) annotated bibliographies for elementary and secondary school students. Chapter 14, on Arab Americans, is new and was written expressly for this edition. The chapter on Arab Americans in the previous edition was reprinted from another publication.

Recommended grade levels are designated for the student resources in the student bibliographies. Although the bibliographies are selective, no book is appropriate for all purposes and settings. You should examine each book carefully before assigning it to your students. The annotations can help in this screening process.

The appendixes are designed to help you obtain information and materials for classroom use. Appendix A is a chronology of key events in the history of ethnic groups in the United States. Appendix B describes Web sites for teaching about ethnic diversity. Appendix C annotates videotapes and CD-ROMs suitable for teacher education and for student use. Appendix D lists the Carter G. Woodson Award books, awarded annually by the National Council for the Social Studies. Appendix E cites twenty classic and landmark books in ethnic literature.

Acknowledgments

I am grateful to a number of colleagues and friends for their help in the preparation of this edition of *Teaching Strategies for Ethnic Studies*. Carlos F. Diaz contributed Chapters 6 (Native Hawaiians) and 12 (Cuban Americans). Virgie O. Chattergy and Amrita N. Zahir updated the bibliographies in Chapter 6. Amrita N. Zahir also helped to update Chapter 6. Jerome L. Ruderman is the original author of Chapter 9 (Jewish Americans); Hallie Esbin Rosen revised it for this edition. Paula Hajar wrote Chapter 14 (Arab Americans). I would like to thank Alixa Naff and Michael Suleiman for their thoughtful comments on Chapter 14 that enabled the author to strengthen it.

I was able to complete this seventh edition in a timely way because of the help I received from four individuals who annotated most of the books for students and teachers. I am greatly indebted to Lyn Miller-Lachmann, editor of *Multicultural Review,* for annotating most of the children's books that appear in the chapters of Parts III through V. Jennifer Outhouse, Caroline Tamayo, and Amrita N. Zahir, research assistants at the Center for Multicultural Education at the University of Washington, annotated most of the books for teachers in Parts III through V.

I am grateful to Patricia A. Banks, my daughter, for preparing a number of the tables in this book that are based on the 2000 U.S. Census. I would like to thank Cristine Hinman—who assists me in the daily operation of the Center for Multicultural Education—for her creative and thoughtful work on the Internet resources that comprise Appendix B, and I want to thank the reviewer of the seventh edition H. Prentice Baptiste, New Mexico State University.

Warm thanks to Myrna Breskin of Chestnut Hill Enterprises for her editorial assistance with this book. I am grateful to Cherry A. McGee Banks—my intellectual and spiritual partner—for over three decades of encouragement, caring, and intellectual support. Our daughters, Angela and Patricia, give us hope for the future.

James A. Banks

PART ONE

Goals, Concepts, and Instructional Planning

Part I of this book discusses the basic instructional problems in teaching ethnic content and integrating it into the curriculum. Chapter 1 reviews some of the major trends in teaching ethnic content and argues for a need to expand the definition of ethnic studies and to include content about a range of ethnic groups in the multicultual curriculum. The problem of formulating goals for the multicultural curriculum and the interdisciplinary, conceptual approach to teaching are discussed in Chapter 2, in which I state that the major goal of the multicultural curriculum should be to help students develop decision-making skills so that they can become effective change agents in society.

To help students develop effective decision-making skills, the multicultural curriculum must help them master higher-level concepts and generalizations. Chapter 3 discusses key concepts that can be used to organize a sound multicultural curriculum. The final chapter in Part I, Chapter 4, discusses practical ways to plan, organize, and teach multicultural units and lessons. The actual steps to follow in order to gain the needed content background, to identify key concepts and generalizations, and to choose ethnic content are discussed. Valuing strategies and social action projects are also discussed in Chapter 4.

1 The Multicultural Curriculum

Rationale, Trends, and Goals

This chapter describes the nature and complexity of ethnic diversity in U.S. society. It also discusses emerging demographic trends, current developments in multicultural education in the nation's schools, and the goals of a multicultural curriculum. An important goal of the multicultural curriculum is to help students view events, concepts, issues, and problems from diverse cultural and ethnic perspectives.

The Persistence of Ethnicity in American Society

Americans have always held tightly to the idea that ethnic cultures would melt or vanish. Consequently, a strong assimilationist idea has dominated U.S. society since the British gained control of most American institutions early in the nation's history. The assimilationist idea envisions a society in which ethnicity and race are not important identities. Group identities and affiliations would be based primarily on such variables as social class, politics, education, and other interests. The assimilationist idea that deeply influenced U.S. life is symbolized by the melting pot concept. This concept was celebrated in Zangwill's play, *The Melting Pot*, staged in New York City in 1908.

Even though the strong assimilationist idea in U.S. society contributed greatly to the making of one nation out of diverse ethnic and immigrant groups, it has not eradicated ethnic and cultural differences and is not likely to do so in the future. Ethnic differences persist in U.S. society for several important reasons. Discrimination prevents many individuals and groups with particular ethnic, racial, and/or cultural characteristics from attaining full structural inclusion in U.S. society (Jones, 1997; Winant, 1994). Ethnic cultures and communities often help individuals satisfy important human needs (Takaki, 1998). Ethnicity also persists because of continuing immigration to the United States (U.S. Census Bureau, 2001).

Immigration to the United States has increased markedly since the Immigration Reform Act, enacted in 1965, became effective in 1968. Most new

3

immigrants are coming from Spanish-speaking Latin American nations and from Asia rather than from Europe, the continent from which most American immigrants came in the past. Between 1981 and 1998, about 75% of the legal immigrants to the United States came from nations in Asia and Latin America (Riche, 2000). Nearly 20% of immigrants to the United States came from Europe during this period, and about 4% came from Africa (Riche). Most Asian immigrants came from China, the Philippines, India, and Korea. Mexico and nations in the Caribbean were the leading sources of immigrants from the Americas (U.S. Census Bureau, 2001).

The population of ethnic groups of color is increasing at a much faster rate than is the general population. People of color made up about 29% of the U.S. population in 2000 (U.S. Census Bureau, 2001). If current demographic trends continue, they are expected to make up 38% of the U.S. population by 2025 and 47% by 2050 (Martin & Midgley, 1999).

The Hispanic population increased much faster than the rest of the population and other ethnic groups between 1990 and 2000. It increased 57.9%, from 22.4 million in 1990 to 35.3 million in 2000 (Guzmán, 2001; Schmitt, 2001). The rapid growth in the Hispanic population between 1990 and 2000—and the much slower rate of growth in the African American population—caused the Hispanic population to become slightly larger than the African American population (see Table 1.1). The rapid growth in the Hispanic population resulted from a high rate of immigration from Latin America and from a high birth rate. Table 1.1 shows the population of the major ethnic groups in the United States in 1980, 1990, and 2000.

Although frequently done in the popular media, it is misleading to view Hispanics or Latinos as a single ethnic or cultural group because they speak the same language (Ovando & McLaren, 2000). Extensive cultural, ethnic, and racial differences exist both among and within the various Hispanic groups, such as those from Mexico, Cuba, Puerto Rico, El Salvador, the Dominican Republic, Colombia, and Venezuela. Most Hispanics view themselves as Mexicans, Puerto Ricans, or Cubans rather than as Hispanics.

The Asian American population increased 41% between 1990 and 2000—from 7.4 to 10.2 million. Even though Chinese Americans remain the largest group of Asian Americans, the Asian Indian population grew the most between 1990 and 2000; it doubled to 1.7 million. The growth in the Asian Indian population between 1990 and 2000 makes it the third-largest Asian American population. The Filipinos were the second-largest Asian American group in 2000, with a population of 1.85 million (Kulish, 2001; see Table 13.2).

The Demographic Imperative

The ethnic texture of the United States is changing substantially. The U.S. Census projects that ethnic minorities—including African Americans, American Indians and Alaska Natives, Asian and Pacific Islanders, and persons of

TABLE 1.1 Population of Ethnic Groups in the United States, 1980, 1990, and 2000

Ethnic Group	1980 Population	1990 Population	2000 Population
Total	226,504,825	248,710,000	281,421,906
White Americans*	188,340,790	199,686,000	211,460,526
African Americans	26,488,218	29,986,060	34,658,190
Hispanics	14,608,673	22,354,000	35,305,818
Mexican Americans	8,740,439	13,496,000	20,640,711
Puerto Ricans	2,013,945	2,728,000	3,406,178
Cubans	803,226	1,044,000	1,241,685
Other Spanish Origin		5,086,000	10,017,244
Jewish Americans		5,981,000	6,000,000
American Indians	1,361,869	1,878,000	2,475,956 **
Eskimos	42,149	57,000	
Aleuts	14,177	24,000	
Asians or Pacific Islanders		7,274,000	10,242,998 ***
Chinese Americans	812,178	1,645,000	2,432,585
Filipino Americans	781,894	1,407,000	1,850,314
Japanese Americans	716,331	848,000	796,700
Korean Americans	357,393	799,000	1,076,872
Asian Indians	387,223	815,000	1,678,765
Vietnamese Americans		615,000	1,122,528
Native Hawaiians and Pacific Islanders	172,346	211,000	140,652
Guamanian or Chamorro			58,240
Samoan			91,029
Other Pacific Islander			109,914

* This figure includes the 48% of Hispanics who classified themselves as White in the 2000 Census.
** This figure for the 2000 Census includes both American Indians and Alaskan Natives.
*** This figure for the 2000 Census includes Asian Americans only, not Pacific Islanders.

Source: U.S. Census Bureau (2001). *Table DP-1. Profile of General Demographic Characteristics for the United States: 2000.* [On line] Available at Web site: *http://www.census.gov*

Hispanic origin—will make up 47% of the U.S. population by 2050 (Martin & Midgley, 1999). The changing ethnic texture of the U.S. population has major implications for all of the nation's institutions, including schools, colleges, universities, and the workforce. These institutions must be restructured and transformed in order to meet the needs of the diverse groups who will work in and be served by them.

The demographic characteristics of the nation's student population are also changing greatly. The percentage of White students in the nation's schools is gradually decreasing while the population of students of color is increasing. In 1982, Whites made up about 73% of the nation's student population; in 1998 they made up 63% (Pratt, 2000). Pallas, Natriello, and McDill (1989) project that by 2020 White students will make up 54.5% of the nation's school population and that students of color will make up 45.5%.

The population of the nation's schools is also coming increasingly from low-income families. The number of children in poverty is growing in the United States and is expected to continue to grow in the future. The percentage of children in poverty increased from 16.2% in 1979 to 18.7% in 1998 (Terry, 2000).

American classrooms are experiencing the largest influx of immigrant students since the period from 1880 to 1924 (Eck, 2001). Between 1991 and 1998, about 7.6 million legal immigrants made the United States their home (Riche, 2000). Most of these immigrants (74.7%) came from nations in Latin America (43.8%) and Asia (30.9%); only 14.9% came from nations in Europe (U.S. Immigration and Naturalization Service, 2000; see Table 1.2).

A large but undetermined number of illegal or undocumented immigrants also enters the United States each year. The influence of an increasingly ethnically diverse population on the nation's schools, colleges, and universities is, and will continue to be, enormous. In fifty of the nation's largest urban public school systems, African Americans, Hispanics, Asian Americans, and other non-White students made up 76.5% of the student population in 1992 (Council of the Great City Schools, 1994). In some of the nation's largest cities and metropolitan areas, such as Chicago, Los Angeles, Washington, D.C., New York, Seattle, and San Francisco, half or more of the public school students are students of color. In California, the population of students of color in the public schools has exceeded the percentage of White students since the 1988/89 school year.

Most teachers now in the classroom or in teacher educational programs are likely to have students from diverse racial, ethnic, cultural, and language groups in their classrooms during their careers. This is true for both inner-city and suburban teachers.

A major goal of multicultural education is to transform the challenges of ethnic, cultural, and racial diversity into educational and societal opportunities. To reach this goal, teachers will need to acquire new knowledge, skills, and attitudes. A major goal of this book is to help teachers to acquire the knowledge and skills needed to function effectively in multicultural classrooms and schools.

TABLE 1.2   Region of Last Residence of Legal Immigrants, Percent Distribution by Decade

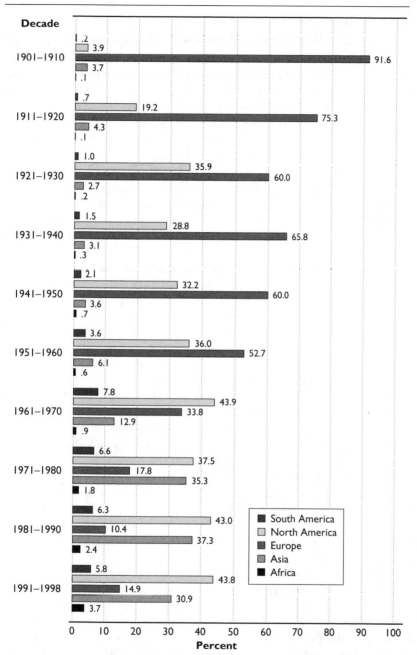

Note: Oceania and unspecified region represent no more than 1 percent of legal immigration each decade.

Source: U.S. Immigration and Naturalization Service, *Statistical Yearbook of the Immigration and Naturalization Service, 1998*. Washington, DC: U.S. Government Printing Office, p. 16.

Diversity: An Opportunity and a Challenge

The cultural, ethnic, racial, and language diversity that the United States and other Western nations are experiencing is both an opportunity and a challenge to their schools, colleges, and universities. In addition to its racial, ethnic, and language diversity, the new immigration since 1968 has made the United States the "most religiously diverse nation on earth" (Eck, 2001). Buddhists, Hindus, Muslims, and Zoroastrians are now significant groups in the United States. The new religious diversity within the United States poses new challenges to the nation's motto, *e pluribus unum*, and to the important phrase that begins the Constitution, "We, the people of the United States." "The people," as Eck insightfully points out, are not just Christian, but are religiously quite diverse. Consequently, when the issue of religion in the schools is raised, educators must ask, "Whose religion?" This important question seems to have eluded the many Americans who think of religion in the United States as primarily Christian.

When groups with different religions, cultures, and languages interact within a society, ethnocentrism and religious bigotry as well as other forms of institutionalized rejection and hostility usually occur. Ample examples of these forms of group hostility and rejection exist in every nation characterized by racial, cultural, and religious diversity (Eck, 2001; Fredrickson, 1997; Kymlicka, 2001; Marx, 1998). In several nation-states throughout the world—including the United States, the United Kingdom, and Germany—the incidents of bigoted attacks on ethnic and cultural minorities increased during the late 1980s and early 1990s (Banks & Banks, 2001; Castles & Davidson, 2000; Figueroa, 2001). Some observers link the increase in overt bigotry to the serious economic transformations that are occurring in the Western nations.

Ethnic, cultural, language, and religious diversity is also an opportunity. It can enrich a society by providing novel ways to view events and situations, to solve problems, and to view our relationship with the environment and with other creatures. The exploitation of the environment is a serious problem in most developed nations, partly because of how Westerners have traditionally viewed their relationship with the earth. Traditional Indian cultures in North America viewed the earth as sacred and had deep reverence for other living creatures (George, 1989; Philip, 1996).

The challenge to Western societies and their schools is to try to shape a modernized, national culture that has selected aspects of traditional cultures coexisting in some kind of delicate balance with a modernized postindustrial society. In the past, in their singular quest for modernity and a technocratic society, the Western nation-states tried to eradicate traditional cultures and thus alienated individuals and groups from their first cultures and languages. This approach to shaping a unified nation-state has created alienation and has deprived individuals and groups of some of the most important ways in which people satisfy their needs for symbolic meaning and community. It has also resulted in the political and cultural oppression of some racial and ethnic groups within society and has consequently caused them to focus on their own particular needs and goals rather than on the overarching goals of the nation-state (Castles & Davidson, 2000; Kymlicka, 2001).

Westernized nation-states will be able to create societies with overarching goals that are shared by diverse groups only when these groups feel that they have a real stake and place in their nation-states and that their states mirror their own concerns, values, and ethos. A multicultural curriculum that reflects the cultures, values, and goals of the groups within a nation will contribute significantly to the development of a healthy nationalism and national identity.

The Complexity of Ethnicity in American Society

Ethnicity is an integral but complex part of American life. To acquire a sophisticated knowledge of the United States, students must master facts, concepts, generalizations, and theories related to the intricate, complex nature of race and ethnicity in American society. Although ethnicity is a significant part of American life, there is a national American culture and identity shared by all groups in the United States. This national culture resulted (and is resulting) from a series of multiple acculturations (Banks, 2001). Diverse ethnic cultures, such as the Anglo-Saxon Protestant, the African, the Jewish, and the Mexican, influenced each other. The national American culture and identity consist of cultural components that have become universalized and are shared by most people within the nation. These universalized cultural components are products of the ethnic cultures in the United States and the American experience.

While most Americans are members of cultural, ethnic, racial, and language communities, they share an overarching American identity. A goal of the multicultural education curriculum is to foster *unity within diversity* by helping all students to develop a thoughtful commitment to the overarching American identity that we all share while, at the same time, respecting as well as incorporating aspects of their cultural and community identities into the school culture and the curriculum (Banks et al., 2001).

In addition to the national American culture and identity, there are ethnic and other subsocieties and institutions in the United States whose characteristics have not been universalized or become part of the shared national culture. The Anglo-Saxon Protestant subsociety, like other ethnic subsocieties, has cultural elements that are not universalized or shared by other Americans. *Consequently, an individual American is ethnic to the extent that he or she functions within ethnic subsocieties and shares their values, behavioral styles, and cultures.* An individual, however, may have a low level of ethnicity or psychological identification with his or her ethnic group or groups.

In Figure 1.1, the shaded area represents the American national culture shared by all ethnic and cultural groups. Circles A, B, C, and D represent ethnic subsocieties, such as the Anglo-Saxon Protestant, African American, Italian American, and Mexican American subsocieties. A major goal of the multicultural curriculum is to help students develop *cross-cultural competency,* which consists of the abilities, attitudes, and understandings students need to function effectively within the American national culture, within their own ethnic subsocieties, and within and across different ethnic subsocieties and cultures.

Ethnicity and Individuals

Ethnicity becomes even more complex when we try to determine the ethnic group affiliations and identification of individuals. Many individuals in U.S. society not only perceive themselves as members of ethnic groups, but also are

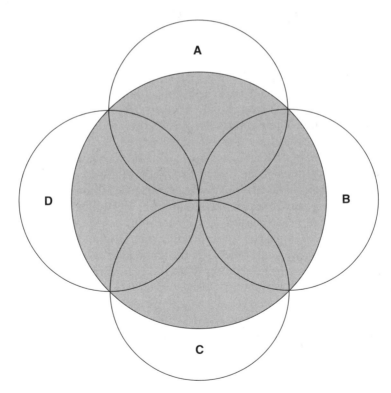

Figure 1.1   Ethnicity and the National American Culture   The shaded area represents the national American culture. Circles A, B, C, and D represent ethnic subcultures.

perceived as members of these groups by individuals outside their ethnic groups. This includes many, but not all, Americans who are Mexican, Polish, Jewish, and Vietnamese. The asterisks in the closed circles in Figure 1.2 represent individuals within these ethnic groups. However, these individuals also perceive themselves and are usually perceived by others to be American, as well as Mexican, Polish, Jewish, or Vietnamese, even though Mexican, for example, may be the first and most important identity for many Mexican Americans.

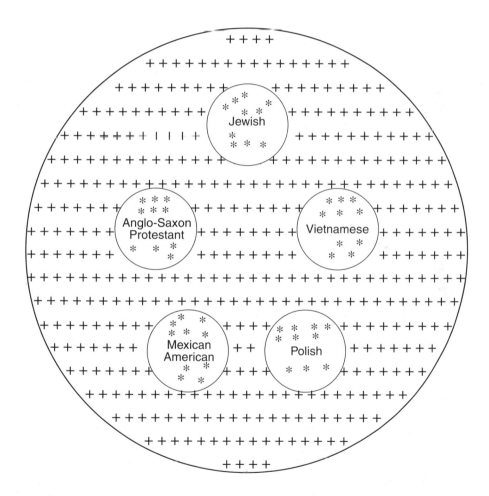

Figure 1.2   Ethnicity and Individuals   The asterisks in the closed circles represent individuals who perceive themselves and who are perceived by other people to be members of clearly delineated ethnic groups. The plus signs [+] represent individuals who perceive themselves and are perceived by most other people to be merely *American*.

Mexican Americans also share a broader American identity and the overarching idealized American values that cement the nation. Many Anglo-Saxon Protestants, such as those who are members of the Brahmin elite in Boston, also see themselves as members of a specific cultural group. Individuals represented by the asterisks in the closed circles in Figure 1.2 are clearly ethnic, from both inside and outside points of view.

Other Americans are more difficult to characterize ethnically because of how they view themselves and how others view them. These individuals are represented by the plus signs in Figure 1.2.

They perceive themselves only as American and do not consciously identify with a clearly defined ethnic group. This group of Americans includes many third- and fourth-generation Irish and Scandinavians, as well as individuals with multiple European heritages. These individuals can best be described as mainstream Americans from sociological and psychological perspectives. Culturally, however, mainstream Americans share many characteristics with Anglo-Saxon Protestants because Anglo-Saxon Protestants have influenced the national culture more than any other American subgroup.

The increase of biracial marriages and births has made racial identification in the United States more complex (Nash, 1999; Root, 2001). Between 1970 and 1992, the number of African American-White couples quadrupled, to 246,000 (Kalish, 1995). Interracial births more than doubled between 1978 and 1992, while total births increased 22 percent. Interracial marriages are also increasing.

In the 2000 Census, respondents were given the option of selecting one or more race categories to indicate racial identities; 2.4% of all respondents—or almost 7 million (6,826,228) people—reported two or more races (U.S. Census Bureau, 2001). Figure 1.3 shows the percentage distribution of the population that selected two or more races, most of whom were younger people. The U.S. Census predicts that more people will choose the "two or more races" category in the future. Kenneth Prewitt, who was director of the 2000 Census, believes that in 15 to 20 years about one fourth of the population will identify themselves as multiracial (cited in Kent, Pollard, Haaga, & Mather, 2001, p. 33).

Ethnic and Cultural Studies: Assumptions and Practices

Many educators realize the importance of ethnicity in U.S. society and the need to help students develop more sophisticated understandings of the diverse ethnic groups that make up the United States and a greater acceptance of cultural differences. Educational institutions at all levels have made some attempts to include more information about ethnic groups in the social studies, language arts, and humanities curricula within the last two decades. However,

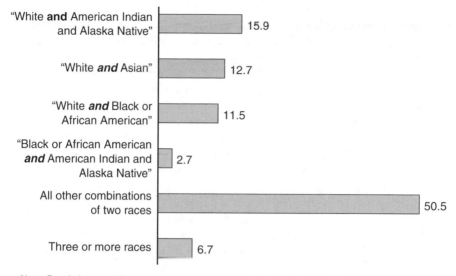

Note: Population reporting two or more races was 2.4 percent of the total population.

Figure 1.3 **Percent Distributition of Population of Two or More Races, Showing the Four Two-Race Combinations Identified by the Office of Management and Budget: 2000.**

Source: U.S. Census Bureau (2001), *Overview of Race and Hispanic Origin* [On-line]. Available: *http://www.census.gov*

some assumptions about ethnic studies and multicultural education have adversely affected the integration of ethnic content into the curriculum.

We need to examine and challenge these assumptions and related school practices and to formulate new assumptions and goals in order for the multicultural education movement to serve as a catalyst for curriculum reform and transformation. The greatest promise of multicultural education is that it will serve as a vehicle for general curriculum reform and transformation. If ethnic content is merely added to the traditional curriculum, which has many problems (Pinar, Reynolds, Slattery, & Taubman, 1995), then efforts to modify the curriculum with ethnic content are likely to lead to a dead end. The total school curriculum should be transformed.

One pervasive assumption many educators embrace is that ethnic studies deals exclusively with groups of color, such as Asian Americans, American Indians, and African Americans. This assumption is widespread within the schools, and school programs often reflect it. In many school ethnic studies units and lessons little or no attention is devoted to the experiences of European American ethnic groups, such as Jewish Americans, Polish Americans, and Italian Americans. This narrow conceptualization of ethnic studies emerged out of the social forces that gave rise to the ethnic studies movement in the 1960s. To conceptualize ethnic studies exclusively as the study of people of color is inconsistent with how sociologists define *ethnicity* (Alba, 1992). It also prevents the development of broadly conceptualized comparative approaches to ethnic studies and multicultural education. Comparative approaches to ethnic studies and multicultural education are needed to help students understand fully the complex role of ethnicity in U.S. life and culture. Conceptualizing ethnic studies exclusively as the study of ethnic groups of color also promotes a kind of we–they attitude among many White students and teachers. Many students think that ethnic studies is the study of them—*the Others*—whereas American studies is the study of "us." Many educators believe that ethnic studies has no place within an all-White classroom.

A related assumption that educators often make about ethnic studies is that only students who are members of a particular ethnic group should study that group's history and culture. Some ethnic studies units and lessons focus on one specific ethnic group, such as Puerto Ricans, African Americans, or American Indians. The ethnic group on which the units and lessons focus is usually either present or dominant in the local school population. Content related to diverse ethnic groups should be an integral part of the curriculum experienced by all students. *Ethnic modification of the total curriculum is essential.*

All students, regardless of their race, ethnicity, or social class, should study about the cogent and complex roles of ethnicity and cross-ethnic relationships and interactions in U.S. society and culture. Most Americans are socialized within ethnic or cultural enclaves and have low levels of cultural and ethnic literacy. Within their communities, people learn primarily about their own cultures and assume that their lifestyles are the legitimate ones and that other cultures are invalid, strange, and different. The school should help students to break out of their cultural enclaves and to broaden their cultural perspectives. Students need to learn that there are cultural and ethnic alternatives within our society that they can freely embrace.

Many educators assume that ethnic studies is essentially additive in nature and that we can create a sound multicultural curriculum by leaving the present curriculum intact and adding ethnic heroes and heroines, such as Martin Luther King, Jr., Cesar Chávez, Sojourner Truth, Pocahontas, and Malinche to the list of mainstream heroes and heroines who are already studied in most schools. Conceptualizing ethnic studies as essentially additive in nature is problematic for several reasons. In too many classrooms throughout the nation, teachers still emphasize the mastery of low-level facts and do not help students master higher levels of knowledge.

Modifying the school curriculum to include ethnic and cultural content provides a tremendous opportunity to reexamine the assumptions, purposes, and nature of the curriculum and to formulate a curriculum with new assumptions and goals. Merely adding low-level facts about ethnic content to a curriculum that is already bulging with discrete and isolated facts about mainstream

American heroes will not result in significant curriculum reform. Isolated facts about Crispus Attucks and the Boston Massacre do not stimulate the intellect any more than do isolated facts about George Washington or Betsy Ross. To integrate ethnic content meaningfully into the total school curriculum, we must undertake more substantial curriculum reform. Adding facts about ethnic heroes and heroines and events of questionable historical significance is not sufficient. Transformation of the curriculum is essential.

An Expanded Definition of Ethnicity

Problems in teaching about ethnic groups result, in part, from the ways in which *ethnicity* and *ethnic groups* in the United States are often conceptualized and defined by teachers and curriculum specialists. They often limit their conceptualization of an ethnic group to an ethnic group of color or to an *ethnic minority* group. Teachers and curriculum specialists must have a more accurate and inclusive definition of an ethnic group in order to integrate ethnic content into the curriculum in more meaningful ways.

What is an *ethnic group*? Individuals who constitute an ethnic group share a sense of group identification, a common set of values, political and economic interests, behavioral patterns, and other culture elements that differ from those of other groups within a society. Members of an ethnic group have a shared sense of peoplehood, culture, identity, and shared languages and dialects. Alba (1992) states that Max Weber's classic definition of an *ethnic group* is still the most useful definition. Weber (cited in Alba) defines an ethnic group as a group whose members "entertain a subjective belief in their common descent because of similarities of physical type or of customs or both, or because of memories of colonization and migration.... It does not matter whether or not an objective blood relationship exists" (p. 16).

An individual is ethnic to the extent that he or she shares the values, behavioral patterns, cultural traits, and identification with a specific ethnic group. Many individuals have multiple ethnic group attachments; others consider themselves "American" rather than ethnic.

An individual's identity with his or her ethnic group varies significantly with the times in his or her life, with economic and social status, and with the situations and/or settings. Ethnicity is very important for some Americans and of little or only symbolic importance to others. Groups based on other factors—such as religion, social class, region, sexual orientation, gender, or occupation—are more important to many individuals. As members of lower socioeconomic ethnic groups attain economic mobility, their social-class interests often become more important to them than their ethnic affiliations.

In this book, ethnic studies is conceptualized broadly, as it is in the *Harvard Encyclopedia of American Ethnic Groups* (Thernstrom, Orlov, & Handlin, 1980). Information, materials, and strategies for teaching about White ethnic groups—such as Italian Americans and Jewish Americans—as well as about the experiences of ethnic groups of color, such as Mexican Americans, Puerto Ricans, and Asian Americans, are included. To conceptualize ethnic and cultural studies more narrowly will result in curricula that are too limited in scope and that will not help students understand fully both the similarities and differences in the experiences of the diverse groups in the United States.

The multicultural curriculum should enable students to derive valid generalizations and theories about the characteristics of ethnic, cultural, and religious groups and to learn how they are alike and different, in both their past and present experiences. Even though it is neither possible nor necessary for the curriculum of a particular school or district to include content about every ethnic group in the United States (there are more than 100), *each curriculum should focus on a range of groups that differ in their racial characteristics, cultural experiences, languages, histories, values, and current problems.* By studying a range of ethnic and cultural groups, students will be able to formulate valid comparative generalizations and theories about the nature of race, ethnicity, and culture in U.S. society. The curriculum can be transformed only when events, concepts, and issues are studied from the perspectives of a range of ethnic, cultural, and religious groups.

Ethnic Minority Groups/People of Color

Even though an ethnic group shares a common set of values, behavioral patterns, culture traits, and a sense of peoplehood, an ethnic minority group can be distinguished from an ethnic group. An *ethnic minority group* has unique physical and/or cultural characteristics that enable people who belong to mainstream groups to identify its members easily and, thus, to treat them in a discriminatory way. Jewish Americans are an ethnic minority group with unique cultural and religious characteristics. African Americans are an ethnic minority group with both unique physical and cultural characteristics.

An ethnic minority group is usually a numerical minority and comprises only a small percentage of the national population. In 2000, ethnic minorities (including Hispanics of all races) in the United States made up 29% of the national population. However, as pointed out previously, the non-White percentage of the U.S. population is growing at a much faster rate than the White population. The U.S. Census projects that by 2050 ethnic groups of color will make up about 47% of the total U.S. population (Martin & Midgley, 1999). The concept *minority* is becoming increasingly misleading and less useful in the United States as the population of people of color becomes closer to that of Whites.

In many school districts and schools, and in the school-age population of California and Hawaii, students of color constitute majorities. In part for this reason, educators and social scientists are increasingly referring to groups such as African Americans, Hispanics, and Asian Americans as *people of color* rather than as ethnic *minorities*. Educators and social scientists are realizing that many terms and concepts used in the past do not accurately and sensitively describe ethnic, racial, and cultural realities today. Although *people of color* is a contested term that some educators find perplexing, it is used often because a more helpful term has not yet been developed.

Ethnic and Cultural Studies: A Process of Curriculum Reform

Ethnic and cultural content should not be studied only by ethnic groups of color or be limited to specialized courses. Rather, ethnic and cultural studies should be viewed as a process of curriculum reform and transformation that will result in the creation of a reformed curriculum based on new assumptions and perspectives. Such a transformed curriculum will help students gain novel views of the American experience and a new conception of what it means to be an American. Because the English immigrants assumed control of most economic, social, and political institutions early in U.S. national history, to Americanize has been interpreted to mean to *Anglicize*. During the height of nativism in the late 1800s and early 1900s, the English Americans defined *Americanization* as *Anglicization* (Higham, 1972). This notion of Americanization is still widespread within U.S. society and schools today. Thus, when we think of American history and American literature, we tend to think of Anglo-American history and of literature written by Anglo-American authors.

Reconceptualizing American Society

Because the assumption that only what is Anglo-American is American is so deeply ingrained in curriculum materials and in the hearts and minds of many students and teachers, we cannot transform the curriculum by merely adding a unit or a lesson here and there about African American, Mexican American, or Italian American history or literature. Rather, we need to examine seriously the conception of American that is perpetuated in the curriculum and the basic canon, assumptions, and purposes that underlie the curriculum.

It is essential to reconceptualize and re-envision how we view American society and history in the school curriculum. We should view American history, literature, art, music, and culture from diverse ethnic and cultural perspectives rather than primarily or exclusively from the point of view of mainstream historians, writers, and artists. Most courses in the curriculum are taught primarily from mainstream perspectives (Levine, 1996; Nussbaum, 1997). Often ethnic and cultural content is added to the mainstream curriculum, which is left intact. I call these types of courses, units, and lessons the *Contributions* and

Additive approaches to curriculum reform (see Figure 1.4). Multicultural education, as a process of curriculum reform, can and often does proceed from the Additive and Contribution approaches to the Transformative and Social Action Approaches.

In courses, units, and activities based on the Contributions and Additive approaches, ethnic content is additive to the major curriculum thrust, which remains mainstream-oriented. Many school districts that have attempted ethnic modification of the curriculum have implemented Contributions and Additive curriculum changes and reforms. Courses on specific ethnic groups, such as African Americans and Mexican Americans—and special units on ethnic groups—are examples of Contributions and Additive types of approaches.

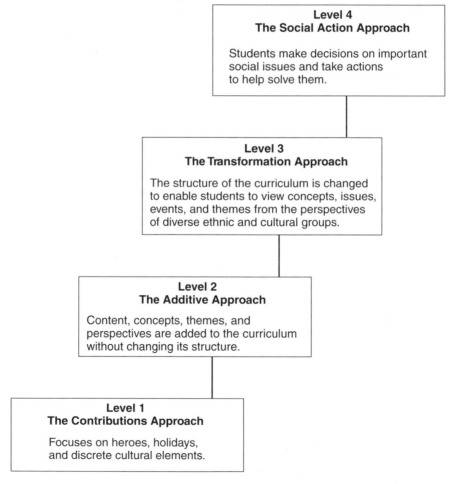

Figure 1.4   Levels of Integration of Ethnic Content

Approaches to Teaching Multicultural Content

I will further discuss the four approaches to the integration of ethnic content into the curriculum. The *Contributions Approach* to integration is one of the most frequently used. This approach is characterized by the addition of ethnic heroes into the curriculum. The heroes and heroines added to the curriculum are viewed from a mainstream-centric perspective and are also usually selected for inclusion into the curriculum using mainstream criteria. Consequently, ethnic heroes and heroines viewed positively by the mainstream society, such as Booker T. Washington, Marian Anderson, and Sacajawea, are most often chosen for study rather than are ethnic Americans who challenged the dominant class and social structure in society, such as W. E. B. Du Bois, Geronimo, and Angela Davis.

The mainstream curriculum remains unchanged in terms of its basic structure, goals, and salient characteristics. This is the easiest approach for teachers to use to integrate the curriculum with ethnic content. However, it has several serious limitations. Students do not attain a comprehensive view of the role of ethnic and cultural groups in U.S. society. Rather, they see ethnic issues and events primarily as an addition to the curriculum and, thus, as an appendage to the main story of the nation's development.

Content, concepts, themes, and perspectives are added to the curriculum without changing its basic structure, purpose, and characteristics in the *Additive Approach*. The content, concepts, and issues added to the curriculum are viewed primarily from mainstream perspectives. This approach is often accomplished by the addition of a book, a unit, or a course to the curriculum without changing it substantially. The Additive Approach allows the teacher to put ethnic content into the curriculum without restructuring it, which takes substantial time, effort, training, and rethinking of the curriculum and its purposes, nature, and goals.

The Additive Approach can be the first phase in a more radical curriculum reform effort designed to restructure the total curriculum and to integrate it with ethnic content, perspectives, and frames of reference. However, this approach shares several problems with the Contributions Approach. Its most important shortcoming is that it usually results in the viewing of ethnic content from the perspectives of mainstream historians, writers, artists, and scientists because it does not involve a restructuring of the curriculum.

The *Transformation Approach* differs fundamentally from the Contributions and Additive Approaches. This approach changes the basic assumptions of the curriculum and enables students to view concepts, issues, themes, and problems from several ethnic perspectives and points of view. The key curriculum issue involved in the Transformation Approach is not the addition of ethnic groups, heroes, heroines, and contributions, but the infusion of various perspectives, frames of reference, and content from different groups that will extend students' understandings of the nature, development, and complexity of the United States and the world.

Mainstream perspectives should be among many different perspectives taught in the various content areas. Only by approaching the study of American society and culture in this way will students obtain a holistic, rather than an ethnocentric, view of our nation's history and culture. A writer's or artist's experience and culture, including his or her ethnic or community culture, cogently influences his or her works and views of the past and present. Feminists call this influence *positionality* (Code, 1991; Tetreault, 2001).

Positionality is used to describe how race, culture, social class, and gender—as well as other personal and cultural factors—influence how we view our society and the world. However, it would be simplistic to argue that there is one mainstream view of history, art, literature, or contemporary events, or one African American view. Wide differences in experiences and perceptions exist both within and across ethnic and cultural groups.

However, people who have experienced a historical event or social event, such as racial discrimination, slavery, or internment, often view the event very differently from people who have watched it from a distance. Accounts written by people who were enslaved or interned provide unique insights and perspectives on these events that cannot be provided by people who did not experience them.

A powerful account of slavery was chronicled by Olaudah Equiano, the son of an Ibo tribal leader who was one of 10 to 12 million Africans captured and enslaved in the Americas (Johnson, Smith, & WGBH Series Research Team, 1998). The insights provided by Yoshiko Uchida (1982) in *Desert Exile*, which describes her experiences in a concentration camp during World War II, could not have been written by someone observing these events from the outside. Individuals who viewed the internment from the outside can also provide unique and important perspectives. Hence, both insider and outsider perspectives (Merton, 1972) should be studied in a sound multicultural curriculum.

Only by looking at events from many different perspectives can we fully understand the complex dimensions of American culture and society. Important goals of the multicultural curriculum are to broaden students' conceptions of what *American* means and to present them with new ways to view and interpret American society, literature, music, and art. Any goals that are less ambitious, while important, will not result in curriculum transformation or enable students to acquire a new conception of the United States and the world.

Table 1.3 contains a lesson that illustrates the transformation approach to teaching. In this lesson, students view Columbus's arrival in the Caribbean from the perspectives of both the Native people (the Arawaks or Taino) and Columbus.

The *Social Action Approach* includes all of the elements of the Transformation Approach and adds components that require students to make decisions and take actions related to the concept, issue, or problem they have studied. Table 1.4 lists possible actions developed by a junior high school

TABLE 1.3   Teaching Multiple Perspectives: Christopher Columbus and the Arawaks

The students are presented with the following excerpts from Christopher Columbus's diary that describe his arrival in an Arawak Indian community in the Caribbean in 1492. These are some of the observations that Columbus makes about the Arawaks:

> *They took all and gave all, such as they had, with good will, but it seemed to me that they were a people very lacking in everything. They all go naked as their mothers bore them, and the women also, although I saw only one very young girl.... They should be good servants and quick to learn, since I see that they very soon say all that is said to them, and I believe that they would easily be made Christians, for it appeared to me that they had no religious beliefs. Our Lord willing, at the time of my departure, I will bring back six of them to Your Highnesses, that they may learn to talk. I saw no beast of any kind in this island, except parrots.*

The students are then encouraged to view Columbus's statement from the perspective of the Arawaks. The Arawaks had an oral culture and consequently left no written documents. However, archaeologist Fred Olsen studied Arawak artifacts and used what he learned from them to construct a day in the life of the Arawaks, which he describes in his book, *On the Trail of the Arawaks*. The students are asked to read an excerpt from Olsen's account of a day in the life of the Arawaks and to respond to these questions:

1. Columbus wrote in his diary that he thought the Arawaks had no religious beliefs. You read about Arawak life in the report by Fred Olsen. Do you think Columbus was correct? Why?
2. Accounts written by people who took part in or witnessed (saw) an historical event are called primary sources. Can historians believe everything they read in a primary source? Explain.

Sources: Jan, C. (1930). *The Voyages of Christopher Columbus*. London: The Argonaut Press. Olsen, F. (1974). *On the Trail of the Arawaks*. Norman: University of Oklahoma Press.

social studies class after studying a unit on the civil rights movements of the 1960s and 1970s.

The four approaches to the integration of ethnic content into the curriculum described above are often mixed and blended in actual teaching situations (see Figure 1.4). The move from the lower to the higher levels of ethnic content integration is likely to be gradual and cumulative. An important goal of teaching about racial, ethnic, and cultural diversity should be to empower students with the knowledge, skills, and attitudes they need to participate in civic action that will help transform our world and enhance the possibility for human survival.

TABLE 1.4   Student Action

After a unit on the civil rights movement of the 1960s and 1970s, Mr. Carson's 7th grade social studies class made this list of actions they could take to help reduce discrimination in their personal lives, school, and community.

1. Making a personal commitment to stop telling racist jokes.
2. Making a commitment to challenge our own racial and ethnic stereotypes either before or after we verbalize them.
3. Compiling an annotated list of books about ethnic groups that we will ask the librarian to order for our school library.
4. Asking the principal to order sets of photographs that show African Americans and other people of color who have jobs that represent a variety of careers. Asking the principal to encourage our teachers to display these photographs on their classroom walls.
5. Observing television programs to determine the extent to which people of color, such as African Americans and Asian Americans, are represented in such jobs as news anchors and hosts of programs. Writing to local and national television stations to express our concern if we discover that people of color are not represented in powerful and visible roles in news or other kinds of television programs.
6. Contacting a school in the inner-city to determine if there are joint activities and projects in which we and they might participate.
7. Asking the principal or the board of education in our school district to require our teachers to attend inservice staff development workshops that will help them learn ways in which to integrate content about ethnic and racial groups into our courses.
8. Sharing some of the facts that we have learned in this unit, such as that by the year 2000, one out of every three Americans will be a person of color, with our parents and discussing these facts with them.
9. Making a personal commitment to have a friend from another racial, ethnic, or religious group by the end of the year.
10. Making a personal commitment to read at least one book a year that deals with a racial, cultural, or ethnic group other than my own.
11. Do nothing; take no actions.

Multicultural Education and Global Education

Students should also study world events, issues, and concepts from a transformative rather than a Eurocentric perspective. The world studies program in schools often uses a Eurocentric approach to examine problems, issues, and concepts. Events and issues are viewed primarily or exclusively from the perspectives of mainstream groups in European nations and cultures. There are many opportunities in the school curriculum to link multicultural education and global education, and to help students view international events, concepts, and issues from the perspectives of the ethnic and racial groups that live in the various nations of the world. Figure 1.5 illustrates how students can study a global event, problem, issue, or concept using a transformative approach.

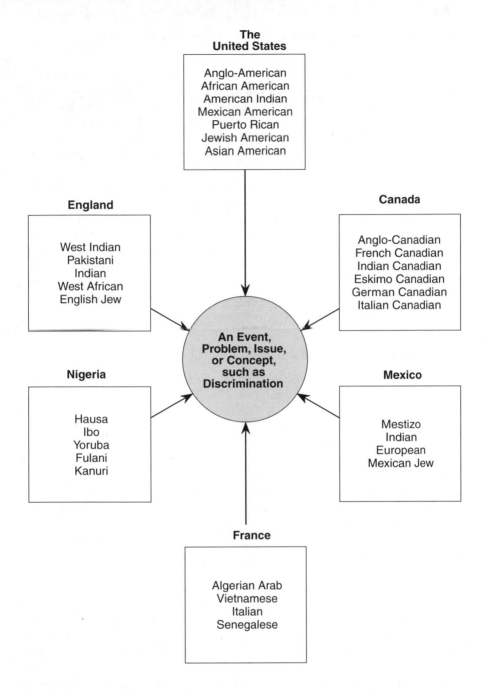

FIGURE 1.5   A Transformative Approach to Global Studies   This figure illustrates
how an event, problem, issue, or concept can be viewed from the perspectives of ethnic
groups within several nations. A study of ethnic perspectives within other nations will
help students gain a global framework for viewing and studying human events and
problems.

It is important to link multicultural education and global education because they share several important goals and because the population of the United States is constantly being changed by the infusion of ethnic and immigrant groups from beyond its borders. Ethnic studies helps students better understand the lands and cultures from which these groups come.

When relating multicultural and global education, it is important for teachers to foster what Kymlicka (1995) calls *multicultural citizenship*. Multicultural citizenship education recognizes and legitimizes the right and need of citizens to maintain commitments to their ethnic and cultural communities as well as to the national civic culture. It also helps students develop a thoughtful global identification. *Cultural, national,* and *global* identifications are interrelated (Banks, 2002). A healthy cultural identification is needed to develop a thoughtful and clarified commitment to the nation-state. A clarified and reflective national identification is needed to become thoughtful citizens of the global community. Figure 1.6 shows the relationship between *cultural, national,* and *global identifications.*

Distinguishing Multicultural and Global Education

Although it is important to link multicultural and global education, it is essential that they not be confused and that one is not substituted for the other. Sometimes, when teachers integrate Mexico, Japan, and Nigeria into their lessons they will claim that these topics constitute multicultural education. Global and multicultural education should be distinguished. Each makes unique and important contributions to the education of students. Multicultural education deals with ethnic, cultural, and gender groups within the United States (Banks & Banks, 2001). Global education deals with nations outside the United States and the interrelationships among nations (Diaz, Massialas, & Xanthopoulos, 1999).

The Goals of the Multicultural Curriculum

Concepts, content, and teaching strategies cannot be identified and selected until goals are clearly defined. The education of effective citizens in a diverse society is the key goal for multicultural education presented in this book. This goal requires that students develop decision-making and social action skills so they can take personal, social, and civic action to make our nation more democratic and humane.

The multicultural curriculum should help students develop the ability to make reflective decisions on issues related to race, ethnicity, and culture and to take *personal, social,* and *civic* actions to help solve the racial and ethnic problems in our national and world societies. Effective solutions to the enormous ethnic and racial problems in our nation and world can be found only by an

A major goal of multicultural citizenship
education should be to help students acquire
a delicate balance of cultural, national,
and global identifications.

FIGURE 1.6   Cultural, National, and Global
Identifications

Source: Reprinted with permission from James A. Banks
(2002). *An Introduction to Multicultural Education* (3rd
ed.) Boston: Allyn and Bacon, p. 87.

active and informed citizenry capable of making reflective personal and public decisions. Chapter 4 discusses decision making and its components in more detail.

The multicultural curriculum should also help students view historical and contemporary events from diverse ethnic and cultural perspectives, clarify their ethnic and cultural identities, and function effectively within their own cultural communities. Individuals must clarify their own ethnic and cultural identities before they can relate positively to people who belong to different racial and ethnic groups. Educators need to foster the development of self-acceptance, but to discourage ethnocentrism. Diversity and unity in a delicate balance should be fostered by the schools.

The multicultural curriculum should also help individuals develop cross-cultural competency: the ability to function within a range of cultures. Although individuals within a pluralistic society must learn to accept their own ethnic and cultural identities and become comfortable with them, they must also learn to function effectively within other cultures and to respond positively to individuals who belong to other ethnic, cultural, language, and religious groups. They also need to learn how to interact with and to resolve conflicts with people from diverse groups. The multicultural curriculum seeks to help individuals gain greater self-understanding by viewing themselves from the perspectives of other cultures.

Another important goal of the multicultural curriculum is to provide students with cultural and ethnic alternatives. Both the White mainstream Protestant and the Filipino American student should be provided with cultural and ethnic options in the school. Historically, the school curriculum has focused primarily on the cultures of Anglo-Saxon Protestants. In many schools the curriculum is primarily an extension of the homes, communities, and cultures of White mainstream students. It often does not present these students with cultural and ethnic alternatives, thereby denying them the richness of the music, literature, art, values, lifestyles, and perspectives that exist among such ethnic groups as Jews, Greeks, Puerto Ricans, and African Americans. Many behaviors and values within these ethnic groups can help mainstream White students to enrich their personal and public lives.

The multicultural curriculum should also try to reduce ethnic and cultural encapsulation and help students develop a better understanding and awareness of their own cultures. Individuals who only know, participate in, and see the world from their unique cultural and ethnic perspectives are denied important aspects of the human experience and are culturally and ethnically encapsulated. These individuals are unable to know and see their own cultures fully because of their cultural and ethnic blinders. The multicultural curriculum seeks to help individuals gain greater self-understanding by viewing themselves from the perspectives of other cultures.

The multicultural curriculum should also help students to expand their conceptions of what it means to be human, to accept the fact that ethnic minority cultures are functional and valid, and to realize that a culture can be evaluated only within a particular cultural context. Because cultures are made by people, there are many ways of being human. By studying this important generalization, students will hopefully develop an appreciation for the capacity of human beings to create a diversity of lifestyles and to adapt to a variety of social and physical environments.

Another important goal of the multicultural curriculum is to help students master essential reading, writing, and math skills. Multicultural content can help students master important skills in the content areas. Multicultural readings and data, if taught effectively, can be highly motivating and meaningful, especially when teachers help students to understand and grapple with the conflicts inherent within cross-cultural teaching and learning (Graff, 1992). Students are more likely to master skills when the teacher uses content that deals with significant human problems, such as race, culture, language, religion, and power within our communities, nation, and world.

Summary

The curriculum within the nation's schools, colleges, and universities should be transformed so that it will accurately reflect the racial, ethnic, cultural, language, and religious diversity within the United States. Schools, colleges, and universities are using various approaches to infuse multicultural content into the curriculum, including the contributions and additive approaches. Each of these approaches has important problems. To respond adequately to the diversity within the nation and the world, the curriculum should be transformed so that it can help students to develop the decision-making, social-action, and cross-cultural skills needed for the twenty-first century.

REFLECTION AND ACTION ACTIVITIES

1. The melting pot concept does not accurately describe the nature of ethnicity in the United States. React to this position by stating whether you agree or disagree with it and why.

2. Make a list of the different ethnic, racial, cultural, and language groups that constitute your ethnic heritage. Compare your list with similar lists made by other individuals in your class or workshop. What conclusions can you derive about ethnicity in U.S. society by analyzing these data?

3. Study the results of the last national or local election. Note particularly the voting patterns of predominantly racial, ethnic, and language communities. What generalizations can you make on the basis of these data? What are the limitations of your generalizations?

4. Interview a curriculum coordinator in one or two local school districts. Ask this individual to describe the school's efforts to implement multicultural education. If the school focuses on some ethnic groups and not on others, ask for an explanation of this practice. How do your findings compare with the trends described in this chapter?

5. According to the author, what should be the goals of the multicultural curriculum? Write, in one sentence or more, what you think should be the goals of the multicultural curriculum. Compare your statement with the goals listed in this chapter. In what ways are your statement and the listed goals alike and different? Why? How are your assumptions about ethnic studies and ethnicity similar to and different from those of the author?

6. Divide into small discussion groups in your class or workshop. Appoint a group leader and a reporter for each group and discuss the following questions in your

groups. When the small-group discussions have ended, the class or workshop should reassemble. Reporters should give a brief summary of each group's discussion. The large group should then react both to the reports and to the following questions:

a. Which of the approaches presented in Figure 1.4 best describes the curriculum in your school or in a school that you have attended or in which you have observed?

b. Do you think it would be desirable to help your school (or a school that you have attended or in which you have observed) move from one approach to another (for example, from the Contributions to the Transformative Approach)?

c. What problems might you, as a teacher, encounter in trying to move your school (or a school that you have attended or in which you have observed) curriculum from one approach to another (for example, moving from Contributions to Transformation)?

d. How might these problems best be overcome?

e. What benefits might result for both you and the students if your school (or the school that you have attended or in which you have observed) changed from one approach to another?

7. Define each of the following concepts and terms and tell why each is important:

the melting pot	contributions approach
ethnic group	additive approach
ethnic minority group	transformation approach
people of color	social action approach
multicultural citizenship	

REFERENCES

Alba, R. (1992). Ethnicity. In E. F. Borgatta & M. L. Borgatta (Eds.), *Encyclopedia of Sociology* (Vol. 2, pp. 575–584). New York: Macmillan.

Banks, J. A. (2001). *Cultural Diversity and Education: Foundations, Curriculum, and Teaching* (4th ed.). Boston: Allyn and Bacon.

Banks, J. A. (2002). *An Introduction to Multicultural Education* (3rd ed.). Boston: Allyn and Bacon.

Banks, J. A., & Banks, C. A. M. (Eds.). (2001). *Handbook of Research on Multicultural Education.* San Francisco: Jossey-Bass.

Banks, J. A., Cookson, P., Gay, G., Hawley, W. D., Irvine, J. I., Nieto, S., Schofield, J. W., & Stephan, W. G. (2001). *Diversity within Unity: Essential Principles for Teaching and Learning in a Multicultural Society.* Seattle: Center for Multicultural Education, University of Washington.

Castles, S., & Davidson, A. (2000). *Citizenship and Migration: Globalization and the Politics of Belonging.* New York: Routledge.

Code, L. (1991). *What Can She Know? Feminist Theory and the Construction of Knowledge.* Ithaca, NY: Cornell University Press.

Council of the Great City Schools. (1994). *National Urban Education Goals: 1992–1993 Indicators Report.* Washington, DC: Author.

Diaz, C. F., Massialas, B. G., & Xanthopoulos, J. R. (1999). *Global Perspectives for Educators.* Boston: Allyn and Bacon.

Eck, D. L. (2001). *A New Religious America: How A "Christian Country" Has Become the World's Most Religiously Diverse Nation.* New York: HarperSanFrancisco.

Figueroa, P. (2001). Multicultural Education in the United Kingdom: Historical Development and Current Status. In J. A. Banks & C. A. M. Banks (Eds.), *Handbook of Research on Multicultural Education* (pp. 778–800). San Francisco: Jossey-Bass.

Frederickson, G. M. (1997). *The Comparative Imagination: On the History of Racism, Nationalism, and Social Movements.* Berkeley: University of California Press.

George, Chief D. (1989). *My Heart Soars.* Blaine, WA: Hancock House.

Graff, G. (1992). *Beyond the Culture Wars: How Teaching the Conflicts Can Revitalize American Education.* New York: Norton.

Guzmán, B. (2001). The Hispanic Population: Census 2000 Brief. U.S. Census Bureau (2001). [On-line]. Available: *http://www.census.gov/*

Higham, J. (1972). *Strangers in the Land: Patterns of American Nativism 1860–1926.* New York: Atheneum.

Johnson, C., Smith, P., & the WGBH Series Research Team. (1998). *Africans in America: America's Journey through Slavery.* New York: Harcourt Brace.

Jones, J. M. (1997). *Prejudice and Racism* (2nd ed.). New York: McGraw-Hill.

Kalish, M. L. (1995). Multiracial Birth Increases as U.S. Ponders Racial Definitions. *Population Today, 23*(4), pp. 1–2.

Kent, M. M., Pollard, J. H., Haaga, J., & Mather, M. (2001, June). First glimpses from the 2000 U.S. Census. *Population Bulletin,* vol. 56, no. 2. Washington, DC: Population Reference Bureau.

Kulish, N. (2001, May 14). The New Demographics: U.S. Asian Population Grew and Diversified, Census Shows. *Wall Street Journal,* p. B4ff.

Kymlicka, W. (1995). *Multicultural Citizenship: A Liberal Theory of Minority Rights.* New York: Oxford University Press.

Kymlicka, W. (2001). *Politics in the Vernacular: Nationalism, Multiculturalism, and Citizenship.* New York: Oxford University Press.

Levine, L. W. (1996). *The Opening of the American Mind: Canons, Culture, and History.* Boston: Beacon Press.

Martin, P., & Midgley, E. (1999). *Immigration to the United States.* Washington, DC: Population Reference Bureau.

Marx, A. W. (1998). *Making Race and Nation: A Comparison of the United States, South Africa, and Brazil.* New York: Cambridge University Press.

Merton, R. K. (1972). Insiders and Outsiders: A Chapter in the Sociology of Knowledge. *American Journal of Sociology 78*(1), 9–47.

Nash, G. (1999). *Forbidden Love: The Secret History of Mixed-Race America.* New York: Henry Holt.

Nussbaum, M. C. (1997). *Cultivating Humanity: A Class Defense of Reform in Liberal Education.* Cambridge: Harvard University Press.

Ovando, C. J., & McLaren, P. (Eds.). (2000). *The Politics of Multiculturalism and Bilingual Education.* New York: McGraw-Hill.

Pallas, A. M., Natriello, G., & McDill, E. L. (1989). The Changing Nature of the Disadvantaged Population: Current Dimensions and Future Trends. *Educational Researcher 18*(5), 16–22.

Philip, N. (1996). *Earth Always Endures: Native American Poems.* New York: Viking.

Pinar, W. F., Reynolds, W. M., Slattery, P., & Taubman, P. M. (1995). *Understanding Curriculum: An Introduction to the Study of Historical and Contemporary Curriculum Discourses.* New York: Peter Lang.

Pratt, R. (Ed.). (2000). *The Condition of Education, 2000.* Washington, DC: U.S. Government Printing Office.

Riche, M. F. (2000). *America's Diversity and Growth: Signposts for the 21st Century.* Washington, DC: Population Reference Bureau.

Root, M. P. P. (2001). *Love's Revolution: Interracial Marriage.* Philadelphia: Temple University Press.

Schmitt, E. (2001, April 1). U.S. Now More Diverse, Ethnically and Racially. *New York Times,* p. 1, 20ff.

Takaki, R. (1998). *A Larger Memory: A History of Our Diversity, with Voices.* New York: Little Brown.

Takashima, S. (1971). *A Child in Prison Camp.* Montreal, Canada: Tundra Books.

Terry, D. (2000, August 11). U.S. Child Poverty Rate Fell as Economy Grew, But Is above 1979 Level. *New York Times,* p. A10.

Tetreault, M. K. (2001). Classrooms for Diversity: Rethinking Curriculum and Pedagogy. In J. A. Banks & C. A. M. Banks (Eds.), *Multicultural Education: Issues and Perspectives* (4th ed., pp. 152–173). New York: John Wiley & Sons.

Thernstrom, S., Orlov, A., & Handlin, O. (Eds.). (1980). *Harvard Encyclopedia of American Ethnic Groups.* Cambridge: Harvard University Press.

Uchida, Y. (1982). *Desert Exile: The Uprooting of a Japanese-American Family.* Seattle: University of Washington Press.

U.S. Census Bureau. (2000). *Statistical Abstract of the United States* (120th ed.). Washington, DC: U.S. Government Printing Office.

U.S. Census Bureau. (2001). [On-line]. Available: *http://www.census.gov/*

U.S. Immigration and Naturalization Service. (2000). *Statistical Yearbook of the Immigration and Naturalization Service, 1998.* Washington, DC: U.S. Government Printing Office.

Webster's Third New International Dictionary. (1986). (Unabridged). Springfield, MA: Merriam-Webster.

Winant, H. (1994). *Racial Conditions: Politics, Theory, Comparisons.* Minneapolis: University of Minnesota Press.

ANNOTATED BIBLIOGRAPHY

Banks, J. A. (2002). *An Introduction to Multicultural Education* (3rd ed.). Boston: Allyn and Bacon.

This brief book introduces preservice and practicing education to the major issues and concepts in multicultural education. It includes sample lessons, an evaluation checklist, and a bibliography.

Banks, J. A. (2001). *Cultural Diversity and Education: Foundations, Curriculum and Teaching* (4th ed.). Boston: Allyn and Bacon.

This book discusses the historical, conceptual, and philosophical issues in multicultural education. It includes an important chapter on "Reducing Prejudice in Students: Theory, Research, and Strategies."

Banks, J. A., & Banks, C. A. M. (Eds.). (2001). *Handbook of Research on Multicultural Education.* San Francisco: Jossey-Bass.

In 47 chapters and 882 pages, the leading scholars in multicultural education and related disciplines discuss the history, philosophy, practice, and future of the field. An important reference book for libraries and staff-development collections.

Banks, J. A., & Banks, C. A. M. (Eds.). (2001). *Multicultural Education: Issues and Perspectives* (4th ed.). New York: John Wiley & Sons.

A group of scholars in multicultural education discuss educational issues and strategies related to ethnicity, race, gender, social class, religion, and exceptionality in this introduction to multicultural education.

Banks, J. A., Cookson, P., Gay, G., Hawley, W. D., Irvine, J. I., Nieto, S., Schofield, J. W., & Stephan, W. G. (2001). *Diversity within Unity: Essential Principles for Teaching and*

Learning in a Multicultural Society. Seattle: Center for Multicultural Education, University of Washington.

This publication describes twelve research-based principles that can be used to create school environments that reflect the diversity within U.S. society. It can be downloaded as a pdf file. Print copies can be ordered from the Center. See the Center for Multicultural Education Web site: http://depts.washington.edu/centerme/home.htm

Beykont, A. F. (Ed.). (2000). *Lifting Every Voice: Pedagogy and Politics of Bilingualism.* Cambridge, MA: Harvard Education Publishing Group.

This book consists of an informative and thoughtful collection of essays on teaching and learning a second language.

Bigelow, B., & Peterson, B. (Eds.). (1998). *Rethinking Columbus: The Next 500 Years.* Milwaukee, WI: Rethinking Schools.

An excellent and thought-provoking selection of articles and documents that can be used to teach about Columbus, using a transformative approach.

hooks, b. (1994). *Teaching to Transgress: Education as the Practice of Freedom.* New York: Routledge.

bell hooks, the noted African American feminist, describes education as the practice of freedom in this book that describes a liberating pedagogy, a powerful strategy for multicultural teaching.

Loewen, J. W. (1995). *Lies My Teacher Told Me: Everything Your American History Textbook Got Wrong.* New York: The New Press.

The author critiques twelve leading high school American history textbooks and gives his own perspective on historical events.

Smelser, N. J., Wilson, W. J., & Mitchell, F. (Eds.). (2001). *America Becoming: Racial Trends and Their Consequences,* Vols. 1 and 2. Washington, DC: National Academy Press.

This two-volume work is an excellent and comprehensive source for information about immigration trends and the social, economic, and political developments of the various U.S. ethnic groups.

Takaki, R. (1993). *A Different Mirror: A History of Multicultural America.* Boston: Little, Brown.

Takaki provides new perspectives on the development of America that are important for teachers and students.

Todorov, T. (1982). *The Conquest of America: The Question of the Other.* New York: HarperCollins.

A thoughtful and informative book that provides perceptive insights into Columbus, Cortés, and the concept of the "Other." An important book for gaining a new perspective on America.

Van Ausdale, D., & Feagin, J. R. (2001). *The First R: How Children Learn Race and Racism.* Lanham, MD: Rowman & Littlefield.

An informative book about children's racial attitudes that includes an excellent review of the research on children's racial attitudes.

Wilkins, R. (2001). *Jefferson's Pillow: The Founding Fathers and the Dilemma of Black Patriotism.* Boston: Beacon Press.

The author describes how the founding fathers wrote about freedom and justice while, at the same time, owning slaves and internalizing the institutionalized racism of their culture and time.

2 Developing a Conceptual Multicultural Curriculum

The key goal of the multicultural curriculum should be to help students develop decision-making and citizen-action skills. The decision-making process consists of several components, including knowledge, values, the synthesis of knowledge and values, and action designed to implement the decision made. However, the knowledge that comprises reflective decision making must have certain characteristics. It must be scientific, higher-level, conceptual, and interdisciplinary. Reflective decision makers must identify the sources of their values, determine how these values conflict, identify value alternatives, and choose freely from among the alternatives. They act only after identifying alternative courses of action, ordering them according to personal values, and expressing a willingness to accept the possible consequences of their actions.

This chapter focuses on the knowledge components of decision making. A presentation of the interdisciplinary conceptual approach is followed by a discussion of four categories of knowledge: *facts, concepts, generalizations,* and *theories.* You must be able to identify the categories of knowledge in order to structure interdisciplinary and conceptual lessons and units. Chapter 3 discusses concepts you can use to organize multicultural lessons and units. The valuing and social action components of the multicultural curriculum are discussed in Chapter 4. Key issues related to the selection and evaluation of multicultural teaching materials are also discussed in Chapter 4.

The Interdisciplinary–Conceptual Approach

A decision-making curriculum is not only characterized by the sequential development of higher-level ideas; it is also *interdisciplinary.* In such a curriculum, concepts, when feasible and appropriate, are viewed from the perspectives of several disciplines and subject areas, such as the various social sciences, art, music, literature, physical education, communication, the physical and biological sciences, and mathematics.

It is necessary for students to view events and situations from the perspectives of several disciplines because any one discipline gives them only a partial understanding of issues and concepts related to ethnic and cultural diversity in society. Concepts such as *discrimination* and *ethnic diversity* are not merely sociological; they also have multiple dimensions. They have economic, political, legal, cultural, and moral aspects. The values and experiences of people of color are reflected in their literature, art, music, drama, dance, communication styles, and foods. Dominant ethnic groups within a society also express issues related to ethnic diversity and respond to these issues in their artistic and cultural forms. Students must view concepts and issues related to ethnic groups from diverse disciplinary perspectives in order to gain a complete understanding of the experiences of the diverse cultural and ethnic groups in the United States and the world.

Studying Culture: An Example of the Interdisciplinary–Conceptual Approach

When students study a concept such as *culture,* they can gain a comprehensive understanding only by viewing ethnic cultures from the perspectives of the various social sciences and by examining the expressions of ethnic cultures in literature, music, drama, dance, art, communication, and foods. Content and insights from science and mathematics can also be incorporated into an interdisciplinary study of cultures. The next section discusses special issues involved in incorporating science and mathematics into the multicultural curriculum.

Concepts such as *culture* can be used to organize units and activities related to ethnicity that are interdisciplinary and cut across disciplinary lines. Other concepts, such as cultural assimilation, acculturation, and values, can also be analyzed and studied from an interdisciplinary perspective. However, it is neither possible nor desirable to teach each concept in the curriculum from the perspectives of all disciplines and curricular areas. Such an attempt would result in artificial relationships and superficial learnings by students.

There are many excellent opportunities within the curriculum for teaching concepts from an interdisciplinary perspective. Interdisciplinary teaching, however, requires the strong cooperation of teachers in the various content areas. Team teaching will often be necessary, especially at the high school level, to organize and implement interdisciplinary units and lessons. Table 2.1 contains key questions that students can pursue when they study cultures from an interdisciplinary perspective. Figure 2.1 illustrates the process.

Incorporating Elements from Science and Mathematics into the Multicultural Curriculum

Incorporating elements from science and mathematics into the multicultural curriculum is difficult for most teachers. Issues related to science and mathematics can be incorporated into the multicultural curriculum in at least three

TABLE 2.1 **Studying Ethnic Cultures from an Interdisciplinary Perspective**

Discipline or Curriculum Area	Key or Focus Question
Social Studies	In what ways are the cultures of ethnic groups such as African Americans, Jewish Americans, and Mexican Americans similar and different? Why?
Reading and Literature	How do the fiction and other literary works by American ethnic authors reveal characteristics and components of their cultures?
Music	What does the music of an ethnic group reveal about its values, symbols, and culture?
Drama	What do plays written by ethnic authors reveal about their culture?
Physical Education	How do ethnic groups express their cultures, values, aspirations, and frustrations in their dances and creative movements?
Art	What does the art of an ethnic group reveal about its lifestyles, perceptions, values, history, and culture?
Communication (Language Arts)	How does the language of an ethnic group express and reflect its values and culture? What can we learn about an ethnic group by studying its symbols and communication styles, both verbal and nonverbal?
Home Economics	What do ethnic foods reveal about an ethnic group's values and culture? What can we learn about an ethnic culture by studying its foods?
Science	How do the physical characteristics of an ethnic group influence its interactions with other groups, intragroup relationships, and its total culture?
Mathematics	What is the relationship between the number system used within a society and its culture? What do the symbol systems within a culture reveal about it? Historically, what contributions have different ethnic groups made to our number system?

ways: (1) ways related to content; (2) ways related to perspectives, paradigms, and concepts; and (3) ways related to equity issues (Atwater, 1994; Banks, 1995; Secada, 1992; Secada, Fennema, & Adajian, 1995).

Some content related to science and mathematics can be incorporated into the multicultural curriculum. In science, the biological basis of skin color and

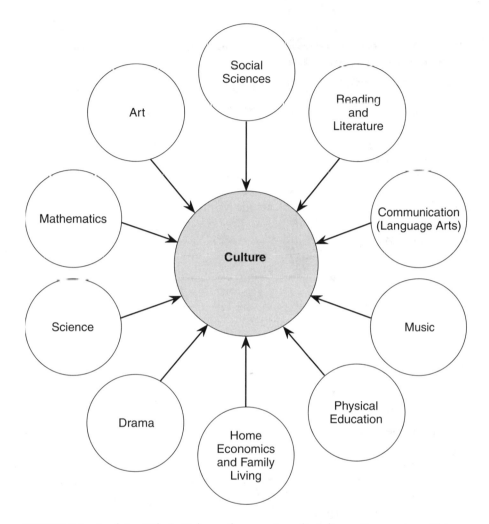

FIGURE 2.1   Studying Ethnic Cultures from an Interdisciplinary Perspective   This figure illustrates how a concept such as *culture* can be viewed from the perspectives of a number of disciplines and areas. Any one discipline gives only a partial understanding of a concept, social problem, or issue. Thus, multicultural units and lessons should be interdisciplinary and cut across disciplinary lines.

the other physical characteristics of various racial groups can be studied. However, when the biological basis of race is studied, students should be helped to understand that race is largely a *socially constructed* concept or category even though scientists have attempted to formulate different racial categories (Banks, 1995; Gould, 1996; Harding, 1998; Selden, 1999). Health issues and diseases related to various ethnic groups are other appropriate subjects for science in the multicultural curriculum.

The experience of various ethnic and cultural groups in science, in both past and contemporary society, is another appropriate study for science in the multicultural curriculum. The lives of African American scientists such as Daniel Hale Williams and Ernest E. Just should be examined in the scientific component of the multicultural curriculum. These individuals made significant contributions to science despite the blatant discrimination they experienced. Contemporary scientists from diverse groups should also be studied.

Content related to mathematics in the multicultural curriculum can highlight the role played by groups such as the Egyptians and Aztecs in the development of theory and practice in mathematics (Mason, 1962; Sertima, 1986). In the film *Stand and Deliver,* Mr. Escalante uses his knowledge of Aztec contributions to mathematics to motivate his Mexican American students to study calculus. Mr. Escalante reminds his students that their ancestors, the Aztecs, made significant mathematical breakthroughs. Students can also examine the experiences of mathematicians today from various cultural and racial groups.

Another important way to view science and mathematics in the multicultural curriculum is to examine the basic concepts, paradigms, and perspectives used in science and mathematics and the influence these paradigms, concepts, and perspectives have had and still have on various ethnic and cultural groups (Banks, 1995; Gould, 1996; Harding, 1998; Selden, 1999). This can be done more readily in science than in mathematics. Darwin's theory of evolution as well as other scientific theories—such as the genetic theory of intelligence—have historically been used, and are being used today, to support scientific racism (Gould, 1996; Herrnstein & Murray, 1994). Students can examine scientific racism from both a historical and contemporary perspective (Banks, 1995).

Levins and Lewontin, using a Marxist dialectic, argue that scientists act within a social context and from a philosophical perspective that is inherently political (1985). Students can examine the Levins and Lewontin thesis and determine the extent to which it is applicable to their science textbooks and readings. Students can also study such questions as these: What major assumptions, concepts, and perspectives do scientists use today that are related to the experiences of ethnic groups? What major influence are these assumptions, concepts, and perspectives having on the experiences of ethnic groups? Students can also examine how applied mathematics is being used to influence societal issues and practices.

When examining how scientists have constructed ideas about the low IQs of African Americans and other ethnic groups historically and today, the students can examine the arguments set forth by Herrnstein and Murray in *The Bell Curve* (1994) about the inferior intellectual abilities of Blacks and can discuss questions such as these: Why did Herrnstein and Murray create their theory? What groups in society benefit from it? What groups in society are hurt by it? Why are theories such as the one by Herrnstein and Murray created and popularized by the mass media when many scientists have serious doubts about them? The students can read critiques of the Herrnstein and Murray theory in *The Bell Curve Debate,* edited by Jacoby and Glauberman (1995).

A third, and perhaps the most important, way in which science and mathematics teachers can include multicultural content in their curricula is by examining equity issues in science and mathematics and by modifying their teaching techniques and expectations in order to enhance the academic achievement of students of color and of women. Researchers have indicated that students of color and female students often do not achieve as well as White males in higher-level mathematics and science courses (Belenky, Clinchy, Goldberger, & Tarule, 1986).

Students of color and female students also take fewer high-level mathematics and science courses than do White males. Researchers have suggested that these situations result in part from low teacher expectations and from the teaching styles used in science and mathematics courses that are inconsistent with how many students of color and female students learn (Belenky, Clinchy, Goldberger, & Tarule, 1986; Cohen & Lotan, 1997). To make their teaching multicultural, science and mathematics teachers should encourage their students of color and their female students to enroll in higher-level courses, provide these students with support and encouragement, and modify their teaching techniques to make them more consistent with the learning styles of students of color and female students. Fullilove and Treisman (1990) have found that cooperative teaching and learning strategies can help students of color to learn advanced calculus.

The Forms of Knowledge

I have illustrated how a key concept such as culture can be viewed from diverse disciplinary perspectives. To identify and select key concepts such as culture, you must be familiar with the nature of knowledge and its various forms: *facts, concepts, generalizations,* and *theories.* These major knowledge forms and the contribution that each can make to an interdisciplinary and conceptual multicultural curriculum are discussed next.

Facts

Facts are low-level, specific empirical statements about limited phenomena. Facts may be considered the lowest level of knowledge, and they have the least predictive capacity of all of the knowledge forms. In multicultural studies, as in all academic areas and disciplines, facts are the building blocks of knowledge. Students must master facts in order to learn higher levels of knowledge. Examples of facts are:

- The Chinese immigrants who came to San Francisco in the 1800s established the *hui kuan.*

- More than 131,600 legal immigrants came to the United States from Mexico in 1998.
- Between 1991 and 1998, 7,605,000 legal immigrants from Europe settled in the United States.

A careful study of these facts about U.S. ethnic groups reveals several characteristics of factual statements. First, facts are *empirical* statements, or statements that can be tested with available data or data that can be obtained. By carefully studying and analyzing historical documents and statistical data, a social scientist can determine whether the Chinese immigrants who came to the United States in the 1800s actually established *hui kuan* societies. It is important to stress that factual statements are capable of verification or testing; however, many statements presented as facts, especially in multicultural studies, are, on closer scrutiny, normative or value statements that cannot be tested or can be tested only with great difficulty. An example of such a statement is "Indians were hostile." This statement is actually a misleading stereotype masquerading as a factual statement.

Because factual statements are limited in explaining causal relationships, students need to master higher levels of knowledge in addition to facts. Facts should not be the end goal of instruction because they are very limited. Many teachers end units by testing students primarily for their mastery of facts. Because facts, in and of themselves, do not encompass a large quantity of data, they have little transfer value, are quickly forgotten by students, and do not, if they are the end goal of instruction, help students to gain in-depth understandings of society.

However, to say that facts are limited in the contribution they can make to students' understanding of social events and problems is not to say that they are not important and that they do not have a proper role in instruction—quite the contrary. Factual statements are important in teaching. If you keep their limitations in mind and use them judiciously, they can contribute to student learning. Facts are the foundations of the higher levels of knowledge: *concepts, generalizations,* and *theories.* Without learning facts, as I later illustrate, students will not be able to master concepts and generalizations. However, you are justified in teaching facts only if they are used to help students develop higher forms of knowledge or to make decisions. Thus, for every fact you select for inclusion in the curriculum, you should have a concept, generalization, or theory in mind that the fact is intended to help the students develop. Facts taught randomly and in isolation have little instructional value. Yet, they can become powerful instructional tools if they are carefully selected and taught.

Concepts

Concepts are words or phrases that enable us to categorize or classify a large class of observations and thus to reduce the complexity of our environment. In structure and function, concepts differ from facts, generalizations, and theories. Both facts and generalizations are empirical *statements;* a theory consists of a system of interrelated generalizations and principles. However, concepts are special constructs because they are necessary for the formulation of the other categories of knowledge and are contained in all facts, generalizations, and theories. Because concepts are contained in all other forms of knowledge, students cannot understand a fact, generalization, or theory unless the concepts contained within them are meaningful.

The following are some of the key concepts discussed in Chapter 3:

Cultural assimilation   Immigration
Acculturation   Power
Race   Values
Culture

Even though concepts are contained in all facts, generalizations, and theories, they are unique because they can also encompass a large range of facts and generalizations. A complete theory can be formulated about a single concept, such as cultural assimilation or discrimination. Some concepts are rather concrete, such as *street;* others are more abstract, such as *megalopolis.* Some concepts, such as *city,* are somewhere between these two extremes. We might call these kinds of concepts *intermediate-level* concepts. Thus, if we arrange these concepts into a hierarchy, it would look like this:

megalopolis
city
street

In this example, *megalopolis* is the highest-level concept because it consists of a region made up of several cities and their surrounding areas. *City* is the next-level concept because a city contains many streets. Of course, there are parallel concepts that are more concrete than *street.*

Concepts encompassing generalizations are often more abstract (or at a higher level) than are concepts that are contained in the generalizations encompassed. Also, the concepts contained in facts are often less abstract than those used to classify those facts. The same is true for theories. The example below illustrates how a higher-level concept, *immigration,* can be used to categorize a number of facts. The facts, of course, contain many concepts.

HIGHER-LEVEL CONCEPT

Immigration
Facts being categorized or grouped under concept:

- Between 1820 and 1979, 36,267,000 European immigrants came to the United States.
- By 1860, there were 34,933 Chinese in the United States.

- In 1900, 24,326 Japanese lived in the United States.
- Between 1991 and 1996, 236,500 people from India immigrated to the United States.

Higher-level concepts can also encompass or classify generalizations (see discussion below for definition of a generalization). In the next example, the concept *culture* is used to categorize a number of generalizations at varying levels of abstraction.

CONCEPT

Culture

Generalizations being categorized or grouped under concept:

- An ethnic minority group usually acquires some of the values, behaviors, and beliefs of the dominant ethnic groups within a society.
- Dominant ethnic groups usually acquire some of the cultural characteristics of ethnic minority groups.
- African Americans have made a number of contributions to American music.

In many cases, some concepts are clearly at a higher level than are others. For example, city is a higher-level concept than street because a city contains many streets. However, because a concept appears in a factual statement does not necessarily mean that it is a lower-level or concrete concept. Study this factual statement:

More than 36,000 Chinese immigrants arrived in the United States in 1998.

This factual statement contains the higher-level concept, *immigrant*. As previously illustrated, the concept *immigration* can be used to categorize a number of facts. The distinguishing characteristic of a higher-level concept is that it can categorize a number of facts and generalizations. This is true even though that same concept may sometimes appear within factual statements. By identifying higher-level concepts, you will be able to help students relate discrete facts and data to form generalizations about ethnicity, which they can apply when studying ethnic and cultural groups both within the United States and in other nations. Table 2.2 illustrates how key concepts can be used to do a comparative study of ethnic groups within the United States and in other nations.

Table 2.3 illustrates one strategy for teaching a concept. This strategy is called "Lesson Plan for Attaining a Concept." Try teaching this lesson to a group of students or to a group of your classmates or colleagues in your workshop. After teaching this lesson, respond to this question: What are the advantages of using a conceptual approach to teaching?

TABLE 2.2   A Comparative Study of Ethnic Groups in Different Nations

Key Concepts and Related Key Questions	Filipino Americans (USA)	British Pakistanis	French Canadians	Nigerian Ibos	Mexican Indians	French Algerians
Origins Is the group native or did it migrate or immigrate to its current location? If an immigrant group, what caused the immigration?						
Discrimination Is the group experiencing discrimination? If so, what kinds? If not, why not?						
Culture What are the group's unique cultural and ethnic characteristics?						
Assimilation To what extent is the group assimilated both culturally and structurally?						
Economic Status Is the group facing economic problems or does it have a secure economic status?						

(continued)

TABLE 2.2 Continued

Key Concepts and Related Key Questions	Filipino Americans (USA)	British Pakistanis	French Canadians	Nigerian Ibos	Mexican Indians	French Algerians
Education Are the group's youths experiencing problems in the schools? Why or why not?						
Power What role does the group play in the political system? Has it been able to organize and to exercise political power effectively?						
Ethnic Revitalization Is the group experiencing or has it experienced an ethnic revitalization movement? Explain.						

42

TABLE 2.3   Lesson Plan for Attaining a Concept

1. Write "Rite of Passage" on the board. Ask the students to repeat the words.

2. List these examples of rites of passage on the board and tell the students, "These are examples of rites of passage":

Marriage ceremony

Christening ceremony

Funeral

Vision quest among the Zuni Indians

Baptism

Bar Mitzvah

Bas Mitzvah

3. Ask the students to describe what these examples of the concept have in common. Put the list on the board.

4. Help the students to identify and state the critical attributes of "rite of passage."

5. Ask the students to write a definition of *rite of passage* using the list of key attributes that they formulated above. Their definitions should be a variation of this one: "Ceremonies that mark a critical transition in the life of an individual from one phase of the life cycle to another."*

Follow-up Activity: Ask the students to interview parents and other family members to find out what rites of passages have taken place in their families. Ask them to share at least one family rite of passage in which they have participated or observed. Ask the students: "What important functions do rites of passage play for individuals, families, and societies?"

*This definition is from Theodorson, G. A., & Theodorson, A. G. (1979). *A Modern Dictionary of Sociology.* New York: Barnes and Noble, p. 350.

Generalizations

A generalization contains two or more concepts and states the relationship between them. Like empirical facts, generalizations are scientific statements that can be tested and verified with data. Generalizations are useful tools in instruction because they can be used to summarize a large mass of facts and to show the relationship between higher-level concepts that students have mastered. Like concepts, generalizations vary greatly in their level of inclusiveness. There are low-level generalizations, which are little more than summary statements, and there are high-level generalizations, which are universal in applicability. To illustrate levels of generalizations, we study one fact listed earlier in this chapter and state generalizations at various levels that encompass it.

FACT:
The Chinese immigrants who came to San Francisco in the 1800s established the *hui kuan*.

Lower-Level Generalization:
Chinese immigrants in America established various forms of social organizations.

Intermediate-Level Generalization:
All groups that have immigrated to the United States have established social organizations.

Highest-Level or Universal Generalization:
In all human societies, forms of social organizations are created to satisfy the needs of individuals and groups.

A study of these examples indicates that a generalization is a higher-level statement than a fact because a generalization encompasses a number of facts. The fact noted above tells us only that Chinese Americans established one kind of social organization, the *hui kuan*. The lower-level generalization in our example reveals that Chinese Americans established a variety of social organizations. Thus, the lower-level generalization encompasses not only the fact about the *hui kuan* but also the following facts:

- Chinese immigrants in America formed organizations called "clans."
- The Chinese Benevolent Association is a confederation of clans and secret societies.
- Secret societies emerged within Chinese communities in the United States.
- The Chinese secret societies provided help to Chinese Americans and obtained control of gambling in Chinese American communities.

The next generalization in the example—an intermediate-level generalization—encompasses facts not only about Chinese Americans but also about all immigrants and migrants in the United States. Thus, this generalization is at a higher level of abstraction because it encompasses more facts than the lower-level generalization. For example, the intermediate-level generalization, in addition to encompassing the facts about Chinese American organizations, encompasses the following facts:

- Puerto Ricans established the Puerto Rican Forum to help solve the problems of Puerto Rican migrants in New York City.
- Jewish Americans founded the Anti-Defamation League of B'nai B'rith to help mitigate anti-Semitism in the United States.
- In 1921, Spanish-speaking Americans formed the *Orden Hijos de America* (Order of the Sons of America) to train its members for U.S. citizenship.

- Japanese immigrants in America created the Japanese Association to provide services for its members.
- The National Urban League was founded in 1911 to help African American southern migrants adjust to city life.

The last generalization is the highest form of generalization possible because it encompasses all the other facts and generalizations above it, and it applies to all human societies in the past and present. Note that it does not contain a reference to any particular people, region, or culture. One way to determine whether a generalization is written at the highest possible level is to ascertain whether it is limited to a particular people, culture, or historical era. A generalization of wide applicability contains few or no exceptions and can be tested and verified, to varying degrees, within any human culture. The highest-level generalization in the example states that in every past and present human society, one can find examples of social organizations. This generalization has been tested and verified by social scientists. Whether they studied a preliterate tribe in New Zealand or the cultures in Medieval Europe, social scientists found types of social organizations such as the family and some kind of kinship system. It is true that the forms these organizations take vary greatly both within and between cultures, but nevertheless they exist.

It is necessary for you to be able to identify and write generalizations at various levels in order to incorporate ethnic content into the curriculum. During initial planning, you should identify generalizations of the highest order so that you can then select content samples from a variety of cultures to enable students to test them. If you start planning by identifying lower-level or intermediate-level generalizations, you will be greatly limited in the content that you can select to exemplify the generalizations. For example:

Chinese immigrants in America established various forms of social organization.

If you selected this generalization to organize instruction, you would not be able to help students derive generalizations related to the organizations that other ethnic groups, such as Anglo-Saxon Protestants, Mexican Americans, Jewish Americans, and Arab Americans, have formed in the United States.

You should begin planning by identifying high-level concepts and generalizations (often called key or organizing generalizations in this book) and then should select lower-level concepts and generalizations related to the chosen content *samples*. This type of planning is necessary in order to help students develop higher-level statements, one of the ultimate goals of instruction. Chapter 4 discusses procedures you can use to identify high-level concepts and generalizations that can form the core of a sound multicultural curriculum.

We have noted that generalizations range from the concrete to those that are universal in application. A fact related to a Chinese American institution, the *hui kuan,* was chosen to illustrate how a single fact can be encompassed by generalizations at three different levels. The choice of three levels was an arbitrary decision; generalizations at fewer or more levels could have easily been written. For example, Hilda Taba has identified four levels (or orders, as she calls them) of generalizations (Taba, Durkin, Fraenkel, & McNaughton, 1971). Because generalizations exist at many different levels, it is not necessary for you to spend undue time trying to devise elaborate schemes for classifying levels of generalizations.

However, to plan effective units and lessons, you should know that generalizations exist at many different levels, that all generalizations are at a higher level than facts, and that the highest-order or -level generalizations should be identified during the initial stages of unit planning.

Earlier in this chapter, I said that a generalization is a statement capable of being tested or verified. This is true; but because human behavior is so complex, generalizations in the social and behavioral sciences are always tentative statements and can never be proven to be 100% correct. Almost always, social science generalizations will have some exceptions. Because social science generalizations tend to be tentative and nonconclusive, they often contain qualifying words.

Study this generalization: *(When an ethnic minority group is oppressed and it sees no legitimate ways to alleviate its problems, rebellions will sometimes occur.)* The word *sometimes* qualifies this generalization because in many situations an ethnic minority group may feel oppressed and see no legitimate ways to alleviate its problems, yet ethnic rebellions may not occur. Japanese Americans, when they were forced to leave their homes during World War II and were sent to internment camps, did not resist or rebel as a group, although some individuals did resist internment. One social scientist has hypothesized that most Japanese Americans cooperated with the federal government because of the norms within their culture toward authority and because they did not believe that resistance would succeed (Kitano, 1976). On the other hand, many African Americans who felt oppressed in U.S. cities in the late 1960s violently rebelled. The particular times, the culture of a group, and the group's perceptions of its social and economic status greatly influence how it will respond to an oppressive situation. This example is used merely to illustrate that students should be taught how tentative social science conclusions and generalizations are and *should learn that social knowledge is constantly changing and is never absolute.*

Generalizations are important in instruction because they enable students to make predictions; the predictive capacity of generalizations varies directly with their degree of applicability and amount of empirical support. Generalizations that describe a large class of behaviors and that have been widely verified are the most useful for making predictions. We have called these types of generalizations *high-level* or *organizing* generalizations. Generalizations enable students not only to predict behavior with a fairly high degree of accuracy, but also to solve problems in novel situations.

Theory

Theory is the highest form of knowledge and is the most useful for predicting human behavior. I stated that a *concept* is a word or phrase used to categorize or classify facts, data, and other forms of information and knowledge. A *generalization* is a statement that shows the relationship between two or more concepts that can be empirically verified. A review of the definitions of these terms is important because a theory consists of a number of interrelated generalizations. The generalizations within a theory constitute a deductive system and are logically interrelated. The generalizations contained within a theory are also high-level and *universal-type* generalizations; they are not low-level ones. A theory is called a *deductive* system because when several generalizations within a theory are stated, the concluding ones can be logically derived. In other words, when given some propositions within a theory, a conclusion can be derived from the stated generalizations. An empirical theory has the following characteristics:

- It consists of a set of interrelated lawlike propositions or generalizations that are testable.
- The propositions must show the relationship between variables or concepts that are clearly defined.
- The propositions must constitute a deductive system and be logically consistent: unknown principles must be derivable from known ones.
- The propositions must be a source of testable hypotheses.

The following example of a theory illustrates how the deductive process works. Gordon's (1964) theory of cultural and structural assimilation has heavily influenced the field of ethnic studies. Here are the four major generalizations within this theory:

1. With regard to *cultural behavior*, differences of social class are more important and decisive than are differences of ethnic group.

2. With regard to *social participation* in primary groups and primary relationships, people tend to confine these to their own social class segment within their own ethnic group, that is, the *ethclass*.

3. With a person of the same social class but of a different ethnic group, one shares behavioral similarities but not a sense of peoplehood.

4. With those of the same ethnic group but of a different social class one shares a sense of *peoplehood* but not behavioral similarities (pp. 52–53; emphases added).

Gordon's theory satisfies our criterion of a theory: *a system of high-level interrelated generalizations that constitute a deductive system.* In the first generalization in the theory, Gordon hypothesizes that in terms of cultural behavior, social class is more important than ethnicity. By cultural behavior, he means such things as the values a person holds, his or her speech patterns, and occupational aspirations.

This generalization suggests that an upper-class African American individual's clothing, values, and foods are likely to be more similar to those of an upper-class White than to those of a lower-class African American. The second generalization in the theory suggests that an upper-class Mexican American, while sharing cultural characteristics with White Anglo-Saxons, is more likely to participate in the private clubs and cliques of other upper-class Mexican Americans than in Anglo-Saxon private clubs and social cliques. The theory hypothesizes that even though upper-status individuals within different ethnic groups share similar values and behavior, their close, primary group relationships are largely confined to members within their ethnic groups of the same social class. This is also true for lower-class members of ethnic groups. Gordon presents much compelling evidence in his book to support the generalizations that comprise his theory.

Gordon's theory (1964) meets the criterion of a theory because, when given generalizations one and two of his theory (presented above), one can logically derive generalizations three and four. To do so, however, it might be necessary to know how he defines two key concepts in his generalizations: *ethclass* and *sense of peoplehood*. He defines *ethclass* as the "subsociety created by the intersection of the vertical stratifications of ethnicity with the horizontal stratifications of social class" (pp. 52–53). Thus, lower-middle-class Vietnamese Americans constitute an ethclass. By *sense of peoplehood*, Gordon means "an individual's identification with a group that shares a common culture, religious beliefs, and values" (p. 23). He contends, for example, that African Americans in all social classes share an ethnic identification.

Grand and Middle-Range Theories

Social science has few *grand* theories. Grand theories try to explain all of behavior. Freudian psychology is an example of a grand theory in social science. As Merton (1968) points out, most theories in social science are what he calls "theories of the middle range." Gordon's theory is middle range because it tries to explain only behavior related to cultural assimilation. Although Gordon's theory of assimilation has much explanatory power, it was created almost forty years ago; ethnic and race relations have changed in significant ways since Gordon first constructed his theory. Gordon's theory needs to be examined in light of new findings and studies in social science. Heath and McLaughlin (1993), for example, found that, for many of the teenagers they studied, ethnicity or race was not their primary or most important identity. These youth often formed social groupings that cut across racial and ethnic lines.

Using Theories in Teaching

To help students fully understand the ethnic experience in the United States, you should, whenever possible, help them relate generalizations to a theoretical system. Generalizations have much more meaning when they are studied within a theoretical framework than when studied in isolation.

Because of their specialized structure and function, a complete theory can be structured around a single concept. Gordon's theory of *cultural and structural assimilation* is an example of a theory formed around the concept of assimilation. Cultural assimilation occurs when one ethnic group attains the values and behavior patterns of another ethnic group. Usually, the ethnic minority group attains the cultural characteristics of the dominant ethnic group. Structural assimilation occurs when one ethnic group participates in the primary groups, such as private clubs and social cliques, of another ethnic group (Gordon, 1964). Gordon concludes that, even though widespread cultural assimilation has taken place in U.S. society, little structural assimilation has occurred because ethnic groups within U.S. society, including dominant ethnic groups and people of color, participate mainly in the primary groups of their own ethnic communities. He maintains that our society has a high degree of cultural assimilation but is characterized by *structural pluralism*. Although Gordon's theory probably explains large classes of ethnic behavior in the United States, the research by Heath and McLaughlin (1993) indicates that his theory must be interpreted within the context of U.S. society in the twenty-first century.

An Effective Multicultural Curriculum

Major goals of an effective multicultural curriculum are to help students develop the ability to make reflective decisions on personal and public issues and to take successful action. Integrating the curriculum with ethnic content can be viewed as a process of curriculum reform. During this process, the entire curriculum is transformed to enable students to view events, concepts, and issues from diverse ethnic and cultural perspectives.

The multicultural curriculum is broadly conceptualized and includes the study of a wide range of ethnic groups. These groups are studied using a comparative approach. The multicultural curriculum is also conceptual and interdisciplinary. Major concepts, when feasible and appropriate, are studied from the perspectives of disciplines such as the various social sciences, art, literature, communication, and the physical and biological sciences. Figure 2.2 summarizes the characteristics of an effective multicultural curriculum. The next

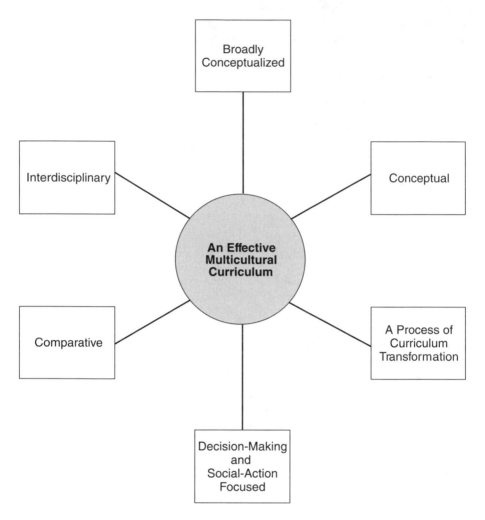

FIGURE 2.2   The Components of an Effective Multicultural Curriculum   The
effective multicultural curriculum must be conceptual, broadly conceptualized,
interdisciplinary, comparative, decision-making and social-action focused, and
viewed as a process of curriculum transformation.

chapter (Chapter 3) presents key concepts that can be used to plan and organize a multicultural curriculum.

Summary

The conceptual approach can best facilitate the integration of ethnic content
into the curriculum and into the various subject areas. Using this approach, the

teacher selects key concepts, such as culture, power, and discrimination, and then identifies content samples that can be used to help students attain these ideas. The conceptual approach allows the teacher to use content samples from several different disciplines and, thus, to teach in an interdisciplinary way.

When identifying concepts for a conceptual multicultural curriculum, you should make sure that a balanced approach is taken and that people of color are not depicted only or primarily as victims. They should also be described as people who helped to shape their own destinies, who built ethnic institutions, and who played major roles in attaining their civil rights. It is necessary to teach such concepts as prejudice, discrimination, and racism. However, it is also essential to teach such concepts as protest, empowerment, interracial cooperation, and ethnic institutions in order to portray a full and accurate view of the experiences of ethnic groups in the United States.

REFLECTION AND ACTION ACTIVITIES

1. Label each of the following a *fact, concept,* or *generalization* and justify each label:
   a. acculturation
   b. In every human society there is a conflict between unlimited wants and limited resources.
   c. assimilation
   d. In 1827 Vincente Guerrero became president of Mexico.
   e. Ethnic cultures, values, and behavior are undergoing constant change.
   f. On September 22, 1862, President Lincoln issued a statement that has been called the Preliminary Emancipation Proclamation.
   g. In 2000, Mexicans made up 58.5 percent of the Hispanic population in the United States.
   h. During the 1960s and 1970s, people of color strove less for cultural assimilation and more for cultural pluralism.
   i. cultural pluralism
   j. ethnic group

2. Here is a higher-level generalization: *Most foreigners who voluntarily immigrated to the United States were seeking better economic, political, and social opportunities.* Examine several of the books on ethnic groups contained in the bibliographies in Parts II–V and write several factual statements and lower-level generalizations that this generalization will encompass.

3. Examine several of the books in the bibliographies in Parts II–V and find a number of factual statements and generalizations that these concepts will encompass: cultural assimilation, structural assimilation, protest, discrimination.

4. Tell whether each of these statements is normative or empirical, and why:
   a. The American colonists should not have taken land away from the American Indians.
   b. Irresponsible African Americans rioted in many American cities in the 1960s.
   c. Many Mexican immigrants entered the United States illegally.
   d. Japanese Americans should not have been sent to relocation camps in 1942.

    e. Many Puerto Ricans migrate to the United States mainland each year.
    f. Many Chinese Americans live in ghettos in U.S. cities.

5. What do you think should be the role of the following categories of knowledge in a sound multicultural curriculum? Why?
    a. facts
    b. concepts
    c. generalizations
    d. theories

6. Examine several books dealing with people of color (see the annotated bibliographies in Parts II–V of this book) and identify a theory related to ethnic groups. Can this theory be taught to a group of elementary or high school students? Why or why not? If you think it can be taught to a group of students, develop a plan for teaching it. If you are a classroom teacher or a student teacher, implement your teaching plan and evaluate its effectiveness.

7. Make a list of your close friends. Note their *ethnic, religious,* and *racial backgrounds.* Compare your list with similar lists made by other individuals in your class or workshop. What conclusions can you make about structural assimilation in U.S. society on the basis of the responses made by you and your classmates or fellow workshop participants?

8. If your parents are first- or second-generation U.S. immigrants, make a list of their values and lifestyles that are different from your own. If your parents are not first- or second-generation immigrants, interview individuals whose parents are and compare their values and lifestyles with those of their parents. What tentative generalizations can you make about cultural assimilation in U.S. society by studying these data?

9. Define each of the following terms and tell why each is important:

knowledge	ethclass
reflective decision	cultural assimilation
fact	structural assimilation
concept	intermediate-level generalization
generalization	high-level generalization
theory	high-level concept
normative statement	low-level concept
empirical statement	

REFERENCES

Atwater, M. M. (1994). Research on Cultural Diversity in the Classroom. In D. L. Gabel (Eds.), *Handbook of Research on Science Teaching and Learning* (pp. 558–576). New York: Macmillan.

Banks, J. A. (1995). The Historical Reconstruction of Knowledge about Race: Implications for Transformative Teaching. *Educational Researcher, 24*(2), 15–25.

Banks, J. A. (2001). Multicultural Education: Historical Development, Dimensions, and Practice. In J. A. Banks & C. A. M. Banks (Eds.), *Handbook of Research on Multicultural Education* (pp. 3–24). San Francisco: Jossey-Bass.

Belenky, M. F., Clinchy, B. M., Goldberger, N. R., & Tarule, J. M. (1986). *Women's Ways of Knowing: The Development of Self, Voice, and Mind.* New York: Basic Books.

Cohen, E. G., & Lotan, R. A. (Eds.). (1997). *Working for Equity in Heterogeneous Classrooms.* New York: Teachers College Press.

Fullilove, R. E., & Treisman, P. U. (1990). Mathematics Achievement among African American Undergraduates at the University of California, Berkeley: An Evaluation of the Mathematics Workshop Program. *The Journal of Negro Education, 59*(3), 463–490.

Gordon, M. M. (1964). *Assimilation in American Life.* New York: Oxford University Press.

Gould, S. J. (1996). *The Mismeasure of Man* (Revised & expanded ed.). New York: Norton.

Harding, S. (1998). *Is Science Multicultural? Postcolonialisms, Feminisms, and Epistemologies.* Bloomington: Indiana University Press.

Heath, S. B., & McLaughlin, M. W. (Eds.). (1993). *Identity & Inner-City Youth: Beyond Ethnicity and Gender.* New York: Teachers College Press.

Herrnstein, R. J., & Murray, C. (1994). *The Bell Curve: Intelligence and Class Structure in American Life.* New York: The Free Press.

Jacoby, R., & Glauberman, N. (Eds.). (1995). *The Bell Curve Debate: History, Documents, Opinions.* New York: Times Books.

Kitano, H. H. L. (1976). *Japanese Americans: The Evolution of a Subculture* (2nd ed.). Englewood Cliffs, NJ: Prentice-Hall.

Levins, R., & Lewontin, R. (1985). *The Dialectical Biologist.* Cambridge: Harvard University Press.

Mason, S. F. (1962). *A History of the Sciences.* New York: Collier Books.

Merton, R. K. (1968). On Sociological Theories of the Middle Range. In R. K. Merton. *Social Theory and Social Structure* (Enlarged ed., pp. 39–72). New York: Free Press.

Secada, W. G. (1992). Race, Ethnicity, Social Class, Language, and Achievement in Mathematics. In D. Grouws (Ed.), *Handbook of Research on Mathematics Teaching and Learning* (pp. 623–660). New York: Macmillan.

Secada, W. G., Fennema, E., & Adajian, L. B. (Eds.). (1995). *New Directions for Equity in Mathematics Education.* New York: Cambridge University Press.

Selden, S. (1999). *Inheriting Shame: The Story of Eugenics and Racism in America.* New York: Teachers College Press.

Sertima, I. V. (Ed.). (1986). *Blacks in Science: Ancient and Modern.* New Brunswick, NJ: Transaction Books.

Taba, H., Durkin, M. C., Fraenkel, J. R., & McNaughton, A. H. (1971). *A Teacher's Handbook for Elementary School Studies: An Inductive Approach* (2nd ed.). Reading, MA: Addison-Wesley.

ANNOTATED BIBLIOGRAPHY

Banks, J. A., & Banks, C. A. M. (with Clegg, A. A., Jr.). (1999). *Teaching Strategies for the Social Studies: Decision-Making and Citizen Action* (5th ed.). Boston: Allyn and Bacon.

Chapter 3 of this book is a detailed discussion, with illustrations, of the nature and teaching of concepts, generalizations, and theories. Part IV discusses value inquiry, decision making, citizen action, and evaluation strategies.

Davidson, N. (Ed.). (1990). *Cooperative Learning in Mathematics: A Handbook for Teachers.* Menlo Park, CA: Addison-Wesley.

Research indicates that cooperative learning can enhance the academic achievement of some students of color. This book contains twelve articles that describe cooperative activities teachers can use in mathematics.

Secada, W. G., Fennema, E., & Adajian, L. B. (Eds.). (1995). *New Directions for Equity in Mathematics Education*. New York: Cambridge University Press.

An excellent and thoughtful collection of articles that discuss many different issues and programs related to increasing the achievement of ethnic minorities and women in mathematics.

Stephan, W. (1999). *Reducing Prejudice and Stereotyping in Schools*. New York: Teachers College Press.

An informative and research-based discussion of prejudice and stereotyping by one of the major researchers in the field.

Valdes, G. (2001). *Learning and Not Learning English: Latino Students in American Schools*. New York: Teachers College Press.

This sensitive and informative ethnographic study describes some of the major issues and problems related to the experiences of the increasing number of U.S. students who learn English as a second language.

Zinn, H. (2001). *Howard Zinn on History*. New York: Seven Stories Press.

An insightful collection of essays that challenge mainstream interpretations of U.S. history and provide a transformative perspective on American history.

3

Key Concepts for the Multicultural Curriculum

The multicultural curriculum should help students master higher levels of knowledge so that they can better understand race and ethnic relations and develop the skills and abilities needed to make reflective personal and public decisions. Sound multicultural lessons and units focus on higher-level concepts and generalizations and use facts primarily to help students master higher forms of knowledge and make decisions. Students must be able to make reflective decisions in order to take thoughtful personal, social, and civic action.

Criteria for Selecting Interdisciplinary Concepts

Within the various academic fields and disciplines is a wide range of concepts from which you might select when planning the multicultural curriculum. What criteria can you use when selecting concepts to organize multicultural units and lessons? First, you should consider whether the concept will help explain some significant aspect of the history, culture, and contemporary experiences of a range of ethnic groups in U.S. society. The experiences of ethnic groups in the United States have been characterized by a number of salient events, expressions, and themes, such as discrimination, protest and resistance, cultural assimilation, and acculturation. Consequently, these themes are highly appropriate organizing concepts for the multicultural curriculum.

Higher-level concepts that are capable of encompassing a wide range of data and information should also be selected for the multicultural curriculum. *Culture* is a more powerful concept than *language* because it can be used to organize and teach more information.

Concepts chosen for the multicultural curriculum should also be *interdisciplinary*. Interdisciplinary concepts are capable of encompassing facts, generalizations, and examples from several disciplines and areas. It is necessary to select interdisciplinary concepts because the curriculum should help students view and interpret events and situations from the perspectives of several disciplines. When students view events and situations from the perspective of a single discipline, they can acquire, at best, only a partial understanding of the event or situation they are studying.

When *social protest,* for example, is studied only from the perspective of political science, students learn that social protest occurs when alienated groups within a political system organize to push for political and social change. However, students need to study protest from other disciplinary perspectives to understand it fully (see Figure 3.1). During the civil rights movement of the 1960s, African Americans expressed protest not only in politics but also in their literature, songs, dances, art, and language. Thus, students need to examine social protest in these forms of communication to fully understand Black protest in the 1960s.

Some concepts are important to the structure of a particular discipline but cannot function successfully in an interdisciplinary role. Rhythm, melody, harmony, and tone color are important concepts in music. Key concepts in art include form, line, and shape. However, because these concepts are highly specific to their particular disciplines, they are not effective interdisciplinary concepts. However, both music and art, as well as dance and language, are forms of communication and culture. Music and art also have themes or convey central messages to the perceiver: so do a play, a dance, and many examples of human behavior. Consequently, communication, culture, and theme are effective interdisciplinary concepts because they can help students develop generalizations by studying examples drawn from the social sciences and the humanities.

When selecting organizing concepts for multicultural lessons, you should give some attention to the developmental level of your students. Young children can understand discrimination easier than they can understand institutionalized racism, in part because almost every child has been the victim of some kind of discrimination. He or she may have been the new child in the classroom, may be fat or thin, or may have had some other characteristic that other students singled out for ridicule. Young children can also understand discrimination more easily than institutionalized racism because discrimination is a more well-defined, less abstract, and less ambiguous concept than is institutionalized racism.

In the primary and middle school grades, you should focus on concepts that can be taught using concrete examples, such as similarities, differences, culture, race, discrimination, and ethnic group. A number of outstanding children's books, annotated in Parts II through V, are available that you can use successfully to teach these concepts. Open-ended stories and role-playing situations, many of which are described in Parts II through V, can make these concepts real and meaningful to young children.

Children's books are also a powerful tool for teaching concepts to students in the primary and intermediate grades. *A Jar of Dreams,* by Yoshiko Uchida (1982), is a moving story that vividly describes examples of discrimination directed against eleven-year-old Rinko and her family. *Songs of the Trees* by Mildred D. Taylor (1975) and *Through My Eyes* by Ruby Bridges (1999) can

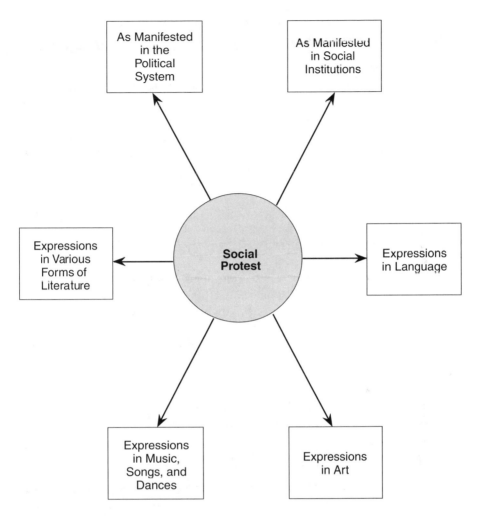

FIGURE 3.1 Viewing Social Protest from an Interdisciplinary Perspective   This figure illustrates how a concept such as social protest must be viewed from diverse disciplinary perspectives in order for students to understand its total political, social, and artistic ramifications.

also be used to teach about discrimination and its effects on its victims. *Through My Eyes* describes how a young girl led the desegregation of the public schools in New Orleans and how these events influenced her life. *The Journal of Wong Ming-Chung: A Chinese Miner,* by Lawrence Yep (2000), focuses on immigration. It tells the story of a ten-year-old boy who comes to California to help his uncle during the Gold Rush.

The students' previous experience with concepts and content related to race and ethnicity is an important consideration when selecting concepts for study. Concepts such as institutionalized racism, ethnic separatism, ethnic revitalization movement, and colonialism are so complex and emotional that they are often inappropriate for students who are studying race and ethnicity for the first time. More concrete and less controversial concepts are appropriate for such students. A student who is not familiar with such basic concepts as ethnic group, ethnic minority group, people of color, discrimination, and prejudice will have a difficult time understanding and appreciating abstract concepts such as institutionalized racism and ethnic separatism. These concepts should be studied only after students have mastered the basic concepts in ethnic studies.

Interdisciplinary Concepts

Concepts drawn from various behavioral science disciplines that can be used effectively to organize interdisciplinary units and lessons are discussed below. The social and behavioral sciences are a rich source of interdisciplinary concepts because behavioral scientists study a wide range of human behavior. Art, music, dance, foods, language, and literature are expressions of concepts studied by behavioral scientists. Table 3.1 summarizes the major concepts discussed in this chapter. Table 3.2 illustrates how key concepts such as those in the following discussion can be used to plan and implement a comparative study of ethnic groups. Table 3.3 describes nine key concepts that can be used to organize a focused study of an ethnic group in the United States.

Culture, Ethnicity, and Related Concepts

Culture.   *Culture* is the key concept in cultural anthropology. It is an essential concept in ethnic studies because an ethnic group is a type of cultural group. Culture consists of the behavior patterns, symbols, institutions, values, and other human-made components of society. It is the unique achievement of a human group that distinguishes it from other groups. Even though cultures are in many ways similar, a particular culture constitutes a unique whole.

There is tremendous debate and controversy within anthropology about the meaning of culture. Some anthropologists do not consider tools and other artifacts examples of culture and believe that the meaning and interpretation of these elements are what constitute culture. Bullivant (1993) defines *culture* as a program for survival; Geertz (cited in Kuper, 1999) defines it as "an ordered system of meaning and symbols" (p. 98).

The U.S. culture is comprised of many smaller groups. These microcultural groups share many characteristics with the national culture but have

TABLE 3.1   Key Concepts

Culture, Ethnicity, and Related Concepts	Culture
	Ethnic group
	Ethnic minority group
	Stages of ethnicity
	Ethnic diversity
	Cultural assimilation
	Acculturation
	Community culture
Socialization and Related Concepts	Socialization
	Prejudice
	Discrimination
	Race
	Racism
	Ethnocentrism
	Values
Intercultural Communication and Related Concepts	Communication
	Intercultural communication
	Perception
	Historical bias
Power and Related Concepts	Power
	Social protest and resistance
The Movement of Ethnic Groups	Migration
	Immigration

Note: This table contains a list of high-level concepts that can be used to develop units and lessons that draw content, examples, and information from several disciplines. These concepts are defined and illustrated in this chapter.

some distinguishing characteristics that set them apart from other groups. Thus, it is possible to describe the U.S. culture, as well as the various microcultures that constitute it, such as Appalachian culture, Southern culture, and gay culture.

Ethnic Group and Ethnic Minority Group.   Ethnic groups are types of microcultural groups within the United States that have unique characteristics that set them apart from other cultural groups. Many microcultural groups are voluntary groups, but an ethnic group is usually an involuntary group, although individual identification with the group may be optional. An ethnic group has a historic origin and a shared heritage and tradition. The origins of the group preceded the creation of the nation-state or were external to the nation-state. An ethnic group also has an ancestral tradition, and its members share a sense of peoplehood and an interdependence of fate. It has some value

TABLE 3.2 An Interdisciplinary Study of Ethnic Groups

Key Concepts and Related Questions	American Indians	Mexican Americans	African Americans	Jewish Americans	Filipino Americans	Puerto Ricans
Culture: What ethnic cultural elements are present in the group's culture today? How is the group's culture reflected in its music, literature, and art?						
Ethnic Enclave: To what extent are members of the group concentrated within particular geographical regions?						
Racism and Discrimination: To what extent is the group a victim of racism or other forms of discrimination?						
Communication: To what extent do members of the group encounter problems when communicating with other ethnic groups?						
Self-Concept: How have the group's societal experiences affected the self-concepts of its members?						
Power: To what extent does the group exercise power within the ethnic community? Within the economic system? Within the larger society?						

Note: This table illustrates how a data retrieval chart organized around key concepts can be used by the teacher to plan and implement a comparative study of ethnic groups.

TABLE 3.3   Organizing Concepts for a Focused Study of an Ethnic Group

The experience of each ethnic group in the United States can be viewed and compared using a few key concepts and themes. Below are nine concepts that can be used to study the experiences of an ethnic group.

Origins and Immigration

It is important to examine the origins and immigration pattern of an ethnic group in the United States.

Shared Culture, Values, and Symbols

Most ethnic groups in the United States have unique cultures and values that resulted from an interaction of their original culture with the host culture in the United States, from ethnic institutions created partly as a response to discrimination, and from their social-class position.

Ethnic Identity and Sense of Peoplehood

A shared sense of peoplehood and ethnic identity is one of the most important characteristics of an ethnic group in the United States. This shared sense of identity results from a common history and current experiences.

Perspectives, World Views, and Frames of Reference

Members of the same ethnic group often view reality in a similar way and differently from other groups within a society. This results largely from their shared sense of peoplehood and identity described above.

Ethnic Institutions and Self-Determination

Many ethnic institutions were formed by ethnic groups in the United States in response to discrimination and segregation. Many of these institutions continue to exist today because they help ethnic groups to satisfy unique social, cultural, and educational needs.

Demographic, Social, Political, and Economic Status

When studying a U.S. ethnic group, its current demographic, social, political, and economic status needs to be determined. The economic and educational status of an ethnic group can change. New immigration can change the demographic and economic profile of an ethnic group.

Prejudice, Discrimination, and Racism

Prejudice, discrimination, and racism have been major themes and issues in the history and contemporary experiences of U.S. ethnic groups, particularly those of color.

(continued)

TABLE 3.3   Continued

Intraethnic Diversity

Even though ethnic groups share a culture, values, a sense of identity, and a common history, there are tremendous differences within ethnic groups. These important differences must always be kept in mind when ethnic groups are studied, or new stereotypes and misconceptions may arise.

Assimilation and Acculturation

The experiences of ethnic groups in the United States have been and still are characterized by widespread cultural assimilation on the part of ethnic minority groups and ethnic minority cultures. The influence of ethnic minority cultures on the mainstream culture should be examined as should the assimilation of minority groups into the mainstream culture.

orientations, behavioral patterns, and interests, often political and economic, that differ from those of other groups within society. Ethnic groups tend to have an influence, often substantial, on the lives of their members. Anglo-Saxon Protestants, Italian Americans, and Irish Americans are examples of ethnic groups.

An ethnic minority group is an ethnic group with several distinguishing characteristics. Although an ethnic minority group, like an ethnic group, shares a common culture, a historic tradition, and a sense of peoplehood, it also has unique physical and/or cultural characteristics that enable individuals who belong to other ethnic groups to identify its members easily, often for discriminatory purposes. Ethnic minority groups also tend to be a numerical minority and to exercise minimal political and economic power. Vietnamese Americans are an ethnic minority group with unique physical and cultural characteristics. Non-White ethnic minority groups, such as Vietnamese Americans and African Americans, are often called *people of color.* Jewish Americans, another ethnic minority group, are distinguished on the basis of their religious and cultural characteristics.

Culture, ethnic group, ethnic minority group, and people of color are essential concepts for the multicultural curriculum and should be introduced in the primary grades. You can introduce the concept of culture by showing the students a menorah, an engagement ring, and the numeral "5." By asking the students what these objects have in common, and by class discussion and the use of more examples, you can help your students formulate a definition of culture. When introducing the concept of culture, you should emphasize the *meanings* that artifacts and cultural elements have to individuals and groups and how they use and interpret them.

After the students have studied culture, they can then be introduced to the concept of microcultural group. Ethnic group and, later, ethnic minority group can be introduced using appropriate examples. When you introduce *ethnic group* you should help students understand that individuals are members of many different groups, such as religious, kinship, and economic groups, and that an ethnic group is only one of the many groups to which individuals belong.

A person's attachment to and identity with these various groups varies with the individual, the times in one's life, and the situations and settings in which one finds oneself. Depending on experiences, social class, and many other variables, ethnicity may be important to an individual or it may be unimportant. Students should be helped to understand that, just because they think an individual is a member of a particular ethnic group, that does not mean that the individual has a strong identity with his or her ethnic group or that ethnicity is important in his or her life. Ethnicity is rather unimportant in the lives of many highly assimilated and upper-status members of ethnic groups but tends to be a cogent factor in the lives of many lower-class ethnic individuals.

The Stages of Cultural Identity: A Typology

We often assume that ethnic groups are monolithic and have rather homogeneous needs and characteristics. Rarely is sufficient attention given to the enormous differences within ethnic groups. We also tend to see ethnic groups as static and unchanging. However, ethnic groups within modernized democratic societies are highly diverse, complex, and changing entities. I have developed a typology that attempts to describe some of the differences that exist between individual members of ethnic and cultural groups. The typology assumes that individual members of ethnic and cultural groups are at different stages of development and that these stages can be identified and described.

The typology is an ideal-type construct in the Weberian sense and constitutes a set of hypotheses based on the existing and emerging theory and research and on my observations and study of ethnic and cultural behavior (Banks, 2001). The typology is presented here because it can be used as a departure point for classroom discussions of race, ethnicity, and culture. However, *its tentative and hypothetical nature should be emphasized in class discussions.*

Stage 1: Cultural Psychological Captivity

During this stage, the individual has internalized negative ideologies and beliefs about his or her ethnic or cultural group that are institutionalized within the society. Consequently, the Stage 1 person exemplifies cultural self-rejection and low self-esteem. The individual is ashamed of his or her cultural group and identity during this stage and may respond in a number of ways, including avoiding situations that lead to contact with other cultural groups or striving aggressively to become highly culturally assimilated.

Stage 2: Cultural Encapsulation

Stage 2 is characterized by cultural encapsulation and cultural exclusiveness, including voluntary separatism. The individual participates primarily within his or her own cultural community and believes that his or her cultural group is superior to that of others. Many Stage 2 individuals, such as many Anglo-Saxon Protestants, have internalized the dominant societal myths about the superiority of their group and the innate inferiority of other groups and races. Many individuals who are socialized within all-White suburban communities and who live highly ethnocentric and encapsulated lives may be described as Stage 2 individuals. Alice Miel (with Kiester, 1967) describes these kinds of individuals in *The Shortchanged Children of Suburbia*.

Stage 3: Cultural Identity Clarification

At this stage, the individual is able to clarify personal attitudes and cultural identity, reduce intrapsychic conflict, and develop positive attitudes toward his or her cultural group. The individual learns to accept self, thus developing the characteristics needed to accept and respond more positively to outside cultural groups. Self-acceptance is a requisite for accepting and responding positively to other people.

Stage 4: Biculturalism

Individuals within this stage have a healthy sense of cultural identity and the psychological characteristics and skills needed to participate in their own culture, as well as in an outside cultural group. The individual also has a strong desire to function effectively in two cultural communities. We may describe such an individual as *bicultural*.

Stage 5: Muliculturalism and Reflective Nationalism

Stage 5 describes the idealized goal for citizenship identity within a culturally diverse nation. The individual at this stage is able to function, at least at minimal levels, within several cultural communities and to understand, appreciate, and share the values, symbols, and institutions of several cultures. Such multicultural perspectives and feelings, I hypothesize, help the individual to live a more enriched and fulfilling life and to formulate more creative and novel solutions to personal and public problems.

Stage 6: Globalism and Global Competency

Individuals within Stage 6 have clarified, reflective, and positive cultural, national, and global identifications and the knowledge, skills, attitudes, and abilities needed to function in different cultural communities within their own nation as well as in cultures within other nations. These individuals have the ideal delicate balance of cultural, national, and global identifications, commitments, literacy, and behaviors. They have internalized the universalistic ethical values and principles of humankind and have the skills, competencies, and commitments needed to act on these values.

Characteristics of the Typology. The Stages of Cultural Identity Typology is an ideal-type construct and should be viewed as dynamic and multidimensional rather than as static and unilinear. The characteristics within the stages exist on a continuum. Thus, within Stage 1, individuals are more or less culturally psychologically captive; some individuals are more culturally psychologically captive than others.

The division between the stages is blurred rather than sharp. Thus, a continuum exists between as well as within the stages. The culturally encapsulated individual (Stage 2) does not suddenly attain clarification and acceptance of personal cultural identity (Stage 3). This process is gradual and developmental. Also, the stages should not be viewed as strictly sequential and unilinear. I am hypothesizing that some individuals may never experience a particular stage. However, I also hypothesize that once an individual experiences a particular stage that person is likely to experience the stages above it sequentially and developmentally. However, individuals may experience the stages upward, downward, or in a zigzag pattern. Under certain conditions, for example, the bicultural (Stage 4) individual may become multicultural (Stage 5); under new conditions the same individual may again become bicultural (Stage 4), culturally identified (Stage 3), and culturally encapsulated (Stage 2). For example, many individual members of northern White ethnic groups became increasingly more culturally encapsulated as busing for school desegregation gained momentum in northern cities such as Boston during the 1970s.

Figure 3.2 illustrates the dynamic and multidimensional characteristics of the development of cultural identity among individuals. Note especially the arrowed lines, which indicate that continua exist both horizontally and vertically.

Ethnic Diversity

Students should learn that there are many different ethnic cultures in our society, and that these differences are not likely to vanish. Events cause them to emerge in each new generation. This concept is the antithesis of the melting pot theory. When studying about ethnic differences in the United States, students should be helped to understand that, even though we have not experienced a true melting pot, most ethnic groups have acquired many mainstream American cultural characteristics. The mainstream culture has also incorporated many components of ethnic minority cultures, such as African American music. This process is still taking place. Consequently, both ethnic cultures and the mainstream culture are being transformed as they interact.

Many ethnic individuals are *bicultural;* that is, they usually acquire traits of mainstream American culture but also retain many of their ethnic characteristics. Even though the more upwardly mobile members of ethnic groups tend to be less ethnic than are lower-class members, this generalization is nevertheless valid. A highly acculturated Chinese American, for example, will often marry

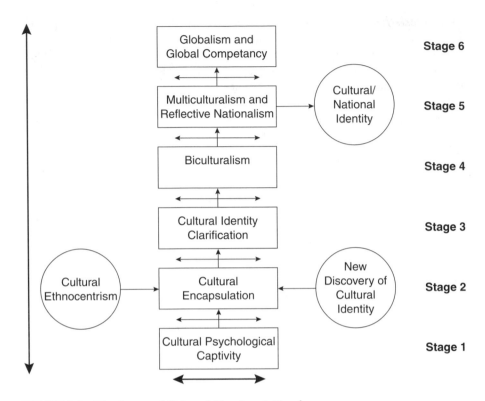

FIGURE 3.2   The Stages of Cultural Identity: A Typology

another Chinese person, eat Chinese foods, and belong to Chinese social organizations. Many ethnic youths attend public schools during the day and a language or ethnic school after regular school hours or on the weekend. Most African Americans who obtain college degrees speak standard English on their jobs and in other settings where it is appropriate to conform to the dominant society's norm. However, when socializing with less assimilated relatives and friends, they often use many words and phrases that linguists call Black English or Ebonics (Smitherman, 2000). Upwardly mobile Mexican Americans will eat "Anglo-Saxon steak" at fancy Anglo restaurants with their Anglo friends, but they often drive to Spanish-speaking neighborhoods to eat foods such as enchiladas and chiles rellenos.

In other words, ethnic individuals acquire those mainstream cultural traits necessary for them to survive in the wider society but often retain many elements of their ethnic cultures. The more upwardly mobile an individual is, the more likely he or she is to acquire mainstream cultural traits. The acquisition of mainstream Anglo-American speech, behavior, and values is necessary for upward mobility in the United States because mainstream Americans control entry to most social, economic, and political institutions.

When studying about ethnic differences, students should learn that cultural differences exist within as well as between various ethnic groups. Too many Americans think of groups of color as monolithic, and they find it difficult to understand why conflict exists within these groups. *(It is very important for students to study about the differences that exist within ethnic groups.)* When many mainstream Americans are introduced to an African American or an Asian American, certain stereotypic images often emerge. They often assume that all African Americans know something about the Black inner-city community because of their personal experiences and can tell them how the Black community feels about busing or interracial marriage. Many people assume that all Asian Americans are stoic, shy, and have a high scientific aptitude.

It is true that we can associate certain general characteristics with the various American ethnic groups. However, within these groups, individuals embrace these characteristics to varying degrees. Some deliberately attempt to reject them. When we meet an individual and know only that he or she is a Mexican American, and nothing else, there are but a few conclusive statements we can accurately make about that person.

Mexican Americans, like Asian Americans and African Americans, are a highly diverse group. Some Mexican Americans identify strongly with this group's political movement and wish to be called Chicanos. Others, especially those in the upper classes, tend to identify more strongly with their Spanish heritage and consider the word *Chicano* pejorative and insulting. Such individuals are more likely to prefer the term *Latin American* or *Spanish American* and to reject their Indian heritage. Some Mexican Americans consider themselves Spanish, even though their biological traits may be identical to others who consider themselves Chicanos or Mexican Americans. Forty-eight percent of Latinos classified themselves as White in the 2000 Census (U.S. Bureau of the Census, 2001).

The tremendous differences that exist within various ethnic groups often make it difficult for many mainstream Americans to understand why many Japanese Americans are anti-Korean, why the *Nisei* (first-generation Japanese American) often express disappointment about the values and lifestyles of the *Sansei* (second generation), or why some upwardly mobile Mexican Americans disdain Mexican migrant workers. Intragroup differences and conflict exist within dominant ethnic groups as well as within minority groups. However, Americans tend to understand why a German American corporation president might disdain a German American dishwasher. The African American, however, who openly wonders about what life is like in the Black inner city may be considered an oddity by many mainstream Americans. Class differences within the African American community are deepening as the income gap between those who are very poor (the so-called underclass) and the up-wardly mobile Blacks increases. About 35% of African Americans are mem-bers of the middle-class (Blackwell, 1997).

Cultural Assimilation

When a member of an ethnic minority group acquires the behavior patterns, lifestyles, values, and language of the mainstream culture, we say that she has become culturally assimilated. *Cultural assimilation* is the process by which an individual or group acquires the cultural traits of a different ethnic or cultural group. Because the dominant group controls most of the social, economic, and political institutions in a society, members of ethnic minority groups must ac-quire its cultural traits to move up the social and economic ladder. When studying this concept, it is important for students to learn that, although people of color may become totally assimilated culturally (i.e., in cultural char-acteristics they may become indistinguishable from Anglo-Saxon Protestants), they will still be victims of discrimination and racism because of their different physical characteristics.

A widespread misconception is that Mexican Americans and African Amer-icans experience discrimination because they often have meager educations and live in inner-city communities. Even though it is true that many Mexican Amer-icans and African Americans are members of the lower socioeconomic classes, and that all lower-class individuals are treated differently than middle- and upper-class people, it is also true that Mexican Americans and African Ameri-cans with high educational levels and incomes frequently experience discrimina-tion because of their color. Because American racism is based largely on skin color, no degree of cultural assimilation eliminates it. A number of popular books describe the racism experienced by middle-class African Americans (Cose, 1993; Feagin & Sikes, 1994).

Some discussion of forced assimilation and cultural genocide should take place when students study cultural assimilation. Assimilation often occurs when a minority group "voluntarily" acquires the behavior patterns and lifestyles of the dominant group in order to attain social mobility and occupational success. I use the word *voluntarily* here reluctantly because, without some degree of cul-tural assimilation, a group that is very different culturally may not be able to survive in a particular culture. However, in the history of the United States, some forms of cultural assimilation that took place were totally nonvoluntary and might be called *forced* assimilation because the cultures of certain groups were deliberately destroyed (cultural genocide). These groups were forced to acquire the language, lifestyles, and values of the dominant culture.

Individuals and groups who refused to accept the dominant culture were sometimes the victims of severe punishments, such as death. The cultures of Af-rican groups were deliberately destroyed by the slave masters. This cultural de-struction began on the slave ships. Historians have documented that systematic and deliberate attempts were made to destroy Indian cultures (Brizan, 1998; Wilson, 1997). These efforts were highly successful. Many of the cultural elements of these groups now exist only in the pages of history, and sometimes not even there because they were often destroyed before they could be recorded.

Acculturation. When an Anglo-Saxon Protestant eats chow mein and a Chinese American sees a Shakespearean play, we say that acculturation is occurring because two different ethnic groups are exchanging cultural elements and complexes. Although the exchange of cultural traits is widespread within U.S. society, we often think of the cultural traits that ethnic minorities acquire from dominant ethnic groups, but we hear too little about the cultural traits that dominant groups have acquired from ethnic minorities. Because this is the case, you should highlight the ethnic minority cultural traits that have been acquired by mainstream Americans.

Students should study the contributions that African Americans have made to American music, especially their spirituals, blues, and jazz (DjeDje & Meadows, 1998). American cultural traits of Indian origin are rarely mentioned in schoolbooks. Indian contributions to American culture include the selection of sites for many American cities, as well as dress styles, tobacco, foods, and values related to the veneration and preservation of the earth. In two popular books, Weatherford (1988; 1991) describes the contributions Native Americans made to the world (*Indian Givers*) and to the United States (*Native Roots*).

All American ethnic groups, including people of color, have contributed material elements (such as foods and fashions), as well as nonmaterial traits (such as values and norms), to mainstream American culture. Students can use a data retrieval chart similar to the one illustrated in Table 3.2 to record examples of contributions that various groups have made to American life. This type of chart is a convenient tool for studying cultural contributions as well as other aspects of ethnic group life in the United States.

Community Culture. Most Americans grow up in communities in which ethnic and cultural values, lifestyles, language patterns, and behavior patterns differ from those of many other groups. This is as true for Puerto Ricans who grow up in East Harlem as it is for Anglo-Saxon Protestants who are raised in wealthy suburban neighborhoods such as Mercer Island, Washington, and Forest Park, Illinois. We usually do not think that middle-class or wealthy White suburbs have a unique culture because the culture within them constitutes the dominant one in the United States. However, Miel (with Kiester, 1967) in *The Shortchanged Children of Suburbia,* and Henry (1963; 1971), in *Culture against Man* and *Pathways to Madness,* describe some of the unique cultural traits of middle-class mainstream U.S. communities.

Because most Americans grow up in ethnic or cultural enclaves, they are *culturally encapsulated.* Ethnic minority groups, in order to attain social and economic mobility, are usually forced out of their ethnic encapsulation. However, mainstream Americans, who control entry to most social, economic, and political institutions, often spend their entire lives within their own unique cultural communities. The cultures of other groups remain foreign, nonhuman, and exotic to them. These groups are viewed as "the Other." African Americans who grow up in small southern rural communities often think that everyone eats sweet potato pie, chitterlings, and hog head and black-eyed peas to celebrate New Year's Day. Without this kind of New Year's meal, bad luck will be imminent. When these African Americans migrate to northern and western cities and begin to participate in social institutions that have other norms and values, they discover, sometimes abruptly, that their world is not the entire world, and that, not only do many people not eat sweet potato pie, but they have serious questions about people who eat hog intestines.

A sound multicultural curriculum should help all students—from both majority and minority groups—to break out of their cultural and ethnic enclaves and learn that there are many ways to live and survive and that, because an individual has a different lifestyle, he or she is not inferior or superior. Many youths of color tend to devalue their ethnic cultures when they begin to participate in the mainstream society. Mainstream students should learn that there are different ways of living that are as legitimate and functional as their own. I am not suggesting that the school should attempt to force different lifestyles on students. However, the school should help release students from *cultural* and *ethnic* encapsulation so that they can learn to appreciate cultural differences and, thus, learn how to live with people who speak a different dialect or language, eat different foods, and value things they may not value. We can learn to respect and appreciate different cultures without choosing to participate in them. Participation should be an individual decision, but cultural understanding and empathy for other people should be fostered by the school.

Socialization and Related Concepts

Socialization.   *Socialization* describes the process by which people become human. Sociologists, who use socialization as their central concept, assume that, even though people are born with the physical capacities to become human, they are capable of becoming many things. People can acquire the characteristics of other animals if they grow up with them and not with other human beings. Sociologists assume that people acquire human traits and characteristics only by interacting with the human group. The group makes use of norms and sanctions to ensure that the individual acquires the attitudes, values, and behavior patterns it deems appropriate.

Socialization and related concepts, such as values and norms, are important in multicultural education because they provide useful insights that help us understand how individuals acquire prejudices and ethnocentric values, and how people learn to discriminate against other groups. Socialization theory teaches us that children are not born with racial antipathies. Children learn these attitudes from the adults in their environment early in life (Stephan, 1999; Van Ausdale & Feagin, 2001).

Modern sociological research and theory dispel old notions, such as the racial and cultural difference theory, which held that individuals have an instinctive fear and dislike of people who are physically and culturally different from them. The theory that explains prejudice as emerging from a traumatic experience has also been discredited. Negative attitudes toward certain ethnic groups are institutionalized within our society. Children acquire them by interacting with "significant others" in their environment and reading books in school, watching television, and going to their places of worship (Stephan, 1999; Van Ausdale & Feagin, 2001). Most institutions within our society, including the schools, reinforce and teach negative lessons about America's ethnic groups of color. Students need to understand the relationship between socialization, prejudice, racism, and discrimination.

Prejudice and Discrimination. Prejudice is a set of rigid and unfavorable attitudes toward a particular group or groups that are formed in disregard of facts. The prejudiced individual responds to perceived members of these groups on the basis of his or her preconceptions, tending to disregard behavior or personal characteristics that are inconsistent with his or her biases. Individuals who are anti-Semitic will argue that Jews are loud and rudely aggressive no matter how many Jews they meet who do not have these characteristics. Prejudiced people see the world through a set of blinders and refuse to perceive people, incidents, and groups that do not reinforce their negative attitudes and stereotypes.

Although prejudice and discrimination are highly related and are usually associated, they are different concepts, but are often confused. Prejudice is a set of *attitudes,* whereas discrimination consists of differential *behavior* directed toward a stigmatized group. Rose defines discrimination "as the differential treatment of individuals considered to belong to particular groups or social categories" (Rose, 1974, p. 102).

You can use Merton's typology (1949) with students in the middle, upper, and high school grades to help them better understand discrimination. His typology makes it clear that a prejudiced individual will not necessarily discriminate and that an individual who is not prejudiced may discriminate. Merton's typology clarifies the extent to which discrimination is contextual, situational, and related to the social settings in which individuals function. Merton identifies four types of persons:

Type I: The unprejudiced nondiscriminator or all-weather liberal. This individual believes in racial equality and acts on her beliefs.

Type II: The unprejudiced discriminator or fair-weather liberal. This is a person of expediency. She does not have personal prejudices but will discriminate when it is easier or more profitable to do so.

Type III: The prejudiced nondiscriminator or fair-weather illiberal. This person does not believe in racial equality but does not discriminate because of laws or external factors that negatively sanction racial discrimination.

Type IV: The prejudiced discriminator or the all-weather illiberal. This is the bigot who is not ashamed of her attitudes and who acts on her prejudices and beliefs.

When using Merton's typology with students, point out that it is an ideal-type conceptualization. This means that no actual individual is a pure example of any of Merton's four types. Rather, the typology can be used to think of and to classify individuals who approach one of the types. Students can also use Merton's typology to describe individuals they encounter in their readings, media presentations, or in their social settings. They can use it to analyze and think about their own behavior and attitudes toward other racial and ethnic groups.

Race.   Physical anthropologists attempt to divide the human species into sub-groups on the basis of biological traits and characteristics. They use the concept of *race* to differentiate among the various human subgroups. However, anthropologists have had considerable difficulty trying to structure valid racial categories because of the wide variety of traits and characteristics that human groups share, the extensive mixture among groups, and because the racial categories they have formulated are socially constructed. Consequently, the schemes they have developed for classifying human races vary greatly in number and in characteristics.

Montagu (1997), who calls race "man's most dangerous myth" and "one of the most tragic" (p. 41), seriously questions the validity of the concept of race and believes it has been a highly destructive factor in the history of humankind. He writes: "The myth of race refers not to the fact that physically distinguishable populations exist, but rather to the belief that races are populations or peoples whose physical differences are innately linked with significant differences in mental capacities, and that these innate hierarchical differences are measurable by the cultural achievements of such populations, as well as by standardized intelligence (IQ) tests" (p. 44).

In most societies, the *social significance of race is much more important than the presumed physical differences among groups.* The social definitions of race also reveal the arbitrariness of the concept and why it might well be humankind's most dangerous and tragic myth. In the United States, any individual with any acknowledged Black African blood is classified as Black, regardless of that person's phenotype (Davis, 1991). Many such persons, of course, look completely Caucasian and classify themselves as White. The majority of them accept the racial category imposed on them by society. We have no reliable statistics of how many such individuals "pass" as White.

Jacobson calls races "invented categories" (1998, p. 4). Omi and Winant (1994) state that the "determination of racial categories is…an intensely political process" (p. 3). Their theory of racial formation "emphasizes the social nature of race, the absence of any essential racial characteristics, the historical flexibility of racial meanings and categories…and the irreducible political aspects of racial dynamics" (p. 4).

In early Mexico, the Spaniards invented so many concepts and terms for different types of racial mixtures that the cumbersome system of racial classification eventually became so complex and dysfunctional that it died of its own weight (Hunt & Walker, 1974). Partly as a result, the attitudes toward differences in skin color and in physical characteristics are considerably more flexible in Latin America than they are in the United States. In Puerto Rican society today, for example, individuals with a wide range of skin colors are regarded as White. Other variables, such as social status, income, education, and hair texture are important in determining an individual's racial designation (Flores, 1993). In Mexico, the rural Indian can become a Mestizo by moving from the village to the city, becoming assimilated into the dominant Mestizo culture, and learning to speak Spanish (van den Berghe, 1978). By exploring the complex ramifications of the social meaning of race both in the United States and in other nations, students will be able to gain a better understanding of both its arbitrariness and political implications.

Racism. Racism is closely related to the idea of race. Racism is a belief that human groups can be validly grouped on the basis of their biological traits and that these identifiable groups inherit certain mental, personality, and cultural characteristics that determine their behavior. A corollary belief is that some biological groups, such as Caucasians, have superior mental and behavioral traits and that others, such as African Americans and Indians, are mentally and culturally inferior. Van den Berghe (1978) defines racism as "any set of beliefs that organic, genetically transmitted differences (whether real or imagined) between human groups are intrinsically associated with the presence or the absence of certain socially relevant abilities or characteristics, hence that such differences are a legitimate basis of invidious distinctions between groups socially defined as races" (p. 11).

Racism, however, is not merely a set of beliefs but is practiced when a group has the power to enforce laws, institutions, and norms based on its beliefs that oppress and dehumanize another group. Gay (1973) stresses the behavioral aspects of racism: "It is an extension of an attitude into an action. Although the focus of attention is on *behavior,* attitudes are of crucial importance for they are the motivating forces which determine the nature of the actions one takes" (p. 30). In a racist society, the political, economic, and social systems reflect and perpetuate racism; thus, racism is institutionalized.

Even though ethnocentrism is found in all human societies, racism is not. The kind of racism that exists in the modern world is a rather recent historical development. In the ancient world, different groups and peoples were often the victims of oppression or were enslaved. However, discrimination was rarely done on the basis of racial characteristics. Rather, it was usually based on religious, cultural, political, and social-class differences. Social scientists have noted that, with few exceptions, racism as we know it today was not practiced up through the seventeenth century (Montagu, 1997). According to van den Berghe (1978), however, racism "has been independently discovered and rediscovered by various peoples at various times in history" (p. 21). However, he notes that it was not until the nineteenth century that racism became an elaborate ideology distinguishable from ethnocentrism. Racism developed in the modern world to justify the exploitation and enslavement of aboriginal peoples by Europeans when they began their explorations into Africa, the Caribbean, and the Americas.

The European explorers and slave owners were Christians who needed an ideology to justify slavery when it was attacked. They needed an ideology they could view as consistent with both their religious beliefs and economic institutions. The arguments they structured eventually blossomed into an elaborate racist ideology. According to van den Berghe (1978): "Racism was congruent with prevailing forms of capitalist exploitation, notably with slavery in the [Americas] and incipient colonial expansion in Africa. There is no question that the desire to rationalize exploitation of non-European peoples fostered the elaboration of a complex ideology of paternalism and racism" (p. 17). Montagu (1974) echoes the same point: "The idea of 'race' was, in fact, the deliberate creation of an exploiting class which was seeking to maintain and defend its privileges against what was profitably regarded as an inferior social caste" (p. 39).

When students study racism, they can try to determine the extent to which it is institutionalized within U.S. society, such as in the mass media or within schools and churches, and how racism is manifested in employment and in housing. The students can also discuss whether they are unconscious participants within an institutionalized racist system and what they might be able to do to change the system. Gay (1973) has distinguished *individual, cultural,* and *institutionalized* racism. Fruitful activities for students are to attempt to formulate working definitions for each of these concepts and to identify examples of them (Feagin & Vera, 1995).

Ethnocentrism.   Most ethnic groups within a society tend to think that their culture is superior to the culture of other groups. This is especially true of the most powerful and dominant groups. In U.S. society, Anglo-Saxon Protestants are the dominant group. Many of them feel that their culture is superior to the cultures of other groups and define *culture* as those aspects of *their* culture that they value highly, such as European classical music and paintings by the European masters.

Students must understand *ethnocentrism* to comprehend fully the complex dimensions of American racism and the separatist movements that have emerged within ethnic minority groups. Although some minority persons, because of their socialization, tend to have low self-concepts and value the mainstream culture over their own, ethnocentrism among people of color escalated in the late 1960s. Some African Americans, Mexican Americans, and Asian Americans extolled the virtues of their cultures and demanded separatism and independent institutions. It may be that some degree of ethnocentrism is necessary for a group to attain cohesion and a strong identity, and that separatism is, as Sizemore (1972) has suggested, a necessary step toward inclusion within the larger society. However, you can ask students this question: How much cultural and political separatism can a society experience and remain cohesive? If this question is raised, several related ones should also be posed: If a society needs some common goals in order to survive, what groups within it should determine these goals? How might we change our society so that each ethnic group can influence policy that shapes common societal goals? At present, dominant groups determine most societal goals and the means to attain them. However, ethnic groups of color made it clear during the 1960s and 1970s that they will not accept this kind of power arrangement without protest and conflict. These kinds of questions and problems, related to ethnocentrism, should constitute a vital part of the multicultural curriculum.

Values. Those elements within a culture to which individuals and groups attach a high worth are called *values*. Within a social system are values that influence the group's feelings toward foods, human life, behavior patterns, and attitudes toward people who belong to outgroups. Sociologists have studied how values develop within societies and how they are inculcated by individuals in a community. Values, like attitudes and beliefs, are learned from the groups in which the individual is socialized; we are not born with a set of values and do not derive them independently. Groups use norms and sanctions to inculcate individuals with the pervasive values within their culture or microculture.

Even though there are some common values embraced by most U.S. communities (such as a respect for the lives of those regarded as human beings and loyalty toward national symbols such as the U.S. flag and the Constitution), these shared values are often defined and perceived differently within various ethnic microcultures, or they take diverse forms. Other values are important in some ethnic communities and largely absent in others.

The Nisei usually endorse many traditional Japanese values, including personal control, the samurai ethic, a high respect for authority, the achievement ethic, and a strong sense of family obligation (Tamura, 1994). Family obligation in traditional Japanese cultures was often considered more important than personal freedom. Although many of the Nisei values have eroded among the Sansei because the Sansei are highly culturally assimilated, important vestiges of these values remain in Japanese communities today, especially among the aged. Some of these values, such as a high respect for authority and a strong sense of family obligation, conflict with mainstream American values. In mainstream U.S. society, authority is often challenged. It is rarely concentrated in one family member. Mainstream Americans also tend to be highly individualistic rather than group oriented.

Values in ethnic minority communities are often different from those in mainstream U.S. society. In the traditional Puerto Rican family, the girl was highly protected, and the father was the undisputed head of the family. The family was also a highly interdependent unit. Uncles, aunts, and other relatives were often considered integral parts of the family unit. This type of extended family was also common among African Americans in the Deep South. As African Americans and Puerto Ricans become more urbanized and more heavily represented in the middle classes, these aspects of their cultures diminish. However, the extended family is still a part of these ethnic cultures. Puerto Rican girls in New York City often do not have the same freedom to come and go with boys as do their Anglo-American peers.

When American Indians are studied in school, students are often introduced to certain stereotypic components of their cultures, such as tipis, baskets, canoes, or moccasins. These physical elements were parts of the cultures of certain American Indian groups, but they were by no means the most essential parts of them. Thus, students gain a superficial view of Indian cultures when they study only tangible cultural elements. *The essence of a culture can be understood only by studying its central values and their relationships to the daily lives of the people.*

The Indian view of people and their relationship to the universe must be studied to understand Indian values toward people and nature. Indian groups tended to look on the universe as a whole, with every object having a sacred life; to separate people from nature was antithetical to the Great Spirit, for to the Great Spirit all was life.

It is the values and related lifestyles of ethnic communities that constitute their essence, not chow mein, basket weaving, sombreros, or soul food. These values and related behavioral characteristics and perspectives should be emphasized in the curriculum, not exotic cultural elements whose major outcome is the reinforcement of stereotypes. However, I am not suggesting that tangible cultural elements should not be studied, but that they should not be emphasized. Even though the study of ethnic values should constitute a large part of the multicultural curriculum, it is important to realize that the values of all of America's ethnic groups are slowly changing, especially in urban areas. People of color are becoming urbanized at a faster rate than are mainstream Americans. It is also important to remember that highly assimilated and higher-status members of ethnic minority groups may share few, if any, characteristics with their more humble brothers and sisters. Despite these caveats, ethnic values are an integral part of life in the United States and add strength and diversity to the national culture. This significant message should be communicated to students in all grades.

Intercultural Communication and Related Concepts

Communication. Social science literature is replete with definitions of *communication.* A person whose behavior and symbols are perceived and interpreted by another individual are common to these many definitions. When an individual communicates, he or she uses symbols that are interpreted by the perceiver. Successful communication occurs when both the sender and receiver of the symbols interpret them in a similar way. Communication is unsuccessful when the sender and receiver of the symbols interpret them differently.

Individuals who are socialized within the same culture or microculture are more likely to have shared meanings of symbols than are individuals who are socialized within different microcultures, cultures, and nations. The wider the differences in cultures or microcultures between individuals, the more ineffective communication is likely to be. A middle-class Australian is less likely to interpret correctly the symbols made by a lower-class African American than is a middle-class mainstream American.

Intercultural Communication. In response to the increased communication between nations and world cultures (caused in part by new technological developments and a heightened interest in ethnic minorities in the United States), a new field, *intercultural communication,* has emerged. This field draws concepts and generalizations from various disciplines and studies the variables involved in communication across cultures. The field is also known as cross-cultural communication, interethnic communication, and transracial communication. Lustig and Koester (1993) define *intercultural communication* as "a symbolic, interpretive, transactional, contextual process in which people from different cultures create shared meanings" (p. 51). Communication often fails across cultures because the message producer and the receiver have few shared symbols and have been socialized within environments in which the same symbols are interpreted differently.

Intercultural communication is an important concept in multicultural studies. It helps explain many of the conflicts and misunderstandings that often occur between ethnic groups in the United States. During the 1960s, many African Americans interpreted Black power symbols positively and viewed them as symbols of racial pride and political efficacy. Whites often viewed Black power negatively and considered it threatening and a form of Black racism. In 1995, Whites and African Americans, as groups, viewed affirmative action differently. Most African Americans (82%) indicated that affirmative action programs were still needed. Whites, by a narrow majority (52%), indicated that affirmative action programs were no longer needed (Benedetto, 1995).

Cross-cultural communication can be improved when individuals from different cultures begin to interpret symbols in similar ways and when they have a strong desire to communicate effectively. When teaching about intercultural communication, you can identify many examples of barriers to effective communication across ethnic boundaries on radio and television news programs and in local and national newspapers and magazines. The class can use role-playing and discussion techniques to explore ways in which cross-ethnic and cross-racial communication can be improved.

Perception.   Social scientists define *perception* as the "complex process by which people select, organize, and interpret sensory stimulation into a meaningful and coherent picture of the world" (Berelson & Steiner, 1964, p. 88). This concept helps us better understand the factors that influence how individuals come to know and interpret their physical and social environments. Many factors influence how people view their world. Social and cultural factors are cogent variables. In our society, race, ethnic group membership, and social class often influence how people see and interpret events, situations, and social issues. An African American civil rights leader and a mainstream U.S. corporation president are likely to view the high unemployment rate among African American youths quite differently.

Cultural, ethnic, and racial variables affect the perception of the historian, the writer, and the artist, as well as the layperson. Culture and ethnicity may have a cogent influence on a particular historian, writer, or artist, or practically no influence. The individual's level of identification with his or her cultural or ethnic group will highly influence whether his or her work will be affected by culture or ethnicity. Ethnicity tends to be a strong factor in people's lives in a society characterized by inequality and high levels of ethnic discrimination; it tends to be a less important factor in a society in which the various ethnic groups experience social and economic equality. The United States is highly stratified along racial, social class, and ethnic lines. Consequently, culture, ethnicity, and race are cogent factors that often influence members of both dominant and minority groups, including the members of these groups who are historians, writers, and artists.

Historically, American history and literature written by mainstream Americans have been mainstream-centric and have interpreted events and situations primarily from mainstream perspectives (Phillips, 1918/1966). Often, minority group cultures were not regarded as worthy of inclusion in literature anthologies, American history textbooks, and in music and art textbooks. Within the last three decades, many mainstream American historians and writers have attempted to include more about ethnic groups in their works. However, often their interpretations of the experiences of other ethnic groups are mainstream-centric, although more benign than in the past. Since the 1970s, more historical, sociological, and artistic works by people of color have been produced (Andrews, Foster, & Harris, 1997; Gonzales, 1999; Smitherman, 2000; Takaki, 1998). Many of the perspectives presented in these works are refreshing, and add a vital component to our academic, artistic, literary, and social worlds.

Historical Bias.   The social, cultural, and ethnic variables that influence how historians perceive their data result in *historical bias*. A historian's view of the past is influenced by her culture, personal biases, purposes for writing, availability of data, and the times in which she lives and writes (Appleby, Hunt, & Jacob, 1994). Because the historian can never totally reconstruct past events and is unable to report all the data he or she uncovers about particular events, she must use some criteria to determine which aspects of an event to report. The historian must also interpret historical events. History cannot be written without presenting interpretations and points of view. Because this is the case, it is important for you to teach students about the biases in all historical writing and how to recognize and analyze them.

It is especially important for you to teach students how to analyze historical materials that are related to America's ethnic groups of color. Prior to the 1970s, most histories of minority groups were written by mainstream historians. They often wrote histories of ethnic minorities that legitimized the dominant social and economic structure and that often depicted minorities negatively (Phillips, 1918/1966). Mainstream American writers and social scientists often perpetuated myths and stereotypes about ethnic minorities to explain why they "deserved" the low status in society to which they were most often assigned. Many of the stereotypes and myths that were constructed in early historical and social science research are still widespread within U.S. society; for example, African Americans were enslaved because they were uncivilized and lazy; slavery would not only civilize them, but would also deliver their souls to God; Indians were savages who had to be civilized by Whites in order to survive; Japanese Americans were a threat to national survival during World War II and thus had to be confined to relocation camps for national security. Some mainstream historians and social scientists are gatekeepers of the status quo; they generate research legitimizing the myths and stereotypes that dominant groups create about powerless groups to justify their status (Herrnstein & Murray, 1994; Jensen, 1969; Tucker, 1994).

Throughout human society, history has been written by the victors and not by the vanquished. Thus, most students in our schools study histories of American Indians and African Americans that were written by American mainstream historians who most often had little empathy or understanding of those cultures. Because this is the case, you should help students view the experiences of ethnic minority groups from their perspectives. I am not suggesting that the histories of ethnic minorities written by mainstream writers should be banned from the schools. However, the study of America must also be seen through the eyes of the vanquished, because students now study it primarily from the viewpoints of the victors. Even though both views can add to our understanding of the American experience, we must stress other viewpoints because mainstream views of American history are so widespread within our schools and the larger society. Only by trying to see this nation from the viewpoints of marginalized peoples will we be able to understand fully its complexity.

Histories and social science accounts written by ethnic minority writers, like the writings of dominant groups, reflect particular points of view and biases. However, students need to study these writings seriously in order to gain a "balanced" perspective on U.S. life and history.

Power and Related Concepts

Power.   The ethnic experience within the United States cannot be understood without considering the role that the struggle for power among competing ethnic groups has played in shaping American history. History and contemporary social science teach us that in every past and present culture individuals have had, and still have, widely unequal opportunities to share fully in the reward systems and benefits of their society. The basis for unequal distribution of rewards is determined by elitist groups in which power is centered. Almost every decision made by people in power, including economic policy, is made to enhance, legitimize, and reinforce their power. Powerful groups not only make laws, but they also determine which traits and characteristics are necessary for full societal participation. They determine necessary traits on the basis of the similarity of such traits to their own values, physical characteristics, lifestyles, and behavior. At various periods in history, powerful groups have used celibacy, gender, ethnicity, race, and religion, as well as many other variables, to determine which individuals and groups would be given or denied opportunities for social mobility and full societal participation.

In colonial America, male Anglo-Saxon Protestants with property controlled most social, political, economic, and military institutions. These were the men who wrote the Declaration of Independence and the United States Constitution (Wilkins, 2001). They excluded from full participation in decision making those people such as African Americans and American Indians who were different from themselves. Our founding fathers had a deep suspicion of and contempt for individuals who were culturally and racially different. They invented and perpetuated stereotypes and myths about excluded groups to justify their oppression (Wilkins, 2001). The United States, like all other nations, is still controlled by a few powerful groups who deny individuals opportunities to participate in society on the basis of how similar such individuals are to themselves.

Money and power in the United States are highly concentrated; the gap between the rich and the poor widened for much of the 1980s and 1990s. The share of the nation's wealth held by the wealthiest households (0.5%) rose sharply in the 1980s after declining for 40 years. In 1976, this segment of the U.S. population held 14% of the nation's wealth. In 1983, it held 26.9% (Phillips, 1990). In 1997, 12.7% of Americans, which included a higher percentage of African Americans and Hispanics (8.5% of non-Hispanic Whites, 26.0% of African Americans, 27.1% of Hispanics), were living in poverty (U.S. Census Bureau, 2001).

When studying about power relationships in American society, students can be asked to hypothesize about how we can make our nation an open society and, thus, more consistent with our national ideology. They can define an open society as one in which rewards and opportunities are not necessarily evenly distributed, but are distributed on the basis of the knowledge and skills that each person, regardless of his or her ethnic characteristics, can contribute to the fulfillment of the needs of society. Students should be asked to discuss which of their hypotheses are most sound and how actions based on them might be implemented, and to state their limitations.

Social Protest and Resistance. Throughout U.S. history, movements have emerged within ethnic communities to protest social conditions, political policies, and economic practices that were considered unjust and unconstitutional. The types of protest have varied widely, from the actions of individual Japanese Americans to resist the internment during World War II to the race riots that occurred in U.S. cities in the 1960s. Groups tend to resort to extreme methods of protest such as riots and rebellions when they feel that the political system is oppressive, that there are no legitimate channels for the alleviation of their grievances, that there is some cause for hope, or that their protest movement might succeed. When studying about social protest, it is important for students to understand that such movements occur only when oppressed people feel that there is a cause for hope. For example, students can derive this generalization when studying the Black protest movements of the 1960s. This movement emerged partly because prior policies aimed at reducing discrimination had occurred. These included the desegregation of the armed forces by President Harry S. Truman, the laws that desegregated many southern state universities, and the historic *Brown* v. *Board of Education* Supreme Court decision in 1954, which legally outlawed *de jure* school segregation. These events were necessary precedents to the Black civil rights movement of the 1960s.

Many people think that the ethnic protests of the 1960s were the first of their kind in U.S. history. Even though it is true that ethnic protests reached their zenith during these years, ethnic groups have protested discrimination and racism throughout U.S. history. Black protest actually began on the slave ships on the journeys from West Africa to the Americas. Slave uprisings and mutinies often occurred on these ships. Many slaves also committed suicide by throwing themselves into the Atlantic rather than acquiesce to bondage. Protest by African Americans continued during and after slavery. Slave uprisings, led by such individuals as Denmark Vesey, Gabriel Prosser, and Nat Turner, sometimes resulted in the mass murder of Whites (Aptheker, 1943/1987; Genovese, 1979).

Near the turn of the century, Black organizations emerged to fight systematically for civil rights, including the National Association for the Advancement of Colored People (NAACP) and the National Urban League. Other ethnic groups have also continually fought for their rights. Such organizations as the Anti-Defamation League of B'nai B'rith, the Japanese American Citizenship League, the League of United Latin-American Citizens, and the Puerto Rican Forum were organized to work for the civil rights of various ethnic groups in a systematic way. Oppression of any human group is likely to lead to organized protest and resistance. Such protest and resistance have emerged within all of America's ethnic minority groups, although the forms and styles of that protest have reflected the unique cultural values, lifestyles, and histories of the particular groups.

The Movement of Ethnic Groups

Migration and Immigration

When individuals or groups move within a nation in which they are natives or citizens, we say that they are *migrants*. Individuals or groups who settle in a foreign country are called *immigrants*. Thus, migration describes the movement of individuals and groups within a nation, and immigration describes the settlement of people in a foreign nation. These two concepts must be studied in the multicultural curriculum because all groups that comprise the United States, except for a few such as American Indians, Eskimos, Aleuts, and Native Hawaiians, immigrated to this land from a foreign nation or migrated from Puerto Rico. We call Puerto Ricans migrants rather than immigrants because they became U.S. citizens with the passage of the Congressional Jones Act of 1917. Archeological theories and evidence indicate that some American Indians immigrated to the Americas from Asia via the Bering Strait. Although this evidence is strongly endorsed by some anthropologists, it is inconclusive. Many American Indians believe that they were created in the Americas by the Great Spirit.

When studying these two concepts, students can formulate hypotheses about why very large numbers of immigrants entered the United States in the nineteenth century. Between 1820 and 1930, about 38 million immigrants came to the United States, most of them from Europe. Students might hypothesize that many individuals and groups came to the United States to avoid religious and political persecution and to improve their economic conditions. When studying statistics on immigration to the United States, students can be asked to note the countries from which most immigrants came and to explain why. For example, between 1820 and 1979, 6,985,000 German immigrants entered the

United States. During the same period, only 3,038,000 immigrants came from the entire continent of Asia, and 36,267,000 came from the rest of Europe. Only 142,000 came from Africa. An investigation into why many more immigrants came from Europe than from Asia and Africa will lead students to discover that our immigration policies, until they were reformed in 1965, were designed to keep this nation largely White and to keep out non-Whites.

A study of immigration to the United States since the Immigration Reform Act of 1965 reveals that the source of immigration to the United States has changed substantially since that time (see Table 3.4). Nearly 60% of the immigrants to the United States between 1951 and 1960 were from nations in Europe. Europeans comprised only 20% of the immigrants to the United States between 1981 and 1998 (Riche, 2000). About 75% of the legal immigrants that settled in the United States during this period came from nations in Latin America and Asia.

During their study of the immigration and migration of ethnic groups, students can profitably compare and contrast the reasons why various groups immigrated and the kinds of experiences they had in their new country. The special case of African immigrants to the United States should be highlighted. This group differed from all the other immigrant groups because their immigration was forced. They were also the only group enslaved on their arrival in the Americas. All the other groups of immigrants voluntarily came to the Americas, although many were escaping abject poverty, religious persecution, and political repression. Many of the early immigrants to the Americas were indentured servants who had few rights. However, most White indentured servants were eventually able to obtain their freedom.

When studying about the southern and eastern European immigrants to the United States, students can note how each group experienced discrimination and lived in urban ghettos, and how many of them eventually became culturally assimilated, attained social mobility, and moved to the suburbs of cities such as New York, Boston, and Chicago. Groups like Italians and Poles discriminated against African Americans and Mexican Americans when these groups started migrating to large cities after the two world wars.

European immigrant groups, especially the southern and eastern ones, were often the victims of discrimination and racist ideologies, but the racism they experienced never reached the proportions it did in the South against African Americans or on the West Coast when Asian immigrants started arriving there in the 1800s. It is important for students to realize that, even though certain classes of European immigrants, such as lunatics, convicts, and idiots, were prevented from entering the United States in the 1800s, the first national group that was totally excluded from the United States was non-White. The Chinese Exclusion Act of 1882 completely stopped Chinese immigration to the United States for several decades. In the 1920s, the number of southern and eastern European immigrants entering the United States was reduced to a

TABLE 3.4 Immigrants by Country of Birth: 1981 to 1998

Country of Birth	1981–90, Total	1991–96, Total	1997	1998
All countries	7,338.1	3,146.2	798.4	660.5
Europe[1]	705.6	875.6	119.9	90.8
France	23.1	16.9	2.6	2.4
Germany	70.1	43.7	2.7	5.5
Greece	29.1	10.0	1.0	0.9
Ireland	32.8	54.9	1.0	0.9
Italy	32.9	14.7	2.0	1.8
Poland	97.4	130.2	12.0	8.5
Portugal	40.0	17.1	1.7	1.5
Romania	38.9	34.3	5.5	5.1
Soviet Union, former[2]	84.0	339.9	49.1	30.2
Armenia	(NA)	[3]320.8	2.1	1.1
Azerbaijan	(NA)	[3]312.3	1.5	0.5
Belarus	(NA)	[3]321.4	3.1	1.0
Russia	(NA)	[3]370.4	16.6	11.5
Ukraine	(NA)	[3]316.1	3.3	7.4
Uzbekistan	(NA)	[3]316.1	3.3	0.6
United Kingdom	142.1	95.0	10.7	9.0
Yugoslavia	19.2	31.7	10.8	8.0
Asia[1]	2,817.4	1,914.9	265.8	219.7
Afghanistan	26.6	3.6	1.1	0.8
Bangladesh	15.2	35.4	8.7	8.6
Cambodia	116.6	11.9	1.6	1.4
China	[4]388.8	268.7	41.1	36.9
Hong Kong	63.0	52.9	5.6	5.3

Country of Birth	1981–90, Total	1991–96, Total	1997	1998
Syria	20.6	16.6	2.3	2.8
Taiwan	([4])	76.8	6.7	7.1
Thailand	64.4	36.1	3.1	3.1
Turkey	20.9	15.7	3.1	2.5
Vietnam	401.4	317.8	38.5	17.6
North America[1]	3,125.0	2,740.7	307.5	253.0
Canada	119.2	90.7	11.6	10.2
Mexico	1,653.3	1,651.4	146.9	131.6
Caribbean	892.7	655.4	105.3	75.5
Cuba	159.2	94.9	33.6	17.4
Dominican Republic	251.8	258.1	27.1	20.4
Haiti	140.2	114.4	15.1	13.4
Jamaica	213.8	109.8	17.8	15.1
Trinidad and Tobago	39.5	41.1	6.4	4.9
Central America[1]	458.7	342.8	43.7	35.7
El Salvador	214.6	147.7	18.0	14.6
Guatemala	87.9	70.3	7.8	7.8
Honduras	49.5	41.9	7.6	6.5
Nicaragua	44.1	50.4	6.3	3.5
Panama	29.0	16.9	2.0	1.6
South America[1]	455.9	344.0	52.9	45.4
Argentina	25.7	17.1	2.0	1.5
Brazil	23.7	32.4	4.6	4.4
Chile	23.4	11.4	1.4	1.2
Colombia	124.4	81.7	13.0	11.8

Country				
India	261.9	236.5	38.1	36.5
Iran	154.8	79.4	9.6	7.9
Iraq	19.6	26.8	3.2	2.2
Israel	36.3	22.9	2.4	2.0
Japan	43.2	39.9	5.1	5.1
Jordan	32.6	5.1	4.2	3.2
Korea	338.8	114.1	14.2	14.3
Laos	145.6	37.8	1.9	1.6
Lebanon	41.6	29.9	3.6	3.3
Pakistan	61.3	70.5	13.0	13.1
Philippines	495.3	348.5	49.1	34.5
Ecuador	56.1	45.2	7.8	6.9
Guyana	95.4	53.6	7.3	4.0
Peru	64.4	66.7	10.9	10.2
Venezuela	17.9	16.2	3.3	3.1
Africa[1]	192.3	213.1	47.8	40.7
Egypt	31.4	28.0	5.0	4.8
Ethiopia	27.2	30.9	5.9	4.2
Ghana	14.9	18.0	5.1	4.5
Nigeria	35.3	37.9	7.0	7.7
South Africa	15.7	14.2	2.1	1.9
Other countries[5]	41.9	31.0	4.5	10.9

[In thousands (7,338.1 represents 7,338,100). For fiscal years ending Sept. 30. For definition of *immigrants*, see text of this section.]

NA Not available   [1]includes countries not shown separately.   [2]Includes other republics and unknown republics, not shown separately.   [3]Covers years 1992–1996.   [4]Data for Taiwan included with China.   [5]Includes unknown countries.

Source: U.S. Census Bureau. (2000). *Statistical Abstract of the United States: 2000* (120th Ed.). Washington, DC: U.S. Government Printing Office, p. 10.

trickle because discrimination against them became intense and widespread. Non-White groups were virtually excluded from the United States. Only groups from northern and western Europe were favored by the "national origins" quota system that was enacted by Congress in 1921 and tightened in 1924. The quota was based on percentage of residents of a particular nationality in the United States in 1920.

The McCarran Act of 1952 relaxed some of the earlier restrictions but made the national origin parts of the law even more severe. Significant immigration reform did not occur until the Immigration Act of 1965, which amended the Immigration and Nationality Act of 1952. This act became effective in 1968. The 1965 act removed the national origin quotas and liberalized U.S. immigration policy.

Summary

This chapter has discussed a number of high-level concepts that can be used effectively to organize and teach multicultural units and lessons. I suggested that key concepts selected for the multicultural curriculum should be able to function successfully in an interdisciplinary role, should help explain some significant aspects of the cultures and experiences of ethnic groups, and should be able to encompass a wide range of data and information. When choosing concepts for the multicultural curriculum, you should also consider your students' developmental levels and their prior experiences with content related to race, ethnicity, and culture. Chapter 4 discusses ways in which the multicultural curriculum can be planned and organized.

REFLECTION AND ACTION ACTIVITIES

1. Identify a racial, ethnic, or religious problem in your community, such as a controversy over affirmative action, the question of open housing, or discrimination directed against a particular religious or ethnic groups, such as Arab Americans after the September 11, 2001, bombing of the World Trade Center in New York City and the Pentagon in Washington, D.C. List concepts and generalizations from several disciplines that might help students understand the problem. What strategies and materials would you use to teach the problem to students?

2. State the advantages of interdisciplinary multicultural lessons and units. What problems might you encounter in trying to structure these kinds of lessons and units? How might you resolve them?

3. Examine several of the books dealing with specific ethnic groups listed in the bibliographies of this book. Identify and list cultural traits that are unique to different ethnic communities. What is the origin of these cultural traits? Why do they continue to exist? Are they unique to particular ethnic groups or merely associated with lower-class status or a certain region? Explain your responses.

4. After reading a book on each of the major ethnic groups, make a list of the types of cultural and physical differences existing within them. Explain why these differences emerged and why they still exist.

5. Make a list of the major occupations in which most American Indians, Mexican Americans, Asian Americans, Puerto Rican Americans, and African Americans work (see U.S. Census Bureau on line at: *http://www.census.gov/*

   Note the percentages of each group working in the major occupations identified. Carefully study the data you have gathered. What generalizations and conclusions can you make about the occupational status of ethnic groups of color in U.S. society? What factors explain their occupational status?

6. Using a map of your city or community, pinpoint the regions in which the various ethnic groups live with different colored markers to represent each major racial or ethnic group. What conclusions and generalizations can you make about where different racial or ethnic groups are concentrated in your community? What factors explain their location patterns?

7. Locate several conflicting accounts of slavery or the U.S.-Mexican War and develop an inquiry lesson to teach students how personal biases influence the writing of history.

8. Study the treatments of the major ethnic groups in your basal social studies, language arts, or other textbooks. What conclusions can you make? What materials and strategies can you use to extend textbook treatments of ethnic groups? How?

9. List examples of racial and ethnic discrimination you have seen and/or experienced. Why did the discrimination occur? How might this type of discrimination be reduced? How did you respond to it? Explain.

10. Watch several television programs during the week that have ethnic minority characters. Also study the treatment of ethnic groups such as African Americans and Mexican Americans in a newspaper or news magazine for a one-week period. Write a three- to five-page paper summarizing your observations about the treatment of ethnic minorities on television and in the printed sources you examined. Did you find any examples of racism? Explain.

    A helpful book for this activity is Carlos E. Cortés (2000), *The Children Are Watching: How the Media Teach about Diversity*. New York: Teachers College Press.

11. Try to think of several examples of problems that result from communicating across different ethnic cultures. Develop and write a lesson plan for teaching the concept of intercultural communication to students.

12. Define each of the following terms and tell why each is important:
    high-level concept
    interdisciplinary
    conceptual curriculum
    microculture
    ethnic group
    socialization
    intercultural
    communication

REFERENCES

Andrews, W. L., Foster, F. S., & Harris, T. (Eds.). (1997). *The Oxford Companion to African American Literature.* New York: Oxford University Press.

Appleby, J., Hunt, L., & Jacob, M. (1994). *Telling the Truth about History.* New York: Norton.

Aptheker, H. (1943/1987). *American Negro Slave Revolts.* New York: International Publishers.

Banks, J. A. (2001). *Cultural Diversity and Education: Foundations, Curriculum and Teaching* (4th ed.). Boston: Allyn and Bacon.

Benedetto, R. (1995, July 25). Affirmative Action Divides Blacks, Whites. *USA Today.* Section A, p. 1.

Berelson, B., & Steiner, G. A. (1964). *Human Behavior: An Inventory of Scientific Findings.* New York: Harcourt, Brace and World.

Blackwell, J. A. (1997). *The Black Community: Diversity and Unity* (3rd ed.). New York: Addison-Wesley Longman.

Bridges, R. (1999). *Through My Eyes.* New York: Scholastic.

Brizan, G. (1998). *Grenada: Island of Conflict.* London: Macmillan Education.

Bullivant, B. M. (1993). Culture: Its Nature and Meaning for Educators. In Banks, J. A., & Banks, C. A. M., (Eds.), *Multicultural Education: Issues and Perspectives* (pp. 29–47). Boston: Allyn and Bacon.

Clark, K. B., & Clark, M. P. (1940). Skin Color as a Factor in Racial Identification of Negro Pre-School Children. *Journal of Social Psychology, 11,* 159–167.

Cose, E. (1993). *The Rage of a Privileged Class.* New York: HarperCollins.

Davis, F. J. (1991). *Who Is Black? One Nation's Definition.* University Park: Pennsylvania State University Press.

DjeDje, J. C., & Meadows, E. S. (Eds.). (1998). *California Soul: Music of African Americans in the West.* Berkeley: University of California Press.

Feagin, J. R., & Sikes, M. P. (1994). *Living with Racism: The Black Middle-Class Experience.* Boston: Beacon Press.

Feagin, J. R., & Vera, H. (1995). *White Racism: The Basics.* New York: Routledge.

Flores, J. (1993). *Divided Borders: Essays on Puerto Rican Identity.* Houston: Arte Público Press.

Gay, G. (1973). Racism in America: Imperatives for Teaching Ethnic Studies. In J. A. Banks (Ed.), *Teaching Ethnic Studies: Concepts and Strategies* (pp. 27–49). Washington, DC: National Council for the Social Studies.

Genovese, E. D. (1979). *From Rebellion to Revolution: Afro-American Slave Revolts in the Making of the Modern World.* Baton Rouge: Louisiana State University Press.

Gonzales, M. G. (1999). *Mexicanos: A History of Mexicans in the United States.* Bloomington: Indiana University Press.

Goodman, M. E. (1964). *Race Awareness in Young Children.* New York: Collier Books.

Henry, J. (1963). *Culture against Man.* New York: Vintage Books.

Henry, J. (1971). *Pathways to Madness.* New York: Random House.

Herrnstein, R. J., & Murray, C. (1994). *The Bell Curve: Intelligence and Class Structure in American Life.* New York: Free Press.

Hunt, C. L., & Walker, L. (1974). *Ethnic Dynamics: Patterns of Intergroup Relations in Various Societies.* Homewood, IL: Dorsey Press.

Jacobson, M. F. (1998). *Whiteness of a Different Color: European Immigrants and the Alchemy of Race.* Cambridge: Harvard University Press.

Jensen, A. R. (1969, Winter). How Much Can We Boost IQ and Scholastic Achievement? *Harvard Educational Review, 39,* 1–123.

Kuper, A. (1999). *Culture: The Anthropologist's Account.* Cambridge: Harvard University Press.

Lustig, M. W., & Koester, J. (1993). *Intercultural Competence across Cultures*. New York: HarperCollins.

Merton, R. K. (1949). Discrimination and the American Creed. In R. M. MacIver (Ed.), *Discrimination and National Welfare* (pp. 99–126). New York: Harper & Row.

Miel, A., with Kiester, E., Jr. (1967). *The Shortchanged Children of Suburbia*. New York: American Jewish Committee.

Montagu, A. (1997). *Man's Most Dangerous Myth: The Fallacy of Race* (6th ed.). Walnut Creek, CA: AltaMira Press.

Oliver, D. L. (1964). *An Invitation to Anthropology: A Guide to Basic Concepts*. Garden City, NY: National History Press.

Omi, M., & Winant, H. (1994). *Racial Formation in the United States: From the 1960s to the 1990s* (2nd ed.). New York: Routledge and Kegan Paul.

Phillips, K. (1990). *The Politics of Rich and Poor*. New York: Random House.

Phillips, U. B. (1918/1966). *American Negro Slavery*. Baton Rouge: Louisiana State University Press.

Riche, M. F. (2000). *America's Diversity and Growth: Signposts for the 21st Century*. Washington, DC: Population Reference Bureau.

Rose, P. I. (1974). *They and We: Racial and Ethnic Relations in the United States* (2nd ed.). New York: Random House.

Sizemore, B. A. (1972, January). Is There a Case for Separate Schools? *Phi Delta Kappan, 53,* 281–284.

Smitherman, G. (2000). *Talkin That Talk: Language, Culture, and Education in African America*. New York: Routledge.

Stephan, W. (1999). *Reducing Prejudice and Stereotyping in Schools*. New York: Teachers College Press.

Takaki, R. (1998). *A Larger Memory: A History of Our Diversity, with Voices*. New York: Little, Brown.

Tamura, E. H. (1994). *Americanization, Acculturation, and Ethnic Identity*. Urbana: University of Illinois Press.

Taylor, M. D. (1975). *Song of the Trees*. New York: Dial.

Trager, H. G., & Yarrow, M. R. (1952). *They Learn What They Live*. New York: Harper.

Tucker, W. H. (1994). *The Science and Politics of Racial Research*. Urbana: University of Illinois Press.

Uchida, Y. (1982). *A Jar of Dreams*. New York: Atheneum.

U.S. Census Bureau. (2001). [On-line]. Available: *http://www.census.gov/*

U.S. Immigration and Naturalization Service. (1993). *Statistical Yearbook of the Immigration and Naturalization Service, 1992*. Washington, DC: U.S. Government Printing Office.

Van Ausdale, D., & Feagin, J. R. (2001). *The First R: How Children Learn Race and Racism*. Lanham, MD: Rowman & Littlefield.

van den Berghe, P. L. (1978). *Race and Racism: A Comparative Perspective* (2nd ed.). New York: John Wiley.

Weatherford, J. (1988). *Indian Givers: How the Indians of the Americas Transformed the World*. New York: Fawcett Columbine.

Weatherford, J. (1991). *Native Roots: How the Indians Enriched America*. New York: Fawcett Columbine.

Wilkins, R. (2001). *Jefferson's Pillow: The Founding Fathers and the Dilemma of Black Patriotism*. Boston: Beacon Press.

Wilson, S. M. (Ed.). (1997). *The Indigenous People of the Carribbean*. Gainesville: University Press of Florida.

Yep, L. (2000). *The Journal of Wong Ming-Chung: A Chinese Miner*. New York: Scholastic.

ANNOTATED BIBLIOGRAPHY

Moses, R. P., & Cobb, C. E., Jr. (2001). *Radical Equations: Math Literacy and Civil Rights.* Boston: Beacon Press.

> *The authors make a convincing case that the right to acquire math literacy in the United States is a basic civil right. The first author of this book is the founder of the Algebra Project.*

Okihiro, G. Y. (2001). *Common Ground: Reimaging American History.* Princeton: Princeton University Press.

> *A perceptive and sensitive historian describes transformative and visionary ways to interpret and view American history.*

Root, M. P. P. (2001). *Love's Revolution: Interracial Marriage.* Philadelphia: Temple University Press.

> *An important and informative book by a leading psychologist who specializes in the nation's growing interracial population.*

Smith, L. (1949/1994). *Killers of the Dream.* New York: Norton.

> *This classic by the Southern White writer and activist is powerful and engaging reading. It provides keen insights that will help teachers think about racism today and the responsibility of Whites to help eliminate it.*

Van Ausdale, D., & Feagin, J. R. (2001). *The First R: How Children Learn Race and Racism.* Lanham, MD: Rowman & Littlefield.

> *This book summarizes important research about the development of children's racial attitudes.*

4 Planning the Multicultural Curriculum

The multicultural curriculum should help students develop the ability to make reflective personal and public decisions. A curriculum focused on decision making must be conceptual and interdisciplinary and based on higher levels of knowledge. The preceding chapter, "Key Concepts for the Multicultural Curriculum," presents criteria and examples of concepts that you can use to organize multicultural units and lessons.

This chapter discusses ways to organize a decision-making curriculum after you have selected appropriate concepts and content. It also presents other components of an effective multicultural curriculum, including valuing and personal, social, and civic action. Steps you can take to select and evaluate instructional materials are also discussed.

Identifying Key Concepts and Organizing Generalizations

When planning multicultural lessons and units that have a comparative approach and focus, you or a curriculum committee should start by identifying key concepts. These concepts should be higher-level ones that can encompass numerous facts and lower-level generalizations. They should have the power to organize a great deal of information and to explain significant aspects of the experiences and histories of ethnic groups. These concepts should also be able to function successfully in an interdisciplinary role.

After you or a curriculum committee has selected key concepts from several disciplines, at least one organizing generalization related to each concept should be identified. Each organizing generalization should be a higher-level statement that explains some aspects of human behavior in all cultures, times, and places. It should not contain references to any particular culture or group but should be a universal type of statement capable of being scientifically tested. Table 4.1 presents a list of key concepts and related organizing generalizations that can be

TABLE 4.1 Key Concepts and Organizing Generalizations

Key Concept	Organizing Generalization
Acculturation	Whenever ethnic groups have extended contact, exchange of cultural traits occurs between minority and majority groups, as well as between different ethnic groups.
Intercultural communication	Individuals and groups socialized within different ethnic cultures are often unable to communicate effectively because they interpret the meanings of symbols differently. Ineffective communication frequently results in conflict between ethnic groups.
Perception	In a society stratified along racial and ethnic group lines, ethnicity and race tend to influence cogently how individuals see and interpret events, situations, and public issues.
Racism	Powerful groups that hold racist beliefs usually structure institutions, laws, and norms that reflect their beliefs and oppress the victims of racism.
Power	Within an ethnically stratified society, individuals and power groups struggle for power and influence. Power struggles often lead to social change.
Immigration–migration	In all cultures, individuals and groups have moved to seek better economic, political, and social opportunities. However, movement of individuals and groups has been both voluntary and forced.

used to plan a multicultural conceptual curriculum incorporating the experiences of a range of ethnic and cultural groups.

Identifying Intermediate-Level Generalizations

After an organizing (universal-type) generalization is identified for each key concept chosen, an intermediate-level generalization that relates to each organizing generalization should be formulated. An intermediate-level generalization applies to a nation, to regions within a nation, or to groups comprising a particular culture. Table 4.2 presents an intermediate-level generalization for *immigration–migration,* a key concept listed in Table 4.1. In an actual curriculum, intermediate-level generalizations would be identified for each organizing

TABLE 4.2   Generalizations Related to Immigration–Migration

Key Concept

Immigration–migration

Organizing Generalization

In all societies, individuals and groups have moved to seek better economic, political, and social opportunities. However, movement of individuals and groups has been both voluntary and forced.

Intermediate-Level Generalization

Most individuals and groups who immigrated to the United States and who migrated within it were seeking better economic, political, or social opportunities. However, movement of individuals and groups to and within the United States has been both voluntary and forced.

Low-Level Generalizations

Indians: Most movements of Indians within the United States was caused by forced migration and genocide.

Mexican Americans: Mexicans who immigrated to the United States came primarily to improve their economic condition by working as migrant laborers in the western and southwestern states.

European Americans: Most southern and eastern Europeans who immigrated to the United States came primarily to improve their economic status.

African Americans: Large numbers of Blacks migrated to northern and western cities in the early 1900s to escape lynchings and economic and political discrimination in the South.

Asian Americans: Most Asian immigrants who came to the United States in the 1800s expected to improve their economic conditions and return to Asia. During World War II, Japanese Americans were forced to move from their homes to federal internment camps.

Puerto Ricans: Puerto Ricans usually come to the U.S. mainland seeking better jobs; they sometimes return to the island of Puerto Rico because of American racism and personal disillusionment experienced on the mainland.

Indochinese Americans: Most Indochinese Americans, unlike most American immigrant groups, came to the United States because of political developments in their native lands.

generalization selected and shown in Table 4.1. However, the example in Table 4.2 is limited to save space.

Determining which Ethnic Groups to Study

Selecting a Range of Groups.   When an intermediate-level generalization has been identified for each key concept, you must decide which ethnic groups will be selected for study. A range of groups should be included in comparative multicultural units and lessons in order to teach significant concepts related to U.S. ethnic groups and to illustrate both the differences and similarities in their experiences, cultures, and histories. Groups that differ in racial characteristics, levels of assimilation, social-class status, and in the periods and circumstances of immigration to or migration within the United States should also be studied in the multicultural curriculum.

Units that include ethnic groups that have been successful educationally and economically, such as Jewish Americans and Japanese Americans, and those who still face massive social and economic problems, such as American Indians and Mexican Americans, can illustrate the enormous range in the experiences of ethnic groups in the United States. However, when ethnic groups such as Jewish Americans and Japanese Americans are studied, you should help students understand that, although Jewish Americans and Japanese Americans have experienced tremendous educational and social mobility, members of these groups are often victims of discrimination and sometimes face identity problems related to their ethnicity (Dershowitz, 1997; Tamura, 1994). Thus, these groups share some characteristics with lower-status ethnic groups such as American Indians, African Americans, and Mexican Americans.

Studying ethnic groups such as Chinese immigrants and Cuban Americans can illustrate the differences and similarities of two ethnic groups who came in large numbers to the United States at different points in history and for different reasons. The first Chinese immigrants came to the United States in the 1800s hoping to get rich quickly and return to their homeland. Most of the Cubans who settled in the United States between 1959 and 1970 came to escape a communist form of government (Olson & Olson, 1995). African Americans provide an interesting contrast to these groups. They were the only ethnic group that was forced to come to America and who came in chains.

The experiences of Jewish Americans in the United States have also been unique. Jews comprise a White ethnic, cultural, and religious group that has experienced high levels of educational and economic mobility but still retains significant aspects of their ethnic culture and identity (Brodkin, 1998). In 2000, about 48% of Jews still married within their own ethnic group (see Chapter 9). Usually, White ethnic groups become mainstream Americans when they attain high levels of educational and economic mobility (Waters, 1990). American Indians, Eskimos, Aleuts, and Native Hawaiians differ from most other ethnic groups because they can claim America as their native land. Indochinese Americans can be studied to illustrate the problems faced by ethnic groups displaced by a modern war and relocated in an alien and highly industrialized society.

Studying Groups That Illustrate Key Concepts. No single multicultural curriculum can include a study of each American ethnic group. The number is much too large to be manageable. There are more than 100 ethnic groups in the United States (Thernstrom, Orlov, & Handlin, 1980). In addition to the groups of color who, since the 1960s, have urged educators to include more information about their histories and cultures in the curriculum, some White ethnic groups—such as Italian and Polish Americans—are also urging teachers to include the study of their experiences and histories in the school curriculum. Arab Americans—a growing and important population within the United States (McCarus, 1994)—also deserve attention in the school curriculum. Teachers need to help undercut the pernicious stereotypes about them that are institutionalized within the United States and other Western societies (Bayoumi & Rubin, 2000).

A major goal of the multicultural curriculum is to help students master key concepts that will help them make better decisions and become more effective citizens in a pluralistic democratic society. *Thus, the focus should be on helping students master key concepts that highlight major themes in the experiences of racial, ethnic, language, and cultural groups in the United States.* Within a conceptual curriculum, which particular groups are selected for study becomes a secondary, though important, consideration. The experiences of the groups selected for study should be the best examples of particular concepts.

It is essential that students master certain concepts, such as *race, racism, prejudice,* and *discrimination* if they are to gain a full understanding of U.S. society and history. Racism has been a decisive force in the United States since its beginning and is still a major force in the United States today (Schuman, Steeh, Bobo, & Krysan, 1997). Consequently, students must study this concept in a sound multicultural curriculum. When studying racism, students will need to examine the histories and contemporary experiences of ethnic groups of color such as African Americans, American Indians, Mexican Americans, and Asian Americans. Racism emerged to justify the enslavement of African Americans and was later developed into a full-blown ideology used to defend the exploration and exploitation of America and its native peoples (Banks, 1995).

Racism is still a major problem in U.S. society. A study of various ethnic groups that are victimized by institutionalized racism will help students develop a better understanding of this complex problem and the ability to reason about it thoughtfully. The different forms of prejudice and discrimination that exist in U.S. society also merit serious study by students in all grades, kindergarten through the university level. Research by Glock, Wutnow, Piliavin, and Spencer

(1975) indicates that students who are more cognitively sophisticated and who can reason more logically about prejudice are likely to express fewer prejudices than are less cognitively sophisticated students. Gabelko and Michaelis (1981), influenced by the Glock et al. findings, developed a handbook of activities to help students reason more logically about prejudice and, thus, to reduce it.

A study of the experiences of Jews in the United States can facilitate an examination of the forms of prejudice and discrimination in contemporary U.S. society. Research indicates that anti-Semitism is still a problem in American society (Brodkin, 1998). It warrants open examination by students within democratic classrooms.

Concepts such as *cultural assimilation* and *structural assimilation* are also important in the multicultural curriculum. A study of groups of color, such as African Americans and Filipino Americans, can illustrate how some members of these groups have become *culturally* assimilated but have been denied *structural* assimilation, or the ability to participate freely in most U.S. institutions because of their physical characteristics. However, the study of White ethnic groups, such as Irish Americans and German Americans, can illustrate how these groups have attained high levels of cultural and structural assimilation (Ignatiev, 1995). Often, members of these groups are indistinguishable from other mainstream Americans (Alba, 1990).

When studying cultural and structural assimilation, students can also examine such groups as Polish Americans and Italian Americans. By studying these groups, students can see how some White ethnic groups are experiencing particular levels of cultural and structural assimilation but still retain many ethnic institutions. Individuals within these ethnic groups often participate in ethnic communities and institutions (Pula, 1995).

Other factors will also influence which ethnic groups you or the curriculum committee selects for study, including your interests and academic background and the ethnic groups represented in your class, school, and local community. However, units and lessons should not be limited to a study of local ethnic groups. Puerto Rican students should have the opportunity to study their own ethnic culture. They also need to learn about other ethnic cultures in order to understand more fully their own ethnic culture and the total human experience. Learning only about one's own culture is encapsulating and restricting. As Edward T. Hall has perceptively stated, "The future depends on [humankind's] transcending the limits of individual cultures" (Hall, 1977, p. 2).

Identifying Low-Level Generalizations

When key concepts and organizing generalizations have been selected and the ethnic groups to be studied have been identified, low-level generalizations related to each ethnic group should be stated. Identifying a low-level generalization for each group will ensure that specific information about each group will be included in the teaching units and lessons that will be developed later. Table 4.2 presents low-level generalizations related to seven major ethnic groups and to the key concept, *immigration–migration.*

Organizing generalizations are universal statements that omit references to specific peoples, cultures, and places. Intermediate-level generalizations refer to a particular nation, to regions within a nation, and to a particular culture. Low-level generalizations differ from both organizing and intermediate-level generalizations in that they apply to specific groups or microcultures within a culture and a nation.

Concepts and Generalizations in the Multicultural Curriculum

To help you plan the multicultural curriculum, I have identified five key concepts related to ethnic groups and related intermediate-level generalizations. To save space, related organizing generalizations are not stated. However, these can be inferred from the generalizations given. For example, the first concept is *conflict.* The related organizing generalization, which encompasses the two statements below it, is: *Throughout history conflict has arisen between and among groups in all societies.* Although organizing generalizations are not given below, they are important because they enable you to incorporate content from other nations for comparative purposes and to help students appreciate the power of high-level ideas. Table 4.3 shows how the students can use a data-retrieval chart to study the key concepts below and *immigration–migration,* which is in Table 4.2.

CONFLICT

(The words and phrases in capitals are concepts; the statements that follow them are related generalizations).

Conflict exists among different generations and subgroups within ethnic minority groups. These conflicts are especially evident in values, goals, and methods of protest.

CULTURAL DIVERSITY

There is wide diversity among and within various ethnic groups. The extent of group identification by members of ethnic groups varies greatly and is influenced by many factors, such as skin color, social class, and personal experiences.

VALUES

Many values within ethnic minority communities differ from those of mainstream Americans, even though their values are changing, especially as people of color become more culturally assimilated.

TABLE 4.3 Using Selected Key Concepts for a Comparative Study of American Ethnic Groups

Key Concepts	American Indians	Mexican Americans	African Americans	Jewish Americans	Vietnamese Americans	Puerto Ricans	Cuban Americans
Conflict: Within group: With other groups:							
Cultural Diversity: Within group:							
Values: Unique: Shared with others:							
Social Protest: Types used: Results of:							
Immigration– *Migration:* Reasons for: When: Results of:							
Assimilation: Cultural: Structural:							

SOCIAL PROTEST

At various times in history, movements within ethnic minority groups emerge to develop more pride in their groups, to shape new identities, to gain political power and control of institutions, and to shatter stereotypes. The intensity, scope, and type of movements have varied widely from group to group and have been influenced by the unique histories, values, cultures, and lifestyles of ethnic groups.

ASSIMILATION

As ethnic groups become more assimilated and attain higher socioeconomic status, they tend to abandon certain elements of their traditional cultures. However, they sometimes reclaim aspects of their cultural heritage once they are secure in middle- or upper-class status. This assimilation usually occurs in the third generation.

Teaching Strategies and Materials

Once you or the curriculum committee has identified the key concepts and generalizations that can serve as a framework for a multicultural curriculum or unit and has stated lower-level generalizations related to the experiences of ethnic groups in the United States, you (or the committee) can then identify the materials and teaching strategies necessary to help students derive the concepts and their related generalizations. A wide variety of teaching strategies, content, and materials can be used to teach ethnic content, many of which are described in the chapters on ethnic groups in this book (Chapters 5 through 14).

The sample generalization about immigration–migration in Table 4.2 can be effectively taught using content related to the forced westward migration of the Cherokee, which occurred in 1838 and 1839. This poignant migration is often called "The Trail of Tears."

Simulation, role-playing, as well as other strategies described in Parts II through V, can be used to teach effectively about immigration and other key concepts identified in this chapter. The six key concepts and organizing generalizations presented in Table 4.1 can be taught at every level within a spiral conceptual curriculum and developed at increasing levels of complexity with different content samples. At each level K–12 materials related to a range of ethnic groups should be used as content samples to teach students key social science concepts and generalizations. Figure 4.1 illustrates how six key concepts can be spiralled within a conceptual curriculum at eight different levels. This same curriculum design, of course, can be used in a K–12 program, an 8–12 curriculum, or with any levels.

Planning Lessons

To assure that every lower-level generalization identified in the initial stages of planning is adequately developed within a unit, the teacher can divide a sheet

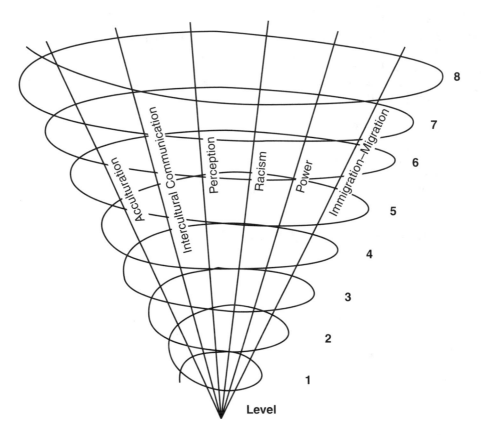

FIGURE 4.1   Six Key Concepts Spiralled within a Conceptual Curriculum at Eight Different Levels   This diagram illustrates how information related to America's ethnic groups can be organized around key concepts and taught at successive levels at an increasing degree of complexity.

of paper in half and list the key concepts and the organizing, intermediate-level, and lower-level generalizations on one side of it and the strategies and materials needed to teach the ideas on the other half (see Table 4.4).

The Value Component of the Multicultural Curriculum

Although higher-level scientific knowledge is necessary for reflective decision making on ethnic and racial problems, it is not sufficient. To make reflective decisions, citizens must also identify and clarify their values and relate them to

TABLE 4.4   Key Ideas and Teaching Strategies

Key Ideas	Activities
Key Concept: Immigration–Migration **Organizing Generalization:** In all cultures, individuals and groups have moved to different regions in order to seek better economic, political, and social opportunities. However, movement of individuals and groups has been both voluntary and forced. **Intermediate-Level Generalization:** Most individual and groups who have immigrated to the United States and who have migrated within it were seeking better economic, political, and social opportunities. However, movement of individuals and groups within the United States has been both voluntary and forced. **Lower-Level Generalization:** During World War II, Japanese Americans were forced to move from their homes to internment camps.	1. Reading aloud selections from Takashima, *A Child in Prison Camp*. 2. Discussing how Shichan, Yuki, and Mother felt when David and Father were taken away. 3. Viewing and discussing the drawings in *A Child in Prison Camp*. 4. Viewing and discussing the photographs in Conrat and Conrat, *Executive Order 9066: The Internment of 110,000 Japanese Americans*. 5. Hypothesizing about why Japanese Americans were interned. 6. Comparing textbook accounts of the internment with accounts in *Executive Order 9066* and *Within the Barbed Wire Fence: A Japanese Man's Account of His Internment* by Takeo U. Nakano. 7. Reading selections from the novel *Journey to Topaz*, by Yoshiko Uchida, and discussing the experiences of the Sakane family during internment. 8. Viewing and discussing the videotape *Family Gathering* (New York: New Day Films). In this videotape, a Japanese American woman comes to terms with her family's World War II internment. 9. Summarizing and generalizing about the forced migration (internment) of Japanese Americans during World War II.

the knowledge they have derived through the process of inquiry. Values education today is often referred to as *character education* (Lickona, 1991). However, to be consistent with the notion of values education in this book, character education must enable students to think critically about values and to make values choices freely. A didactic approach to character education will not enable students to undertake the kind of value analysis that is essential for reflective decision making and action.

Because many ethnic and racial problems within our society are rooted in value conflicts, the school should play a significant role in helping students to identify and clarify their values and to make moral choices reflectively. Although the school has a tremendous responsibility to help students make moral choices thoughtfully, teachers often fail to help students deal with moral issues reflectively.

Some teachers treat value problems like the invisible person; they deny their existence. They assume that if students know all the "facts," they can resolve value problems. Such teachers may be said to practice the cult of false objectivity. Other teachers use an evasion strategy: when value problems arise in the classroom, they try to change the subject to a safer topic. A frequently used approach to value education in the elementary and high school is the inculcation of values considered "right" by adults or the indoctrination of these values. Such values as honesty, justice, truth, freedom, equality, and love (as defined by teachers) are taught with legendary heroes and heroines, stories, rituals, and patriotic songs. This approach to value education—which is the way that character education is conceptualized by some educators—is unsound and inconsistent with a democratic classroom and society.

The school should promote democratic values such as human dignity, justice, and equality. However, these values cannot be taught in a didactic fashion. Didactic approaches to moral education are unsound because they fail to help students learn a process for handling value conflicts and dilemmas. Often, individuals must choose between two equally "good" values, such as freedom and equality. In a democratic pluralistic nation such as the United States, values such as freedom and equality are often interpreted differently by different individuals and groups. The values themselves are also often in conflict.

During the mid-1990s, many African Americans, Mexican Americans, American Indians, and women argued that affirmative action programs were necessary for them to attain equal employment opportunities because of past discrimination (Edley, 1996). White males often opposed affirmative action and felt that it denied them equality and justice. In 1995, Governor Pete Wilson of California became a visible and influential leader in an anti-affirmative action movement that resulted in the end of affirmative action in the state's colleges and universities (Orfield, 2001). Affirmative action is a highly contentious issue because of the different ways that various interest groups view and interpret it (Edley, 1996; Ezorsky, 1991).

Because of the different ways in which various ethnic and racial groups often interpret the same values, such as justice, equality, and freedom, and because of the conflicts inherent in these values, teaching students in a didactic manner that they should value honesty, freedom, or justice is ineffective. Rather, students should be taught a *process* for identifying value conflicts, analyzing them, and for resolving value conflicts and dilemmas.

Students should also be helped to make reflective moral choices and learn how to justify their moral decisions. All values are not equally valid. Some values, such as inequality, racism, and oppression, are clearly inconsistent with human dignity and other American creed values that are set forth in the basic legal and constitutional documents of the United States. Although standards that guide a person's life must be freely chosen from alternatives after thoughtful consideration of their consequences, students who choose or hold values that conflict with human dignity and other American creed values should be helped to see how their values conflict with democratic values and ideologies.

Students should also be helped to understand and predict the possible consequences of the values they embrace. The major goal of moral education should be *to help students develop a process for identifying value conflicts, resolving them, and rationally choosing and defending their moral choices.* This is the only approach to value education that is consistent with democratic teaching and learning. Serious value problems arise in the classroom when ethnic groups are studied. Students of color often have important value questions about their ethnic cultures, their identities, and about effective strategies to use to effect social and political change. Public issues such as poverty, affirmative action, and discrimination in housing and employment pose controversial and complex moral dilemmas.

Approaches to Moral Education

A number of models, approaches, and theories related to value education have been developed that you can use to organize and teach value inquiry lessons. These include the public issues approach developed by Oliver and Shaver (1966) and Newmann (1970), the values clarification approach conceptualized by Simon, Harmin, and Raths (1991), and the cognitive-developmental approach developed by Lawrence Kohlberg (1975). The next section presents a brief summary of the cognitive-developmental approach developed by Kohlberg and a value inquiry model that I have developed.

The Cognitive-Developmental Approach to Moral Education

Kohlberg (1975) hypothesized that an individual's ability to reason morally develops sequentially in a series of definite stages and that these stages are found in all nations and cultures. He identified three levels of moral development: (1) the preconventional, (2) the conventional, and (3) the postconventional. Each level has two stages. The six stages constitute a hierarchy: each higher stage is a more sophisticated and more rational form of moral reasoning (see Table 4.5).

The theory assumes that an individual's stage of moral development can be determined and that moral education must be based on the student's stage of moral reasoning. A major goal of moral education, according to Kohlberg, is to stimulate students by using moral dilemmas to move to the next higher stage of moral development.

TABLE 4.5   A Summary of Kohlberg's Stages of Moral Development

Level 1: Pre-Conventional

At this level an individual's moral reasoning results from the consequences of actions (punishment, reward, exchange of favors) and from the physical power of those in positions of authority.

Stage 1:   Decisions result from a blind obedience to power, an attempt to avoid punishment, or an attempt to seek rewards.

Stage 2:   Decisions result from a desire to satisfy one's own needs and occasionally the needs of others. Individuals view reciprocity as a matter of "You scratch my back and I'll scratch yours." Reasoning involves little consideration of loyalty, gratitude, or justice.

Level 2: Conventional

At this level an individual's moral reasoning involves consideration of the interest of others (family and peers) and a desire to maintain, respect, support, and justify the existing social order.

Stage 3:   Decisions result from a desire to please and help others and receive their approval in return. Behavior is frequently judged by intention—"He means well" becomes important for the first time.

Stage 4:   Decisions result from a desire to maintain the existing authority, rules, and social order. Right behavior consists of doing one's duty.

Level 3: Post-Conventional

At this level an individual's moral reasoning incorporates moral values and principles that have validity and application beyond the authority of groups. Moral reasoning becomes more comprehensive and reflects universal principles.

Stage 5:   Decisions result from recognition of an individual's rights within a society that has a social contract. As a result the individual's reasoning emphasizes the "legal point of view," but with an emphasis on the possibility of changing laws.

Stage 6:   Decisions result from an obligation to universal ethical principles that apply to all [human-]kind. The universal principles of justice, reciprocity, and equality of human rights, and respect for the dignity of human beings as individuals serve as a basis for individual reasoning.

Source: From "An Application of Kohlberg's Theory of Moral Development to the Social Studies Classroom," by Ronald E. Galbraith and Thomas M. Jones, 1975, *Social Education, 39*, p. 17. Copyright 1975 by National Council for the Social Studies. Reprinted by permission.

Kohlberg believed that students cannot understand levels of moral reasoning that are more than one stage higher than their own. However, instruction below a student's stage of moral development will not stimulate her to think at the next higher stage. Kohlberg's research indicated that, when students are engaged in discussions about moral dilemmas in which they are required to reason at one stage above their current stage, moral development and growth occur. Two basic assumptions of Kohlberg's theory are that an individual must proceed through the stages sequentially and that none can be skipped.

The theory assumes that there is an indirect relationship between chronological age and level of moral development. Very young children, according to the theory, tend to reason at the lower levels. As individuals grow older, they tend to reason at the higher levels. However, Kohlberg found that most individuals he studied were not able to reason beyond Stage 4. Kohlberg used open-ended stories that present moral dilemmas and discussion related to the dilemmas to stimulate students to think at higher stages of moral development. The nature and quality of the subsequent discussion are an extremely important part of this teaching strategy. Kohlberg used stories similar to "What Should the Vinsons Do?"

What Should the Vinsons Do?

Mr. and Mrs. Vinson are strong advocates of civil rights in the local community. Mr. Vinson testified in favor of school desegregation when the U.S. Commission on Civil Rights held hearings on school desegregation in Northtown two years ago. A year ago the Northtown Public Schools were ordered by a federal judge to implement immediately a plan for desegregating its public schools. The plan was implemented when school opened in September. Lincoln School, which had been an all-White school, was the first school that African American students attended. These students *are bused from the Vinsons' neighborhood.*

The Vinsons' daughter, Tessie Mae, who is eight, is one of the students being bused to the Lincoln School each day. Tessie Mae gets up at 6:30 A.M. so that she can catch the bus in front of her house at 7:30 A.M. Last week, just one month after school opened, a ten-year-old African American girl was beaten by a White mob at Lincoln School. Rumors say that some White parents are coming to school with guns. The climate of the school is tense and hostile. A racial incident occurs at the school almost daily. Several days last week White parents greeted the buses bringing Black children to Lincoln School by throwing rocks and eggs at them. Anti-Black graffiti are on the walls of Lincoln's halls.

The Vinsons are worried about their daughter and are seriously considering taking her out of Lincoln School. However, the leaders of the National Association for the Advancement of Colored People (NAACP), which initiated the legal suit that resulted in the court order forcing the Northtown schools to desegregate, are strongly urging African Americans to keep sending their children to Lincoln. These leaders feel that, if African American parents stop sending their children to Lincoln, they will be doing exactly what many of the Whites want them to do and that they will be defeating the desegregation plan. The NAACP is urging the African American community to stand up for what it believes in: an equal education for African American children.

Question: Should the Vinsons take Tessie Mae out of Lincoln School?

A Value Inquiry Model

I have developed a value inquiry model that is presented in detail in *Teaching Strategies for the Social Studies,* 5th ed. (Banks & Banks, with Clegg, 1999), that you can use to help students to identify value conflicts, examine them reflectively, and choose and defend their moral choices. The model is reprinted below (in list form), along with a sample lesson illustrating how it can be used when discussing value problems related to race and ethnicity.

1. Defining and recognizing value problems: observation–discrimination.
2. Describing value-relevant behavior: description–discrimination
3. Naming values exemplified by behavior described: identification–description, hypothesizing
4. Determining conflicting values in behavior described: identification–analysis
5. Hypothesizing about sources of values analyzed: hypothesizing (citing data to support hypotheses)
6. Naming alternative values to those exemplified by behavior observed: recalling
7. Hypothesizing about the possible consequences of the values analyzed: predicting, comparing, contrasting
8. Declaring value preference: choosing
9. Stating reasons, sources, and possible consequences of value choice: justifying, hypothesizing, predicting

Value Inquiry Lessons: Examples

For value inquiry lessons, you can use case studies clipped from the daily newspaper, such as incidents related to racial profiling, housing discrimination, and affirmative action. Ethnic literature and open-ended stories are excellent resources for value inquiry. Below, I will use an open-ended story, "Seed of Distrust," to show an example of a value inquiry lesson. Photographs, role-playing activities, and case studies related to ethnic events can also be used effectively.

An Open-Ended Story.   Open-ended stories present problem situations. If carefully chosen or written, they are excellent tools for stimulating class discussions of issues related to race and ethnicity, as well as other human relations problems. After reading an open-ended story to the class, you can have the students identify the problems within it, the values of the characters, the courses of action they might take to resolve the problems, and the possible consequences of the proposed solutions. The students can also act out or role-play solutions to the problems.

Role-Playing in the Curriculum by Fannie R. Shaftel and George Shaftel (1982) includes several open-ended stories that deal with intergroup problems. The story reprinted below is from this book. Questions that can be used with the story are also provided.

Seed of Distrust

Betty was all excited when she ran into the apartment. "Mother, will you iron my green dress tonight?"

"I was planning to do it Saturday night, honey, so you'd have it for Sunday School."

"But I'll need it!"

"What's the rush?"

"Nora's invited me to a party tomorrow after school."

"Oh. I see," her mother said slowly, as if thinking hard. "Nora's the little girl on the second floor?"

"Yes. She's real nice."

Betty's sister Lucy, who was a sophomore in high school, asked, "Does her mother know?"

"Know what?" Betty asked.

"Nora's White. Isn't she?"

"Sure!"

"Does her mother know she's invited you?"

"Of course! I m-mean. I guess so."

"Does her mother know you're Black?" [Or Mexican, or Puerto Rican, etc.]"

"Sure!"

"You mean you think so?"

"Y-Yes," Betty stammered.

"Better make sure," Lucy said, and turned back to the math she was studying.

"I'll iron your dress, honey," Betty's mother said reassuringly. "You'll look real nice."

"Uh-huh," Betty said dully. "Thanks, Mom."

And then, next day, after lunch, the thing happened—Nora met Betty in the hall, outside the fifth-grade room.

"Betty. I've been hunting for you," Nora said urgently. "Listen. My Aunt Dorothy phoned last night. She's arriving today for a visit. My grandma's coming over to see her, and mother's making a dinner for the whole family, cousins and all. You see? We've got to postpone my party. Until next week, maybe. I'll let you know!"

Betty looked at her, blank-faced.

"Don't bother," Betty said. "Don't bother at all." And Betty turned and walked away, her back very straight. For an instant Nora just stood and stared. Then she ran. She caught Betty's arm and stopped her.

"Betty, what's the matter? Why're you talking like that?" (pp. 383–384)

(Copyright © 1982 by Prentice-Hall. Reprinted by permission.)

Questions
1. What is the main problem in this story?
2. What do you think of these characters: Betty, Lucy, Nora? Why? What kinds of things and people do you think are important to each of them? Why?
3. Do you think that Lucy should have asked Betty if Nora's mother knew that she was an African American? Why or why not?
4. Do you think Nora told the truth about the family dinner? Why or why not?
5. What are some courses of action that Betty can take? What should Betty do? Why? What would you do if you were Betty? Why? What might be the consequences of your action? Why?

Providing Opportunities for Personal, Social, and Civic Action

People of color in all regions of the United States are victims of institutionalized racism, poverty, and political powerlessness. When you identify concepts and generalizations, you should select those that will help students make decisions and take personal, social, or civic actions that reduce prejudice and discrimination in their personal lives, in the school, and, when possible, in the other social settings in which they function. Primary grade students cannot take actions that will reduce discrimination in the larger society. However, they can make a commitment to not tell or laugh at racist jokes, to play with and make friends with students from other racial, ethnic, and religious groups, and to read books that describe children from other racial, ethnic, and religious groups. Middle, upper grade, and high school students can also take personal and social actions within the school community to improve race and ethnic relations (Lewis, 1991).

Teachers must play an active role in getting students to undertake personal and social action to improve race relations in their personal lives and in the institutions in which they function. To improve race relations in the classroom, you can structure interracial work and study groups, making sure that students of color have equal-status roles in these groups (Cohen, 1994). Research has indicated that when students from different races and social classes have equal status within interracial work and study groups, these groups can improve interracial attitudes and help students of color increase their academic achievement (Slavin, 2001). A number of researchers, such as Slavin (2001) and Cohen (1994), have published works that will enable you to structure cooperative groups that will help students develop more positive intergroup and interracial attitudes. If you structure groups within the classroom that improve students' interracial and ethnic attitudes, the students will be more likely to take actions in their personal lives outside of the classroom that will make their lives more interracial and multicultural.

After they have mastered higher-level knowledge related to racial and ethnic problems and have clarified their values, you can ask your students to list *possible actions* they can take to help improve race relations in their personal lives, in the school, and in the other institutions in which they function. Also ask them to list the *possible* consequences of each action they identify. Students should participate in action activities and projects only after they have studied the issues related to the action from the perspectives of the social sciences and humanities, analyzed and clarified their values regarding them, identified the possible consequences of their actions, and expressed a willingness to accept them.

Figure 4.2 is a graphic you can use when asking students to list possible actions and consequences they can take when planning action and participation projects and activities.

Finding Student Resources

Hundreds of children's books are published each year. Consequently, you will find it necessary to rely on bibliographies published periodically by professional and ethnic organizations to locate the most recent books. Some of the best bibliographies that list books on ethnic groups are published by public and private organizations, such as state departments of education, school systems, civil rights organizations, public libraries, and professional organizations.

One of the most comprehensive periodic publications that contains critical reviews of children's books dealing with ethnic groups is *Multicultural Review,* published quarterly by the Greenwood Publishing Group, located in Westport, Connecticut. *Multicultural Review* also contains feature articles as well as reviews of videotapes and other audiovisual materials. *Multicultural Perspectives,* a quarterly publication of the National Association for Multicultural Education, includes a column on "Multicultural Resources" that periodically includes a discussion of materials for students, including films, videotapes, and books. Most of the materials included in the column are for teachers and other professionals. *Teaching Tolerance,* a magazine published twice a year by the Southern Poverty Law Center, is distributed to teachers without charge. This magazine also has a Web site (*www.TeachingTolerance.org*). It includes helpful ideas for teaching about diversity as well as books and other materials for use with students. The National Women's History Project in Windsor, California,

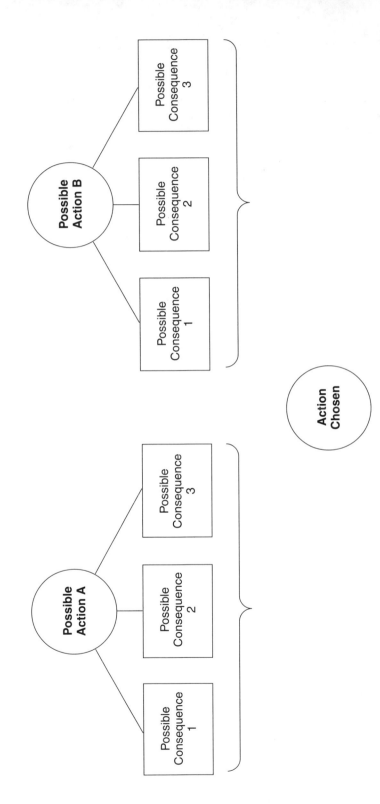

FIGURE 4.2 Possible Actions and Consequences

publishes a periodic *Women's History Catalog* that includes some excellent materials on women of color for students and teachers.

A book-length work that includes valuable annotations and information on children's books about diverse ethnic groups is *The New Press Guide to Multicultural Resources for Young Readers,* edited by Daphne Muse (1997). This comprehensive guide, which includes an index, consists of 688 pages.

Rethinking Schools, an excellent and informative periodic publication targeted for a teacher audience, contains perceptive and serious reviews of both student and teaching materials related to diversity. Rethinking Schools is located in Milwaukee, Wisconsin. Its Web site address is <*www.Rethinkingschools.org*>. AACP, in San Mateo, California, markets books and materials on Asian Americans. It publishes a comprehensive catalog periodically. *Quarterly Black Review of Books* is published six times per year in New York City. It reviews books for children and adults.

Several publishers specialize in books on ethnic groups of color. An example is Arte Publico Press at the University of Houston, which specializes in books on Latinos. Publishers that specialize in multiethnic books include Children's Book Press (San Francisco), Lee & Low Books (New York City), The New Press (New York City), and Northland Publishing (Flagstaff, AZ). You should check their Web sites and obtain copies of their periodic catalogs.

Social Education, the official journal of the National Council for the Social Studies, publishes an annual supplement on notable children's books. *The Booklist,* published by the American Library Association, the *Bulletin of the Center for Children's Books,* published by the University of Chicago Press for the University's Graduate School of Librarianship, *School Library Journal,* published by R. R. Bowker, and *Horn Book* are periodic publications that contain reviews of children's books. *The Language Arts,* published by the National Council of Teachers of English, occasionally publishes articles that discuss children's books. The Council periodically issues special publications on books dealing with ethnic groups.

Magazines and newspapers, such as *Ebony* and *The New York Times,* also publish book lists and reviews of children's books periodically. You should check these sources. Finally, browsing in the children's section of local bookstores in large cities can lead to the discovery of a gold mine of recent children's books. The salesperson in charge of children's books is usually willing and able to help the browsing teacher or school librarian.

Guidelines for Evaluating and Selecting Multicultural Materials

Some of the books and other materials on ethnic groups published each year are insensitive, inaccurate, and written from mainstream and insensitive perspectives and points of view. Nevertheless, good materials on each group are published annually. Identifying them requires a considerable amount of time and careful evaluation and selection. The books discussed in the following pages suggest criteria that will help teachers, curriculum specialists, and librarians evaluate and select ethnic studies resources for classroom and library use.

One useful way to select excellent books on ethnic themes for children and young adults is to examine carefully the new works of authors who have established reputations for writing sensitive and excellent books for children and young adults. African American authors, such as Lucille Clifton, Virginia Hamilton, Walter Dean Myers, and Mildred D. Taylor, have written excellent books that accurately depict African American culture in sensitive ways. Other authors of color have also written sensitive and powerful books about their particular groups, such as the late Yoshiko Uchida (Japanese American), Laurence Yep (Chinese American), Virginia Driving Hawk Sneve (American Indian), and Nicholasa Mohr (Puerto Rican). Some writers who are not members of the ethnic groups they write about have also established excellent reputations for writing and editing outstanding books. Both Dorothy Sterling and Milton Meltzer have edited outstanding books on African Americans.

Books and other materials should accurately portray the perspectives, attitudes, and feelings of ethnic groups. Certain values, aspirations, and viewpoints are prevalent in American ethnic communities. Books should honestly and accurately reflect these perspectives and feelings, both through characters and in the interpretations of events and situations. One of the best ways to assure that books describe the perspectives of ethnic groups is to use books written by them. In *The Magic Paintbrush,* Lawrence Yep (2000) describes how eight-year-old Steve turns to art to cope with the death of his parents and the destruction of his home in a fire. Yoshiko Uchida (1982) tells the powerful story of her family's internment in *Desert Exile: The Uprooting of a Japanese-American Family.* In her autobiography written for young people, Rosa Parks (with Haskins, 1992) gives her view on her arrest that triggered the Montgomery Bus Boycott. Her account refutes often-repeated accounts that state that she did not give up her seat because she was tired.

Fictional works should have strong ethnic characters. Many books have characters of color who are subservient, weak, and ignorant. Papa, Mama, Aunt Waka, and Rinko are strong characters with whom the reader can empathize in *A Jar of Dreams* by Yoshiko Uchida (1981). The reader learns about the further adventures of Rinko in the sequels to this book, *The Best Bad Thing* (1985a) and *The Happiest Ending* (1985b).

Books should describe settings and experiences with which all students can identify and yet should accurately reflect ethnic cultures and lifestyles. The *Moon Lady* by Amy Tan (1992), *Finding the Greenstone* by Alice Walker (1991), *Drylongso* by Virginia Hamilton (1992), and *The Patchwork Quilt* by Valerie Flournoy (1985) each describe authentic ethnic cultures within the context of universal stories with which all children can identity.

The protagonists in books with ethnic themes should have ethnic character-istics but face conflicts and problems that are universal. The characters in *Dragon's Gate* by Laurence Yep (1993), *The Best Bad Thing* by Yoshiko Uchida (1985a), and *The Road to Memphis* by Mildred D. Taylor (1990) have authentic ethnic characteristics and values yet describe universal human problems.

The illustrations in books should be accurate, ethnically sensitive, and technically well done. Many books have beautiful photographs or drawings that are inaccurate. Excellent and powerful illustrations are in these titles: *Love Flute*, story and illustrations by Paul Goble (1992); *Lift Ev'ry Voice and Sing—The African American National Anthem,* by James Weldon Johnson, il-lustrated by Spivey Gilchrist (1995); and *African Animals ABC,* written and il-lustrated by Philippa-Alys Browne (1995).

Ethnic materials should not contain racist concepts, clichés, phrases, or words. Many books contain words, phrases, and statements that have negative connotations even though these books might have many other strengths. Books on Eskimos sometimes present them as carefree, happy people who have no serious human problems. Some books on Indians either state or imply that all Indians lived in tipis, were hostile to European settlers, and were sav-ages. Words such as *savage, squaw, hostile, primitive,* and *uncivilized* can alert you to a possibly insensitive book or resource, although their use in a book does not necessarily mean that it is insensitive. An author might use these words for the sake of historical accuracy, to depict the language of bigots, or for other justifiable reasons. The teacher or librarian must judge the use of words and phrases within the total context of the book or resource. Neverthe-less, you should watch for these kinds of words when evaluating instructional materials. You should also be sensitive to stereotypes of ethnic groups that are subtle. Subtle ethnic stereotypes are more frequent in books today than are blatant ones.

Factual materials should be historically accurate. Books that present inac-curate information about ethnic groups confuse students and reinforce stereo-types. They can also be the source of misconceptions and stereotypes. Examples of accurate informational books about ethnic groups are *The Middle Passage: White Ships/BlackCargo* by Tom Feelings (1995); *Stubborn Twig: Three Gener-ations in the Life of a Japanese American Family* by Lauren Kessler (1994); and *The Chinese American Family Album* by Dorothy and Thomas Hoobler (1994).

Multiethnic resources and basal textbooks should discuss major events and documents related to ethnic history. Events such as the removal of Indians to Indian Territory in the 1800s and the large migrations of Puerto Ricans to the U.S. mainland that began in the 1920s should be included in every compre-hensive U.S. history textbook. Key legal documents such as the Treaty of Guadalupe Hidalgo (1848) and the Chinese Exclusion Act of 1882 should be included. To be able to determine which key events and documents should be included in basic factual sources, you will need to read at least one general book and a comprehensive chapter on each of the major ethnic groups.

In addition to the guidelines suggested above, you should determine the age level for which a particular book might be appropriate. Both interest and reading level should be considered. Some books are excellent for adult reading but are inappropriate for school use; others are fine for older readers but inappropriate for young children. The type of classroom situation should also be considered when selecting multicultural materials. A particular book might be appropriate for use with some classrooms but not with others. You should bear in mind whether your class is, for example, all African American, all American Indian, all Asian, all White, or ethnically integrated. You should also consider how you will use each resource. Some books are excellent for basic information but will not give students a feeling for the ethnic group. Other books have excellent illustrations but poor and distorted texts. Some excellent books, such as *Desert Exile* and *In Nueva York* by Nicholasa Mohr (1977), are not appropriate for all students, all purposes, and in all kinds of settings. You should exercise sound judgment, sensitivity, integrity, and insight when selecting and evaluating multicultural materials for class use. In the final analysis, only you can determine which materials can best help to achieve your teaching goals.

Summary

This chapter has described the steps you need to take to structure a multicultural curriculum focused on decision making. These steps include (1) the identification of key concepts and generalizations, (2) the formulation of intermediate-level generalizations, and (3) the identification of lower-level generalizations related to the ethnic groups selected for study. Once these steps are completed, you can then proceed to structure lessons and gather materials. When formulating lessons, you should make sure that lessons include value inquiry exercises as well as social-action and participation activities when these are appropriate. Examples of value inquiry lessons and social participation activities were discussed.

Prior to implementing a multicultural curriculum, you should plan a reading program that includes (1) one or two general books on ethnic groups in the United States, and (2) at least one survey book or comprehensive chapter on each of the major ethnic groups. Recommended books in both categories are in the bibliography of this chapter. The selection and evaluation of student materials is a challenging task. Guidelines and resources for completing this task were given.

Part I of this book deals with the goals of the multicultural curriculum and procedures for planning and organizing instruction. Parts II through V present historical overviews of ethnic groups in the United States and strategies and materials for teaching about them.

REFLECTION AND ACTION ACTIVITIES

Respond to the following *Ethnic Literacy Test* and discuss your responses, giving reasons for them, with your classmates or colleagues. Determine your Ethnic Literacy Score by comparing your responses with the answers given at the end of the test. How might you use this test with your students to stimulate research and discussion? What sources might they use to check their responses? Administer this test, in part or whole, to your class. Adapt it to your students' reading and grade levels. How well did they do on the test? Why?

ETHNIC LITERACY TEST

Directions: Indicate whether each of the following statements is TRUE or FALSE by placing a "T" or "F" in front of it.

1. The U.S. Census projects that people of color will make up about 47% of the United States population by 2050.
2. The first Chinese immigrants who came to the United States worked on the railroads.
3. In 2000, the population of African Americans in the United States exceeded the national population in Canada, as well as that of Australia.
4. Puerto Ricans on the island of Puerto Rico became U.S. citizens in 1920.
5. In 2000, Mexican Americans made up 58.5% of the Hispanics in the United States.
6. Between 1820 and 1930, 15 million immigrants came to the United States.
7. White Anglo-Saxon Protestants are the most powerful ethnic group in the United States.
8. Rosh Hashanah, which in Hebrew means "end of year," is a Jewish holiday that comes early in the fall.
9. While most Arabs are Muslims, Arabs make up no more than than 20% of the Muslims in the world.
10. The first law to limit immigration to the United States was passed in 1882 to restrict the number of African immigrants.
11. Puerto Ricans in New York City tend to identify strongly with African Americans in that city.
12. In the 2000 Census, about 7 million people, or 2.4% of the population, identified with two or more racial groups.
13. Most African Americans came from the eastern parts of Africa.
14. The internment of the Japanese Americans during World War II was opposed by President Franklin D. Roosevelt.
15. The 2000 U.S. Census indicated that the Hispanic population slightly exceeded the African American population.
16. Between 1990 and 2000 the Chinese population increased more than any other group of Asian Americans.
17. Congress passed a Removal Act that authorized the removal of Indians from the east to west of the Mississippi in 1830.
18. A Japanese settlement was established in California as early as 1869.

19. The United States acquired a large part of Mexico's territory under the terms of the Treaty of Guadalupe Hidalgo in 1848.
20. Agriculture dominates the economy of the island of Puerto Rico.
21. The first Africans to arrive in North America came on a Dutch ship that landed at Jamestown, Virginia, in 1619.
22. Whites made up about 72% of the U.S. population in 2000.
23. *Paper sons* is a custom that is associated with Chinese Americans.
24. There were less than two million American Indians, Eskimos, and Aleuts in the United States in 2000.
25. Some of the bloodiest riots involving African Americans and Whites occurred in the early 1900s.
26. Between 1991 and 1998, over 300,000 immigrants came to the United States from Africa.
27. The United States acquired the island of Puerto Rico from Spain in 1898.
28. There are only 438 Japanese surnames.
29. Chinese immigrants to the United States became distinguished for their outstanding work on truck farms.
30. The 2000 U.S. Census indicated that 14.5% of Latinos were Central and South Americans, which was larger than the percentage of Puerto Ricans.
31. A third-generation Japanese American is called a Sansei.
32. About 251,700 Iranians immigrated to the United States between 1981 and 1998.
33. About one-fifth of Native Americans lived on reservations and trust lands in 1990.
34. Most Chinese immigrants to the United States came from western China.
35. Eleven Italian Americans were lynched in New Orleans in 1892.
36. Nativism directed against southern and eastern European immigrants was intense when the Statue of Liberty was dedicated in 1886.
37. In 2000 there were more than one million Cubans living in the United States.
38. More than 283,000 Haitians immigrated to the United States between 1981 and 1998.

Answers to Ethnic Literacy Test
1. T 2. F 3. T 4. F 5. T 6. F 7. T 8. F. 9. T 10. F. 11. F 12. T
13. F 14. F. 15. T 16. F 17. T 18. T 19. T 20. F 21. T 22. T
23. T 24. F 25. T 26. T 27. T 28. F 29. F. 30. T. 31. T. 32. T.
33. T. 34. F. 35. T. 36. T. 37. T. 38. T.

REFERENCES

Alba, R. D. (1990). *Ethnic Identity: The Transformation of White America*. New Haven: Yale University Press.
Banks, J. A. (1995). The Historical Reconstruction of Knowledge about Race: Implications for Transformative Teaching. *Educational Researcher, 21*(2), 15–25.
Banks, J. A., & Banks, C. A. M., with Clegg, A. A., Jr. (1999). *Teaching Strategies for the Social Studies* (5th ed.). New York: Longman.
Bayoumi, M., & Rubin, A. (Eds.). (2000). *The Edward Said Reader*. New York: Vintage Books.
Brodkin, K. (1998). *How Jews Became White Folks and What That Says about Race in America*. New Brunswick: Rutgers University Press.

Browne, P. A. (1995). *African Animals ABC*. San Francisco: Sierra Club Books for Children.

Cohen, E. G. (1994). *Designing Groupwork: Strategies for the Heterogeneous Classroom* (2nd ed.). New York: Teachers College Press.

Dershowitz, A. M. (1997). *The Vanishing American Jew: In Search of Jewish Identity for the Next Century*. New York: Little, Brown

Edley, C., Jr. (1996). *Not All Black and White: Affirmative Action and American Values*. New York: Hill and Wang.

Ezorsky, G. (1991). *Racism and Justice: The Case for Affirmative Action*. Ithaca, NY: Cornell University Press.

Feelings, T. (1995). *The Middle Passage: White Ships/Black Cargo*. Illustrated by the author. New York: Dial Books.

Flournoy, V. (1985). *The Patchwork Quilt*. Illustrated by J. Pinkney. New York: Dial.

Gabelko, N. H., & Michaelis, J. U. (1981). *Reducing Adolescent Prejudice: A Handbook*. New York: Teachers College Press.

Glock, C. Y., Wutnow, R., Piliavin, J. A., & Spencer, M. (1975). *Adolescent Prejudice*. New York: Harper and Row.

Goble, P. (1992). *Love Flute*. New York: Bradbury Press.

Hall, E. T. (1977). *Beyond Culture*. Garden City, NY: Doubleday.

Hamilton, V. (1992). *Drylongso*. Illustrated by J. Pinkney. New York: Harcourt.

Hoobler, D., & Hoobler, T. (1994). *The Chinese American Family Album*. New York: Oxford University Press.

Ignatiev, N. (1995). *How the Irish Became White*. New York: Routledge.

Johnson, J. W. (1995). *Lift Ev'ry Voice and Sing*. Illustrated by J. S. Gilchrist. New York: Scholastic.

Kessler, L. (1994). *Stubborn Twig: Three Generations in the Life of a Japanese American Family*. New York: Dutton.

Kohlberg, L. (1975, October). Moral Education for a Society in Moral Transition. *Educational Leadership, 33*, 46–54.

Lewis, B. A. (1991). *The Kids' Guide to Social Action*. Minneapolis: Free Spirit.

Lickona, T. (1991). *Educating for Character: How Our Schools Can Teach Respect and Responsibility*. New York: Bantam Books.

McCarus, E. (Ed.). (1994). *The Development of Arab-American Identity*. Ann Arbor: University of Michigan Press.

Mohr, N. (1977). *In Neuva York*. New York: Dial.

Muse, D. (Ed.). (1997). *The New Press Guide to Multicultural Resources for Young Readers*. New York: The New Press.

Newmann, F. N., with Oliver, D. W. (1970). *Clarifying Public Controversy: An Approach to Teaching Social Studies*. Boston: Little, Brown.

Oliver, D., & Shaver, J. P. (1966). *Teaching Public Issues in the High School*. Boston: Houghton Mifflin.

Olson, J. S., & Olson, J. E. (1995). *Cuban Americans*. New York: Twayne.

Orfield, G. (Ed.). (2001). *Diversity Challenged: Evidence on the Impact of Affirmative Action*. Cambridge, MA: Harvard Education Publishing Group.

Parks, R., with Haskins, J. (1992). *Rosa Parks: My Story*. New York: Dial.

Pula, J. S. (1995). *Polish Americans: An Ethnic Community*. New York: Twayne.

Rodriguez, C. (1991). *Puerto Ricans Born in the U.S.A.* (Rev. ed.). Boulder, CO: Westview.

Schuman, H., Steeh, C., Bobo, L., & Krysan, M. (1997). *Racial Attitudes in America: Trends and Interpretations* (Rev. ed.). Cambridge: Harvard University Press.

Shaftel, F. R., & Shaftel, G. (1982). *Role-Playing in the Curriculum* (2nd ed.). Englewood Cliffs, NJ: Prentice-Hall.

Simon, S. B., Harmin, M., & Raths, L. E. (1991). *Values and Teaching: Working with Values in the Classroom* (Rev. ed.). Columbus, OH: Charles E. Merrill.

Slavin, R. E. (2001). Cooperative Learning and Intergroup Relations. In J. A. Banks & C. A. M. Banks (Eds.), *Handbook of Research on Multicultural Education* (pp. 628–634). San Francisco: Jossey-Bass.

Tamura, E. H. (1994). *Americanization, Acculturation, and Ethnic Identity.* Urbana: University of Illinois Press.

Tan, A. (1992). *The Moon Lady.* Illustrated by G. Schields. New York: Macmillan.

Taylor, M. (1990). *The Road to Memphis.* New York: Puffin (Penguin).

Thernstrom, S., Orlov, A., & Handlin, O. (Eds.). (1980). *Harvard Encyclopedia of American Ethnic Groups.* Cambridge: Harvard University Press.

Totten, H. L., & Brown, R. W. (1994). *Culturally Diverse Library Collections for Children.* New York: Neal-Schuman.

Uchida, Y. (1981). *A Jar of Dreams.* New York: Atheneum.

Uchida, Y. (1982). *Desert Exile: The Uprooting of a Japanese-American Family.* Seattle: University of Washington Press.

Uchida, Y. (1985a). *The Best Bad Thing.* New York: Atheneum.

Uchida, Y. (1985b). *The Happiest Ending.* New York: Atheneum.

Walker, A. (1991). *Finding the Greenstone.* New York: Harcourt.

Waters, M. C. (1990). *Ethnic Options: Choosing Identities in America.* Berkeley: University of California Press.

Yep, L. (1993). *Dragon's Gate.* New York: HarperTrophy.

Yep, L. (2000). *The Journal of Wong Ming-Chung: A Chinese Miner.* New York: Scholastic.

Yep, L. (2000). *The Magic Paintbrush.* Illustrated by S. Wang. New York: HarperCollins.

BIBLIOGRAPHY

Multiethnic References

Eck, D. (2001). *A New Religious America: How a "Christian Country" Has Become the World's Most Religiously Diverse Nation.* New York: HarperCollins.

Jacobson, M. F. (1998). *Whiteness of a Different Color: European Immigrants and the Alchemy of Race.* Cambridge: Harvard University Press.

Malcomson, S. L. (2000). *One Drop of Blood: The American Misadventure of Race.* New York: Farrar, Straus, Giroux.

Rimers, D. M. (1992). *Still the Golden Door: The Third World Comes to America* (2nd ed.). New York: Columbia University Press.

African Americans

Franklin, J. H., & Moss, A. A., Jr. (2000). *From Slavery to Freedom: A History of Black Americans* (8th ed.). New York: Knopf.

Hine, D. C., & Thompson, K. (1998). *A Shining Thread of Hope: The History of Black Women in America.* New York: Broadway Books.

Horton, J. O., & Horton, L. E. (2001). *Hard Road to Freedom: The Story of African America.* New Brunswick: Rutgers University Press.

American Indians

Champagne, D. (1994). *Native America: Portrait of the Peoples.* Detroit: Visible Ink Press.

Hunt, S. (1999). *Illustrated Atlas of Native American History.* Edison, NJ: Chartwell.

Marks, P. M. (1998). *In a Barren Land: American Indian Dispossession and Survival.* New York: William Morrow.

Arab Americans

Kamalipour, Y. R. (Ed.). (1995). *The U.S. Media and the Middle East: Image and Perception.* Westport, CT: Praeger.

Naff, A. (1985). *Becoming American: The Early Arab Immigrant Experience*. Carbondale: Southern Illinois University Press.
Suleiman, M. (Ed.). (1999). *Arabs in America: Building a New Future*. Philadelphia: Temple University Press.

Asian Americans

Chan, S. (1991). *Asian Americans: An Interpretive History*. New York: Twayne.
Cordova, F. (1983). *Filipinos: Forgotten Asian Americans, 1773–1963*. Dubuque, IA: Kendall/Hunt.
Kitano, H. L., & Daniels, R. (1995). *Asian Americans: Emerging Minorities* (2nd ed.). Englewood Cliffs, NJ: Prentice-Hall.
Takaki, R. (1998). *Strangers from a Different Shore: A History of Asian Americans* (Rev. ed.). Boston: Little, Brown.
Wu, J. Y., & Song, M. (Eds.). (2000). *Asian American Studies: A Reader*. New Brunswick, NJ: Rutgers University Press.

Hispanic Americans

Gonzales, M. G. (1999). *Mexicanos: A History of Mexicans in the United States*. Bloomington, IN: Indiana University Press.
Meier, M. S., & Ribera, F. (1993). *Mexican Americans/American Mexicans: From Conquistadors to Chicanos* (Rev. ed.). New York: Hill and Wang.
Olson, J. S., & Olson, J. E. (1995). *Cuban Americans*. New York: Twayne.
Rodriguez, C. E. (1991). *Puerto Ricans Born in the U.S.A.* (Rev. ed.). Boulder, CO: Westview.

European Americans

Berrol, S. C. (1995). *Growing Up American: Immigrant Children in America: Then and Now*. New York: Twayne.
Dinnerstein, L., & Reimers, D. M. (1990). *Ethnic Americans: A History of Immigration* (3rd ed.). New York: HarperCollins.
Jones, M. A. (1992). *American Immigration* (2nd ed). Chicago: University of Chicago Press.
Pula, J. S. (1995). *Polish Americans: An Ethnic Community*. New York: Twayne.

Jewish Americans

Cohen, S., & Eisen, A. (2000). *The Jew within: Self, Family, and Community in America*. Bloomington, IN: Indiana University Press.
DeLange, N. (1997). *The Illustrated History of the Jewish People*. San Diego: Harcourt Brace.
Howe, I. (1998). *World of Our Fathers: The Journey of the East European Jews to America and the Life they Found and Made*. New York: Schocken.

PART TWO

The First Americans and African Americans

Concepts and Strategies

This part consists of content, concepts, teaching strategies, and materials for teaching about American Indians, Native Hawaiians, and African Americans. Although different in many ways, these groups share some important experiences. American Indians and Native Hawaiians are native to the land that is now the United States. African Americans were one of the first groups to come to America from a distant land. They were the only group to come in chains. Each of these groups has deep roots in America.

American Indians and Native Hawaiians are two of the nation's smallest ethnic groups (2000 population—2,475,956 [this figure includes Native Alaskans] and 140,652, respectively). African Americans have been in the past the nation's largest ethnic minority group (2000 population—34,658,190). African Americans comprised about 12.3% of the nation's population in 2000. Collectively, the various Hispanic ethnic groups slightly exceeded the population of African Americans in 2000 (35,305,818).

Despite the tremendous differences in the sizes of the populations of African Americans, Indians, and Native Hawaiians, the experiences of these groups have often been characterized by common concepts and themes, such as racism, discrimination, protest, and resistance. A study of these three ethnic groups will help students better understand the long journey toward freedom in the United States. It might also help them renew their commitment to justice and equality.

CHAPTER

5

American Indians

Concepts, Strategies, and Materials

The earth was created by the assistance of the sun, and it should be left as it was.... The earth and myself are of one mind.

—Chief Joseph, Nez Perce

Popular images about American Indians and Eskimos are widespread and often stereotypic, contributing to students' misunderstandings of Indian and Eskimo cultures. Older Western movies shown on television contribute greatly to the stereotypic image of American Indians within U.S. society. Statements made in schools by educators, such as "Sit like an Indian," also contribute to the perpetuation of Indian stereotypes. Even though popular books in the 2000s do not include the blatant stereotypes of the "hostile" Indian often found in books in the past, they usually present history from a Western-centric point of view and perspective. Popular books often call the Americas *the New World*, implying, if not stating, that Columbus "discovered" America, and describe the migration of European Americans from the eastern to the western part of the United States as "The Westward Movement."

These approaches to the study of American history and culture are Eurocentric and mainstream-centric because they imply that American civilization did not exist until the Europeans first arrived in the late fifteenth century. They consequently deny the existence of the Native American cultures and civilizations that had existed in the Americas for centuries before the Europeans came.

Archaeologists estimate that human beings have lived in the Americas for at least 40,000 years. These peoples had established complex civilizations before the Europeans arrived in the fifteenth century. These cultures included elaborate irrigation works and massive artificial mounds crowned with temples. The

Olmec in Mexico, the Chavin in Peru, and the civilizations of Teotihuacan, the Maya, the Toltecs, and Aztecs were important American civilizations before the Europeans arrived in the Americas (*Hammond Past Worlds*, 1988, p. 205).

A major goal of American Indian curriculum content should be to help students to view the development of the Americas—and of U.S. society in particular—from the point of view of the Native Americans. For example, the movement of the European Americans from the eastern to the western part of the United States was not, from the Indian point of view, a westward movement. The Lakota Sioux did not consider their homeland the west but the center of the universe. Students should be helped to understand key events, concepts, and issues from different ethnic and cultural perspectives. "The Westward Movement" had very different meanings for the migrating European Americans and for the Indians whose homelands were being invaded. To Indian people, it could more appropriately be called "An Age of Doom" or "The Great Invasion" rather than "The Westward Movement." By helping students to view concepts, events, and issues from diverse cultural and ethnic perspectives, we can help them become critical thinkers and more compassionate citizens of the nation-state. Content about American Indians can contribute greatly to these important and generic educational goals.

Early Life in the Americas

When the European explorers arrived in the Western Hemisphere in 1492, it was populated by many different cultures and groups that became collectively known as "Indians" to Europeans. Columbus thought that he had reached India when he landed in San Salvador in 1492. This misnaming of the aboriginal peoples of the Americas by the Europeans foreshadowed the misunderstandings, distrust, and hostility that later developed between the two groups.

The early history of American Indians is still somewhat of a mystery to scientists. Archaeologists are trying to unravel their early history by digging up fossils that give clues to early human life in the Americas. Occasionally, landmark archaeological discoveries are made, enabling scientists to learn more about early people in the Western Hemisphere. In 1927, near Folsom, New Mexico, scientists found a point embedded between the ribs of a Pleistocene bison that early Americans used for hunting. This finding proved that men and women were in the Americas when Ice Age animals were roaming freely on this continent. Similar points were found at a dig near Clovis, New Mexico, in 1932. Scientists were able to date the points to 9200 B.C. by using Carbon 14 (Ceram, 1971).

The Origins of American Indians

We do not know exactly when people first came to the Americas. However, archaeologists have ruled out the possibility that human beings evolved in the Western Hemisphere because no fossils of pre-Homo Sapiens have been found

AMERICAN INDIANS: HISTORICAL PERSPECTIVE

Important Dates	Events
1513	Juan Ponce de León landed on the Florida peninsula while en route from Puerto Rico. The relationship between Europeans and North American Indians began.
1565	The Spaniards established the St. Augustine colony in Florida, the first settlement organized by Europeans in present-day United States.
1637	Connecticut colonists killed more than 500 Indians when the Pequot tribe tried to stop the colonists from invading their territory. This event is known as the Pequot War.
1675–76	King Philip, a Wampanoag chief, led a coalition of Indian troops that nearly defeated the English colonists. However, his forces were eventually beaten and his body dismembered by the colonists.
1680	The Pueblos rebelled against the Spaniards and drove them from Pueblo territory. Many Spaniards were killed during the uprising.
1754–63	The French and Indian War occurred. It was one of a series of wars in which the French and the British struggled for control of the eastern part of North America. Each nation vied for Indian support.
1784	A group of Indians suffered a crushing defeat at Fallen Timbers in Ohio on August 20. In 1795, they were forced to sign a treaty that ceded large segments of their lands in the Northwest Territory to Whites.
1812	The War of 1812, a war between the United States and Britain, caused deep factions among the Indian tribes because of their different allegiances. The Indian allies of the British were severely punished by the United States when the war ended.
1824	The Bureau of Indian Affairs was established in the War Department.
1830	Congress passed a Removal Act that authorized the removal of Indians from east to west of the Mississippi and stated conditions under which removal could be legally undertaken.

Important Dates	Events
1831	The Supreme Court recognized Indian tribes as "domestic dependent nations" within the United States. In an 1832 decision, the Court declared that such nations had a right to self-government.
1838–39	The Cherokee were forcefully removed from Georgia to Indian Territory in present-day Oklahoma. Their poignant journey westward is recalled as the "Trail of Tears."
1864	The Colorado militia killed nearly 300 Cheyennes in a surprise attack at Sand Creek, after the Cheyenne leaders had negotiated an armistice. This incident is known as the Sand Creek Massacre.
1871	A congressional act prohibited the making of further treaties with Indian tribes.
1876	Sioux tribes, under the leadership of Sitting Bull, wiped out Custer's Seventh Cavalry at Little Big Horn. This was one of the last victories for Indian tribes.
1881	Helen Hunt Jackson's *A Century of Dishonor* was published. It was the first influential book to dramatize the plight of Indian peoples in the United States.
1886	The brave Apache warrior, Geronimo, surrendered to U.S. forces in September 1886. His surrender marked the defeat of the southwest tribes.
1887	Congress passed the Dawes Severalty Act, which was designed partially to terminate the Indian's special relationship with the U.S. government. It proved to be disastrous for Indians.
1890	Three hundred Sioux were killed at Wounded Knee Creek in South Dakota.
1924	The Snyder Act made American Indians citizens of the United States.
1928	The Meriam Survey recommended major changes in federal policy relate to Indian affairs. Many of its recommendations were implemented in subsequent years.
1934	The Wheeler-Howard Act made it possible for Indians to reestablish aspects of their traditional cultures, including tribal lands and governments.

Important Dates	Events
1944	The National Congress of American Indians was organized by Indians.
1946	The Indian Claims Commission was established to hear cases related to possible compensations due Indians for loss of land and property.
1948	Indians were granted the right to vote in New Mexico and Arizona.
1954	Congressional acts terminated the relationship between the federal government and several Indian tribes, including the Klamath tribe in Oregon, the Menominee of Wisconsin, and the California Indians.
1969	*Custer Died for Your Sins: An Indian Manifesto* by Vine DeLoria, Jr., was published. This book represented a significant point in the Indian civil rights movement. N. Scott Momaday won the Pulitzer Prize for *House Made of Dawn*.
1970	President Richard M. Nixon made a statement advocating Indian self-determination.
1972	Congress restored the Menominee tribe of Wisconsin to federal-trust status.
1973	Members of the American Indian Movement and other Indians occupied Wounded Knee, South Dakota, to dramatize the Indian's condition in the United States.
1975	The Indian Self-Determination Act recognized the autonomy of Indian tribes and their special relationship with the federal government.
1978	The Indian Freedom of Religion Act was passed. This act granted Indians the right to practice their religious beliefs.
1979	The Supreme Court upheld the fishing rights claims of the Indian tribes of Washington state.
1980	The Passamaquoddy and Penobscot tribes of Maine received a settlement of their land claims after a long and difficult legal battle.

Important Dates	Events
1989	Native American tribal groups were successful in convincing the Smithsonian Institution to develop a policy that will allow it to return the remains of their ancestors to them. Native American tribes felt that the remains of their ancestors were being desecrated by the Smithsonian as well as by other museums.
1990	The Native American Graves Protection and Repatriation Act was enacted. It requires federal agencies to return human remains and other objects to tribes that request them.
1991	Native Americans were honored by the renaming of the Custer Battlefield to the Little Bighorn National Monument.
2000	The U.S. Census revealed that the American Indian and Alaska Native population was 2,475,956 or 0.9% of the U.S. population.

on the American continent (Josephy, 1991). No remains of the closest cousins of human beings, the great apes, have been found in the Americas, either. Despite these theories, however, many Indian groups believe that they were created by the Great Spirit in the Americas. Archaeologists believe that the ancestors of American Indians originally came from Asia. However, when and how they came is a matter of controversy among archaeologists.

A decade ago, most archaeologists would have used the Bering Strait theory to explain how the people first reached the Western Hemisphere. The body of water separating Siberia and Alaska today is called the Bering Strait. This theory holds that, at various times in prehistory, this water receded and a landmass, called Beringia, bridged present-day Siberia and Alaska. The early ancestors of the Native Americans, according to this theory, walked across this stretch of land while hunting animals and plants to eat.

Today some scientists are rethinking the Bering Strait theory. Instead of arriving 14,000 years ago as many scientists used to believe, some think that humans arrived in the Americas 15,000, 20,000, or even 30,000 years ago (Parfit & Garrett, 2000). Some scientists are suggesting that some of the ancestors of Indians came to America by boat, which is challenging the theory that they all walked across Beringia.

The Indian Population before the Europeans Came

There is as much controversy about the size of the Indian population when the Europeans arrived in the Americas in the fifteenth century as there is about when the Indians crossed Beringia to reach the Americas. The population estimates vary greatly. In 1924, Rivet (cited in Stuart, 1987) estimated the Western Hemisphere population to have been 40 to 50 million and the North American population to have been 2 to 3.5 million when the Europeans arrived. Mooney (cited in Stuart, 1987), in 1928, estimated the Indian North American pre-Columbian population to be 1,153,000. In 1939, Kroeber estimated the Western Hemisphere population to be 8,400,000 and the North American continent population to be 900,000 (Stuart, 1987).

In the 1960s and 1970s, researchers such as Dobyns (1976) and Denevan (1976) seriously challenged the estimates by Mooney (1928) and Kroeber (1934), and made much higher estimates. Dobyns believes that the Americas were heavily populated when the Europeans arrived. In 1966, Dobyns estimated that the Western Hemisphere population at contact was 90,043,000 and that the North American population was 9,800,000 (Stuart, 1987). Dobyns and Denevan estimate that the population north of the Rio Grande was at least 10 million when the Europeans first came to the Americas.

The Diversity of Indian Cultures

Although the word *Indian* often connotes a stereotypic image in the popular mind, Indian peoples are quite diverse, both physically and culturally. Their skin color, height, hair texture, and facial features vary greatly.

It is not possible to determine exactly how many languages were spoken in the Americas before the Europeans came or to determine how many people spoke each language. Two frequently accepted estimates of the number of languages spoken are 1,800 and more than 2,000 (Harris & Levey, 1975). Anthropologists have tried, with great difficulty, to categorize Indian languages into six major language families.

How Indians survived also varied widely. Some groups, like the tribes of the subarctic, did not practice agriculture but obtained food by fishing and hunting. Agriculture was the basis of the sedentary communities and complex cultures of the southwest Indians.

Political institutions in Indian cultures were also quite diverse. Highly sophisticated confederations were common among the northeast tribes, such as the Creek Confederacy and the League of the Iroquois. These confederations contrasted strikingly with political life within the California tribes. These tribes usually had no formal political institutions, but were organized into small family units that were headed by men who had group responsibilities but little authority over others. Warring and raiding were important aspects of the Apache culture. However, the Hopi, who called themselves "the peaceful ones," were one of the most tranquil peoples on Earth. Social class had little meaning among the southwest tribes, but it was extremely important in the northwest Pacific Coast cultures. Food, hunting methods, house types, clothing, tools, and religious ceremonies also varied greatly among and within various American Indian cultural groups (Hunt, 1999).

Similarities in Indian Cultures

Although American Indian cultures are highly diverse, they are similar in many ways. Some of their similar characteristics, especially those related to core values, make up "Indianness" or what is uniquely "Indian." Indian cultures were and are based on a deep spirituality that greatly influences all aspects of life. Because Indians see people existing within a spiritual world that includes all other living things, they see themselves living in harmony with all beings on earth. They view the universe as a harmonious whole, with every object and being having a sacred life: to separate human beings from nature is antithetical to the Great Spirit, for to the Great Spirit all is life.

The tribes of the northwest Pacific Coast believed in many spirits. They sought the protection of these spirits through various ceremonies and rituals. American Indians often called on the help of the spirits in their daily lives. Shamans, who played a key role in many Indian religions, helped them gain contact with the spiritual world. The southwest tribes had a rich and elaborate year-round sequence of ceremonials including songs, dances, and poetry. The Hopi performed dances to bring rain. The Apaches engaged in special dances and ceremonies to gain the support of the spirits before undertaking raids or going into war. Many Indian groups often sought contact with the spirits by going on a vision quest. Spiritual beliefs and ceremonies permeated every aspect of Indian life (Stripes, 2001).

American Indians had a deep respect and reverence for the earth and for all other living things. They believed that people must not harm the earth and should regard it as sacred. Many Indian religious leaders were often shocked by the ways in which the White people's agriculture defiled the Mother Earth. Forbes (1973) has summarized these beliefs:

> The Earth our Mother is holy and should be treated as such...all forms of life are our brothers and sisters and have to be respected.... Life itself is a holy, sacred experience...we must live our lives as a religion, that is, with constant concern for spiritual relationships and values...we must live lives that bring forth both physical and spiritual 'beauty.' All life has the potentiality of bringing forth Beauty and Harmony, but [humans] in particular [have] also the ability to bring forth ugliness and disharmony (pp. 208–209).

In their literature and speeches, American Indians often bemoaned how the Whites destroyed and defiled the earth, as in this passage by a Winto elder (cited in McLuhan, 1971):

> The White people plow up the ground, pull down the trees, kill everything. The tree says, 'Don't. I am sore. Don't hurt me.' But they chop it down and cut it up.

The spirit of the land hates them. They blast our trees and stir it up to its depths.... How can the spirit of the earth like the White man?... Everywhere the White man has touched it, it is sore (p. 15).

The Indian conception of the earth and their relationship to the land differed greatly from the Europeans' and was a source of conflict among the cultures. The Indians believed that people could use the earth as long as they treated it with respect, but they could not sell it anymore than they could sell the air or the sea. When, in exchange for gifts, American Indians gave Europeans permission to use their lands, many did not realize that from a European viewpoint they were also giving up their own rights to use the lands. The Europeans regarded the earth as a commodity that could be broken into parts and owned by individuals. To the American Indian, the earth was sacred and, consequently, could never be owned by human beings.

Indian people also had a deep respect for the rights and dignity of the individual. Decisions in Indian councils and confederacies were usually based on group consensus. Deliberations were often long and decisions of governing bodies slow because consensus had to be attained. The Creek Confederacy reached all of its decisions by consensus. However, each nation within the confederacy maintained its autonomy and was not bound to a decision with which it did not agree. The Europeans learned a great deal from the American Indians about representative government and the rights and dignity of the individual, which they incorporated into the major constitutional documents on which U.S. democracy is based.

Leaders of groups within the subarctic tribes had little authority over their followers. This was characteristic of Indian societies. Leaders were rarely deified as they were in Europe, the Middle East, and Asia. There were few hierarchical political organizations in the Americas. Leaders often had to earn the respect of others by becoming outstanding warriors, acquiring a special ability to communicate with the spirits, or learning to perform some other service the community needed and valued. Communities were usually democratic, with no kings or other kinds of rulers. However, there were important exceptions to these generalizations. The Inca Empire of Peru was one of the most totalitarian states that ever existed in human history.

Because of their feudalistic background, the Europeans looked for kings among the Indians and assumed that Indian chiefs had absolute authority over their tribes. The European settlers created tremendous problems by imposing their conceptions of the nation-state on Indian societies. They made treaties with chiefs and assumed that they were binding on their tribes. They did not understand that the chief's authority was usually limited by the tribal council. He had little power that the tribe did not grant him. This cultural conflict between the Europeans and Indian groups haunted their relationships for centuries.

Early Contact with Europeans

The Indians' earliest contacts with the Europeans were usually friendly and generally involved trade. The French, the English, and the Dutch exchanged European goods and tools for furs. This exchange of goods was initially beneficial for both groups. The furs greatly increased the Europeans' wealth; the European goods and tools made life easier for the Indians. Eventually, the Indians began to consider the European goods necessities rather than luxuries. What had begun as a mutually beneficial trade relationship was destined to cause disaster for the Indians.

Indians acquired rum, guns, gunpowder, horses, and other goods from the Europeans. Tribes that wanted European goods but had depleted the supply of fur-producing animals on their lands began to invade the territories of other tribes to obtain furs for trade. These invasions led to skirmishes and eventually to wars. European goods made intertribal warring more likely and possible. It was rather easy for the tribes that had European guns and gunpowder to defeat tribes lacking these supplies. Thus, the Europeans, through trade and other schemes (discussed later), initiated divide-and-conquer tactics among the Indian tribes in New England. Indian wars, raids, and attacks were greatly intensified by the presence of the Europeans.

The League of the Iroquois began an aggressive campaign to gain a monopoly of the European trade and to dominate competing tribes. The League had eliminated hundreds of Hurons and forced those remaining into captivity in 1649. The Iroquois were feared by tribes throughout New England. They eventually dominated the Delawares, the Nanticokes, and other groups of Algonkian-speaking tribes by 1680. The League became so powerful that the British regarded it as a power to be reckoned with.

Indian and European Wars

From about 1540 to the 1790s, no one power was dominant in the Indian territory that had been invaded by the Europeans in the Northeast. The Swedes and the Dutch had been driven from the area before 1700. However, the French, Spanish, and English struggled for control of the region. The Indians also tried to maintain their power. The power struggle became more intricate and intense when the British colonies entered the contest. Until the American Revolution, the Indians were unable to tell which of the warlike European nations, if any, would become the dominant power. The Indians probably thought that a balance of power would eventually be established in the region, in which they would be a major participant.

The European wars and struggles for power deeply influenced Indian policy and political institutions. In each war with European people, the Indians had to decide which group, if any, they would support. Each of the powers competed for Indian alliance and support. Although the Indians often tried to maintain a policy of neutrality, this became increasingly difficult as the European nations aggressively vied for their support. The Creeks and the Cherokees fought on the side of the French, against the British, in the French and Indian War. The French were defeated, and their Indian allies were severely punished by the British for helping the enemy. The Indians were also weakened by their severe losses during the war.

The European wars caused deep factionalism within the Indian tribes and confederations. In the War of 1812, the various tribes became deeply divided over whether they should support the United States or the British. The treaties ending the American Revolution and the War of 1812 stunned and angered Britain's Indian allies. Neither treaty acknowledged the decisive roles the Indians had played in these wars. After the American Revolution, the British granted the colonists lands that were occupied by their Indian allies. The British had pitted Indian tribes against each other and then ignored these allies' self-interests when the fighting stopped. In time, the Indians began to see the futility of becoming involved in the European wars and became increasingly committed to a policy of neutrality. Alexander McGillivray, the Creek diplomat, used the Europeans' tactics and pitted the colonists against the Spaniards by astutely negotiating.

The Decline of the League of the Iroquois

The League of the Iroquois was deeply affected by the European wars and was eventually destroyed by the factionalism caused by the wars. The League, the French, and the British were the three major powers in the Northeast in the first decades of the 1700s. Factionalism developed within the League over the positions it should take in the European wars. One of the nations, the Senecas, fought on the side of the French in the French and Indian War. The other nations supported the British. Even greater disunity developed within the League when the American Revolution began. Some of the nations supported the British; others were sympathetic to the colonists. Internal splits developed within several of the nations over this issue. The colonists looted and burned Iroquois villages after the Revolution and flaunted their newly gained power.

The fate of the Iroquois was later experienced by other tribes. The Iroquois had warred against other Indian tribes in order to obtain furs to trade and had fought as allies in the European wars. Their confederation was later destroyed because of splits caused by the European wars. The Indian nations did not realize that they had a common fate in the Northeast, and that the future of one Indian nation was intricately tied to the future of all Indian tribes. Culturally and politically, the Indians were separate and distinct groups. However, the Whites saw them as a group that had to be pushed west of the Mississippi and ultimately conquered or destroyed.

Treaties and Indian Removal

The relationship between Indians and European settlers had developed into a pattern by the time of the American Revolution. The initial contact usually involved trade, whereby Indians acquired tools and firearms and the Europeans obtained furs. These initial events usually pitted Indian tribes against each other as they competed for the European trade and for the lands containing fur-producing animals. When the furs had been depleted, the Europeans began an aggressive drive to obtain the lands the Indians occupied. The Indians often formed confederations and alliances to fight back the European invaders or extended the functions of existing confederations. Ironically, however, the Indians' involvement in the White people's wars usually disrupted these confederations. Indians adamantly resisted the attempts by the Whites to displace them. They fought defensive wars, such as the King Philip's War in 1675 and the Black Hawk War in 1832. Indian uprisings also occurred, like the Sioux uprising in 1862 and the Little Crow uprising in 1863.

Despite the Indians' aggressive and bold resistance, the Europeans were destined to win the struggle. The Whites retaliated with shocking massacres, like Sand Creek in 1864, biological warfare, and massive wars in which men, women, and children were killed and, often, dismembered and scalped. After Indian resistance was crushed, Whites legitimized the taking of Indian lands by convincing the Indian leaders to sign treaties. Indian chiefs were frequently offered gifts or other bribes to sign treaties. Once an Indian group had signed a treaty, the Whites schemed to remove them from their land. Often the Indians were forced west of the Mississippi into Indian Territory (present-day Oklahoma), land the Whites considered uninhabitable. If only a few Indians remained after the conquest, they were often absorbed by local tribes or forced onto reservations.

This cycle was repeated many times as the White settlers pushed westward. When Whites went farther west, Indians were forced to sign new treaties granting Whites the lands earlier treaties had assured them. Some Indian groups, like the Winnebagos, were forced to move as many as six times during a period of thirty years. No aspects of U.S. history are more poignant than the accounts of the making and breaking of Indian treaties by Whites and the forced removal of Indians across the United States. This prediction by a Cherokee newspaper describing how Whites would obtain Indian land in Texas highlights how treaties were often made (cited in Hagan, 1961):

> A Commissioner will be sent down to negotiate, with a pocket full of money and his mouth full of lies. Some chiefs he will bribe, some he will flatter, and some he will make drunk: and the result will be...something that will be called a treaty (p. 99).

The Westward Journeys

Some Indian tribes, realizing the futility of resistance, moved westward without force. Others, however, bitterly resisted removal and were removed by military troops. Generally, the tribes that had to be removed at gunpoint suffered the most. However, they all suffered greatly. The Winnebagos, who offered little resistance, were shifted from place to place between 1829 and 1866. About half of them perished during the perpetual sojourn. The Seminoles, who signed a removal treaty in 1832, violently resisted removal. Hostilities began in 1835 and continued for seven years. The United States lost nearly 1,500 men and spent more than $50 million in its attempts to crush the Seminoles' resistance. Most of the Seminoles were eventually forced to move to Indian Territory. However, several hundred remained in the Florida Everglades, where their descendants live today.

The Georgians began an aggressive drive to remove the Cherokees from their homeland when gold was discovered on Cherokee land in 1829. The Cherokees initiated a court battle against removal. In 1832, the Supreme Court ruled that the Cherokees had a right to remain on their land. However, this ruling by the high court did not halt the determined efforts of the Georgians and President Andrew Jackson to remove the Cherokees. Harassed and pressured, part of the tribe finally signed a removal treaty in 1835. Even though only a minority of the tribe's leaders signed the treaty, the Cherokees were forced to move to Indian Territory. During the long march from Georgia to Oklahoma in 1838 and 1839, almost one fourth of the Cherokees died from starvation, diseases, and the perils of the journey. Their long westward journey is recalled as the "Trail of Tears." The Creeks were forced to sign a treaty in 1832, which gave the Whites rights to their lands east of the Mississippi. Nearly half of the Creeks perished during the migration to and during their early years in the West.

Like the White people's wars, removal caused deep factions within the various Indian tribes and nations. Some leaders felt that it was in their best interests to cooperate with the White authorities; others believed that removal should be resisted until the bitter end. These splits within the tribes intensified when the Indians arrived in the West and hastened the disintegration of their institutions that had begun before removal.

In retrospect, it is clear that Indian people either had to relocate or be exterminated. The federal government legitimized Indian removal with the Removal Act of 1830. This act legalized Indian removal and specified the conditions under which Indians could be removed legally. The act provided funds for removal and authorized an exchange of lands for displaced Indians. The act stipulated that the tribe's consent must be obtained, but made little difference in the actual removal of Indians. Local officials continued to use any possible tactics to convince Indians to sign treaties and to move westward.

Indians in the West

Much tension developed in the western territories when the eastern tribes reached their destinations. Many of the eastern tribes were forced to settle in territories occupied by the plains Indians. The plains tribes had acquired the White people's guns and horses and were tough fighters when the eastern tribes began to settle in their territories. When competition for the buffalo became acute, they fought and raided the eastern tribes. The U.S. government failed to provide the eastern tribes military protection as it had promised when they were forced to settle in the West.

The conquest and displacement of tribes that took place in the East later occurred west of the Mississippi. However, the conquest of the plains tribes and other western tribes took place in a shorter period of time. The powerful Sioux nations of the northern plains were defeated and forced onto reservations within twenty-seven years. The Comanche of the southern plains had been conquered by the White settlers by 1873. Writes Spicer (1969): "The other plains tribes presented about the same picture as the Comanche or the Sioux: a twenty or twenty-five year period of intensive warfare both with other tribes and the Americans, a period of unsettled and sometimes desperate conditions as they were forced on reservations and finally unhappy acceptance of the new way" (p. 87).

When the United States acquired most of the territory that now comprises the Southwest from Mexico in 1848 (see Chapter 10 on Mexican Americans), the southwestern tribes quickly learned that their new conquerors were enemies, not friends. The Spaniards had never completely conquered the southwestern tribes: they had retained a great deal of their culture and many institutions. Indians such as the Pueblos and the Pimas had hoped that the United States would protect them from the Navajos and the Apaches. However, the new government's goals were to conquer all of the tribes and to place them on reservations. The California gold rush of 1849 hastened the defeat of the western tribes. A congressional act in 1871 that prohibited further treaties indicated that Indian resistance had been broken and that the Indians were now considered a conquered and defeated people. The act declared that in the future, "no Indian nation or tribe within... the United States shall be acknowledged or recognized as an independent nation, tribe, or power" (cited in Josephy, 1991, pp. 339–340). This act represented a major change in federal policy in Indian affairs and reversed the policy declared by the Supreme Court in 1831. The Court ruled in 1831 that the "Cherokees and other Indians were dependent domestic nations...definable political entities within the United States" (Spicer, 1969, p. 66). The 1871 Congressional act closed an important chapter in Indian history. When he surrendered in 1877, Chief Joseph of the Nez Perce said:

> Hear me, my chiefs, I am tired; my heart is sick and sad. From where the sun now stands, I will fight no more forever.

Messianic Movements: The Utopian Quests

Indians had been conquered by the late 1880s, and vigorous efforts to eradicate their cultures, values, and ways of life were already under way. Many were forced to live on reservations that were operated by superintendents and government agents who ruled the Indians with an iron hand and stifled all their efforts for self-initiative. Confined to reservations (some of which were fenced in), many were forced to farm, which they considered women's work. In their desperation, Indians turned to religious prophets who promised a return to the traditional ways and the extermination of Whites and their life-styles. Messianic leaders who heralded the end of White domination emerged within many of the eastern and western tribes.

As early as the 1760s, a prophet arose among the Delawares. He urged his followers to reject European goods and return to their old way of life. Tensk-watawa, a Shawnee, experienced a revelation in 1805 that told him that White Americans would be destroyed by a natural catastrophe. Tenskwatawa and his brother, Tecumseh, taught the Shawnees to hold firm to their lands and refuse to relinquish them to the Whites. Handsome Lake began preaching among the Sen-ecas around 1800 after the League of the Iroquois had been broken up. He urged the Senecas to remain neutral in the White people's wars, not to indulge in the White vices, and to live by his moral code. Handsome Lake became important to those Senecas who were trying to resist cultural domination by the Whites.

As Whites began to conquer Indian tribes in the West, prophets who envi-sioned a utopian future emerged among the western tribes. In 1855, a prophet called Smohalla began preaching among the Wanapum Indians in the Oregon Territory. Like the eastern prophets, Smohalla preached that the White people would be eliminated and that their way of life was detrimental. He believed that the way the White people farmed harmed Mother Earth.

A Paiute prophet named Wovoka began having visions in 1885. He preached that a natural catastrophe would destroy White people and that the Indians' an-cestors would return. The White authorities became alarmed about Wovoka's re-ligion and its ritualistic "Ghost Dance." It spread rapidly among the Great Plains Indians and eventually reached the Lakota on the Pine Ridge Reservation in South Dakota. A frightened Indian agent called soldiers to the reservation in 1890. When a misunderstanding arose between the soldiers and Big Foot follow-ers, the soldiers killed 300 Sioux at Wounded Knee Creek. This incident shocked the nation and wiped out the Ghost Dance among most Indian tribes.

American Indians and Federal Policy

When the Indians had been thoroughly subjugated and placed on reservations, White authorities began efforts to "civilize" them; *civilize* meant to make them as much like Whites as possible. The goal of federal policy was to assimilate the Indians quickly into the mainstream society. No attempt was made to give them a choice or to encourage them to retain elements of their cultures. Efforts were made to make Indians farmers and to give their children White people's educa-tion. Indian children were sent to boarding schools far away from home reserva-tions so that the authority of their parents would be undermined (Lomawaima,

1994). The schools were a dismal failure. When Indian children left them, they were frequently unable to function well either in their ethnic communities or within the mainstream society. What the schools tried to teach had almost no relevance to life on the reservations. The schools also failed to teach Indian children the White people's culture. The quality of the teachers and the curricula were very poor.

Policymakers felt that they had to break up the Indians' communally held tribal lands and make individual allotments to family heads in order to make Indians independent and successful farmers. That this would violate Indian cultures and traditions was not a major concern. In 1887 Congress passed the Dawes Severalty Act. Designed to make Indians independent and to terminate their special relationship with the federal government, the act was destined to have the opposite effect. The act authorized the president to break up tribal lands and to make individual allotments to family heads. Each family head was to receive 160 acres; minors, 80 acres each. "Surplus" land was to be sold on the open market. The government was to hold the land in trust for 25 years. Citizenship was to be granted to family heads when they received their allotments. Many tribes adamantly opposed the act from the beginning.

The results of the act were disastrous for Indians. Many Whites bought or leased lands from Indians at outrageously low prices or obtained land from them in extralegal ways. Some Whites persuaded their Indian friends to will them their lands. Indians who made such wills often turned up mysteriously dead shortly after finalizing the will. A 1906 Congressional act gave the federal government more authority to supervise the administration of the Dawes Act. However, schemes for obtaining the Indian land developed more rapidly than government policies to safeguard it. Many Indians became poverty-stricken during the period in which the act was in effect. Indians lost about 90 million out of a total of 138 million acres of land between 1887 and 1932.

It was clear by the late 1920s that the Dawes Act had failed. It had not only resulted in the loss of millions of acres of tribal land but had also increased, rather than decreased, the role of the federal government in Indian affairs. The Meriam Report, published in 1928, recommended major reforms in federal Indian policy, including the abandonment of the allotment plan and the consolidation of Indian land for use by the tribes. John Collier, who became commissioner of Indian affairs in 1933, believed that tribal land should be reestablished, as well as Indian government and other aspects of Indian culture. In 1934 Congress passed an act sanctioning the new federal policy. Termination had failed; the government would now take a more active role in Indian affairs and urge Indians to reestablish aspects of their cultures. The Wheeler-Howard Act of 1934 brought a halt to the allotment of Indian lands, made it possible for tribes to acquire additional lands, and granted American Indians the right to local government based on their traditional cultures.

By the 1950s, advocates for the termination of the federal government's role in Indian tribal affairs were again dominant in the nation's capital. In

1953, the federal government stated its intent to abolish the federal role in tribal affairs and to treat Indians the same as other Americans in House Concurrent Resolution 108. During the 1950s, Congress passed several laws that gave the states additional responsibilities for Indian affairs. A 1954 termination bill ended the relationship between the federal government and the Klamath tribe in Oregon. The tribe and its reservation were abolished. However, the termination was disastrous for the Klamaths because they had not achieved economic independence when it began. The Menominee Reservation in Wisconsin was also terminated during the 1950s.

Self-Determination and the Challenge to Termination

Most Indians are strongly committed to their tribal groups and to the continuation of their special legal relationship with the federal government. They feel that only in this way can they, a relatively small group, acquire their political rights and justice. Indians believe that they are too few to exercise significant political power. Most Indian leaders remained strongly committed to self-determination and against termination during the period of the 1950s and 1960s, when a termination policy was pursued by the federal government. However, termination received a severe blow when President Richard Nixon stated his Indian policy in 1970. He said (cited in Spicer, 1980):

> Self-determination among the Indian people can and must be encouraged without the threat of eventual termination.... This is the only way that self-determination can effectively be fostered. This, then, must be the goal of any new national policy toward the Indian people: to strengthen the Indians' sense of autonomy without threatening the sense of community.... We must assure the Indian that he can assume control of his own life without being separated involuntarily from the tribal group. And we must make it clear that Indians can become independent of federal control without being cut off from federal concern and federal support (p. 120).

The challenge to termination and the support of Indian self-determination continued throughout the 1970s. According to the U.S. Commission on Civil Rights (1981), "The executive branch repudiated the policy of termination and successive administrations adopted a policy of Indian self-determination— a policy favoring Indian control over decision-making and promoting tribal interest" (p. 180). In 1975, the Indian Self-Determination Act made it clear that Indians could "control their relationships both among themselves and with non-Indian governments, organizations, and persons." The 1978 Indian Child Welfare Act provides for tribal jurisdiction and Indian community involvement in the adoption and foster placement of Indian children.

Fishing Rights and Land Claims

Tremendous controversies developed during the 1970s over both Indian fishing rights in the state of Washington and the land claims of Indian tribes in the states that originally made up the thirteen colonies. The fishing-rights controversy arose because of treaties signed by the federal government and Indians in the Washington Territory in the 1850s. The Indians gave up vast land claims in return for specific federal promises. One was a recognition of Indian fishing rights. The Indians were promised that they "could continue to fish where they always had fished, exclusively on reservation and in common with the citizens of the territory at the Indians' usual and accustomed grounds and stations off reservation" (U.S. Commission on Civil Rights, 1981, p. 180).

As the supply of fish grew smaller, the state of Washington began to regulate fishing in a way that favored non-Indian fishing and violated the Indians' treaty promises. Some Indians were jailed for fishing in ways that violated state law. However, these Indians felt that their fishing was legal because of the terms of the nineteenth-century treaties. When the Indians took their cases to the courts, they won major legal victories. In 1974, Judge George Boldt ruled in a federal District Court that the Indians had separate rights to a significant share of the fish and that the state should protect their rights and not interfere with them. The Boldt decision evoked a storm of controversy among the non-Indians of Washington state and led to personal attacks on Judge George Boldt.

The non-Indian fishermen strongly rejected the Boldt decision and worked to get the case to the Supreme Court. They hoped that the high court would reverse the Boldt decision. The Supreme Court ruled on the controversial case on July 2, 1979, and upheld the decision made by Judge Boldt.

In 1790, the U.S. Congress enacted the Indian Trade and Intercourse Act, also known as the Nonintercourse Act of 1790. This act, which is still in effect, requires the federal government to supervise the transfer of Indian lands to non-Indians in states that formerly made up the original thirteen colonies. This act was designed to maintain friendly relationships between Whites and Indians. Most of the land in these states was transferred from Indians to non-Indians without the required federal supervision. During the 1970s, a number of eastern Indian tribes went to court to claim that their lands had been transferred illegally and to demand redress and compensation for the illegal transfer of their lands.

The Passamaquoddy and Penobscot tribes of Maine took legal actions to regain more than ten million acres of land in the state of Maine. Their claim made up one half of the state and included land inhabited by 350,000 non-Indians. This property was valued at $25 million. After a long and difficult battle, these tribes received a settlement of their claim in 1980.

Other tribes that have made land claims, with varying results, include the Oneidas in New York state, the Mashpee tribe in Massachusetts, the Schaghiticoke tribe in Connecticut, and the Narrangansetts in Rhode Island. The Narragansetts received a rather rapid settlement of their claim. They made their claim in 1976 and received a settlement in 1978. Congress provided the funds to carry out the 1,800-acre settlement.

American Indians Today

The Indian Population

Once known as the "vanishing Americans," the American Indian population has increased at every Census count since 1940. The Indian population in 1940 was 345,000. The first complete census of American Indians was conducted in 1890. There were 248,000 Indians counted that year. The biggest increase in the Indian population since 1890 occurred between the 1970 and the 1980 Censuses. The Indian population increased 42% during that ten-year period, from 793,000 to 1,364,000 (U.S. Bureau of the Census, 1993). A number of factors other than the increase in the number of births over deaths may have accounted for this dramatic increase in the Indian population. These factors may have included improvements in the way the Census Bureau counted people in 1980, the wider use of self-identification to obtain information about ethnic group membership, and the greater tendency for people to identify as Indian in 1980 than in 1970 (U.S. Bureau of the Census, 1993). In 2000, the American Indian and Alaskan Native population was 2,475,956 (U. S. Census Bureau, 2001).

The 1990 Census identified about 500 American Indian tribes and bands (U.S. Bureau of the Census, 1993). These tribes and bands varied greatly in size. The Cherokee, the Navajo, the Chippewa, and the Sioux were the only tribes that included more than 100,000 people. About 16% of all Indians identified as Cherokee; about 12% identified as Navajo; and 6% each as Chippewa and Sioux. Figure 5.1 shows the ten largest American Indian tribes in 2000 and their populations. The four states with the largest Indian populations in 2000 were California (324,938), Oklahoma (262,931), Arizona (252,270), and New Mexico (171,507) (U.S. Census Bureau, 2001).

Indians in Urban Communities

American Indians have become increasingly urbanized since the 1950 Census. In 1950 about 56,000 Indians, or 16% of the total population, lived in urban areas and cities. That number had increased to 146,000, or 28% of the population, in 1960. In 1980, about 49% of Indians lived in urban areas (Snipp, 1991). This was a 4% increase from 1970. In 1990, 22.3% of American Indians, Eskimos, and Aluets lived on reservations and trust lands; 10.2% lived on tribal jurisdiction statistical areas; and most (62.3%) lived in other parts of the United States (see Figure 5.2). About 60% lived in urban areas. In 2001, nearly two thirds of Indians lived in cities and towns off reservations (Edwards, 2001).

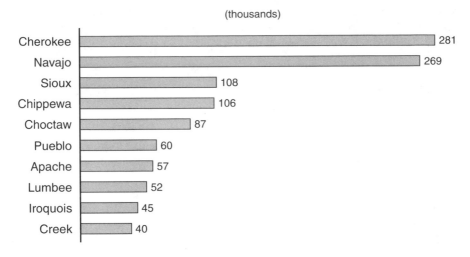

FIGURE 5.1   Ten Largest Indian Tribes: 2000

Source: Data Sets: Census 2000 Summary File 1 (SF 1) 100-Percent Data (http://www.census.gov)

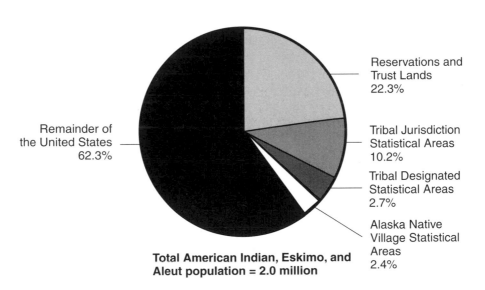

FIGURE 5.2   American Indian, Eskimos, and Aleuts by Type of Areas: 1990

Source: U.S. Bureau of the Census. (1993, September). *We, the First Americans.* Washington, DC: U.S. Government Printing Office, p. 7.

Even though about two thirds of American Indians lived off reservations in 2001, many reports, statistical sources, and other kinds of informational sources focus on the minority of Indians who live on reservations. Detailed studies of urban Indians are scarce. Wax (1971) includes a chapter, "Indians in the Cities," in his dated, but informative book, *Indian Americans: Unity and Diversity.* After a general discussion of Indians in cities, Wax discusses several case studies of urban Indian communities, including the Sioux in Rapid City, Iowa, the Tuscarora (a branch of the Iroquois) in New York state, and the Indians in Minneapolis.

Wax (1971), as well as other authors, such as Sorkin (1978) and Bolt (1987), point out that many Indians have a difficult time adjusting to life in urban communities. Often cut off from families and reservation benefits, they have trouble getting jobs, health and medical care, and good schooling for their children. Reservation Indians who migrate to urban areas tend to settle in towns and cities near reservations and to maintain contacts with their kin on the reservation. They frequently settle near reservations, such as in Gallup, New Mexico, Rapid City, South Dakota, and Ponca City, Oklahoma.

When teaching about Indians in the cities, you should not gloss over the enormous problems that urban Indians often have. However, you should remember that there is tremendous diversity within Indian urban communities. White, in a study summarized by Wax (1971), identified three social classes among Indians in his study of the Indians in Rapid City, South Dakota. He called one group "middle class mobiles." These individuals constituted what White called "the Mixed-blood elite." They were upwardly mobile and not highly identified with the full-blood Indians who lived on the reservation. He called another group "upper middle class White Indians." These individuals were descendants of upwardly mobile mixed-blood families. They occasionally identified with a female Indian ancestor. The final group of urban Indians that White identified were lower-class, rural, and reservation Indians who faced tremendous problems in the urban environment.

In a revealing and interesting study of Indians living in an urban community in a Great Lakes area city, Jackson (2001) found that the people she studied were trying to reconnect with their Indian pasts. To assimilate into White society, their parents had denied their Indian heritages and not revealed them to their children. Jackson described these children as having "holes in their hearts" because of the pain they experienced from being cut off from their Indian heritages. Jackson stated that urban Indians, who tend to be dispersed rather than concentrated in cities, form Indian organizations that cut across tribal lines.

Indians Face the Future

American Indians are in a unique demographic, cultural, legal, and historical situation. In 2000, Indians and Alaskan Natives numbered 2,475,956. They are increasing, rather than vanishing, Americans. However, they are never likely to be a powerful political force because of their relatively small population in a nation that numbers more than 280 million people. Yet, they have treaty rights to land and a special relationship with the federal government that no other ethnic group has. Consequently, they are able to exercise considerable power in the courts. When they do, however, as with fishing rights and land claims, they often evoke considerable hostility among non-Indians.

By most measures, Indians are one of the nation's poorest and least educated ethnic groups. Yet they own lands that contain rich resources that are of enormous value to this nation (Dorris, 1981). The challenge that Indians face today is how to marshal their legal claims and resources in ways that will help them to attain the full benefits of U.S. citizenship.

Teaching Strategies

To illustrate how content related to Indians can be used to integrate the curriculum, exemplary strategies are identified for teaching these concepts at the grade levels indicated: *cultural traditions* (primary grades), *cultural diversity and similarity* (intermediate and upper grades), and *federal policy* (high school grades).

Primary Grades

CONCEPT

Cultural Traditions
Generalization: Cultural traditions such as potlatches help us to remember and celebrate our past, to express caring and kindness, and to fulfill obligations and expectations.

1. Ask the students to list some of the ways that we show kindness and caring to family members and to friends. Responses might include: (1) with warm and cordial greetings such as "good morning and "good bye"; (2) saying "thank you" and "excuse me," helping family members with chores; and (3) helping a friend who is in trouble. Write their responses on the board or butcher paper.
2. Tell the children that we have special days that we celebrate. On these special days we give gifts to family members and friends to show kindness and caring, to fulfill expectations, and to satisfy obligations. Ask the children to name some of the special days on which we give or receive gifts. Responses might include birthdays, Valentine's Day, weddings, Christmas, and Chanukah. List their responses on the board or butcher paper.
3. Ask the children to name the people to whom we usually give or from whom we usually receive gifts on these special days. Responses will probably include family members and friends. List their responses on the board or butcher paper.
4. Ask the children: "Why do we usually give or receive gifts on these special days to family members and friends and not to strangers or to people we do

not know?" By using questions and discussion, help the students to develop and state the idea that "gift giving is a way of continuing our cultural traditions and expressing caring and kindness for family members and friends and of fulfilling obligations and expectations."

5. Tell the students that some American Indian and Eskimo groups have special occasions for giving gifts called *potlatches*. Explain that *potlatch* is from the Indian word *pat shotl*, which means 'giving' (Tucker, 1995). Read or phrase in your own words the description of *potlatches* that Mark Tucker, a Yup'ik Eskimo from Emmonak, Alaska, wrote in 1990:

> At a potlatch, one village invites another village to watch some dancing and to accept gifts.... Alaska native villages have sponsored this kind of potlatch as far back as anyone can remember. The Indians of the Northwest Coast also hold potlatches to celebrate the completion of a new totem pole or to celebrate the building of a new house by members of the clan. [Explain what a *totem pole* is to the students and show them pictures of some. Excellent photographs of totem poles are in Bruggmann & Gerber (1987), *Indians of the Northwest Coast*].
>
> Once a child attains a certain age, the parents and grandparents prepare a "first dance" [like a debut] for that child. The mother and grandmothers make such gifts as yarn gloves, socks, mittens, hot plate holders and aprons. The father and grandfathers make things like spears, spear throwers, harpoons, ice picks, fish traps and ulus.
>
> When the child is ready to dance, his family hands out these gifts to the family of the person whose name was handed down to the child. It is a Yup'ik custom that a newborn child is named after the last elder in the village to die. After the potlatch, the child is allowed to dance as many songs as he or she wants at any social event (pp. 193–194).

6. Summarize the lesson by pointing out how the traditions of giving gifts within mainstream U.S. society are in some ways similar to traditions within American Indian and Eskimo groups to show caring and kindness and to fulfill obligations and expectations. *Potlatches* are also unique and different in many ways from giving traditions within mainstream society. However, stress similarities so that the students will understand the ways in which gift giving is a tradition shared by human groups. The students can learn about other important characteristics of *potlatches*, such as their relationship to social status and about their spiritual aspects, in later grades.

Intermediate and Upper Grades

CONCEPT

Cultural Diversity and Similarity
Generalization: Indian cultures used both different and similar means to satisfy common human needs and wants.

1. Ask the students to name some things they think all human beings need in order to survive and satisfy unique human wants. Their responses will probably

include "food," "a place to live in," and "clothing." Probing questions might be necessary to bring out that people also have such needs as the need to explain unknown phenomena in the universe, for government, and for self-esteem.

2. List the student responses on the board and, with the class, group them into specific categories, such as food, shelter, clothing, government, family, religion, and economy.

3. Ask the students to name some institutions and means used in our society to meet the needs they have identified and categorized. Write their responses, in abbreviated form, on the board. Tell the class that in this unit they will be studying about how four earlier cultures in North America satisfied these same human needs in ways different from the ways in which we usually satisfy them today.

4. Before introducing the four cultures, develop, with the class, key questions related to each category. The students will use the questions as guides when studying the four cultures. Examples are as follows:

   a. Food
      (1) What kinds of foods did the people eat?
      (2) Were they primarily hunters and gatherers or farmers?
      (3) How was the food usually prepared? By whom?

   b. Government
      (1) Who or what group made major decisions and laws?
      (2) How were major decision makers chosen?
      (3) How were rules and laws enforced?

   c. Economy
      (1) What goods and services were produced?
      (2) How were they produced? By whom? For whom?
      (3) How were goods and services exchanged? Was some form of money used? Barter?

5. The students should record the key questions in their notebooks. They will use them as guides when examining the four cultures.

6. Introduce the four cultures the class will study. When selecting four Indian cultures for the unit, try to select cultures (1) that have both similarities and differences that the students will be able to see clearly, and (2) for which you have adequate and high quality student books and resources. To assure cultural diversity, select the four groups from four different geographical areas, such as the Southeast, the Northwest, the Southwest, and California. This unit could be taught with as few as two groups. However, generalizations are more powerful when they are developed from a larger content sample. On the other hand, it is difficult for elementary students to study more than four cultures in one unit. In our example, we have chosen the Iroquois (a northeastern Indian group), the Haida (Northwest), the Hopi (Southwest), and the Pomo (California). These four groups clearly illustrate both the similarities and diversity that existed within Indian cultures.

7. Ask the students to construct a data-retrieval chart (like the one illustrated in Table 5.1) that includes: (1) the categories and key questions they identified earlier, and (2) the names of the four groups. As they read and discuss each group, they should complete the blank spaces in the chart. When the chart is com-

TABLE 5.1 Data Retrieval Chart for Comparing and Contrasting Four Cultures

Categories and Related Questions	Iroquois	Haida	Hopi	Pomo
Food (Questions)				
Shelter (Questions)				
Clothing (Questions)				
Government (Questions)				
Family (Questions)				
Religion (Questions)				
Economy (Questions)				

pleted, ask the students key questions that will enable them to formulate this generalization: *Indian cultures used both different and similar means to satisfy common human needs and wants.* Excellent sources for factual information about various Indian tribes are Hoxie (1996), *Encyclopedia of North American Indians,* and Hunt (1999), *Illustrated Atlas of Native American History.*

8. Show the students the videotape *Weave of Time: The Story of a Navajo Family 1938–1986.* This videotape shows four generations of change in one Navajo family over a period of nearly fifty years. Ask the students to compare the changes over the four generations in the Navajo family with changes over the generations in their own families.

VALUING ACTIVITY

Speeches and selections that highlight traditional Indian values can evoke reflective value discussion and reasoning in the classroom. Rich and powerful sources of Indian speeches and statements are found in *Great Documents in American Indian History,* edited by Wayne Moquin with Charles Van Doren (1973), and *Touch the Earth: A Self-Portrait of Indian Existence,* edited by T. C. McLuhan (1971). The following statement was made by Chief Standing Bear (1933), a Sioux born in 1868. The teacher can read this statement to the class and/or project it using an overhead or opaque projector. He or she can then ask the questions that follow the selection and discuss them with the class. The teacher should encourage the students to give reasons for their responses and to defend rationally their moral choices.

The Lakota Was a True Naturalist—A Lover of Nature

He loved the earth and all things of the earth, the attachment growing with age. The old people came literally to love the soil and they sat or reclined on the ground with a feeling of being close to a mothering power. It was good for the skin to touch the earth and the old people liked to remove their moccasins and walk with bare feet on the sacred earth. Their [tipis] were built upon the earth and their altars were made of earth. The birds that flew in the air came to rest upon the earth and it was the final abiding place of all things that lived and grew. The soil was soothing, strengthening, cleansing, and healing.

That is why the old Indian still sits upon the earth instead of propping himself up and away from its life-giving forces. For him, to sit or lie upon the ground is to be able to think more deeply and to feel more keenly; he can see more clearly into the mysteries of life and come closer in kinship to other lives about him.... Kinship with all creatures of the earth, sky, and water was a real and active principle. For the animal and bird world there existed a brotherly feeling that kept the Lakota safe among them and so close did some of the Lakotas come to their feathered and furred friends that in true brotherhood they spoke a common tongue. The old Lakota was wise. He knew that a man's heart away from nature becomes hard; he knew that lack of respect for growing, living things soon led to lack of respect for humans too. So he kept his youth close to its softening influence (pp. 192–197).

Questions

1. What are the main values of the Lakota (tribal name for the Sioux) that are revealed in this statement by Chief Standing Bear?
2. In what ways might these values of the Lakota have conflicted with the values of the Europeans who settled in North America?
3. What problems do you think developed between the Lakota and the Europeans because of their value differences? Why?
4. How do traditional Lakota values, as revealed in the statement by Chief Standing Bear, conflict with many modern-day American values?
5. Do you think it is possible for individuals who endorse traditional Lakota values, such as those revealed in Chief Standing Bear's statement, to function successfully within a highly modernized nation such as the United States? Why or why not? What conflicts might such individuals experience? How might they resolve them?
6. Do you think that traditional Lakota values, as revealed in the Chief's statement, could help strengthen a modernized nation such as the United States? Why or why not? If so, in what ways?
7. Which of the traditional Lakota values revealed in Chief Standing Bear's statement do you personally endorse? Which do you reject? Are you willing to act on those that you endorse? Why or why not?
8. When did you last act on the values in the statement that you endorse? When do you plan to act on them again?

High School Grades

CONCEPT

Federal Policy
Generalization: Most federal policy on Indian affairs was made without Indian input and usually sought Indian assimilation and the termination of federal–tribal relationships.

1. To gain an understanding of the legal relationship Indian tribes have with the federal government, the students should examine some of the Indian treaties made between the United States government and Indian tribes. These treaties were usually made when Indian tribes were forced to cede their territories and to relocate on reservations. They were granted reservation land in exchange for their land. Several such treaties are reprinted in Chapter 2 of *Of Utmost Good Faith,* edited by Vine Deloria, Jr. (1971).

2. Shortly after Indians had been conquered and forced onto reservations in the late 1800s, efforts were begun by the federal government to terminate its special relationship with the tribes, to force them to give up most aspects of their cultures, and to force assimilation into the dominant culture. These goals of federal policy were implemented in the Dawes Severalty Act of 1887. Ask the students to research the arguments, both pro and con, that preceded the passage of the act.

   a. Although many White liberals favored the passage of the act, most Indian tribes opposed it. When the bill was being debated in Congress, representatives of the Five Civilized Tribes sent a strong message to Congress opposing its passage. Ask the class to read and discuss this statement, which is reprinted in *Of Utmost Good Faith,* edited by Vine Deloria, Jr. (1971).

   b. White allies of Indians strongly supported the passage of a bill, such as Dawes, that would break up tribal lands and allot them to individual household heads. They felt that such a bill would enable Indians to assimilate into the dominant culture. In 1884, the Indian Rights Association of Philadelphia, whose members were White friends of the Indian, issued a pamphlet strongly advocating the passage of an allotment bill. Ask the students to read and discuss excerpts from this pamphlet, reprinted in *The Indian and the White Man,* edited by Wilcombe Washburn (1964). The class should then compare the statement sent to Congress by the Five Civilized Tribes and the excerpt from the pamphlet. They should discuss the merits and weaknesses of the two positions.

3. Ask several students to role-play a debate between those who favored the Dawes bill and those who opposed it.

4. Ask the students to research these questions: "What effects did the Dawes Severalty Act have on Indian people?" "On White society?" "How do you think Indian life might be different today if the bill had failed in Congress?" "Why?" Two books, Alvin M. Josephy, Jr. (1991), *The Indian Heritage of America,* and Edward H. Spicer (1969), *A Short History of the Indian in the United States,* contain good discussions of the disastrous effects of the act on Indian tribes.

5. Because of the loss of millions of acres of tribal lands and the severe poverty of Indians, it was clear by the 1920s that the Dawes Act had been a colossal failure. John Collier, who became Commissioner of Indian Affairs in 1933, outlined a new federal policy for Indians. Ask the students to read and discuss his statement, "A New Deal for the Red Men," in Washburn (1964) and the federal act of 1934 that embodied the new federal policy, the Wheeler-Howard Act, in Deloria (1971).

6. Ask the class to research the effects the Wheeler-Howard Act has had on Indian life and on the larger society. They can share their research findings by using role-playing, debates, or group discussion techniques.

7. Heated arguments for the termination of federal–tribal relationship surfaced again in the 1950s. Ask the class to prepare research reports on these topics:
   a. The House Concurrent Resolution 108, 83rd Congress, 1st session, passed on August 1, 1953, called for the termination of the federal role in Indian affairs.
   b. How termination policy affected these tribes and the conditions of the termination policy in each case:
      (1) the Klamaths of Oregon
      (2) the Menominees of Wisconsin
      (3) the Alabamas and the Coushattas in the South

8. Ask the class to study the various debates on termination that took place in the 1960s and 1970s between Indians and federal officials. An interesting argument against termination by an Indian is that of Earl Old Person (Blackfoot). See "Testimony against Proposed Congressional Legislation, 1966," reprinted in *Great Documents in American Indian History,* edited by Moquin and Van Doren (1973).

9. To conclude this unit, ask the students to divide into three groups and pretend that they are three different reservation tribes that have legal relationships with the federal government. Each tribe must unanimously decide, in the Indian tradition, whether they will terminate or maintain their legal relationship with the federal government. When the role-playing is over, the class should reassemble and discuss the decisions of each tribe and the process and arguments they experienced in reaching them.

REFERENCES

Bolt, C. (1987). *American Indian Policy and American Reform: Case Studies of the Campaign to Assimilate the American Indians.* London: Allen and Unwin.

Bruggmann, M., & Gerber, M. (1987). *Indians of the Northwest Coast.* New York: Facts on File.

Ceram, C. W. (1971). *The First Americans: A Story of North American Archaeology.* New York: Mentor Books.

Chief Luther Standing Bear. (1933). *Land of the Spotted Eagle.* Boston: Houghton Mifflin.

Deloria, V., Jr. (Ed.). (1971). *Of Utmost Good Faith.* San Francisco: Straight Arrow Books.

Denevan, W. M. (1976). *The Native Population of the Americas in 1492.* Madison: University of Wisconsin Press.

Dobyns, H. F. (1976). *Native American Demography: A Critical Bibliography.* Bloomington: Indiana University Press.

Dorris, M. A. (1981, Spring). The Grass Still Grows, the Rivers Still Flow: Contemporary Native Americans. *Daedalus 110,* 43–69.

Edwards, B. (2001, January 31). *Morning Edition with Bob Edwards: Who is Indian?* [On-line]. Available: *http://www.npr.org/programs/morning/010131.cfoa.html*

Forbes, J. D. (1973). Teaching Native American Values and Cultures. In J. A. Banks (Ed.). *Teaching Ethnic Studies: Concepts and Strategies* (pp. 201–225). Washington, DC: National Council for the Social Studies.

Hagan, W. T. (1961). *American Indians.* Chicago: University of Chicago Press.

Hammond Past Worlds: The Times Atlas of Archaeology. (1988). Maplewood, NJ: Hammond.

Harris, W. H., & Levey, J. S. (Eds.). (1975). *The New Columbia Encyclopaedia.* New York: Columbia University Press.

Hoxie, F. E. (Ed.). (1996). *Encyclopedia of North American Indians.* Boston: Houghton Mifflin.

Hunt, S. (Ed.). (1999). *Illustrated Atlas of Native American History.* Edison, NJ: Chartwell.

Jackson, D. D. (2001). "This Hole in Our Heart": The Urban-Raised Generation and the Legacy of Silence. In Susan Lobo & Kurt Peters (Eds.), *American Indians and the Urban Experience* (pp. 189–206). Walnut Creek, CA: Altamira Press.

Josephy, A. M., Jr. (1991). *The Indian Heritage of America* (Enlarged ed.). Boston: Houghton Mifflin.

Kroeber, A. L. (1934). Native American Population. *American Anthropologist, 36,* 1–25.

Lomawaima, K. T. (1994). *They Called It Prairie Light: The Story of Chilocco Indian School.* Lincoln: University of Nebraska Press.

McLuhan, T. C. (Ed.). (1971). *Touch the Earth: A Self-Portrait of Indian Existence.* New York: Pocket Books.

Mooney, J. M. (1928). *The Aboriginal Population of America North of Mexico.* In J. R. Swanton (Ed.), *Smithsonian Miscellaneous Collections* (Vol. 80, no. 7). Washington, DC.

Moquin, W., with Van Doren, C. (Eds.). (1973). *Great Documents in American Indian History.* New York: Praeger.

Parfitt, M., & Garrett, K. (2000). The Dawan of Hamans: Hunt for the First Americans. *National Geographic, 198*(6), 40–67.

Snipp, C. M. (1991). *American Indians: The First of This Land.* New York: Russell Sage Foundation.

Sorkin, A. L. (1978). *The Urban American Indians.* Lexington, Mass.: D.C. Heath.

Spicer, E. H. (1969). *A Short History of the Indians in the United States.* New York: Van Nostrand Reinhold.

Spicer, E. H. (1980). American Indians: Federal Policy toward. In S. Thernstrom, A. Orlov, & O. Handlin (Eds.), *Harvard Encyclopedia of American Ethnic Groups* (pp. 114–122). Cambridge: Harvard University Press.

Stripes, J. (2001). Native Americans: An Overview. In G. T Kurian, M. Orvell, J. E. Butler, & J. Mechling (Eds.), *Encylopedia of American Studies* (Vol. 3, pp. 197–204). New York: Grolier Educational.

Stuart, P. (1987). *Nations within a Nation: Historical Statistics of American Indians.* New York: Greenwood Press.

Tucker, M. (1995). Contemporary Potlatches. In A. Hirschfelder (Ed.), *Native Heritage: Personal Accounts by American Indians 1790 to the Present* (pp. 193–194). New York: Macmillan.

U.S. Bureau of the Census. (1993, September). *We, the First Americans.* Washington, DC: U.S. Government Printing Office.

U.S. Census Bureau. (2001). [On-line]. Available: *http://www.census.gov/*

U.S. Commission on Civil Rights. (1981). *Indian Tribes: A Continuing Quest for Survival.* Washington, DC: Author.

Washburn, W. E. (Ed.). (1964). *The Indian and the White Man.* New York: Doubleday.

Wax, M. L. (1971). *Indian Americans: Unity and Diversity.* Englewood Cliffs, NJ: Prentice-Hall.

The World Atlas of Archaeology. (1985). New York: Portland House.

A N N O T A T E D   B I B L I O G R A P H Y

Books for Teachers

Especially Recommended

Brown, J. E. (2001). *Teaching Spirits: Understanding Native American Religious Traditions.* New York: Oxford University Press.

This thematic book uses contemporary and historic examples to describe the diversity of Native American religious traditions and the common themes in Native American cultures.

Cates, G. (2001). *Indian Country.* New York: Grove Press.

This pictorial work of art makes visible the often invisible, misrepresented, and stereotyped Native American people and culture. The intermingling of photographs and personal narratives captures the diversity and beauty of American Indians.

Champagne, D. (Ed.). (1999). *Contemporary Native American Cultural Issues.* Walnut Creek, CA: AltaMira Press.

This book describes the complexity and diversity of Native American culture by addressing both the contemporary issues facing Native American nations and the multitude of future possibilities.

Deloria, P. J. (1998). *Playing Indian.* New Haven: Yale University Press.

This provocative book spans history from the Boston Tea Party to the present in order to illustrate how non-Indians have inflicted a dichotomous reality on Indian people by simultaneously embracing and rejecting them throughout history.

Gonzalez, M., & Cook-Lynn, E. (1999). *The Politics of Hallowed Ground: Wounded Knee and the Struggle for Indian Sovereignty.* Chicago: University of Illinois Press.

This analysis of the historic and recent events surrounding the 1890 massacre at Wounded Knee illuminates the long-standing struggle of Native people to recover their history and sacred lands.

Harvey, K. D., & Harjo, L. D. (1998). *Indian Country: A History of Native People in America.* Golden, CO: North American Press.

This rich teaching resource includes historical informative on Native American groups as well as lesson plans and a comprehensive bibliography.

Hoxie, F. E. (Ed.). (1996). *Encyclopedia of North American Indians.* Boston: Houghton Mifflin.

An excellent, comprehensive reference work that is a valuable source of information on the various Natives American cultures and tribes.

Hoxie, F. E., Mancall, P. C., & Merrell, J. H. (Eds.). (2001). *American Nations: Encounters in Indian Country, 1950 to the Present.* New York: Routlege Press.

This collection challenges the many common misconceptions of Native peoples by providing the reader with rich narratives of those who have actively counteracted these misconceptions through negotiation, accommodation, debate, and resistance.

Waldman, C. (1999). *Encyclopedia of Native American Tribes.* New York: Checkmark Books.

This comprehensive reference guide covers over 150 tribes with illustrations, maps, and glossaries that enable the reader to navigate the rich history of Native peoples and civilizations.

Other References

Allen, P. G. (1998). *Off the Reservation: Reflections on Boundary-Busting, Border-Crossing, Loose Canons.* Boston: Beacon Press.

This collection of essays describes relationships between the larger global community with the eco-spiritual and multicultural heritage of Native peoples.

Archuleta, M. L., Child, B. J., & Lomawaima, K. T. (Eds.). (2000). *Away from Home: American Indian Boarding School Experience.* Pheonix: Heard Museum.

Text and pictures provide a vivid historical glimpse of the boarding school experience for Native Americans. The reader experiences a strong sense of the diversity of individual experiences of Native Americans in boarding schools.

Bataille, G. M. (Ed.). (2001). *Native American Representations: First Encounters, Distorted Images, and Literary Appropriations.* Lincoln: University of Nebraska Press.

Leading critics of Native American literature and culture examine the meaning of the depictions and distortions of Native Americans over the past five centuries.

Battiste, M. (Ed.). (2000). *Reclaiming Indigenous Voice and Vision.* Vancouver: UBC Press.

This collection of primarily indigenous authors focuses on the cultural restoration of Native peoples by providing new frameworks for understanding the process of colonization and its role in the lives of indigenous peoples.

Bensen, R. (Ed.). (2001). *Children of the Dragonfly: Native American Voices on Child Custody and Education.* Tucson: University of Arizona Press.

This anthology combines the voices of contemporary and classic authors to describe the struggle for cultural survival amidst the U.S. and Canadian long-standing tradition of removing Native American children from their homes.

Bol, M. C. (1998). *North, South, East, West: American Indians and the Natural World.* Pittsburgh, PA: Carnegie Museum of Natural History and Roberts Rinehart Publishers.

This visual collection of American Indian culture combines text and photographs.

Churchill, W. (1998). *Fantasies of the Master Race: Literature, Cinema and the Colonization of American Indians.* San Francisco: City Light Books.

This collection of essays analyzes the manner in which American Indians have been represented in literature and film, revealing a long history of national denials and misrepresentations of Native Americasns.

Cleary, L., & Peacock, T. (1998). *Collected Wisdom: American Indian Education.* Boston, MA: Allyn and Bacon.

This book, based on the collective voices of both Indian and non-Indian teachers of Indian students, describes a holistic approach to the educational issues facing Indian students.

Cook-Lynn, E. (2001). *Anti-Indianism in Modern America: A Voice from Tatekaya's Earth.* Urbana: University of Illinois Press.

This book links historical and current practices and policies of genocide to illustrate how Native American cultures are still victims of colonialism.

Dubin, L. S. (1999). *North American Indian Jewelry and Adornment: From Prehistory to the Present.* New York: Harry N. Abrams.

With over 1,200 illustrations and corresponding text, this excellent classroom reference book reveals the diverse and rich history of Native American adornment as a medium of cultural expression.

Frazier, I. (2000). *On the Rez.* New York: Farrar, Straus and Giroux.

This fictional book provides a humorous, yet truthful, glimpse into the current realities of American Indians and the tenacious survival of Native cultures.

Garrett, M. (1998). *Walking on the Wind: Cherokee Teachings for Harmony and Balance.* Rochester, VT: Bear and Company.

This collection of stories combines the wisdom of medicine men's teachings and the author's knowledge of counseling. The powerful messages contained in this book are appropriate for all grade levels and can help people find balance and harmony in their lives.

Halliday, J., & Chehak, G. (2000). *Native Peoples of the Northwest: A Travelers Guide to Land, Art and Culture.* Seattle: Sasquatch Books.

> *This guidebook provides the reader with a detailed and user-friendly resource on the rich Native-owned and -operated destinations in the Pacific Northwest.*

Hazen-Hammond, S. (1997). *Timelines of Native American History: Through the Centuries with Mother Earth and Father Sky.* New York: Perigee.

> *This user-friendly reference book documents the rich Native American history from 20,000 BC up to the current time in a concise and truthful presentation.*

Hirschfelder, A. (2000). *Native Americans: A History in Pictures.* New York: Dorling Kindersley.

> *This collection of magnificent archive photographs and moving narratives provides a compelling profile of the social, economic, and spiritual life of Native Americans.*

Hull, M. (2000). *Sun Dancing: A Spiritual Journey in the Red Road.* Rochester, VT: Inner Traditions International.

> *This inspiring book recounts the real-life spiritual journey of a White man invited to participate in the sacred Lakota spiritual ceremony, the Sun Dance. His story documents the power of the Lakota spiritual practice, as well as the reluctance of Native Americans to share their sacred ceremonies with outsiders.*

Hunsaker, J. B. (2001). *Sacagawea Speaks: Beyond the Shining Mountains with Lewis and Clark.* Guilford, CO: Globe Pequot Press.

> *This historical account of the life of Sacagawea uses first-person narrative to present the author's interpretation of this well-known Native American's life.*

Jacobs, S., Thomas, W., & Lang, S. (Eds.). (1997). *Two-Spirit People: Native American Gender Identity, Sexuality, and Spirituality.* Chicago: University of Illinois Press.

> *Using narrative and academic text, this book describes sex roles, sexuality, and gender in Native American communities.*

LaDuke, W. (1999). *All Our Relations: Native Struggles for Land and Life.* Cambridge, MA: South End Press.

> *The voice of this highly acclaimed Native environmental activist, as well as local Native activist, presents a detailed and thoughtful account of Native American resistance to environmental and cultural degradation.*

Lobo, S., & Peters, K. (Eds.). (2001). *American Indians and the Urban Experience.* Walnut Creek, CA: AltaMira Press.

> *This collection combines multiple genres, such as poetry, scholarship, and art, to capture the rich and diverse experiences of Native Americans who live in urban communities. It is one of a series of books that focuses on urban Indians edited by Troy Johnson and Duane Champagne and published by AltaMira Press. Other books in the series include* Contemporary Native American Political Issues, *edited by Troy Johnson (1999) and* Contemporary Native American Cultural Issues, *edited by Duane Champagne (1999).*

Marks, P. M. (1998). *In a Barren Land: American Indian Dispossession and Survival.* New York: William Morrow.

> *A thoughtful and informative account of how the Native peoples of America were stripped of their land and their ways of life.*

Morton, R. (Ed.). (1996). *Powwow.* New York: Harry N. Abrams.

> *This rich collection of brilliant color portraits and personal narratives of diverse powwow dances in full regalia illuminates the shared spiritual significance of the Native American powwow.*

Swisher, K. G., & Tipperconnic III, J. (Eds.). (1999). *Next Steps: Research and Practice to Advance Indian Education.* Charleston, WV: ERIC/CRESS.

> *This collection of chapters by noted American Indian educators discusses the reality and future direction of American Indian education from two perspectives: tribal self-determination and the need to move toward an educational approach built on the strengths of tribal cultures.*

Wilkins, D. E. (2002). *American Indian Politics and the American Political System.* Lanham, MD: Rowman and Littlefield.

> *This book provides a comprehensive overview of the historical and contemporary relationship between tribal governments and American politics. American Indian activism, economic development, media treatment, and individual and collective cultural identity are described throughout this text.*

Books for Students

(Note: These designations are used throughout this book: **Primary, grades 1–3; Intermediate, 4–6; Middle School, 7–8; High School, 9–12**)

Bierhorst, J., (Ed.). (1998). *The Deetkatoo: Native American Stories about Little People.* Illustrated by H. Coy. New York: Morrow.

> *The noted folklorist offers 22 stories, from 15 tribal groups, that feature small humans with special powers. (Intermediate and Up)*

Bruchac, J. (1998). *The Heart of a Chief.* New York: Dial.

> *A contemporary Abenaki preteenager gains confidence when he takes sides in a controversy over development on his reservation. (Intermediate/Middle School)*

Bruchac, J. (2000). *Pushing up the Sky: Seven Native American Plays for Children.* Illustrated by T. Flavin. New York: Dial.

> *Seven plays by Bruchac adapt folktales from the Abenaki, Tlingit, Cheyenne, Ojibway, Cherokee, Snohomish, and Zuni traditions for classroom performance. (Intermediate)*

Bruchac, J. (2000). *Sacagawea: The Story of Bird Woman and the Lewis and Clark Expedition.* San Diego: Harcourt.

> *The historic expedition is narrated from both the explorers' point of view and that of their Shoshone guide. (Middle School/High School)*

Bruchac, J., & Begay, S. (2001). *Navajo Long Walk.* Washington, DC: National Geographic Society.

> *Shonto Begay's stunning illustrations portray the forced journey of the Navajo People in 1864 while Joseph Bruchac's text tells the events that led to the tragedy and its aftermath. (Intermediate/Middle School)*

Child, B. J. (1998). *Boarding School Seasons: American Indian Families, 1900–1940.* Lincoln: University of Nebraska Press.

> *The Ojibwe author presents hundreds of letters from children and their parents, contrasted with those of boarding school officials, as part of this accessible historical work that challenges boarding school apologists, past and present. (High School)*

Deloria, V., Jr. (1999). *Spirit and Reason: The Vine Deloria, Jr., Reader.* Golden, CO: Fulcrum.

> *A collection of essays by the respected Native educator and writer, who touches on such diverse topics as stereotypes in film, tribal politics, activism, and teaching the next generation. (High School)*

Dorris, M. (1996). *Sees behind Trees.* New York: Hyperion.

A boy with poor eyesight uses his ingenuity to prove himself in a rite-of-passage challenge. Dorris is the author of another work of historical fiction for older elementary readers, Morning Girl (Hyperion, 1992), which presents a twelve-year-old Taino girl who tries to understand why she and her brother view the world so differently. (Intermediate)

Dunn, A. M. (1997). *Grandmother's Gift: Stories from the Anishinabeg.* Mount Horeb, WI: Midwest Traditions.

The author offers 40 traditional and contemporary stories that illustrate the history, heritage, and values of her people. Humor is a major element, as are concerns about the Earth, family, social justice, and respect for others. This is a companion to Dunn's earlier title, When Beaver Was Very Great (Midwest Creations, 1995). (Intermediate)

Echo-Hawk, R. C., & Echo-Hawk, W. R. (1994). *Battlefields and Burial Grounds: The Indian Struggle to Protect Ancestral Graves.* Minneapolis: Lerner.

An informative book on an important topic. (Middle School/High School)

Erdoes, R., & Ortiz, A. (Eds.). (1998). *American Indian Trickster Tales.* New York: Viking.

The final collaboration of the noted folklorists presents a well-annotated and indexed collection of trickster tales from a variety of Native cultures. An important companion work to Erdoes's and Ortiz's classic American Indian Myths and Legends *(Pantheon, 1985). (Middle School and Up)*

Erdrich, L. (1989). *The Birchbark House.* New York: Hyperion.

The acclaimed Ojibwe writer depicts one year in the life of a seven-year-old girl growing up in the eighteenth century on an island in what is now Lake Superior, dealing with life, death, and change. (Intermediate/Middle School)

Grace, C. O., & Bruchac, M. M. (2001). *1621: A New Look at Thanksgiving.* Washington, DC: National Geographic Society.

The story of Thanksgiving is told from a Wampanoag perspective, with Wampanoag traditions and English colonial records used to challenge today's stereotypes and oversimplifications. (All ages)

Gravelle, K. (1997). *Growing Up: Where the Partridge Dreams Its Wings.* Illustrated with photos by S. R. Poole. Danbury, CO: Franklin Watts.

This attractive photo essay features two young cousins who live on the Akwesasne Mohawk Reserve in Quebec. (Intermediate)

Hamm, D. J. (1997). *Daughter of Suqua.* Morton Grove, IL: Albert Whitman.

A Native child in the early twentieth century observes the changes brought about by allotment and boarding schools; the writer effectively communicates the characters' sense of foreboding and grief. (Intermediate/Middle School)

Harjo, J. (2000). *The Good Luck Cat.* Illustrated by P. Lee. San Diego: Harcourt.

A girl fears the worst when her cat, who has already used up her nine lives, cannot be found. Among the cat's earlier mishaps is being locked in a hot car trunk during a powwow, and other details of the girl's Native heritage enhance this contemporary story written by the noted Muscogee poet. (Primary)

Hogan, L. (1998). *Power.* New York: W. W. Norton.

Written for adults, this coming of age story by the Chickasaw novelist and poet describes 16-year-old Omishto, torn between her white-identified mother and her aunt, whose traditional practices expose her and Omishto to a devastating hurricane and the ire of animal rights activists. (High School)

Hoyt-Goldsmith, D. (1998). *Lacrosse: The National Game of the Iroquois.* Illustrated with photos by L. Migdale. New York: Holiday House.

Accurate information, clear writing, and lively photographs distinguish this photo essay that presents a 13-year-old lacrosse player of Onandaga heritage and the popular game that originated with the Iroquois and maintains a key place in their culture. (Intermediate)

Hucko, B. (1996). *Where There Is No Name for Art: The Art of Tewa Pueblo Children.* Seattle: School of American Research/University of Washington Press.

Artworks by Tewa children ages five to twelve are featured along with a discussion of Native concepts of art; readers will have their own notions of art challenged in this visually beautiful and accessibly written book. Winner of the 1997 Carey McWilliams award. (High School)

Lacapa, K., & Lacapa, M. (1994). *Less than Half, More than Whole.* Illustrated by M. Lacapa. Flagstaff, AZ: Northland.

This is an excellent book that can be used to explain racial identity to children. Tony realizes that he is neither a White like his friend Scott, nor 100% Indian like Will. Tony's realization that he is more than whole is comforting to children who have ever felt "different." Michael Lacapa has also adapted and illustrated several traditional Apache stories for young readers, including The Flute Player *(Northland, 1990). (Primary)*

Lomawaima, K. T. (1994). *They Called It Prairie Light: The Story of Chilocco Indian School.* Lincoln: University of Nebraska Press.

Lomawaima (Hopi) offers an oral history of the Chilocco Indian Agricultural School that reveals the many facets of student resistance to assimilationist efforts at the Indian boarding schools. (High School)

Malotki, E., comp. (1998). *Hopi Animal Tales.* Lincoln: University of Nebraska Press.

This exhaustive compilation of traditional animal tales features the Hopi alphabet, an extensive glossary, and source notes. (All ages)

Martin, J. W. (1999). *Native American Religion.* Series: *Religion in American Life.* New York: Oxford University Press.

The diverse traditions and common themes of indigenous religions in the present-day United States are discussed, as are the impact of the encounter with Christianity and contemporary debates over religious freedom for traditional observances. (Middle School/ High School)

McMillan, B. (1998). *Salmon Summer.* Illustrated with photos by the author. Boston: Houghton Mifflin.

The author/photographer chronicles a summer that an Aleut father and son spend together fishing for salmon. (Primary/Intermediate)

Mercredi, M. (1997). *Fort Chipewyan Homecoming: A Journey to Native Canada.* Illustrated with photos by D. McNally. Series: *We Are Still Here.* Minneapolis: Lerner.

The author's 12-year-old son, a "city kid," spends the summer with his Chipewyan relatives; he hunts, fishes, and experiences life on the land. (Primary/Intermediate)

Monture, J. (1996). *Cloudwalker.* Golden, CO: Fulcrum.

Eight engaging short stories portray relationships between Native youngsters and their elders; the title story presents the experiences of Mohawk construction workers who walked the girders to build New York City's skyscrapers. (Intermediate/Middle School)

Nichols, R. (1998). *A Story to Tell: Traditions of a Tlingit Community*. Illustrated with photos by D. B. Kraus. Series: *We Are Still Here*. Minneapolis: Lerner.

> *The Tewa author and Tlingit photographer team up to describe a reunion between the photographer's mother and niece, as young Marissa learns Tlingit history through her grandmother's stories. (Primary/Intermediate)*

Perry, R. J., comp. (1998). *Life with the Little People*. Illustrated by C. Scott. Greenfield Center, NY: Greenfield Review Press.

> *An entertaining collection of tales about the "Indian leprechauns" from the Muscogee, Cherokee, and Chickasaw traditions. (All ages)*

Rendon, M. (1996). *Powwow Summer: A Family Celebrates the Circle of Life*. Illustrated with photos by C. W. Bellville. Minneapolis: Carolrhoda.

> *In beautifully written text accompanied by expressive photos, the Anishinabe author describes a family preparing for and attending powwows, which serve as a place to honor the dead and the living. Another good introduction to powwows is Susan Browne's (Assiniboine) Drumbeat, Heartbeat: A Celebration of the Powwow (Lerner, 1995), which presents the Fourth of July powwow on the Northern Cheyenne Reservation. (Primary/ Intermediate)*

Rose, L. (1999). *Grandchildren of the Lakota*. Illustrated with photos by C. W. Bellville. Series: *The World's Children*. Minneapolis: Carolrhoda.

> *The Lakota author and grandmother describes her extended family and offers a well-written discussion of Lakota history, the boarding school experience, and the importance of children to Lakota families today. (Primary/Intermdeiate)*

Smith, C. L. (2000). *Jingle Dancer*. Illustrated by C. Van Wright and Y-W. Hu. New York: Morrow.

> *A young girl borrows jingles from relatives and older friends so that she can have a dress in which to dance at the powwow; in return, she promises to dance for all those women who cannot. (Primary)*

Smith, C. L. (2001). *Rain Is Not My Indian Name*. New York: HarperCollins.

> *In this heartfelt novel by a young Muscogee author, a 14-year-old girl struggles with her grief over the sudden deaths of her mother and her best friend and with the expectations others have of her because she is Indian. (Middle School)*

Sneve, V. D. H. (1997). *The Trickster and the Troll*. Lincoln: University of Nebraska Press.

> *The acclaimed Lakota author combines the trickster Iktomi of Lakota legend and the outcast troll featured in Norwegian mythology (the heritage of her husband) in a series of tales that explores both cultures and the experience of dispossession that both mythic figures have in common. (Intermediate and Up)*

Sneve, V. D. H.. (2000). *Grandpa Was a Cowboy and an Indian and Other Stories*. Lincoln: University of Nebraska Press.

> *This collection of brief stories retells traditional legends and myths, depicts moments in the history of the Plains Indians, and portrays the intergenerational bonds that serve as a model and support structure for Indian youth. (High School)*

Sterling, S. (1997). *My Name is Seepeetza*. Toronto: Douglas & McIntyre.

> *The Salish author describes the bleak environment of the Indian boarding schools and the joy and warmth Seepeetza experiences with her family during the long summer vacations. (Middle School/High School)*

Tallchief, M., as told to R. Wells. (2000). *Tallchief: America's Prima Ballerina*. Illustrated by G. Kelley. New York: Viking.

The ballerina, of Osage heritage, tells of her childhood on the reservation and the early years of her career. (Primary/Intermediate)

TeCube, L. (1999). *Year in Nam: A Native American Soldier's Story*. Lincoln: University of Nebraska Press.

The Apache author describes his service with the army and how his boyhood on the reservation helped him to fight a "war without fronts." (High School)

Updyke, R. (1997). *Jim Thorpe: The Legend Remembered*. Gretna, LA: Pelican.

This biography of the gifted Native American athlete describes his success in a variety of sports and offers a history of Native people in a time of transition in the early part of the twentieth century. (Intermediate/Middle School)

Viola, H. J. (1998). *It Is a Good Day to Die: Indian Eyewitnesses Tell the Story of the Battle of the Little Bighorn*. New York: Crown.

Drawing from other published sources, Viola presents a variety of perspectives on the famous battle. (Middle School)

Walters, E. (1998) *War of the Eagles*. Victoria, BC: Orca Books.

Jed, a Tsimshian boy, saves an injured eagle and tries to help his best friend Tadashi, a Japanese Canadian who is facing persecution at the beginning of the Second World War. (Middle School)

Yamane, L. (1997). *Weaving a California Tradition: A Native American Basketweaver*. Illustrated with photos by D. Aguiar. Series: *We Are Still Here*. Minneapolis: Lerner.

The author, herself an Ohlone basketweaver, describes the life of a contemporary Native child who learns the art. (Primary/Intermediate)

Yamane, L. (1998). *The Snake That Lived in the Santa Cruz Mountains and Other Ohlone Stories*. Berkeley, CA: Oyate.

Seven traditional stories will delight readers of all ages. Yamane's earlier volume of traditional Ohlone pourquoi tales is entitled When the World Ended, How Hummingbird Got Fire, How People Were Made: Rumsien Ohlone Stories *(Oyate, 1995). (All ages)*

Yue, C., & Yue, D. (2000). *The Wigwam and the Longhouse*. Boston: Houghton Mifflin.

Cultural differences between the early Algonquin and Iroquois peoples are explored through the design, construction, and use of their signature dwellings. (Intermediate)

6

Native Hawai'ians

Concepts, Strategies, and Materials

You must not think that this is anything like olden times, that you are the only chiefs and can leave things as they are. Smart people have arrived from the great countries that you have never seen. They know our people are few in number and living in a small country; they will eat us up.

—Davis Malo, 1837

The experiences of Native Hawai'ians parallel those of other indigenous peoples whose cultures and traditional lifestyles were drastically altered by European contact.[1] Like the American Indians, the numbers of Native Hawai'ians were sharply reduced in the past two centuries. Their culture was initially modified and finally overwhelmed by European and American settlers.

Native Hawai'ians often found it difficult to assume a viable role in a Hawai'ian society in which Western practices were foreign to them. Values that, for centuries, had been hallmarks of Native Hawai'ian culture were often counterproductive in a Hawai'ian society run by foreigners. This conflict inevitably led to helplessness and despair for some of Hawai'i's original inhabitants.

This chapter was contributed by **Carlos F. Diaz,** Professor of Education, Florida Atlantic University, Boca Raton, Florida. Professor Diaz is the editor of *Multicultural Education in the 21st Century* (Longman, 2001) and co-author of *Global Perspectives for Educators* (Allyn and Bacon, 1999). The bibliographies at the end of this chapter were done by **Virgie O. Chattergy,** Professor of Education, University of Hawaii, Manoa and **Amrita N. Zahir,** Research Assistant, Center for Multicultural Education, University of Washington.

Yet, the culture of Hawai'i has shown remarkable resiliency despite the great odds against its survival. The Hawai'ian Renaissance of the 1970s indicated that a new consciousness of what it means to be Hawai'ian had developed. The Hawai'ian independence movement in the late twentieth and early twenty-first centuries has shown that, at least for some Hawai'ians, there is dissatisfaction with the political status quo and their role in it. For some Native Hawai'ians, the American dream has borne fruit. For most, it has been largely deferred, and they remain the most economically disadvantaged group in Hawai'i. Students should be aware that, although small in number, Native Hawai'ians have made unique and lasting contributions to the American saga.

In 1778, Captain James Cook's expedition landed on the Islands that he named the Sandwich Islands, now called the state of Hawai'i. There, Cook found as many as 800,000 people living in relative isolation (Stannard, 1989). Since that time, Hawai'ian history has been fraught with the paternalism of Europeans and Americans, often to the detriment of Native Hawai'ians. This story is one of broken promises and the exploitation of Native Hawai'ians by foreigners that, in some ways, is similar to the plight of American Indians.

Until foreigners started coming to Hawai'i, Native Hawai'ians did not have a word for *race*. There were two groups, Hawai'ians and strangers. They called themselves *kanakas* and referred to strangers as *haoles*. This total unimportance of race was to change with the coming of Europeans. The word *haole* came to mean "White" instead of "stranger" as Whites became more prevalent on the Islands. The Hawai'ian people were forced to deal with an alien White economic, social, and legal system that they did not understand.

Native Hawai'ians: Before European Contact

In the early subsistence economy of Hawai'i, the survival of Hawai'ians depended on a communal effort to reap the maximum benefits from the Islands' scarce resources. The Hawai'ians were an agricultural and fishing people with a complex socioreligious structure. The Islands were governed by the *ali'i*, who were powerful chiefs. The power of these chiefs was legitimized by the priest, or *kahuna*, who interpreted the religious doctrine set forth in the *kapu*. The common people, or *maka'ainana*, were extremely devoted to their chiefs. The high chief, or *ali'inui*, was the supreme ruler over his territory and was expected to provide protection for his people. People had the freedom to move to the district of another chief, but rarely did so. Although sharing was a predominant practice, there was a considerable difference between the lifestyles of the chiefs and the common people.

There were two Hawai'ian customs that would lead to inevitable conflict with *haoles* in the future. One was a system of sharing and bartering, in which products were exchanged from one island to another. The Hawai'ians did not use currency, and therefore the accumulation of wealth in a market economy

NATIVE HAWAI'IANS: A HISTORICAL PERSPECTIVE

Important Dates	Events
1778	The beginning of European contact. Captain James Cook's expedition landed on the Hawai'ian Islands.
1795	The rise to power of King Kamehameha I, who united the Hawai'ian people under one ruler. This marked the beginning of the Kamehameha dynasty.
1820	The breaking of taboo against eating *kapu* by King Kamehameha II, which signaled the end of the ancient Hawai'ian religion as a state religion. The first missionaries arrived in Hawai'i from New England.
1835	King Kamehameha III granted an American firm the first long-term lease for a sugar plantation.
1845	The Great Mahele; all the land on the Islands was divided among the king and 245 chiefs.
1893	Queen Liliuokalani was overthrown in a bloodless revolution led by American planters. The Republic of Hawai'i was established, with Sanford B. Dole as president. This government lasted until annexation by the United States.
1920	The Hawai'ian Homes Commission was started to benefit the native Hawai'ians. Very little of this land was used for its stated purpose. (By the 1930s, the commission was leasing half of its land to corporations or to non-Hawai'ians.)
1954	For the first time since Hawai'i became a territory, the Democratic party captured a majority in both houses of the legislature.
1959	Hawai'i became the fiftieth state of the United States.
1974	George Ariyoshi was the first non-*haole* elected governor of Hawai'i.
1975	The U.S. Congress passed a law recognizing Native Hawai'ians as a Native American group.
1976	The voyage of the Hawai'ian canoe Hokule'a from Hawai'i to Tahiti reinforced pride in the Polynesian roots of Hawai'ian culture. Daniel Akaka became the first Native Hawai'ian member of the U.S. House of Representatives.

Important Dates	Events
1977	The first edition of the newsletter *Native Hawai'ian* was published, marking a growing Hawai'ian consciousness movement.
1978	The Office of Hawai'ian Affairs was established by the state government to help Native Hawai'ians secure their rights.
1980	The Hawai'ian tourist industry suffered its first decline since 1949. This fueled debate about diversification of the Hawai'ian economy.
1984	Hawai'i celebrated twenty-five years of statehood.
1986	John D. Waihee, the first Hawai'ian governor of Hawai'ian ancestry, took office.
1993	President Clinton signs PL 103-150 into law, officially apologizing to the Hawai'ian people for the overthrow of the Hawai'ian monarchy.
1995	Seven hundred people demonstrate at the state capitol to pass a 600 million-dollar settlement to allow faster development of Hawai'ian homelands.
2000	The U.S. Supreme Court rules in *Rice vs. Caytano* that eligible voters in elections for Office of Hawai'ian Affairs trustees could not be limited to Native Hawai'ians.
2001	Senators Akaka and Inouye and Representative Abercrombie file bills to recognize Native Hawai'ians as a governing entity as well as for other purposes.

as we know it was unknown. The other custom was the notion that the land belonged to the gods, and therefore belonged to everyone and could not be owned. The earliest visitors to the Islands found the natives willing to share whatever they had. After all, that was the Hawai'ian way.

European Contact

The propensity of Hawai'ians to share eventually helped to seal their demise. Besides providing provisions for ships, Hawai'ians were quite willing to share their women, and Whites were eager to become intimate with them. These casual contacts over a long period of time had a decimating effect on the Islands' population. The venereal diseases introduced by European and American sailors found little natural resistance among the Hawai'ians and, along with measles, cholera, and alcoholism, took a deadly toll.

An estimated 300,000 people inhabited the Hawai'ian Islands at the time of European contact. By 1840, only about 100,000 Hawai'ians remained. Many Native Hawai'ians were naturally alarmed at what was taking place due to contact with the *haoles*. According to David Malo (cited in Jacobs & Landau, 1971), a Native Hawai'ian writer espoused this viewpoint: "The ships of the White man have come and smart men have arrived from the great countries.... They know our people are few in number and living in a small country; they will eat us up" (p. 22). His prophecy came true eventually, but at that time it fell on deaf ears. When David Malo died, he was buried at his request in Lahaina, next to a school where he had received his education from missionaries.

The paternalism of *haoles* began with sea captains, who needed the Islands as a place to replenish supplies and repair their ships. Often, chiefs were given a few metal items in return for supplies. As commercialism grew and the chiefs saw more European goods, there began to be a desire for these items. Sandalwood, which was plentiful on the Islands, was in great demand for carving as well as for its aromatic qualities. It could be bought in Hawai'i for 1 cent per pound and sold lucratively in Canton, China, for 34 cents per pound (Kent, 1983, p. 18). As the Yankee traders increased their demands for sandalwood, many chiefs forced their subjects to cut more of the mountain trees and haul the lumber down steep slopes. Some chiefs also became fervent consumers of Western goods and kept their subjects away from their own food-producing activities in order to satisfy the sandalwood trade and their own avarice. This continued until the slopes of Hawai'i were nearly denuded of sandalwood trees. Today, they are scarce on the Islands.

The ascension to power of King Kamehameha I marked the rise of the Kamehameha dynasty. According to Day (1968), "One of Kamehameha's greatest qualities was his ability to attract many White men to his service and retain their loyalty for years or even a lifetime" (p. 44). Even though Kamehameha was skillful in retaining power, this practice proved disastrous in the long run for his heirs because often the *haole* advisers put their own interests ahead of the Hawai'ian people they were supposed to help.

Kamehameha I is often regarded as one of the greatest Hawai'ian monarchs because he conquered populations of other islands and unified the entire island chain under one rule. The weapons and technology he had obtained through contact with Westerners were of great assistance in this campaign.

After the death of Kamehameha I in 1819, he was succeeded by his son, Liholiho. During the reign of Liholiho (Kamehameha II), he was pressured into abolishing the *kapu* system of taboos. This had far-reaching effects on

Hawai'ian society. Although the *kapu* system was often oppressive, and sometimes abused, its elimination began an erosion of Native Hawai'ian culture with no satisfactory substitutes provided.

Besides the traders and the confidants of chiefs, another group entered the Hawai'ian scene to lend its paternalistic hand. In 1820, the first groups of missionaries arrived in the Islands from New England. Their goal was to Christianize the natives, but in most cases their influence far surpassed the religious realm. According to Jacobs and Landau (1971), "Under increased influence of the missionaries of the king, more haoles were given the right to lease land for commercial enterprises. But these men did not want merely to lease the land, they wanted to own it outright so they could sell or lease it to others" (p. 26).

A further blow to the survival of Hawai'ian culture was dealt in 1848, when King Kamehameha III took the suggestions of his foreign advisors and decided to redistribute the land of the Hawai'ian Islands. This act by the king was known as the *Great Mahele*. Kent (1983) notes that, under its provisions, "60% of the land was allocated to the crown and government, 29% to the 208 chiefs, and less than 1% to 11,000 commoners" (p. 31).

After the Great Mahele, there was a steady decline in subsistence farming among the Native Hawai'ian people. Alien concepts such as land deeds and property taxes clashed with the traditional Hawai'ian view that land was for the use and enjoyment of all the people. Slowly, even small plots of land owned by Native Hawai'ians passed into the hands of the *haoles*. This loss of control over their land by Native Hawai'ians somewhat parallels the saga of American Indians.

As the sandalwood trade faded, the Hawai'ian economy began to rely more on supplying whaling ships with meat, vegetables, and water. Hawai'i also became a convenient location to make any repairs needed by whaling vessels on their long voyages. With the income earned from these activities, Hawai'i imported manufactured goods, mainly from the United States. When whaling in the Pacific began to decline, the Hawai'ian economy shifted to plantation agriculture.

During each of these phases, the Hawai'ian economy was being controlled by forces thousands of miles away from the Islands. The interests and needs of the Native Hawai'ian population were inconsequential when compared to the potential for large profits.

The plantation system began to flourish in the latter part of the nineteenth century. Native Hawai'ians worked in the cane fields as laborers but were not as productive as plantation owners had expected. The dawn-to-dusk labor in the cane fields and rigid production quotas were difficult adjustments for Native Hawai'ians. Lacking a significant economic niche on their islands, and slowly losing political control, the Native Hawai'ian population continued to decline.

From a population of 71,019 in 1853, the Hawai'ian population, including those of mixed ancestry, had dropped to 39,504 by 1896 (Lind, 1980).

During this period, planters were importing field labor to the Hawai'ian Islands from nearly the entire world. The first major group was the Chinese, soon followed by the Japanese, Portuguese, Koreans, Puerto Ricans, and immigrants from other nations.

The planters' strategy was to keep any one nationality of laborers from becoming too numerous and, thus, to thwart any type of labor organization. George H. Fairfield (cited in Takaki, 1983), manager of the Makee Sugar Company, stated the planters' strategy as follows: "Keep a variety of laborers, that is of different nationalities, and thus prevent any concerted action in case of strikes, for there are few, if any, cases of Japanese, Chinese, and Portuguese entering into a strike as a unit" (p. 24). Largely as a result of these methods, Hawai'i's population was transformed into a multicultural one.

As the plantation economy matured, a Big Five emerged among planters that would eventually dominate the Hawai'ian economy for decades: Hackfield and Company (AMFAC), C. Brewer and Company, Theo Davis Company, Castle and Cooke, and Alexander and Baldwin.

The nature of the sugar and pineapple plantations of the nineteenth and early twentieth centuries required a large concentration of land and capital, as well as a disciplined work force. Such large-scale operations also required that the political climate of Hawai'i be conducive to the interests of planters.

The practice of surrounding the Hawai'ian monarch with *haole* advisors created a facade of political sovereignty by the latter part of the nineteenth century. In 1873, the Hawai'ian throne was denied to Queen Emma by a group of planters who bribed, cajoled, and threatened electors into giving the crown to David Kalakaua. Pro-Emma supporters stormed the courthouse to register their outrage. This group was dispersed by U.S. Marines and British sailors whose assistance was requested by planter Charles Bishop to "quell the riotous mob" (Kent, 1983, p. 45).

In 1877, the planter oligarchy rewrote the Hawai'ian constitution and presented it to King Kalakaua for his signature under a state of armed siege. The constitution the king signed became known as the "bayonet constitution" to Hawai'ians. It made the king a ceremonial monarch, disenfranchised most Native Hawai'ians through strict property requirements, excluded all Asians from voting by declaring them aliens, and gave the vote only to U.S. citizens. After this action, the remaining days of pretended sovereignty were numbered.

Annexation

To paint a picture of something other than imperialistic motives by the United States in annexing Hawai'i would be doing a severe injustice to the facts. American military leaders saw Hawai'i as a coaling station for the Pacific fleet. As Jacobs and Landau (1971) note, "The strength and influence of the pro-annexation Americans grew in Hawai'i and on the mainland, where the concepts of expansion and 'manifest destiny' were attracting a growing number of adherents" (p. 29). The latter doctrine, having reached the Pacific shore, seemed to have had its sights set on Hawai'i. The American planter oligarchy viewed annexation as an opportunity to guarantee, in perpetuity, the largest market for Hawai'ian agricultural products. Expansionist, military, and economic motives worked to end the last vestiges of Hawai'ian autonomy.

The first attempt at the deposition of the monarchy came on January 17, 1893. This coup was supported by U.S. troops (although not officially) and was led by Lorrin P. Thurston, a Honolulu publisher. U.S. minister John L. Stevens gave an order to disembark 162 troops, ostensibly to protect American life and property. The troops had the coercive effect of forcing the queen's resignation. Controversy has always surrounded the issue of whether Minister Stevens acted on his own or on direction from the U.S. government. Writes Imperatore (1992), "A review of Stevens' correspondence with the U.S. Secretary of State implies premeditation with the action simply awaiting opportunity" (p. 263).

Queen Liliuokalani ruled Hawai'i from 1891 to 1893. Her overthrow was an event from which Hawai'ians never recovered. The queen did not order her troops to battle the insurgents because the odds were overwhelmingly against her and she trusted the fairness of the United States. After losing her throne, the queen wrote a desperate plea to President Cleveland to have it restored. President Cleveland sent an emissary, James Blount, to investigate the overthrow of the queen. After receiving a report critical of the coup leaders, President Cleveland urged Sanford B. Dole and the conspirators to return the queen to her throne. Dole responded to Cleveland by telling him not to interfere in Hawai'ian affairs (Imperatore, 1992).

The Republic of Hawai'i was established, with Sanford B. Dole as its first and only president. Annexation by the United States was imminent. In 1898, under President William McKinley, the Islands became part of the territorial possessions of the United States. Manifest Destiny had triumphed again. The *haoles* who had once come as guests had managed to usurp the entire kingdom. Richard Olney (cited in Wright, 1972), the secretary of state at that time, summarized the situation: "Hawai'i is ours," he said, "but as I look back upon the first steps in this miserable business and as I contemplate the means used to complete the outrage, I am ashamed of the whole affair" (p. 21).

From Territory to State

Once Hawai'i became a territory of the United States, its political and economic affairs were managed by forces on the mainland or by island elites responding to powerful people on the mainland. The territorial governorship of Hawai'i was a powerful position. The governor was appointed by the president of the United States. This appointment was heavily influenced by the recommendation of the Hawai'ian elite. The economy of the territory depended on favorable legislation from the U.S. Congress to subsidize Hawai'ian sugar and other agricultural products. The opening of the Panama Canal made it much easier for Hawai'ian products to reach markets on the east coast of the United States. Favorable subsidies and market shares from the U.S. Congress made Hawai'i nearly totally reliant on sugar.

The Big Five corporations ran the economy of the Islands through a variety of interlocking directorates and the vertical integration of business. To the average Native Hawai'ian, this world of Merchant Street was alien and remote. The original inhabitants of Hawai'i found themselves on the bottom rung of a plantation society with little hope of improving their situation.

Prince Jonah Kuhio Kalanianaole became the territorial delegate to the Congress by serving the interests of plantation owners. However, his frustrations would sometimes emerge, as they did in 1912, when he told a Hawai'ian audience (cited in Kent, 1983), "Under the political conditions in the territory, a man doesn't own his soul" (p. 45).

Native Hawai'ians' need for land was supposed to be reconciled in 1921 with the passage of the Hawai'ian Rehabilitation Act. Under the auspices of the Hawai'ian Homes Commission, 200,000 acres of land were to be distributed to landless Hawai'ians for small-scale farming. Most of the land actually distributed was not suitable for farming. Eventually, it passed into the hands of large plantation interests (Parker, 1989). The large amount of acreage devoted to export crops like sugar and pineapples meant that the traditional small-scale farming of the Native Hawai'ian was nearly a relic from the past. Hawai'i had become a major importer of food from the mainland, although historically it had been self-sufficient in food. Once again, actions intended to improve living conditions for Native Americans resulted in benefits for other groups.

The plantation economy continued earning large profits with the support of the Republican party, which had dominated island politics for the first fifty years of the twentieth century. On some plantations, managers monitored the actions of their workers by hanging pencils by strings from the ceilings of the voting booths. By noting in which direction the string moved, party preference could be determined. Anyone voting for a Democrat would be fired (Shaplen, 1982).

After World War II, political leaders in Hawai'i seriously began to discuss seeking statehood from the U.S. Congress. It was argued that becoming a state would guarantee the large U.S. market for Hawai'ian products. Hawai'ian leaders also believed that statehood would significantly increase the tourist industry and that many new construction and service jobs would be created.

While economic predictions turned out to be, in general, correct, Native Hawai'ians did not share proportionately in the new prosperity. As Joseph Keoloha, Chairman of the State Office of Hawai'ian Affairs, observed, "Statehood was the final act following the confiscation of our land and the overthrow of our Queen, and Native Hawai'ians have mixed feelings about it" (Chrysler, 1984, p. 40).

Native Hawai'ians Today

Social Class and Politics

Present-day Hawai'i is a polyglot of peoples with varied backgrounds. There are sizable communities of Chinese Americans and Japanese Americans. There is a Korean American population that originally came to work in the pineapple and sugar cane estates. Filipinos and Portuguese also came as agricultural workers. There are also a few thousand African Americans in Hawai'i, as well as the still powerful *haoles*. Americans of Japanese ancestry have been especially successful in the political arena. Chinese Americans have become business leaders in many areas.

Upward mobility by Asian Americans in Hawai'i contrasts sharply with their status as primarily agricultural workers one or two generations ago. This change in status has caused some interethnic discord and ill feelings. Many Native Hawai'ians who perceived the *haoles* as the holders of all-powerful positions often see Japanese Americans in their place. Other groups besides Hawai'ians who find themselves disproportionately represented in the lower economic classes realize that the ethnic caste system of the big plantation era still exists in a modified form.

Dissatisfaction bred by this earlier caste system caused a major political movement. Organizers tried to convince workers that their future would best be served by identifying politically with their working-class brethren regardless of their ethnic origin. This movement achieved its first major success in 1954, when the Democratic party broke the traditional Republican control in both houses of the territorial legislature. The man given a major share of the credit for this triumph was John A. Burns, who would play an important role in Hawai'i's future politics by lobbying vigorously for statehood and by becoming governor.

The 1954 victory was viewed generally as the beginning of a progressive movement in Island politics. By 1970, the Democrats were the solidly entrenched party, and John Burns was a candidate for a third term as governor. The main opposition within the Democratic party came from Tom Gill, who had been lieutenant governor under Burns. Gill charged that what may have started out as progressive political forces in 1954 had now become a power structure that was working together with the business and economic interests they originally opposed. The Gill campaign had a strong issue orientation, capitalizing on respect for Hawai'i's fragile environment. Governor Burns, with a network of loyal supporters on several islands, relied primarily on a media campaign and was successful in winning a third term.

In 1974, George Ariyoshi became the first non-*haole* governor of Hawai'i. He was later reelected to second and third terms of office. Governor Ariyoshi was followed by John D. Waihee in 1986. Governor Waihee became the first person of Hawai'ian ancestry to hold this office and was reelected in 1990. Ben Cayetano was elected governor in 1994 and reelected in 1998. Neither major political party in Hawai'i has a homogeneous political base. To make a viable appeal to a diverse society, each party has had leaders who represent most of Hawai'i's major ethnic groups.

The issues that are likely to dominate Hawa'ian politics in the foreseeable future are land use, tourism, economic diversification, Native Hawai'ian self-determination, and the preservation of Hawai'i's fragile natural environment. Today, 55% of all land in Hawai'i is privately owned (Hawai'i State, 1996), and 95% of that land is held by 70-odd corporations or individuals (Bank of Hawai'i Reports, 1999, 2001; Shaplen, 1982). The zoning and distribution of land are likely to evoke strong feelings among many Hawai'ians. Tourism is clearly Hawai'i's largest source of income. In 1959, Hawai'i had only about 243,000 visitors each year. By the mid- and at the end of the 1990s, that number had reached nearly 7 million (Bank of Hawai'i Reports, 1999, 2001; Trask, 1992, p. 34) and has become a business worth nearly $11 billion annually (Hunter, 1994).

Some critics of the tourist-dependent economy note that visitors cannot be relied on as a stable source of income. Hawai'i's tourist revenues were very adversely affected following the attacks on the World Trade Center and the Pentagon on September 11, 2001, as the overall air travel volume declined globally. While the longer-term economic impacts of the terrorist attacks is not yet entirely clear, economists in Hawai'i forecast the restoration of tourism as it had been prior to the tragic events of September 11th. They do, however, forecast a slowdown of Hawai'i's overall economic growth rate and current stability (Bank of Hawai'i Reports, 2001).

There are many viewpoints, but no clear consensus on exactly how to diversify Hawai'i's economy. Agricultural land is too expensive for farming to ever regain its former prominence. Transportation and labor costs work against Hawai'i becoming a major manufacturing center. Meanwhile, tourism remains the mainstay of the economy while Hawai'ians attempt to reach a consensus on new directions for the Islands' economic future.

Adapting Native Hawai'ian Values

The Hawai'ian spirit of *Aloha Aina* (love for the land) has had a resurgence in response to growing developments through language revitalization, land restoration, and independence movements in the 1970s (Castanha, 1996; Kamana & Wilson, 1996; Tabrah, 1980). These activist movements finally led to the creation of the Office of Hawai'ian Affairs in 1978 by an amendment to the state constitution (Castanha, 1996).

The traditional value of *ohana* is a cooperative system of social relationships found within an extended family. A study in a Hawai'ian community near Honolulu found that the spirit of *ohana* still permeates the lives of Native Hawai'ians. This study noted the following (cited in Howard, 1974): "Our research continually affirmed that the overwhelming proportion of the people find gratification in their lifestyle. If wages were higher, most would continue to invest in a lifestyle similar to the one they are currently leading" (p. 226).

This value of *ohana* is sometimes counterproductive to Hawai'ian children attending school, where cooperation on academic work may be perceived as "cheating." Also, Hawai'ian youngsters do not particularly relish the peer competition engendered in many school situations and, consequently, they often do not respond well to competitive tasks.

The Hawai'ian value of *kokua* undergirds a traditional economic system based on cooperation with some element of competition. Under this system, one expression of *kokua* (cooperation) should be repaid with another expression of *kokua*. In this manner, the status of the individual is enhanced (Ogawa, 1978). As the trend toward development continues in a state with limited natural resources, the spirit of *kokua* might point the way toward an accommodation among competing groups.

Another Hawai'ian value that could prove helpful in a multiethnic and growing society is *ho'oponopono*. Literally, this means 'setting to right of wrongs' (Ogawa, 1978, p. 579). In early Hawai'i, *ho'oponopono* meant that all people had an opportunity to speak out on a problem until a solution was reached that would be binding on all parties. This ancient tradition could possibly be adapted to modern Hawai'i and become a valuable tool for building consensus on a difficult issue.

The Hawai'ians Today and Tomorrow

Proper classification of Native Hawai'ians is difficult because the overwhelming majority of them are part Hawai'ian. Estimates vary as to the number of part-Hawai'ians. According to the 2000 Census, 282,667 people identified themselves as at least part Native Hawai'ian or Pacific Islander, an increase of 74.2% from 1990. But 113,539 described themselves solely as a member of that group, a decrease of 30% (Dingeman & Bricking, 2001). These figures contrast sharply with the estimated 800,000 Native Hawai'ians on the Islands when Captain Cook first visited in 1778.

Under current law, only people with 50% or more Hawai'ian blood are entitled to land and to medical and legal benefits. Perhaps no more than 60,000 of the state's 1,200,000 people can prove that pedigree (Egan, 1990, p. 29A; U.S. Census Burau, 2000a). An issue in Hawai'i is whether to lower the 50% requirement in order to allow more people to qualify for any program designated for Native Hawai'ians. Even if the current policy is followed, the matter of establishing Hawai'ian lineage to meet the 50% requirement often leaves the Office of Hawai'ian Affairs in a quandary.

The average Native Hawai'ians fall far below their White counterparts in the area of economic prosperity. They generally live in communities whose facilities are substandard (Bricking, 2001), and comprise a disproportionately high percentage of school dropouts and police arrests.

Native Hawai'ians have generally not adapted to the competitive nature of the dominant Western society. Rather, they are oriented toward affiliation, not competition. Friendship and family harmony, especially sibling relationships, are important social aspects of Native Hawai'ians. Research indicates that Hawai'ian school children achieve better when they are evaluated collectively rather than individually (McIntyre, 1996; Tharp & Yamauchi, 1994; Yamauchi, Ceppi, & Lau-Smith, 2000). Kathryn Au (1981) and Roland G. Tharp (1982), working in the Kamehameha Early Education Program (KEEP), found that both student participation and standardized achievement test scores increased when classroom teachers use strategies consistent with the cultures of Native Hawai'ian students and used the children's experiences in reading instruction.

The research described above has influenced the creation of schools whose curricula are based on Hawai'ian values. First among such schools was the Kamehameha School, a K–12 private school for children of Hawai'ian ancestry founded in the 1970s (Clarke et al., 1996; Tharp & Yamauchi, 1994; Yamauchi, Ceppi, & Lau-Smith 2000). The more recent charter school movement has further made it possible to offer publicly funded school programs based on bilingual and bicultural curricula. This offers the possibility for Native Hawai'ian students to acquire a strong background in Hawai'ian language and culture while, at the same time, developing traditional mainstream academic skills such as individual and field independent learning styles.

The Black civil rights movement, the anti-Vietnam protests, and the other movements for civil rights during the 1960s and 1970s stimulated the rise of the Hawai'ian sovereignty movement, which has political as well as cultural aims (Castanha, 1996). Beginning in the 1970s, a militant grassroots movement for Native Hawai'ian rights began. A primary goal of these nationalist groups is to return lost economic and political power to people of Hawai'ian ancestry. Castanha (1996) gives an overview of the Hawai'ian sovereignty movement:

> In the 1980s and 1990s, major sovereignty organizations...formed to demand the return of lands, self-governance and independence based on the international rights of self-determination. In 1985, the Institute for the Advancement of Hawaiian Affairs...was created...In 1991, Hui Na'auao, a coalition of 47 Hawaiian groups focusing on sovereignty education, was organized...In 1992 The 'Ohana Council of Hawaiian Kingdom...commenced. Also in 1992, the restored Kingdom of Hawai'i began (p. 8).

Along with the Hawai'ian sovereignty movement, there has been a revision in Hawai'ian history that does not consider the whole era of Hawai'ian monarchy to be a glorious age of benevolent rule. Among some of these Hawai'ian nationalists, Kamehameha III is viewed as a ruler who broke up the traditional system of land ownership and started the Islands on their steady slide toward *haole* control. Queen Liliuokalani is viewed as a great monarch who tried to retain power in the hands of Hawai'ians while facing insurmountable odds.

This militancy is reflected in the formation of such groups as the *Kokua* and the Hawai'ians. Membership in the *Kokua* is limited to non-*haoles*. This group espouses a Third World outlook. The Hawai'ians limit their membership to people with at least some Hawai'ian blood. Their ideology is more moderate than the *Kokua*. The existence of these two groups has had little impact on the economic status of most Native Hawai'ians.

Another manifestation of this militancy was the Free Kahoolawe movement in the mid-1970s. Kahoolawe, a small island owned by the military six miles off the coast of Maui, had been used for bombing practice since World War II. The movement began with an occupation of the island by a group of Hawai'ians joined by people from nearly all segments of Hawai'i's population. The goal of the Free Kahoolawe movement was the return of the island to state government jurisdiction and public access (Tabrah, 1980). In 1994, the Free Kahoolawe movement succeeded, and the U.S. Navy returned Kahoolawe to the State of Hawai'i. The Hawai'ian legislature designated Kahoolawe as a cultural and educational preserve. The Free Kahoolawe movement was a precursor to the conflicts between the residents of Vieques Island in Puerto Rico and the U.S. Navy over the use of that island for maneuvers and as a bombing range.

There can be little doubt that a true Hawai'ian Renaissance occurred in the 1970s. This trend represented a sharp contrast to predictions that the Hawai'ian culture was slowly being extinguished. The renaissance went beyond a renewal of interest in cultural activities. It resulted in a new economic and political consciousness, an increasing involvement with other Pacific Island peoples (Kanahele, 1982) as well as an effort to revitalize the Hawai'ian language. Resulting from the latter were Hawai'ian immersion K–12 school programs and the development of new undergraduate and graduate programs in Hawai'ian studies and Hawai'ian language (Warschauer & Donaghy, 1997). Overall it can be said that the Hawai'ian Renaissance arrived at a propitious time, when Native Hawai'ian culture was being practiced less and less.

The issue of sovereignty for Native Hawai'ians has received added attention in recent years. Dudley and Agard (1990) chronicle the history of the Hawai'ian sovereignty movement and discuss various forms of possible Native Hawai'ian sovereignty. Among the variations are: (1) the American Indian model, (2) a broader model of "nation within a nation" that American Indians enjoy, or (3) restoration of the Hawai'ian nation.

There are strong differences of opinion on Hawai'ian sovereignty among Hawai'i's people, even among Native Hawai'ians. Those who favor it generally see the movement as a way to right historical wrongs. Those who oppose it often say that it will polarize Native Hawai'ians from non-Hawai'ians or are concerned that the outcome may not be fair to non-Hawai'ians.

A Hawai'ian Sovereignty Elections Council was to conduct an election in 1996 with the electorate being limited to persons of Hawai'ian ancestry over the age of 18. This election was successfully challenged by a rancher from the big island, Fred Rice, in the case of *Rice v. Cayetano*. The Supreme Court ruled that the electorate for Office of Hawai'ian Affairs (OHA) trustees could not be limited to persons of Hawai'ian ancestry. Subsequently, an election was held with the full electorate eligible and most of the trustees elected were individuals of Hawai'ian ancestry.

Native Hawai'ians are vitally concerned with the future of their Islands' natural environment. High real estate prices in Hawai'i promote vertical expansion of new dwellings, but the environment of the Islands is particularly fragile. Foreign investment is playing an ever-increasing role in Hawai'i's economy. Will absentee landlords be appropriately concerned with the environmental impact of development, particularly if such measures reduce profit margins? These quality-of-life issues are important to all Hawai'ians and are particularly salient to Native Hawai'ians, whose culture is inextricably tied to the land.

Hawai'i is sometimes presented as the personification of the aloha spirit. This is a misrepresentation to some degree. Hawai'i is more ethnically harmonious than some societies. However, it is not an ethnic or a racial paradise. The future of racial and ethnic distinctions in Hawai'i is unclear. The Native Hawai'ians' out-marriage rate is among the highest of any group on the Islands (Hawai'i State, 1996). In a strictly biological sense, the Native Hawai'ian population is being dissolved into other groups. Current census data show that only 6.6% of the Hawai'ian population indicated that they were Native Hawai'ians. In contrast, 21.4% indicated that they were two or more races (U.S. Census Bureau, 2000b). Matching these numbers with the movement toward independence and a continued revitalization of Hawai'ian language and values, a more optimistic outlook is that the culture of the Native Hawai'ians is, to some extent, enriching the lives of all the inhabitants of these beautiful islands.

Teaching Strategies

The concept of expansion can be illustrated in many ways. The Native Hawai'ians provide a classic case of the displacement of a native population because they were an obstacle to the expanding forces. Their story can be related to other native inhabitants who suffered a similar fate.

CONCEPT

Expansion
Generalization: As a nation expands to obtain territory, often the rights of the native population are not protected.

1. After giving the students sufficient background information about the Native Hawai'ians, ask them to make a list of factors that apply both to the Native Hawai'ians and the American Indians. These factors can include both past and present situations. Afterwards, these points can be grouped, classified, and discussed.

2. Organize your students into small groups and present them with this hypothetical situation: One person in the group would be chosen to supervise and control the financial affairs of all the members. What problems might develop with such an arrangement? A tape could be made of their reactions. Later, this tape could be replayed and compared to what occurred between American advisers and Hawai'ian rulers.

3. Role-play the following situation, which occurred in Hawai'i in 1845. The *haole* adviser to the King is trying to persuade him to grant some land to Mr. Farmer, a prospective planter. Kaeo opposes the entire proposition. After the role-play situation, ask the students the questions that follow. The role descriptions are as follows:

> **King Kamehameha III:** He is indecisive over what to say to the planter. Yet, he greatly respects the advice of his *haole* counsel, Mr. George Bennett.
>
> **George Bennett:** Adviser to the king and a good friend of Mr. Farmer, whose interests he protects. He has been a missionary for nearly twenty years.
>
> **Floyd S. Farmer:** Planter and business tycoon. He intends to start sugar plantations in Hawai'i because of the predictably warm weather.
>
> **Kaeo:** A Native Hawai'ian and a member of the king's court. He vehemently opposes the granting of any more land to *haoles*.

Questions
1. Did George Bennett succeed in persuading the king to grant the land to Mr. Farmer? If so, why? If not, why?
2. Was Kaeo successful in his opposition to the land deal? Why or why not?
3. Did Mr. Farmer tell the king his plans for using native labor? Why or why not?
4. Did the king decide to grant the land lease to Mr. Farmer? If he did, what were his reasons? If he did not, why not?
5. Did Mr. Bennett use his position as a missionary to help his argument? Why or why not?

CONCEPT

Adaptation

Generalization: When a native culture finds itself surrounded by a dominant culture, it becomes increasingly difficult to maintain the native culture.

Read the following story to the class and ask the questions that follow.

A Hawai'ian Dilemma

The old ramshackle house had stood relatively unchanged since the family had obtained it more than forty years ago from the Hawai'ian Homes Commission. Around it were the two acres of vegetables that had provided subsistence for the Panui family during that time. Mary Panui lived on the property along with her sons, George and Eddie. Mr. Panui had died five years before and, since that time, things had not been the same. One afternoon George was weeding one of the vegetable patches when Eddie returned from a day in town. Feeling that he deserved some help, George asked his brother. "Hey, aren't you going to help out around here?"

Eddie answered, "No, I have gotten a job in town with the tourist agency. I will drive the mainland *haoles* around during the day, and in the evenings I will dance at the luaus."

George couldn't believe his ears. After all of those years that their father had taught them to respect their Hawai'ian heritage, his brother was suddenly changing. "Eddie, how can you do a thing like this?" George wondered. "It would have broken Dad's heart, and anyway, what will mother say?"

Eddie looked at his brother casually and said, "I have been weeding taro root all of my life and I'm tired of it. I know Dad would probably say that I'm putting our culture up for sale but it's the only way to get ahead!"

The two brothers entered the home where Mary Panui was cooking dinner and told her of their conversation. The old woman with the creased brow was also unhappy with what Eddie was considering. However, she could not deny that the vegetable gardens would never provide more than a subsistence living.

Seeing his mother caught up in the dilemma, George tried one last time. "Eddie, can you imagine yourself in one of those flowered shirts selling shell necklaces to the tourists? Where is your pride?"

Eddie thought for a moment and answered smugly, "Pride doesn't fill your wallet: when will you realize that?"

With that, George started out of the door but stopped short and told his brother, "I may never have much money to my name, but I'll never be a practicing Hawai'ian!"

Questions

1. What would you have done if you had been Eddie Panui?
2. Do you feel Eddie's brother is justified in calling him a practicing (commercialized) Hawai'ian?
3. Can you think of other ethnic groups in other settings that have had their culture commercialized? If so, how much was this trend sanctioned or resisted by the group?

REFERENCES

Au, K. (1980). Participation Structures in a Reading Lesson with Hawaiian Children. *Anthropology and Education Quarterly, 11*(2), 91–115.

Bank of Hawaii. (1999). *Annual Economic Report, Vol. 48.* [On-line]. Available: *http://www.boh.com*

Bank of Hawaii. (2001). *Hawaii Economic Trends.* [On-line]. Available: *http://www.boh.com/econ/*

Bricking, T. (2001, April 30). Census Finds Hawai'ians Remain in Poorest Areas. *Honolulu Advertiser.*

Castanha, A. (1996). The Hawaiian Sovereignty Movement: Roles and Impacts on Non-Hawaiians. Master's Thesis, University of Hawaii. [On-line]. Available: *http://www.hookele.com/non-hawaians/abstract.html*

Chrysler, K. M. (1984, August 27). Hawai'i: Youngest State Finds Its Place in the Sun. *U.S. News and World Report*, p. 40.

Clarke, M. A., Davis, A., Rhodes, L. K., & DeLott Baker, E. (1996). Conceptual framework and literature review: Minority status and school success. In *Creating Coherence: High Achieving Classrooms for Minority Students* (HACMS). University of Colorado at Denver, Research Report, Chapter VI. [On-line]. Available: *http://carbon.cudenver.edu/~wdavis/chapt6 _min.html*

Day, A. G. (1968). *Hawai'i and Its People*. New York: Meredith Press.

Dingeman, R., & Bricking, T. (2001, March 20). Census Lists More Native Hawai'ians Than Ever. *Honolulu Advertiser.*

Dudley, M. K., & Agard, K. K. (1990). *A Call for Hawai'ian Sovereignty*. Honolulu: Na Kane O Ka Malo Press.

Egan, T. (1990, January 20). Blood and Benefits: Hawai'i to Vote on Ancestral Rights. *Miami Herald*, p. 29A.

Hawai'i Grappling with Sovereignty Movement. (1994, June 3). *Miami Herald*, p. 7A.

Hawai'i State. Department of Business, Economic Development and Tourism, *The State of Hawai'i Data Book: A Statistical Abstract, 1996*. In *Native Hawai'ian Data Book, 1998*: Table 3.1. [On-line]. Available: *http://oha.org/databook/tab3-01.98.html*

Hawai'i State. Department of Health. *Vital Statistics Supplement, 1996*. In *Native Hawaiian Data Book, 1998;* Table 1.32. [On-line]. Available: *http://oha.org/databook/tab1-32.98.html*

Howard, A. (1974). *Ain't No Big Thing: Coping Strategies in a Hawai'ian American Community*. Honolulu: University Press of Hawai'i.

Hunter, B. (Ed.). (1994). *The Statesman's Year Book, 1994–1995* (131st ed.). New York: St. Martin's Press.

Imperatore, W. (1992, November/December). The Deposing of the Hawai'ian Monarch: The Changing Narrative in Textbooks. *The Social Studies*, 261–266.

Jacobs, P., & Landau, S., with Pell, E. (1971). *To Serve the Devil: Colonials and Sojourners* (Vol. 2). New York: Vintage.

Kamana, K., & Wilson, W. H. (1996). Hawaiian language programs. In G. Cantoni (Ed.), *Stabilizing Indigenous Languages*. Flagstaff: Center for Excellence in Education, Northern Arizona University. [On-line]. Available: *http://www.ncbe.gwu.edu/miscpubs/stabilize/ additional/hawaiian.htm*

Kanahele, G. (1982). *Hawai'ian Renaissance*. Honolulu: Project Waiaha.

Kent, N. J. (1983). *Hawai'i: Islands under the Influence*. New York: Monthly Review Press.

Lind, A. (1980). *Hawai'i's People*. Honolulu: University Press of Hawai'i.

McIntyre, T. (1996). Does the Way We Teach Create Behavior Disorders in Culturally Different Students? *Education and Treatment of Children*, 19(3), 354–370.

Ogawa, D. (1978). *Kodomo No Tame Ni*. Honolulu: University Press of Hawai'i.

Parker, L. S. (1989). *Native American Estate: The Struggle over Indian and Hawai'ian Lands*. Honolulu: University Press of Hawai'i.

Population Reference Bureau. (2000). *United States Population Data Sheet of the Population Reference Bureau*. Washington, DC: Author.

Shaplen, R. (1982, September 6). A Reporter at Large: Islands of Disenchantment. *New Yorker*, p. 85.

Stannard, D. E. (1989). *Before the Horror: The Population of Hawai'i on the Eve of Western Contact*. Honolulu: University of Hawai'i, Social Science Research Institute.

Tabrah, R. (1980). *Hawai'i: A Bicentennial History*. New York: Norton.

Takaki, R. (1983). *Pau Hana: Plantation Life and Labor in Hawai'i*. Honolulu: University Press of Hawai'i.

Tharp, R. G. (1982). The Effective Instruction of Comprehension: Results and Description of the Kamehameha Early Childhood Education Program. *Reading Research Quarterly*, 17(4), 503–527.

Tharp, R. G., & Yamauchi, L. A. (1994). Effective Instructional Conversation in Native American Classrooms. *Educational Practice Report, 10.* [On-line]. Available: *http://www.ncbe.gwu.edu/miscpubs/ncrcdsll/epr10.htm*

Trask, H. K. (1992). Racism against Native Hawai'ians at the University of Hawai'i. *Amerasian Journal, 18*(3), 33–50.

U.S. Census Bureau, Census 2000a Redistricting Data (P.L. 94-171) Summary File; compiled by the Hawaii State Department of Business, Economic Development and Tourism, Hawaii State Data Center. [On-line]. Available: *http://www.hawaii.gov/dbedt/census2k/pltable3.html*

U.S. Bureau of the Census: Census 2000b; Summary File 1. Proximity Census 2000 School District General Demographic Characteristics Profile Geographic Area: State of Hawaii. [On-line]. Available: *http://proximityone.com*

Warschauer, M., & Donaghy, K. (1997). Leokï: A Powerful Voice of Hawaiian Language Revitalization. *Computer Assisted Language Learning, 10*(4), 349–362. [On-line]. Available: *http://www.gse.uci.edu/markw/leoki.html*

Woerner, B. (2000, August). Big Island's Charter Schools. *Waimea Gazette* p. [On-line]. Available: *http://www.k12.hi.us/~bwoerner/ipcs/bigislandcharters.html*

Wright, T. (1972). *The Disenchanted Isles.* New York: Dial Press.

Yamauchi, L. A., Ceppi, A. K., & Lau-Smith, J. -A. (2000). Teaching in a Hawaiian Context: Educator Perspectives on the Hawaiian Language Immersion Program. *Bilingual Research Journal, 24*(4), [On-line]. Available: *http://brj.asu.edu/v244/articles/art5.html#theory*

ANNOTATED BIBLIOGRAPHY

Books for Teachers

Especially Recommended

Benham, M. K. P., & Heck, R. H. (1998). *Culture and Educational Policy in Hawai'i: The Silencing of Native Voices.* Mahwah, NJ: Lawrence Erlbaum.

This book presents the educational history of public schools in Hawai'i. The authors analyze how dominant Western policies have debased Hawai'ian culture and its sovereignty and discuss how historical trends in the U.S. education system have, overall, served to assimilate Native groups.

Eyre, D. L. (2000). *By Wind, by Wave: An Introduction to Hawai'i's Natural History.* Honolulu: Bess Press.

This book presents the stories of 17 animals, and from this perspective examines the close interrelationships among ocean, plants, animals, and people in Hawai'i.

Frazier, F. N. (2000). *Kamehameha and His Warrior Kekuhaupi'o.* Honolulu: Kamehameha Schools Press.

This book is the translation of a series of newspaper articles written in Hawai'ian by Stephen Desha from 1920 to 1924 about the Hawaiian martial art practices of Kekuhapi'o, King Kamehameha's bodyguard.

Fuchs, L. H. (1961). *Hawai'i Pono.* New York: Harcourt, Brace and World.

Perhaps the most highly regarded book on the social history of Hawai'i, it covers the period from annexation through statehood.

Kawena Puku'i, M., & Curtis, C. (1996). *Hawai'i Island Legends: Pikoi, Pele and Others.* Honolulu: Kamehameha Schools Press.

This book is a collection of Hawai'i's most important legends and folktales.

Lowe Hasegawa, R. (1998). *David Kalakaua*. Honolulu: Kamehameha Schools Press.

This book presents the story of Kalakaua, the seventh monarch of Hawai'i and the first who was not from the Kamehameha line. The text is accompanied by illustrations.

Morgan, J. R. (1996). *Hawaii: A Unique Geography*. Honolulu: Bess Press.

This book offers an exploration of Hawai'i's natural and cultural landscapes and addresses the impact of the state's geography on social, economic, cultural, and political events.

Rayson, A. (1994). *Modern Hawai'ian History*. Honolulu: Bess Press.

This book is a historical documentary, based on oral history and the study of primary documents to address Hawaii's modern history, beginning with the overthrow of the monarchy in the nineteenth century.

Rayson, A., & Bauer, H. (1997). *Hawai'i: The Pacific State* (4th ed.). Honolulu: Bess Press.

This book provides a complete and up-to-date history of Hawai'i from the formation of the islands, the arrival of the first Hawai'ians, the European arrival in Hawai'i, the shift from monarchy to territory, and the political evolution through both world wars to the current sovereignty movement. The book further covers island holidays and festivals.

Williams, J. S. (1997). *From the Mountains to the Sea: Early Hawaiian Life*. Honolulu: Kamehameha Schools Press.

This book describes the life and activities of people on the Hawai'ian Islands before Western contact. The text is accompanied by illustrations.

Other Books

Andrade, E., Jr. (1996). *Unconquerable Rebel: Robert W. Wilcox and Hawai'ian Politics 1880–1903*. Niwot, CO: University Press of Colorado.

Scholars tracing the development of the Hawai'i Sovereignty Movement will be intrigued by this period of the state's history as presented by the author through the life of an individual who dominated the political landscape of the era.

Aoude, I. G. (Ed.). (1999). *The Ethnic Studies Story: Politics and Social Movements in Hawaii—Essays in Honor of Marion Kelly*. Honolulu: University of Hawaii Press.

This book presents a variety of interdisciplinary essays that address contemporary social, cultural, and political movements in Hawai'i.

Becket, J., & Singer, J. (1999). *Pana Oahu: Sacred Stones, Sacred Land*. Honolulu: University of Hawaii Press.

This book presents a photographic collection and contextual information of ancient sacred sites in Hawaii. The authors address the function of these sites as well as the history behind the abolition of traditional Hawai'ian religion.

Beechert, A. M., & Beechert, E. D. (Eds.). (2000). *From Kona to Yenan: The Political Memoir of Koji Ariyoshi*. Honolulu: University of Hawaii Press.

This book is the biographical portrait of Koji Ariyoli, the editor of one of Hawai'i's daily newspapers. Ariyoshi became the leading voice for labor concerns in the postwar conflicts between labor unions and the Hawai'ian elites.

Bird, A. J., Goldsberry, S., & Kanekoa Bird, J. K. (Eds.). (1982). *The Craft of Hawaiian Lauhala Weaving*. Honolulu: University of Hawaii Press.

This book offers a brief history of and instructions for the craft of Lauhula weaving, an ancient Hawai'ian tradition.

Boylan, D. (2000). *John A. Burns: The Man and His Times*. Honolulu: University of Hawaii Press.

This book presents the biography of John A. Burns who strongly influenced Hawai'ian politics from 1945 to 1970. Working together with labor leaders and Japanese American war veterans, Burns forged the Democratic Party that would later on become important for the promotion of social change in Hawaii.

Calder, A., Lamb, J., & Orr, B. (Eds.). (1999). *Voyages and Beaches: Pacific Encounters, 1769–1840*. Honolulu: University of Hawaii Press.

This interdisciplinary collection of essays examines how the Pacific was shaped by the European conquest and discusses how the Pacific Islands absorbed and were transformed by this impact.

Chinen, J., Kane, K. O., & Yoshinaga, J. N. (1997). *Women in Hawaii: Sites, Identities, and Voices*. Honolulu: University of Hawaii Press.

This anthology is a collection of art, poetry, literary criticism, and personal essays that reflect a wide variety of women's stories from a sociological, historical, political, and cultural perspective.

Chock, E., Harstad, J. R., Lum, D. H. Y., & Teter, B. (Eds.). (2000). *Growing Up Local: An Anthology of Poetry and Prose from Hawaii*. Honolulu: University of Hawaii Press.

This collection presents works of a variety of Hawai'ian authors who describe what it means to be Hawai'ian.

Clark, J. R. K. (2001). *Hawaii Place Names: Shores, Beaches, and Surf Sites*. Honolulu: University of Hawaii Press.

This book presents the history of place names associated with the ocean and beaches.

Clarke, J., & Dods, D. (Eds.). (1996). *Artists/Hawaii*. Honolulu: University of Hawaii Press.

This book provides portraits of 22 artists of Hawaii's contemporary arts community.

Cordy, R. (2000). *Exalted Lies the Chief*. Honolulu: Mutual Publications.

Blending archaeology, history, and oral history, the author provides the readers with a broad perspective of Hawai'i's history from the eighteenth century to the present. Of note are the years prior to the unification of the Islands by King Kamehameha because there is very little known today about those years.

Cox, J. H., & Davenport, W. H. (1988). *Hawaiian Sculpture* (2nd ed.). Honolulu: University of Hawaii Press.

This book is the first comprehensive study of the Hawai'ian sculptural tradition. Over 60 illustrations depict the wooden sculptures of human figures created by unknown artists.

Daws, G. (1976). *Shoal of Time*. Honolulu: University of Hawai'i Press.

This is a complete interpretive history of Hawai'i from European contact to statehood. Still popular reading today.

Dudley, W. C., & Lee, M. (1998). *Tsunami!* Honolulu: University of Hawaii Press.

This book examines the tsunami phenomenon and its impact on Hawai'i.

Dye, B. (1997). *Merchant Prince of the Sandalwood Mountains: Afong and the Chinese in Hawaii*. Honolulu: University of Hawaii Press.

This book presents the results of documentary research and interviews about Chun Afong, Hawai'i's first Chinese millionaire. By way of this biography, the role of the Chinese in nineteenth century Hawai'i is explored.

Dye, B. (1998). *Hawaii Chronicles II: Contemporary Island History from the Pages of Honolulu Magazine*. Honolulu: University of Hawaii Press.

This collection of articles examines individuals who have, politically or culturally, made a difference in Hawai'i's history since WW II and, in this way, provides the context for current political events.

Dye, B. (2000). *Hawaii Chronicles III: World War Two in Hawaii.* Honolulu: University of Hawaii Press.

This book examines, through a selection of newspaper articles, how Hawai'ians experienced the human and social impact of WW II events on their islands.

Forbes, D. W. (1992). *Encounters with Paradise: Views of Hawaii and Its People.* Honolulu: University of Hawaii Press.

This book offers an extensive overview and examination of how Hawaii has been seen and painted from the eighteenth to the mid-twentieth century by artists throughout the world.

Frazier, F. N. (2001). *The True Story of Kaluaikoolau: As Told by His Wife, Piilani.* Honolulu: University of Hawaii Press.

This book presents the English translation of the story of Koolau, who became a legendary figure on Kauai. Following the overthrow of Queen Lilioukalani, Koolau, who in 1892 had fled into a mountainous valley after contracting leprosy in order not to be killed, became a powerful symbol of resistance. The story of his last years was told by his wife and published in Hawai'ian in 1906.

Hara, M., & Okja Keller, N. (Eds.). (2000). *Intersecting Circles: The Voices of Hapa Women in Poetry and Prose.* Honolulu: University of Hawaii Press.

This book presents the voices of mixed-race women and their experiences of growing up.

Hawaii Nikkei History Editorial Board. (1998). *Japanese Eyes/American Heart: Personal Reflections of Hawaii's World War II Nisei Soldiers.* Honolulu: University of Hawaii Press.

This book is a collection of personal thoughts of Hawaii's Nisei soldiers as recorded in diaries and letters sent home.

Ito, K. L. (1999). *Lady Friends: Hawai'ian Ways and the Ties that Define.* Ithaca, NY: Cornell University Press.

This book describes Hawai'ian customs through the eyes of a university professor who lived with a series of Hawai'ian families. There is a particularly valuable chapter on Ho'oponopono (to make right, to correct) that gives a detailed description of the Hawaj'ian form of conflict resolution.

Judd, W. F. (1998). *Hawai'i Joins the World.* Honolulu: Mutual Publishing.

A rich resource for historians trying to understand the events that helped shape the transformation of the Hawai'ian Islands from Polynesian feudalism to become part of the Western world. The evolution was fraught with conflicts and challenges. The book covers the first half of the nineteenth century, which, according to the author, were the most turbulent years of Hawai'ian history.

Juvik, S. P., Juvik, J. O., & Paradise, T. R. (1998). *Atlas of Hawaii, Deluxe Edition* (3rd ed.). Honolulu: University of Hawaii Press.

This atlas offers in six sections an excellent overview on the geographical, physical, biological, cultural, and social aspects of Hawai'i.

Kanahele, G. (1995). *Waikiki: 100 BC to 1900 AD: An Untold Story.* Honolulu: Queen Emma Foundation. Distributed by University of Hawaii Press.

In writing this first comprehensive depiction of the evolution of Waikiki, the author draws from archeological findings and the works of Hawai'ian historians and scholars. He weaves myths and legends into these sources to produce a fascinating story of one of Hawai'i's most well-known locations. The book is especially rich in historical and cultural information about life in Hawai'i in general prior to Captain Cook's arrival in the Islands.

Kanahele, G. (1999). *Emma, Hawai'i's Remarkable Queen*. Honolulu: Queen Emma Foundation Publication. Distributed by University of Hawaii Press.

Considered to be a complete biography of Queen Emma's life and the time in which she lived, this is a rich source book for anyone interested in understanding the legacies established by the Queen, which include a school, a church, and a hospital.

Kapulani Landgraf, A. (1994). *Na Wahi Pana O' Ko'olan Poko: Legendary Places of Ko'olan Poko*. Honolulu: University of Hawaii Press.

This book presents a collection of photographs as well as textual descriptions of the Hawai'ian island O'ahu as a response to the current urban development of this once primary and sacred place of culture and worship.

Lebra, J. C. (1999). *Shaping Hawai'i: The Voices of Women*. Honolulu: Goodale Publication.

Using oral history as a way of recording and reporting on these octogenarians' stories of life in Hawai'i, the author succeeds in weaving a rich tapestry of various ethnic experiences. Women's voices from different major ethnic groups in Hawai'i are presented against the historical, sociocultural contexts within which they lived.

Linnekin, J. (2000). *Sacred Queens and Women of Consequence: Rank, Gender, and Colonialism in the Hawai'ian Islands*. Ann Arbor, MI: University of Michigan Press.

An intriguing analysis of the Hawai'ian Islands during the first century of Western contact. The author examines the various roles and status of women with reference to different social units and presents these within historical events of the period.

Linnekin, J. R., & Poyer, L. (1990). *Cultural Identity and Ethnicity in the Pacific*. Honolulu: University of Hawaii Press.

This book examines, from a historical and ethnographic perspective, how Oceanic societies were organized prior to the arrival of the Europeans.

Mast, R. H., & Mast, A. B. (1997). *Autobiography of Protest in Hawaii*. Honolulu: University of Hawaii Press.

This book explores political activism in Hawai'i by recording the voices of 35 progressive activists about their experiences that led them to become activists.

Nordyke, E. C. (1999). *Pacific Images: Views from Captain Cook's Third Voyage*. Honolulu: University of Hawaii Press.

This book is a collection of pictorial and textual descriptions of Cook's voyage through the Pacific.

Nunes, S. S., & Nunes-Atabaski, S. (1999). *The Shishu Ladies of Hilo: Japanese Embroidery in Hawaii*. Honolulu: University of Hawaii Press.

This book offers an overview of the teachings of Japanese embroidery (shishu) in Hawai'i from the 1930s to the 1960s. The authors describe how materials and embroidery motifs changed across the time span and how this art helped women in the stitching community to develop an ethnic identity.

Okamura, J. (Ed.). (1996). *Filipino History, Identity, and Community in Hawaii*. Honolulu: University of Hawaii Press.

This book is a collection of essays on the culture and experience of Filipino Americans in Hawai'i.

Osborne, T. J. (1998). *Annexation, Hawai'i: Fighting American Imperialism*. Waimanalo, HI: Island Style Press.

A detailed and objective presentation of the events about the annexation of the Islands. The book focuses on the years 1893 to 1898 because these years witnessed the most heated debate on the subject. Although the book presents both sides of the issue, the author highlights the resistance to the attempts at annexation that eventually happened five years later.

Paik Moriarty, L. (1986). *Ni'ihau Shell Leis.* Honolulu: University of Hawaii Press.

This book introduces the social and cultural history of the use of shells for adornment and currency in pre- and post-war Hawai'i. Instructions for how to make a shell lei are included.

Patterson, W. (2000). *The Ilse: First-Generation Korean Immigrants in Hawaii, 1903–1973.* Honolulu: University of Hawaii Press.

This book is the first comprehensive social history of the first-generation Korean immigrants to Hawai'i.

Rauzon, M. J. (2000). *Isles of Refuge: Wildlife and History of the Northwestern Hawaiian Islands.* Honolulu: University of Hawaii Press.

This book offers an overview of the animal and plant wildlife of the Northwestern Hawai'ian islands through photographs, illustrations, and textual information. The volume brings together the natural and cultural history of Hawai'i's Northwest.

Reinecke, J. E. (1997). *The Filipino Piecemeal Sugar Strike of 1924–1925.* Honolulu: University of Hawaii Press.

This book provides an important part of the history of plantations and sugar production in Hawai'i.

Rensel, J., & Rodman, M. (Eds.). (1997). *Home in the Islands: Housing and Social Change in the Pacific.* Honolulu: University of Hawaii Press.

This book is a collection of interdisciplinary essays on the relationship and interaction between human beings and their housing.

Sakamoto, E. (2000). *Aloha Las Vegas and Other Plays.* Honolulu: University of Hawaii Press.

This book presents three plays that offer a constructed image of life in Hawai'i from 1959 to 1994.

Schutz, A. J. (1995). *The Voices of Eden: A History of Hawaiian Language Studies.* Honolulu: University of Hawaii Press.

This book offers an important contribution to Hawai'ian history as the author examines the Islands' linguistic past.

Stanton, J. (Ed.). (1997). *A Hawai'i Anthology.* Honolulu: University of Hawai'i Press.

A collection of literary pieces showcases young writers' reflections. It includes the work of local authors from different ethnic backgrounds who give us a glimpse of Hawai'i in earlier years and includes a section devoted to the rich traditions of story and song that are central to Hawai'ian culture.

Stephan, S. J. (2001). *Hawaii under the Rising Sun: Japan's Place for Conquest after Pearl Harbor.* Honolulu: University of Hawaii Press.

A provocative, historical analysis that challenges the belief that the Japanese had intended to invade the Hawai'ian islands.

Stewart, R. (2000). *Leper Priest of Molokai: The Father Damien Story.* Honolulu: University of Hawaii Press.

This biography examines the life and achievements of the missionary priest Father Damien, who lived in the leper settlement of Molokai.

Stewart Williams, J. (1998). *Princess Bernice Pauahi Bishop.* Honolulu: Kamehameha Schools Press.

This book is the biography of the last survivor of the Kamehameha dynasty and benefactress of the establishment of the Kamehameha Schools.

Takabuki, M. (1998). *An Unlikely Revolutionary: Matsuo Takabuki and the Making of Modern Hawaii.* Honolulu: University of Hawaii Press.

This book presents the autobiography of one of the key figures behind Hawaii's political and economic transformation from an agricultural society to a competitive, modern community.

Trask, H. -K. (1999a). *From a Native Daughter: Colonialism and Sovereignty in Hawaii.* Honolulu: University of Hawaii Press.

This book critically addresses the concerns about the abuse of Native Hawai'ian rights, institutional racism, and gender discrimination. The author further examines the moral and political rationale for Hawai'ian self-determination and sovereignty.

Trask, H.-K., (1999b). *Light in the Crevice Never Seen* (2nd ed.). Corvallis, OR: Calyx Books.

This book offers the poetry of an indigenous Hawai'ian rights activist and addresses the social realities that affect Native Hawai'ians today.

Twigg-Smith, T. (1998). *Hawai'ian Sovereignty: Do the Facts Matter?* Honolulu: Goodale Publication.

Adding to the debate on the subject of sovereignty, the author questions the accuracy of the advocates of the movement and challenges their interpretation of historical events. As a fifth-generation resident of Hawai'i and a descendent of one of the first missionaries who arrived in 1920, the author claims that facts have been ignored by zealous activists. His intent is to provide another perspective.

Weinstein, M. (Ed.). (1982). *Social Process in Hawai'i* (Vol. 29). Honolulu: The University of Hawai'i Press.

The entire volume is useful for its contribution to our knowledge about the major ethnic groups in Hawai'i. This overview of race and ethnic relations in Hawai'i is recommended for any student of race relations.

Wichman, F. B. (1998). *Kauai: Ancient Place-Names and Their Stories.* Honolulu: University of Hawaii Press.

This book provides a resource guide to Kauai as well as a history of place names.

Wood, H. (1999). *Displacing Natives.* Lanham: Rowman & Littlefield.

This book examines how the journals of Captain Cook, Hollywood films, commercialized hula, the Waikiki development scheme, and the appropriation of a traditional legend by White Hawai'ians have displaced and continue to colonize Native culture.

Young, K. G. T. (1998). *Rethinking the Native Hawaiian Past.* New York: Garland.

This book proposes a study of Hawai'ian history from a Native-centered historiography. By changing this focus, new information can be brought to the social organization of the traditional Hawai'ian polity.

Books for Students

Alameida, R. K. (1997). *Na Mo'olelo Hawaii'io ka Wa Kahiko: Stories of Life in Old Hawaii.* Honolulu: Bess Press.

This book offers a collection of forty-five traditional Hawai'ian legends, including the creation myths and stories about the people of old Hawai'i. The stories are written at a fourth-grade reading level. (Intermediate)

Beamer, W. D. (1984). *Talking Story with Nona Beamer.* Honolulu: The Bess Press.

A collection of favorite stories of Hawai'i told by a well-known and popular Hawai'ian composer and choreographer. A unique feature is the author's original, easy-to-learn chants created to capture the essence of some of the stories. (Primary/Intermediate)

Dunford, B. (1987). *The Hawai'ians of Old*. Honolulu: The Bess Press.

A revised edition of the author's earlier book on selected segments of Hawai'ian lifestyles. The book introduces various occupations of early Hawai'ians, the Islands themselves, and their flora and fauna. She details the varied ways in which early Hawai'ians entertained themselves through sports, music, and talk stories about their mythical heroes. The glossary and reference list are useful additions to the book. (Middle School/High School)

Galuteria, P. (1991). *Lunalilo*. Honolulu: Kamehameha Schools, Bernice Pauahi Bishop Estate.

A story about one of the seven monarchs who ruled Hawai'i. It chronicles his birth, his life, and his short reign. The young king was very popular with his people, and the author captures this feeling in this book. (Intermediate)

Gomes, B. (1984). *Maile and the Marvelous One*. Taiwan: Press Pacifica.

This imaginative and fanciful story is about a Hawai'ian mongoose, Maile, who is teased for being a dreamer. She becomes the pride of the family when she meets and befriends the "Aumakua," the Marvelous One, protector of Hawai'i's land and people. The Aumakua is disguised as a snake to test the mongoose's ability to trust. (Primary)

Guard, D. (1984). *Hale-Mano: A Legend of Hawai'i*. Milbrae, CA: Dawne-Leigh.

This charming Hawai'ian legend is about Hale-Mano's adventures, foremost of which was winning the love of a princess. (Intermediate)

Harden, M. J. (1999). *Voices of Wisdom: Hawai'ian Elders Speak*. Kula, HI: Aka Press.

This is an illustrated work of the views of 22 Hawai'ian elders as told to the author. It also contains two interviews with younger Hawai'ians in a section titled "The next generation." This is an excellent source for a "first person" view of Hawai'ian culture. (High School)

Kane, H. K. (1987). *Pele*. Honolulu: The Kawainui Press.

Accompanied by attractive drawings and illustrations, this book presents various aspects of the mythology of Pele, the goddess of Hawai'i's volcanoes. The book also provides some background information on the Island of Hawai'i's formation and the Volcano National Park. (Primary/Intermediate)

Lowe, R. H. (1993). *Lili'uokalani*. Honolulu: Kamehameha Schools, Bernice Pauahi Bishop Estate.

The story of the last reigning monarch, Queen Lili'uokalani, written for young children. A chronology of major events is presented in simple language and story line for easy and fast reading. (Middle School)

MacKenzie, M. K. (Ed.). (1991). *Native Hawai'ian Rights Handbook*. Honolulu: Native Hawai'ian Legal Corporation (distributed by the University Press of Hawai'i).

A manual written to inform readers of fundamental issues relative to the sovereignty movement in Hawai'i. The essays center on the rights of native Hawai'ians to their land and water resources, federal programs, and trusts. It is written in a straightforward manner, devoid of technical and legal language, and, with guidance, is readable at the high school level. (High School)

McBarnet, G. (1987). *Fountain of Fire*. Puunene, HI: Ruwanga Trading.

A simple and charming story about a young girl who lives in a community threatened by volcanic eruptions. Easy to read and attractively presented with many pictures. The author gives his readers a feel for what life is like when a volcano erupts in Hawai'i. (Primary)

Menton, L., & Tamura, E. (Eds.). (1989). *A History of Hawai'i*. Honolulu: University Press of Hawai'i.

A textbook of Hawai'ian history, from precolonial Hawai'i to the present. The emphasis placed on highlighting issues of concern to the state and its people makes this a better than average traditional text for high school students. (High School)

Perry, Y. N. (1994). *The Other Side of the Island.* Santa Barbara, CA: Daniel and Daniel.

> *A collection of short stories by the author, who depicts local Hawai'ian scenes with poignancy as she weaves story after story of people and events taking place in the Islands. The book should appeal to young adults and families sympathetic to the Hawai'ian lifestyle. (High School)*

Salisbury, G. (1992). *Blue Skies of the Sea.* New York: Delacorte Press.

> *A collection of short stories that captures the ambience of a fanciful life in Hawai'i. Written by a descendant of early missionaries, the author scripts an adventuresome tale from the perspective of a fictionalized family whose members, no doubt, were inspired by his own. Delightful reading for high school students or young adults. (High School)*

Stanley, F. (1991). *The Last Princess: The Story of Princess Ka'iulani of Hawai'i.* Illustrated by D. Stanley. New York: Four Winds Press.

> *A beautifully illustrated and informative biography of the princess who never ruled her kingdom. (Primary/Intermediate)*

Summers, C. C. (1988). *The Hawai'ian Grass House in Bishop Museum.* Honolulu: Bishop Museum Press.

> *An informative description of the style of houses people in Hawai'i built and lived in before the turn of the century. (Intermediate)*

Tuen, C. S. (1988). *How Maui Slowed the Sun.* Honolulu: University Press of Hawai'i.

> *A delightfully retold story of the legend of Maui, the boy who forced the sun to slow down to help his people accomplish more with a longer day. This version is appealing to young children because the story line is simple, the vocabulary is at their level, and the colorful drawings accompanying the story are attractive. (Primary)*

Veary, N. (1989). *Change We Must.* Honolulu: Water Margin Press.

> *Reflections on life in Hawai'i through the eyes of the author, who grew up in a Hawai'i of another era, "a place that was extremely different from what we know today." It is a book that informs and inspires. (Primary)*

Westervelt, W. D. (1987). *Myths and Legends of Hawai'i: Ancient Lore Retold.* Honolulu: Mutual Publishing.

> *Selected folktales from ancient Polynesian lore retold for the enjoyment of today's readers. (High School)*

CHAPTER

7

African Americans

Concepts, Strategies, and Materials

It is a peculiar sensation, this double-consciousness, this sense of always looking at one's self through the eyes of others.... One feels his twoness—an American, a Negro; two souls, two unreconciled strivings; two warring ideals in one dark body, whose dogged strength alone keeps it from being torn asunder.

—William E. B. Du Bois (1903/1973)

Africans have had a unique experience in the Americas. They came with the earliest European explorers and settlers and were gradually enslaved in the North American colonies in the 1600s. When the eighteenth century began, slavery was flourishing in North America. The African experience in the United States has strikingly revealed the gross discrepancies between American ideals and reality. Throughout their history, African Americans have called on America to make its dream a reality. Their cries have usually fallen on deaf ears. African American history and culture must be studied to enable students to understand and appreciate fully the great conflicts and dilemmas in American society and to develop a commitment to help make America's ideals a reality.

African Explorers in America

Africans have been in America for many centuries. Inconclusive evidence suggests that they established a colony in Mexico long before Columbus's voyage in 1492. Africans were with the first Europeans who explored America. Africans had been living in Europe for many years when European explorations of

AFRICAN AMERICANS: HISTORICAL PERSPECTIVE

Important Dates	Events
1565	Africans helped to establish a colony in St. Augustine, Florida.
1619	The first Africans arrived in the English North American colonies.
1808	The slave trade was legally ended, but illegal slave trading began.
1829	David Walker published his *Appeal*, in which he harshly denounced slavery and urged slaves to take up arms and rebel.
1831	Nat Turner led a slave revolt in which nearly 60 Whites were killed.
1850	The Fugitive Slave Act, which authorized the federal government to help capture runaway slaves, was enacted. It helped pave the way to the Civil War.
1857	The Supreme Court ruled in the *Dred Scott Decision* that slaves did not become free when they moved to free territory. It also held that African Americans were not and could not be citizens.
1861–62	Congress enacted several Confiscation Acts designed to prevent the Confederacy from using slaves in its war efforts.
1863	Many African Americans in New York City were attacked and killed by largely Irish mobs that were protesting the draft laws and expressing anti-Black feelings.
	On January 1, 1863, President Lincoln issued the Emancipation Proclamation, which freed slaves in those states fighting the Union.
1865	Slavery was legally abolished throughout the United States by the enactment of the Thirteenth Amendment to the Constitution.
1866	The Fourteenth Amendment, which made African Americans United States citizens, was enacted. The Civil Rights Act of 1866 was enacted. It extended the African American's civil liberties in several areas.
1870	The Fifteenth Amendment was enacted. It enabled many African Americans to vote.

Important Dates	Events
1876	In the disputed Hayes-Tilden election, Hayes's supporters promised that he would remove the remaining federal troops from the South. This bargain symbolized the extent to which northern Whites had abandoned the southern African Americans.
1896	In a historic decision, *Plessy v. Ferguson,* the Supreme Court ruled that "separate but equal" facilities were constitutional.
1905	W. E. B. Du Bois and a group of African American intellectuals organized the Niagara Movement to promote civil rights for African Americans.
1910	The National Association for the Advancement of Colored People (NAACP) was organized. It successfully fought for African American legal rights.
1911	The National Urban League was founded to help the Black urban migrant adjust to city life and find jobs.
1914	Marcus Garvey organized the Universal Negro Improvement Association. Garvey urged African Americans to return to Africa.
1917	One of the worst riots in U.S. history occurred in East St. Louis, Illinois. Thirty-nine African Americans were killed.
1919	A series of riots occurred in a number of cities during the "Red Summer" of 1919. One of the most serious occurred in Chicago, in which 38 people lost their lives.
1943	White violence directed at African Americans led to a serious riot in Detroit, in which 34 people were killed.
1954	In a landmark decision, *Brown v. Board of Education,* the Supreme Court ruled that school segregation was inherently unequal.
1955	African Americans in Montgomery, Alabama, began a boycott of the city's buses that ended bus segregation there in 1956.
1957	Martin Luther King, Jr., and a group of Baptist ministers organized the Southern Christian Leadership Conference (SCLC). National guardsmen were required to help integrate Central High School in Little Rock, Arkansas.

Important Dates	Events
1960	On February 1, 1960, the sit-in movement, which desegregated public accommodation facilities throughout the South, began in Greensboro, North Carolina.
1961	The Congress of Racial Equality (CORE) led Freedom Rides throughout the South to desegregate interstate transportation.
1963	More than 200,000 people participated in a "March on Washington for Freedom and Jobs."
	In a Birmingham demonstration, led by Martin Luther King, Jr., civil rights demonstrators were violently attacked by the police.
1992	Carol Mosely Braun (Democrat, Ill.) became the first African American woman elected to the U.S. Senate.
1993	Toni Morrison was the first African American woman and the eighth woman to receive the Nobel Prize for Literature.
2001	President George W. Bush appointed Condoleezza Rice National Security Adviser, Roderick Paige Secretary of Education, and Colin L. Powell Secretary of State. These were the highest positions that African Americans held in any president's administration.

America began. The Moors, a North African people, invaded Europe in 711. They eventually conquered and ruled Spain. Other Africans were brought to Europe as slaves beginning in the 1400s. These Africans worked in private homes as servants, in banks and shipyards, and in mercantile establishments.

Diego el Negro was with Columbus on his last voyage to America in 1502. When Balboa arrived at the Pacific Ocean in 1513, his crew included a Black man, Nuflo de Olano. Africans explored present-day Kansas in 1541 with Coronado. Africans were also with many of the other early Spanish expeditions to the Americas. Estevanico, a Moor, is one of the most famous early Black explorers. Arriving in America in 1529, he explored present-day New Mexico and Arizona and paved the way for later Spanish explorations of the Southwest.

In addition to exploring America, Africans were among its first non-Indian settlers. Some of the settlers of the ill-fated South Carolina colony in 1526, San Miguel de Guadalupe, were African. Africans helped to establish

St. Augustine, Florida, in 1565, the oldest non-Indian settlement in the United States. A number of colonies were established by Africans and the French. These groups settled in the Mississippi Valley in the seventeenth century.

The Slave Trade

The Arabs invaded Africa and enslaved Africans long before Europeans arrived on the continent. The European nations became involved in the African slave trade when they started trading with Africa in the 1400s. In the mid-fifteenth century, European monarchs sent explorers to Africa to obtain such goods as skins and oils. Many of these explorers brought back these wares as well as African slaves and gold as gifts for their rulers. These gifts greatly pleased the European monarchs. As more and more Europeans explored Africa and brought Africans back to Europe, the slave trade gradually gained momentum. Black slavery never became widespread in Europe, but it grew by leaps and bounds when Europeans started settling in America in the 1600s. Europeans developed large plantations in the West Indies that grew crops such as sugar, indigo, cotton, and tobacco. Sugar production reigned supreme over all other crops. To produce increasing amounts of sugar, the Europeans brought thousands of Africans to the West Indies.

The slave trade became highly lucrative. European nations competed aggressively to monopolize it. At first, the Portuguese dominated the slave trade. Portugal was eventually challenged by the Dutch. Gradually, more and more nations gained a toehold in Africa. However, England was dominating the slave trade when it peaked in 1700. The European nations greatly benefited from the slave trade. They obtained many raw materials from Africa that helped them to attain high levels of industrial growth. The ships that left Europe carried small items to use for exchange with the Africans. While in Africa, they picked up wares such as gold, ivory, and dyewood as well as captives. The ships usually traveled from Africa to the West Indies, where the captives were sold and exchanged goods acquired. The goods were taken back to Europe. The journey from the West Coast of Africa to the West Indies was known as the "Middle Passage" because it was only part of a route that eventually led back to Europe.

When the slave trade in the West Indies began, European nations granted monopolies to a few favorite companies, such as the Dutch West India Company and the Royal African Company of England. Later, when these nations realized that they could make more money by allowing companies to compete, the monopoly system was abandoned. Before the monopolies ended in the late 1600s, the European colonists in North America were not able to obtain nearly as many Africans as they wanted. The major companies sold most of their Africans on the more profitable markets of the West Indian sugar plantations. However, the

North American colonists were able to buy as many Africans as they wished when monopolies ended. The smaller companies were eager to trade with them.

Whereas the slave trade was profitable for European nations and contributed to their industrial growth and development, it was disastrous for the West African nations. When the trade first began, African rulers sold captives and criminals. Most of the captives had been taken from other tribes during warfare. There was no concept of "Africans" among the diverse groups that lived in Africa in the seventeenth century. The peoples of Africa identified with their clans or tribal groups, not with the continent (Ladson-Billings, 1994). As the Europeans sought more and more Africans, these sources became inadequate. The African rulers were so fascinated with the trinkets, rum, firearms, and other items they received in exchange for captives that they started warring to obtain captives, using the firearms they received from Europeans. Warring became increasingly frequent and destructive as the Europeans' desire for captives soared. As warring increased, some groups had to sell captives to acquire the firearms they needed to protect themselves. These wars adversely affected African political stability. The slave trade also drained off many of Africa's strongest and most productive young men and women. The slave traders wanted only healthy captives who could survive the horrible middle passage and the backbreaking work on the plantations in America.

The Beginning of Bondage

The captive's life was terrifying, brutal, and shocking. Slave catchers, who were usually Africans, raided the interior of the West African coast looking for captives from other tribal groups. When Africans were caught, they were chained together and marched long distances, often hundreds of miles, to the European forts near the coast. Here they waited, sometimes for months, to be forced onto ships headed for America. The captives adamantly resisted bondage. Some of them escaped on the long march to the forts. Others jumped overboard once the ships were at sea. Mutinies occurred, both on the African shore and in mid-ocean. In 1753 a group of captives seized a ship bound for America, killed the White crew, and forced the ship back to Africa. In 1839, the *Amistad*, a slave ship, was brought into New London, Connecticut, by a group of Africans who had revolted against their captors. Cinque, the young African leader, and his followers were granted their freedom by the U.S. Supreme Court (Ladson-Billings, 1994).

Conditions on the slave ships were degrading and dehumanizing. The captured Africans were packed into the ships like sardines. They were chained together with iron ankle fetters. The space for each slave was so small that they were forced to lie down in the ship. Because of the crowded and filthy conditions on the ships, diseases were rampant and took many lives. Many Africans died from scurvy, dysentery, and smallpox. Sometimes everyone on a ship was blinded by ophthalmia. Africans who became very sick were dumped into the ocean because dead Africans were worthless on the American slave market. More than half of the Africans sometimes died during the journey. Some historians estimate that one out of every eight captives died in the middle passage and never reached the Americas. This painful trip usually took from forty to sixty days.

Slavery in North America

The first Africans to arrive in the English North American colonies came in 1619 on a Dutch ship. These twenty Africans were not slaves but, like most of the Whites who came to the colonies during this period, were indentured servants. To pay for their passage to America, indentured servants agreed to work for their sponsors for a specified period of time. When they had completed their period of service, they became free. At first, the English colonists met their labor needs with indentured servants. Increasingly, the colonists began to feel that they were not obtaining enough workers with this system and that slavery had many more advantages. For one thing, indentured servitude was more expensive than slavery. The servants had to be provided certain goods and services, and eventually they became free. With slavery, the worker received few benefits and remained a servant for life. Also, the slaves' children would also be slaves. Clearly, slavery was a more profitable system than indentured servitude. The colonists deliberately decided to replace indentured servitude with African slavery for economic reasons.

Slavery existed in practice in most of the colonies long before it acquired legal status. The legal institutionalization of slavery was a gradual process. By 1630 in Virginia, laws and legal cases were beginning to evolve that would culminate in the legalization of slavery. In that year, a court sentenced a White man to a whipping for having sex with an African woman. The Virginia House of Burgesses passed a law in 1643 limiting the years for White indentured servants but not for African servants. The House enacted a law in 1662 that declared that children would inherit their mother's status. This law reversed English common law, which held that children inherited their father's status. A 1667 law enacted by the House enabled Christians to be slaves. A law passed in Maryland in 1664 openly declared that Blacks and their children would be slaves in that colony. By the end of the seventeenth century, slavery existed in fact as well as in law in Colonial America.

American slavery was a unique institution in human history. It was designed to dehumanize Africans and to convince them that they were inferior and deserved the treatment they received. It was also designed to enable Whites to make maximum profits from African labor and to reinforce White supremacy. All of the laws, customs, and norms that developed around slavery reflected and reinforced its major goals. Slaves were regarded as property who should cater to the whims and wishes of their masters. A number of arguments and traditions emerged to justify slavery and to ensure its continuation. Because of their treatment of Blacks, and because of constant attempts by the captives to resist bondage, Whites developed a chronic fear of slave rebellions and retaliation. Sometimes, especially after a slave rebellion or when one was rumored, White fears of slave insurrections and uprisings became chronic, paranoid, and widespread. Consequently, the slave codes were made more severe and the institutions and norms supporting bondage were revitalized.

Attempts by Whites to deny the African captives humanity and to oppress them are reflected in the numerous slave codes enacted in colonies from New York to Georgia. These codes varied from colony to colony but tended to be most severe in the southern colonies. However, all of them were degrading and designed to reinforce bondage. In some colonies, slaves could not form groups without the presence of a White; they could not carry or own firearms, testify in court against a White person, or be taught to read or write. Some colonies prevented them from owning property or drinking liquor and did not recognize their marriages as legal. They were forbidden from leaving the plantation unless they had a special pass. Punishment for crimes was severe, although some planters did not welcome the death penalty because it deprived them of profitable workers. Slaves were subject to the death penalty for such crimes as rape, arson, and robbery.

Slaves worked in a wide variety of occupations, especially in the northern colonies. They worked as laborers and house servants in New England, and also as skilled artisans. Many skilled slaves in the North hired themselves out and saved enough money to buy their freedom. Few skilled slaves in the South were allowed to keep the money they earned hiring themselves out. Although slaves in the South worked in many different jobs, especially in the cities, where many were skilled artisans, most worked on the large plantations owned by a few rich members of the southern aristocracy. Life on these large plantations, which specialized in such crops as tobacco and cotton, was hard and painful. Often driven by a merciless overseer and a driver, the slaves worked from sunup to sundown. They usually lived in mud-floor shacks on the plantation that were cold in the winter and hot in the summer. Their food consisted mostly of hominy and fatback. Their clothing was limited. Men usually had little more than two shirts and two pairs of trousers.

Even though Whites tried to deny the slaves a human existence, Africans succeeded in developing a sense of community and a social life quite apart from the world of Whites. Slaves had stable marriages, even though they were not legally recognized by White society. These marriages usually occurred after long courtships. The family was important to the slaves. Family members taught their children how to survive the harsh White environment, as well as how not to submit totally to the whims of the master. Black fathers openly disapproved of the ways Whites treated their families. However, these men usually obeyed the master so that they could avoid severe punishment or death. Many slave families that had developed strong bonds of love and kinship were broken up when their master sold family members to different buyers or sold only some members of the family. Some slaves escaped to search for members of their families when they were sold.

Most African captives never totally submitted to slavery or accepted it. They resisted it in both covert and blatant ways. To avoid work, slaves would sometimes feign illness. They sometimes destroyed farm equipment deliberately or cut up the plants when they were hoeing crops. A few slaves maimed themselves to avoid work. Some domestic slaves put poison in their masters' foods and killed them. Other slaves escaped. The number of runaways increased greatly when the Civil War began and when the Emancipation Proclamation was issued in 1863. Many slaves were helped to the North and Canada by a loosely organized system known as the Underground Railroad. Free Blacks, many of whom were escaped slaves, made numerous trips to the South to help Blacks escape. Africans such as Harriet Tubman and Josiah Henson helped hundreds of slaves follow the North Star to freedom. Many slaves traveled by night and were helped by "conductors" of the Underground Railroad. Other slaves escaped alone. These lone and brave captives were determined to escape bondage at any cost.

African captives also resisted slavery by rebellion (Genovese, 1979). Even though most slave uprisings were unsuccessful, partly because of slave informers, historical records indicate that at least 250 occurred (Aptheker, 1987). One of the most ambitious slave uprisings was planned by Gabriel Prosser in 1800. Prosser and a group of about 1,000 slaves armed themselves and headed for Richmond, Virginia. A heavy rainstorm stopped the rebels, and the authorities in Richmond, who had been alerted, were armed and waiting for them. Gabriel Prosser and 30 of the other captives died at the end of a rope.

Denmark Vesey, a free Black in Charleston, South Carolina, planned an insurrection in 1822. The group he led armed themselves and were prepared to take Charleston's two arsenals. The revolt was crushed before it got started, and the participants were hanged. The most successful slave revolt of the antebellum period was led by Nat Turner in 1831. Turner was a highly imaginative African American preacher who felt that he was destined by God to free his people from bondage. Turner organized and armed a crew that killed about sixty Whites, including his master and family. The Turner rebels caught their victims by surprise. Whites crushed the rebellion after it had raged for forty-eight hours. When they were seized, Turner and nineteen other rebels were hanged.

The Abolitionists

The first societies organized to agitate for the abolition of slavery were formed during and after the American Revolution. The earliest was founded in Philadelphia in 1775. The Quakers were the leading figures in this society. However, slavery was hotly debated among the Quakers. There were also Quakers in the South who owned slaves (Ladson-Billings, 1994). Other abolitionary societies were formed during this period. Most of the members of these early societies were propertied men who were sympathetic to the South. They spoke kindly of the South, were soft-spoken, and felt that slave owners who freed their slaves should be compensated. They advocated a gradual abolition of slavery. Because of the tactics they used, many Southerners supported these societies. These abolitionists did not believe in or practice social equality. Women and African Americans were excluded from their organizations.

The abolitionary societies organized in the 1800s were much more militant and aggressive than the earlier ones. They harshly denounced slavery and slave owners and demanded an immediate end to slavery. These groups were unpopular in both the North and the South. They became known as militants and extremists. Both Whites and Blacks participated in these societies, although the Whites, who did not believe in racial equality, tried to keep the African Americans in the background. Frederick Douglass, Robert Purvis, and Sojourner Truth were some of the leading African American abolitionists (Quarles, 1969; Yee, 1992).

One of the most militant societies was the American Anti-Slavery Society, organized in 1833. Although this society vigorously denounced slavery, it kept Blacks in the background. In its early years, it had no African American lecturers. Most of the policy was made by Whites. Members of the society discouraged African Americans when they started editing their own newspapers and lecturing. They wanted only a few Blacks to be visible in the organization for symbolic purposes. The African American abolitionists harshly condemned the White abolitionists, accusing them of discriminating against Blacks in their businesses and their daily lives.

The African American abolitionists often went their separate ways (Quarles, 1969). They edited newspapers and gave moving speeches giving Black views of abolition. Despite objections from White abolitionists such as William Lloyd Garrison, Frederick Douglass edited and published a paper, the *North Star*. Black abolitionists also expressed their views in the series of conventions they held in the antebellum period. At the National Negro Convention in 1843, Henry Highland Garnet gave a controversial speech in which he urged slaves to rise up and fight for their freedom. He later worked with William G. Allen to edit a newspaper, *The National Watchman*. Sojourner Truth and Harriet Tubman were also important African American abolitionists. Truth worked with other abolitionists such as William Lloyd Garrison and Frederick Douglass. She also became active in the women's rights movement. Harriet Tubman was one of the most successful "conductors" on the Underground Railroad. She helped more than 300 captives escape to freedom.

As was to be the case in later years, African American and White participants in Black liberation movements in the 1800s often had different goals and aims, and they used different approaches. These divergent goals and methods inevitably led to conflict and hostility between these groups.

The Colonization Movement

In the early nineteenth century, an intense movement developed among Whites to deport African Americans to another country. The motives of the advocates of colonization varied. Some saw themselves as humanitarians and felt that, because of White racism, African Americans would never be able to achieve equality in the United States. They believed that Blacks would have a much better chance in another nation. Other advocates of colonization were supporters of slavery and wanted to deport free Blacks because they felt that non-slave Blacks were a threat to slavery. Many southern Whites eagerly supported the American Colonization Society, organized in 1816 by a group of eminent White Americans.

Many influential Whites, such as Francis Scott Key and Henry Clay, supported colonization. A region in West Africa, named Liberia, was acquired by American colonizationists in 1822. Despite the enthusiastic support for the movement, it did not succeed. Fewer than 8,000 African Americans had immigrated to Liberia by 1852. Many of these were captives who had been granted their freedom on the condition that they immigrate to Africa. The colonization movement failed primarily because most African Americans were strongly against it. The American Colonization Society made its plans and solicited support from eminent White Americans but ignored the feelings of African Americans. African American leaders denounced the society, which often condoned racist practices, in loud terms. They argued that they would not leave the United States because their ancestors had helped to build the nation. They consequently had a right to live in the United States by birthright. The free African Americans who strongly opposed colonization saw it as an attempt by slave owners to get rid of them and, thus, make slavery more safe and secure. These leaders argued that their fate rested with the fate of their enchained brothers and sisters.

A few African Americans who became disillusioned with the United States began to advocate colonization. However, some of the leaders, such as Martin Delany, strongly criticized the American Colonization Society. Delany felt that the society's members were "arrogant hypocrites." He correctly perceived the White colonizationists' motives as being quite different from his. African American colonizationists wanted to leave the United States because they had become disillusioned and frustrated. Most White colonizationists hoped to deport African Americans so that they could get rid of a racial group they did not want in the United States.

From time to time, small groups of despairing African Americans thought seriously about colonization and sometimes took concrete actions to realize their aspirations. Paul Cuffe took thirty-eight Blacks to Sierra Leone in 1815. In 1859, Martin D. Delany obtained a piece of land in Africa for an African American settlement. A Black colonization group, the African Civilization Society, was organized by a group of eminent African Americans in 1858. Despite these attempts, African American colonizationists had no more success than White colonizationists because most African Americans were determined to remain in the United States. Back-to-Africa advocates emerged later in the nineteenth and twentieth centuries, but their cries continued to fall on deaf ears. Marcus Garvey was a strong advocate of African colonization in the 1930s.

Nonslave African Americans

Not all African Americans were slaves, either in the North or South, during the antebellum period. Many African Americans in the North hired themselves out and earned their freedom. Some in New England sued for their freedom in courts and won it. Some bondsmen were awarded their freedom after service in the Revolutionary War. A few African Americans were descendants of Black indentured servants and were never slaves. In the South, some slave masters left wills freeing their slaves on their deaths. Often these slaves were their children or other blood relatives that resulted from forced sex with Black women captives. Some southern slaves were given their freedom after meritorious service to their communities. Others obtained their freedom by escaping. In both the North and the South, nonslave Blacks were harassed and demeaned and were often treated as if they were slaves. When Whites saw African Americans, they assumed that they were slaves. Nonslave Blacks had to prove that they were free. Free Blacks had to carry papers, which they usually had to purchase, that certified their freedom. However, they were often captured and enslaved whether they carried "free" papers or not.

Many of the legal limitations imposed on slaves also governed the nonslave African Americans. In many parts of the South, nonslave Blacks were forbidden to form groups without the presence of a White, were prohibited from testifying against a White, and were not allowed to own a gun or a dog. In the North, they were denied the franchise and prohibited by law from migrating to such states as Illinois, Indiana, and Oregon. The free African American could settle in other old northwest states only after paying bonds up to a thousand dollars. Southerners regarded free African Americans as a nuisance and a threat to slavery. They blamed them for most of the slave rebellions and for encouraging slaves to escape. For these reasons, many southern Whites eagerly supported the movement to deport free Blacks to Africa.

Nonslave northern Blacks played an extremely important role in African American life. They strongly protested the racism and discrimination Blacks experienced. The Negro Convention Movement served as an important protest forum. Black conventions were held from 1830 up to the beginning of the twentieth century. At most of them, the delegates issued cogent statements demanding an end to racism in various areas of American life. The colonization movement, discrimination in northern schools, and segregation in the church were targets of Black protest.

Free African Americans also organized significant institutions, including the numerous self-help and mutual aid societies from which most of today's Black insurance companies grew. One of the earliest mutual benefit societies, the African Union Society, was organized in Newport, Rhode Island, in 1780. Like many similar societies organized later, it helped its members when they were out of work, gave them decent burials, and set up an apprentice program that trained young Blacks to be skilled artisans. Other mutual aid societies included the Masonic Order organized by Prince Hall in 1787 and the Grand United Order of Odd Fellows, established in 1843. These organizations were extremely important within the Black community.

African Americans also organized their own churches. African Americans were forced to sit in separate pews in White churches and were sometimes interrupted in the middle of prayers if they were seated in the "wrong" sections. These kinds of indignities led Blacks such as Richard Allen and Absalom Jones to organize independent Black churches. In 1794, two Black Methodist churches were founded in Philadelphia, St. Thomas Protestant Episcopal Church and the Bethel African Methodist Episcopal Church. African American Methodist churches soon spread to many other cities. African American Baptists also established independent churches. The Black church became an extremely important institution in African American life. It trained most Black protest leaders, opened schools for Black children, gave Blacks practice in self-governance and increased their self-respect. The church and the fraternal orders, which were affiliated with the church, were the key institutions within Black America. Today, the African American church still performs many of its historic functions and remains an important institution.

The Civil War and Reconstruction

African Americans viewed the Civil War as the God-sent conflict that would emancipate them from bondage. However, they were virtually alone in this view. Most White Americans, including President Lincoln and the U.S. Congress, viewed the war as a conflict to preserve the Union. When news of the war spread, northern Blacks rushed to recruiting stations and tried to enlist in the armed forces. Their services were rejected. Leaders thought that the war would last only ninety days. The war dragged on for four long years. When it became evident that the war would last much longer than was originally thought, the Union, and later the Confederacy, reluctantly allowed African Americans to take up arms.

Congress and President Lincoln took a number of steps to weaken the Confederacy. They realized that the slaves were being used to help the Confederate forces to maintain their strength. Consequently, Congress enacted a number of laws that undermined the Confederacy. In 1861, Congress enacted legislation enabling it to free slaves who were used to help the Confederate forces. In the summer of 1862, Congress passed a bill that freed slaves who had escaped and authorized the president to use Black troops. President Lincoln also used his authority to weaken the Confederacy. On September 22, 1862, he announced that slaves in rebel states would be freed on January 1, 1863. Lincoln kept his promise and issued the Emancipation Proclamation, freeing those slaves in rebel states on January 1, 1863. Although African Americans and abolitionists rejoiced when the Emancipation Proclamation was issued, legally it did no more than the act that was passed by Congress in 1862. The thousands of slaves in states not fighting the Union were not freed, but the proclamation did give African Americans a moral uplift and motivated more captives to escape. However, captives had been escaping in large numbers ever since northern soldiers started coming to the South.

After four bitter years and the bloodiest war in U.S. history up to that time, General Lee surrendered at Appomattox on April 9, 1865, and the Civil War ended. On April 14, 1865, Lincoln was assassinated by John Wilkes Booth, and Andrew Johnson became president. President Johnson, like Lincoln, favored a lenient plan for readmitting the southern states back into the Union. However, the Republican Congress wanted to gain a toehold in the South so that the Republican party could win future presidential elections. To obtain their objective, they franchised the newly freed African Americans so that they would develop an allegiance to the Republican party. In a series of acts, Congress gave Black men the right to vote and extended their civil rights, thereby endearing the Republicans to them. In 1865, Congress enacted the Thirteenth Amendment, which abolished slavery throughout the United States, and passed a Civil Rights Act in 1866 that made African Americans citizens and granted them certain legal rights. The Fourteenth Amendment, enacted in 1866, also recognized Blacks as citizens. The Reconstruction Act of 1867 divided the South into five military districts and required the Confederate states to enact constitutions that would be approved by Congress and to ratify the Fourteenth Amendment before they could be redacted into the Union. The South considered the Reconstruction Act especially galling.

Because they could now vote and run for public office, a number of African Americans held elected offices for brief periods during Reconstruction. Most of them held minor local offices. However, twenty-two served in the U.S. Congress, two as U.S. senators. Black elected officials were too few in number and their tenure too brief for them to play a leading role in shaping policy. However, the South established its most enlightened state constitutions during Reconstruction and enacted some of its most humane social legislation. For years after Reconstruction, southern apologists justified southern violence by arguing that the South was reacting to the former Black control of the southern states. However, African Americans never controlled any of the states' legal bodies and none were elected governors.

The Rise of White Supremacy

The Republicans' plan to grab the Black man's vote was successful. Blacks in large numbers voted for the Republican presidential candidate in the election of 1868. However, by 1876 the Republicans, who were dominated by northern industrial interests, had new interests and no longer needed Blacks to attain them. In fact, African Americans stood in their way. Northern industrialists were now interested in extending their trade in the South and consequently wanted to court the southern Whites. To appease southern Whites, northern Whites decided to leave the fate of Blacks up to the South. The handling of the Hayes-Tilden election in 1876 indicated the extent to which northern Whites had abandoned African Americans. In that disputed election, an Electoral Commission named the Republican candidate, Hayes, president. To placate the South, Hayes's supporters promised White southerners that when he became president, Hayes would remove all of the remaining federal troops from the South.

Hayes kept this promise when he became president. By the time that the last federal troops were removed from the South, southern Whites were reestablishing their control of state governments throughout the South and had aggressively begun their campaigns to make African Americans chattel even though slavery had been legally abolished. One of the first acts of the state legislatures was to disenfranchise African Americans. A motley collection of ingenious methods were used to keep Blacks from voting. The Democratic primary election, the grandfather clause, literacy tests, and the poll tax were among the many ways in which African Americans, and, inadvertently, some poor Whites, were prevented from voting.

Determined to "put Blacks in their place," violence against African Americans became rampant. The goals of this violence were to intimidate African Americans to keep them from voting and to reestablish the caste system that had existed before the Civil War. African Americans became victims of a rash of riots that swept through the South between 1866 and 1898. When African Americans tried to obtain the right to vote in New Orleans in 1866, a riot erupted in which forty-eight Blacks were killed. A riot broke out in Savannah, Georgia, in 1872 when Blacks tried to end segregation on the city's streetcars. Thirty African Americans were killed in a riot that erupted in Meridian, Mississippi, in 1871. Forty-six died in a Memphis riot in 1866. Even though Blacks were usually innocent victims in these riots, they struck back at Whites in the Charleston Riot of 1876.

The Ku Klux Klan was reorganized in 1915 and became a prime leader of anti-Black violence. The lynching of African Americans also became widespread.

About 100 Blacks met their death each year at the end of a rope during these difficult years.

Southern state legislatures also enacted most of their Jim Crow laws during this period. Laws were passed requiring segregation in schools, parks, restaurants, theaters, and in almost all other public accommodation facilities. Tennessee passed a Jim Crow railroad car act in 1881. Most of the other southern and border states soon followed Tennessee's lead. In a series of cases, the Supreme Court upheld and legitimized the South's Jim Crow laws. In 1883 it ruled that the Civil Rights Act of 1875 was unconstitutional. In the *Plessy v. Ferguson* case of 1896, it upheld a Louisiana law that required segregation in railroad cars. The Court ruled that literacy tests and poll taxes required for voting were constitutional. It stripped the Fourteenth and Fifteenth Amendments of all their meaning as far as African Americans were concerned and encouraged White southerners to enact more racist laws.

Many African Americans expected to receive forty acres and a mule after the Civil War. However, most of the land confiscated from southern plantation owners was either given back to them or to other members of the southern aristocracy. Few African Americans were able to obtain land. Most of them became bound to the land and to White landowners in the sharecropping system. The sharecropper's life was similar to that of a slave's. In theory, a sharecropper received a share of the crop. However, Black sharecroppers, who had to buy their merchandise from their boss's store, were severely cheated. Each year, when the crops were harvested, they found themselves further and further in debt and required to stay on the land until they paid their bill. The sharecropper's status was little better than that of a slave's and in some ways worse.

To make the system even more like slavery, southern state legislatures enacted a series of laws between 1865 and 1866 that became known as the Black Codes. These laws were similar to the old slave codes. In some states, Blacks could not testify in court against Whites, carry guns, or buy some types of property. African Americans who were unemployed could be arrested. Those who were unable to pay their fines were hired out. In some places, Black workers could not leave the farm without permission. By the beginning of the twentieth century, White southerners had totally succeeded in reestablishing White supremacy, reducing African Americans to the status of peons. Black hopes born during the Civil War had been almost completely shattered. When the twentieth century opened, African Americans were deeply disillusioned and saw little hope for the future. They attempted to solve their problems by migrating north, still in search of the American Dream.

Migration and City Life

After the Civil War, large numbers of African Americans began to migrate to urban areas in the South and to settle in the Southwest (Lemann, 1991). Because of the widespread discrimination they faced in the United States, some African Americans established all-Black towns. Nearly thirty such towns were established near the turn of the century, including Mound Bayou, Mississippi, in 1887 and Langston, Oklahoma, in 1891. Many African Americans also wanted to make Oklahoma an all-Black state, but this idea never materialized.

Although many African Americans settled in the South and Southwest, most who migrated near the turn of the century settled in large cities in the Midwest and East (Adero, 1993). New York City's Black population doubled between 1900 and 1910. During the same period, Chicago's increased by more than 30%. African Americans migrated to northern cities in large numbers in the early 1900s because of the severe economic, political, and social conditions in the South. Southern states had stripped African Americans of most of their legal rights. Disastrous floods, the boll weevil, and the sharecropping system combined to make life on the southern plantations nearly intolerable. The beginning of World War I had nearly stopped immigration from southern and eastern Europe. Consequently, northern manufacturers badly needed laborers. Some of them sent agents to the South to lure Blacks to the North. Black newspapers, such as the *Chicago Defender,* described the North as a land of milk and honey and urged African Americans to leave the South. These forces led nearly one-half million southern Blacks to head for the North during and immediately after World War I. This mass migration to the North greatly disturbed southern Whites because it deprived them of a cheap source of labor. They tried to stop Blacks from going North, but their efforts were useless.

When the African Americans arrived in midwestern and eastern cities, they had a rude awakening. Life in these cities was extremely difficult. African Americans were the victims of White violence and experienced gross discrimination in housing and employment. Many Blacks who moved into White communities were beaten and their homes were bombed. Because of a variety of techniques used by real estate agents, Blacks were excluded from many neighborhoods. Consequently, the Black urban community grew by leaps and bounds because African Americans were forced to live in areas that were predominantly Black. Also, many Blacks preferred to live in communities that had established Black churches, clubs, and fraternal orders.

As African Americans competed with Whites for housing and jobs, conflict and tension developed between them. Whites were determined to keep Blacks from their jobs and out of their communities. White aggression and violence in the early 1900s led to some of the bloodiest riots that the United States had experienced. One of the worst riots occurred in East St. Louis in 1917. The riot was started when a group of Whites fired into a Black neighborhood and Blacks retaliated. Thirty-nine African Americans and nine Whites were killed. During the same year, riots also occurred in Philadelphia and Chester, Pennsylvania. More than 20 riots occurred in cities throughout the United States in 1919. The gifted writer James Weldon Johnson called that summer the "Red Summer" because of the blood that ran in city streets. The most tragic riot that summer occurred in Chicago. The riot started when a Black youth was drowned after being chased by a group of Whites at a segregated beach on Lake Michigan. The riot lasted for almost two weeks. When it ended, 38 people had been killed, 23 of them Black. More than 1,000 homes were destroyed and 537 people were injured. In 1919, riots also occurred in such cities as Washington, D.C., and Longview, Texas.

World War I

As with other wars, African Americans enthusiastically supported World War I and were impressed with President Wilson's high-sounding rhetoric about fighting the war to "make the world safe for democracy." African Americans took Wilson seriously and joined the armed forces in massive numbers. However, it was not long before they realized that White Americans intended African Americans to be second-class citizens in the military. The discrimination that Black soldiers experienced during the war was blatant. When the United States first entered the war, no training camps were established for African American soldiers. Many Black professionals, like doctors, were made privates in the army. Most Black soldiers were given noncombatant assignments, although some fought on the battlefield. A tragic incident that occurred in Houston, Texas, in 1917 symbolized to African Americans more than anything else the status of the Black soldier. When a group of Black soldiers tried to board a segregated streetcar, a fight occurred in which twelve civilians died. Thirteen of the soldiers were sentenced to die, and fourteen were sent to prison for life. The fate of these soldiers shocked and dismayed the African American community.

Organizations

During these trying times a number of African American institutions and organizations emerged to help African Americans adjust to city life and to fight racism and discrimination in the courts. W. E. B. Du Bois, a militant spokesman for Black rights, and a group of Black intellectuals founded the Niagara Movement in 1905. The men in this movement issued a strong statement denouncing American racism. The Niagara Movement was short-lived. However, the National Association for the Advancement of Colored People (NAACP), organized in 1910, was an outgrowth of it. Although most of the officers of the NAACP were White, Black people strongly supported it. The NAACP concentrated on improving the African American's legal status. Under its leadership, the legal status of Blacks greatly improved. A group of social workers founded the National Urban League in 1911 to help Black migrants adjust to city life and to find employment. The Urban League worked against enormous odds because of job discrimination. However, it experienced some gains.

Whereas the NAACP and the National Urban League appealed greatly to middle-class and upwardly mobile African Americans, Marcus Garvey's Universal Negro Improvement Association (UNIA), organized in 1914, was a movement that strongly attracted the Black poor. Garvey preached Black pride and urged African Americans to return to Africa because they would never have equality in the United States. He also urged Blacks to establish businesses and to improve their own communities. The UNIA operated a number of businesses, including restaurants, grocery stores, and a hotel. Garvey was contemptuous of light-skinned and middle-class African Americans because he felt that they wanted to associate with Whites instead of other Blacks. The leading Black spokesmen and organizations were threatened by Garvey. Partly as a result of their efforts, he was jailed for irregularities in the handling of his Black Star Line. More than any other leader during this period, Garvey helped the lower-class African American to feel proud of being Black.

The Harlem Renaissance

During the 1920s and 1930s, African American artists, writers, and musicians produced some of their best work. Like their counterparts in the 1960s, they deliberately tried to reflect the African American cultural heritage in their works. They emphasized Black pride and strongly protested racism and discrimination. Gifted poets, such as Claude McKay and Countee Cullen, penned angry poems that reflected Black aspirations and frustrations. Other African American writers during this period, such as Langston Hughes, Jean Toomer, and Zora Neale Hurston, wrote outstanding novels. African American musicians further developed blues and jazz. These two types of music became recognized throughout the world.

World War II and the Years After

African Americans did not expect World War II to bring them any great gains. Their memories of World War I were still too vivid and poignant. However, the war created additional jobs in the large cities, and masses of southern Blacks migrated during and after the war years. Many Blacks migrated to the West Coast as well as to the North. More than 150,000 African Americans left the South each year between 1940 and 1950. Black city migrants encountered problems similar to those experienced by African Americans who had migrated in earlier decades. Segregation in housing was still increasing. Many manufacturers with government contracts to make war-related materials refused to hire Blacks or hired them only for the lowest-paying jobs. President Roosevelt refused to take action to stop job discrimination until A. Philip Randolph threatened to march on Washington with 100,000 African Americans. To prevent the march, Roosevelt issued an executive order that outlawed discrimination in defense-related jobs and set up a federal committee on fair employment.

Violence and riots also erupted in the cities. The most serious riot during this period occurred in Detroit in the summer of 1943. It lasted for more than thirty hours. When the riot was over, thirty-four people were dead, twenty-five of them Black. During the same summer, riots also occurred in Los Angeles and in the Harlem district of New York City. These riots, especially the one in Detroit, greatly alarmed U.S. politicians. Mayors in many cities formulated commissions to study the causes of the racial outbreaks and to recommend ways to eliminate their causes.

President Truman

President Harry S. Truman, who won the presidential election in 1948 with heavy Black support, took a number of steps to improve race relations and helped to pave the way for the civil rights movement that reached its height in the 1960s. With the use of executive orders, he desegregated the armed forces and created a Committee on Civil Rights that investigated the condition of African Americans. The committee's publication, *To Secure These Rights*, recommended total integration in U.S. society. Truman also ordered industries doing business with the federal government to end discrimination. These measures were mainly symbolic and did not seriously affect the African American's status in the United States. However, they contributed significantly to setting an atmosphere of racial tolerance and the rising expectations of African Americans.

The Supreme Court

More important than Truman's action in improving race relations during the 1940s and 1950s were the actions of the U.S. Supreme Court. During the decades after the Civil War, the Supreme Court had consistently made decisions that denied African Americans civil liberties and legitimized and legalized racist practices. It now began to rule in favor of civil rights. In a series of cases, most of which were led or supported by the NAACP, the Court ruled for greater civil liberties for African Americans, thus reversing its racist tradition. In 1946, the Court ruled against segregation in interstate commerce, and made a negative ruling regarding the restrictive covenants in 1948. In a number of cases related to African Americans attending segregated White universities in the southern and border states, it consistently ruled that Black Americans should be provided a higher education equal to that of Whites in their home states. These rulings forced many states to integrate their state universities. However, many of them created "instant" professional schools for African Americans. The landmark decision of this period was the *Brown v. Board of Education of Topeka* decision of 1954, which ruled that school segregation is inherently unequal. Perhaps more than any other single event, this decision by the high court helped pave the way for the civil rights movement of the 1960s and 1970s.

The Civil Rights Movement of the 1960s and 1970s

In the 1960s, African Americans began a fight for their rights that was unprecedented in the nation's history. However, the civil rights movement of the 1960s was closely related to the heritage of Black protest in America, marked by the slave rebellions and uprisings. Black Americans have always protested, and in ways consistent with the times in which they lived. David Walker, W. E. B. Du Bois, Ida B. Wells, and Ella Baker are a few of the many eminent African Americans who strongly protested against American racism through the years. Individuals like Martin Luther King, Jr., Malcolm X, and Fannie Lou Hamer joined this long family of protest leaders in the 1960s. The Black protest in the 1960s was unique in our history because the times were different. Black protest tends to reflect the times in which it occurs.

During the late 1940s and 1950s, events that occurred to elevate Black people's hopes for a better life in the United States included the actions of President Truman, the *Brown* decision of 1954, and the Civil Rights Act of 1957. As African Americans saw more and more signs indicating that social, economic, and political conditions were improving, they became increasingly impatient with their caste status. Signs of the African American's second-class status were rampant throughout the South when the Montgomery bus boycott began in 1955. The boycott was conceptualized and planned by Jo Ann Gibson Robinson and the Women's Political Council, a group of civic-minded African American women in Montgomery. Robinson gives her accounts of these events in her memoir edited by Garrow (1987).

The boycott started when Rosa Parks, a Black seamstress, was jailed for refusing to move to the back of a city bus. Montgomery Blacks decided that they had taken enough and that they would fight the city's bus company until it eliminated segregation. They began a boycott of the bus line that did not end until a federal court outlawed racial segregation on Montgomery buses a year later. Martin Luther King, Jr., the young preacher who led the boycott, became the country's most influential civil rights leader and remained so until he was assassinated in 1968. Under his leadership and influence, the civil rights movement used direct action and nonviolent tactics to protest racism and discrimination in all areas of American life, including housing, education, and politics.

The civil rights movement actually began when four African American students—who sat down at a segregated lunch counter at a Woolworth's store in Greensboro, North Carolina, on February 1, 1960—refused to leave when they were not served. They had launched the sit-in movement. Within a short time, the sit-in movement had spread throughout the South, and African American college students were desegregating lunch counters and other public accommodation facilities in many cities below the Mason-Dixon line. African American student activists formed the Student Nonviolent Coordinating Committee (SNCC) in 1960 to coordinate their protest activities.

The student protests stimulated other civil rights groups to become more active. The Congress of Racial Equality (CORE), which had been organized since 1942, sponsored a number of freedom rides to Alabama and Mississippi in 1961 to test interstate transportation laws. The CORE riders were the victims of much hostility and violence. Many of them were beaten and jailed, and some of the buses in which they rode were burned. In 1957, King and a group of Black ministers organized the Southern Christian Leadership Conference (SCLC). SCLC trained its volunteers to use civil disobedience tactics and led numerous mass demonstrations. In 1963, King led a demonstration in Birmingham to protest racism and discrimination. The demonstrators were the victims of blatant police violence that was viewed throughout the United States and the rest of the world on television. Mass demonstrations culminated in the summer of 1963, when more than 200,000 people participated in the March on Washington for Freedom and Jobs.

These demonstrations resulted in some small but significant legal gains for African Americans. The historic March on Washington helped to rally public opinion for support of the Civil Rights Act, which finally passed in 1964 after much filibustering in Congress. A voting rights act was enacted in 1965 after King led demonstrations in Selma, Alabama. As a result of this act, which authorized federal workers to oversee elections in the South, the number of African American voters increased sharply in some southern states and counties. However, the mass of African Americans remained poor and without political power. By 1965, many young African American leaders, such as Stokely Carmichael and H. Rap Brown, who had been staunch supporters of nonviolent resistance, began to raise serious questions about this approach and to urge more militant action and different goals.

During a civil rights demonstration in 1966, Carmichael issued a call for "Black Power," and both the phrase and the ideas it signified spread throughout Black America like wildfire. Carmichael had coined a term that described a mood already pervasive within Black America. The concept of Black Power emerged during a time when the civil rights movement was losing momentum and when African Americans were becoming increasingly frustrated with the gains they had acquired using civil disobedience tactics. Black Power had different meanings for most Whites than for most African Americans. To most African Americans, it meant political power, pride in Blackness, Black control of schools and communities, and Black self-help organizations. To most

Whites, the concept meant retaliatory violence and "Black racism." Malcolm X candidly articulated the concept to the Black masses. Black organizations such as the Black Panther party, which was organized in Oakland, California, in 1966, tried to implement the concept. The Panthers attempted to protect the Black community and organized free lunch programs for African American children. The Nation of Islam (Black Muslims) also reflected the concept in its businesses, farms, schools, and weekly newspaper.

Black frustrations, which reached new highs in the mid- and late 1960s, were manifested in a series of tragic race riots in U.S. cities. Unlike the earlier riots in which Whites attacked Blacks, these riots were different because they involved little contact between Whites and Blacks. Rather, urban Blacks directed their attacks toward the symbols of White society within their communities. They burned buildings owned by absentee landlords and looted stores run by merchants who they believed cheated them. The prestigious Kerner Commission, which was appointed by President Lyndon B. Johnson, concluded in 1968 that the riots were caused by the White racism that was rooted deeply in American life. Riots occurred in cities from New York to Los Angeles. Two of the most serious occurred during the summer of 1967 in Newark and Detroit. Twenty-three people lost their lives in the Newark riot; forty-three died in the Detroit outbreak. As in all of the riots during the 1960s, most of the victims were African Americans killed by White law officials. The Kerner Commission concluded in its massive report on the rebellions, "Our nation is moving toward two societies, one White, one Black—separate and unequal" (*Report of the National Advisory Commission on Civil Disorders*, 1968, p. 1).

Women in the Civil Rights Movement

With a history of activism and opposition to oppression trailing them, Black women embraced their legacy of active resistance and worked toward ending racial oppression during the civil rights movement. Despite sexism throughout U.S. society and within the civil rights movement itself, many Black women participated in organizational segments of the movement. Others provided direct and indirect leadership in civil rights organizations.

Black women formed the foundation of the organizational segment of the civil rights movement (Payne, 1993). In many civil rights organizations, they coordinated activities and also mobilized groups. These groups were often composed of large numbers of Black women who participated in voter registration, boycotts, and demonstrations. These grassroots activities, which took place throughout the South, enabled large numbers of African Americans to participate in and gain empowerment from the civil rights movement.

Although the civil rights movement worked against discrimination and exclusion, sexism existed within most of its organizations (Standley, 1993). Despite the small representation of women's leadership in some civil rights groups, a few women secured visible posts and others led groups indirectly. For example, Ella Baker helped to form and served as the chief advisor of the Student Nonviolent Coordinating Committee from 1960 to 1964. Fannie Lou Hamer was a cofounder of the Mississippi Democratic Freedom Party and ran as a candidate for Congress under the party's name. Septima Clark greatly influenced the civil rights movement through her role as the director of education and teaching for the Southern Christian Leadership Conference. She traveled throughout the South to educate African Americans in literacy and helped in voter registration.

Other women played significant roles in the civil rights movement through leadership in lesser-known organizations. Jo Ann Gibson Robinson and the other members of the Women's Political Council provided the organizational support for the Montgomery bus boycott (Garrow, 1987). Before the boycott they exposed the abuses against Blacks that occurred when they rode the city buses. In rural communities, women formed business cooperatives such as the Madison County Sewing Firm and the Hopedale Sewing Project. These small corporations provided jobs for women who had been fired for participating in civil rights activities (Crawford, 1993).

Black women's participation in civil rights activities placed in jeopardy not only their lives but also the livelihood of their families. They could lose their jobs and homes and become victims of terrorist activities. Black women who participated in the civil rights movement faced serious personal, social, and political challenges, which they were willing to take.

African Americans Today: Progress and Problems

Several major trends can be identified in the social, economic, and political condition of African Americans since the civil rights movement of the 1960s. African Americans experienced significant economic gains relative to Whites during the 1960s. During the 1970s the economic condition of African Americans relative to Whites stagnated. During the last two decades, African Americans have experienced both gains and setbacks.

Data released by the U.S. Census Bureau and the Joint Center for Political and Economic Studies indicate that African Americans made educational, economic, and political progress between 1990 and 2000. However, these data also indicate that the Black community still faces important challenges.

Significant progress was noted in educational attainment. Blacks were close to parity with Whites in high school graduate rates, but the gap between college graduates was wide. By 2000, 77% of African Americans age 25 and over had completed high school, compared to 88% of Whites. The high school completion rate for individuals between 25 to 29 was 89% for African Americans and 90% for White, a four-percentage point difference (U.S. Census Bureau, 2001). The proportion of non-Hispanic Whites with at least a bachelor's degree (28%) was almost twice that of African Americans (15%) (McKinnon & Humes, 2000).

Other indices of progress in 2000 indicated that 25% of African American women and 18% of men worked in managerial and professional occupations. The 2000 median household income for African Americans was $30,400—in real terms the highest ever recorded (compared to $45,900 for Non-Hispanic Whites). Also, half of African American *married-couple families* had incomes of $50,000 or more, compared with 60% for their White, non-Hispanic counterparts. Forty-seven percent of African Americans were homeowners (U.S. Census Bureau, 2001).

Even though African Americans continue to make progress in many areas of American life, they still face serious challenges. Only 28% of *all Black families*—compared to 52% of all non-Hispanic White families—had incomes of $50,000 or more in 1999. Estimates by the U.S. Census in 2000 indicated that less than one-half (47%) of all African American families were married-couple families. Forty-five percent were maintained by women with no spouse present, while 8% were maintained by men without a spouse (U.S. Census Bureau, 2001). The comparable figures for non-Hispanic White families are: 82% were married-couple families, 13% were maintained by women with with no spouse present, and 5% were maintained by men with no wife present.

A large proportion of African American families and children continue to be victims of poverty. About 34.5 million Americans were living in poverty in 1998; 9.1 million were African Americans and 15.8 million were non-Hispanic Whites. The poverty rate was 13% for the total population, 26% for African Americans, and 8% for non-Hispanic Whites (McKinnon & Humes, 2000). Thirty-seven percent of African American children under 18 lived in poverty, compared to 19% for all children and 11% for non-Hispanic White children. Three times more African American children lived in poverty than non-Hispanic White children.

A number of factors contribute to the large percentage of African American families and children that still live in poverty. One important factor is the substantial changes in the economy. Most low-skilled workers were able to obtain well-paying jobs a generation ago. However, as the U.S. economy has been transformed, fewer low-skilled jobs are available. Increasingly, available jobs require technical skills and knowledge. Black workers are disproportionately concentrated among low-skilled workers. The movement of many jobs out of the central cities and into the suburbs, as well as racial discrimination, are additional factors that have slowed the economic progress of African Americans.

African Americans in the Political System

African Americans have made substantial gains in politics since the voting rights legislation that resulted from the civil rights movement of the 1960s and 1970s. Their progress in politics is a direct result of African Americans being able to vote and run freely for office. Elected African American officials increased from a few dozen in 1940 to more than 6,800 in 1988 (Jaynes & Williams, 1989). In 1990 there were 300 African American mayors, 10% of whom were mayors of cities with at least 400,000 people (Shearer, 1990).

African Americans experienced both gains and losses in politics between 1990 and 2000. The lone Black U.S. Senator—Carol Mosley-Braun (Democrat-Illinois)—lost the election in her state and consequently her seat in the Senate. However, in January 1999 there were 39 African Americans in the House of Representatives. At the state level, there were 1 governor, 156 state senators, and 427 representatives. Two African Americans were county executives; 794 were members of county governing boards. In 1999, there were 450 Black mayors and 3,498 members of city governing bodies (Joint Center for Political and Economic Studies, 1999).

Perhaps the biggest political setback for African Americans during the last decade were the problems they experienced voting in the 2000 Florida election and the rejection of a large number of their votes. An important outcome of their problems was the election of George W. Bush for president. After the election the U.S. Commission on Civil Rights conducted three days of hearings into allegations of voting irregularities and racial discrimination in voting. The Commission concluded that African Americans experienced discrimination in the 2000 presidential election in Florida (U.S. Commission on Civil Rights, 2000). Among its findings were:

> Black voters in Florida were 10 times more likely than non-Black voters to have their ballots rejected; 14.4% of Florida's Black voters cast ballots that were rejected, compared to about 1.6% of non-Black voters; about 11% of Florida voters were African American; Blacks cast 54% of the spoiled ballots.

Social Class within the African American Community

A substantial number of African Americans have been able to enter the middle class as a result of opportunities and possibilities that resulted from the civil rights movement of the 1960s and 1970s (Cose, 1993). One of the most important developments in the social and economic situation of Blacks since the 1960s has been the development of substantial social class differences within the African American community and the increase of class differentiation (Wilson,1987). Significant social class variation has existed within the African American community for many decades.

However, class variation within the African American community has never been as steep, nor have African Americans ever been as separated as much in terms of neighborhoods and communities on a social class basis. New careers, opportunities, and possibilities opened up for African Americans as a result of the civil rights movement and the affirmative action policies that followed it. Many of the African Americans who had the education and other skills to take advantage of these opportunities are now functioning in mainstream institutions as physicians, college professors and administrators, business people, and corporation heads. Many of these individuals, like their White peers, have joined the exodus to the suburbs and are sending their children to predominantly White suburban public schools or to elite private schools. However, despite their social class mobility and high levels of acculturation, the Black middle class still experiences racism and discrimination (Feagin & Sikes, 1994).

African Americans from all cultures, social classes, and walks of life experience institutional racism and discrimination. The shared experiences of African Americans reinforce their sense of identity and peoplehood. Also, most middle- and upper-class African Americans want their children to know and to feel comfortable with other Blacks and with Black culture. Consequently, a number of middle- and upper-class African Americans encourage their children to attend historically Black colleges such as Fisk, Spelman, Morehouse, Howard, and Hampton.

Little careful work has been done on social class variation within the African American community. Most articles and research on African Americans focus on the bulk of them who are low-income. The wide social class variation within the African American community must be described in order to present an accurate description of Blacks in contemporary American life.

The New Century

When the new century began, African Americans were hopeful about their progress but deeply concerned about the large number of Black children living in poverty and about the conservative political forces in American society that were achieving significant political victories at all levels of government. However, a consensus was developing within the African American community that it must and can take the leadership for its own improvement and that it has the resources to do so.

These resources have to be mobilized. African Americans have a significant middle class that functions in many of the nation's leading institutions. They have Black colleges with a distinguished record of academic excellence, and they have a strong tradition of self-help that has built impressive institutions and businesses. African Americans are working to help themselves and are thinking deeply about their future—and their children's future—in America.

Teaching Strategies

To illustrate how content related to African Americans can be used to integrate the curriculum, exemplary strategies are identified for teaching these concepts at the grade levels indicated: *tradition* (primary grades), *Black protest* (intermediate and upper grades), and *separatism* (high school grades).

Primary Grades

CONCEPT

Tradition
Generalization: African American songs and music are an important part of their cultural traditions and are passed down from generation to generation.

1. Ask the students, "What special days do you celebrate in your families?" List their responses on the board or butcher paper. Answers might include birthdays, Kwanza, Chinese New Year, Chanukah, the Fourth of July, and Thanksgiving.
2. Select several of their responses, such as birthdays, the Fourth of July, and Thanksgiving. Ask the children to give their ideas about why these special days are celebrated in their families. Ask them, "Which of the special days celebrated in your families are also celebrated (1) in other families? (2) in school? (3) throughout the nation? Ask: "Why are these special days also celebrated by these other groups?"
3. Help the students to develop and state the idea that we celebrate these special days because they help us to remember and to honor important events in our personal histories (birthdays), the histories of our families (family reunions), or in the history of our nation (Thanksgiving and the Fourth of July).
4. Explain that the celebration of these special days helps us to remember and to honor our heritages and traditions. Explain that traditions are important ideas, events, and memories that are handed down from one generation to the next. Say, "Not only do families and nations have traditions, but so do groups of Americans such as African Americans, Mexican Americans, Japanese Americans, and Jewish Americans."
5. Tell the students that an important part of the heritage and traditions of African Americans is the song "Lift Ev'ry Voice and Sing," written by James Weldon Johnson and set to music by his brother, J. Rosamond Johnson. Tell the class that the song is often referred to by African Americans as the "Black National Anthem." Remind them that our national anthem is "The Star-Spangled Banner" by Francis Scott Key. Ask the students, "Why do you think that 'Lift Ev'ry Voice and Sing' is sometimes referred to as the 'Black National Anthem'?"
6. Working with the music teacher in your school, introduce your students to "Lift Ev'ry Voice and Sing" by James Weldon Johnson. A beautifully illustrated version of the song makes up the book *Lift Ev'ry Voice and Sing* by Johnson (1995), with moving illustrations by Jan Spivey Gilchrist.
7. Before teaching the students to sing the song, teach the words to them as a poem. Discuss the meaning of each stanza in the song. After the students have discussed each stanza in the song, summarize the lesson by explaining that the song describes the history and struggle of African Americans in the United States and that it is an important part of their traditions. Conclude the unit by teaching the students to sing "Lift Ev'ry Voice and Sing."

Intermediate and Upper Grades

CONCEPT

Black Protest

Generalization: African Americans have protested against racism and discrimination throughout their history in America. The forms of protest reflected the times in which they occurred.

1. Begin this unit by showing and discussing with the students Part I of the videotape series *Eyes on the Prize* (or a similar one). In the discussion, focus on the reasons Black protest emerged and the forms that it took during the years covered in this videotape, 1954 to 1956.

2. Tell the students the story of the slave mutinies that occurred both on the West African coast and in mid-ocean. Herbert Aptheker (1987), *American Negro Slave Revolts,* and Eugene D. Genevese (1979), *From Rebellion to Revolution: Afro-American Slave Revolts in the Making of the Modern World,* are well-researched and highly regarded sources of information on slave rebellions. Ask the students to act out, in role-play situations, the stories they have heard. After the role-play situations, ask them to hypothesize by responding to the following questions. Write their responses on the board.

   a. Why do you think the slaves were captured?
   b. Why do you think they started mutinies?
   c. Why didn't the mutinies end the slave trade?
   d. Do you think it was right for slaves to be captured? Why or why not?
   e. Do you think it was right for slaves to rebel? Why or why not?

   After the students have responded to these questions, read to them, or ask them to read, selections on the slave trade so that they can test their hypotheses.

3. Ask three different groups of students to research the following three topics:
   a. The Gabriel Prosser revolt of 1800
   b. The Denmark Vesey revolt of 1822
   c. The Nat Turner revolt of 1831

   To help them guide their research, ask the groups to focus on the following questions:
   a. Where did the revolt occur?
   b. Why did the revolt occur?
   c. Who led the revolt?
   d. Was the revolt successful? Why or why not?
   e. How were the rebels punished? Why were they punished?

   Discuss the questions above with the entire class when the groups have presented their research. List the students' responses on the board. Through questioning, help the student see how the slave insurrections were both alike and different, and why, of the three rebellions, only the Turner revolt was successful. After the class discussion, ask each group to plan and present to the class a dramatization showing the sequence of events in the rebellion they studied.

4. African Americans were active in the abolitionist movement and in the Underground Railroad, a loosely organized system that helped many slaves escape to the northern states and to Canada. Ask individual students to research the lives of and to "become," in a dramatization, one of the following people.

David Walker   James Forten
Henry Highland Garnet   Frederick Douglass
Robert Purvis   Harriet Tubman
Sojourner Truth

When the dramatizations are presented, discuss the following questions with the class:

a. Why did African American abolitionists oppose slavery? How did their views differ from those of White abolitionists? Why did White abolitionists discriminate against Black abolitionists? Excellent sources on the Black abolitionists are Shirley J. Yee (1992), *Black Women Abolitionists* and Benjamin Quarles (1969), *Black Abolitionists*.

b. What was the Underground Railroad? How did it help slaves escape? Who were some of the outstanding "conductors" on the railroad? What risks did captives take when they escaped? Why did they take them? If you had been a slave, would you have tried to escape? Why or why not?

5. Ask individual students or groups of students to research the following organizations and movements and to describe ways in which they protested racism and discrimination:

a. The Negro Convention Movement (1800s)
b. The Niagara Movement (1905)
c. The National Association for the Advancement of Colored People (1910)
d. The National Urban League (1911)
e. The Universal Negro Improvement Association (1914)
f. The Black church in the 1800s

When their research is complete, the students should share it with the class. The class should discuss how these organizations and movements expressed discontent with the plight of African Americans, the actions they took to improve it, and the successes and failures they experienced and why.

6. Have the class role-play a civil rights conference in 1966 in which leaders of the organizations listed below debate the future directions of the movement. Each organizational representative should be thoroughly familiar with his or her organization's philosophical position in 1966. By that year the civil rights movement was becoming increasingly radicalized, and deep factions had developed within the various organizations.

Southern Christian Leadership Conference (SCLC)
National Association for the Advancement of Colored People (NAACP)
National Urban League
Congress of Racial Equality (CORE)
Student Nonviolent Coordinating Committee (SNCC)
Black Panther party
Revolutionary Action Movement (RAM)

7. Have the students role-play a meeting of the following people after a serious racial rebellion in a major city in 1967. These people have met to decide what can be done to eliminate the causes of city riots. Ask individual students to play specific roles. To structure this activity more tightly, write a role description for each character on a three-by-five-inch index card and give the cards to the student role-players.

   Roles are as follows:

   The mayor of the city
   An SCLC spokesperson
   An NAACP spokesperson
   A National Urban League spokesperson
   A CORE spokesperson
   A SNCC spokesperson
   A Black Panther party spokesperson
   A RAM spokesperson
   A young person who has participated in a riot

8. To enable the students to summarize this unit and to derive the key generalizations stated above, have them complete the data retrieval chart in Table 7.1.

VALUING ACTIVITY

Read the following story to the class and ask the questions that follow.

Trying to Buy a Home in Lakewood Island

About a year ago, Joan and Henry Green, a young African American couple, moved from the West Coast to a large city in the Midwest. They moved because Henry finished his Ph.D. in chemistry and took a job at a big university in Midwestern City. Since they have been in Midwestern City, the Greens have rented an apartment in the central area of the city. However, they have decided that they want to buy a house. Their apartment has become too small for the many books and other things they have accumulated during the year. In addition to wanting more space, they want a house so that they can receive breaks on their income tax, which they do not receive living in an apartment. The Greens also think that a house will be a good financial investment.

The Greens have decided to move into a suburban community. They want a new house and most of the houses within the city limits are rather old. They also feel that they can obtain a larger house for their money in the suburbs than in the city. They have looked at several suburban communities and have decided that they like Lakewood Island better than any of the others. Lakewood Island is an all-White community comprised primarily of lower-middle-class and middle-class residents. There are a few wealthy families in Lakewood Island, but they are the exceptions rather than the rule.

Joan and Henry Green have become frustrated because of the problems they have experienced trying to buy a home in Lakewood Island. Before they go out to

TABLE 7.1 Black Protest: Data Retrieval Chart

Form of Protest, Organization, or Movement	Goal of Protests	Ways of Protest	Results of Protests
Slave mutinies			
Slave rebellions (in USA)			
Black abolitionary movement			
Underground Railroad			
Niagara Movement			
NAACP			
National Urban League			
SCLC			
CORE			
SNCC			
Black Panther party			
RAM			

look at a house, they carefully study the newspaper ads. When they arrived at the first house in which they were interested, the owner told them that his house had just been sold. A week later they decided to work with a realtor. When they tried to close the deal on the next house they wanted, the realtor told them that the owner had raised the price $10,000 because he had had the house appraised since he had put it on the market and had discovered that his selling price was much too low. When the Greens tried to buy a third house in Lakewood Island, the owner told them that he had decided not to sell because he had not received the job in another city that he was almost sure that he would receive when he had put his house up for sale. He explained that the realtor had not removed the ad about his house from the newspaper even though he had told him that he had decided not to sell a week earlier. The realtor the owner had been working with had left the real estate company a few days ago. Henry is bitter and feels that he and his wife are victims of racism and discrimination. Joan believes that Henry is paranoid and that they have been the victims of a series of events that could have happened to anyone, regardless of their race.

Questions

1. Do you think that the Greens were discriminated against in Lakewood Island? Why or why not?
2. What should the Greens do? Why?
3. If you were the Greens, what would you do? Why?
4. What can the Greens do to determine if they are victims of discrimination?

High School Grades

CONCEPT

Separatism
Generalization: Black separatist movements emerge when African Americans experience acute discrimination and a heightened sense of racial pride.

1. Either through choice or force, Black separatism has always existed in America. Most of the social life of the slaves was confined to their communities. One of the earliest manifestations of Black separatism was the colonization movement led by African Americans. To begin this unit, ask several students to prepare and present research reports on the following topics:
   a. Martin R. Delany
   b. Paul Cuffe
   c. The African Colonization Society

   When the reports are presented to the class, the following questions should be discussed:
   a. Why did colonization movements emerge among African Americans?
   b. Were these movements popular and successful? Why or why not?
   c. Why did back-to-Africa movements fail to appeal to most African Americans?
   d. If early Black-led colonization attempts had succeeded, how do you think the subsequent history of African Americans would have been different?

2. Because of discrimination and the need for group solidarity, a number of African American organizations emerged in the 1800s. Ask a group of students to prepare short papers on the following topics and present them to the class in a panel discussion on separate Black institutions in the 1800s.

> The Black church
> Black fraternal and self-help organizations
> Black businesses
> Black schools and colleges
> The Negro Convention Movement

Role-play a Negro Convention in the 1800s in which the participants draft a position statement detailing their major grievances about the plight of African Americans and a plan of action for social change. All of the delegates to the simulated convention must reach agreement on the position statement they prepare. The student role-players will need to be thoroughly familiar with the Negro Convention Movement and the various points of view that were presented in the series of Negro Conventions held in the 1800s.

3. The Niagara Movement was a Black protest organization organized in 1905 by W. E. B. Du Bois and a group of Black intellectuals. Ask a group of students to prepare a research report on this movement and present it to the class.

4. Most of the national civil rights organizations in the early 1900s were interracial. Ask the students to do required readings on the history and development of the NAACP and the National Urban League. When they have completed the readings, they should compare and contrast these two organizations with the Niagara Movement and earlier Black protest movements and organizations such as the Negro Convention Movement. Particular attention should be paid to (1) reasons the organizations emerged, (2) people who made major policy decisions and held key positions within them, (3) types of problems that arose within the organizations, (4) the major goals of the organizations, and (5) ways in which the organizations succeeded or failed and why. While studying these organizations, the students should compare and contrast the ideas and actions of Booker T. Washington and W. E. B. Du Bois. To conclude this activity, ask two students to role-play a debate between Washington and Du Bois on the kind of education needed by African Americans. Two excellent references for this last exercise are *Up from Slavery* by Booker T. Washington and *The Souls of Black Folk* by W. E. B. Du Bois.

5. Ask a group of students to prepare a panel discussion on the ideas and actions of Marcus Garvey and the Universal Negro Improvement Association. Ask them to focus on the following questions:
   a. What social, economic, and political conditions made Garvey's movement particularly appealing to low-income African Americans?
   b. How did Garvey's ideas help to improve low-income Blacks' feelings about themselves?
   c. Why was Garvey's back-to-Africa movement unsuccessful?
   d. Why did conflict develop between Garvey and other Black leaders?
   e. Why was Garvey ultimately crushed as a leader?
   f. What was the main significance of Garvey's movement? The classic biography of Garvey is *Black Moses* by E. D. Cronon. Another excellent book for

this activity is *Marcus Garvey and the Vision of Africa* edited by John Henrik Clarke.

6. When the Black Revolt emerged in 1960, its major goal was to desegregate public accommodation facilities and other institutions. Action tactics and court battles achieved much desegregation. However, by 1965, many African Americans, especially young Black activists, were disillusioned with the attainments of the movement and realized that integration alone would not eliminate the African American's major social, economic, and political problems. These young activists felt that both the goals and tactics of the movement should be changed. They issued a call for Black Power.

Ask the entire class to read excerpts from *Black Power: The Politics of Liberation in America,* by Stokely Carmichael and Charles V. Hamilton. Discuss each excerpt with the class. The following questions and exercises can help guide class discussion and student research.

a. What did the concept "Black Power" mean? Did it mean the same things to African Americans and White Americans?

b. Compare and contrast the goals of the Black Power movement and the goals of civil rights organizations like SCLC and the NAACP in the early 1960s.

c. What kinds of economic, political, and social institutions were implied by the concept of Black Power?

d. Compare and contrast the views of the following people:

David Walker	W. E. B. Du Bois
Martin R. Delany	Stokely Carmichael
Richard Allen	Malcolm X
Prentice Hall	Angela Y. Davis
Paul Cuffe	Jesse Jackson
Marcus Garvey	Fannie Lou Hamer

7. Ask the students to research the Afrocentric movement in the 1990s and to state how it is similar to and different from early Black separatist movements. The ideas and work of Molefi K. Asante (1988) should be examined.

8. Conclude the unit by asking the students to present a dramatization that shows how Black separatism has developed and changed from the 1700s to the 1990s.

REFERENCES

Adero, M. (Ed.). (1993). *Up South: Stories, Studies and Letters of This Century's African-American Migrations.* New York: New Press.

Aptheker, H. (1987). *American Negro Slave Revolts* (40th anniv. ed.). New York: International Publishers.

Asante, M. K. (1988). *Afrocentricity.* Trenton, NJ: Africa World Press.

Cose, E. (1993). *The Rage of a Privileged Class.* New York: HarperCollins.

Crawford, V. (1993). Beyond the Human Self: Grassroots Activists in the Mississippi Civil Rights Movement. In V. Crawford, J. A. Rouse, & B. Woods (Eds.), *Women in the Civil Rights Movement: Trailblazers & Torchbearers 1941–1965* (pp. 13–26). Bloomington: Indiana University Press.

Du Bois, W. E. B. (1903/1973). *The Souls of Black Folk.* Millwood, NY: Kraus-Thomas Organization.

Feagin, J. R., & Sikes, M. P. (1994). *Living with Racism: The Black Middle-Class Experience.* Boston: Beacon Press.

Garrow, D. (Ed.). (1987). *The Montgomery Bus Boycott and the Women Who Started It: The Memoir of Jo Ann Gibson Robinson.* Knoxville: University of Tennessee Press.

Genovese, E. D. (1979). *From Rebellion to Revolution: Afro-American Slave Revolts in the Making of the Modern World.* Baton Rouge: Louisiana State University Press.

Jaynes, G. D., & Williams, R. M., Jr. (1989). *A Common Destiny: Blacks and American Society.* Washington, DC: National Academy Press.

Johnson, J. W. (1995). *Lift Ev'ry Voice and Sing.* Illustrated by J. S. Gilchrist. New York: Scholastic.

Joint Center for Political and Economic Studies. (1999, January). Number of Black Elected Officials in the United States, by State and Office. [On-line]. Available: *http://jointcenter.org/*

Ladson-Billings, G. (1994). Review of *Teaching Strategies for Ethnic Studies,* 5th ed. Madison: University of Wisconsin, unpublished (prepared for 6th edition revision).

Lemann, N. (1991). *The Promised Land: The Great Black Migration and How It Changed America.* New York: Knopf.

McKinnon, J., & Humes, K. (2000, March). The Black Population in the United States: Population Characteristics. Washington, DC: U.S. Census Bureau. [On-line]. Available: *http://www.census.gov/*

McKinnon, J., & Humes, K. (2000, September). The Black Population in the United States: Population Characteristics. U.S. Census Bureau. [On-line]. *http://www.census.gov*

Payne, C. (1993). Men Led, but Women Organized: Movement Participation of Women in the Mississippi Delta. In V. Crawford, J. A. Rouse, & B. Woods (Eds.), *Women in the Civil Rights Movement: Trailblazers & Torchbearers 1941–1965* (pp. 1–11). Bloomington: Indiana University Press.

Quarles, B. (1969). *Black Abolitionists.* New York: Oxford University Press.

Report of the National Advisory Commission on Civil Disorders. (1968). New York: Bantam Books.

Shearer, L. (1990, January 7). The Rise of Black Mayors. *Parade,* p. 14.

Standley, A. (1993). The Role of Black Women in the Civil Rights Movement. In V. Crawford, J. A. Rouse, & B. Woods (Eds.), *Women in the Civil Rights Movement: Trailblazers & Torchbearers 1941–1965* (pp. 183–202). Bloomington: Indiana University Press.

U.S. Census Bureau (2001, February 22). Census Bureau Releases Update on Country's African American Population. [On-line]. Available: *http://www.census.gov/Press-Release/www/2001/cb01–34.html*

U.S. Commission on Civil Rights. (2001, June 8). Voting Irregularities in Florida during the 2000 Presidential Election (Draft Report). [On-line] Available: *http://www.usccr.gov/*

Washington, B. T. (1956/1901). *Up From Slavery.* New York: Bantam. (origional work published 1901).

Wilson, W. J. (1987). *The Truly Disadvantaged: The Inner City, the Underclass, and Public Policy.* Chicago: University of Chicago Press.

Yee, S. J. (1992). *Black Women Abolitionists: A Study in Activism, 1828–1960.* Knoxville: University of Tennessee Press.

ANNOTATED BIBLIOGRAPHY

Books for Teachers

Especially Recommended

Andrews, W. L., Foster, F. S., & Harris, T. (Eds.). (1997). *The Oxford Companion to African American Literature.* New York: Oxford.

A comprehensive (866 pages) and informative reference work that focuses on the lives and careers of more than 400 African American writers. An excellent and useful reference book.

Appiah, K. A., & Gates, H. L., Jr. (Eds.). (1999). *Africana: The Encyclopedia of the African and African American Experience.* New York:

This ambitious reference work (2,095 pages), years in the making, includes information and articles about Africans throughout the world. It contains a gold mine of information that is visually appealing and engaging because it is illustrated with photographs, some of which are in color.

Franklin, J. H., & Moss, A. A., Jr. (2000). *From Slavery to Freedom: A History of Black Americans* (8th ed.). New York: McGraw-Hill.

This comprehensive history of African Americans is still one of the best. The senior author is one of the most highly regarded American historians in the United States.

Gates, H. L., Jr., & McKay, N. Y. (Eds.). (1997). *The Norton Anthology of African American Literature.* New York: Norton.

This massive (2,665 pages) and comprehensive anthology includes every genre of African American literature—such as spirituals, the blues, folktales, and poetry—from the arrival of Blacks in America to the contemporary period. It also includes an excellent chronology of African American literature.

Hine, D. C. (Ed.). (1993). *Black Women in America: An Historical Encyclopedia* (2 vols.). Brooklyn, NY: Carlson.

The definitive work on the experiences of African American women in the United States. An essential reference for school, college, and university libraries.

Hine, D. C., & Thompson, K. (1998). *A Shining Thread of Hope: The History of Black Women in America.* New York: Broadway Books.

A highly readable historical overview of the sojourn of Black women in America. The first author is the best-known expert on the history of African American women in the United States.

Johnson, C., Smith, P., & the WGBH Series Research Team. (1998). *Africans in America: America's Journey through Slavery.* New York: Harcourt Brace.

This sensitively crafted book includes primary documents in which African captives in America poignantly describe the human costs of this degrading institution.

Marable, M., & Mullings, L. (Eds.). (2000). *Let Nobody Turn Us Around: Voices of Resistance, Reform, and Renewal.* New York: Rowman & Littlefield.

This rich and thoughtful collection of documents includes selections that describe the experiences of Blacks in the United States from 1978 to 1998. The documents are excellent for teaching, especially in the upper and high school grades.

Nesbett, P. T. (2001). *Jacob Lawrence: The Complete Prints (1963–2000).* Seattle: University of Washington Press.

This book consists of prints by Jacob Lawrence—America's preeminent African American artist—completed during the last four decades of his life. An excellent source to teach from or to browse.

Salzman, J., Smith, D. L., & West, C. (Eds.). (1996). *Encyclopedia of African-American Culture and History* (5 vols.). New York: Macmillan.

This outstanding, seminal, and comprehensive reference work covers all aspects of African American history and culture. This five-volume set is rich in biographies as well as in thematic essays on such topics as the Harlem Renaissance, intellectual life, and inventors. This encyclopedia should be in every school and university library.

Other References

Beals, M. P. (1994). *Warriors Don't Cry: A Searing Memoir of the Battle to Integrate Little Rock's Central High School*. New York: Pocket Books.

A moving and poignant account of the desegregation of Little Rock's Central High School by one of the nine African American students who first enrolled.

Franklin, J. H., & McNeil, G. R. (Eds.). (1995). *African Americans and the Living Constitution*. Washington, DC: Smithsonian Institution Press.

This book consists of a collection of informative essays about African Americans and the U.S. Constitution.

Guy-Sheftall, B. (Ed.). (1995). *Words of Fire: An Anthology of African-American Feminist Thought*. New York: New Press.

This richly textured and comprehensive anthology documents the experiences of African American women from 1831 to the present. Edited by a leading authority in Black women's studies, it also is appropriate for high school students.

Honey, M. K. (1999). *Black Workers Remembered: An Oral History of Segregation, Unionism, and the Freedom Struggle*. Berkeley: University of California Press.

The struggles and hopes of the lives of African American workers are vividly described in this book by a caring and sensitive labor historian.

Hurston, Z. N. (1978). *Their Eyes Were Watching God*. Urbana: University of Illinois Press.

First published in 1937, this novel about the love between an African American man and woman is a classic.

Jenkins, A. H. (1995). *Psychology and African Americans: A Humanistic Approach* (2nd ed.). Boston: Allyn and Bacon.

The author examines issues that concern contemporary African Americans from a humanistic psychological point of view.

Lewis, J., with D'Orso, M. (1998). *Walking in the Wind: A Memoir of the Movement*. New York: Simon & Schuster.

A riveting and powerful memoir of the civil rights movement of the 1960s and 1970s by one of its most prominent leaders who became a Representative from Georgia, John Lewis.

Moses, Robert P., & Cobb, C. E., Jr. (2001). *Radical Equations: Math Literacy and Civil Rights*. Boston: Beacon.

Robert Moses attained fame for his Project Zero, which successfully teaches algebra to inner-city African American youths. He and Cobb argue that the learning of math is a civil right because math skills are needed for survival in an Internet society.

Segal, R. (1995). *The Black Diaspora*. Boston: Faber and Faber.

An ambitious, important and informative historical study of Blacks worldwide.

Spivey, D. M. (1999). *The Peppers, Cracklings, and Knots of Wool Cookbook: The Global Migration of African Cuisine*. Albany: State University of New York Press.

The foods of Africans and their descendants worldwide are described in this interesting and unusual book. It describes the characteristics of African food in different regions of the world and includes recipes for making tasty dishes.

Stewart, J. C. (1998). (Eds.). *Paul Robeson: Artist and Citizen*. New Brunswick, NJ: Rutgers University Press.

This illustrated book contains a number of well-crafted essays on Robeson—the noted but often forgotten athlete, actor, and singer—whose story needs to be told to today's stu-

dents. His life teaches important lessons about the depth and complexity of racism in American society.

Taylor, Q. (1998). *In Search of the Racial Frontier: African Americans in the American West, 1528–1990.* New York: Norton.

In this much-needed, carefully researched, and engaging book, the nation's preeminent historian of African Americans in the West describes their sojourn. Also see L. D. deGraaf, K. Mulroy, & Q. Taylor (Eds.). (2001). African Americans in California. *Seattle: University of Washington Press.*

Waters, M. C. (1999). *Black Identities: West Indian Immigrant Dreams and American Realities.* Cambridge: Harvard University Press.

This important and careful study by a Harvard sociologist will help students to understand the ethnic diversity within the Black community. Too often, the diversity within the African American community is not acknowledged or recognized.

Yee, S. J. (1992). *Black Women Abolitionists: A Study in Activism, 1828–1860.* Knoxville: University of Tennessee Press.

This informative book examines the activism and work of Black women abolitionists in the nineteenth century.

Books for Students

Adler, D. A. (1999). *A Picture Book of George Washington Carver.* Illustrated by D. Brown. New York: Holiday House.

This book introduces young readers to the noted scientist through lively text and attractive illustrations. Another recent book in the series by the same author presents civil rights lawyer and Supreme Court Justice Thurgood Marshall. (Primary)

Barnwell, Y. M. (1998). *No Mirrors in My Mother's House.* Illustrated by S. Saint James. San Diego: Harcourt.

A singer with the a capella quartet, Sweet Honey in the Rock, offers a picture book based on one of the group's signature songs, which depicts the love between a girl and her grandmother. A CD is included. (All ages)

Bial, R. (1997). *The Strength of These Arms: Life in the Slave Quarters.* Illustrated with photos by the author. Boston: Houghton Mifflin.

Compelling photographs convey the deprivations of slavery and the domestic life of slaves. Other books for this age group that contrast the "big house" with the slave quarters include Paul Erickson's Daily Life on a Southern Plantation, 1853 *(Dutton, 1997) and* Christmas in the Big House, Christmas in the Quarters, *by Patricia and Fredrick McKissack (Scholastic, 1994). (Intermediate/Middle School)*

Black, W. B. (1998). *Slaves to Soldiers: African-American Fighting Men in the Civil War.* Danbury, CO: Frankin Watts.

An extensive history of African American involvement on land and sea in Civil War battles. (Intermediate/Middle School)

Bolden, T. (1998). *And Not Afraid to Dare: The Stories of Ten African-American Women.* New York: Scholastic.

These brief but multidimensional biographies will inspire readers to want to learn more about important African American women from the eighteenth century to the present. (Middle School/High School)

Bridges, R. (1999). *Through My Eyes.* New York: Scholastic.

The young girl who desegregated the New Orleans public schools in 1960 tells how she felt during that tense and fateful time and how those events have affected her life since. Bridges's story is told in compelling language for younger readers in the picture book The Story of Ruby Bridges *(Scholastic, 1995) by noted psychologist and author Robert Coles, illustrated by George Ford. (Intermediate)*

Bryan, A. (1997). *Ashley Bryan's ABC of African American Poetry.* Illustrated by the author. New York: Atheneum.

A beautifully illustrated introduction to African American poetry, written for the youngest readers. (Primary)

Butler, J. (1998). *A Drawing in the Sand: The Story of African American Art.* Illustrated by the author. Madison, WI: Zino Press.

A stunningly illustrated work that is both Butler's autobiography as an artist and a history of and homage to the Black artists who served as his inspiration. (Intermediate and Up)

Clinton, C. (Ed.). (1998). *I, Too, Sing America: Three Centuries of African American Poetry.* Illustrated by S. Alcorn. Boston: Houghton Mifflin.

An accessible introduction to the works of 25 major African American poets, from the mid-eighteenth century to the present, illustrated with Alcorn's haunting woodcuts. Female poets are well represented. (Middle School/High School)

Collier, B. (2000). *Uptown.* Illustrated by the author. New York: Henry Holt.

Watercolors and collage depict a vibrant Harlem neighborhood as well as its rich history in this winner of the 2001 Coretta Scott King award for illustration. (Primary)

Curtis, C. P. (1995). *The Watsons Go to Birmingham—1963.* New York: Delacorte.

A family trip from Michigan to Alabama to see relatives becomes a frightening journey into history when nine-year-old Kenny Watson and his younger sister become witnesses to the Sixteenth Street Church bombing in Birmingham that killed four girls. A 1996 Newbery honor book. (Intermediate and Up)

Curtis, C. P. (1999). *Bud, Not Buddy.* New York: Delacorte.

A ten-year-old African American boy runs away from a cruel foster home to search for his musician father during the depths of the Great Depression. Winner of the 2000 Coretta Scott King award and the 2000 John Newbery Medal for outstanding writing in a children's book. (Intermediate/Middle School)

Curtis, G. (1998). *The Bat Boy and His Violin.* Illustrated by E. B. Lewis. New York: Simon & Schuster.

A boy who loves to play the violin must stand up to his father, a baseball coach who makes the youngster serve as the team's bat boy. A sensitive exploration of a conflict between a father and son who have different interests and dreams. (Primary)

Draper, S. M. (1997). *Forged by Fire.* New York: Simon & Schuster.

After his loving aunt dies, Gerald returns to his drug-addicted mother's home, where he tries to save his younger half-sister from an abusive situation. Winner of the 1998 Coretta Scott King award for writing, this is the second in a trilogy about a group of working-class and middle-class African American teens in a Cincinnati high school. The other titles are Tears of a Tiger *(Simon & Schuster, 1994), which explores the teens' reaction to a drunken driving accident that kills a popular basketball player and leaves a teammate to live with the guilt, and* Darkness before Dawn *(Simon & Schuster, 2001), which portrays a girl who must deal with the grief following her boyfriend's suicide. (High School)*

Draper, S. M. (1999). *Romiette and Julio.* New York: Simon & Schuster.

Family and friends oppose a romance between an African American girl and a Latino boy in a tale based on the classic Shakespeare play and reminiscent of West Side Story. *(Middle School)*

Duggleby, J. (1999). *Story Painter: The Life of Jacob Lawrence.* Illustrated with paintings by J. Lawrence. San Francisco: Chronicle Books.

An appealing, accessible biography of the noted twentieth-century artist, beautifully illustrated with Lawrence's paintings. (Intermediate and Up)

English, K. (1999). *Francie.* New York: Farrar, Straus & Giroux.

An African American girl volunteers to tutor a classmate in the South in the 1950s and risks her own and her family's safety when she helps him to escape after he is falsely accused of attacking a White man. A harrowing account of life in the era of Jim Crow. (Middle School)

Feelings, T. (1995). *The Middle Passage: White Ships/Black Cargo.* Illustrated by the author. New York: Dial Books.

The moving drawings in this book provide powerful insights into the journey of the captured Africans to the Americas. It also contains a personal statement by the author/artist and an introduction by John Henrik Clarke. (Middle School and Up)

Flake, S. (1998). *The Skin I'm In.* New York: Hyperion.

A middle schooler agonizes over her dark skin in this novel that explores issues of physical appearance and self-esteem. (Middle School)

Fradin, D. B., & Fradin, J. B. (2000). *Ida B. Wells: Mother of the Civil Rights Movement.* New York: Clarion.

The life of the early twentieth-century journalist, civil rights activist, and crusader against lynching is presented. Graphic visuals and racist epithets make this book a better choice for the high school level. Other books by the Fradins include Bound for the North Star: True Stories of Fugitive Slaves *(Clarion, 2000). (High School)*

Hamilton, V. (1993). *Many Thousand Gone: African Americans from Slavery to Freedom.* New York: Knopf.

With a poignant text, this book traces African American resistance to slavery from its beginnings to the Emancipation Proclamation by means of more than thirty individual profiles and stories. (Intermediate)

Hansen, J. (1997). *I Thought My Soul Would Rise and Fly: The Diary of Patsy, a Freed Girl.* Series: *Dear America.* New York: Scholastic.

A self-educated freed slave must make a new life for herself in the South during the period of Reconstruction. Education and dreams for a future in freedom are also themes of another work in this series, Patricia McKissack's A Picture of Freedom: The Diary of Clotee, a Slave Girl *(1997). (Intermediate/Middle School)*

Hansen, J. (2000). *The Heart Calls Home.* New York: Walker.

Obi, a runaway slave who fought in the Union Army, searches for his wife and young child at the end of the Civil War. This book is the last in a trilogy that includes Which Way Freedom? *(Walker, 1986) and* Out from this Place *(Walker, 1988). (Middle School/High School)*

Hansen, J., & McGowan, G. (1998). *Breaking Ground, Breaking Silence: The Story of New York City's African Burial Ground.* New York: Henry Holt.

This gripping account explores the controversy over the recently discovered burial ground in Lower Manhattan at the same time as it reveals the lives of African Americans in an earlier era. A good companion to this title is William L. Katz's Black Legacy: A History of New York's African Americans *(Simon & Schuster, 1997). (Middle School/High School)*

Haskins, J. (1997). *Bayard Rustin: Behind the Scenes of the Civil Rights Movement.* New York: Hyperion.

This clearly written, informative book is both a biography of a dedicated but less visible civil rights activist and a history of the movement as a whole. In the same vein, Haskins chronicles the history of school desegregation in Separate But Not Equal: The Dream and the Struggle *(Scholastic, 1997). (Middle School/High School)*

Haskins, J., & Benson, K. (2000). *Out of the Darkness: The Story of Blacks Moving North, 1890–1940.* Series: *Great Journeys.* Tarrytown, NY: Marshall Cavendish/Benchmark Books.

The story of the Great Migration of African Americans moving from the South to the North in search of economic opportunities and freedom from racial terror is told. Also in this series is They Came in Chains: The Story of the Slave Ships, *by Milton Meltzer (2000). (Middle School/High School)*

Hewett, L. (1996). *Soulfire.* New York: Dutton.

A group of African American boys in an urban high school face a variety of challenges. Hewett continues to present the adolescent lives of African Americans in her other realistic novels, Lives of Our Own *(Dutton, 1998) and* Dancer *(Dutton, 1999). (Middle School)*

Hoobler, D. R., & Hoobler, T. (1995). *The African American Family Album.* New York: Oxford University Press.

The African American experience is described in captivating and involving photographs, documents, and text. (Middle School/High School)

Howard, E. F. (2000). *Virgie Goes to School with Us Boys.* Illustrated by E. B. Lewis. New York: Simon & Schuster.

Little sister Virgie is now old enough to walk to school with her brothers, attend classes for the first time, and stay over for the entire week because the school is so far away. Set in rural Tennessee in the late 1800s, this story from the author's family history is accompanied by a photo of Virgie and her brothers. Family photos also enhance the Tenth Anniversary Edition of Aunt Flossie's Hats *(and Crab Cakes Later) (Simon & Schuster, 2001), which presents Aunt Flossies's stories of growing up in Baltimore, Maryland, in the early 1900s. (Primary)*

Igus, T. (1998). *I See the Rhythm.* Illustrated by M. Wood. San Francisco: Children's Book Press.

Winner of the 1999 Coretta Scott King Award for illustration, this book showcases Michelle Wood's artwork, inspired by three centuries of African American music. (All ages)

Johnson, A. (1998). *Heaven.* New York: Simon & Schuster.

Poetic writing and memorable characters distinguish this novel about a fourteen-year-old girl living in a cozy small town who learns hard lessons about identity, loss, and the lies adults tell to protect children. Winner of the 1999 Coretta Scott King Award for writing. In the same year, Angela Johnson received a Coretta Scott King honor citation for her collection of poetry for teens, The Other Side: Shorter Poems *(Orchard, 1998). (Middle School)*

Johnson, D. (1999). *Sunday Week.* Illustrated by T. Geter. New York: Henry Holt.

African Americans, urban and suburban, of diverse religious traditions, engage in a variety of activities that build up to Sunday worship. (Primary)

Joseph, L. (1998). *Fly, Bessie, Fly.* Illustrated by Y. Buchanan. New York: Simon & Schuster.

An appealing picture-book biography of the African American woman aviation pioneer who lived in the early twentieth century. Also recommended is Reeve Lindbergh's biography in verse, Nobody Owns the Sky *(Candlewick, 1996). (Primary/Intermediate)*

Karenga, M. (1998). *Kwanzaa: A Celebration of Family, Community and Culture.* Los Angeles: University of Sankore Press.

> The details about the celebration of Kwanzaa are described by the creator of the holiday in this beautifully illustrated and information-packed book. (All ages).

Katz, W. L. (1999). *Black Pioneers: An Untold Story.* New York: Simon & Schuster.

> The author of several acclaimed books on African Americans in the West returns with a lively, readable history of free African Americans and escaped slaves who made new lives in the Old Northwest Territories between the American Revolution and the Civil War. (Middle School)

Lyons, M. E. (1999). *Talking with Tebe: Clementine Hunter, Memory Artist.* Boston: Houghton Mifflin.

> This fascinating biography of the self-taught folk artist, who died in 1988 at the age of 102, is based on magazine and newspaper articles and taped interviews. (Intermediate/ Middle School)

Mays, O., with A. Govenar. (2000). *Osceola: Memories of a Sharecropper's Daughter.* Illustrated by S. W. Evans. New York: Hyperion/Jump at the Sun.

> An elderly woman recalls her childhood as a sharecropper in East Texas and tells the story of her grandfather, a former slave. Poems from the Civil War period and blues lyrics add to this remarkable and original work of oral history. (Intermediate and Up)

McKissack, P., (2000). *Color Me Dark: The Diary of Nellie Lee Love, the Great Migration North.* Series: *Dear America.* New York: Scholastic.

> Nellie's family moves from Tennessee to Chicago after her uncle's death in a lynching, but up North in the 1910s the family continues to encounter racism. (Intermediate/Middle School)

McKissack, P., & McKissack, F. (1998). *Let My People Go: Bible Stories Told by a Freeman of Color.* Illustrated by J. E. Ransome. New York: Atheneum.

> A retelling of twelve Old Testament stories that draws parallels between the experiences of the Hebrews and the history of African Americans. (Intermediate and Up)

McKissack, P., & McKissack, F. (1999). *Black Hands, White Sails: The Story of African American Whalers.* New York: Scholastic.

> A lively nonfiction account of African Americans who worked in the whaling industry in the nineteenth century. (Intermediate/Middle School)

Miller, W. (2000). *Tituba.* Illustrated by L. Jenkins. San Diego: Harcourt.

> The story of the West Indian slave accused of witchcraft in the Salem witch trials is presented in a format and style appropriate to picture-book readers. Miller is also the author of the sensitively written picture-book biography of the famous writer Zora Neale Hurston, Zora Hurston and the Chinaberry Tree *(Lee & Low, 1994). (Primary/Intermediate)*

Myers, W. D. (1997). *Harlem.* Illustrated by C. Myers. New York: Scholastic.

> A vividly rendered, poetic reconstruction of the life, culture, and history of New York City's preeminent African American neighborhood, well illustrated by Christopher Myers, the son of the acclaimed author Walter Dean Myers. (Primary)

Myers, W. D. (1999). *Monster.* New York: HarperCollins.

> A gripping account of a sixteen-year-old boy accused of being an accomplice in a murder, this novel won the first Michael L. Printz award for excellence in young adult literature. Another recommended recent work by Myers, a pioneering author of young adult books about the African American experience, is 145th Street: Short Stories *(Delacorte, 2000). (Middle School/High School)*

Nelson, M. (2001). *Carver: A Life in Poems*. Asheville, N.C.: Front Street Books.

Renowned poet Marilyn Nelson recounts in a collage of poems the public and spiritual life of the chemist, inventor, and Tuskegee Institute professor. Winner of 2002 Newbury and Coretta Scott King honor awards. (Middle School and Up)

Okutoro, L. O. (Ed.). (1999). *Quiet Storm: Voices of Young Black Poets*. New York: Hyperion.

Poems by young people, ages thirteen to twenty-one, explore Black pride, identity, relationships, urban life, and dreams for the future. (Middle School/High School)

Parks, R., with Haskins, J. (1997). *I Am Rosa Parks*. New York: Dial.

The famed civil rights activist tells of her past struggles and continuing work for social justice in lyrical language understandable to students at the elementary level. This book contains much of the same information, though written for younger readers, as Rosa Parks: My Story *(Dial, 1992). (Primary/Intermediate)*

Patrick, D. L. (1999). *The Longest Ride*. New York: Henry Holt.

A fifteen-year-old runaway slave working as a cattle driver vows to find and free the rest of his family in the final days of the Civil War. High school students looking for adult level books on this topic would enjoy Allen B. Ballard's Where I'm Bound *(Simon & Schuster, 2001), which portrays a Union Army scout who journeys behind enemy lines to free family members trapped on a Mississippi plantation. (Middle School/High School)*

Pinkney, A. D. (2000). *Let It Shine: Stories of Black Women Freedom Fighters*. Illustrated by S. Alcorn. San Diego: Harcourt.

Biographies of African American women who led slaves to freedom, spoke out against lynching and other forms of oppression in the Jim Crow era, and played a role in the civil rights movement and contemporary struggles are profiled along with allegorical portraits of the subjects. (Intermediate/Middle School)

Pinkney, S. L. (2000). *Shades of Black: A Celebration of Our Children*. Illustrated with photos by M. C. Pinkney. New York: Scholastic.

Photographs with descriptive and inspirational accompanying text capture the unique and diverse physical characteristics of African American children. (All ages)

Porter, C. (1999). *Imani All Mine*. Boston: Houghton Mifflin.

A teenager living in a Buffalo, New York, housing project struggles to be a good mother for her daughter despite little emotional support or help from her mother. (High School)

Robinet, H. G. (1998). *Forty Acres and Maybe a Mule*. New York: Atheneum.

After the end of the Civil War, a freed slave and his family struggle to hold on to their land and their rights. (Middle School)

Robinson, A. B. L. (1997). *A Street Called Home*. Illustrated by the author. San Diego: Harcourt.

The author chronicles the migration of her grandparents from the South to Columbus, Ohio, in the 1940s, the lives they made, and the colorful characters they encountered in their new home. (Primary/Intermediate)

Siegelson, K. L. (1999). *In the Time of the Drums*. Illustrated by B. Pinkney. New York: Hyperion/Jump at the Sun.

On a plantation in coastal South Carolina, a grandmother tells her grandson stories of their Ibo people of West Africa, and the two attempt to liberate a boatload of newly arrived slaves from their homeland. The story is based on a legend of the Gullah people. Brian Pinkney won the 2000 Coretta Scott King award for his haunting scratchboard illustrations. (Primary)

Smalls, I. (1996). *Irene Jennie and the Christmas Masquerade: The Johnkankus.* Illustrated by M. Rosales. Boston: Little, Brown.

Through a slave girl who longs to spend Christmas with her parents, Smalls introduces the Johnkankus, a popular musical and dance tradition that originated in the West Indies and spread to North Carolina plantations in the eighteenth and nineteenth centuries. (Primary)

Smalls, I. (1999). *Kevin and His Dad.* Illustrated by M. Hays. Boston: Little, Brown.

In this simple story told in rhymes, a young boy spends a day with his father, cleaning house, playing baseball, seeing a movie, and talking. (Primary)

Steptoe, J., comp. (1997). *In Daddy's Arms I Am Tall: African Americans Celebrating Fathers.* Illustrated by J. Steptoe. New York: Lee & Low.

Javaka Steptoe's expressive illustrations and well-chosen poems by noted African American literary figures celebrate the relationships between fathers and their children. Winner of the 1998 Coretta Scott King award for illustration. (All ages)

Stroud, B. (1996). *Down Home at Miss Dessa's.* Illustrated by F. Marshall. New York: Lee & Low.

Along with other members of the community, two young sisters help take care of an elderly neighbor who is recovering from an accident. Stroud depicts the warmth and closeness of an African American community in the South in the 1940s. (Primary)

Taylor, M. D. (2001). *The Land.* New York: Penguin Putnam.

This prequel to Taylor's classic Roll of Thunder, Hear My Cry *(1976) describes Paul Edward's life as a mixed-race slave on his father's plantation, his efforts to purchase his own farm in Reconstruction-era Mississippi, and his struggle to establish his identity as a person of biracial heritage. Winner of the 2002 Coretta Scott King Award. (Middle School/High School)*

Taylor, T. (1998). *The Flight of Jesse Leroy Brown.* New York: Avon.

A fast-paced, readable biography of the first African American naval aviation cadet, whose determination made him a major figure in the integration of the armed forces after World War II. (High School)

Thomas, J. C. (1997). *I Have Heard of a Land.* New York: HarperCollins.

An African American family in the South sets out for the Oklahoma Territory in search of freedom and opportunity after the Civil War. Based on a family story. Thomas is also the author of a classic book of children's poetry that explores the richness of culture and family, Brown Honey in Broomwheat Tea *(HarperCollins, 1993). (Intermediate)*

Weatherford, C. B. (2000). *The Sound That Jazz Makes.* Illustrated by E. Velásquez. New York: Walker.

Readers take an illustrated journey through moments in African American musical history; the author and illustrator present the many musical and cultural events that contributed to the evolution of jazz. (All ages)

Williams, S. A. (1999). *Girls Together.* Illustrated by S. Saint James. San Diego: Harcourt.

The final children's book by the acclaimed poet and writer who died in 1999 celebrates a friendship among five girls who venture out from the projects to play in a neighborhood with trees. (Primary)

Williams-Garcia, R. (1995). *Like Sisters on the Homefront.* New York: Lodestar.

When fourteen-year-old Gayle and her infant son are sent from New York City to her strict relatives in Georgia to straighten her out, her life and attitude begin to change. Gayle appears as a character in Williams-Garcia's debut novel, Blue Tights *(Lodestar,*

1987), *which was one of the first contemporary young adult novels to address issues of body image and skin tone among African Americans. (Intermediate)*

Winter, J. (1999). *Fair Ball! 14 Great Stars from Baseball's Negro Leagues.* Illustrated by the author. New York: Scholastic.

Through lively text and color illustrations, readers learn of 14 major figures of the Negro Leagues. (All ages)

Woodson, J. (2000). *Miracle's Boys.* New York: Putnam.

Three boys struggle to survive, overcome their grief, and make a life together after the death of their parents. Winner of the 2001 Coretta Scott King award for writing. (Intermediate and Up)

PART THREE

European Americans

Concepts and Strategies

Part III consists of content, concepts, teaching strategies, and materials for teaching about European Americans. Most Americans are of European origin and descent. In 2000, the White, non-Hispanic population of the United States numbered about 202.3 million people and comprised about 72% of the nation's population. However, the percentage of the nation's population of European ancestry had declined significantly since 1900, when it comprised 87.7% of the population. Demographers predict that the percentage of White non-Hispanic Americans in the U.S. population will continue to decline in future years. It is predicted that they will make up about 62% of the nation's population in 2025 and 53% in 2050 (Martin & Midgley, 1999).

White Americans of European descent are increasing at a slower rate than are other ancestry groups. The total population of the United States increased 12% between 1990 and 2000, while the White non-Hispanic population increased only 4%. This difference resulted primarily because a disproportionate number of Whites are middle class (and therefore have fewer children) and because Europeans comprised only 14.9% of the immigrants to the United States between 1991 and 1998 (U.S. Census Bureau, 2000). Even though they are becoming a smaller percentage of the nation's population, Americans of European origin and descent still comprise the overwhelming majority of the nation's population and have the most influence on its culture, values, and ethos. A study of the sojourn of European immigrants across the Atlantic and of their journey in America is essential to a sound multicultural curriculum.

CHAPTER

8

European Ethnic Groups

Concepts, Strategies, and Materials

The poorest, the most miserable came here because they had no future over there. To them, the streets of America were paved in gold. They had what the Finns called kuum, *the American fever.*

—Andy Johnson, an immigrant
From Studs Terkel, *American Dreams: Lost and Found*

Between 1820 and 1998, about 64,599,082 legal immigrants entered the United States. Most of them (37,400,991, or about 61%) were Europeans who belonged to many different religious, political, and cultural groups (U.S. Immigration and Naturalization Service, 2000). The making of one society from so many different ethnic and nationality groups is one of the most amazing chapters in human history. Yet, social scientists, and therefore classroom teachers, have largely ignored the role of ethnicity in U.S. history and modern society. U.S. social scientists have been preoccupied with theories of assimilation and the melting pot concept. Nevertheless, scholars in the United States have given more attention to ethnicity as a variable in American life since the ethnic protest movements in the 1960s. However, a significant gap exists between scholarship and the school curriculum. The European ethnic experience is infrequently taught in the schools.

European ethnic groups should be included in a sound multicultural curriculum because the processes of acculturation and assimilation, which they have experienced and which many European ethnic groups are still experiencing, must be considered when students formulate concepts and generalizations about ethnicity and race in U.S. society. European Americans, like other Americans, often experienced ethnic rage, changed their names, and denied their ethnic heritages to gain social and economic mobility and to realize the American dream.

It is also important for students to study European ethnic groups because individuals of European origin comprise the bulk of the nation's population (about 72% in 2000) and Europeans continue to make up a significant proportion of the immigrants to the United States. Between 1981 and 1998, 14,943,200 immigrants entered the United States. Of these, about 11.9% were Europeans. Even though 11.9% is a significant drop in the percentage of European immigrants that settled in the United States in the decades prior to 1968, the number of European immigrants settling in the United States is still sizable.

The European immigrants who have entered the United States since 1981 are diverse in national origins and cultures. Table 8.1 shows the number of European immigrants who entered the United States between 1981 and 1998 from selected nations. As Table 8.1 indicates, a large number of immigrants came from the Soviet Union, the United Kingdom, and Poland. The challenge to Communism that Poland experienced in the late 1980s and in 1990 and the second revolution that Russia experienced in 1990—in which the old political order crumbled—may have been factors that pushed immigrants from Poland and the various nations within the former Soviet Union (Bateman & Egan, 1993). Significant numbers of immigrants also came from Germany, Ireland,

TABLE 8.1   European Immigrants to the United States from Selected Nations: 1981–1998

Country of Birth	Number	Percentage of Total Immigration	Percentage of European Immigration
Soviet Union, former	503,200	3.4	28.1
United Kingdom	256,800	1.7	14.3
Poland	248,100	1.7	13.8
Germany	125,000	0.8	7.0
Ireland	89,600	0.6	5.0
Romania	83,800	0.6	4.7
Yugoslavia	69,700	0.5	3.9
Portugal	60,300	0.4	3.4
Italy	51,400	0.3	2.9
France	45,000	0.3	2.5
Greece	41,000	0.3	2.3
Total Percentage of European Immigration 1981–1998		11.9	

Source: U.S. Census Bureau (2000). *Statistical Abstract of the United States: 2000* (120th Ed.). Washington, DC: U.S. Government Printing Office.

EUROPEAN ETHNIC GROUPS: HISTORICAL PERSPECTIVES

Important Dates	Events
1565	Pedro Menéndez Avilés founded St. Augustine, Florida, on the site of an Indian village.
1607	English immigrants established their first permanent American colony at Jamestown, Virginia.
1620	The Pilgrims came to America from England on the *Mayflower* and established a settlement at Plymouth, Massachusetts.
1623	The Dutch West India Company settled New Netherland as a trading post.
1683	The first German immigrants to North America settled in Pennsylvania.
1718	The Scots-Irish began immigrating to the American colonies in large numbers.
1729	The Pennsylvania Colony increased the head taxes charged to entering immigrants to discourage further foreign settlement.
1798	A Federalist-dominated Congress enacted the Alien and Sedition Acts to crush the Republican party and harass aliens.
1803	The British Passenger Act was enacted to discourage immigration.
1825	Great Britain repealed laws that prohibited immigration. The first group of Norwegian immigrants arrived in the United States.
1845–49	A series of potato blights in Ireland caused thousands of its citizens to immigrate to the United States.
1855	The antiforeign Know-Nothing movement reached its zenith and had a number of political successes in the 1855 elections. The movement rapidly declined after 1855. Castle Garden immigrant depot opened in New York.
1863	The Irish working classes expressed discontent with the Civil War and hostility toward urban Blacks in the New York draft riots, which lasted for four days.

Important Dates	Events
1882	A congressional immigration act established a head tax of 50¢ and excluded lunatics, convicts, idiots, and people likely to become public charges.
1883–85	An economic depression escalated nativistic feelings in the United States.
1885	The Foran Act outlawed the immigration of contract laborers.
1886	The Haymarket Affair in Chicago significantly increased fear of foreign "radicals" and stimulated the growth of nativistic sentiments in the United States.
	The Statue of Liberty was dedicated as nativism soared in the United States.
1891	Eleven Italian Americans were lynched in New Orleans during the height of American nativism after being accused of murdering a police superintendent.
1892	Ellis Island opened and replaced Castle Garden as the main port of entry for European immigrants.
1894	The Immigration Restriction League was organized in Boston by intellectuals to promote the passage of a bill that would require entering immigrants to pass a literacy test. The passage of the bill was urged to restrict immigration from southern and eastern Europe.
1899	William Z. Ripley's *The Races of Europe* was published. Ripley divided European people into three major racial groups, thus giving the nativists intellectual justifications for their movement.
1901–10	Almost 9 million immigrants entered the United States, most of whom came from southern and eastern Europe. This mass immigration intensified significantly the activities of nativistic groups.
1907	A congressional act extended the classes of immigrants excluded from the United States. Victims of tuberculosis and individuals who had committed certain kinds of crimes were added to the list.

Important Dates	Events
1911	The Dillingham Commission, formed in 1907, issued its forty-one volume report in which it strongly recommended a literacy test for entering immigrants and made a marked distinction between the "old" and "new" immigrants.
1916	Madison Grant, a well-known naturalist, published *The Passing of the Great Race in America.* This popular book gave the nativists more ammunition.
1916–19	The movement to Americanize aliens was widespread and intense.
1917	A comprehensive immigration bill was enacted that established the literacy test for entering immigrants, added to the classes of those excluded, and increased the head tax from $4 to $8. This act was a major victory for the nativists.
1919–20	During the height of antiradical attitudes in America, hundreds of alien radicals were captured and deported in a movement led by A. Mitchell Palmer.
1921	The Johnson Act signaled a turning point in American history. It set up a nationality quota system and imposed the first numerical limits on European immigration to the United States.
1924	The Johnson-Reed Act established extreme quotas on immigration and blatantly discriminated against southern and eastern European and non-White nations.
1927	Two Italian radicals, Nicola Sacco and Bartolomeo Vanzetti, were executed during a period of extreme antiradical sentiment in America. Their execution set off a wave of reactions throughout the Western world.
1952	The McCarran-Walter Act, which allegedly removed radical barriers to immigration, essentially continued the policy established in 1924 and was in some ways more restrictive.
1954	The closing of Ellis Island marked the end of mass European immigration to the United States.
1965	A new immigration act, which became effective in 1968, abolished the national origins quota system and liberalized significantly U.S. immigration policy.

Important Dates	Events
1984	Presidential and vice-presidential candidates of both major political parties appeared at the National Italian American Foundation dinner, indicating the continued importance of ethnicity to U.S. politicians.
1986	The Centennial of the Statue of Liberty was commemorated.
1990	The Immigration Act of 1990 made some significant changes in immigration law. It set immigration to 675,000 annually (beginning in 1995) to consist of these categories: 480,000 family-sponsored; 140,000 employment-based; and 55,000 "diversity immigrants."
	Ellis Island National Immigration Museum opened to honor the nation's immigrants.
1991	After disorder and fighting, the Communist USSR fell, leaving its former republics to create democracy in the chaotic aftermath.
1991–98	A significant number (386,327) of immigrants from nations in the former Soviet Union settled in the United States.

and Romania between 1981 and 1998. Canada was also a major source of White immigrants; 231,700 Canadians immigrated to the United States between 1981 and 1998.

Spaniards in the Americas

Spain was the first European nation to establish permanent settlements in the Americas. Spanish ships arrived in the Americas in 1492 under the leadership of Christopher Columbus. In 1496, Columbus and his brother Bartholomew founded the city of Santo Domingo on the island of Hispaniola. Santo Domingo was the first permanent continuing European settlement in the Americas. A number of Spanish explorers, including Coronado, Cortez, Cabeza de Vaca, and Ponce de Leon, followed Columbus. These and other Spaniards explored and settled in the Americas. In 1526, San Miguel de Gualdape, a Spanish colony in South Carolina, was established by Lucas Vasquez de Ayllon. Another Spaniard, named Pedro Menendez de Aviles, founded the oldest permanent city in the United States, St. Augustine, Florida, in 1565. These early Spaniards influenced the language, religion, and other cultural aspects of the Americas.

Even though their influence in the Americas was great, few Spaniards came to the Americas. It has been estimated that no more than 300,000 Spaniards came to the Americas during the entire three colonial centuries, and many of these people stayed only a short time. Many of the Spaniards who remained in America fathered children with Indian women. These unions produced a new ethnic group in the Americas, the *mestizos* (see Chapter 10 on Mexican Americans). Today, the number of Spanish-born Americans is still small. Between 1991 and 1998, only 14,677 people immigrated to the United States from Spain (U.S. Immigration and Naturalization Service, 2000).

More Europeans Come to America

Europeans began settling in America in significant numbers in the 1600s. The economic, social, and political conditions existing in Europe caused many of its inhabitants to cross the Atlantic searching for a new home. The main causes of the waves of immigrations were the drastic economic and social changes occurring in Europe. Serfdom had been the basis of European society for centuries. Most people were peasants who earned their living by farming. Throughout Europe, the old relationships between peasants and the land were changed and the peasants suffered severely. The land owned by the village was divided into individual plots. With each succeeding generation, the land was further divided. Eventually, the plots of land became so small that younger sons were unable to make a living. Some peasants suffered when land holdings were consolidated by the landlords.

The peasants became landless or feared the loss of land and their place in the social order because they were attached to the land. Without it, they were unable to make a living or maintain a sense of being. The tremendous population growth Europe experienced in the seventeenth and eighteenth centuries increased the peasants' problems. Famine and crop failures also caused many people to immigrate.

The early settlers were a diverse group, although most of them were peasants. Many were unable to pay for their passage and became indentured servants in order to make the journey. However, merchants, artisans, professionals, and laborers comprised a small, but significant, part of the immigrants during the entire colonial period. Vagrants and convicts, who were unwanted by European nations, were also among the first settlers.

Although the bulk of the first European immigrants came to North America primarily for economic reasons, some came for religious and political reasons. Most European nations had established churches associated with the state. Religious dissenters who wanted to practice other religions sometimes immigrated to America. The Separatists who arrived in the colonies in 1620 on the Mayflower were seeking a place where they could freely practice their religion. The Jewish immigrants who settled in North America during the colonial period also were seeking religious and political freedom.

Once the European immigrations were under way, the movement itself produced forces that stimulated it. The letters settlers sent back to friends and relatives in Europe extolling the opportunities in America were a cogent factor that pulled more Europeans to America (Kamphoefner, Helbich, & Sommer, 1991). Guidebooks about wages and living conditions in America were distributed in Europe by travel and shipping agents and helped to motivate thousands of Europeans to immigrate.

The rise of the industrial revolution and scientific farming in the nineteenth century also stimulated European immigration to America. The development of industry put many artisans out of work. Modern farming methods displaced many farmers. These displaced workers tried to solve their problems by immigrating to America. Ship companies eager to get passengers, and U.S. states and railroad companies that wanted to settle sparsely populated areas in the nation, recruited European immigrants. European governments either discouraged or legally prohibited immigration in the 1600s and 1700s. However, these obstacles to immigration were largely removed in the nineteenth century. This, too, encouraged Europeans to immigrate. The development of more efficient and inexpensive ocean transportation also stimulated European immigration in the nineteenth century.

Although all of these factors contributed to European immigration to America, it was the search for a chance to earn a better living that caused most European immigrants to come to the United States. The tide of immigration rose and fell with economic conditions in the United States. When times were good, the immigrants came in great numbers. When depression set in, immigration dropped significantly. During some brief periods, the number of immigrants returning to Europe actually exceeded the number that arrived. Historians estimate that about one third of the immigrants returned to Europe (Vecoli & Sinke, 1991). The key role that economic factors played in the European immigrations to North America make them similar to other mass movements to the United States from such nations as Canada, Mexico, the Philippines, China, and Japan.

Although some religious and political dissenters came to America so that they could freely practice their beliefs, this aspect of European immigration has been greatly exaggerated and oversimplified in textbooks and in the popular mind. Most came mainly for economic reasons. Most who were religious and political dissenters also hoped to improve their economic lot. The widespread belief that most of the first European settlers in America loved freedom and liberty has also been grossly exaggerated. The Puritans and other religious dissenters who settled in North America were not liberty-loving people but were doctrinaire groups who believed that their religions were the only true and valid ones. They were as intolerant of religious differences as those who protected the official churches in Europe (Jones, 1992). Their aim was to find a place where they could practice *their* religions freely and not to build a nation in which all religions would be tolerated.

Religious freedom and toleration developed in North America not because of the goals and wishes of the early colonists, but because the motley collection of religious groups that came to America competed for and won the right to practice their beliefs. The same is true about American democracy and the colonists. The colonists were Europeans in mind and spirit. They tried hard to establish European institutions and beliefs on American soil. They were not liberty-loving citizens who had a deep belief in democracy. Quite the contrary was true. They were the products of a hierarchical and class-structured society and had internalized these beliefs (Jones, 1992). That they failed to establish a highly stratified society in America was not because they did not try. Rather, a form of democracy emerged in the United States in part because the social and economic conditions that developed in North America made it impossible to establish a new Europe and fostered the development of a more open society. The ideas of the Enlightenment—which found a fertile ground in the British colonies—combined with the unique social, economic, and political conditions in the United States to produce American democracy.

The Passage to America

Especially in the seventeenth century, the journey from the peasants' European homes to the American port cities was hard and hazardous (Handlin, 1951). The peasants made the decision to come to America only after much thought. Often, only the threat of starvation or the loss of status compelled them to attempt the difficult journey. The trip was also expensive, especially during the first immigrations. Thus, even after they made the decision to come to America, they often had to save money for a long time before they could begin the trip.

The immigrants' first step in the journey to America was taking a long trip, usually by foot, to a European city that had a seaport from which ships sailed to America. Not everyone who started out was able to complete this stage of the journey. Many of those who made it to the European port cities were tired and battered. Once they arrived in the port city, the immigrants had to wait for weeks, and sometimes months, before the ship departed for America. The ship captains waited until the ships were full of goods and human cargo before they sailed for North America because the fuller ship was more profitable. During the long wait, the immigrants became restless and tired. Some were not able to board the ship when it was finally ready to depart. As each day went by during the long wait for the American departure, the food the immigrants had stored for the journey steadily dwindled. Renting a room at the European port city also took a large part of the meager funds they had saved for the trip.

Finally, the day came when the ship headed for America. The immigrants' joy at the departure was to be short-lived. The conditions on the ships were depressing and harsh. To maximize his profits, the ship captain packed the people in like sardines. Each family was assigned an extremely small space on the ship. The family spent most of its time in these dark, crowded compartments. Diseases were rampant on the vessels and took many lives. Dysentery, cholera, yellow fever, and smallpox were some of the more common ship diseases. The journey was long, often taking more than a month. Many families barely had enough food to last throughout the journey. Eventually, European nations passed laws requiring ship owners to provide a certain amount of food for the trip. However, ship captains who wanted to profit thought of many ingenious ways to evade these weakly enforced laws.

The Atlantic journey, especially before the time of the steamship, was a tremendous shock to the European immigrants. The family disruption that continued when they reached America began on the ship. Almost wholly dependent on the ship's crew, the father was unable to exercise his traditional role as leader and master of the family. The mother could not function in her traditional role, either. When food was getting scarce, she had to try to keep the family fed. These transatlantic conditions severely strained family relationships.

The immigrants who survived the journey eventually landed at an American port city. The landing was eagerly awaited and celebrated. However, the immigrants still had some hurdles to overcome. They had to be checked and questioned by American immigration officials before they could travel freely in America. Wrong answers to questions or poor health could mean further questioning by officials and boards, a stay in a hospital, or even a trip back to Europe. In the earliest years, the inspection focused on physical health and ability to work. Gradually, questions related to the immigrant's morals and political beliefs were added. In 1917, Congress enacted a law requiring immigrants to demonstrate literacy in some language before they could enter the United States.

Many of the immigrants were broken, both financially and physically, when they arrived at American seaport cities. Some were the sole survivors in their families. Broken and lonely, some found asylum in poorhouses. Many immigrants who had planned to settle elsewhere never left the port cities in which their vessels landed. Thousands who had planned to settle elsewhere stayed in cities like Milwaukee, Chicago, and St. Louis. Some of the first settlers found work on construction projects in cities. Later, railroad construction provided work for immigrants. When the industrial revolution began, factory work became available. In all these lines of work, the immigrants were paid low wages and were exploited by their employers. Many of the immigrants settled in urban areas. However, a large percentage of the nineteenth-century immigrants settled on farms and became successful farmers. Many Germans,

Scandinavians, Dutch, and Belgians settled in farm areas in the Midwest and successfully farmed (Vecoli, 1994).

The Urban Ghetto

Most European immigrants settled in cities, like most migrants from rural areas today. They had neither the means nor the desire to settle in rural areas. Like their modern counterparts, the new immigrants settled in blighted and dilapidated areas that became ethnic ghettos. Irishtowns, Germantowns, and Little Italys developed in most of the cities in the Northeast and Midwest. Ethnic organizations, like schools, newspapers, and churches, emerged within these communities. The immigrants, especially the more recent arrivals, usually lived in rundown housing near the business and manufacturing districts that had been vacated by suburban-bound, upwardly mobile residents when the manufacturing district sprawled outward into their communities.

When the upwardly mobile left the inner city, their old mansions were converted into multiple-family dwellings for the immigrants. The multiple-dwelling units became a source of quick profit for the owners. Little was done to make these dwellings comfortable. Profit, not comfort, was what the slum landlord sought. When these neighborhoods were deserted by the old residents, they were also forsaken by the street cleaners and sanitation crews. The smells from the garbage were pungent. The immigrants' habits of throwing garbage out of the window and keeping animals in their back yards made these communities even more unpleasant. High-rise apartments went up in some of the ethnic communities. Most of these buildings were crowded and uncomfortable. Many did not have interior plumbing or central heating. Some of the earliest ones had no toilets. There were only two toilets on each floor in some later apartment buildings. To help pay the rent, some families took in lodgers.

The immigrants looked forward to the day when their income would permit them to leave the ghetto and join the exodus to the suburbs. For most ethnic groups, this day eventually came. However, as one ethnic group vacated the ghetto, another group replaced it. In New York City, Italians took over old Irish neighborhoods. Jews from Russia and Poland occupied districts where the Germans had lived. After World War II, many of the urban areas that had been occupied by European ethnic groups received a large number of African Americans from the South, Mexican Americans from the Southwest, and migrants from Puerto Rico.

Immigrant Political Action

The participation of the immigrants in the urban political machines, though significant, was not the total of their importance in the U.S. political process. Early in U.S. political history, when the number of immigrants in U.S. cities became substantial and their votes had the power to sway or determine election outcomes, politicians became increasingly sensitive to the concerns and wishes of immigrant groups. Even politicians like Theodore Roosevelt and Woodrow Wilson, who felt rather negatively about the "new" immigrants, were forced on occasion to say positive things about them publicly. However, it was difficult for President Wilson to convince the southern and eastern European immigrants that he had had a change of heart.

Nevertheless, the major political parties began to vie aggressively for immigrant support and to include references to immigrants in their political platforms that reflected the specialized concerns of ethnic groups in the United States. These groups had many special concerns and aspirations, usually related to U.S. foreign policy and the ways in which the United States was treating their "Mother" countries. Although many European immigrants did not have much of a sense of nationality when they arrived in the United States, intense nationalist movements developed among them. According to Jones (1960), "There was a tendency among Irish political refugees as well as German Forty-eighters, to look upon themselves as exiles and to use the United States simply as a base for promoting European causes…. [These movements] afforded a means of group identification and self-assertion" (pp. 141–142).

Although the actions of these political refugees were probably extreme, most European immigrant groups did continue to see themselves as Europeans. The immigrants formed many groups to campaign aggressively for European causes and to sway U.S. foreign policy. In World War I, German Americans criticized Wilson's actions toward Germany and the Irish Americans became bitter because of Wilson's pro-British actions. The Irish voted strongly against Wilson in the subsequent election. The militant actions by some European American groups, especially German Americans, caused many Americans to question seriously their loyalties to the United States. However, even though some of these movements were radical and aggressively nationalistic, the most radical ones were unable to attract mass support because of the deep conservatism of most immigrants.

Anglo-Saxon Cultural Dominance

The early European settlements were highly ethnically mixed. English, Scots-Irish, Germans, French Huguenots, Africans, and Jews were among the earlier colonists. Writes Bailey (1961):

> The population of the thirteen colonies, though basically Anglo-Saxon, was perhaps the most mixed that could be found anywhere in the world. Counting [Africans], nearly 40% was of non-English origin, although New England boasted more native born and persons of English blood than the other sections. Of the 56 signers of the Declaration of Independence in 1776, 18 were non-English, and 8 of these had been born outside the colonies" (p. 67).

Ethnic conflict also developed early in the colonies. The English were dominant during the first years of colonial settlement. Consequently, they shaped the basic social and political institutions of Colonial America. The English cultural dominance of the colonies was challenged by subsequent groups, but it remained the dominant social and political force in American life. Because of English political and cultural dominance, Anglo-Saxon culture became the ideal by which all subsequent ethnic groups were judged and by which levels of assimilation and acculturation were judged. To become *acculturated* became synonymous with acquiring Anglo-Saxon Protestant lifestyles, values, and language. The English language was dominant in almost every American colony by 1775.

Early in American colonial life, non-English groups began to be evaluated negatively. The New England colonies, which were predominantly English, took steps to bar the settlements of Roman Catholics. The French Huguenots became the focal point of English hostility. Later, the Scots-Irish and the German immigrants were the victims of English antagonism. An English mob prevented a group of Irish immigrants from landing in Boston in 1729. Several years later, another mob destroyed a new Scots-Irish Presbyterian church in Worcester, Massachusetts. The attitude that English culture and institutions were superior to all others profoundly shaped American life and was extremely significant in the nativistic movements that emerged after the Civil War. However, when the southern and eastern European immigrants began their mass exodus to the United States in the late 1800s, public opinion leaders extended the supposedly superior traits of the English to all northern and western European "races." (In the nineteenth century, Europeans were considered to belong to several races, such as the Teutonic, the Alpine, and the Mediterranean. The races of northern and western Europe were considered superior to the races in southern, central, and eastern Europe.) This extension was necessary to enable the old immigrants to band together to condemn the new immigrants. However, race assumed a new meaning when the southern and eastern European groups attained acceptable levels of assimilation in the twentieth century. All White races became one (Brodkin, 1998). Racial hostilities could now focus on non-White ethnic groups, such as African Americans, Asian Americans, Mexican Americans, and American Indians. Whites of southern and eastern European descent joined former adverse White ethnic groups to exclude people of color from full participation in U.S. life.

The Southern and Eastern European Immigrants

Before 1892, most European immigrants who came to America were from northern and western European nations, such as England, Germany, France, and Scandinavia. Northern and western Europeans exceeded the number of immigrants from other parts of Europe up to the last decades of the nineteenth century. However, by 1896, a major change had taken place in the source of European immigrants to the United States. Most European immigrants to America now came from southern, eastern, and central Europe. Austria-Hungary, Italy, and Russia sent the largest number of new immigrants. However, substantial numbers also came from such countries as Greece, Romania, Bulgaria, and Finland. Fifteen million European immigrants arrived in the United States between 1890 and 1914, most of them from southern and eastern Europe.

When immigrants from southern and eastern Europe began coming to the United States in significant numbers, a number of arguments evolved that were designed to distinguish them from immigrants who had come earlier from the northern and western parts of Europe. The southern and eastern immigrants became known as the "new" immigrants; the earlier immigrants were referred to as the "old" immigrants. The mass media, intellectuals, and politicians perpetuated the myth that the new immigrants were inferior to the older ones, that they caused major problems in the cities, and that steamship companies and U.S. industries eager for unskilled labor were the main causes of the new traffic. The Dillingham Commission, formed to investigate immigration in 1907, concluded that there was a fundamental difference in both the character and the causes of the new and old immigrations.

Repetition of this myth became evidence of its validity. It was eagerly embraced by writers, historians, and policymakers and significantly influenced the racist immigration legislation enacted in the 1920s. The nativistic movements reached their zenith in the 1920s and chose the southern and eastern European immigrants as their chief targets. Only the Asian immigrants in California were more harshly criticized. The distinctions made between the old and the new immigrants were artificial and based on inaccurate information and false assumptions. The southern and eastern European immigrants came to the United States for the same reasons that the earlier immigrants had come: to improve their economic conditions and to seek religious and political freedom. Steamship lines and U.S. industries played no greater role in stimulating immigration from southern and eastern Europe than they had in stimulating immigration from other parts of Europe. In both cases, their influence was rather meager and has been grossly exaggerated.

The types of new immigrants who came from southern and eastern Europe, like the older immigrants, were highly diverse. Some southern and eastern Europeans came to the United States for temporary work, not because of something unique about them, but because the new steamship lines had so greatly reduced the length of the Atlantic trip that it was practical and possible to come to the United States for seasonal work.

Southern and eastern European immigrants were judged as being innately inferior to older Americans partly because they started coming to the United

States when the notion that the United States should be an asylum for the oppressed peoples of Europe was beginning to wane. When the Statue of Liberty was dedicated in New York City in 1886, many Americans had lost faith in the poetic words penned by Emma Lazarus about Europe's "huddled masses." They had also begun to question the melting pot theory and to raise serious questions about whether Europeans could be as readily assimilated as they had originally believed. The doubts about the new immigrants were not caused by their inability to be assimilated, but by the conditions and conceptions of foreigners emerging within American life. Thus, the rush of southern and eastern European immigrants to the United States was poorly timed. The internal conditions in the United States were giving birth to distinctly antiforeign attitudes. A scapegoat was needed to blame for urban blight, political corruption in the cities, and economic recession. The new immigrants were vulnerable and convenient targets. Consequently, they were judged intellectually and culturally inferior to the old immigrants and declared unassimilable. That they were an inferior "race" became widely accepted both in the intellectual community and in the popular mind.

Nativistic Movements

As early as 1727, nativistic feelings toward the Germans in Pennsylvania ran high. (*Nativism* was a movement designed to restrict immigration to the United States and to protect the interests of the native-born. It was an extreme form of nationalism and ethnocentrism.) To discourage further foreign settlement in the colony, Pennsylvania passed a statute in 1729 increasing the head tax on foreigners, allegedly to prevent persons likely to become public charges from entering the colony. Other antiforeign legislation emerged in the eighteenth century. In 1798, Congress, dominated by the Federalists, passed the Alien and Sedition Acts to crush the Republican party by destroying its large base of immigrant support. These acts were also designed to silence criticism of the Federalists and to harass European immigrants. The Alien and Sedition Acts lengthened the time required to become a U.S. citizen from five to fourteen years and gave the president almost unlimited control over the behavior of immigrants, virtually nullifying the freedoms of speech and the press.

Nativistic sentiments continued to ebb and flow during the eighteenth and nineteenth centuries, although their most violent expressions did not arise until the late nineteenth and early twentieth centuries (Bennett, 1988). Nativism reached its zenith in the 1920s, culminating with the passage of the Johnson-Reed Act in 1924. The Know-Nothing movement, which emerged in the 1840s and reached its climax in 1855, was one of the most successful nativistic movements in the nineteenth century. The various secret organizations constituting this movement, such as the Order of United Americans and the Order of the Star-Spangled Banner, were strongly anti-Catholic and agitated for an extension of the period required for an immigrant to become a U.S. citizen and for the election of only "Americans" to political office. The movement, which became less secretive in 1855 and openly called itself the American Party, enjoyed tremendous political successes in a number of states in the 1855 elections. However, the Know-Nothing movement died as quickly as it had emerged. Conflict over slavery within the American Party severely strained and weakened it. Nativistic sentiments in the United States in the 1850s were not strong enough to sustain the Know-Nothing movement.

By the late 1800s, anti-Chinese agitation on the West Coast was virulent, and race ideologies emerged to justify it (Takaki, 1993). The concept of the inferiority and superiority of various races became rampant in the West. In 1882, Congress passed the Chinese Exclusion Act, the first immigration bill specifically designed to exclude a particular race. Although many Americans viewed the case of the Chinese as separate from European immigration, the anti-Chinese act gave impetus to antiforeign attitudes throughout U.S. society. Three months after the anti-Chinese bill was passed, Congress enacted a bill further restricting the classes of Europeans who could enter the United States. Convicts, idiots, and lunatics, as well as those who might become public charges, were excluded.

Nativism grew more and more intense as the fear soared of a Catholic takeover of the federal government and of foreign radicals. The big jump in the number of southern and eastern European immigrants entering the United States in the 1900s added fuel to the fire. Cries of "100% Americanism" and "America for Americans" became widespread. Agitations for antiforeign legislation became intense, especially legislation that would exclude foreign "radicals" and require immigrants to pass a literacy test.

Congress, responding to pressure in 1885, passed the Foran Act, which prohibited the importation of contract labor from Europe. Violence also erupted during these turbulent times. Italians and Jews were frequently the victims of violent and outrageous acts. Eleven Italians were murdered in a mass lynching in New Orleans in 1891, when they were accused of killing a police superintendent. Riots directed at Jews in Chicago increased public paranoia about foreign "radicals." Congress further extended the classes of immigrants excluded from the United States in 1907. Imbeciles and victims of tuberculosis were now added to the list.

Nativistic movements, which were directed against most Irish Catholics and German radicals in the 1850s, began to focus increasingly on southern and eastern European immigrants as masses of them arrived in U.S. cities. The intellectual community legitimized the racist myths about the innate inferiority of southern and eastern Europeans (Tucker, 1994). William Z. Ripley was one of the leading intellectual nativists. His book, *The Races of Europe,* published in 1899, divided Whites into three major races: the Teutonic, the Northern blondes; the Alpine, the central race of stocky roundheads; and the Mediterranean, dark and slender longheads (Higham, 1972). The Teutonic was the superior race. Ripley warned against a racial mixture that would pollute the superior race with southern and eastern European racial groups.

Madison Grant (1916), a well-known naturalist, also argued for racial purity in his popular book, *The Passing of the Great Race in America*, published in 1916. Ripley and Grant, as well as other intellectuals and writers in the early twentieth century, provided the nativists with the scientific and intellectual justifications for their movements and issued a ringing plea for restrictive legislation (Higham, 1972; Smedley, 1993). As in other periods of mass hysteria in America, social and physical scientists justified and legitimized prevailing social attitudes and myths (Tucker, 1994).

When the twentieth century opened, nativist sentiments and attitudes had gained tremendous momentum in U.S. life. They did not subside until they culminated in the extreme restrictive legislation enacted in the 1920s. The Dillingham Commission, which issued its report in 1911, noted that the new European immigrants were essentially different from the old and strongly recommended the passage of a bill that would require immigrants to pass a literacy test. Agitation for a literacy test bill became intense, but the advocates of the bill faced repeated opposition in Congress and from President Wilson. As the United States prepared to enter World War I, nativism—directed especially at German Americans—became intense. Patriotic groups demanded that all aspects of German culture, including music and the names of streets and schools, be eradicated in the United States. Although most German Americans were loyal citizens during this period, they were often the victims of harassment. However, the abuses they endured were less severe than those suffered by Japanese Americans during World War II (see Chapter 13).

Just before the United States entered World War I, the literacy bill advocates finally mustered enough congressional votes to override a second Wilson veto, and the literacy bill was passed on February 5, 1917. Adult immigrants now had to be able to read a passage in some language before they could enter the United States. The bill was comprehensive. It codified existing legislation and added vagrants, chronic alcoholics, and psychopaths to the list of excluded aliens. The head tax was increased from $4 to $8 (Higham, 1972). Although nativists celebrated their victory, they began immediately to plan strategies to restrict further immigration to the United States.

Campaigns to "Americanize" aliens already in the United States became a national passion during World War I. When the war ended, Congress was pressured again to enact restrictive legislation. The law requiring immigrants to pass a literacy test did not halt immigration as the nativists had thought. In fact, it reduced it very little. Consequently, nativists pushed for a quota system to restrict immigration. Antiforeign groups and organizations experienced tremendous growth in memberships. The Ku Klux Klan grew greatly in the South and Midwest. It had more than 2½ million members by 1923. The phenomenal growth of the Klan was symptomatic of pervasive antiforeign attitudes in U.S. life.

Eventually, the nativistic forces gained congressional victories. The Johnson Act, enacted in 1921, marked a turning point in the history of American immigration. The Johnson Act established a nationality quota system and imposed the first numerical limits on immigration from European nations. The quota system was based on the various nationality groups in the United States. The most important immigration bill of this period was enacted in 1924, the Johnson-Reed Act. The quotas this act set were severe and blatantly discriminated against southern and eastern European and non-White nations. It stopped Asian immigration completely. After 1927, the act allowed only 150,000 Europeans to enter the United States each year, and they were "parceled out in ratio to the distribution of national origins in the White population of the United States in 1920." Because Europeans from the North and West represented the largest percentages of Whites in the United States in 1920, the authors of the Johnson-Reed Act had thought of an ingenious way to limit severely the number of immigrants from southern and eastern Europe, while assuring that a significant number were allowed to enter from the North and West. Nativism had triumphed, and an important chapter in U.S. history had been closed.

Subsequent Immigration Acts

There was little change in U.S. immigration policy from 1924 until the outbreak of World War II. A number of Europeans were displaced by the events of World War II and sought asylum as refugees in the United States. After much debate, a Displaced Persons Act was passed in 1948, which permitted about 400,000 refugees to enter the United States during a four-year period. The Mc-Carran-Walter Act, passed in 1952, allegedly to remove racial barriers to immigration, essentially continued the policy established in 1924 and was, in some ways, more restrictive. In 1953, Congress passed a temporary measure, the Refugee Relief Act, to enable refugees from Communist nations to settle in the United States. However, major reform in U.S. immigration policy was not made until 1965. President John F. Kennedy had strongly urged Congress to pass an enlightened immigration act. After much discussion and vigorous debate, the bill finally became a reality during the Johnson administration on July 1, 1968. This act abolished the national origins quota system and allowed 170,000 persons to enter the United States each year from the Eastern Hemisphere and 120,000 from the Western Hemisphere. Technical skill and family ties, rather than country of origin, became the major criteria for admitting immigrants to the United States. This bill was a major victory for liberal-thinking Americans and is a tribute to American democratic ideals.

Congress enacted a comprehensive immigration bill, the Immigration Reform and Control Act, on November 6, 1986 (U.S. Immigration and Naturalization Service, 1998). This act allowed aliens who had been in the United States illegally since January 1, 1982, to attain temporary and then permanent resident status. It also established sanctions for employers who knowingly hired illegal aliens. The Immigration Act of 1990 initiated a major overhaul of immigration law. It increased immigration to a flexible limit of 675,000 annually, beginning in 1995. The 675,000 level was to consist of 480,000 family-sponsored immigrants, 140,000 employment-based immigrants, and 55,000 "diversity immigrants" (U.S. Immigration and Naturalization Service, 1998).

European Ethnic Groups in U.S. Society

The mass settlement of Europeans in North America was a unique phenomena in human history. Almost 60 million immigrants (59,795,158) entered the United States between 1820 and 1992 (U.S. Department of Justice, 1998). Most came from Europe, and represented many religious, political, and cultural groups. Yet the United States, by forcing the immigrants to acquire the culture of the dominant society, was able to prevent the Balkanization of America and to establish a unified society. The immigrants paid a heavy price for cultural assimilation and acculturation. Nevertheless, a rather culturally homogeneous society emerged, although ethnicity is still a viable but complex force in U.S. life.

When European immigrants arrived on America's shores, their thoughts, feelings, aspirations, and attitudes were decidedly European. Many immigrants aggressively tried to build European institutions in the United States. They tried to maintain their religious life by building churches similar to those in Europe. They established parochial schools, ethnic newspapers, ethnic theaters, and self-help organizations in their attempts to hold onto the old order. Some groups, such as the German Americans, created ethnic colonies, where their European cultures and ethnic kinships could flourish. Despite the concerted efforts by the immigrants to establish European institutions in the United States, these attempts were, by and large, destined to fail. Forces within American life worked against them and eventually eroded or greatly modified most European cultures in the United States.

The public schools, the U.S. press, and U.S. political institutions played key roles in mitigating the attempts to establish and maintain European institutions on U.S. soil. By the beginning of the nineteenth century, the English dominated most U.S. institutions, such as the schools, the courts, and the popular press. The immigrants and their children often found it necessary to acquire Anglo-Saxon cultural traits before they were allowed to participate fully in U.S. society. School teachers demeaned foreign languages; employers often preferred to hire assimilated immigrants. European Americans, especially the second generation, often responded to these cogent forces by becoming ashamed of their ethnic cultures, deliberately denying them, such as by Anglicizing or changing their surnames, and actively seeking to assimilate. Many second- and third-generation immigrants became—in mores, values, and outlook—similar to Anglo-Saxon Protestants. These immigrants paid a tremendous psychological price for denying their cultures, languages, and identities. However, as Greenbaum (1974) has perceptively written, the larger society shamed the immigrants into abandoning their ethnic cultures, but held out to them the hope of economic and structural inclusion into the mainstream society. White ethnic groups, unlike people of color, were able to attain full inclusion into the mainstream society and to experience social-class mobility once they were culturally identical to Anglo-Saxon Protestants.

The New Ethnicity

During the 1950s, social scientists expected most ethnic characteristics eventually to disappear in the United States and a modernized, shared culture to evolve. In this common national culture, social class would persist but factors such as race and ethnicity would be largely unimportant.

Glazer and Moynihan, in their 1963 pathbreaking book *Beyond the Melting Pot* (1970), presented one of the first theoretical arguments that the melting pot conception of the United States was inaccurate and incomplete. They argued that ethnicity in New York was important and that it would continue to be important for both politics and culture. Significantly, they included case studies of the persistence of ethnicity among three White ethnic groups: the Jews, Italians, and Irish of New York City. They described how ethnicity persisted among these groups in politics and family structure.

During the 1960s, the civil rights movement emerged. This movement made ethnicity more legitimate. African Americans made claims on the federal government and other institutions because of the historic discrimination they experienced in the United States. The Black civil rights movement stimulated ethnic revitalization movements among other ethnic groups, such as American Indians and Mexican Americans, and among White ethnic groups, such as Jews, Poles, Italians, and Greeks. Southern, eastern, and central European ethnic groups were the most active participants in the White ethnic revitalization movements that emerged in the early 1970s.

These ethnic groups, through leaders and organizations, began to articulate ways in which they had been victims of ethnic stereotypes and discrimination, and how their histories and cultures had been omitted from history books and the school curriculum. They argued that, like Blacks, Indians, and Mexican Americans, they needed public policies that would enable them to acquire more equity and cultural democracy. Michael Novak, an articulate theologian and humanist, became the most prolific speaker and writer for what he called the "unmeltable ethnics." His book, *The Rise of the Unmeltable Ethnics,* published in 1971, signaled the birth of the "new pluralism" among White ethnic groups.

In this widely reviewed and quoted book, Novak identified the "unmeltable ethnics" (Poles, Italians, Greeks, and Slavs), tried to explain how they were both different from and culturally alienated from Anglo-Saxon Protestants, and described how they were victims of discrimination, cultural arrogance, and the intellectual community. In moving prose, Novak also described how he and other Slavs were forced to deny their cultural identities. He wrote (1971): "The estrangement I have come to feel derives not only from a lack of family history. Early in life, I was made to feel a slight uneasiness when I said my name.... Liberal education tends to separate children from parents, from their roots, from their history, in the cause of a universal and superior religion" (pp. 64, 69).

Novak (1971) urged opinion leaders and politicians to recognize and respect the cultures of the White ethnics and predicted that they would be a powerful political force during the 1970s. He called the 1970s "the decade of the White ethnics." While Novak was arguing for the civil rights of White ethnics and attempting to mobilize them politically, researchers such as Andrew M. Greeley and William C. McCready were studying the extent to which ethnicity had survived among White ethnic groups, including the Irish Americans. In their 1974 article, they described significant differences among the Anglo-Saxons, the Irish, and the Italians on personality variables, political participation, and attitudes toward sexuality and drinking. Publications that focused on the new ethnicity of White ethnic groups also emerged. *Ethnicity*, a journal published between 1974 and 1982, included a number of articles describing the cultural differences among White ethnic groups.

The ethnic revitalization movements among White ethnic groups during the 1970s evoked considerable controversy. Some scholars argued that the White ethnic movement was not genuine but was a racist political movement designed to divert attention from the legitimate needs of ethnic groups of color, such as African Americans and Mexican Americans. Other critics argued that the movement was a "me-too," contrived movement. Critics of the new ethnic movements included scholars such as Orlando Patterson (1977), a Harvard sociologist, and distinguished historian Arthur Mann. Wrote Mann (1979): "The White ethnic revival was the product of a seriously divisive movement in history. Like previous revivals in America and elsewhere, secular as well as religious, the 1960s–1970s movement rested on the belief that the only way out for a troubled people lay in the return to a previous but languishing heritage" (pp. 41–42). Two anthropologists, Stein and Hill (1977), published a book-length work on the White ethnic movement in which they harshly criticized it. They wrote: "The New Ethnicity, then, is both a symptomatic expression of a disintegrated life and an attempt to cope with this sense of personal disintegration through regression to an earlier stage in individual development" (p. 9).

Scholars and civil rights leaders who defended the White ethnic movement argued that it was a genuine movement that had emerged in response to cultural assaults, discrimination, and epithets used to describe White ethnics by the liberal press. White ethnic leaders argued that those who dismissed the new pluralism as a "racist movement" had completely misunderstood its nature and complexity and were using a code word to dismiss it summarily.

White Ethnic Groups Today: Into the Twilight of Ethnicity?

Most of the fervor of the ethnic revival movement of the 1970s has disappeared. Most European Americans, as they were in the 1970s, were continuing down the road toward assimilation into the mainstream society. The ethnic movement among White ethnic groups during the 1970s involved primarily ethnic leaders and intellectuals and not common men and women. As Alba (1985) indicates, the fact that ethnic leaders and intellectuals were able to articulate their rage and concerns in the mainstream media and intellectual community indicated that White ethnic groups had attained a significant level of structural inclusion into the mainstream society.

A lasting legacy of the White ethnic movement, and of the ethnic movements in the 1970s, is that ethnicity is more legitimate in the United States today than it was before the 1970s. Many Poles, Italians, and Yugoslavs no longer feel that they need to change their names or to become completely alienated from their ethnic culture in order to realize the American dream and attain economic and social mobility. Many social, political, and scholarly organizations are working to secure visibility and rights for European ethnic groups, including organizations such as the Illinois Consultation on Ethnicity in Education and the American Italian Historical Association. While many members of White ethnic groups are becoming more assimilated into the mainstream society, continuing immigration from Europe infuses some European ethnic groups, such as Greeks and Italians, with heavy doses of ethnic culture each year. Even though groups like the Greeks and Italians may have entered the twilight of ethnicity, as Alba (1985) claims, new infusions of immigrants and various political and social events continue to renew ethnicity in the United States. The large number of immigrants that arrived in the United States from the nations of the former Soviet Union between 1990 and 1998 is the most recent example of how White ethnic groups and cultures are continually becoming parts of the United States.

Teaching Strategies

To illustrate how content related to European Americans can be used to integrate the curriculum, exemplary strategies are identified for teaching these concepts at the grade levels indicated: *cultural contributions* (primary grades), *immigration* (intermediate and upper grades), and *nativism* (high school grades).

Primary Grades

CONCEPT

Cultural Contributions
Generalization: Our ancestors came from many different nations and belonged to many ethnic groups. All of these groups made outstanding contributions to American life.

1. To collect the information needed for this unit, duplicate the following letter and give each child one to take home. Tell the pupils to ask their parents to complete the form and return it to you the next day.

Name of Child _____

Ethnic Groups

English	Jewish (Specify nation)
Scottish	African American
Welsh	American Indian
German	Mexican American
Irish	Asian American (Specify nation)
Italian	Puerto Rican
Polish	Other(s) (Please specify)
Russian	

Dear Parents:

To help our students understand and appreciate the contributions all ethnic groups have made to American life, we are studying about ethnic groups and their role in America. I want to make sure that we study the ethnic heritages of all of my students. To do this, I need your help. Would you please study the list above and place an "X" by the group indicating your child's ethnic heritage. If your child has a mixed heritage, such as "English" and "Russian," please check both of these. However, please try to limit your checks to three by checking only the main strains in your child's ethnic heritage. The list above is based on the categories used by the U.S. Bureau of the Census. They represent the largest ethnic groups in the United States. However, many American ethnic groups are not included. If your child's ethnic heritage is not listed, please check "Other" and fill in the name(s) of your child's ethnic group(s), such as "Spanish" or "French."

Please send this form back to me tomorrow morning. Thank you very much for your cooperation. I am sure that your response will help us to have a much better unit.

Sincerely,

Ms. Rosa Rivera
Third Grade Teacher

2. When you have received the forms from the parents, make a table, showing the ethnic groups represented in your class. Put the table on butcher paper and list the children's names under the appropriate ethnic categories. Your table might look like Table 8.2.

3. Discuss the table with the students, noting that our ancestors came from many different nations. Using a primary globe, locate and write the names of some of the nations and continents from which the children's ancestors came, such as Great Britain, Africa, and Germany. Discuss these nations and continents with the students.

4. Using the photographs in a book such as *Ellis Island: An Illustrated History of the Immigrant Experience* by Ivan Chermayeff, Fred Wasserman, and Mary J. Shapiro (1991), tell the students the story of the great immigrations from Europe. Point out some of the reasons the immigrants came, how they came, and how they settled in the United States. The special case of the African Americans, as well as immigrants from other nations of color, should also be discussed.

5. Make another table on butcher paper listing the major ethnic groups represented in your class and other major U.S. ethnic groups. Under each major group, list some famous Americans and the fields in which they have made outstanding contributions to American life. Your table might look like Table 8.3. Many books contain information about the ethnic backgrounds of famous Americans (see the annotated bibliographies in this chapter and in other chapters in Parts II through V of this book).

TABLE 8.2 Our Ethnic Heritages

English	Irish	Italian	German	African American	Polish
Susie	Cathy	Roy	*Pete	Jack	Linda
John	*Pete	Pat	Ray	Sam	Terry

*Pete has both Irish and German ancestors. Some of the children might be listed under several categories.

TABLE 8.3 Famous Ethnic Americans

English	Italian	African American	Polish
George Washington, *President*	Joe DiMaggio, *Baseball player*	Benjamin Banneker, *Scientist*	Helena Modjeska, *Actress*
Benjamin Franklin, *Scientist*	Frank Sinatra, *Singer*	Martin L. King, *Civil rights leader*	Edmund S. Muskie, *U.S. Senator*

6. After you have completed the Famous Ethnic Americans table, making sure that all the children's ethnic heritages are represented, discuss the table with the students, and help them to formulate, in their own words, the following generalization: *Our ancestors came from many different lands and groups, and all these groups made many outstanding contributions to American life.*

   Make sure that each child knows at least one famous person who belongs to his or her ethnic group. This exercise must be modified in classrooms in which there is only one ethnic group. Use some famous Americans from the students' own ethnic group, but also select heroes and heroines from at least five or six other ethnic groups not represented in your classroom.

Intermediate and Upper Grades

CONCEPT

Immigration

Generalization: Europeans immigrated to the United States for various economic, political, and social reasons. Their experiences in the United States were both similar and different.

1. To help the students gain the needed content background to study American immigration, assign appropriate readings that will enable them to answer the following questions about the first or old immigrants to America:
   a. What European nations did the first immigrants to America come from during the colonial period?
   b. Why did they come?
   c. Was America like they expected? If so, in what ways? If not, why not? Explain.
2. After the students have completed their reading assignments, discuss the three questions above with the class. During the discussion, list on the board the reasons that various groups immigrated to the United States. When the reasons have been listed, group them, with the class, into three or four categories, such as "economic," "political," and "social" reasons.
3. Ask the students to read about the new immigrants who came to the United States from Europe in the late 1800s and early 1900s. These immigrants came primarily from southern and eastern Europe and included Ukrainians, Russian Jews, Poles, Italians, Greeks, and many other groups. The students should discuss the same three questions about these immigrants that they had discussed after reading about the old immigrants.
4. After the students have read and discussed the old and new immigrants, they should compare and contrast these groups. The following questions can be used to guide discussion:
   a. Did the old and new immigrants come to the United States for similar or different reasons? Explain.
   b. How did the new immigrants differ from the old? Why?
   c. How did American life differ at the times when the old and new immigrants came to America? How did this difference affect the adjustment of the newly arrived immigrants?

    d. Both the old and the new immigrants experienced problems on the trip across the Atlantic. How were these problems similar and different?

    e. How were the problems of settlement and finding jobs in America similar and different for the two groups of immigrants?

    f. Ethnic conflict developed early during the settlement of European nationality groups in America. What problems of prejudice and discrimination were experienced by the various groups? Which groups of immigrants were discriminated against the most? The least? Why?

    The students can summarize this phase of the unit by making a data-retrieval chart to summarize and compare information about major ethnic groups representing old and new immigrants, similar to Table 8.4.

5. To help the students gain a feeling for the harshness of the journey across the Atlantic that the immigrants experienced, read aloud to them Chapter 2, "The Crossing," in Oscar Handlin (1951), *The Uprooted*. The class can develop a dramatization of the passage as described in Handlin and present it in a school assembly. The entire class should be involved in writing and presenting the dramatization.

6. European immigrants in the United States often wrote to their friends and relatives in Europe describing the wonders of America and, occasionally, their problems. These two books contain letters that German and Norwegian immigrants wrote home: Walter D. Kamphoefner, Wolfgang Helbich, and Ulrike Sommer (1991), *News from the Land of Freedom: Immigrants Write Home;* Solveig Zempel (1990), *In Their Own Words: Letters from Norwegian Immigrants*.

    Read and discuss selected letters from these two books (or similar ones) with the class. Ask the students to pretend that they are new European immigrants in the United States in the 1800s. They should write to a friend or relative in Europe telling about their experiences. This activity can be correlated with the language arts.

7. Have the students role-play the situation below, which involves a poor Italian farmer and an agent of a steamship company who tries to persuade the farmer to immigrate to the United States. After the role-playing situation, ask the students the questions that follow.

Mr. Pareto, a Poor Italian Farmer in Southern Italy in the 1800s
Mr. Pareto is in his thirties. He is a hard worker and is close to his family, which includes his wife, eight children, and both of his parents. For the past three years, Mr. Pareto has been unable to feed and clothe his family well because of severe crop failures. He has heard about the greatness of America and has often thought about going there. However, he knows that his father feels he should stay in Italy so that he can depend on him in his old age. He also realizes that, if he goes to America, he will have to leave his wife and children in Italy.

Mr. Rossi, an Agent for a Steamship Company That Makes Trips to America
Mr. Rossi tries to persuade Italian men to immigrate to America. The more men that he can persuade to go to America on his company's steamship line, the more money he makes. He goes up to Mr. Pareto at the village market and

TABLE 8.4 Generalizing about the Old and New European Immigrants

	Old Immigrants				New Immigrants Southern and Eastern		
	English	Irish	Germans		Italians	Jews	Poles
Reasons for immigrating							
Kinds of people in group							
Problems on Atlantic journey							
Problems of settlement							
Prejudice and discrimination experienced							
Immigration laws in European country of origin							
Relationships *within* the nationality group							

tells him about the wonders of America and why he should go there. He tells him that he can obtain a job quickly in America and become a wealthy man. He knows that if Mr. Pareto goes to America he will not be able to take his family. However, Mr. Rossi tells Mr. Pareto that he will be able to send for his family within two or three months after he arrives in America.

Questions
1. Did Mr. Rossi persuade Mr. Pareto to go to America? Why or why not?
2. If Mr. Pareto goes to America, what do you think will happen to his family?
3. If Mr. Pareto stays in Italy, how do you think he will take care of his family?
4. How do you think his wife, parents, and children will react if Mr. Pareto goes to America? Why?
5. What else can Mr. Pareto do besides stay in his Italian village or immigrate to America?
6. If you were Mr. Pareto, would you immigrate to America? Why or why not? Explain.
7. Conclude this unit by viewing and discussing a videotape about European immigration.

VALUING ACTIVITY

Many European immigrants, especially those from southern and eastern Europe, changed their names and adopted Anglo-American culture characteristics so that they could assimilate more quickly into the dominant society and experience rapid social, economic, and political mobility. Other immigrants, however, even though they were the victims of affronts by the larger society, tried to hold onto their names and ethnic cultural characteristics in America. In the following selection, written in 1939, a Polish American tells why he did not want to change his name. Read the selection to your students and ask them the questions that follow the selection.

I Was Ashamed of My Name

Twenty-odd years ago I was ashamed of my Polish name and heritage. To the boys in the neighborhood I was the lone "dirty Polack." This rankled, burned, and developed in me a bitter sense of inferiority. There was no Poland...I was no Polack! I was American! I didn't want to be a Polack! I would not go to a Polish school! If my parents spoke to me in Polish, I would answer in English. I dreamed of going West, changing my name to Edward R. Edwards, and being American. The end of the war and the Versailles Treaty brought some consolation. Now there was a Poland! True, we didn't hear much about it, but we knew it was there. We had found peace.

In high school, a teacher who had trouble with my name started calling me Scott. Others followed suit. I tried to convince people my name wasn't Scott but Kostyra. Some refused to accept the more difficult name. Mail came to my home for me addressed to Scott. My parents soundly berated me, because they considered the pseudonym an insult to them. I was in a quandary (*Polish American Review,* 1939).

Questions
1. What problems did Kostyra face?
2. Why do you think it was difficult for his family to accept a new name for him?
3. Why was Kostyra ashamed of his Polish name?
4. Why do you think some Americans refused to call Kostyra by his Polish name?
5. Do you feel that an individual should change his or her name under any circumstances? Why or why not? If so, under what circumstances?
6. What are some things that Kostyra could have done to solve his problems? What were probable consequences of each course of action?
7. What do you think Kostyra should have done? Why?
8. If you had been Kostyra, what would you have done? Why?
9. Have you ever been in a situation similar to the one that Kostyra was in? If so, what did you do? Why?

High School Grades

CONCEPT

Nativism
Generalization: Negative feelings toward immigrant groups emerged early in colonial America. However, American nativism did not become widespread until the late nineteenth and early twentieth centuries. It eventually led to a virtual halt to European immigration.

1. Ask the students to read Chapter 2, "Ethnic Discord and the Growth of American Nationality," in Maldwyn Allen Jones (1992), *American Immigration,* and Chapter 1, "A Colonial Heritage," in David H. Bennett (1988), *The Party of Fear: From Nativist Movements to the New Right in American History,* and be able to discuss the following questions when they have finished the reading:
   a. Antiforeign attitudes were present in the early American colonies. What groups were the main victims of these negative feelings?
   b. What forms did nativism take in Colonial America? What acts and laws were passed in Colonial America that reflected antiforeign attitudes?

   When the students have completed these readings, discuss the above questions with the class. They will discover that the Irish, French, Huguenots, Catholics, and Germans were the main targets of early antiforeign attitudes in America. Record their responses to the questions above, in summary form, on the board.
2. Ask individual students or groups of students to prepare reports on the following topics and present them to the class.
   - The Know-Nothing movement in the 1850s
   - The Chinese Exclusion Act of 1882

- The Immigration Act of 1882, which excluded certain classes of European immigrants
- The Immigration Restriction League, formed in 1894
- The Foran Act of 1885
- The Haymarket Affair, 1886
- The Lynching of eleven Italians in New Orleans, 1891
- William Z. Ripley's *The Races of Europe*, published in 1899
- The Dillingham Commission, which issued its report in 1911
- The 1917 Immigration Act
- Madison Grant, *The Passing of the Great Race in America*, published in 1916
- The Johnson Act of 1921
- The Johnson-Reed Act of 1924
- The McCarran-Walter Act of 1952
- The Immigration Act of 1965
- The Immigration Reform and Control Act of 1986
- The Immigration Act of 1990

The books by Jones (1992) and Bennett (1988), cited above, are two excellent sources for information about the above topics. When the students are sharing their reports, help them identify some causes of nativistic movements. These causes should be noted on the board and in the students' notebooks. They include anti-Catholic attitudes, fear of foreign "radicals," economic recession and depression, the mass of new immigrants that arrived in the United States in the late 1800s and early 1900s, the belief that aliens were taking jobs away from American citizens, and the popularity of beliefs about the innate inferiority of southern and eastern European immigrants perpetuated by such writers as William Z. Ripley and the well-known naturalist Madison Grant.

3. Heated debates took place in Congress, as well as in other public forums, about the passage of a bill that would require immigrants to pass a reading test before they could enter the United States. Two opposing views of the literacy test are found in Chapter 8 of Oscar Handlin (1959), *Immigration as a Factor in American History*. Samuel Gompers defends the test and President Woodrow Wilson opposes it. Read these two accounts to the class. Ask the students to role-play a session of Congress in 1917 in which the bill is discussed. Different students should argue for and against the bill. After the speeches on the floor, the students should vote for or against the bill. After the voting, they should discuss why their final vote was similar to or different from the Congressional vote in 1917.

4. Anthropologists and physical scientists divided Whites into various races in the 1800s (Tucker, 1994). William Z. Ripley (1899) and Madison Grant (1916) popularized these views and argued that southern and eastern European immigrants were innately inferior to immigrants from the northern and western parts of Europe. Ask the class to compare the views of these writers with the racial views of contemporary scientists such as Richard J. Herrnstein and Charles Murray (1994). Excellent critiques of the views of Herrnstein and Murray are found in *The Bell Curve Debate: History, Documents, Opinions*, edited by Russell Jacoby and Naomi Glauberman (1995).

5. Social and physical scientists blamed the new immigrants for political corruption, urban blight, crime, and large welfare rolls. Ask the students to study writings about the immigrants during the 1800s and to compare these writ-

ings with writings today about ethnic minorities such as African Americans, Mexican Americans, and Puerto Ricans. The class can discuss the ways in which the old and new criticisms are alike and different and why they are alike and different. Oscar Handlin (1959), *The Uprooted*, Maldwyn A. Jones (1992), *American Immigration,* and David H. Bennett (1988), *The Party of Fear: From Nativist Movements to the New Right* contain information and references that will help students to carry out this activity.

6. The Johnson-Reed Act of 1924 marked the end of an era in the history of American immigration because it put a virtual end to immigration and discriminated blatantly against southern and eastern European immigrants and non-White nations. Duplicate a copy of this act for the class and ask them to discuss its legal, moral, and political implications. The students can then compare the Johnson-Reed Act with these acts: the McCarran-Walter Act of 1952, the Immigration Act of 1965, the Immigration Reform and Control Act of 1986, and the Immigration Act of 1990.

Students can also compare nativism near the turn of the century directed against southern, central, and eastern European immigrants with the nativism that is directed against Asians and Hispanics today. For example, a number of states with large Hispanic populations have passed referenda that make English the official state language. In 1994, California voters passed Proposition 187, an initiative that denies undocumented workers and their children schooling and nonemergency medical care. You can conclude this unit by asking the students to write a five- to ten-page paper on "Nativism as a Factor in American Society: Today and Yesterday." This activity can be correlated with English or the language arts.

REFERENCES

Alba, R. D. (1985). *Italian Americans: Into the Twilight of Ethnicity.* Englewood Cliffs, NJ: Prentice-Hall.

Bailey, T. A. (1961). *The American Pageant: A History of the Republic* (2nd ed.). Boston: D.C. Heath.

Bateman, G., & Egan, V. (1993). *Encyclopedia of World Geography.* New York: Barnes & Noble.

Bennett, D. H. (1988). *The Party of Fear: From Nativist Movements to the New Right in American History.* Chapel Hill: University of North Carolina Press.

Brodkin, K. (1998). *How the Jews Became White Folks & What That Says about Race in America.* New Brunswick: Rutgers University Press.

Chermayeff, I., Wasserman, F., & Shapiro, M. J. (1991). *Ellis Island: An Illustrated History of the Immigrant Experience.* New York: Macmillan.

Glazer, N., & Moynihan, D. P. (1970). *Beyond the Melting Pot: The Negroes, Puerto Ricans, Jews, Italians, and Irish of New York City* (2nd ed.). Cambridge: M.I.T. Press.

Grant, M. (1916). *The Passing of the Great Race.* New York: Charles Scribner's Sons.

Greeley, A. M., & McCready, W. C. (1974, April). Does Ethnicity Matter? *Ethnicity, 1,* 91–108.

Greenbaum, W. (1974, August). America in Search of a New Ideal: An Essay on the Rise of Pluralism. *Harvard Educational Review, 44,* 411–440.

Handlin, O. (Ed.). (1951). *The Uprooted: The Epic Story of the Great Migrations That Made the American People.* New York: Grosset and Dunlap.

Handlin, O. (Ed.). (1959). *Immigration as a Factor in American History.* Englewood Cliffs, NJ: Prentice-Hall.

Herrnstein, R. J., & Murray, C. (1994). *The Bell Curve: Intelligence and Class Structure in American Life.* New York: Free Press.

Higham, J. (1972). *Strangers in the Land: Patterns of American Nativism 1860–1925.* New York: Atheneum.

Jacoby, R., & Glauberman, N. (Eds.). (1995). *The Bell Curve: History, Documents, Opinions.* New York: Times Books/Random House.

Jones, M. A. (1960). *American Immigration.* Chicago: University of Chicago Press.

Jones, M. A. (1992). *American Immigration* (2nd ed.). Chicago: University of Chicago Press.

Kamphoefner, W. D., Helbich, W., & Sommer, U. (Eds.). (1991). *News from the Land of Freedom: Immigrants Write Home.* Ithaca, NY: Cornell University Press.

Mann, A. (1979). *The One and the Many: Reflections on the American Identity.* Chicago: University of Chicago Press.

Martin, P., & Midgley, E. (1999). Immigration to the United States, Population Bulletin, vol. 54, no. 2. Washington, DC: Population Reference Bureau.

Novak, M. (1971). *The Rise of the Unmeltable Ethnics: Politics and Culture in the Seventies.* New York: Macmillan.

Patterson, O. (1977). *Ethnic Chauvinism: The Reactionary Impulse.* New York: Stein and Day.

Polish American Review. (1939, July).

Ripley, W. Z. (1899). *The Races of Europe: A Sociological Study.* New York: D. Appleton.

Smedley, A. (1993). *Race in North America: Origin and Evolution of a Worldview.* Boulder, CO: Westview Press.

Stein, H. F., & Hill, R. F. (1977). *The Ethnic Imperative: Examining the New White Ethnic Movement.* University Park: Pennsylvania State University Press.

Takaki, R. (1993). *A Different Mirror: A History of Multicultural America.* New York: Little, Brown.

Terkel, S. (1980). *American Dreams: Lost and Found.* New York: Pantheon.

Tucker, W. H. (1994). *The Science and Politics of Racial Research.* Urbana: University of Illinois Press.

U.S. Bureau of the Census. (1994). *Statistical Abstract of the United States* (114th ed.). Washington, DC: U.S. Government Printing Office.

U.S. Census Bureau [On-line]. Available: *http://www.census.gov*

U.S. Immigration and Naturalization Service. (1998). *Statistical Yearbook of the Immigration and Naturalization Service, 1998.* Washington, DC: U.S. Government Printing Office.

U.S. Immigration and Naturalization Service. (2000). *1998 Statistical Yearbook of the Immigration and Naturalization Service.* Washington, DC: U.S. Government Printing Office.

Vecoli, R. J. (1994). *Review of Teaching Strategies for Ethnic Studies* (5th ed.). (Comments prepared for author's revision of text for this 6th edition).

Vecoli, R. J., & Sinke, S. (Eds.). (1991). *A Century of European Migrations 1830–1930.* Urbana: University of Illinois Press.

Zempel, S. (Ed.). (1990). *In Their Own Words: Letters from Norwegian Immigrants.* Minneapolis: University of Minnesota Press.

ANNOTATED BIBLIOGRAPHY

Books for Teachers

Especially Recommended

Alba, R. (1990). *Ethnic Identity: The Transformation of White America.* New Haven, CT: Yale University Press.

> *In this informative, thoughtful, and provocative book, Alba uses data from in-depth interviews with more than 500 people to examine the impact of ethnicity on the lives of White*

ethnics. He argues that ethnic specific characteristics, such as those of Polish American and Italian American origin, are increasingly less important. However, a new collective White ethnic identity and group has emerged, which he calls "European Americans."

Bennett, D. H. (1988). *The Party of Fear: From Nativist Movements to the New Right in American History.* Chapel Hill: University of North Carolina Press.

This is a sweeping and comprehensive history of nativism and antidemocratic groups in American society, the most comprehensive book on the topic since the publication of John Higham's Strangers in the Land: Patterns of American Nativism 1860–1925, *first published in 1963.*

Fuchs, L. H. (1990). *The American Kaleidoscope: Race, Ethnicity, and the Civic Culture.* Hanover, NH: University Press of New England.

A rich, informative and comprehensive treatment of the ethnic diversity that constitutes American society and culture.

Howard, G. R. (1999). *We Can't Teach What We Don't Know: White Teachers, Multiracial Schools.* New York: Teachers College Press.

This book offers a healing vision for the future of education in pluralistic nations, and it engages the reader on a journey of personal and professional transformation. The author's lively stories and compelling analysis reveal what it means to be a culturally competent White teacher in racially diverse schools.

Jacobson, M. F. (1999). *Whiteness of a Different Color: European Immigrants and the Alchemy of Race.* Cambridge: Harvard University Press.

The author examines the ways in which Whiteness has been constructed historically in the United States. The ways in which race construction relates to power are effectively and perceptively described. This is an excellent and well-crafted book.

Waters, M. C. (1990). *Ethnic Options: Choosing Identities in America.* Berkeley: University of California Press.

This important sociological study examines the ethnic identities of fourth, fifth, and later generations of European Americans.

Other References

Boscia-Mul, P. (1999). *Authentic Ethnicities: The Interaction of Ideology, Gender, Power, and Class in the Italian-American Experience.* Westport, CT: Greenwood Press.

This is based on an empirical study of a three-generation sample of Italian Americans. The author argues that people's relationship with their ethnic culture is always a strategic compromise, through which class and gender emerge as two fundamental variables in the way people identify with, manipulate, or are constrained by ethnic ideologies. The findings of this study challenge many commonplace understandings about Italian Americans and about ethnicity as a social phenomenon and means of identification.

Coan, P. M. (1997). *Ellis Island Interviews: In Their Own Words.* New York: Checkmark Books.

This book compiles over 100 firsthand accounts of the last surviving immigrants who entered America through Ellis Island, as well as some of the employees who interacted with the over 12 million immigrants from Europe, the British Isles, and the Middle East who entered between 1892 and 1954.

Dezell, M. (2000). *Irish America: Coming into Clover: The Evolution of a People and a Culture.* New York: Doubleday.

This insightful book reexamines Irish American identity in a way that skillfully interweaves history and reporting, observation and opinion, and sensitivity and humor. It goes well beyond the stereotypical portrait of Irish American culture.

Fine, M., Weis, L., Powell, L. C., & Wong, L. M. (Eds.). (1997). *Off White: Readings on Race, Power, and Society.* New York: Routledge.

This book places Whiteness at the center of analysis: Whiteness as race, as privilege, as social construction. The contributors from the fields of education and psychology unravel the racial hierarchies that shape our society by challenging the White norm that pervades our schools, communities, social research, and political movements.

Gladsky, T. S., & Gladsky, R. H. (1997). *Something of My Very Own to Say: American Women Writers of Polish Descent.* New York: Columbia University Press.

This collection of essays and representative selections of literature enlarges the history of American women's literature. Polish and American scholars reflect on questions of gender and ethnicity that have framed the experiences of all women, but particularly those of Polish descent.

Gribbean, A. (Ed.). (1999). *The Great Famine and the Irish Diaspora in America.* Amherst: University of Massachusetts Press.

A volume of original essays that commemorates the 150th anniversary of the 1.5 million Irish exodus to the United States between 1845 and 1855.

Hayden, T. (2001). *Irish on the Inside: In Search of the Soul of Irish America.* London: Verso.

The denial by the author's family of its Irish heritage served as the catalyst for this exploration of the cultural losses brought about by the assimilation of the Irish into mainstream American culture. In this book, he argues that too much assimilation leaves Irish Americans with a weak sense of their ethnic identity.

Hegi, U. (1997). *Tearing the Silence: On Being German in America.* New York: Touchstone.

This award-winning novelist shares the powerful and provocative oral histories of postwar German immigrants in a way that captures these long-silent voices as they confront their silence surrounding the Holocaust and the struggles of living between two cultures.

Laurino, M. (2000). *Were You Always an Italian? Ancestors and Other Icons of Italian America.* New York: W.W. Norton.

The author sifts through the stereotypes of Italian Americans to deliver a realistic and humorous examination of third-generation ethnic identity in a way that captures the Italian immigrant experience in the United States.

Logue, P. (2000). *Being Irish: Personal Reflections on Irish Identity Today.* Dublin: Oak Tree Press.

A diverse group of over 100 individuals share the essence of their Irish self-identity in a way that illuminates and celebrates the diversity within the Irish American community.

Lovell, O. S. (1999). *The Promise of America: A History of the Norwegian American People.* Minneapolis, MN: University of Minnesota Press.

This author tells the story of the thousands of Norwegian immigrants in the United States from a historical perspective that offers new understandings of the Norwegian American in the past and present.

Luebke, F. C. (Ed.). (1998). *European Immigrants in the American West: Community Histories.* Albuquerque: University of New Mexico Press.

This collection of essays explores the rural and urban settlement patterns of European immigrants during the nineteenth and early twentieth centuries by analyzing their comparative histories and the maintenance of their communities.

Morreale, B., & Carola, R. (2000). *Italian Americans: The Immigrant Experience.* Berkeley: Publishers Group West.

An oversized and beautifully illustrated history of the Italian sojourn in the United States. It contains striking color and black-and-white photographs as well as an informative text. The photographs are excellent for teaching.

Mucha, J. (1996). *Everyday Life and Festivity in a Local Ethnic Community.* New York: Columbia University Press.

This book describes the process by which everyday Polish community life was transformed in the United States.

Padden, M., & Sullivan, R. (1999). *May the Road Rise to Meet You: Everything You Need to Know about Irish American History.* New York: Plume.

Using an entertaining and informative question-and-answer format, this accessible reference book provides a comprehensive view of the Irish American experience.

Pula, J. S. (1995). *Polish Americans: An Ethnic Community.* New York: Twayne.

This book describes the complexities of Polish American history and culture by using central themes that have bound Polish Americans into an identifiable community, often referred to as "Polonia."

Ray, C. (2001). *Highland Heritage: Scottish Americans in the American South.* Chapel Hill, NC: University of North Carolina Press.

The author examines how and why we use memories of our ancestral pasts to provide a sense of identity and community in the present. This book is an original and insightful examination of what it means to be Scottish in the American South.

Schiavo, G. (2000). *Four Centuries of Italian-American History.* New York: Center for Migration Studies.

This illustrated volume provides an impressive wealth of historical information that describes the role and contributions of Italians in U.S. history.

Stave, B. M., Sutherland, J. F., & Salerno, A. (1999). *From the Old Country: An Oral History of European Migration to America.* Hanover, NH: University Press of New England.

This book contains a tapestry of firsthand testimony detailing the late nineteenth and early twentieth centuries' great wave of European immigrants to the United States. It provides a third-generation perspective on the experiences of the Irish, Scandinavian, Italian, and other European immigrant groups.

Talarico, R. (2000). *The Journey Home: Eleven Italian-American Narratives and "An Utterance of Joy."* West Lafayette, IN: Bordighera.

This book consists of informative narratives by Italian Americans.

Thandeka. (1999). *Learning to Be White: Money, Race, and God in America.* New York: Continuum.

This book describes the origins of White identity by using the personal memories of European Americans. This study of the process through which they learned of and accepted their Whiteness demonstrates the privilege and shame that often accompanies being White.

Books for Students

Aliki. (1998). *Marianthe's Story: Painted Memories/Spoken Words.* Illustrated by the author. New York: Greenwillow.

This picture book, presented in an unusual format with each side a separate story, chronicles the first days in America of a contemporary immigrant from a war-torn country. It is based on the noted children's author/illustrator's own experience as a refugee from Greece in the late 1940s. (Primary)

Bartoletti, S. C. (2000). *A Coal Miner's Bride: The Diary of Anetka Kaminska.* Series: *Dear America.* New York: Scholastic.

Thirteen-year-old Anetka's arranged marriage to a crude and unloving coal miner finances her family's passage from Poland to the United States in 1896. (Middle School)

Bartone, E. (1993). *Peppe the Lamplighter.* Illustrated by the author. New York: Lothrop.

A story about an Italian American boy who takes a job lighting the gas street lamps. The illustrations are striking and powerful. (Primary)

Bogomolny, A. (Ed.). (1999). *New to North America: Writing by U.S. Immigrants, Their Children and Grandchildren.* Santa Cruz, CA: Burning Bush.

This general anthology collects three generations of immigrant experiences from a variety of cultures. Poems, stories, and essays portray immigrants' and descendants' lives from 1840 to the present. (High School)

Bunting, E. (1999). *I Have an Olive Tree.* Illustrated by K. Barbour. New York: HarperCollins.

A seven-year-old Greek American girl journeys to the land of her mother's birth to place a memorial for her grandmother in an olive tree. (Primary)

Chermayeff, I., Wasserman, F., & Shapiro, M. J. (1991). *Ellis Island: An Illustrated History of the Immigrant Experience.* New York: Macmillan.

This is an excellent and attractive teaching resource that includes photographs, many in color, of people, artifacts, and documents. (All ages)

Colicchio, J. (2000). *High Gate Health and Beauty.* Berkeley, CA: Creative Arts.

Written for adult readers, this coming-of-age story features a group of working-class Italian American teenagers who live in an ethnically diverse and changing urban neighborhood in New Jersey. (High School)

Denenberg, B. (1997). *So Far from Home: The Diary of Mary Driscoll, an Irish Mill Girl.* Series: *Dear America.* New York: Scholastic.

In the midst of the potato famine of the 1840s, an Irish girl travels to Lowell, Massachusetts, to work as a spinner in a textile mill. (Intermediate/Middle School)

Durban, W. (2000). *The Journal of Otto Peltonen: A Finnish Immigrant, Hibbing, Minnesota, 1905.* Series: *My Name Is America.* New York: Scholastic.

Fifteen-year-old Otto comes to America with his family in search of farmland but experiences danger and labor strife in the iron ore mines of northern Minnesota. (Intermediate/Middle School)

Erickson, J. H. (1999). *Orthodox Christians in America.* Series: *Religion in American Life.* New York: Oxford University Press.

This series title explores the religion of immigrants from Greece, Russia, Ukraine, Belarus, and other places in Eastern Europe, the Balkans, and the Caucasus. (Middle School/High School)

Gaspar, F. X. (1999). *Leaving Pico.* Hanover, NH: University Press of New England.

A coming-of-age story featuring a Portuguese American boy growing up in a fishing village on the Massachusetts coast. (High School)

Gundisch, K. (2001). *How I Became an American.* Chicago: Cricket Books.

The immigration of a family from Austria–Hungary to the United States in the late nineteenth century is told from the perspective of a 10-year-old boy. Translated from German, this book won the 2002 Mildred L. Batchelder Award.

Hoobler, D., & Hoobler, T. (1994). *The Italian Family Album.* New York: Oxford University Press.

This rich and appealing book contains captivating period photographs as well as diaries, letters, interviews, and other period sources. Other titles in The American Family Album *Series on European Americans include* The German Family Album *(1995), and* The Irish

Family Album *(1995). Each of the titles in* The American Family Album *series is similar in reading level, design, and appearance. (Middle School and Up)*

Hoobler, D., & Hoobler, T. (1997). *The Scandinavian Family Album.* New York: Oxford University Press.

This excellent series title traces the history, immigration patterns, and family and community life of immigrants from Norway, Sweden, Finland, Denmark, and Iceland, most of whom settled in the upper Midwest. (Middle School and Up)

Joselit, J. W. (2001). *Immigration and American Religion.* Series: *Religion in American Life.* New York: Oxford University Press.

This series title traces the role of religion in the lives of immigrants from the colonial period through successive waves of migration from Ireland and southern and eastern Europe up to the present. (Middle School/High School)

Kelley, W. (2000). *The Sweet Summer.* Louisville, KY: Westminster John Knox Press.

A young Irish American man, the only White on an all-Black Air Force boxing team, gets a firsthand view of prejudice and of African American culture when his team tours the South in the early 1950s. (High School)

Lorbiecki, M. (1997). *My Palace of Leaves in Sarajevo.* Illustrated by H. Tauss. New York: Dial.

A Bosnian Muslim girl corresponds with her cousin, who lives in the United States and whose family is trying to bring her and her family to safety. (Intermediate)

Maestro, B. (1995). *Coming to America: The Story of Immigration.* Illustrated by S. Ryan. New York: Scholastic.

This book tells the story of immigrating to the United States. (Intermediate)

Murphy, J. (2001). *Pick and Shovel Poet: The Journeys of Pascal D'Angelo.* New York: Clarion.

A sensitive and moving account of D'Angelo's life that focuses on his migration from an impoverished village in Italy to the United States in 1910 at the age of 16, his work as a manual laborer, and the birth of his poetic talent as a chronicler of the immigrant experience. (Middle School/High School)

Murphy, J. (1998). *West to a Land of Plenty: The Diary of Teresa Angelino Viscardi.* Series: *Dear America.* New York: Scholastic.

After the family's business in Jersey City fails, an Italian American girl, her parents, and her siblings endure a harrowing journey to the Idaho Territory in 1883. (Intermediate/Middle School)

Raphael, M. (2001). *Streets of Gold.* New York: Persea.

A fourteen-year-old Polish teenager and her older brother must remain alone in the United States when her parents are sent back to their home country because her younger sister has tuberculosis. Realistic details of both Poland and New York City at the turn of the twentieth century characterize this novel. (Middle School/High School)

Rosenberg, L. (1999). *The Silence in the Mountains.* Illustrated by C. Soentpiet. New York: Orchard.

In this emotionally powerful story, an immigrant from the Caucasus misses the mountains of his former land but finds peace in the hills near his new home. (Primary)

Sakson-Ford, S. (1999). *The Czech Americans.* Series: *The Immigrant Experience.* Philadelphia, PA: Chelsea House.

This series title traces the history of Czechs in the United States from the mid-1700s through the largest wave, beginning in the late 1800s, up to the present. (Middle School/High School)

Silverman, R. (1997). *A Bosnian Family.* Series: *Journey between Two Worlds.* Illustrated with photos by S. Silverman. Minneapolis: Lerner.

Clear text and attractive color photographs present a family of Bosnian Muslim refugees who fled their war-torn country in 1994 for a new life in the United States. (Intermediate)

Suwyn, B. J. (1997). *The Magic Egg and Other Tales from Ukraine.* Englewood, CO: Libraries Unlimited.

The folklorist offers 33 tales grouped into four categories—animal stories, pourquoi stories, moral tales, and legends and fairy tales—along with source notes and other cultural information. (Intermediate and Up)

Watson, M. (1996). *The Butterfly Seeds.* Illustrated by the author. New York: Morrow.

Immigration to America separates Jake from his grandfather, but planting the butterfly seeds along with other immigrants in his diverse neighborhood helps Jake to remember. (Primary)

Woodruff. E. (1997). *The Orphan of Ellis Island.* New York: Scholastic.

A lonely Italian American boy living in a foster home reconnects with his immigrant ancestors on a class trip to Ellis Island and learns about the hardships that they faced. (Intermediate)

Yezerski, T. (1998). *Together in Pinecone Patch.* Illustrated by the author. New York: Farrar, Straus & Giroux.

Irish American immigrant children and their Polish American counterparts clash in a dusty coal mining town in Pennsylvania at the turn of the twentieth century. (Primary/Intermediate)

9

Jewish Americans

Concepts, Strategies, and Materials

The journey of the Jews to success in America is part of American history; the survival of their Jewishness, and what definition of it they fashion or invent, is the stuff of Jewish history.

—Arthur Hertzberg

About 6 million Jewish Americans live in the United States, comprising about 2.2% of its population (Singer, 1999, 2000). They constitute a religious, cultural, and ethnic minority group that originated in the land that is, today, Israel. They are a diverse group, living in each of the fifty states, with about 58% in the Northeast and Midwest and 42% in the South and West. The population movement has generally been from the Northeast and Midwest to the South and West (Singer 1999, 2000).

Jewish Americans have been an integral part of American history since the days of Columbus, and they have contributed significantly in the arts and sciences, medicine, education, law, and other fields. American culture has been enriched by the works of Jewish novelists, playwrights, and critics who write from a Jewish perspective and on Jewish themes. Yet, the role of Jews in American history clearly transcends a mere listing of their contributions. Their presence is

This chapter was written by **Jerome L. Ruderman,** former Department Head, Frankford High School, Philadelphia, Pennsylvania. It was revised by **Hallie Esbin Rosen,** who worked for fourteen years for the Anti-Defamation League as Regional Education Director and facilitator for *A World of Difference.* She is the author of several discussion guides and manuals including *Confronting Anti-Semitism: A Facilitator's Manual* (2000).

intimately intertwined with many fundamental themes and concepts that have characterized American history, such as religious freedom, the achievement of civic equality, and the struggle of a group to maintain its ethnic identity while assimilating into the U.S. mainstream.

Historical Roots

Jewish history, from Biblical times to the settlement of the first Jews in America, is a vast, complicated story, woven into nearly 4,000 years of Western civilization. In the year A.D. 70, conquering Romans crushed the Jewish state in Palestine, driving most, but not all, of its inhabitants into exile. Many fled to Babylonia, where they established a community that soon outshone Palestine as a center of Jewish life. By the ninth century, the hub of the Jewish world had shifted to Spain, where the cooperative attitudes of the Moors encouraged a golden age of Jewish scholarship, literature, and science. This lasted until the thirteenth century, when Christian brutality against Jews replaced the tolerant Moorish rule. Entire Jewish communities were decimated, and countless numbers of Jews were forced or frightened into the Catholic church. Many professed Christianity but secretly adhered to Judaism. They were derisively referred to by the Spanish as *Marranos* (pigs). In 1492, the Spanish monarchs expelled the entire Jewish community, and nearly 150,000 Jews left Spain. A few made their way to America, where they laid the foundations of the Jewish community in America, which in time was to become the largest Jewish population in the world. Today approximately 46% of the world's Jews live in the United States, compared with 31% in Israel (Singer 2000).

The earliest Jews (*Marranos*) to reach America arrived with Christopher Columbus in 1492. By the sixteenth century, Marranos were prominent in Portuguese Brazil, particularly in the city of Recife. In 1630, that city fell to the liberal Dutch, and Marranos joyfully abandoned the mask of Christianity. In 1654, when the Portuguese reconquered the city, they gave Jews the choice of baptism or exile. Most chose exile. Twenty-three of them found their way to the Dutch colony of New Amsterdam. Since then, Jewish immigration to the United States has been nearly continuous.

The Colonies

In New Amsterdam, Governor Peter Stuyvesant wished to expel the Jews, but the Dutch West India Company disagreed. He was ordered to permit them to remain as long as they did not become a burden on the colony. However, Stuyvesant confined them to homes in a narrow street that came to be known as "Jews' Alley." He denied them equality with other people in New Amsterdam, even refusing them permission to build a synagogue. The Jews, nonetheless, formed a

JEWISH AMERICANS: HISTORICAL PERSPECTIVE

Important Dates	Events
1492	The Jews were expelled from Spain. Jews accompanied Columbus on his first voyage to America.
1654	Twenty-three Jewish immigrants from Brazil arrived in New Amsterdam. They established the first Jewish settlement in North America.
1730	The first synagogue in North America was completed in New Amsterdam.
1740	An act of Parliament exempted Jews from saying the words, "on the true faith of a Christian," in the naturalization oath, enabling them to become citizens in English colonies.
1774	Francis Salvador was elected to the South Carolina Provincial Congress. He was the only Jewish delegate to any representative assembly in colonial times.
1786	The Virginia Statute of Religious Freedom was passed. It guaranteed religious equality to Jews in Virginia and became a model for other colonies.
1787	The Constitution of the United States barred religious tests for federal office.
1791	The First Amendment of the Bill of Rights prohibited congressional establishment of religion in the United States.
1809	Jacob Henry, a Jew, was allowed to retain his seat in the North Carolina House of Commons despite a state law limiting office holding to Protestants.
1815	The Congress of Vienna nullified the rights of German Jews, causing thousands to immigrate to the United States.
1826	The Maryland "Jew Bill" was passed. It ended religious tests against Jews in Maryland.
1848	The Revolution of 1848 in Europe caused many German Jews to come to America as political refugees.
1862	Rabbis were permitted to serve as U.S. military chaplains. General Ulysses S. Grant issued General Order No. 11, which expelled Jews as a class from the Department of the Tennessee.

Important Dates	Events
1868	The Fourteenth Amendment was adopted. Subsequent court decisions broadened it to guarantee religious equality in the states.
1877	Joseph Seligman, a Jewish manufacturer, and his family were excluded from a resort hotel, foreshadowing the pattern anti-Semitism was to take in the United States.
1881–82	Discriminatory legislation and *pogroms* (government-sponsored attacks) against Russia's Jews spurred wholesale immigration to America.
1885	The Pittsburgh Platform was enunciated by Reform Jews. It stated their principles and beliefs.
1886	The Jewish Theological Seminary was founded by leaders of Conservative Judaism.
1914	Louis D. Brandeis became the leader of the American Zionist movement.
1915	Leo Frank, a Jew, was lynched in Georgia, a result of anti-Semitic hatred.
1924	The Johnson-Reed National Origins Quota Act drastically curtailed Jewish immigration to the United States.
1930–40	Anti-Semitism, stimulated by Nazi propaganda, reached alarming levels in the United States.
1939–46	Six million Jews were killed by the Nazis during World War II.
1948	President Harry S. Truman recognized the State of Israel immediately after its establishment.
1967	Jewish Americans strongly supported Israel during the Six Day War.
1973	Jewish Americans contributed huge sums of money to Israel when the Yom Kippur War broke out.
1976	Jews throughout the world took pride in the heroic Israeli commando raid on Entebbe airfield in Uganda. This action freed hostages held by Palestinian terrorists.

Important Dates	Events
1978	First woman rabbi was ordained.
1979	Egypt's President Anwar el-Sadat and Israel's Premier Menachim Begin signed a peace treaty, together with President Carter, in a White House ceremony a few months after a thirteen-day conference at Camp David.
1981	Pressure generated by the New Right and Christian Right troubled many Jewish Americans as the "moral majority" and similar groups challenged the concept of separation of church and state.
1982	Many Jewish Americans were privately critical of Israel's military thrust into Lebanon to end PLO terrorism, which thus reflected a shift from unquestioned support to criticism of the Begin government.
1985	American Jews were shocked by President Reagan's visit to a military cemetery in Bitburg, Germany, which contains the graves of forty-seven members of the Waffen SS (Hitler's elite armed guard).
1986	Elie Weisel was awarded the Nobel Peace prize.
1993	Israel signed a peace agreement with the Palestine Liberation Organization (PLO). The United States Holocaust museum was opened in Washington, D.C. Ruth Bader Ginsberg was appointed to the United States Supreme Court. *Schindler's List* was released and received several Academy Awards.
1994	Israel and Jordan signed a peace agreement. Steven Breyer was appointed to the United States Supreme Court.
1995	Israeli Prime Minister Yitzhak Rabin was assassinated at a Tel Aviv peace rally.
1997	Secretary of State Madeline Albright learned that at least 3 of her grandparents were Jewish and that they had perished in the Holocaust.
2000	Senator Joseph Lieberman ran and loss as the first Jewish American nominated as the Democratic Vice Presidential candidate.

congregation (1656) and worshipped in private homes. With the transfer of power to the British in 1664, their status gradually improved. A synagogue was permitted, and was completed in 1730. Ten years later, Parliament exempted Jews from saying the words "upon the true faith of a Christian" in the oath required for naturalization in the English colonies.

Jews were welcomed in other colonies such as Rhode Island, Pennsylvania, Georgia, and South Carolina. There, under the enlightened leadership of men like Roger Williams, William Penn, James Oglethorpe, and John Locke, Jewish communities were established. But, even in these colonies, Jewish participation in civic life was limited. Throughout the entire colonial period only one Jew, Francis Salvador of South Carolina, was elected (1774) to a representative congress or assembly. Nonetheless, Jews slowly gained the rights of domicile, trade, and religious organization. Where restrictions against them existed, they were usually ignored.

In some colonies, however, Jews were barred altogether. No Jewish community developed in Massachusetts, for example, until after the American Revolution. Virginia and Maryland, too, were unfriendly to Jews. Maryland was actually one of the last states to lift restrictions against Jews (1826).

Biblical Influence

Ironically, though few Jews lived in New England, Jewish influence there was pervasive and penetrating. The Puritan theocracy was modeled after that of ancient Israel, its early legal codes were patterned after the Law of Moses, and daily life and religious practices were influenced by the Hebrew Bible and the Judaic tradition. In New England, as was true throughout the colonies, there was considerable interest in the Hebrew language. Intelligent laymen studied it and frequently assembled collections of Hebraica. At Harvard and Yale, proficiency in Hebrew was required for graduation. In the eighteenth century, the New England clergy, often in the forefront of the drive for independence, frequently referred to the democratic principles in the Hebrew Bible, as did political pamphleteers like Thomas Paine. In their hands it became a political, as well as a religious, text.

The American Revolution

At the outbreak of the Revolution, Jewish Americans numbered about 2,000 of a total population of 2 million. Many were merchants and traders. Others were doctors, manual laborers, candlemakers, watchmakers, shoemakers, silversmiths, wigmakers, bakers, or butchers. Like other colonists, Jews participated in a wide range of professions and occupations. The notion of Jews as a homogeneous population was as erroneous then as it is today.

When fighting broke out, most Jews participated in the struggle for independence, even those of the merchant–shipowner class, whose commercial interests were in England. A few Jews were loyalists, but the majority participated as enlisted men and officers in the American army. Bernard Gratz of Philadelphia and other Jewish merchants signed nonimportation agreements. Aaron Lopez of Newport donated much of his personal fortune to the Continental cause. He and other shipowners outfitted their vessels with cannons and dispatched them against British ships. In Philadelphia, Haym Salomon was undoubtedly the most competent bill broker in America. As Broker to the Office of Finance, he sold bills of exchange and government notes for the highest possible prices and the lowest commissions. His son and the sons and grandsons of numerous Jews of the Revolutionary period served in the War of 1812.

Uriah Phillips Levy is perhaps the best known of these men. He ultimately reached the rank of Commodore in the U.S. Navy, despite a lifetime struggle to overcome anti-Semitism. Levy is best remembered for his crusade to end corporal punishment in the Navy and for preserving Thomas Jefferson's home, Monticello, as a national shrine.

A result of the Revolution was that the colonists were no longer subjects of a king, but enfranchised citizens of their own country. Important as that was for the colonists in general, it was even more important for the Jews because it legitimized the rights and privileges they had won. It was the first time in the history of Western civilization that they had been a legitimate part of the body politic, no longer excluded from the civic life of the community because of their religion. This transformation was eloquently expressed in 1790 by George Washington in a letter to the Jews of Newport, Rhode Island, in which he wrote, "happily the government of the United States, which gives to bigotry no sanction, to persecution no assistance, requires only that they who live under its protection should demean themselves as good citizens."

Equality in the States

Constitutional guarantees of freedom of religion implicit in the Revolution were not automatically or universally guaranteed by the federal Constitution. Its protections were limited to suffrage and office-holding at the federal level. The states were as free as ever to impose religious tests that, in some cases, remained on the statute books long after the adoption of the Constitution. In Pennsylvania, state office-holding was limited to Christians; in New Jersey and North Carolina, it was restricted to Protestants. Not until the adoption of the Fourteenth Amendment in 1868 was a significant attempt made to limit the power of the states in this regard. Even then, it was many years before the Supreme Court wrote interpretations of the Fourteenth Amendment supporting the rights of religious minorities in the states. Thus, the struggle for full equality was thrown back to the states. In Virginia, Jefferson and Madison led the way with the Virginia Statute of Religious Freedom in 1786. By 1790, New York, Georgia, Pennsylvania, and South Carolina, states with established Jewish communities, had passed similar laws. Others tarried well into the nineteenth century.

In North Carolina, in 1809, Jacob Henry, a Jew, was reelected to the state House of Commons. He was challenged on the grounds that his election violated a state requirement that all public officials be Protestant and accept the divine authority of the Christian Bible. After a spirited defense, he was permitted to retain his seat, but only by a legal subterfuge. The law itself was not changed regarding Jewish Americans until 1868, when the North Carolina state constitution, which also enfranchised African Americans, was adopted by a Reconstruction government.

Similarly, the Maryland Constitution of 1776 required "a declaration of belief in the Christian religion" in order to hold state office. A protracted struggle by Maryland Jews, with the aid of a gentile, Thomas Kennedy, who was a member of the state legislature, resulted in the Maryland "Jew Bill" in 1826. It provided that any citizen could qualify for any public office by declaring "his belief in a future state of rewards and punishments." Though still a religious test of sorts, it was not specifically aimed at Jews. By the end of the Jacksonian period, the few religious disabilities that remained were largely unenforced and a friendly attitude toward Jewish Americans prevailed.

German–Jewish Immigration

Though German Jews had predominated in the colonies since 1728, the years from 1820 to 1880 are considered the period of German-Jewish immigration. During those sixty years, about 200,000 Jews came to the United States from Germany and neighboring countries, where for centuries Jews had been vulnerable to recurring outbursts of mass hysteria and violence by the surrounding Christian population. Often confined to ghettos and forbidden to enter many skilled trades and farming, Jews had developed a close-knit society that emphasized study of the Bible and frequently turned to trade and commerce. In the eighteenth century, the Enlightenment and the reforms of Napoleon battered down their civic disabilities, and the Jews entered the secular worlds of France and Germany. However, their emancipation was short-lived. In 1815, the Congress of Vienna sought to nullify their newly won rights, causing thousands to depart for America. They were actually part of an exodus of about 5 million Germans who sought political freedom and economic opportunity in the United States. After the Revolution of 1848, the number who came as political refugees increased.

The German immigrants spread out across the country, though most settled in the Ohio and Mississippi valleys. Many of them, Christians as well as Jews, turned to peddling, an occupation that required no training and little capital and that served the needs of rural and frontier America. From these humble beginnings, some peddlers managed to accumulate enough capital to acquire a cart, then a horse and wagon, and finally a small store, which in some cases evolved into modern department stores. Some stores founded by Jewish peddlers are Bamberger's, Bloomingdale's, Filene's, Magnin's, Gimbel's, and Macy's (a dry goods business that Isidor and Nathan Straus turned into a giant department store). Other Jewish immigrants remained in the growing cities of the East and were frequently engaged in tailoring or shoemaking or dealt in secondhand clothing or dry goods.

A small number of Jews went West and became part of the saga of the frontier as buffalo hunters, ranchers, newspapermen, mayors (Galveston, Texas, had a Jewish mayor in 1850), miners, explorers, traders, artists, and photographers. Solomon Nunes Carvalho was a prominent Jewish artist and photographer who traveled with John Charles Fremont. Levi Strauss manufactured strong, copper-riveted denim trousers (Levi's) for the gold miners in California. By the mid-1850s, San Francisco had about 4,000 Jews.

The German-Jewish community in the nineteenth century was characterized by the multitude and variety of voluntary, self-help organizations that it established to meet a variety of social and political needs. A "Hebrew Benevolent Society" usually served many purposes in small communities. In larger cities, specific societies met specific needs, such as care of orphans or the poor. Five Jewish fraternal orders were born. The best known was B'nai B'rith in 1843. The Young Men's Hebrew Association (YMHA) was established at this time, as were a number of Jewish hospitals that provided kosher food to Jewish patients and training for Jewish medical students. During the Civil War, they admitted so many non-Jewish casualties that they became nonsectarian and have remained so to the present day.

Early attempts at Jewish schools met with little success. As public schools became popular, Jewish students attended them during the day and Jewish religious schools in the late afternoon or on Saturday or Sunday morning. This is still the most common form of Jewish education in the United States.

In 1843, the Reverend Isaac Leeser of Philadelphia founded a monthly publication, *The Occident*. Other Jewish periodicals appeared; the most important was that of Rabbi Isaac Mayer Wise, an outstanding Jewish leader and the father of Reform Judaism in America.

Reform Judaism

Most German Jews established their own congregations rather than join the existing Spanish congregations whose ritual and liturgy differed somewhat from their own. Consequently, between 1850 and 1870 the number of congregations in the United States rose from 37 to 189.

Among the new congregations, demands were soon heard for shorter religious services, elimination of Sabbath observance, the use of English rather than Hebrew for prayer, modified dietary laws, and elimination of many traditional restrictions that had been part of Jewish tradition for centuries. Their demands were answered by the Reform movement, which, having begun in Germany, found fertile ground in America. Its leader, Rabbi Isaac Mayer Wise, preached that Judaism must adapt to the American environment or it would die. Not withstanding the bitter opposition of traditionalists, who felt it wrong to tamper with sacred law and tradition, the new movement had become so much a part of Jewish life in America by 1885 that a panel of Reform rabbis met in Pittsburgh to codify their principles and beliefs. While adhering to the moral teachings of Judaism, the "Pittsburgh Platform" rejected traditional practices "not adapted to the views and habits of modern civilization."

The Civil War

Before and during the Civil War, Judaism took no common position on the question of slavery. Then, as now, individual Jews and congregations were entirely free of hierarchical control. Pronouncements by individuals, even rabbis, represented no more than their personal opinions, which varied from those of fanatical abolitionists like Michael Heilprin of Philadelphia to champions of slavery like Judah P. Benjamin, Secretary of State in the Confederate government and an intimate and influential adviser of Jefferson Davis.

Jewish merchants, whatever their inclination, played only a minimal role in the Atlantic slave trade. In the seventeenth century they were excluded from the Spanish and Portuguese colonies and banned from the French West Indies, areas of major slave trade activity. In the next century, when the slave trade was dominated by England, France, and Holland, Jewish names are virtually absent from the records. In general, geography determined the allegiance of American Jews, whose attitudes toward slavery reflected the culture in which they lived. Many Southern Jews, sensitive to proslavery pressures and concerned about anti-Semitism, prudently accepted the status quo. Others, steeped in the traditions of the South, embraced the Confederate cause promptly and enthusiastically. But Jews were not major slaveholders. Over 90% of the American slave population was concentrated in plantation districts where Jews were a rarity. Those who did hold slaves generally lived in cities and owned small numbers of domestic servants. In the North, many Jews were recent immigrants from Germany whose experience with persecution usually pitted them against slavery. When the fighting broke out, Jews in the North and South flocked to their respective colors. More than 6,000 Jewish soldiers and officers served in the Union forces, and several thousand Jews fought for the Confederacy, including 24 known staff officers.

Of greater significance than the number of Jewish participants in the war was the growth of anti-Semitism during this period. Though anti-Semitism had been present in American society since 1654, when the first Jews arrived in

New Amsterdam, it was not until the Civil War that it became a national issue. The first incident occurred early in the war as Jewish soldiers in the Union army sought to have rabbis ordained as military chaplains. A furor of protest ensued as certain Protestant groups objected. In December 1861, the Reverend Arnold Fischel visited President Lincoln, who rectified the injustice.

But anti-Semitism would not be stilled. In December 1862, Ulysses S. Grant issued General Order No. 11. It expelled "the Jews, as a class" from the Department of the Tennessee without trial or hearing (the Department of the Tennessee was the district controlled by Grant's armies). Violators would be jailed until they could be deported as prisoners. Jews sent letters and telegrams to Jewish leaders all over the country. Cesar Kaskel, one of those deported, visited President Lincoln in Washington to protest. Lincoln was sympathetic. He directed Grant to cancel the infamous order.

The press of the country was divided. Newspapers supporting the administration generally defended Grant. Some printed anti-Jewish invective previously unheard in America. The *New York Times* condemned the order as "one of the deepest sensations of the war." Jewish Americans were stunned when the Senate and House of Representatives failed to pass resolutions castigating Grant's action. Partisan arguments in both houses obscured the moral and legal aspects of the matter. Grant never apologized for the order, but as president he displayed no antagonism toward Jewish Americans. Rather, he supported Jewish causes on a number of occasions and appointed Jews to public office.

In the Confederacy, verbal attacks against Jews were widespread. Jews were frequently accused of speculating in all manner of merchandise, thereby causing the horrendous wartime inflation that paralyzed the South. A Jewish stereotype became the Confederacy's scapegoat, whereas the real causes of inflation, insufficient industrial base, heavy wartime demands on industry, and a successful Union blockade, were ignored.

Postwar Anti-Semitism

The years following the Civil War witnessed the emergence of the chief forms of anti-Semitism that Jewish Americans have had to contend with: discrimination in certain professions and occupations and exclusion from certain residential areas, social clubs, fashionable resorts, private schools, and universities, particularly medical schools. Such anti-Semitic discrimination became more striking in the 1920s, 1930s, and 1940s.

As early as 1867, attempts by a number of insurance companies to deny Jews fire insurance became a public issue. Ten years later, Joseph Seligman, an eminent Jewish clothing manufacturer, and his family were excluded from a fashionable hotel in Saratoga, New York. At about the same time, the president of the Long Island Railroad declared, "We do not like Jews as a class."

These incidents and the pattern of discrimination they foreshadowed must be viewed against a background of the improved social and economic status of Jews in America. By 1877, most Jews had left the ranks of the working class. But their rapid rise from humble origins made them abhorrent to high society. Moreover, thousands of eastern European Jews began immigrating to the United States after 1880. Their foreignness undoubtedly stimulated nativist tendencies and added to the determination of the White Anglo-Saxon Protestants in the country to exclude all Jews from their ranks.

Although anti-Semitism has never been an instrument of governmental policy in the United States, as has been the case in Europe, and though violence has never been a serious problem for Jewish Americans—even Grant's order produced no physical violence against them—the pattern of bigotry and hatred that characterized the post-Civil War years did lead to the Georgia lynching in 1915 of a Jew named Leo Frank.

Conservative, Reconstructionist, and Orthodox Judaism

By 1885, Reform Judaism had deviated drastically from received Jewish tradition. Even before that year, traditionalists, alarmed at its growing strength, had organized a countermovement that became known as Conservative Judaism. By 1886, it was strong enough to found the Jewish Theological Seminary in New York City. Though it made some concessions to the modern world, Conservative Judaism remained faithful to the core of Jewish law and ancestral traditions.

The early organizational efforts of Conservative Judaism were unimpressive, but with the arrival of one-half million Orthodox eastern-European Jews by the end of the century, its prospects improved greatly. To many of the American-born children of the Orthodox, the Conservative movement offered an attractive compromise between their middle-class desire for social integration and their attachment to traditional Jewish culture. In 1901, Jewish philanthropists financed the reorganization of the Jewish Theological Seminary, which soon began graduating American-trained rabbis to satisfy the flourishing Conservative movement.

Shortly after this time, the smallest branch of American Judaism began. Reconstructionism, which began in the philosophy of Mordechai Kaplan, a graduate of the Jewish Theological Seminary, saw Judaism as a "religious civilization" emerging from the history and culture of the Jewish people. It is like Reform Judaism in its emphasis on reexamination of religious beliefs and similar to Orthodox Judaism in its commitment to preserve forms and symbols of religious practice.

But it was Orthodox Judaism that benefited most from the immigration of eastern-European Jews. By 1900, most of the 850 congregations in the United States were Orthodox. Two years later, the Union of Orthodox Rabbis was organized to "place Orthodox Judaism in America on a firm basis." One of the educational institutions it supported became the nucleus of Yeshiva University.

Despite the growth of both the Reform and Conservative movements, Orthodox Judaism has maintained a significant place in the American Jewish community. Its numbers were augmented after World War I with the influx of thousands of Orthodox Jews from eastern Europe, many of whom settled in New York City.

The New Immigration

Between 1881 and 1924, more than 2 million Jews left eastern Europe because of anti-Jewish legislation and *pogroms* (government-sponsored attacks) against them. In some years, they came to the United States at the rate of more than 100,000 per year. The vast majority, as was true of other immigrant groups, settled in the northeastern states, particularly in the port cities of New York, Boston, Philadelphia, and Baltimore. Others crowded into the great cities of the Midwest. The Jews moved into densely populated ethnic neighborhoods such as New York's Lower East Side, South Philadelphia, or Chicago's West Side. Data from 1908 to 1924 indicate that only 5% of Jews arriving in the United States returned to Europe, compared to 33% of the general immigration (Thernstrom, Orlov, & Handlin, 1980). Many found work in the new ready-to-wear clothing industry. They were attracted to it, not because of an inherent proclivity for tailoring, but because of the constant demand for cheap labor and the fact that many had had garment experience in Europe. Working conditions were deplorable. The highly competitive contract system and the sweatshops it generated regularly exploited the workers. The sweatshops were dark, airless, unsanitary firetraps in which whole families often worked to meet production quotas. Tuberculosis and other diseases were rampant. Laborers worked from 4:00 A.M. to 10:00 P.M. Men earned $6 to $10 a week; women and children much less.

Such conditions led to the formation in 1888 of the United Hebrew Trades in New York. It was the first organization to introduce Jewish immigrants to the trade union movement. After the turn of the century, Jewish clothing workers organized the powerful International Ladies' Garment Workers Union and the Amalgamated Clothing Workers of America. In 1911, a tragic fire at the Triangle Shirtwaist Factory in New York City underscored the need for better working conditions in the industry. Over the years, the International and the Amalgamated improved conditions and benefits and broke new ground in employer–employee relations. Since the end of World War I there has been a steady exodus of Jewish workers from the garment industry, but the legacy of the once largely Jewish unions remains an important chapter in the history of American labor.

Yiddish

Yiddish was the daily language of most of the eastern-European Jews. Hebrew, the holy tongue, was reserved for prayer and study of the Bible. Though both use the Hebrew alphabet and are written from right to left, they are not the same. Yiddish is similar to German; Hebrew is a Semitic language.

Daily newspapers in Yiddish appeared in several U.S. cities, most notably in New York. They taught the immigrants American history and civics in the language they understood best. Many read Yiddish fiction in America. The stories of Sholom Aleichem, one of the better-known Yiddish writers, inspired the hit Broadway musical *Fiddler on the Roof*. Yiddish theater, too, flourished and attained a high literary and dramatic level, producing a host of Yiddish dramatists. But the flowering of Yiddish was a phenomenon of the immigrant generation. By mid-twentieth century, it had fallen into disuse. Gifted writers like Waldo Frank, Ben Hecht, Ludwig Lewisohn, Michael Gold, and Abraham Cahan wrote about the Yiddish experience in English. The stories of one contemporary Yiddish writer, Isaac Bashevis Singer, are enjoyed in their English translations. Singer was awarded the Nobel Prize for Literature in 1978.

Courses in Yiddish are offered in universities and adult education programs today in an attempt to preserve and revitalize Yiddish culture. The National Yiddish Book Center, founded in 1980, oversees the recovery, collection, and cataloguing of Yiddish books from around the world that would otherwise be thrown away. In 1999, the Center had collected 1.5 million books, instituted a Yiddish library development program, Yiddish musical projects, and a series of public radio broadcasts of Yiddish stories in English translation (Singer et al., 2000).

The Interwar Period

Following World War I, America's traditional hospitality toward immigrants suddenly changed. Undoubtedly, anti-Semitic factors account in part for the series of restrictive immigration laws that, by 1924, virtually stopped Jewish immigration. In that year, the Johnson-Reed National Origins Quota Act blatantly curtailed immigration from eastern Europe, where most Jews lived, from southern Europe, and from non-White countries. Its system of national quotas remained in effect until 1965.

The prosperity of the war years enabled many Jewish Americans to move to newer, middle-class neighborhoods, foreshadowing a later exodus to the suburbs. The less affluent, often more religious Jews tended to remain in older neighborhoods, where eastern-European orthodoxy survived in its purest forms. Kosher restaurants flourished, late afternoon Jewish schools, Yiddish publications, and Orthodox synagogues were abundant. In the newer neighborhoods, indifference, even skepticism, toward Jewish ritual was a common attitude. It seemed to foreshadow the demise of Judaism in America; yet that is not what happened. Instead, most Jewish Americans felt an overriding desire to preserve their Jewish cultural identity and pass it on to their children. This can be seen in their high rate of endogamous marriage and in the growth of congregations and Jewish schools in the newer Jewish neighborhoods during these years.

By 1940, Jewish Americans had transformed themselves from a working-class to a middle-class community of commercial, white-collar, and professional people who established an excellent record of achievement in the sciences, medicine, and other fields of endeavor.

For many Jews, education was a calculated means of social and economic improvement. But a more likely explanation of their drive for education is to be found in Jewish culture itself, which places a high priority on knowledge and learning for its own sake. Education was part of the value system that the Jewish immigrants brought with them, as well as part of the value system that sustained generations of pious Jews in their perpetual study of the Bible.

During these years, anti-Semitism assumed an ominous hue. The Ku Klux Klan reappeared. It burned fiery crosses in front of synagogues and smashed store windows of Jewish merchants. By 1925, it had more than four million members. In 1920, Henry Ford reprinted *The Protocols of the Elders of Zion* in his weekly newspaper, *The Dearborn Independent*. It was a clumsy fabrication, originally published in 1904 in Russia, purporting to be the minutes of a secret meeting of Jewish leaders in Prague, in the last years of the nineteenth century, who plotted the overthrow of the world. Many Americans were prepared to believe it. During the Great Depression, Jewish bankers were accused of controlling world finance. A *Fortune Magazine* survey in 1936 proved conclusively that Jews played, at best, a minimal role in national and international banking, yet the myth persisted. Later, in the 1930s, as the influence of Nazism was increasingly felt in the United States, and attempts to prove that Jews were biologically inferior were imported, anti-Jewish propaganda intensified. Hatemongers, like Father Charles E. Coughlin, the Detroit "radio priest," revived the myth of a Jewish takeover of the world. But they made little headway in the United States, and with the end of World War II, when the full dimensions of the Nazi Holocaust were revealed, anti-Semitism ebbed to its lowest level in years.

Despite periodic ups and downs in reported anti-Semitic incidents due to, for instance, the situation in the Middle East, anti-Semitism in the United States continues at low levels. According to the Anti-Defamation League (2000), which has conducted an Audit of Anti-Semitic Incidents since 1979, through education and the diligent work of law enforcement, anti-Semitic incidents continue to decrease.

Zionism

The two most important events in the history of the Jewish people since their dispersion 2,000 years ago have been the Nazi Holocaust and the creation of the

State of Israel in 1948. Modern political Zionism, as the proposal for the return of the Jewish people to Zion (Palestine) is known, is considered to have begun in 1897, when Theodore Herzl convened the first Zionist Congress in Basel, Switzerland. The Zionist movement in the United States drew its greatest support from the eastern-European Jewish immigrants. A major factor in its growth was the emergence of Louis D. Brandeis as its leader, a role he held at the time of his appointment as associate justice of the U.S. Supreme Court in 1916. Yet, it was the Nazi Holocaust that brought the Zionist goal to fruition (Linenthal, 1995).

Six million of Europe's Jews and five million other people were killed by the Nazis in World War II (Berenbaum, 1993). The majority were systematically murdered in specially built death camps. The commander of Auschwitz estimated that two and one-half million victims were executed at that camp alone, and another one-half million died there of starvation and disease. Had it not been for America's restrictive immigration laws during these years, many lives could have been saved. Only a pitifully small number of Jewish refugees reached the United States in the 1930s. The best known was Albert Einstein. Ships carrying refugees from Germany were actually turned away from U.S. shores and sent back to the Nazi crematoria. The consistent refusal of the United States and other Western nations to accept Jewish refugees led to the near fanatical determination of Zionists the world over to reestablish a homeland in Palestine as a haven for persecuted Jews from any land. It also accounts for the passionate support of contemporary Jews for Israel. After the war, when the culpability of the Western nations in not accepting more refugees became evident, the general public endorsed the Zionist program. When the State of Israel was proclaimed, President Harry S. Truman recognized the new nation immediately. Despite their emotional attachment to Israel, few Jewish Americans have moved to Israel, but Israel has long been a focal point of unity for the American Jewish community, particularly during the Six Day War in 1967 and the Yom Kippur War in 1973. In recent years, however, Israel has become a divisive communal issue. Policies toward the Palestinians, the peace process, and Israel's religious life have all become increasingly controversial, causing mixed feelings for some American Jews (Singer et al., 2000). Despite the growing complexity of this relationship, 80% of Jewish Americans still believe that caring about Israel is a very important part of their Jewish identity (American Jewish Committee, 2000).

Jewish Americans Today

Jews Today

Today, Jewish Americans are enjoying another golden age. At the end of the twentieth century Jewish Americans have been accepted and have thrived in contemporary American society as never before.

Postwar prosperity and the end of educational quotas and social barriers after World War II opened up opportunities for Jews who entered the academic world in disproportionate numbers. By 1990, surveys showed that Jewish men and women had earned higher levels of education than their gentile White counterparts (Carlson, 1999). Jewish women, in particular, have achieved considerably greater levels of education than their non-Jewish contemporaries. Fifty-seven percent of Jewish women are college graduates compared with 19% of all American women (Kosmin, 1992). Institutions that once discriminated against Jews, such as Harvard, Columbia, and Princeton, have all hired Jewish presidents.

Another symbol of Jewish success is the role of Jews in the upper echelons of government. For the first time in American history, the fact that someone was Jewish became irrelevant when being appointed to a high government position. During President Clinton's tenure, there were several Jewish cabinet members and two Jewish Supreme Court justices were appointed, as were numerous Jewish ambassadors. What made many of these appointments noteworthy was how little attention they actually received by the general public.

Being Jewish has also not kept Jews from seeking and securing various elective offices. In 1999 there were 10 Jewish senators and 23 Jewish members of Congress (Singer et al., 2000). While Jewish congressmen in the past tended to represent the largely Jewish districts in New York, this is no longer the case. Jewish members of Congress represent diverse communities all over the United States, even where the Jewish population is miniscule. States like Vermont (0.9% Jewish population) and New Mexico (0.4%) have elected Jews to represent them (Hoffman, 1993). Although his Jewishness was significant, it did not keep Senator Joseph Lieberman from running as the Democratic candidate for vice president in the 2000 presidential election.

American Jews tend to be more liberal than the general population. Despite the shift in the early 1970s, when the U.S. political center moved to the right, carrying many Jews with it, the center of the Jewish political spectrum remained left of the national center. Today, nearly two out of three Jews consider themselves liberal rather than conservative (Kosmin et al., 1991). In 2000, 59% of American Jews affiliated with the Democratic party and 30% with the Independents, compared with 9% who registered Republican (American Jewish Committee, 2000).

Although reasons for their liberal views are unclear, the commitment of Jews to reformist tradition, no doubt, has deep roots in their religious, economic, and political history and is related to their own struggle for equality and security from persecution. The generation of Jews that came after World War II was in the forefront of the civil rights movement and active in liberal politics. Students, professors, and rabbis were especially prominent in the demonstrations, marches, sit-ins, and voter registration campaigns of the 1960s.

Jews have continued to support liberal causes with an emphasis on civil rights. Unfortunately, despite some similar experiences between the African

American and Jewish communities, friction between African Americans and Jews emerged in the mid-1980s and erupted into violence in 1991, when African Americans rioted in Crown Heights, an orthodox Jewish community in Brooklyn, after a Jewish motorist struck and killed an African American youngster. Tension heightened again in 1993, when Khalid Abdul Muhammad, a top aid to Nation of Islam leader Louis Farrakahn, delivered an anti-Semitic speech at Kean College in New Jersey.

In 1995, when Louis Farrakhan led the Million Man March in Washington, D.C., many in the Jewish community, while supportive of some aspects of the march's message, were deeply disappointed when Farrakhan, known for his virulent anti-Semitism, was embraced by many in the civil rights community. Though the golden age of Black–Jewish cooperation seemed over, well-meaning African Americans and Jews sought to quiet the angry voices and repair the damage to Black–Jewish relations (Lerner & West, 1995).

Until the 1970s few Jews occupied positions of genuine power in the country's largest corporations. During the 1990s the wealth of individual Jews significantly grew with 25% of America's richest people being of Jewish background (Marsh, 1996). The per capita income of Jews is nearly double that of non-Jews (Cohen, 1989).

Jewish Americans are unquestionably more secure in U.S. society and more willing to demonstrate, protest, and lobby in their own self interest as never before. Despite this security, 63% of American Jews believe that anti-Semitism is a problem in the United States (American Jewish Committee, 2000). Certainly such groups as the Ku Klux Klan, the American Nazi Party, and the Neo-Nazis are a cause for concern, as is the growing number of Web sites devoted to White supremacy and hate groups that are found on the Internet. While anti-Semitism still exists, people and groups who hate Jews today are largely marginalized and powerless, leaving the daily impact on the lives of American Jews greatly lessened.

Many contend that a major threat to American Jewish life comes, not from those who hate the Jews, but from a culture that is so accepting it has eroded Jewish distinctiveness. In 1990, the Council of Jewish Federations released their 1990 National Jewish Population Study. To date this is the definitive source of data on the Jewish community for the last decade of the twentieth century. Among its many findings, the most astonishing is that the rate of intermarriage in 1990 was found to be 52%, up from 31% in 1974 (Kosmin et al., 1991). This, coupled with other findings of rampant assimilation and a negative birthrate (nonobservant Jews average between 1.5 and 1.6 children per couple), left many in the Jewish community feeling as if Judaism in America would not survive far into the twenty-first century. Not surprisingly, a notable amount of debate and discussion within the Jewish community during the last decade of the twentieth century was about Jewish survival and continuity.

There have been two main responses to the Jewish continuity debate. The first is that communal resources should be used to encourage "outreach" to intermarried and unaffiliated Jews. Others believe that resources should be used to reach "within" the community to those who are already somewhat Jewishly connected. In his book, *The Vanishing American Jew,* Alan Dershowitz (1998) argues that Jews must create a new sense of Jewish identity that focuses on the positive, the 3,500-year-old legacy of Jewish culture, values, and traditions. By accentuating the positive, he contends that the current trend of unbridled assimilation can be reversed.

When the twenty-first century began, fears of the Jewish community's demise were premature. The Jewish community remains an important ethnic and religious group in U.S. society, reflecting a wide diversity of social class, religious commitment, political outlook, and economic status.

Teaching Strategies

To illustrate how content related to Jewish Americans can be used to integrate the curriculum, exemplary strategies are identified for teaching these concepts at the grade levels indicated: *values* (primary and middle and upper grades), *assimilation* (middle and upper grades), *ethnic organizations and institutions* and *ethnic identity* (high school grades).

Primary Grades

CONCEPT

Values
Generalization: The values of Jewish Americans are reflected in their sacred writings and literature.

1. Distribute the following List of Jewish Values to each student. Divide the students into small groups of four or five.
2. In their small groups, have the students discuss each value. For each value, the students should answer the following questions:
   a. What do you think that the value means?
   b. How does it relate to your own life?
   c. Have you ever learned a lesson similar to this value from your family, friends, or religion?
   d. Discuss an example of something you can do in your everyday life that would describe each value.

After these activities, discuss the questions that follow the List of Jewish Values with the whole class.

List of Jewish Values
1. Repairing or perfecting the world (Aleynu Prayer, Prayer Book)
2. You are not required to complete the task, nor are you free to desist from it entirely. (Pirkey Avot, Ethics of the Fathers, Chapter 2, Mishnah 21)

3. Humanity is created "in God's image." (Genesis, Chapter 1, Verse 27)
4. Guard your tongue from speaking evil. (Psalms, Chapter 34, Verse 14)
5. Do not look at the vessel, but rather at what it contains. (Pirkey Avot, Ethics of the Fathers, Chapter 4, Mishnah 27)
6. Love your neighbor as yourself. (Leviticus, Chapter 19, Verse 18)
7. What is hateful to you, do not do to your neighbor. (Tractate Shabbat, Talmud 31 A)
8. If I am not for myself, who will be for me? (Pirkey Avot, Ethics of the Fathers, Chapter 1, Mishnah 14)

Discussion Questions

1. What surprised you about these particular Jewish values? Do you think that these values only apply to American Jews? Explain. What are some of the lessons that these values teach?
2. Have the class prepare a list of things that they can do at their school or at home that would exemplify these values.

Second Strategy

1. Read the following books to the class:
   a. *The Treasure* by Uri Shulevitz (HarperCollinsCanada, 1978): This Caldecott Honor Book tells the story of an elderly man who travels a great distance to find a treasure that is already at his home.
   b. *Keeping Quilt* by Patricia Polaaco (Simon and Schuster, New York, 1988): This autobiography tells the story of one family's keepsake that is passed from generation to generation. It shares family and religious traditions and shows how people can assimilate into a new country while maintaining rituals from their homeland.
2. Ask students to share family traditions and rituals with the class. Have students interview family members to learn the most important values from their own tradition that can be shared with the class.

Middle and Upper Grades

CONCEPT

Values
Generalization: The values of Jewish Americans are reflected in their philosophy and literature.

1. Distribute the handout of Maimonides's Eight Steps of Giving Charity in a scrambled order to each student. Maimonides was a Jewish philosopher.
2. Ask the class to arrange the eight steps in the proper order, from the least to the most virtuous.
3. In small groups have the students explain the order of their lists.
4. In a large group, show the class the eight steps according to Maimonides. Conclude the discussion with the questions that follow *Eight Steps*.

Maimonides's Eight Steps of Giving Charity

1. Give, but grudgingly.
2. Give less than is fitting, but willingly.

3. Give only after being asked to.
4. Give before being asked to.
5. Give in such a way that the giver does not know to whom he or she is giving.
6. Give in such a way that the one who receives does not know who has given to him or her.
7. Give in such a way that neither the giver nor the one who receives knows the identity of the other.
8. The highest form of charity is to help the poor become self-supporting by lending them money, taking them into partnership, or giving them work. In this way there is no loss of self-respect.

Discussion Questions

1. What surprised you about Maimonides's list? How did it compare to your own?
2. Do you agree that the highest form of charity is to help the poor become self-supporting? Why? How does this compare to welfare reform in our society?
3. Ask the students for examples of charity at each level.

Second Strategy

1. Read the story, "If Not Still Higher" (reprinted from *The Case against the Wind and Other Stories* by I. L. Peretz, New York: Macmillan, 1975) to the class.
2. Have students discuss in small groups what particular value(s) are expressed in this story.
3. After the small-group discussions, have a whole-class discussion of the questions that follow the story.

If Not Still Higher

The Rabbi of Nemirov disappeared every morning during High Holy Days Selichoth prayers (prayers asking for forgiveness). Some people thought he went to heaven each morning. One day a Jew from Lithuania came to town. He laughed and assured the people that no one could go to heaven while still alive. But he decided to find out for himself where the rabbi went.

Early the next morning he followed the rabbi to a nearby forest. The rabbi was dressed as a workman. He saw the rabbi chop down a small tree, cut it into sticks, make a bundle of them, and sling them over his shoulder. He then walked to a broken-down hut where a sick, old woman lived.

"Who is it?" called the woman.

"Vassili," answered the disguised rabbi, "I have wood for sale for only six cents." He entered the house without waiting for an answer. The Lithuanian stole in behind him.

"How can a poor widow afford even six cents?" asked the old woman.

"I trust you," replied the rabbi.

"And who will light the fire?" lamented the widow. "I am too weak to get up."

"I will," said the rabbi.

As he lit the fire, the rabbi recited the Selichoth prayers. The Lithuanian watched in silence. From that moment on, he became a follower of the Rabbi of Nemirov. Later, when the people would say their rabbi flew to heaven during Selichoth prayers, he would add quietly, "If not still higher!"

Discussion Questions
1. What puzzled the people of Nemirov?
2. Where did they think their rabbi went each morning during Selichoth prayers? What does this tell about their opinion of him?
3. Was it right for the Lithuanian to follow the rabbi the next day? Explain.
4. What did the Lithuanian find out? How did it influence him? Why?
5. What does the title of the story mean?
6. Why didn't the Rabbi of Nemirov give the old woman the wood for nothing?
7. At which level of Maimonides's list does the rabbi's deed belong? Explain.
8. What important Jewish idea does the story bring out?

Alternative Strategies
1. Have students survey family and friends about the role of giving charity in their lives. Have the students compare the results with Maimonides's Eight Steps of Giving Charity.
2. Have students decide for themselves which of Maimonides's Eight Steps of Giving Charity is the highest. Have students organize a social-action project at their school that exemplifies that particular step of giving (i.e., collecting food for a soup kitchen—the receiver would not know the giver).

CONCEPT
Assimilation
Generalization: While the Jewish community in the United States remains an important ethnic and religious group, there are concerns for its survival in the twenty-first century.

1. Have the students read the letter below that was written to the editor of the Jewish *Daily Forward* (reprinted from *A Bintel Brief*, edited by Isaac Metzker, Garden City, NY: Doubleday, 1971) in 1932 or read the letter aloud to the class.
2. Have the students write down their first thoughts about this letter.
3. After the students have read the letter, ask the questions that follow it.

Dear Editor,

I am an immigrant from Russia, my wife is American-born, and we are both free thinkers. We have two grown children, a son and a daughter, who know they are Jews but never saw any signs of religion or holidays in our home. Even *Yom Kippur* is just another day to us. For the last twenty years we've lived among Christians and we socialize with them. Our children also go around with Gentiles.

Some time ago a Christian girl began to come to our house, seemingly to visit our daughter, but it was no secret to us that she was after our twenty-three-year-old son, with whom she was friendly. We said nothing about it, because we wouldn't have minded having her for a daughter-in-law.

Once the girl invited our son to a party at her house where all the other guests were Gentiles. They were all having a good time until one of the guests, whether in jest or earnest, began to make fun of Jews. I don't know what happened there, but I am sure they didn't mean to hurt my son, because none of them, not even his girlfriend, knew that he is Jewish. But he was insulted and told the girl so. Then he told her that he is Jewish and this was a surprise to her.

My son left the party immediately and from that day on he is changed. He began to ask questions about religion, debated with me about things that formerly hadn't interested him. He wanted to know where I was born, how many Jews there are in the world, why the religious don't eat pork, where the hatred of Jews came from, and on and on. He was not satisfied with my short answers but began to read books looking for more information. My son also berated me for not giving him a Jewish upbringing.

His Gentile girlfriend came to beg him to forgive her. She cried and explained that it was not her fault, but he didn't want to have anything to do with her because, it seems, he was deeply insulted. His head was filled with one thought, Jewishness. He found Jewish friends, he was drawn into a Zionist club and they worked on him so that he has come to me with a suggestion that I give up the business and we all go to Palestine. And since he sees that I am not about to go, he's getting ready to go alone.

At first we took it as a joke, but we see now that he's taking it very seriously. Well, my going is out of the question. I am not that crazy. But what can be done about him? I'm willing to give in to his whim. I'm sure that in Palestine he'll sober up and realize that not everyone who is Jewish must live in Palestine. My wife is carrying on terribly; what do I mean, allowing my son to travel to a wild country [where there is conflict between Arabs and Jews]? She says we should not give him the money for the trip. But our son says he will find a way to reach the Jewish Homeland.

My wife and I are very anxious to hear your opinion.

Respectfully, A Reader

Source: Excerpt from *A Bintel Brief* by Isaac Metzker. Copyright © 1971 by Isaac Metzker. Reprinted by permission of Doubleday & Company, Inc.

Discussion Questions

1. How would you advise the writer of the letter? (The editor replied: "Your son is a very sensitive and thinking person. Since he is an adult you must let him go his way and do what he wants to do.").

2. Describe some of the ways the family in the letter has assimilated to life in the United States.

3. What are the advantages of Jews providing a Jewish upbringing for their children? Likewise, should other cultures, religions, and/or racial groups provide

a certain upbringing for their children? Explain. What should this upbringing include?

4. Why does the son join a Zionist club and want to go to Palestine? How will this solve his problem?

5. In what ways could the son satisfy his need to identify as a Jew without moving to Palestine?

6. Did the son overreact to the anti-Semitic comment? Explain. How else might he have reacted? Has a similar situation happened to you? Explain. How did you react?

7. Where and how do people learn anti-Semitism or any kind of prejudice?

8. If someone in your family made an anti-Semitic comment, how would you react?

9. If someone in your family told an ethnic joke, how would you react?

High School Grades

CONCEPT

Ethnic Organizations and Institutions
Generalization: Jewish Americans, like other U.S. ethnic groups, have created organizations to help them to maintain a sense of community and to fight discrimination.

1. Distribute the handout of Table 9.1 to each student.

2. Have the students complete the chart in Table 9.1 by listing parallel institutions of other ethnic or religious groups in column 2 and similarities and differences in columns 3 and 4.

3. After the students have completed the chart, discuss the following questions.

Discussion Questions

1. What surprised you about the information you found?

2. How are the various organizations funded (grants, private funds, etc.)?

3. Share some of the similarities you found between the various organizations.

4. Why do various ethnic and religious groups feel that it is necessary to maintain these organizations? Do you think they are necessary? Explain.

5. In some cases there may be "overlap" in the kinds of services these organizations provide. Should they merge? Why? Why not?

CONCEPT

Ethnic Identity
Generalization: Jewish identity within the United States is threatened by an increasing rate of intermarriage (which increased from 31% in 1974 to 52% in 1990), a low birthrate, and widespread assimilation among Jewish Americans.

1. Ask the students: Are Jews a nation, an ethnic group, a religious minority, a people, a race, all of these, some of these, or none of these? (The answer is "some of these." Jews are not a race.) The government of Israel in 1958 established a special committee to provide an answer to the perplexing question: "Who is a Jew?" The results were inconclusive. Have students conduct a

TABLE 9.1 Similarities and Differences in Jewish and Non-Jewish Organizations

Jewish Institutions/Organizations	Non-Jewish Institutions/Organizations	Similarities	Differences
YMHA			
Jewish Community Centers			
Jewish Day Schools			
Synagogues			
Jewish Hospitals			
Yiddish Press			
Civil Rights Organizations			
Fraternal Organizations			
Jewish Publication Society			
Service Clubs			
Fund-Raising Organizations			
Organizations for College Students			

survey or do a research paper to see if they can provide an answer. Students should include information about other ethnic groups so that they can conclude whether these groups have difficulty defining themselves.

2. Have students read and report on a book about Jews by a Jewish American author. Reports should tell how individuals or families they read about reconcile their desire to become Americanized with the desire to preserve their Jewish heritage. (These are among the authors the students can choose: Sholom Aleichem, Mary Antin, Pearl Abraham, Saul Bellow, Edna Ferber, Bernard Malamud, Tova Mirvis, Chaim Potok, Irwin Shaw, Leon Uris, Elie Wiesel, and Herman Wouk.)

3. Since 1948, Jewish Americans have become passionate supporters of Israel, despite the fact that few of them or their immediate ancestors were born there or plan to live there. Ask students to write essays that compare Jewish attitudes toward Israel with those of other ethnic minority groups to their country of origin. What similarities or differences exist? How do students account for them?

4. The rate of intermarriage for Jewish Americans has increased dramatically in recent years. Ask students to conduct an informal survey among their friends and families to determine if this is true of other ethnic and religious groups. Discuss and debate the pros and cons of intermarriage.

VALUING ACTIVITY

Read the following story to the class and ask the questions that follow.

Mr. Cohen and the Christmas Tree

Mr. and Mrs. Cohen live in Chicago, where Mr. Cohen owns a small business. The Jewish religion is an important part of their family life. They are members of a synagogue and attend religious services every week. They observe Jewish holidays and customs, and Mrs. Cohen keeps a traditional Kosher home and lights Sabbath candles every Friday evening. Their only son is a college professor. His wife is Jewish but she is from a nonreligious background. They do not follow the Jewish religion closely. They have two children, a girl, eight, and a son, four. They live in a suburb not far from Mr. and Mrs. Cohen.

Last Christmas the Cohens were in their son's neighborhood and dropped in for a surprise visit. When they entered the living room they saw their son trimming a Christmas tree and his two children helping him. Mr. Cohen was furious. His two grandchildren greeted him with "Merry Christmas."

Mr. Cohen did not answer. He did not even take off his coat. He looked at his son and said, "Jews do not have Christmas trees." He took his wife by the arm and they turned to leave. Their son and daughter-in-law begged them to stay, but Mr. Cohen would not change his mind. Mrs. Cohen was confused. She felt her place was with her husband and returned home with him.

Mr. Cohen's son says he had the Christmas tree only for the sake of his children, so they would not feel different from their non-Jewish friends. He assured his father the Christmas tree had nothing to do with religion. He did not consider it wrong having a Christmas tree and felt his father had no right to be angry about it.

Mr. Cohen says his grandchildren are different from Christian children and should feel the difference. He argues that Jews and Gentiles should observe national American holidays, but Christmas is the most important religious holiday of the Christians, and Jews have nothing to do with it. They should not have Christmas trees.

He refuses to visit his son's home and Mrs. Cohen cannot convince him to change his mind.

Questions
1. Who is right, Mr. Cohen or his son?
2. Do you think Mr. Cohen is being unfair to his wife, his son, his daughter-in-law, his grandchildren? Explain.
3. What alternatives are open to Mr. Cohen? To his son?
4. Do you think Mr. Cohen's son should be concerned that his children feel that they are different from other children? Why or why not?
5. Do you think Christians should send or expect to receive Christmas cards from their Jewish friends? Justify your answer.

REFERENCES

American Jewish Committee. (1999, 2000). *Annual Survey of Jewish Opinion*. New York: American Jewish Committee.

Anti-Defamation League. (2000). *Annual Audit of Anti-Semitic Incidents*. New York: Author.

Berenbaum, M. (1993). *The World Must Know: The History of the Holocaust as Told in the United States Holocaust Memorial Museum*. Boston: Little Brown.

Carlson, R. (Ed.). (1999). *American Jewish Desk Reference*. New York: Random House.

Cohen, S. (1989). *The Dimensions of American Jewish Liberalism*. New York: American Jewish Congress, 1989.

Dershowitz, A. (1998). *The Vanishing American Jew*. New York: Simon and Schuster.

Hertzberg, A. (1998). *The Jews in America: Four Centuries of an Uneasy Encounter: A History*. New York: Columbia University Press.

Hoffman, M. (1993, February). More Jews in Congress: Doesn't It Make a Difference? *Moment*, pp. 32–39.

Kosmin, B. (1992, August). The Permeable Boundaries of Being Jewish in America. *Moment*, pp. 30–33, 51.

Kosmin, B., Goldstein, S., Waksberg, J., Lerer, N., Keysar, A., & Scheckner, J. (1991). *Highlights of the CJF 1990 National Jewish Population Survey*. New York: Council of Jewish Federations.

Lerner, M., & West, C. (1995). *Let the Healing Begin: Blacks and Jews*. New York: G. P. Putnam's Sons.

Linenthal, E. T. (1995). *Preserving Memory: The Struggle to Create America's Holocaust Museum*. New York: Viking.

Marsh, A. (1996, October 14). Meet the Class of 1996. *Forbes*, pp. 100–295.

Singer, D. (Ed.). (1999, 2000). *American Jewish Yearbook* (Vol. 99 & 100). New York: American Jewish Committee.

Thernstrom, S., Orlov, A., & Handlin, O. (Eds.). (1980). *Harvard Encyclopedia of American Ethnic Groups*. Cambridge, MA: Harvard University Press.

ANNOTATED BIBLIOGRAPHY

Books for Teachers

Especially Recommended

Abrams, E. (1997). *Faith or Fear: How American Jews Can Survive in a Christian America*. New York: Free Press.

> *In response to current trends of intermarriage, a low birthrate, and declining interest in organized Jewish life, Abrams suggests ways to combat these challenges to the Jewish continuity. The author argues that Fundamentalist Christians are the natural allies of American Jews rather than their enemies.*

Carlson, R. (Ed.). (1999). *American Jewish Desk Reference* (Stevie Jewish Historical Society). New York: Random House.

> *This all-encompassing reference to Jewish life in the United States, from 1654 to the present, contains nearly 900 entries on all aspects of Jewish culture, and brings together the events, personalities, themes, and issues of contemporary Jewish life in the United States.*

Cohen, S., & Eisen, A. (2000). *The Jew Within: Self, Family, and Community in America*. Bloomington, IN: Indiana University Press.

> *In response to current trends of intermarriage and assimilation in the Jewish community, the authors probe beneath the surface to explore the foundations of belief and behavior among moderately affiliated American Jews.*

Goldman, A. (2000). *Being Jewish: The Spiritual and Cultural Practice of Judaism Today*. New York: Simon and Schuster.

> *The former New York Times religion reporter explores the origins and meaning of Jewish ritual and what it means for the contemporary practice of Judaism, from practitioners of Orthodox ways to members of the Reform movement.*

Howe, I. (1998). *World of Our Fathers: The Journey of the East European Jews to America and the Life they Found and Made*. New York: Schocken.

> *This story of over 2 million Jewish immigrants in America in four decades begins with the 1880s. It also provides a detailed look at everything from Yiddish theatre to the Jewish labor movement.*

Kaufman, J. (1998). *Broken Alliance: The Turbulent Times between Blacks and Jews in America*. New York: Scribners'.

> *This is a portrait of the relationship between Blacks and Jews from the strong partnership forged during the Civil Rights Movement of the 1960s to the more recent relationship that includes both collaborations and recriminations.*

Telushkin, J. (1991). *Jewish Literacy*. New York: William Morrow.

> *In 346 short entries, Rabbi Telushkin tells the most important things to know about the Jewish religion, essential trends, concepts, personalities, and culture.*

Other References

Cook, S. D. (Ed.). (1997). *Black-Jewish Relations: Dillard University National Conference Papers*. Franklin, TN: Providence House.

The speeches and essays in this book show how the Black–Jewish alliance played a pivotal role in the Civil Rights Movement.

DeLange, N. (1997). *The Illustrated History of the Jewish People*. San Diego: Harcourt Brace.

The story of Judaism from its earliest beginnings to the present as narrated by eight Jewish historians.

Diamant, A. (1997). *The Red Tent*. New York: St. Martin's Press.

A hugely popular book with Jewish and non-Jewish readers, The Red Tent is the story of Jacob's daughter, Dinah, and his four wives. As Diamant explores the trials and triumphs of ancient women, she brings a foreign world to life as seen through the emotional filter of Dinah's eyes.

Dubner, S. (1998). *Turbulent Souls: A Catholic Son's Return to His Jewish Family*. New York: William Morrow.

Dubner's parents were Jewish, but they both converted to Catholicism before they met. The devout Catholics raised their eight children in their new faith. Dubner eventually uncovered his parents' secret and set out in search of his spiritual and ethnic roots.

Goldberg, J. J. (1997). *Jewish Power: Inside the American Jewish Establishment*. Cambridge, MA: Perseus.

This is a study of Jewish organizations, money, and political power in the United States. Goldberg includes such topics as liberalism and American Jews; Jews and the Cold War; and how Jews vote.

Kamenetz, R. (1997). *The Jew in the Lotus: A Poet's Rediscovery of Jewish Identity in Buddhist India*. North Vale, NJ: Jason Aronson.

Kamenetz, a poet and professor of English, accompanied a group of eight Jewish leaders to Dharamsala in 1990 for a Jewish/Tibetan Buddhist dialogue. He relates encounters with Tibetan leaders, including the Dalai Lama, and with Jewish rabbis and cultural leaders.

Kertzer, M. N., Revised by Hoffman, L. A. (1997). *What Is a Jew?* New York: Simon and Schuster.

Completely revised and reorganized, this guide to the traditions, beliefs, and practices of Judaism, written to inform both Jew and non-Jew, tackles a wide range of subjects in a question-and-answer format.

Nathan, J. (1998). *The Jewish Holiday Kitchen: 250 Recipes from around the World to Make Your Celebrations Special*. New York: Schocken.

By adding over 50 new recipes, Joan Nathan has improved and expanded what is already considered the classic Jewish cookbook.

Susser, B., and Liebman, C. S. (1999). *Choosing Survival: Strategies for a Jewish Future*. New York: Oxford University Press.

The authors examine what happens to Jews and Jewish identity when persecution, anti-Semitism, and gentile hostility no longer endanger them.

Tobin, G., & Simon, K. (1999). *Opening the Gates: How Proactive Conversion Can Revitalize the Jewish Community*. San Francisco: Jossey-Bass.

Opening the Gates explores the roles of intermarriage and conversion in the Jewish community. Tobin and Simon offer strategies to incorporate conversion into the larger vision of building the next Jewish civilization.

Wyman, D. (1998). *The Abandonment of the Jews: America and the Holocaust 1941–1945.* New York: New Press.

A definitive account of American apathy regarding the Jewish plight during the Holocaust.

Books for Students

Adler, D. (1996). *The Kid's Catalog of Jewish Holidays.* Philadelphia: Jewish Publication Society.

Introduces the history and traditions of major Jewish holidays, including games, songs, crafts, stories, poems, riddles, jokes, and a wide variety of recipes, representing foods of several nations. It's well illustrated with sketches, cartoons, and photographs. (Intermediate)

Bat-Ami, M. (1999). *Two Sons in the Sky.* Ashville, NC: Front Street/Cricket.

A love story about a Catholic American teenager in Oswego, New York in 1944 and a young Holocaust survivor living in the Emergency Refugee Camp in Oswego. (High School)

Beerman, C. (1998). *Journey to Ellis Island: How My Father Came to America.* Illustrated by L. McGaw. New York: Hyperion.

The dramatic true story of a young Russian Jewish boy's journey with his mother and sister to America. Illustrated beautifully with evocative paintings and family photographs as well as period art and photos. (Intermediate)

Chametzky, J., Felstiner, J., Flazbaum, H., & Hellerstein, K. (Eds.). (2000). *Jewish American Literature: A Norton Anthology.* New York: W. W. Norton.

This rich anthology reconsiders Jewish American literature from its seventeenth-century origins to its flourishing present. It gathers the work of 145 writers in all genres—fiction, poetry, drama essays, journals, autobiography, song lyrics, and cartoons. (High School)

Cohen, J. (2000). *The Christmas Menorahs: How a Town Fought Hate.* Illustrated by B. Farnsworth. Morton Grove, IL: Albert Whitman.

Describes how people in Billings, Montana joined together to fight a series of hate crimes against a Jewish family. (Intermediate)

Finklestein, N. (2001). *The Other 1492: Jewish Settlement in the New World.* Lincoln, NE: iUniverse.

Describes the causes, events, and aftermath of the expulsion of the Jews from Spain in 1492. (Middle School)

Frank, A. (1995). *The Diary of a Young Girl: The Definitive Edition.* Ed. O. H. Frank & M. Pressler, Trans. S. Massoty. New York: Doubleday.

This new edition of the Diary of Anne Frank *restores passages that previously had been deleted. The new translation is far superior to earlier versions. (High School)*

Greene, B. (1999). *Summer of My German Soldier.* New York: Penguin Putnam.

A twelve-year-old Jewish girl living in a backward Arkansas town forms a destructive friendship with a young German prisoner of war. When rebellious Patty hides the enemy turned friend, the town's communal wrath is swift and sure. (Middle School)

Hest, A. (1997). *When Jessie Came Across the Sea.* Illustrated by P. J. Lynch. Cambridge, MA: Candlewick.

Thirteen-year-old Jessie is given a one-way ticket from her eastern-European shtetl to America. She overcomes the emotion of leaving her grandmother. In America she becomes a dressmaker and, in three years, saves enough money for a ticket for her grandmother. The emotions of separation, hope, and love will appeal to children. Strikingly illustrated. (Primary)

Jafee, N. (2000). *Tales for the Seventh Day: A Collection of Sabbath Stories.* Illustrated by K. Sutherland. New York: Scholastic.

Includes seven tales tied to the Jewish Sabbath but reflective of different cultures and times and of different moods. Jaffee includes a careful introduction outlining the concepts of the Jewish Sabbath as well as an extensive bibliography. (Intermediate)

Kerr, J. (1997). *When Hitler Stole Pink Rabbit.* New York: Putnam.

Recounts the adventures of a nine-year-old Jewish girl and her family in the early 1930s as they travel from Germany to England. (Intermediate)

Kimmelman, L. (2000). *Dance, Sing, Remember: A Celebration of Jewish Holidays.* Illustrated by O. Eitan. New York: Harper Collins.

Explains eleven major Jewish holidays and how they are celebrated. (Primary)

Kluger, S. (1998). *The Last Days of Summer.* New York: Avon/Bard.

The poignant story of Joey Margolis, the only Jewish kid in the building. Though regularly beaten up, he lives a charmed life and establishes a relationship with his hero, Charlie Banks, rookie third-baseman for the Giants. The two have amazing adventures together. (High School)

Koss, A. G. (1998). *How I Saved Hanukkah.* Illustrated by D. deGroat. New York: Dial.

Fourth-grader Maria Feinstein wants to know what Hanukkah is all about. Her curiosity gets her mother into the spirit of the holiday, which leads to a big Hanukkah party for all her friends, Jewish and non-Jewish alike. (Intermediate)

Lasky, K. (1997). *Marven of the Great North Woods.* Illustrated by K. Hawkes. Orlando, FL: Harcourt.

When his Jewish parents send him to a Minnesota logging camp to escape the influenza epidemic of 1918, ten-year-old Marven finds a special friend. (Primary/Intermediate)

Lasky, K. (1998). *Dreams in the Golden Country: The Diary of Zipporah Feldman, a Jewish Immigrant Girl.* New York: Scholastic.

Part of the Dear America series. The story of a Russian immigrant family in New York City in 1903 as told by twelve-year-old Zippy, who records events in her diary. This book deals with the Ellis Island experience as well as sweatshops, unionism, women's suffrage, and religious differences. (Intermediate)

Nye, N. (1999). *Habibi.* New York: Simon and Schuster.

When fourteen-year-old Liyanne Abboud, her younger brother, and her parents move from St. Louis to a new home between Jerusalem and the Palestinian village where her father was born, they face many tensions between Jews and Palestinians. (Middle School)

Polacco, P. (2000a). *The Butterfly.* New York: Penguin Putnam.

During the Nazi occupation of France, Monique's mother hides a Jewish family in her basement and tries to help them escape to freedom. (Intermediate)

Polacco, P. (2000b). *The Trees of the Dancing Goats.* New York: Simon and Schuster.

During a scarlet fever epidemic one winter in Michigan, a Jewish family helps make Christmas special for their sick neighbors by making their own Hanukkah miracle. (Primary)

Potok, C. (1996). *The Chosen.* New York: Random House.

The Chosen chronicles the friendship between Danny Saunders, a boy from a Hasidic family, and the more assimilated Rueven Malter, as they come of age in Williamsburg, Brooklyn. (High School)

Prose, F. (1998). *You Never Know: A Legend of the Lamed Vavniks*. Iluustrated by M. Podwal. New York: Greenwillow Books.

> *Though mocked by the rest of the villagers, poor Schmuel, the shoemaker, turns out to be a very special person. (Primary/Intermediate)*

Rosen, S. (2001). *Speed of Light*. New York: Simon and Schuster.

> *An eleven-year-old Jewish girl living in the South during the 1950s struggles with anti-Semitism and racism, which pervade her small community. (Middle School)*

Ross, K. (1997). *The Jewish Holiday Craft Book*. Illustrated by M. Levine. Brookfield, CT: Millbrook Press.

> *Each of the ten sections in this book focuses on a Jewish holiday and offers introductory information about that particular celebration and instructions for several related crafts. (Primary)*

Schotter, R. (1998). *Purim Play*. Illustrated by M. Hafner. Boston: Little, Brown.

> *This book is not just another repeat of the traditional Purim story about Haman. Frannie and her cousins do the story as a play, in which the unlikable Mrs. Teplitzsky dons a robe and beard to play Haman. She is a big hit and becomes a new friend. (Middle School)*

Schreiber, M., Schiff, A. I., & Klenicki, L. (Eds.). (1998). *The Shengold Jewish Encyclopedia*. Rockville, MD: Schreiber.

> *A revised and updated edition of the Junior Jewish Encyclopedia, first published over forty years ago. Covers American Jewish life, the contemporary Jewish world, and Jewish culture and history. Supported by an interactive Web site with monthly updates. (Middle School/High School)*

Schwartz, H. (2000). *The Day the Rabbi Disappeared: Jewish Holiday Tales of Magic*. Illustrated by M. Passicott. New York: Penguin Putnam.

> *This retelling of twelve traditional tales from Jewish folklore features elements of magic and relates to holidays, including Rosh Hodesh, Sukkot, Tu b'shvat, and Shabbat. (Primary)*

Sender, R. (2000). *To Life*. Illustrated by J. Coon. New York: Simon and Schuster.

> *A Holocaust survivor recounts her liberation from a Nazi concentration camp, search for surviving family members, and a long and difficult ordeal of trying to immigrate with her husband and two children to America. (Middle School)*

Sloan, S. R. (1998). *An Isolated Incident*. New York: Warner.

> *Set on Seward Island in Puget Sound, this murder mystery deals with bigotry and prejudice as the evidence seems to point to Jerry Frankel, a newcomer to the island, and one of a group of Jews protesting the high school's Christmas pageant festivities. (High School)*

Stavens, I. (Ed.). (1998). *The Oxford Book of Jewish Stories*. New York: Oxford University Press.

> *A collection of stories by 52 Jewish writers from around the world. Themes include anti-Semitism, the Holocaust, domestic affairs, Biblical subjects, inter-religious accounts, and ethnic relations. (High School).*

Wing, N. (1996). *Jalapeno Bagels*. Illustrated by R. Casilla. New York: Simon and Schuster.

> *For International Day at school, Pablo wants to bring something that reflects the cultures of both his parents. (Primary)*

Woodruff, E. (1999). *The Memory Coat*. Illustrated by M. Dooling. New York: Scholastic.

> *In the early 1900s, two cousins leave their Russian shtetl with the rest of their family to come to America, hopeful that they will all pass the dreaded inspection at Ellis Island. (Intermediate)*

PART FOUR

Hispanic Americans

Concepts and Strategies

Part IV consists of content, concepts, teaching strategies, and materials for teaching about three major Hispanic groups in the United States: Mexican Americans, Puerto Ricans, and Cuban Americans. Hispanics are one of the nation's fastest growing ethnic groups. The number of Hispanics in the United States grew from 22.4 million in 1990 to 35.3 million in 2000, a 57.9% increase. Mexican Americans are the largest Hispanic group in the United States, and this group is growing faster than are Cubans or Puerto Ricans. Between 1990 and 2000, Mexican Americans increased 52.9%, compared to a 24.9% increase of Puerto Ricans and an 18.9% increase of Cuban Americans. The Hispanic population is growing about five times faster than the rest of the U.S. population; the Hispanic population increased 57.9% between 1990 and 2000, compared to 12% for the total U.S. population (U.S. Census Bureau, 2000). The rapid growth of Hispanics is due primarily to massive immigration and to a high birthrate.

Central and South Americans

A substantial number of immigrants from Central and South America entered the United States between 1990 and 2000. A significant number of these immigrants came from El Salvador, Guatemala, Colombia, Guyana, and Ecuador. Central and South Americans made up 8.6% of the Hispanic population of the United States in 2000 (U.S. Census Bureau, 2000). Figure A shows the percentage distribution of Hispanics in the United States in 2000. Table A shows the population and percentage for each group. It is misleading, however, to conceptualize these diverse groups of immigrants as one people because they have significant cultural, racial, and ethnic differences.

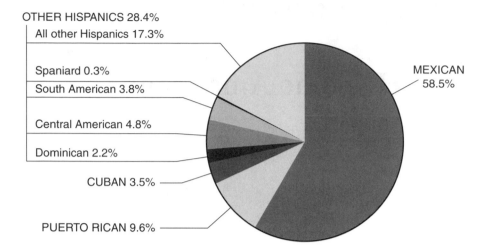

OTHER HISPANICS 28.4%

All other Hispanics 17.3%

Spaniard 0.3%

South American 3.8%

Central American 4.8%

Dominican 2.2%

CUBAN 3.5%

PUERTO RICAN 9.6%

MEXICAN 58.5%

FIGURE A   Percent Distribution of the Hispanic Population by Type: 2000

(For information on confidentiality protection, nonsampling error, and definitions, see *www. census.gov/prod/cen2000/doc/sf1.pdf*)

Source: U.S. Census Bureau (2001). *The Hispanic Population: Census 2000 Brief.* [On-line]. Available: *http://www.census.gov/*

Demographic Characteristics of Hispanics

The Hispanic population, compared to the rest of the U.S. population, is young. The median age of Hispanics in 2000 was 25.9, compared to 35.3 for the non-Hispanic population (U.S. Census Bureau, 2000). The Hispanic population is also highly concentrated in the Southwestern United States. In 2000, 43.5% of Hispanics lived in the West and 32.8% in the South; 14.9% lived in the Northeast; and 8.8% in the Midwest (U.S. Census Bureau, 2000). Table B shows the Hispanic population for selected states in 2000 and the percentage of Hispanics in these states.

Diversity among Hispanics

It is misleading to consider Hispanics as one ethnic group. Even though the various Hispanic groups share a past influenced significantly by Spain and the Spanish language, there are tremendous historical, racial, and cultural differences among and within them. Most Mexican Americans are mestizos, whereas some Cubans and Puerto Ricans are Black. Some Mexican Americans are native to the United States; others, as well as some other Hispanics, arrived in the United States quite recently. Language is probably the most important

TABLE A   Hispanic Population by Type: 2000

Subject	Number	Percent
Hispanic or Latino Origin		
Total population	281,411,906	100.0
Hispanic or Latino (of any race)	35,305,818	12.5
Not Hispanic or Latino	246,116,088	87.5
Hispanic or Latino by Type		
Hispanic or Latino (of any race)	35,305,818	100.0
Mexican	20,640,711	58.5
Puerto Rican	3,406,178	9.6
Cuban	1,241,685	3.5
Other Hispanic or Latino	10,017,244	28.4
Dominican (Dominican Republic)	764,945	2.2
Central American (excludes Mexican)	1,686,937	4.8
Costa Rican	68,588	0.2
Guatemalan	372,487	1.1
Honduran	217,569	0.6
Nicaraguan	177,684	0.2
Panamanian	91,723	0.3
Salvadoran	655,165	1.9
Other Central American	103,721	0.3
South American	1,353,562	3.8
Argentinean	100,864	0.3
Bolivian	42,068	0.1
Chilean	68,849	0.2
Colombian	470,684	1.3
Ecuadorian	260,559	0.7
Paraguayan	8,769	0.0
Peruvian	233,926	0.7
Uruguayan	18,804	0.1
Venezuelan	91,507	0.3
Other South American	57,532	0.2
Spaniard	100,135	0.3
All other Hispanic or Latino	6,111,665	17.3
Checkbox only, other Hispanic	1,733,274	4.9
Write-in Spanish	686,004	1.9
Write-in Hispanic	2,454,529	7.0
Write-in Latino	450,769	1.3
Not elsewhere classified	787,089	2.2

(For information on confidentiality protection, nonsampling error, and definitions, see *www.census.gov/prod.cen2000/doc/sf1.pdf*)

Source: U.S. Census Bureau (2001). *The Hispanic Population: Census 2000 Brief.* [On-line]. Available: *http://www.census.gov/*

TABLE B   Hispanic Population in Selected States (2000)

State	Total Population	Hispanic American Population	Percentage of Total State Population
California	33,871,648	10,966,556	32.4
Texas	20,851,820	6,669,666	32.0
New York	18,976,457	2,867,583	15.1
Florida	15,982,378	2,682,715	16.8
Illinois	12,419,293	1,530,262	12.3
Arizona	5,130,632	1,295,617	25.3
New Jersey	8,414,350	1,117,191	13.3
New Mexico	1,819,046	765,386	42.1
Colorado	4,301,261	735,601	17.1
Georgia	8,186,453	435,227	5.3
Massachusetts	6,349,097	428,729	6.8
Pennsylvania	12,281,056	394,088	3.2
Nevada	1,998,257	393,970	19.7
North Carolina	8,049,313	378,963	4.7
Virginia	7,078,515	329,540	4.7
Connecticut	3,405,565	320,320	9.4
Oregon	3,421,399	275,314	8.0
Maryland	5,296,486	227,916	4.3
Ohio	11,353,140	217,123	1.9
Indiana	6,080,485	214,536	3.5
Utah	2,233,169	201,559	9.0
Wisconsin	5,363,375	192,921	3.6
Kansas	2,688,418	188,252	7.0
Oklahoma	3,450,654	179,304	5.2
Minnesota	4,919,479	143,382	2.9

Source: U.S. Census Bureau, (2001). *The Hispanic Population: Census 2000 Brief.* [On-line]. Available: *http://www.census.gov/*

factor that connects the various Hispanic groups. In 1990, about 78% of Hispanics spoke a language other than English at home. Spanish was spoken by most of the Hispanic non-English speakers (U.S. Bureau of the Census, 1993).The multicultural curriculum should help students understand the ways in which the various Hispanic groups are both alike and different.

REFERENCES

Pallas, A. M., Natriello, G., & McDill, E. L. (1989). The Changing Nature of the Disadvantaged Population: Current Dimensions and Future Trends. *Educational Researcher, 18*(5), 6–22.
U.S. Bureau of the Census. (1993). *We, the American Hispanics.* Washington, DC: U.S. Government Printing Office.

U.S. Census Bureau (2000). *The Hispanic Population: Census 2000 Brief.* [On-line]. Available: *http://www.census.gov/*

ANNOTATED BIBLIOGRAPHY

Flores, L. (Ed.). (1998). *The Floating Borderlands: Twenty-five Years of U.S. Hispanic Literature.* Seattle: University of Washington Press.

An anthology of prose and poetry by contemporary Hispanic writers from the 1970s to the late 1990s.

Garza, H. (2001). *Latinas: Hispanic Women in the United States.* Albuquerque: University of New Mexico Press.

This book presents the major social and political contributions of Hispanic women leaders and activists to American culture and communities for over 150 years. This award-winning study is an important contribution to literature for young Chicana women.

Gonzalez, J. (2000). *A History of Latinos in America: Harvest of Empire.* New York: Penguin Books.

A historical chronicle of Latino immigration to the United States by way of family portraits of immigrant pioneers from Puerto Rico, Mexico, Cuba, Dominica, Central America, Colombia, and Panama.

Gracía, J. J. E., & De Greiff, P. (Eds.). (2000). *Hispanics/Latinos in the United States: Ethnicity, Race, and Rights.* New York: Routledge.

A cross-disciplinary collection of essays by social science scholars that focuses on the question of what it means to be a Hispanic/Latina/o in the United States today.

Hondagneu-Sotelo, P. (2001). *Doméstica: Immigrant Workers Cleaning and Caring in the Shadows of Affluence.* Berkeley: University of California Press.

A sociological study that contributes greatly to the uncovering of the hidden world and work environments of immigrant Latina women who are engaged in the United States as nannies and housecleaners.

Kevane, B., & Heredia, J. (Eds.). (2000). *Latina Self-Portraits: Interviews with Contemporary Women Writers.* Albuquerque: University of New Mexico Press.

This book presents ten interviews with important contemporary Latina writers. The writers talk about their work as well as their personal biographies.

Koss-Chioino, J. D., & Vargas, L. A. (Eds.). (1999). *Working with Latino Youth: Culture, Development, and Context.* San Francisco: Jossey-Bass.

This book presents a model for working with Latino youth within the context of their families, communities, and culture. This culturally assertive and well-researched book is a comprehensive resource for human service practitioners in several disciplines.

Laó-Montes, A., & Dávila, A. (Eds.). (2001). *Mambo Montage: The Latinization of New York.* New York: Columbia University Press.

This book is an analysis of Latino identity against the backdrop of New York's metropolis. It examines Latinization in New York City, a process of social differentiation and site of cultural production pressed by powers from above and below.

Maciel, D. R., Ortiz, I. D., & Herrera-Sobek, M. (Eds.). (2000). *Chicano Renaissance: Contemporary Cultural Trends.* Tucson: University of Arizona Press.

This book examines contemporary Chicano/a art and its function in society over the last two decades.

Martínez, E. (1998). *De Colores Means All of Us: Latina Views for a Multi-Colored Country.* Cambridge: South End Press.

> *An important contribution to the fight for civil rights in a multiracial and multiethnic democracy from the perspective of a Chicana activist in Civil Rights, Women's liberation, and Latino/a empowerment movements.*

Menard, V. (2000). *The Latino Holiday Book: From Cinco de Mayo to Día de los Muertos— the Celebrations and Traditions of Hispanic-Americans.* New York: Malowe.

> *A resource that offers an overview and explanations of the special traditions and celebrations of Hispanic Americans. Each celebration is described in regard to its history, custom, foods, and activities.*

Meyer, N. E. (2001). *Biographical Dictionary of Hispanic Americans* (2nd ed.). New York: Facts on File.

> *This book provides information on Hispanic Americans who have contributed in different ways to American culture.*

Montejano, D. (Ed.). (1999). *Chicano Politics and Society in the Late Twentieth Century.* Austin: University of Texas Press.

> *This book is a compilation of ten specifically commissioned essays that assess the years after the protest movements in the 1960s and 1970s. It offers an excellent look into the complex situation and experience of Mexican Americans.*

Nava, Y. (2000). *It's All in the Frijoles: 100 Famous Latinos Share Real-Life Stories, Time-Tested Dichos, Favorite Folktales, and Inspiring Words of Wisdom.* New York: Fireside Books.

> *This book is an important contribution to the preservation of Latino customs and traditions in American culture.*

Novas, H. (1998). *Everything You Need to Know about Latino History* (Rev. ed.). New York: Penguin Plume.

> *This book presents a mix between pop culture and history, describing how Latino culture has influenced the United States.*

Olmos, E. J., Ybarra, L., & Monterrey, M. (1999). *Americanos: Latino Life in the United States/La Vista Latina en los Estados Unidos.* Boston: Little, Brown.

> *A collection of photographs, bilingual essays, poetry, and commentaries that portray and celebrate Latin heritage in the United States.*

Ramírez, E. C. (2000). *Chicanas/Latinas in American Theatre: A History of Performance.* Bloomington: Indiana University Press.

> *An analysis of how Latino/a theatre has evolved across history and left its mark on the American stage.*

Saldívar-Hull, S. (2000). *Feminism on the Border: Chicana Gender Politics and Literature.* Berkeley: University of California Press.

> *This book provides a contemporary feminist analysis and account of Chicana feminist writings that are currently available. The author compares and defines literary and national borders in light of feminist scholarship and work of women of color in the United States.*

Suro, R. (1998). *Strangers among Us: Latina Lives in Changing America.* New York: Vintage Books.

> *A critical study of the Latino population in America that describes a variety of Latino worlds.*

CHAPTER

10 Mexican Americans

Concepts, Strategies, and Materials

It would be a disservice to portray the future in idealistic terms. Hope is important, but the falsification of reality can immobilize a community.

—Rodolfo Acuña

Mexican Americans are the second largest ethnic group of color in the United States. (African Americans are the largest group.) They are also the largest Hispanic group. Mexican Americans comprised 58.5% of the Hispanics in the United States in 2000. They are increasing at a much faster rate than are the other two major Hispanic groups, Puerto Ricans and Cubans. There were about 20,640,711 Mexican Americans living in the United States in 2000 (U.S. Census Bureau, 2000a), up from about 13.5 million in 1990. The Mexican population increased 52.9% during that ten-year period.

The rapid growth in the Mexican American population results primarily from a higher birthrate, compared to other ethnic and racial groups, and a significant and continuing immigration from Mexico. Between 1981 and 1998, 3,583,200 legal immigrants arrived in the United States from Mexico (U.S. Census Bureau, 2000b). A large, but unknown, number of undocumented Mexican aliens in the United States are not reflected in these Census figures. There is little agreement on how many undocumented Mexican aliens are living in the United States. It is also difficult to determine the extent to which the Immigration Reform and Control Act of 1986, designed to reduce the number of undocumented immigrants who enter the United States each year, has been successful. The act imposes severe penalties on employers who knowingly hire illegal aliens. Under the conditions of this act, employers are required to ask job applicants for proof of citizenship.

The Mexican American population is highly concentrated in the West and Southwest, particularly in California and Texas. In 2000, 66% of all Mexican Americans lived in California and Texas; 41% lived in California, and 25% lived in Texas. Illinois and Arizona had the next largest concentrations of Mexican Americans, about 7% and 5%, respectively. In 2000, about 78% of Mexican Americans lived in the following four states: California, Texas, Illinois, and Arizona. The population and percentage of Mexican Americans in selected states is shown in Table 10.1. Even though Mexican Americans are highly concentrated in California, the Southwest, and Illinois, pockets of them

TABLE 10.1   Mexican American Population in Selected States (2000)

State	Mexican American Population	Percentage of Total State Population
California	8,455,926	25.0
Texas	5,071,963	24.3
Illinois	1,144,390	9.2
Arizona	1,065,578	20.8
Colorado	450,760	10.5
Florida	363,925	2.3
New Mexico	330,049	18.1
Washington	329,934	5.6
Nevada	285,764	14.3
Georgia	275,288	3.4
New York	260,889	1.4
North Carolina	246,545	3.1
Michigan	220,769	2.2
Oregon	214,662	6.3
Indiana	153,042	2.5
Kansas	148,270	5.5
Utah	136,416	6.1
Oklahoma	132,813	3.8
Minnesota	95,613	1.9
Ohio	90,663	0.8
Idaho	79,324	6.1
Missouri	77,887	1.4
Tennessee	77,372	1.4
Virginia	73,979	1.0
Nebraska	71,030	4.2

Source: U.S. Census Bureau, (2001). *The Hispanic Population: Census 2000 Brief.* [On-line]. Available: *http://www.census.gov/*

are found throughout the United States, including the South and the North-west. More than 132,000 lived in Oklahoma in 2000. Washington state, in the Northwest, had (in 2000) the eighth largest population of Mexican Americans, 329,934. Mexican Americans are also becoming increasingly urbanized. Significant numbers are concentrated in large cities such as Los Angeles, Chicago, Milwaukee, and Detroit.

Mexican Americans were in the land that is now the United States before all other American groups, except the American Indians, Aleuts, Eskimos, and Native Hawaiians. Their ancestors had settled in the region that is now the southwestern United States before Jamestown was settled by the English colonists in 1607. They became an ethnic minority when Texas was annexed by the United States in 1845. More of their territory was conquered by the United States during the Mexican American War, which lasted from 1846 to 1848. Their property, civic, and cultural rights were guaranteed by the Treaty of Guadalupe Hidalgo, the treaty that ended the war in 1848. In the decades after 1848, the Treaty was blatantly disregarded, and Mexican Americans were made second-class citizens by Anglo-Americans who migrated and settled in the Southwest. There were about 80,000 Mexicans living in the territory Mexico ceded to the United States in 1848. Most modern Mexican American communities were formed by Mexican immigrants who came to the United States after 1910. The study of the conquest and subjugation of Mexican Americans and their resistance, which greatly intensified in the 1960s, is necessary to understand the nature of U.S. society and the genesis of the ethnic conflict and tensions in American life.

The Spanish Conquest

More than 25 million Indians were living in the Western Hemisphere when the Spanish conquistadores arrived in 1517. There were a wide variety of Indian cultures and groups in the region that is now Mexico. The Mayas and the Aztecs developed some of the most complex societies in the region. Mayan domestication and cultivation of corn significantly influenced agriculture in the Americas. A powerful military state and the most impressive contemporary cities were built by the Aztecs. Tenochtitlan, their capital city, has been called the most modern city in the world at the time of the Spanish conquest.

Hernan Cortés, a Spanish explorer, led an expedition into Mexico in 1519. Before he reached the Aztec capital, he gained military help from other Indian civilizations by negotiation and conquest. After a two-year intermittent struggle with the Aztecs, Cortés finally seized Tenochtitlán on August 13, 1521, and the Aztec empire fell. Despite the Aztecs' military strength, the Spaniards were able to defeat them because they were helped by other Indian nations and had horses and superior firearms. Although the Spaniards were

MEXICAN AMERICANS: HISTORICAL PERSPECTIVE

Important Dates	Events
1519	Hernán Cortés, the Spanish conquistador, and a group of Spaniards arrived in the region that is now Mexico.
1521	Cortés, with the support of thousands of Indian allies, seized the Aztec capital city, Tenochtitlán, and the empire fell.
1598	Juan de Oñate established the first Spanish settlement in what is today New Mexico. The Spanish colonial period began.
1718	New Spain founded the mission and presidio of San Antonio.
1769	Fray Junípero Serra and Gaspar de Portolá established the mission and presidio of San Diego, the first in Upper California.
1810	On September 16, 1810, Father Miguel Hidalgo sounded a battle cry known as the *El Grito de Dolores,* which signaled the beginning of the Mexican revolutionary era that eventually resulted in Mexican independence from Spain in 1821.
1836	Mexico's President Santa Anna and his troops defeated the rebelling Texans at the Alamo. Six weeks later, Santa Anna was defeated by Sam Houston and his Texan troops at San Jacinto. Texas declared itself independent and formed the Lone Star Republic.
1845	The United States annexed Texas, which had declared itself independent from Mexico in 1836. This was one key event leading to the Mexican-American War.
1846	On May 13, 1846, the United States declared war on Mexico and the Mexican-American War began.
1848	The United States and Mexico signed the Treaty of Guadalupe Hidalgo, which ended the Mexican-American War. Mexico lost nearly one third of its territory, and the United States acquired most of the territory that comprises the southwestern states.
1853	James Gadsden, representing the United States, purchased from Mexico 45,532 square miles of additional land, which was rich in copper, and opened a railroad route.
1859	Juan N. Cortina, who became a U.S. citizen under the provisions of the Treaty of Guadalupe Hidalgo, led a series of rebellions against Anglo-Americans in the Lower Rio Grande Valley of South Texas.

Important Dates	Events
1862	On May 5, 1862, French forces that had invaded Mexico were defeated at Puebla by Mexican forces led by Ignacio Zaragosa, a Texas Mexican. May 5 (*Cinco de Mayo*) is an important holiday observed by Mexican Americans.
1877	The El Paso Salt War occurred, in which Mexicans organized and rebelled against Anglos because of a dispute over rights to salt beds.
1910	A revolution starting in Mexico caused thousands of Mexicans to immigrate to the United States looking for jobs and to escape political turmoil and persecution.
1924	Congress established the Border Patrol to monitor traffic across the Mexican-U.S. border. This border had previously been primarily open.
1929	The League of United Latin American Citizens was formed in Harlingen, Texas. Like other earlier Mexican-American civil rights organizations, the League stressed U.S. citizenship and assimilation.
1929–35	Thousands of Mexican immigrants and their families were repatriated to Mexico, most without legal proceedings.
1942	The United States and Mexico made an agreement that authorized Mexicans to work temporarily in the United States. This project is known as the *bracero* program.
1943	The anti-Mexican "zoot-suit" riots occurred in Los Angeles during the summer.
1954	The U.S. Immigration and Naturalization Service began "Operation Wetback," a massive program to deport illegal Mexican immigrants to Mexico.
1965	A grape strike led by César Chávez and the United Farm Workers Association began in Delano, California, a town in the San Joaquin Valley.
	Rodolfo "Corky" Gonzales formed the Crusades for Justice in Denver. This important civil rights organization epitomized the Chicano movement that emerged in the 1960s.
	The U.S. Congress passed an immigration act limiting the number of Mexican immigrants to the United States to 20,000 annually.
1970	La Raza Unida party was organized by José Angel Gutiérrez in Crystal City, Texas.

Important Dates	Events
1976	Jerry Apodaca and Raul Castro were elected governors of New Mexico and Arizona, respectively.
1979	Luis Valdez' play, *Zoot Suit,* was the first Mexican American play produced on Broadway.
1982	Toney Anaya was elected governor of New Mexico.
1986	The Immigration Reform and Control Act of 1986 was passed. Designed to control the entry of undocumented (illegal) immigrants to the United States, it imposed severe penalties on employers who knowingly hired illegal immigrants.
1992	President Bill Clinton named Henry G. Cisneros Secretary of the Department of Housing and Urban Development. President Clinton named Federico Peña Secretary of Transportation.
2000	The 2000 Census indicated that Mexican Americans were the largest (20,640,711) and fastest-growing Hispanic group. Their numbers increased 57.9% between 1990 and 2000.

eventually successful in their conquest of much of the land stretching from southern South America to most of what is today the southwestern United States, this task was not easily accomplished. The Indians living in these areas fought hard to maintain their power and rebelled many times after the Spanish conquest. The Spaniards defeated most Indian groups only gradually and with the loss of many of their men.

The Spanish Settlements

The Spanish settlements in Mexico and what is today the southwestern United States differed in several significant ways from the English colonies in the eastern parts of North America. For a number of complex reasons, more settlers from England than from Spain immigrated to the Americas. This was in part because, at the time of the conquest, Spain had a small population compared to other nations in Europe (Jiménez, 1994). It had, for example, about half the population of France. It is estimated that only about 300,000 Spaniards came to the Americas during three centuries of settlement (McWilliams, 1968). More English than Spanish colonists brought their wives, although a severe shortage of women was also a problem in the original English colonies. In 1619 the London Company sent 100 women who were willing to marry colonists to Virginia. Each man who married one of these women had to pay 54 kilograms (120 pounds) of the best tobacco. The serious shortage of women in the Spanish colonies was not dealt with as successfully as in Virginia. Writes Jiménez (1994):

> It is apparent that between 1493 and 1519 women represented less than 6 percent of all emigrants [to new Spain]. In the next twenty years they hardly surpassed this percentage. More favorable conditions in the colonies and the pressure exercised by the laws to encourage the emigration of women and the marriage of the conquistadors and settlers increased these ratios in the following years (p. 79).

The unique characteristics of the Spanish settlers significantly influenced the physical and cultural development of the new "race" that was formed in the Americas. Because few women came to the colonies from Spain, most of the Spanish men had Indian concubines or wives. The offspring of these ethnically mixed unions were known as *mestizos*. The biological and cultural heritage of the Mexican American includes African strains although it is primarily Spanish-Indian. When they came to the Americas, the Spaniards had had long contact with a group of Africans called Moors. Moors came with the conquistadores to the Americas. Estevanico is perhaps the most famous. Nearly 200,000 African slaves were also brought to Mexico. They were so thoroughly mixed with the Spaniards and Indians by 1900 that they were no longer distinguishable as a separate racial group (Franklin & Moss, 2000). The Mexican's biological heritage is more Indian than Spanish. Although the Spaniards imposed their culture and religion on the Indian nations, many Indian cultural elements survived and greatly influenced the development of Mexican culture. Thus, both the physical traits and culture of the Mexicans are primarily blends of Spanish and Indian influences. Writes McWilliams (1968): "To attempt to unravel any single strand from this pattern and label it 'Spanish' is to do a serious injustice to the Mexican and Indians...through whom...Spanish cultural influences survived (p. 34).

The Texas Revolt

At the beginning of the nineteenth century, Mexico was in a perpetual state of political turmoil. Greatly concerned about the declining population in Texas, the Spanish, and later the Mexican government, encouraged Anglo Americans to settle there by making empresario land grants. The Spanish government gave an empresario grant to Moses Austin in 1821. His son Stephen received a reconfirmation of the original grant from the Mexican government in 1823. Because Texas was geographically close to the United States, it attracted a large number of Anglo immigrants who were interested in Texas's rich resources and open territory. Most Anglo settlers in Texas failed to keep the terms of their land-grant agreements with the Mexican government, such as becoming loyal citizens and Catholics, learning Spanish, and giving up their slaves. They were not interested in Mexican culture but wanted to establish Anglo institutions in the Mexican province and to control it.

Texas Mexicans were angry about President Santa Anna's attempts to centralize his power over the northern Mexican territories. The Anglo immigrants in Texas added fuel to the fire because of their disdain for the Mexican government. By permitting and encouraging U.S. citizens to settle in sparsely inhabited Texas, Mexico had inadvertently set the stage for revolt in the province and its eventual loss to the United States.

By the time Mexico realized that Anglo Mexicans were gaining control in Texas and took steps to undermine their power, antigovernment forces in Texas had already been firmly established. The Mexican government attempted to undermine Anglo power in Texas by abolishing slavery in 1829, by restricting Anglo immigration into Texas, and by enforcing customs regulations at the Texas–U.S. border. These actions greatly angered the Texas Anglo Mexicans and evoked attacks against the central government. Mexican federal troops arrived in Texas in 1835 after Texas proclaimed itself "conditionally independent." These troops were badly defeated. In 1836, President Santa Anna led several thousand Mexican troops into Texas. His army killed 187 Texans at a Franciscan mission in San Antonio called the Alamo. The Mexican army had another victory at Goliad, but they were crushed at San Jacinto on April 21 by Sam Houston and his Texas troops who shouted "Remember the Alamo!" After this victory, Texas sought world recognition of its independence and started the chain of events that eventually led to its annexation by the United States in 1845.

The Mexican American War

When the Mexican government took serious steps to halt Anglo immigration to the Southwest, the United States had begun, in the name of Manifest Destiny, an aggressive campaign to annex all of Mexico's northern territories. The United States began a military conquest when negotiations failed, and then angered Mexico by annexing Texas in 1845. The United States declared war on Mexico in 1846 when a boundary dispute developed between the two nations. The United States had defeated Mexico within two years and occupied California and New Mexico by the end of 1846. Mexico's northern provinces had little allegiance to the nation's capital. Anglo settlers who had a strong toehold in Mexican provinces such as California and New Mexico actively sought Mexico's defeat. Mexico was also greatly weakened by internal strife and its inability to rally internal support for the war.

The Treaty of Guadalupe Hidalgo

After Mexico was defeated by the United States, representatives of the two nations signed a treaty on February 2, 1848, in the Mexican village of Guadalupe Hidalgo. The United States forced Mexico to surrender its claim to Texas, which the United States had annexed in 1845, and to cede about one third of its territory to the United States. This chunk of land included most of the territory now comprising the states of the U.S. Southwest, including Arizona, California, New Mexico, Utah, Nevada, and a section of Colorado. The United States paid Mexico $15 million for this large piece of land.

All Mexicans who remained in this newly acquired territory received the right to become U.S. citizens. Only about 3,000 of the nearly 80,000 people living in the area chose to leave their homes and move to the Mexican side of the border. The treaty guaranteed Mexican Americans "all the rights of citizens of the United States…[and] the free enjoyment of…Liberty and property" (The Treaty of Guadalupe Hidalgo, 1971). Write Meier and Rivera (1972):

> By this treaty the United States gained not only an immense new territory but also a large group of new citizens. Although they were left in their same geographic and cultural setting, these new citizens were now exposed to unfamiliar legal, political, and social institutions…. Guaranteed full protection of property rights, they soon became enmeshed in a web of confusing Anglo laws which required proof of ownership unfamiliar to them (p. 71).

After the Conquest: Oppression and Conflict

After 1848, forces were set in motion that were destined to make the Mexicans in the United States a conquered, powerless, and alienated ethnic minority. Although they were guaranteed property and citizenship rights by the Treaty of Guadalupe Hidalgo, it was only a matter of time before Anglo Americans, through a series of legal and financial maneuvers, had obtained control in all of the southwestern territories, and successfully reduced the native Mexicans to the status of second-class citizens.

The pattern of conquest differed somewhat in the various southwestern territories. Before the Anglos came to New Mexico, a rigid class structure existed that sharply divided the rich and the poor. The Anglos in New Mexico pitted the rich against the poor in order to gain control of the territory. Anglo dominance emerged more gradually in New Mexico than in California and Texas. A mass of Anglos immigrated to California during the gold rush of 1849 and in subsequent years. Mexicans were completely outnumbered. Anglos thoroughly dominated northern California by 1851, but domination of southern California was somewhat delayed because most Anglo immigrants first settled in the northern part of the territory. However, they eventually settled in the south and within a few years expanded their dominance over the entire state. There were more than 30,000 Anglos and only 5,000 native Mexicans in Texas as early as 1834. Anglos had controlled Texas since it became independent as the Lone Star Republic in 1836. This dominance continued after U.S. annexation in 1845.

The Anglo Americans were able to obtain most of the land owned by the Mexicans by imposing a series of legal and financial restraints. Land boundaries in Mexico had been rather loosely and casually defined. Many Mexicans had to appear in Anglo courts to defend their rights to the land they owned. Often they did not have the legal papers proving ownership of their land, and Mexican legal papers did not conform to superimposed U.S. law. In many cases they had to sell their land to pay taxes imposed by the new government or exorbitant fees to Anglo lawyers to argue their cases in court. Legal battles over land titles often dragged out in the courts for years and became expensive. Tactics such as these and the Congressional Land Act of 1851, which required U.S.-recognized proof of land ownership, had the ultimate effect of making the Mexican largely land-less and poverty-stricken.

Rioting, lynchings, burnings, vigilante action, and other forms of violence were directed at the country's "newest aliens" during this period of turmoil and Hispanic defeat in the Southwest. Moore (with Pachon, 1976) contends that "No other part of the United States saw such prolonged intergroup violence as did the Border States from 1848 to 1925" (p. 36). Many Anglo outlaws and social misfits settled in the Southwest during this period. They declared open season on Mexicans and often attacked them just for fun. There was little or no law enforcement in many parts of the Southwest during this period. In 1850, California passed a Foreign Miner's Tax that was designed to drive Mexicans out of the mines.

The Mexican Revolution of 1910 contributed to this atmosphere of hostility and violence. Banditry and filibustering (filibustering is pursuing military activity in a foreign nation for adventure) occurred on both sides of the border. Mexican–Anglo hostility reached new highs. Mexicans considered Anglo Americans "gringos," and Anglos called Mexicans "greasers." By the turn of the century, the Mexicans had been conquered and made foreigners within their homeland. Culturally, politically, and economically they were second-class citizens. Mexican Americans faced the beginning of the twentieth century suffering from a crushing second defeat in the Southwest.

North from Mexico

Early Immigrants

During the early development of agriculture in the Southwest, agribusiness-men depended on a large and cheap labor supply. This labor need was met in the late 1800s by the Chinese immigrants and later by immigrants from Japan and the Philippines (see Chapter 13). The expansion of irrigated farming in the Southwest at the turn of the century coincided with the Mexican Revolution of 1910. Many Mexicans were displaced by the Revolution. They came north to the U.S. Southwest seeking job opportunities. They found jobs in truck farming, in cotton and sugar beet fields, in mines, in industry, and on the railroads. Hundreds of Mexican immigrants worked on the construction of railroad lines that crossed the West. Many Mexican American communities in the Southwest grew up around railroad campsites.

There was no legal agreement between Mexico and the United States that protected the rights of these immigrants. Consequently, they were often blatantly exploited by their employers. They were paid the lowest wages, given the worst jobs, and forced to live in the crudest shacks. Many became migrant workers who followed the crops. The mass of Mexican immigrants to the Southwest depressed wages so drastically that many native Mexican Americans migrated to midwestern cities, such as Detroit, Gary, and Chicago, to obtain higher wages. The large number of Mexican immigrants who came to the Southwest between 1910 and 1930 laid the foundations for most modern Mexican American communities.

Many Anglo groups in the Southwest became alarmed by the large numbers of Mexicans who were entering the United States in the 1920s. Between 1920 and 1929, 498,900 Mexican immigrants entered the United States. Vigorous efforts were made to halt their immigration. Although the legal attempts to stop their immigration failed because of the powerful opposition from agribusinessmen who wanted them for cheap labor, other efforts were successful. The U.S.–Mexican border had historically been an open border, with Mexicans and U.S. citizens crossing it at will. The Border Patrol was established in 1924 by Congress to control traffic across the border.

When the Great Depression hit in 1929, and many Mexicans, like other Americans, lost their jobs and found it necessary to obtain welfare to survive, loud cries were heard against the Mexicans. Mexicans were regarded as "foreigners" who did not deserve welfare benefits. As with other immigrants of color who came before them, attempts were made to deport the Mexicans when their labor was no longer needed. Jobs became increasingly scarce as the dust bowl White immigrants fled to the Southwest to compete for the few available jobs. The U.S. Immigration Service, as well as state, county, and local governments, began an aggressive drive to repatriate immigrants.

In the eagerness to rid the United States of Mexicans in order to cut back on welfare rolls, many Mexican American citizens were "encouraged" or forced to go to Mexico. The civil rights of U.S. citizens of Mexican descent were violated seriously in this unfortunate repatriation movement. More than 64,000 Mexican aliens were returned to Mexico between 1930 and 1934 without the benefits of legal proceedings. The Mexican population in the United States declined from 639,000 to 377,000 between 1930 and 1940 (Moore, with Pachon, 1976, p. 42).

The Bracero Program

When World War II began, a new demand for unskilled labor developed in the United States. Agribusiness leaders spoke vigorously about their desperate need for Mexican labor. Partly as a gesture to help with the war effort, Mexico agreed to a seasonal work program with the United States. The two nations signed an agreement in July 1942 that enabled Mexican citizens to work in the United States during work seasons. They were to return to Mexico when the work season ended. Unlike the earlier Mexican immigrants, these workers came under an agreement that guaranteed them specific conditions relating to such problems as wages, working conditions, transportation, and worker rights.

Although these contract stipulations helped reduce some of the extreme conditions experienced by earlier Mexican immigrants, their wages and living conditions were often depressing. The bracero program formally ended in December 1947. When it terminated, the number of undocumented immigrants crossing the U.S.–Mexican border soared. Smuggling undocumented immigrants across the border became a highly profitable business in which many "men snatchers" engaged and profited (McWilliams, 1968, pp. 178–179).

In 1954, the U.S. Immigration and Naturalization Service began a massive drive known as Operation Wetback to deport undocumented immigrants to Mexico. Operation Wetback grossly violated the civil rights of many Mexicans, as had the repatriation project in the 1930s. Hundreds of Mexican American citizens were arrested and harassed. They were threatened and forced to produce proof of their citizenship. Only a few of the thousands of Mexicans deported had formal hearings. Operation Wetback successfully attained its goal but alienated and outraged many Mexican American citizens. When the project ended, more than a million people had been deported to Mexico.

In 1951, the United States and Mexico jointly accepted a Migratory Labor Agreement known as Public Law 78. This agreement set forth conditions for a new bracero program. It contained conditions similar to the earlier bracero agreement. Public Law 78 was extended for various periods until it ended in December 1964. In 1965, the United States Congress passed a new immigration act, which became effective in 1968, that limited the annual immigration from Western Hemisphere nations to 120,000. Each nation, including Mexico, was given an annual quota of 20,000. This new act solved, at least for the time, problems concerning the number of Mexican nationals that could legally enter the United States.

Because of the chronic economic and population problems in Mexico, large numbers of undocumented Mexican immigrants enter the United States each year. The U.S. Census indicated that 35,305,818 Hispanics lived in the United States in 2000 (U.S. Census Bureau, 2000a). However, the actual number of Hispanics who lived in the United States in 2000 was much higher than this figure because of the large numbers of undocumented immigrants who enter the United States from Mexico each year. The largest foreign-born group in the United States is Mexican Americans. In 1990, more than one in five of the people in the United States who were foreign born were of Mexican origin (U.S. Bureau of the Census, 1993).

Violence and Race Riots

In the 1940s, anti-Mexican feelings and stereotypes were rampant in the Southwest. The stereotypes, which depicted the Mexican American as criminal and violent, were perpetuated by the established Anglo press, especially the newspapers. The anti-Mexican press propaganda inflamed racial feelings and antagonisms toward the Mexican Americans. Anti-Mexican racism was the basic cause of the case of the Sleepy Lagoon and the zoot-suit riots that occurred in Los Angeles in the summer of 1943.

The Sleepy Lagoon Case

A young Mexican American, José Diaz, died mysteriously on August 2, 1942, apparently from a fractured skull. Without seriously seeking the facts of the case, the Los Angeles police immediately arrested twenty-four young men who were thought to be members of a Mexican gang accused of killing Diaz. All of them were charged with murder. A gravel pit, which became a central focus in the case, was dubbed "The Sleepy Lagoon" by a Los Angeles reporter. When seventeen of the twenty-four youths were convicted, the Sleepy Lagoon Defense Committee was organized. The committee, headed by journalist Carey McWilliams, successfully appealed the case. The case was dismissed because of insufficient evidence when the district court of appeals reversed the convictions on October 4, 1944.

The Zoot-Suit Riots

On June 3, 1943, eleven sailors were allegedly attacked by a group of boys in a predominantly Mexican neighborhood in Los Angeles. After this incident, the Los Angeles police conducted a raid that inflamed the community but failed to find the attackers. This incident kicked off a chain reaction resulting in one of the most serious series of race riots that has occurred in the United States. Encouraged by the actions of the police and the pervasive anti-Mexican attitudes in Los Angeles, about 200 sailors began to attack violently Mexican American youths on the night of June 4.

The police responded by arresting the victims of the attacks and keeping their hands off the sailors. The Los Angeles press played its usual role in the conflict; it warned that the dangerous zoot-suiters would retaliate the next night. Some Mexican American youths were referred to as "zoot-suiters" because of their style of dress during the 1940s. The press succeeded in alarming the public and in stirring up anti-Mexican feelings. On the night of June 7, hundreds of Anglos went into the streets and began a massive attack on Mexican American youths. Many zoot-suiters were beaten and stripped naked in the streets. This ruckus continued until military authorities intervened late on the night of June 7. Other riots occurred in cities as far away as Philadelphia, Chicago, and Detroit in the summer of 1943.

The Chicano Movement

Prior to the civil rights movement of the 1960s, *Chicano* was a term used to refer to lower-class Mexican immigrants from rural areas and small towns. The term was viewed negatively by the middle-class and elite Mexican Americans but not by the lower-class people who used it. During the 1960s, leaders of the Mexican American protest and civil rights movement used the term in a positive way to describe their new quest for political, social, economic, cultural, and educational equality. The term *Chicano* was also used to link Mexican American political activists and intellectuals to their Mexican Indian heritage. In the past, their Spanish heritage was usually emphasized. The Chicano movement was broad in scope: it had economic, educational, religious, and cultural goals. The push for bilingual education in the schools was one of its major goals. Including more Mexican American priests and other church officials in the Catholic church hierarchy was another.

The Chicano movement was also political. Its leaders saw political clout as one of the best ways to attain the other goals of the movement. Its leaders, who often differed on tactics, had a variety of goals. Many believed that Chicanos would be able to overcome oppression in the United States only when they had political power and control over the institutions, such as schools and courts, that influenced their lives and destinies.

It is inaccurate to interpret the Chicano movement as a protest force that suddenly arose in the 1960s, or to refer to Chicanos as the "awakening minority," nor can it be viewed in isolation. Often this was done in the 1960s. To understand the Chicano movement fully, we must view it as an important link in the long chain of resistance activities in which Chicanos have been involved since 1848. As historian Rodolfo Acuña (1972) pointed out in the 1970s, "Men like Juan Patron and J. J. Herrerra were the precursors of today's breed of rebels or insurrectionists. In understanding them...and others of their kind, we shall better understand the present, and the words of Reis Lopez Tijerina will take on more significant meaning" (p. 77).

Early Resistance to Anglo Dominance

Mexican Americans have resisted Anglo oppression and colonization since Anglo-Americans conquered and occupied the Southwest. Chicanos such as Juan N. Cortina, Juan Jose Herrerra, and Juan Patron led organized resistance efforts in the 1800s. Cortina issued a "declaration of grievances" and urged Mexican Americans to "exterminate" their oppressors. Many Mexicans responded to the revolutionary calls issued by Cortina, Herrerra, and Patron (Acuña, 1988). Mexican American organizations, such as Las Gorras Blancas, fought Anglo leaders who were illegally taking land owned by Mexican Americans in New Mexico.

Unions and Strikes

In the first decades of the twentieth century, most Mexican Americans worked in agriculture, although many worked in mines, industry, and on the railroads. Farm workers were highly exploited by rich and powerful agribusinessmen. Mexican American workers aggressively opposed their conditions and organized unions and strikes, thus shattering the myth that they were docile workers. The period from 1900 to 1940 was characterized by active Chicano involvement in strikes and union organization. In 1927 the Confederacion de Uniones Obreras Mexicanas was organized in California. This union organized a strike in 1928 in the Imperial Valley. Farm owners and law officials, who formed coalitions, responded violently to the strike. They broke it up by deporting some strikers to Mexico and assaulting and intimidating others.

This pattern was used extensively by farm owners to crush strikes by Mexican Americans. However, strikes and union activities continued in the midst of these oppressive tactics. Meier and Rivera (1972) summarize this period: "Although Mexican Americans gained much labor union experience from 1900 to 1940, their organizations achieved only limited success. Some gains were made in wages and working conditions; however, the hopes and aspirations of Mexican-American workers continued to be frustrated by repression and discrimination" (p. 184).

Civil Rights Organizations

A number of civic, service, and political organizations have been organized since the late nineteenth century to promote the civil rights and interests of Mexican Americans. One of the first was a mutual-aid organization formed in Arizona in 1894, the Alianza Hispano-Americana. These early societies restricted membership to individuals of Mexican descent who were citizens of the United States. They were made up primarily of the middle and upper classes and promoted assimilation by urging their members to become loyal U.S. citizens. Cuellar (Moore, with Cuellar, 1970) argues that these organizations pursued a "politics of adaptation" rather than aggressively pushing for their political rights. They included the Order of the Sons of America, organized in San Antonio in 1921, and the League of United Latin-American Citizens, formed in Corpus Christi, Texas, in 1929.

Mexican Americans became more politicized in the post-World War II period. The organizations emerging during these years reflected acute political awareness and skill. The Community Service Organization, formed in Los Angeles in 1947, stressed political involvement and broad political participation. It organized a number of successful voter registration drives. The American G.I. Forum, founded in 1948, the Mexican American Political Association, organized in 1959, and the Political Association of Spanish-Speaking Organizations, formed in 1960, stressed political involvement. These organizations were direct predecessors of the Chicano movement that emerged in the 1960s.

The Militant Chicano Movement

Mexican Americans' protest activities, which had been going on historically, were intensified in the 1960s and 1970s and became collectively known as the "Chicano movement" (Meier & Ribera, 1993). In addition to being more intense than earlier Mexican American movements, the Chicano movement had other unique characteristics. It was more militant and often used forms of direct confrontation and included a wide range of individuals among its ranks such as intellectuals, students, and community activists. Its goals were also more ambitious than the goals of traditional Mexican American civil rights groups. It sometimes demanded Chicano control of institutions within the Mexican American community. Some of its leaders argued that Chicanos in the United States were a colonized people who had been culturally and politically oppressed. They demanded redress of these grievances.

Chicano leaders also gave more attention to their mixed Mexican heritage than did earlier leaders. Their unique heritage, they argued, was to be celebrated and not denied, as was often done in the past by Mexican Americans who insisted on being viewed as "Spanish" instead of "Mexican." Much emphasis was placed on Mexican culture, values, foods, and, especially, on the speaking of Spanish. They demanded the right to speak Spanish in all U.S. institutions such as the school and church. Some Chicano leaders argued that "revolution" was necessary to liberate them.

Of the many local Chicano civil rights leaders, four young men epitomized the movement in the public view of the U.S.: Cesar Chávez, Reies Lopez Tijerina, Rodolfo "Corky" Gonzales, and José Angel Gutierrez. Chávez headed the United Farm Workers Organizing Committee, unionized farm workers, and successfully led the famous Delano grape strike in 1965, as well as many subsequent farm strikes. Tijerina demanded that Anglos in New Mexico return the lands they had taken from Mexican Americans in the 1800s. He formed the Federal Alliance of Free Cities in 1963 to push for the return of New Mexico lands to Chicanos or compensation to Chicanos for the loss of these lands. An important and militant civil rights group, the Crusade for Justice, was organized in Denver in 1965 by Gonzales. The crusade initiated successful projects related to improved education, better housing, and the elimination of police brutality in the Mexican American community. As a result of the activities of the political party, La Raza Unida, organized in 1970 by Gutierrez, Chicanos exercised unprecedented political power in Crystal City, Texas, in the 1970s, which spread throughout the lower Rio Grande Valley. These four charismatic leaders embodied the hopes and aspirations of millions of Mexican Americans.

Mexican Americans Today

Mexican Americans, like African Americans and other people of color, made important educational and economic gains during the 1960s. However, many of these gains faded during the 1970s and 1980s. This loss during the 1970s and 1980s was caused by a number of factors, including the conservative national policies during the Reagan years and important changes in the U.S. economy. In previous decades, when industrial manufacturing was an important part of the U.S. economy, groups with few skills that were highly concentrated in the lower and working classes, such as Mexican Americans and African Americans, could move to large cities and obtain manufacturing jobs that paid well. There has been a substantial decrease in such jobs in the United States during the last thirty years as the United States and other major Western nations have increasingly become societies characterized by high technology and service occupations. These developments in the economy have had a disproportionately negative influence on job availability for groups heavily concentrated in the lower rungs of the economic and educational ladder, such as Mexican Americans, Puerto Ricans in the United States, and African Americans (Gregory & Sanjek, 1994; Wilson, 1987).

By the late 1980s, the militant Chicano movement of the 1960s had been transformed into more pragmatic forms of political organization. The various Hispanic groups, such as Mexican Americans, Puerto Ricans, and Cubans, were working cooperatively to form political, cultural, and business organizations to push for their collective rights and to improve the economic and educational status of U.S. Hispanics. These organizations included the National Association of Latino Elected and Appointed Officials, the Congressional Hispanic Caucus (comprised of Hispanics in the U.S. Congress), the National Hispanic Chamber of Commerce, the League of United Latin American citizens, and the Hispanic Policy Development Project, an organization that gathers data and analyzes public policy related to U.S. Hispanic groups. Many Mexican American organizations also remained viable, such as the Mexican-American Legal Defense and Education Fund. This organization was making tremendous strides in size, scope, and influence.

Mexican Americans were also reaping benefits in local and state elections and were becoming more conscious of their potential political clout. In 1984, Eligio de la Garza (Texas), Manual Lujan, Jr. (New Mexico), and Matthew G. Martinez (California) were among the eleven Hispanics in the U.S. House of Representatives. Mexican American mayors of large cities included Henry G. Cisneros in San Antonio and Federico Pena in Denver. Toney Anaya was governor of New Mexico. Mexican Americans continued to make visible political gains during the Clinton administration in the 1990s, epitomized by the appointment by Clinton of Henry G. Cisneros as Secretary of Housing and Urban Development in his administration.

In 2001, there were 20 Hispanics in the U.S. House of Representatives; none were in the Senate. All were members of the Congressional Hispanic Caucus, formed in 1976. This is a bipartisan group that works to improve conditions for all Hispanics. Six of the Hispanic House members were from California and six were from Texas. Two were from Florida, while each of these states had one: Arizona, New York, Illinois, New Jersey, Puerto Rico, and Guam.

Despite the political gains they had made by the 1980s and 1990s, Mexican American leaders realized that their ethnic group had more potential political power than it was realizing. The nine states in which Hispanics are concentrated (California, Texas, New York, Florida, Illinois, New Jersey, New Mexico, Arizona, and Colorado) have 193 electoral votes, which is 71% of the 270 needed to put a presidential candidate in the White House. Yet, several factors worked against Mexican Americans realizing their potential political strength, including the low voter turnout rate among them and the fact that a significant percentage of Mexican Americans are not U.S. citizens.

The Mexican American population is becoming increasingly urbanized, although it is less urban than other Hispanic groups. More than 75% of Mexican Americans lived in metropolitan areas in 1960. By 1980, that number had increased about 10%, and about four of every five Mexican Americans lived in metropolitan areas (Bean & Tienda, 1987). In 1990, about 89% of Mexican Americans lived in urban areas.

Large populations of Mexican Americans are concentrated in such cities as Los Angeles, Houston, Dallas, Denver, and Chicago. The Mexican American population, like the African American population, has also become more economically stratified since the 1970s. There have always been middle-class Mexican Americans. However, a new group of middle-class Hispanics developed as a result of the economic and educational opportunities they gained during the civil rights movement of the 1960s and 1970s (Acuña, 1988).

This new middle-class group of Mexican Americans is comprised of professionals and businesspeople. They frequently work in mainstream White institutions and live in predominantly White middle-class communities; consequently, they have little contact with the Hispanic barrio or with lower- and working-class Mexican American communities. The children of this new middle class often have little knowledge of the traditional Mexican American culture in the United States. Acuña (1988) has pointed out that these new middle-class professionals and business people often have an identity with and use the term *Hispanic* to refer to themselves. These new middle-class Hispanics, according to Acuña (1988), are often more interested in business development than social action and see business leaders, rather than social activists, as the important movers and shakers in the Mexican American community.

During the 1980s, which some media writers called "The Decade of the Hispanic," the emphasis in the Mexican American community was often on educational and economic development rather than on the kind of strident social action that characterized the civil rights movement of the 1960s and 1970s. Both Presidents Reagan and George Bush appointed successful and visible Mexican Americans to important federal positions. President Reagan appointed a university president, Dr. Lauro F. Cavazos, to be Secretary of the Department of Education. Cavazos was the first Hispanic appointed to a Cabinet post. Bush kept him in that position when he took office in 1989. In 1983, Reagan made history again when he appointed Linda Chavez to the U.S. Commission on Civil Rights. Both Bush and Carter also appointed a number of Hispanics to important positions in their administrations. President Clinton appointed Henry Cisneros, the former mayor of San Antonio, Secretary of Housing and Urban Development.

Nativism in the 1990s: New Xenophobia

The so-called Decade of the Hispanics was not without its stresses and strains, emergent xenophobia (fear of foreigners), and subtle and sometimes blatant racism. The new xenophobia, nativism, and sometimes racism were triggered by several factors. Among them were the large influx of legal Asian and Latin American immigrants to the United States, the nation's inability to control the large but undetermined number of undocumented or illegal immigrants (some estimates put the figure at 200,000 annually), the radical changes in the U.S. economy discussed previously, and the escalating class schism in U.S. society.

Nativistic sentiments and proposals surfaced during the years of heated discussion that finally resulted in the passage of the Immigration Reform and Control Act of 1986, designed to curb the rapid flow of undocumented (illegal) immigrants who enter the United States each year. It severely penalizes employers who knowingly hire undocumented workers. The enacted bill was a difficult compromise. Some of the voices heard during the strident debates over the proposed bill were decidedly anti-Hispanic in tone. The English-Only movement, which came to the forefront during the 1980s, sometimes uses chilling language reminiscent of the nativistic movements at the turn of the last century. A major goal of this movement is to get enacted in as many states as possible referenda that make English the "official language." What these referenda exactly mean in a legal sense is ambiguous. However, important goals are to halt the growth of bilingual education programs and to send the message to native speakers of languages other than English, such as Spanish, that the only language accepted in the United States is English.

The English-Only movement is fostered by U.S. English, a political action group that has a deep pocket and the endorsement of some influential Americans. The English-Only movement initially targeted states with large Hispanic populations for the passage of English-Only referenda. One of its major successes was the November 1986 passage of Proposition 63 in California. U.S. English knew that the stakes were high in California, and spent more than $700,000 to get Proposition 63 passed there (Crawford, 1989). By the beginning of 1990, U.S. English had been instrumental in getting English-Only referenda enacted in sixteen states, including Arizona, Colorado, and Florida.

California continued to be an influential center of nativistic activities and movements throughout the 1990s, perhaps because of its high concentration of Spanish-speaking and other immigrants. In 1990, nearly one third of the nation's immigrants lived in California. About half of the foreign-born lived in just two states, California and New York (U.S. Bureau of the Census, 1993). In 1994, anti-immigrant feelings surfaced and were sometimes encouraged by politicians, epitomized by the passage of Proposition 187 in California, dubbed by its supporters the "Save Our Children" proposition. This initiative denies undocumented workers and their children schooling and nonemergency medical care (*Encyclopaedia Britannica*, 1995). California Governor Pete Wilson endorsed Proposition 187 and made it a key issue in his reelection campaign, but the Proposition faced a legal challenge immediately after its passage.

Mexican Americans face several important challenges in the years ahead, including the need to increase the educational status of its youth, to close the income gap between Mexican Americans and the total U.S. population, and to work with other Hispanic groups to influence political elections and national policy. There are encouraging signs that the Mexican American community will face these challenges creatively.

Teaching Strategies

To illustrate how content about Mexican Americans can be used to integrate the curriculum, three key concepts have been identified and exemplary strategies are given for teaching them. Strategies are presented for teaching *stereotypes, immigration,* and *social protest* for the primary, intermediate and upper, and high school grades, respectively.

Primary Grades

CONCEPT

Stereotypes

Generalization: People have many stereotypes about what makes a person an American. These stereotypes often cause hurt and harm.

1. Read the following story to the class and ask the questions that follow:

Child from Another Land

Manuel and Maria Gonzales are descendants of Indian, Mexican, and Spanish people who have lived in the state of New Mexico for at least a century. The Gonzaleses are proud to be Americans but are just as proud of their Mexican American heritage. In their upper-middle-class community in the Southwest, their eight-year-old son, Ramon, went to a public elementary school that had a 20% Mexican American population. Ramon felt at home at the school and was sorry when he learned that his father, an engineer, was moving to the Midwest to accept an important job at a well-known computer company. Mrs. Gonzales, a high school English teacher, was also able to get a job in the Midwest city to which the family was moving.

Manuel and Maria were excited about the move to the Midwest because of the opportunity it offered Manuel. Ramon was very sorry to leave his friends and the only home and community he had ever known. He had decided, however, that he would try to make the best of the move. Ramon was the only Mexican American child in the third grade in his new school. There were only five Mexican American children in the entire school. During the first several days in his new school, Ramon fared okay but felt awkward when the teacher had trouble pronouncing his name and several children asked him, "What country are you from?"

Questions

1. How do you think Ramon felt about leaving his friends?
2. How do you think he felt in his new school? Why did he feel that way? Have you ever felt that way?
3. How do you think Ramon felt when the teacher had trouble pronouncing his name?
4. Why did the children ask Ramon, "What country are you from?"
5. Why do you think the children thought Ramon was from another country?

2. Introduce the concept *stereotype* to the students. Tell the students that a stereotype is a rigid and simplified way of thinking about a group of people and that it often causes harm to individuals and groups. Explain to the students how stereotypes lead to prejudice and discrimination. Ask them to list some of the stereotypes of different groups they may have, such as stereotypes about boys, girls, rich people, poor people, and fat people.

3. Explain to the students that the children thought Ramon was from a different country because he was a person of color who had a Spanish name. Explain that the children had a stereotypic notion of what an American is. Tell the students that Americans are of all racial, ethnic, and cultural origins and provide several examples. Also, show them pictures of African Americans, Mexican Americans, and Asian Americans. Summarize the lesson by asking the children to list the hurt and harm that stereotypes cause.

Intermediate and Upper Grades

CONCEPT

Immigration

Generalization: Social, economic, and political conditions have influenced Mexican immigration to the United States. Mexican immigrants in the United States have been the victims of racism, deportation, and labor exploitation.

1. Tell the students that about one million Mexican immigrants came to the United States between 1910 and 1930. Ask them to state hypotheses to explain why so many Mexicans immigrated to the United States during this period. List their responses on the board. When the students have finished stating their hypotheses, ask them to group their hypotheses into several categories, using symbols such as "−" and "+" to indicate statements that should be grouped together. When the statements have been grouped, ask the students to label the groups. The hypotheses might be grouped into such broad categories as "social reasons," "political reasons," and "economic reasons." These categories need not be mutually exclusive. In this initial exercise, you will be teaching your students how to hypothesize and conceptualize, which involves three major steps: listing, grouping, and labeling. (See James A. Banks & Cherry A. McGee Banks (1999), *Teaching Strategies for the Social Studies: Inquiry, Valuing, and Decision-Making*, 4th ed. [New York: Longman], p. 85.)

2. When the first exercise is completed, the students should record their hypotheses and categories in their notebooks. They will need to refer to them later in this exercise when they are tested. The students should now collect and study data to test their hypotheses. Their readings should include information on the Mexican Revolution of 1910 and the tremendous need for agricultural labor that had developed in the Southwest by the turn of the century. The Mexican Revolution caused many displaced Mexican peasants to come to the United States looking for jobs after 1910. The wealthy farmers in the Southwest wanted a large and cheap labor supply.

3. Students should investigate the conditions of the early Mexican immigrants to the United States. Most became migrant workers who followed the seasonal crops. Many of their dreams were shattered in the United States. Their problems are vividly and poignantly revealed in Manuel Gamio (1971), *The Life Story of the Mexican Immigrant*. Ask four students to read and dramatize for the class the accounts by these migratory laborers: Gumersindo Valdez, Juan Berzunzolo, Elias Garza, and Nivardo del Rio. Accounts by these writers are found on pages 141–159 of the Gamio book.

4. When the Great Depression struck in 1929, a movement began to deport Mexican immigrants to Mexico. Ask one student to prepare a class presentation giving the views of the U.S. Immigration Service and another to prepare a report revealing how different segments of the Mexican American community felt about this massive repatriation movement. The class should discuss the problem after these two presentations have been given.

5. Beginning in 1942, Mexican immigrants entered the United States under the terms of an agreement between the United States and Mexico. Ask the students to pretend that it is January 1942 and that the *bracero* bill is being debated in the U.S. Congress. Ask different members of the class to play the roles of various kinds of people in the Mexican American community (old settlers, new immigrants, etc.), Southwest agribusinessmen, and representatives of major unions in the United States. Ask the students playing the assigned roles to argue for or against the bill before the simulated Congress. The class should vote to decide the fate of the *bracero* bill of 1942 after they have heard the arguments. The class should then compare the results of their vote with the bill passed by Congress in 1942.

6. Ask several students in the class to make reports on Public Law 78, the Migratory Labor Agreement, and Operation Wetback, which began in 1954. Conduct a class discussion on the legal, social, and moral implications of these two activities that were implemented by the U.S. government. Particular attention should be given to how they affected U.S. citizens of Mexican descent.

7. During the debates and discussion on the passage of the Immigration Reform and Control Act of 1986, many problems of undocumented immigrants to the United States were revealed. Ask the students to research the debates that took place when the proposed act was being discussed, to describe the main goals of the act, and to determine the extent to which the act has been successful.

8. Because of the economic problems in Mexico today, a large number of people (both documented and undocumented) are entering the United States from Mexico. In 1998, 131,600 legal Mexican immigrants entered the United States. A large but unknown number of undocumented immigrants also enter the United States each year.

   Ask the students to investigate the economic conditions in Mexico today that cause large numbers of Mexicans to leave their nation and head for the United States. Unlike the past, most of these immigrants settle in large U.S. cities such as Los Angeles, Dallas, and Houston. Ask the students to find out what kinds of jobs these immigrants obtain in U.S. cities, the problems they encounter, and their general status in U.S. society.

9. Summarize the unit by asking the students to take out the hypotheses they formulated at the beginning of this unit and evaluate them, using the information they have collected and discussed. They should determine which hypotheses can remain as they were originally stated, which ones must be modified, and which ones must be totally rejected on the basis of the evidence collected.

10. Culminate the unit by showing and discussing a videotape or film on the experiences of Mexican Americans. See Appendix B for the descriptions and annotations of available videotapes and films. In the discussion, focus on social,

economic, and political conditions that have influenced Mexican immigration to the United States.

VALUING ACTIVITY

Read the following story to the class and ask the questions that follow.

The Sanchez Family and the Grape Strike

Mr. and Mrs. Sanchez and their seven children came from Mexico to live in California four years ago. Mr. Sanchez had been told by relatives who had been to the United States that he could make money very quickly if he came to California. When Mr. Sanchez arrived in California, he found that it was hard to make a living working in the fields. Since the Sanchez family has been living in California, the family has had to move many times in order to follow the crops and find work. The family has traveled as far as Texas and Michigan to work in the fields.

The work in the fields is very hard. Everyone in the family, except little Carlos, works in the fields so that the family can make enough money. Even Mrs. Sanchez, who used to stay at home and take care of the home when they lived in Mexico, now must work in the fields. The pay for the work is low. Mr. and Mrs. Sanchez find that they become further and further in debt each year.

The Sanchez family is now living in the San Joaquin Valley in California. The family went to live there to work in the grape fields. For a while everything there was okay. Recently, a lot of things have been happening in the valley that Mr. and Mrs. Sanchez do not fully understand. Most of the field workers have said that they will not go to work next week because the Mexican American Union, led by Juan Gonzalez, who is popular with the workers, has called a strike. The union is demanding that the owners of the grape fields pay the workers more money and give them better worker benefits. The workers who belong to the union are threatening to attack any worker who tries to go to work while the strike is on.

Mr. Sanchez is not a member of the union. He wants very much to go to work next week. He has many bills to pay and needs money for food and clothing. The family simply cannot get by with the small amount of money that the union has promised to give Mr. Sanchez if he joins it and refuses to work next week. Mr. Sanchez also realizes that, if the grapes are not picked within the next two weeks, they will rot. He has heard that these strikes sometimes last for months. His boss told him that if he wants to go to work next Monday morning—the day the strike is to begin—he will protect him from the unionized workers. Mrs. Sanchez thinks that Mr. Sanchez should support the strike so that he can make higher wages in the future.

Questions

1. Do you think that Mr. Sanchez and his family will go to work in the fields next Monday? Why or why not?

2. If Mr. Sanchez does go to work, what do you think will happen to him and his family?
3. If Mr. Sanchez does not go to work in the grape fields next Monday, what do you think he might do to earn money?
4. What do you think Mr. Sanchez should do? Why?
5. What would you do if you were (a) Mr. Sanchez, (b) Mrs. Sanchez, (c) the children? Why?
6. Tell whether you agree or disagree with this statement and why: "The head of a family should never let his or her spouse and children do without the food and clothing they need."

High School Grades

CONCEPT

Social Protest
Generalization: Since the Anglo-American conquest of the Southwest, Mexican Americans have used a variety of means to resist oppression and discrimination. This resistance intensified and assumed new characteristics in the 1960s and 1970s.

1. The teacher can begin this unit by having the students read and dramatize the epic poem of the Chicano movement, *I Am Joaquin/Yo Soy Joaquin,* by Rodolfo Gonzales (1972). This poem is a powerful statement of the history and culture of Chicanos, with emphasis on their oppression and struggle for freedom. Among the many references made in the poem related to social protest are Father Miguel Hidalgo and *El Grito de Dolores of 1810,* Cinco de Mayo, the Treaty of Guadalupe Hidalgo, and the Anglo conquest of the Southwest in the 1800s. This poem will stimulate many questions students can pursue while studying Chicano resistance to oppression. The teacher may also want to show the film based on the poem *I Am Joaquin.*
2. References are frequently made to the Treaty of Guadalupe Hidalgo by Chicano leaders. After students have studied the events that led to the treaty, have them examine the treaty in detail and give their interpretations of it. They should compare their interpretations of the treaty with interpretations given by contemporary Chicano leaders. The complete text of the treaty is found in *A Documentary History of Mexican Americans,* edited by Moquin with Van Doren (1972).
3. Ask a group of students to prepare and present to the class a dramatization portraying the positions and statements of early Mexican American militant leaders, such as Juan Patron, J. J. Herrerra, and Juan N. Cortina.
4. Some of the earliest Chicano resistance activities were unionization and strikes. Ask a group of students to prepare short reports on the various strikes and union activities during the period from 1900 to 1940. The strike in the California Imperial Valley in 1928 should be highlighted.
5. The earliest Mexican American civil rights organizations pursued what Cuellar (Moore with Cuellar, 1970) has called a "politics of adaptation." Mexican

American civil rights organizations became more politicized in the post-World War II period. Militant Chicano organizations emerged in the 1960s. Ask the students to research the goals, tactics, and strategies used by the following Mexican American civil rights groups. They will discover the trends described above.

a. Order of the Sons of America (formed in 1921)
b. League of United Latin-American Citizens (1929)
c. The Community Service Organization (1947)
d. The American G. I. Forum (1948)
e. Federal Alliance of Free Cities (1963)
f. Crusade for Justice (1965)

6. Ask the class to research the following questions: How was the Chicano movement similar to other Mexican American protest movements? How were its goals and strategies different? When did the movement emerge? What problems did it help to solve? What had happened to the movement by the late 1980s? Why? In what ways was the Chicano movement similar to, and different from, civil rights movements that emerged within other ethnic minority communities in the 1960s? What long-term effects do you think the Chicano movement has had and is having on U.S. society?

7. The union activity led by Cesar Chávez during the 1960s and 1970s was an integral part of the Chicano movement. You may begin a study of these events by reading to the class the brilliant and poignant letter that Chávez wrote to E. L. Barr, Jr., president of the California Grape and Tree Fruit League, reprinted in Fusco and Horwitz, *La Causa: The California Grape Strike*. The moving photographs in this book will evoke many questions and comments about the strike. The students can also read the excellently written book on the strike by John Gregory Dunne, *Delano: The Story of the California Grape Strike*.

8. After the students have read and discussed accounts and interpretations of Mexican American resistance and the Chicano movement, ask them to write and present a dramatization on "Mexican American Resistance to Oppression in the United States, 1848 to the Present."

REFERENCES

Acuña, R. (1972). *Occupied America: The Chicano's Struggle toward Liberation*. San Francisco: Canfield Press.

Acuña, R. (1988). *Occupied America: The Chicano's Struggle toward Liberation* (3rd ed.). New York: Harper and Row.

Banks, J. A., with Clegg, A. A., Jr. (1990). *Teaching Strategies for the Social Studies: Inquiry, Valuing and Decision-Making* (4th ed.). White Plains, NY: Longman.

Bean, F. D., & Tienda, M. (1987). *The Hispanic Population of the United States*. New York: Russell Sage.

Crawford, J. (1989). *Bilingual Education: History, Politics, Theory and Practice*. Trenton, NJ: Crane.

Encyclopaedia Britannica. (1995). *1995 Book of the Year*. Chicago: Author.

Franklin, J. H., & Moss, A. A., Jr. (2000). *From Slavery to Freedom: A History of Negro Americans* (8th ed.). New York: McGraw-Hill.

Gamio, M. (1971). *The Life Story of the Mexican Immigrant*. New York: Dover.

Gonzales, R. (1972). *I Am Joaquin/Yo Soy Joaquin*. New York: Bantam.

Gregory, S., & Sanjek, R. (Eds.). (1994). *Race*. New Brunswick, NJ: Rutgers University Press.

Jiménez, A. (1994). The Spanish Colonial Model. In A. Jiménez (Ed.), *Handbook of Hispanic Cultures in the United States: History* (pp. 66–95). Houston: Arte Público/University of Houston.

Kanellos, N. (1994). *The Hispanic Almanac: From Columbus to Corporate America*. Detroit: Gale Research.

McWilliams, C. (1968). *North from Mexico: The Spanish-Speaking People of the United States*. New York: Greenwood Press.

Meier, M. S., & Ribera, F. (1993). *Mexican Americans/American Mexicans: From Conquistadors to Chicanos*. New York: Hill & Wang.

Meier, M. S., & Rivera, F. (1972). *The Chicanos: A History of Mexican Americans*. New York: Hill and Wang.

Moore, J. W., with Cuellar, A. (1970). *Mexican Americans*. Englewood Cliffs, NJ: Prentice-Hall.

Moore, J. W., with Pachon, H. (1976). *Mexican-Americans* (2nd ed.). Englewood Cliffs, NJ: Prentice-Hall.

The Treaty of Guadalupe Hidalgo. In W. Moquin with C. Van Doren (Eds.), (1971). *A Documentary History of Mexican Americans* (pp. 241–249). New York: Bantam.

U.S. Bureau of the Census. (1993). *We, the Foreign Born*. Washington, DC: U.S. Government Printing Office.

U.S. Bureau of the Census. (1994). *Statistical Abstract of the United States: 1994* (114th ed.). Washington, DC: U.S. Government Printing Office.

U.S. Census Bureau (2000a). *The Hispanic Population* (Census 2000 Brief). [On-line]. Available: *http://www.census.gov/*

U.S. Census Bureau (2000b). *Statistical Abstract of the United States: 2000* (120th ed.). Washington, DC: U.S. Government Printing Office.

U.S. Census Bureau (2001). [On-line] Available: *http://www.census.gov/*

Wilson, W. J. (1987). *The Truly Disadvantaged: The Inner City, the Underclass, and Public Policy*. Chicago: University of Chicago Press.

ANNOTATED BIBLIOGRAPHY

Books for Teachers

Especially Recommended

Acuña, R. (1999). *Occupied America: A History of Chicanos* (4th ed.).Boston: Addison-Wesley Longman.

> *The author presents the complex history of Mexican Americans from a variety of sources. The cultural, economic, and political strategies that Chicanos/as used to resist colonization are described by the author. This new edition includes new and updated material and addresses questions of gender.*

Anzaldúa, G. (1999). *Borderlands/La Frontera: The New Mestiza* (2nd ed.). San Francisco: Aunt Lute Books.

> *This book explores the cultural, psychological, sexual, and spiritual borderlands within the self using the U.S. Southwest/Mexican border as a starting point. Written from a Chicana feminist perspective, it has an introduction by scholar Sonia Saldívar-Hull and an interview with Gloria Anzaldúa.*

Bodeen, J. (Ed.). (1999). *With My Hands Full/Con Mis Manos Llenas: Young Latino Voices*. Yakima, WA: Blue Begonia Press.

> *A collection of personal essays, stories, and poems of high school students and parent interviews of families who had migrated to Eastern Washington as farm workers.*

Gamboa, E. (2000). *Mexican Labor & World War II: Braceros in the Pacific Northwest, 1942–1947* (Original ed., 1990). Seattle: University of Washington Press.

An important and unique book that describes the labor history of Mexican migrant workers in the Pacific Northwest.

Gonzales, M. G. (2000). *Mexicanos: A History of Mexicans in the United States.* Bloomington: Indiana University Press.

A comprehensive historical overview of Mexicans in the United States from the ruins of the Aztec civilization until 1998.

Gonzales, M. G., & Gonzales, C. M. (Eds.). (2000). *En Aquel Entonces: Readings in Mexican-American History.* Bloomington: Indiana University Press.

This book offers an interdisciplinary overview of various aspects of Mexican American life experiences and is, at the same time, an introduction to Chicana/o historiography. An anthology of 31 journal articles, it represents the important works in Mexican American history from the 1960s to 2000.

Guerra, J. C. (1998). *Close to Home: Oral and Literate Practices in a Transitional Mexicano Community.* New York: Teachers College Press.

This book offers insight and understanding in the social organization and immigration experiences of Mexican immigrant families. After examining the historical and sociocultural context, the author analyzes and presents the discourse practices that exist in transnational communities.

Martínez, O. J. (2001). *Mexican-Origin People in the United States: A Topical History.* Tucson: University of Arizona Press.

A historical analysis of the social, economic, and political change in the twentieth century for Mexican-Americans in the United States.

Martínez, R. (2001). *Crossing Over: A Mexican Family on the Migrant Trail.* New York: Henry Holt.

A journalistic chronicle about the motivations behind the illegal border crossings and immigration into the United States of an extended Mexican family. The book is a strong portrait of migrant culture and life in the borderlands.

Meier, M., & Ribera, F. (2001). *Mexican Americans/American Mexicans: From Conquistadors to Chicanos* (11th ed.). New York: Hill & Wang.

This revised edition analyzes Mexican history in three phases: prior to the arrival of Columbus and up to the arrival of the conquistadors; the period of Mexican independence through the Mexican-American War and the Treaty of Guadalupe Hidalgo; and the period from 1848 to the present.

Other References

Dávila, A. (2001). *Latinos Inc.: The Marketing and Making of a People.* Berkeley: University of California Press.

A critical exploration of how Latino artifacts, such as salsa dancing or food items, are taken up by corporate marketing as well as mainstream entertainment industries while, at the same time, economic parity and political enfranchisement of Latinos in the United States are lagging behind.

Davis, M. (2001). *Magical Urbanism: Latinos Reinvent the U.S. City.* New York: Verso.

This book examines the Latinization of the United States as well as the militarization and violence at the border crossings.

Gonzales, R. (2001). *Message to Aztlán: Selected Writings of Rodolpho 'Corky' Gonzales.* Houston: Arte Público Press.

A collection of speeches, essays, plays, and poetry written between 1967 and 1980 by one of the leaders of the Chicano civil rights movement.

Hart Treviño, E. (1999). *Barefoot Heart: Stories of a Migrant Child.* Tempe, AZ: Bilingual Press.

An autobiographical account of a childhood and coming of age in a family of migrant farm workers.

Hernández-Castillo, R. A. (2001): *Histories and Stories from Chiapas: Border Identities in Southern Mexico.* Austin: University of Texas Press.

An ethnographic study that captures the changes in the identity formation of a Maya group, the Mam, in Chiapas. The book covers a time span from 1933 to 1994 during the Zapatista movement. A special focus is given to women and their role in the Mam society. This book has a foreword by Renato Rosaldo.

Jaramillo, C. M. (2000). *Romance of a Little Village Girl* (original ed., 1955). Albuquerque: University of New Mexico Press.

An autobiographical memoir that takes the reader through girlhood, marriage, motherhood, and later life of the author in northern New Mexico from the late 1800s to the mid 1950s. The personal story is intercepted by the impact of political and economic events of the times on the Hispanic community of New Mexico as well as interspersed with descriptions of religious and folkloric customs in the area.

Maciel, D. R., & Herrera-Sobek, M. (1998). *Culture across Borders: Mexican Immigration & Popular Culture.* Tucson: University of Arizona Press.

This is a study of how experiences of immigration manifest themselves in art, literature, cinema, songs, and jokes.

Mariscal, G. (Ed.). (1999). *Aztlán and Viet Nam: Chicano and Chicana Experiences of the War.* Berkeley: University of California Press.

An anthology of 60 short stories, poems, speeches, and articles about the U.S. war in Viet Nam from Mexican American perspectives. The writings address the experiences of Chicano soldiers as well as the antiwar movement, the Catholic Church, traditional Mexican American groups, and an emerging feminist consciousness among Chicanas.

McGregor, A., & Wathen, C. (Eds.). (2000). *Remembering Cesar: The Legacy of Cesar Chávez.* Clovis, CA: Quill Driver Books.

A collection of personal accounts that portray the migrant farm worker activist Cesar Chávez in his political struggle for rights and justice. Illustrated by black-and-white photographs.

Muñoz, Jr., C. (2000). *Youth, Identity, Power: The Chicano Movement* (9th ed.). London: Verso.

A study on the origins of the political Chicano movement and radicalism in the U.S. The author was one of the leaders of the 1960s Chicano student movement.

Pardo, M. S. (1998). *Mexican-American Women Activists: Identity and Resistance in Two Los Angeles Communities.* Philadelphia: Temple University Press.

This book analyzes the community work of Mexican American women in two Los Angeles neighborhoods on class, gender, and ethnic concerns.

Pérez, E. (1999). *The Decolonial Imaginary: Writing Chicanas into History.* Bloomington: Indiana University Press.

This book discusses the historical methodology that traditionally has created Chicano history. The author draws on critical and feminist theory to examine the methodological assumptions and offer new approaches to uncover previously silenced voices. A special focus is given to Mexican immigrant women.

Poniatowska, E., & Ortiz, S. (2001). *Questions & Swords: Folktales of the Zapatista Revolution: As Told by Subcommandante Marcos.* El Paso: Cinco Puntos Press.

Two illustrated folktales that recount the Zapatista rebellion against the Mexican government and address its importance for the twenty-first century. The stories are illustrated by the Mexican artists Domitila Dominguez and Antonio Ramirez.

Rebolledo, T. D., & Márquez, M. T. (2000). *Women's Tales from the New Mexico WPA: La Diabla a Pie.* Houston: Arte Publico Press.

This book offers stories, folktales, and interviews with women of Hispanic origin that were collected after the Great Depression as part of the Works Progress Administration, a massive national undertaking to get the nation back to work.

Rodríguez, J., Martinez, R., & Rodríguez, L. (Eds.). (2000). *Eastside Stories: Ganglife in East Los Angeles.* New York: PowerHouse Books.

This photographic and narrative documentary of gang life in East Los Angeles offers insights into the family and community lives of gang members and aspects of life in a large metropolitan area that are rarely portrayed.

Rosales, F. A. (2000). *Testimonio: A Documentary History of the Mexican American Struggle for Civil Rights.* Houston: Arte Público Press.

A historical report from the early 1800s to the modern era that presents documents from a variety of sources that tells the history of Mexican Americans from the angle of civil rights.

Stavans, I. (1999). *The Riddle of Cantiflas: Essays on Hispanic Popular Culture* (2nd ed.). Albuquerque: University of New Mexico Press.

A collection of essays by the author that portray the idols of Mexican popular culture in the United States.

Taylor, L. J., & Hickey, M. (2001). *Tunnel Kids.* Tucson: University of Arizona Press.

This books offers a glimpse into the world and reality of youth who live in the drainage tunnels that connect the twin cities of Nogales, Sonora, and Nogales, Arizona. Through story and photographs the authors document the poverty and uncertainty of these children's lives and futures along the United States–Mexico border.

Tijerina, R. L. (2000). *They Called Me "King Tiger": My Struggles for the Land and Our Rights.* Houston: Arte Público Press.

This book is an autobiographical account and historical document of one of the four central figures in the 1960s Mexican American Civil Rights Movement.

Tuñon-Pablos, J. (1999). *Women in Mexico: A Past Unveiled* (original ed., 1987, in Spanish). Austin: University of Texas Press.

A historical and feminist analysis of the role and identity transformation of Mexican women from Cortés to the 1980s.

Tywoniak, F. E., & García, M. T. (2000). *Migrant Daughter: Coming of Age as a Mexican-American Woman.* Berkeley: University of California Press.

Based on an oral history project, this book is the testimony of a young Mexican American woman's story from farm work to a graduate degree. The portrait captures the negotiation between shifting ethnic identity and cultural allegiances.

Urrea, L. A. (1998). *Nobody's Son: Notes from an American Life.* Tucson: University of Arizona Press.

The author presents us with the third and final part of his memoir that describes his growing up as a biracial and bicultural youth in San Diego.

Vila, P. (2000). *Crossing Borders: Social Categories, Metaphors, and Narrative Identities on the U.S.–Mexico Frontier.* Austin: University of Texas Press.

A sociological and ethnographic study of how the inhabitants of El Paso and Ciudad Juárez define their group identity and distinguish themselves from others.

Books for Students

Ada, A. F. (1996). *Gathering the Sun.* Illustrated by S. Silva. New York: Lothrop.

Vivid and compelling illustrations and lyrical poetry portray the life of a migrant child. (Primary/Intermediate)

Alarcón, F. X. (1997). *Laughing Tomatoes and Other Spring Poems/Jítomates risueños y otros poemas de verano.* Illustrated by M. C. González. San Francisco: Children's Book Press.

The first in a series of whimsical bilingual poetry collections that express the joys of the seasons in the life of a Mexican American child. Along with the poems in English and Spanish, the book features lively, colorful illustrations that capture the mood perfectly. The seasonal series continues with From the Bellybutton of the Moon and Other Summer Poems/Del ombligo de la luna y otros poemas del verano *(Children's Book Press, 1998) and* Angeles Ride Bikes and Other Fall Poems/Los ángeles and an en bicicleta y otros poemas de otoño *(Children's Book Press, 1999). (Primary)*

Anaya, R. (1997). *Maya's Children: The Story of La Llorona.* Illustrated by M. Baca. New York: Hyperion.

A retelling of an ancient Mexican tale featuring the legendary cultural figure La Llorona, the crying woman. (Primary/Intermediate)

Anaya, R. (1999). *My Land Sings: Stories from the Rio Grande.* Illustrated by A. Cordova. New York: Morrow.

A collection of folktales that offers an engaging introduction to the Hispanic cultures of the Southwest. (Intermediate/Middle School)

Anaya, R. (2001). *Elegy on the Death of Cesar Chavez.* Illustrated by G. Enríquez. El Paso, TX: Cinco Puntos Press.

The noted writer offers a poem in honor of the labor and civil rights leader who died in 1993. Luminous color illustrations by graphic artist Gaspar Enríquez make this a book to be cherished by readers of all ages. (Intermediate and Up)

Ancona, G. (1998). *Barrio: José's Neighborhood.* Illustrated with photos by the author. San Diego: Harcourt.

A Mexican American child introduces readers to the diverse people and ways of life in his neighborhood; stunning photographs distinguish this and other Ancona books. Another recent Ancona title that highlights Hispanic heritage is Charro: The Mexican Cowboy *(Harcourt, 1997), which features ranches in Mexico, male and female ranchers at work, and the festival and competition known as the charreada. (Primary/Intermediate)*

Anzaldúa, G. (1996). *Prietita and the Ghost Woman/Prietita y la llorona.* San Francisco: Children's Book Press.

Prietita, the young Mexican American girl featured in Friends from the Other Side *(Children's Book Press, 1993), encounters the ghost woman (or "crying woman") of Mexican legend while looking for herbs for her ill mother. Written in both English and Spanish. (Primary/Intermediate)*

Bertrand, D. G. (1999). *Family, Familia.* Illustrated by P. R. Howard. Houston, TX: Piñata Books.

Young Daniel attends a family reunion in this colorful and appealing bilingual book. (Primary)

Chavarría-Chaírez, B. (2000). *Magda's Tortillas/Las tortillitas de Magda.* Illustrated by A. Vega. Houston, TX: Piñata Books.

In this bilingual picture book, seven-year-old Magda struggles to make tortillas as perfect as the ones her grandmother makes. Children will learn lessons of patience and persistence through this warm intergenerational story. (Primary)

DeAnda, D. (1997). *The Ice Dove and Other Stories.* Houston, TX: Piñata Books.

Four stories reaffirm the importance of family, heritage, and community in the lives of young Mexican Americans. DeAnda presents five additional stories, most focusing on Mexican American children living in the suburbs and children's relationship with animals, in The Immortal Rooster and Other Stories *(Piñata Books, 1999). (Intermediate)*

Garza, C. L. (1999). *Magic Windows/Ventanas mágicas.* Illustrated by the author. San Francisco: Children's Book Press.

The acclaimed artist, creator of Family Pictures/Cuadros de familia *(Children's Book Press, 1992) and* My Family/Mi familia *(Children's Book Press, 1996) returns with this exquisite collection of cut-paper illustrations that highlight favorite childhood memories. Winner of the 2000 Pura Belpré award for illustration. (All ages)*

Harris, Z., and Williams, S. (1998). *Piñatas and Smiling Skeletons: Celebrating Mexican Festivals.* Illustrated by Y. G. Woo. Berkeley, CA: Pacific View Press.

A lively introduction to popular Mexican and Mexican American festivals. (Primary/Intermediate)

Hayes, J. (2000). *Little Gold Star/Estrellita de Oro: A Cinderella Cuento.* Illustrated by G. O. Pérez. El Paso, TX: Cinco Puntos Press.

This bilingual retelling of the classic tale is set among the Hispanic peoples of the American Southwest. (Primary)

Herrera, J. F. (2000). *The Upside Down Boy/El niño de cabeza.* Illustrated by E. Gómez. San Francisco: Children's Book Press.

This sensitive bilingual memoir of the immigrant author's struggle to learn English will make children more aware of the beauty of multiple languages and the needs of children who do not speak English as a first language. Herrera is also the author of the bilingual volume of poetry for children, Laughing Out Loud: Poems in English and Spanish *(Atheneum, 1998), and* Calling the Doves *(Children's Book Press, 1995), a lyrical reminiscence about the author's childhood in California with his mother and father, who were farm workers. (All ages)*

Hoobler, D. T. (1994). *The Mexican American Family Album.* New York: Oxford University Press.

An excellent resource that documents the journey of Mexicans from Mexico to the United States. (Middle School/High School)

Jiménez, F. (1997). *The Circuit: Stories from the Life of a Migrant Child.* Albuquerque: University of New Mexico Press.

Twelve interconnected stories describe the author's precarious childhood as an undocumented migrant agricultural worker and his struggles to express himself through language and art. This compelling memoir is reminiscent of Tomás Rivera's classic depiction of a migrant childhood, Y no se lo tragó la tierra.../And the Earth Did Not Devour Him *(Arte Público, 1991). (High School)*

Martínez, F. (1997). *Spirits of the High Mesa.* Houston, TX: Piñata Books.

A Mexican American boy living in a small New Mexico town comes of age amid the economic, social, and technological changes following the Second World War. (Middle School/High School)

Martínez, V. (1996). *Parrot in the Oven: Mi Vida.* New York: HarperCollins.

Eleven lyrical, sparsely written, and sensitive stories tell of the hard life, family conflicts, and small triumphs of a fourteen-year-old Mexican American boy growing up in an impoverished family in California. Winner of the 1998 Pura Belpré award for writing. (Middle School/High School)

Medina, J. (1999). *My Name Is Jorge on Both Sides of the River: Poems in English and Spanish.* Illustrated by F. Vanden Broeck. Honesdale, PA: Boyds Mills.

Moving poems in English, Spanish, and a combination of the two depict a young boy's anxieties as he adjusts to life in the United States, only to have to return to Mexico in the end. (All ages)

Mora, P. (1997). *Tomás and the Library Lady.* Illustrated by R. Colón. New York. Knopf.

This picture book recounts an episode in the life of Tomás Rivera, a poor migrant child who became a noted writer and educator. The story affirms the role of books and libraries in introducing the larger world and its possibilities to children. (Primary)

Rodríguez, L. J. (1998). *América Is Her Name.* Illustrated by C. Vásquez. Willimantic, CT: Curbstone Press.

A nine-year-old Mexican immigrant girl living in Chicago is inspired to write by a poet who visits her school. Best known for his writing and educational work about street gangs, as described in Always Running: La Vida Loca—Gang Days in L.A. *(Simon & Schuster, 1994), Rodríguez offers a compelling tale for younger children of a boy tempted by a gang in* It Doesn't Have to Be This Way *(Children's Book Press, 2000). (Primary/Intermediate)*

Ryan, P. M. (2000). *Esperanza Rising.* New York: Scholastic.

A wealthy Mexican girl escapes with her remaining family to the United States after the murder of her father, only to encounter illness, poverty, and hardship as migrant farm laborers during the Great Depression. Based on the life of the author's grandmother. (Middle School)

Saénz, B. A. (1998). *A Gift from Papá Diego/Un regalo de Papá Diego.* Illustrated by G. García. El Paso, TX: Cinco Puntos Press.

A Mexican American boy dreams of being reunited with his grandfather in Mexico in a tale enhanced by Gerónimo García's imaginative clay illustrations. (Primary)

Soto, G. (1996). *Snapshots from the Wedding.* Illustrated by S. García. New York: Putnam.

Winner of the 1998 Pura Belpré award for illustration, this book conveys the joy and traditions of a Mexican American wedding. (Primary)

Soto, G. (2000). *The Effects of Knut Hamsun on a Fresno Boy: Recollections and Short Essays.* New York: Persea Books.

A collection of new and previously published essays about family relationships, identity, and the lessons learned in childhood and adolescence. Soto is the author of many other notable works for preteens and teenagers, including Baseball in April and Other Stories *(Harcourt, 1990) and* Neighborhood Odes *(Harcourt, 1992). (Middle School/High School)*

Stevens, J. R. (1999). *Carlos and the Carnival/Carlos y la feria.* Illustrated by J. Arnold. Flagstaff, AZ: Rising Moon/Northland.

> *It's Carlos's birthday and also time for the carnival, and the mischievous youngster and his friend Gloria enjoy a variety of adventures and escapades. One of a bilingual series about a Mexican American youngster that includes* Carlos and the Cornfield/Carlos y la milpa de maíz *(Rising Moon/Northland, 1995) and* Carlos Digs to China/Carlos excava hasta la China *(Rising Moon/Northland, 2001). (Primary/Intermediate)*

11 Puerto Ricans in the United States

Concepts, Strategies, and Materials

> *Colonialism has always played an important role in the Puerto Rican experience. Puerto Rico and the United States are connected through colonial ties, and this gives the [Puerto Rican] migration a unique character.*
>
> —Sonia Nieto

Puerto Ricans are the second largest Hispanic group in the United States. Their 2000 population, 3,406,178, made up 9.6% of the total population of documented Hispanics living in the United States (U.S. Census Bureau, 2001). The Puerto Rican population increased 24.9% between 1990 and 2000, from 2.7 to 3.4 million (U.S. Census Bureau, 2001). This rate of growth was considerably greater than the rate of increase for the total U.S. population and for Whites but below the rate of growth for the total Hispanic population (57.9%). The 24.9% population increase experienced by Puerto Ricans between 1990 and 2000 was due primarily to a high birthrate rather than to migration. Puerto Rican migration to the United States peaked in 1953, with about 75,000 net arrivals. Since that time, net migration between Puerto Rico and the United States has ebbed and flowed with economic conditions in the two nations (see Figure 11.1) (Rodriguez, 1991).

The Puerto Rican population on the U.S. mainland is growing faster than the population in Puerto Rico. In 2000, Puerto Rico's population was 3.9 million (Population Reference Bureau, 2001), compared to a mainland Puerto Rican population of 3.4 million. The island's population increased about 9% between 1990 and 2000, whereas the Puerto Rican population on the mainland

FIGURE 11.1   Migration from Puerto Rico to the United States, 1920–1986

Source: Figure 1.1 from *Puerto Ricans Born in the U.S.A.* by Clara E. Rodriguez. Copyright © 1991 by Westview Press. Reprinted by permission of Westview Press, a member of Perseus Books, L.L.C.

increased about 24.9% (U.S. Census Bureau, 2001). Not all of the people who lived on the island, however, were of Puerto Rican descent. Puerto Rico has a sizable immigrant population, including many Cubans. Some population experts predict that, if the current disproportionate rate of population growth on the island and the mainland continues, the number of Puerto Ricans on the U.S. mainland will equal, if not exceed, the number on the island within the next few decades.

Content about Puerto Ricans should be included in the mainstream curriculum because they are an integral part of U.S. society. Knowledge of their experiences on the mainland can help students master important social science concepts, such as *migration, cultural diversity, racism,* and *colonialism.*

When studying about Puerto Ricans on the U.S. mainland, students can compare and contrast their experiences with those of other migrant and immigrant groups. In some ways, Puerto Rican migration is similar to the movement of other groups to the United States. Puerto Ricans are culturally uprooted, like European immigrants were when they migrate to the United States. However, their migration is also unique in U.S. history in several ways.

When large numbers of Puerto Ricans began to migrate to the U.S. mainland, automation had greatly decreased the need for manual labor in the United States. Unlike other groups, Puerto Ricans are U.S. citizens when they set foot on U.S. soil. Their migration is the first "airborne migration" in U.S. history. Puerto Ricans bring racial attitudes to the United States that are considerably different from those they find here. The study of the complex nature of the Puerto Rican migration and experience on the U.S. mainland provides students with excellent opportunities to formulate generalizations that are essential components of a sound multicultural curriculum.

The Island Background

Puerto Rico

Puerto Rico, called San Juan Baptista by Christopher Columbus, is a beautiful, small tropical island in the Caribbean Sea. The island, which sits on the top of a large underwater mountain, is smaller than the state of Connecticut. It is about 35 miles wide, 100 miles long, and its total area is slightly more than 3,400 square miles. Puerto Rico, which has become one of the favorite vacation places for U.S. tourists, has one of the highest population densities in the world, 1,139 persons per square mile in 2001. Almost four million (3.9 million) people lived on this attractive island in 2001 (Population Reference Bureau, 2001).

Puerto Rico's history is just as interesting as its terrain and demography. During the last four centuries, its fate has been determined by two faraway nations that ruled it the way absentee landlords govern a slum. Spain ruled the country from the sixteenth century up to the Spanish-American War in 1898 when the United States took control. It governed Puerto Rico awkwardly and ambiguously. Although the Commonwealth of Puerto Rico has existed since July 1952, Puerto Rico's relationship with the United States is still shaky and unclear (Trías Monge, 1997). Puerto Rico, which is neither a state nor an independent nation, continues to suffer from the burden of colonialism, and its ambiguous colonialist status is likely to continue for some years to come, especially as cries for independence keep emerging in Puerto Rico, even if they are voiced only by a determined, forceful few. In a plebiscite held in 1993, Puerto Rico's current Commonwealth status won by only a slim margin.

Since 1917, Puerto Ricans have been U.S. citizens. In the period between the two world wars, they started migrating to the mainland in large numbers, mainly to New York City. In 1990, about 39% of all Puerto Ricans lived on the U.S. mainland. About half of the mainland Puerto Ricans were born in the United States. The number of Puerto Ricans on the U.S. mainland is significant and increases at every census count, growing from 900,000 in 1960 to 3.4 million in 2000.

PUERTO RICANS IN THE UNITED STATES: HISTORICAL PERSPECTIVE

Important Dates	Events
1493	Columbus landed on the island of Boriquén, November 19, 1493. Boriquén was the home of the Taíno (or Arawak) Indians, the native inhabitants of Puerto Rico.
1508	Juan Ponce de León became the governor of Puerto Rico.
1511	The Taino Indians unsuccessfully rebelled against the Spanish system of forced labor.
1513	African slaves were introduced on Puerto Rican plantations.
1868	*El Grito De Lares*: a group of Puerto Rican revolutionaries called for independence and planned an unsuccessful revolt.
1873	Slavery was abolished in Puerto Rico.
1898	Spain ceded Puerto Rico to the United States under the terms of the Treaty of Paris, the treaty that formally ended the Spanish-American War.
1900	Under the terms of the Foraker Act, the United States established a government in Puerto Rico in which the president of the United States appointed the governor and the Executive Council. The House of Delegates and the resident commissioner were to be elected by popular vote.
1910	The U.S. Census indicated that there were 1,513 native Puerto Ricans living in the United States.
1917	The Jones Act was passed by the U.S. Congress. It made Puerto Ricans U.S. citizens and subject to the U.S. draft. The act also provided for the popular election of both houses of the Puerto Rican legislature.
1920	11,811 persons born in Puerto Rico were living in the United States. That number increased to 58,200 in 1935.
1937	Twenty people were killed in a tragedy known as the "Ponce Massacre" on Palm Sunday.
1947	The U.S. Congress amended the Jones Act of 1917. Puerto Ricans were granted the right to elect their own governor. The governor was given the right to make most of the appointments for high public offices.

Important Dates	Events
1948	Luis Muñoz Marin became the first elected governor of Puerto Rico. He was governor of Puerto Rico until 1964.
1952	On July 25, Governor Luis Muñoz Marin led the inaugural ceremonies establishing the Commonwealth of Puerto Rico, or the Associated Free State.
1961	ASPIRA of America (now the ASPIRA Association, Inc.) was founded.
1965	With the passage of the Civil Rights Act of 1965, Puerto Ricans in the United States were no longer required to pass an English literacy test to vote in the state of New York.
1967	In a plebiscite, Puerto Ricans voted to maintain the Commonwealth status. Statehood and independence were the second and third choices, respectively.
1970	Herman Badillo was elected to the U.S. House of Representatives. He was the first mainland Puerto Rican elected to Congress.
1971	Cuban representatives to the United Nations proposed a resolution to have U.S. colonialism in Puerto Rico debated during a meeting of the United Nations Trusteeship Council.
1972	The United Nations Decolonization Committee declared that Puerto Rico is a colony of the United States.
1974	The legal case, *ASPIRA of New York, Inc. et al. v. Board of Education of the City of New York, Inc. et al.,* ended when the two parties reached an agreement, legally termed a "consent decree." The Board of Education agreed to provide bilingual instruction for Puerto Rican students.
1992	The New Progressive Party, which supports statehood, won the governorship.
1993	In a plebiscite, Puerto Ricans voted by a narrow margin to maintain the Commonwealth status. Statehood was a close second. Independence received only 4.4% of the vote.
2001	The controversy over U.S. Navy troops in Vieques Island, Puerto Rico, was a poignant reminder to Puerto Ricans on the Islands and the mainland of Puerto Rico's colonial and ambiguous status.

The Taino Indians

Puerto Ricans have three major racial heritages—Indian, African, and Spanish. The island was inhabited by a group of Indians called the Tainos when the Spanish arrived in the fifteenth century. Because they left no written records, little is known about the Tainos, except what archaeologists have been able to detect from potsherds and skulls (Rouse, 1992). Some social scientists believe that there were about 40,000 Tainos on the island when the Spanish arrived and that they had straight black hair and copper-colored skin (Babin, 1971). Their culture was based on farming, hunting, and raising animals. Religion was also an important part of the Taino culture. The Spaniards caught the Indians by surprise and totally without the kinds of weapons they needed to fight men who fought with swords (Wagenheim, 1975).

The Coming of the Spaniards

In search of a new route to India, Columbus arrived in the Americas in 1492. When he came back to the Americas in 1493, he landed on the island of Boriquen, home of the Taino Indians. Columbus's arrival on the island foreshadowed the Spanish takeover. When Juan Ponce de Leon was made governor of the island in 1508, the Spanish occupation of Puerto Rico was well underway. From the time of the arrival of the Spanish conquistadors, life for the native Indians became increasingly more difficult. Eventually, they were almost totally exterminated. The Spanish set up a kind of forced labor, known as the *encomienda* system. Under this system, each Spanish colonizer was given a group of Indians to work for him. The Spanish colonizer was supposed to "teach" the Indians Spanish "culture" in return for their work.

At first, the Indians did not fight back. They thought the Spaniards were immortal. Eventually, a group of Taino Indians decided to find out if the Spanish were actually immortal. They tried to drown a young Spaniard and succeeded. Once they discovered that the Spaniards died like other men, they started fighting back. A number of Indian rebellions occurred in various parts of the island and many Spaniards were killed in these skirmishes. The Tainos also ran away from the Spanish settlements. The conquistadors searched for them, often with little success. So many Indians were killed by the Spaniards and their diseases, and so many escaped from the island, that by 1777 they had all but disappeared from Puerto Rico.

Spanish Rule

By the late nineteenth century, Puerto Rico was one of the most neglected colonies in the Western Hemisphere. For nearly 400 years, Spain had ruled the colony from across the Atlantic like an absentee landlord and had woefully neglected it. Puerto Rico's last series of Spanish governors were incompetent and autocratic. They ineptly governed the island with an oppressive, heavy hand. When Spain and the United States entered the Spanish-American War in 1898, Spain's 400-year neglect of her small Caribbean colony was painfully visible. The masses of the people were peons, and the country's wealth was concentrated in the hands of the small upper class. No middle class existed, most of the people were illiterate, 92% of the children were not in school. Contagious diseases were widespread. Public health facilities were almost totally absent. Nearly 80% of the draftable Puerto Rican males failed the physical test given by the U.S. military during World War I.

Spain's neglect and mistreatment of Puerto Rico had led to an aggressive movement for home rule by the 1800s. In 1868, the famous Lares Revolt occurred. A group of independence advocates took the city of Lares and proclaimed it the "Republic of Puerto Rico." The revolt failed, but the agitation for home rule continued, even though it was often sporadic and poorly organized. Eventually the movement bore fruit. On November 28, 1897, Puerto Rico was granted autonomy by Spain. This proved to be one of the shortest and most meaningless political changes in history. Barely before the new Puerto Rican government could begin to function, U.S. troops landed on the island.

The Spanish-American War

Spain declared war on the United States on April 24, 1898. A truce was signed on August 12 of that same year. Spain was a pushover for the United States. The two nations formally ended the war with the Treaty of Paris, signed on December 10, 1898. At the meeting, the United States reigned supreme. Spain ceded the Philippines and Puerto Rico to the United States and gave up rights to Cuba. The United States also acquired American Guam.

As had been the case for 400 years, nobody asked Puerto Rico about its political future. Its fate was determined by the United States and Spain. After the meeting, Puerto Rico lost the little autonomy that Spain had granted it in 1897 and became a United States possession. Puerto Rican independence leaders were shocked and dismayed. They had thought that their neighbor from the North had come to free them from colonialism. It was a rude awakening to discover that the United States, the "citadel of freedom and democracy," would also subjugate Puerto Rico just as Spain had done.

United States Rule

When the U.S. government took control of Puerto Rico in 1898, it had little experience in governing colonies. In fact, "self-determination of nations" had been one of the main ideas voiced by the U.S. government. However, with the emergence of the doctrine of Manifest Destiny, the United States began to go after foreign lands rather aggressively. It acquired nearly one third of Mexico's territory in 1848 and increasingly saw how important Caribbean possessions would be to it, both financially and militarily. When the United States entered the Spanish-American War, it hoped to acquire a toehold in the Caribbean Sea. By defeating Spain and gaining Puerto Rico, the U.S. government was better able to make claims to supremacy in the Western Hemisphere and show the world that it was a powerful military force.

The U.S. relationship with Puerto Rico was awkward and ambiguous during the first two years of U.S. rule. Military governors from the United States ran the island. This type of government did not prove satisfactory. Congress attempted to establish a more workable relationship with Puerto Rico in 1900. That year it passed the Foraker Act. Under the terms of this act, Puerto Rico became "the People of Puerto Rico." Puerto Ricans were not U.S. citizens nor was the nation independent. The governor and the Executive Council (the Upper House) were to be appointed by the president of the United States. The House of Delegates (the Lower House) and the resident commissioner were to be chosen by popular election. The resident commissioner's job was to present the island's views on issues in the U.S. House of Representatives, although he would be unable to vote. Any action taken by the elected House of Delegates could be vetoed by the U.S. Congress. The Circuit Court of Boston was named the high court for the island. Puerto Rican leaders were shocked by this arrangement, which they interpreted as a slap in the face. They had hoped that, when the United States took over the island, its people would be able to decide their own political destiny with a plebiscite. The Foraker Act shattered their hopes.

The Struggle for Self-Governance

Cries for independence were heard throughout Puerto Rico during the sixteen years that the Foraker Act was in effect. Anti-U.S. feelings continued to grow and spread on the island. The island's factional parties shared the belief that Puerto Rico had been betrayed by the United States. As anti-American feelings escalated, the president and the Congress decided that action had to be taken. The then-resident commissioner in Washington, Muñoz Rivera, wanted to poll Puerto Rico's citizens to determine what they felt should be the political status of the island, but Muñoz's arguments were ignored. Instad, Congress decided to deal with the problem by making Puerto Ricans U.S. citizens with the Jones Act in 1917. This act only further alienated the Puerto Ricans who wanted self-governance on the island. The act not only "forced" citizenship on Puerto Ricans, but it also made them obligated to serve in the U.S. armed forces. Many Puerto Ricans resented the "forced" U.S. citizenship and the fact that they had no voice in the matter. They could resist U.S. citizenship, but resistance meant that they would lose many benefits and become aliens within their homeland. Because of the Jones Act, 140,000 Puerto Ricans fought in World War I.

The Nationalist Party

The Nationalist party, the radical party that strongly advocated the independence of Puerto Rico, emerged out of the forces that opposed how the United States was handling Puerto Rico's affairs. The party leaders felt, with some justification, that the major Puerto Rican parties were too sympathetic to U.S. interests and that party members could not deal with the United States effectively by using traditional means such as the ballot and appealing to the U.S. conscience. Pedro Albizu Campos emerged as the militant leader of the party. A graduate of Harvard, Albizu knew U.S. politics well. The party became a target of the Puerto Rican and U.S. governments, who considered it extreme and dangerous.

At a parade sponsored by the Nationalist party on Palm Sunday, March 21, 1937, a shot fired into a crowd resulted in a massacre in the streets of Ponce. When the Nationalists' initial request for a parade permit to march in San Juan was denied, they decided to move the parade to Ponce. The mayor of Ponce granted the parade request because the Nationalists agreed to keep the march peaceful. Despite a last-minute attempt by Governor Blanton Winship to prevent the parade, the Nationalists marched. The marchers did not carry arms, but the police were heavily armed. In the ruckus that occurred after the shot was fired, 20 people lost their lives and more than 100 were wounded. A inquiry by the Brookings Institution revealed that the police instigated the gunfire and were excessively brutal (Nieto, 1995). This infamous event in Puerto Rican history is known as the "Ponce Massacre." It symbolizes the independence struggle in Puerto Rico.

Luis Muñoz Marin: Governor of Puerto Rico, 1948–1964

Between 1900 and 1946, Puerto Rico was headed by a series of fifteen U.S. governors appointed by the president of the United States. With only a few exceptions, they were unimpressive men, and differed little from the Spaniards who had ruled Puerto Rico prior to 1898. Medical, educational, and economic conditions on the island reflected poor leadership. By 1940, conditions in Puerto Rico were not substantially different from conditions in 1898. Persistent expressions of dissatisfaction with the governors by Puerto Rican leaders led the United States to grant Puerto Rico the opportunity to elect its own governor in 1947. In 1948, Senator Luis Muñoz Marin was elected governor of Puerto Rico. He was the first elected governor in Puerto Rico's history.

The Commonwealth of Puerto Rico

Muñoz was destined to change decisively the course of Puerto Rican history. More changes occurred in Puerto Rico during his sixteen years as governor than had taken place during the previous four centuries of Spanish rule. Without question, Muñoz's influence on the island was unprecedented. Like any political leader who gets things done and shapes history, he was a charismatic and controversial figure.

Once in office, Muñoz took a position on the polemical status question. He favored what later became known as the Commonwealth or the *Estado Libre Asociado* (Free Associated State). With this status, Puerto Rico would maintain a tie with the United States, but would have a degree of governmental autonomy. Muñoz fought hard to make the Commonwealth a reality. The people approved it in a plebiscite on June 4, 1951. Muñoz led an inauguration ceremony for the Commonwealth of Puerto Rico on July 25, 1952.

The Commonwealth did not solve the status question, and the controversy continued. Both statehood and independence advocates opposed the new status. Many people refused to go to the polls, claiming that the plebiscite was a hoax because the voters were presented with only two choices. They had to vote either to maintain the status quo or to initiate the proposed Commonwealth. Thus, the meaning of the plebiscite was bitterly debated. To this day, the status question is still one of the hottest political issues on the island and it tends to dominate and overshadow other issues (Trías Monge, 1997).

Urbanization and Operation Bootstrap

Muñoz also set Puerto Rico on a new economic course. He felt that income from the island's three main cash crops—sugar, tobacco, and coffee—was inadequate to support Puerto Rico. Muñoz wanted to industrialize the island by luring U.S. manufacturers to set up plants in Puerto Rico. He formed "Operation Bootstrap" to attract U.S. industry to Puerto Rico. He offered generous benefits, such as lower wages and tax exemptions for up to ten years. Many U.S. companies established plants in Puerto Rico under this program. Like most changes that Muñoz implemented, the program was both successful and controversial. The changes that Operation Bootstrap stimulated in Puerto Rico were truly amazing. By 1971, the program had recruited 2,000 plants and millions of dollars in investments. Income from manufacturing was more than three times that from agriculture, although agriculture was still important in the island's economy. The island's per capita income jumped from $188 a year in 1940 to $1,234 a year in 1969.

The Operation Bootstrap reforms and modernization of Puerto Rico that occurred during the 1940s, 1950s, and 1960s were mixed blessings. Urbanization brought the usual problems in housing and created a new poverty class: the urban poor. Although Operation Bootstrap was designed to help solve the problem of unemployment, it actually increased it. Industrialization displaced small farmers, who migrated to the cities and became unemployed. Many Puerto Ricans left the island and migrated to the U.S. mainland to look for work. Migration from the island to the United States peaked during the 1950s, at a time when Operation Bootstrap was booming.

The Puerto Rican economy remains precarious. The island has a high level of unemployment. Even when Operation Bootstrap was booming, the large numbers of Puerto Ricans who migrated to the United States each year helped maintain a healthy economy on the island. Urbanization has pulled many families to the cities looking for work and has created city slums, housing congestion, and other problems associated with urban growth. The percentage of persons living below the poverty level in Puerto Rico is considerably above the percentage for Puerto Ricans on the U.S. mainland. In 1997, the U.S. Census Bureau estimated that 20% of children on the U.S. mainland and 60% of children age 5 to 17 in the Commonwealth of Puerto Rico were living in poverty (U.S. Census Bureau, 2000).On the U.S. mainland in 2000, the poverty rate for non-Hispanic Whites was 7.7%, 23.6% for African Americans, and 22.8% for Hispanics.

Although urbanization created a middle class in Puerto Rico and bedroom suburban communities, Muñoz's critics correctly note that Operation Bootstrap brought the greatest benefits to the upper class and to U.S. industrialists. U.S. companies take the bulk of the money they earn on the island back to the United States. Many of them are now deserting Puerto Rico for nations in Asia where they can find cheaper labor. Urbanization in Puerto Rico, like so many other developments, has done little to change the living conditions of the poor, except perhaps to show them how to live poor "urban" rather than poor "rural" style. Despite the mixed blessings of the Muñoz reforms, his sixteen-year reign made a tremendous difference in Puerto Rico's present and future.

Controversy on Vieques Island

The U.S. Navy conducted land, sea, and air exercises on Vieques Island in Puerto Rico in the late 1990s and in 2001. When a security guard was accidently killed in one of the Navy's exercises in 1999, many residents on the island became angry and were reminded of what they interpret as Puerto Rico's colonial relationship with the United States. In a local and non-legally binding referendum on the Island on July 29, 2001, 68% of the residents of Vieques Island favored an immediate end to the exercises on the small island. Civil rights advocates on both the Island and the Mainland, many members of the Hispanic Congressional Caucus, as well as Governor Calderon of Puerto Rico, publicly opposed the exercises and said they should be ended.

Responding to the protests against the exercises and pressure, President Bush agreed to withdraw the Navy from Vieques Island in May, 2003. However, the September 11, 2001 tragedies that occurred at the World Trade Center in New York City and at the Pentagon in Washington, D.C., were used by some supporters of the exercises to bolster their argument. Wrote Grayson (2001) on the editorial page of the *Wall Street Journal*: "With America at war, the future of Vieques must be considered. Congress should act immediately to spike the Nov. 6 referendum and quash plans to boot the Navy in 2003" (p. A15). The controversy on Vieques Island, no matter how it is settled, opened deep wounds about the status of Puerto Rico with the United States.

Life on the Mainland

The Migration

After the United States gained control of Puerto Rico, the stage was set for the mass movement of islanders to the U.S. mainland. A few Puerto Ricans, such as cigar makers and merchant seamen, had settled in New York before the 1920s; but Puerto Ricans did not begin to migrate to the United States in significant numbers until the 1920s and 1930s. When Mills, Senior, and Goldsen (1967) published their pioneering study in 1950, most Puerto Ricans in New York City had come during the years between the two great world wars. The number of Puerto Ricans migrating to the United States decreased considerably during World War II because of the closing of transportation routes between New York and Puerto Rico.

After the war, the number of Puerto Ricans migrating to the United States increased. In 1945, only 22,737 Puerto Ricans came to the United States, but that number increased to 101,115 in 1947. Puerto Rican migration to the United States has always reflected economic trends. A significant number of migrants usually return to the island when the mainland economy is depressed. During the Great Depression of the 1930s, the net migration back to the island reached 8,694 people in a four-year period (Mills, Senior, & Goldsen, 1967). *Net migration* is the difference between the number of Puerto Ricans who enter the United States and the number who leave within a specific time period. It can be a positive (+) or a negative (−) figure. When the U.S. economy is booming, Puerto Rican migration usually increases and return migration decreases considerably.

Rodriguez (1991) describes three major periods of Puerto Rican migration to and from the U.S. mainland. The first significant number of migrants arrived between 1900 and 1945. Most of these migrants settled in New York City. The second period of migration took place between 1946 and 1964. During this period, the largest number of migrants from Puerto Rico settled in the U.S. mainland. Rodriguez (1991) calls the third period of Puerto Rican migration, from 1965 to the present, "the revolving-door migration." During this period, migration to the mainland has varied with economic developments on the island and the mainland. Migrants have also dispersed to other regions in the United States, such as New Jersey, Illinois, and California.

The lack of legal barriers is a major factor in Puerto Rican migration to and from the U.S. mainland. The Jones Act of 1917 made Puerto Ricans U.S. citizens. As U.S. citizens, they can move freely from the island to the mainland and within various parts of the United States. Their migration to the United States is not limited by restrictive quotas, as is the case in Mexico and in the various Asian nations. Many Puerto Ricans take advantage of their freedom of movement and migrate to the United States. Although the movement of Puerto Ricans to the mainland has many of the sociological characteristics of an immigration, Puerto Ricans are technically migrants rather than immigrants because they are citizens of the United States.

Easy and inexpensive transportation to the mainland also facilitates Puerto Rican migration. In the 1930s, Puerto Ricans could make a boat trip from San Juan to New York City in the relatively short period of three and a half days, and for as low as $40 (Chenault, 1938). After World War II, plane transportation from the island became more available and inexpensive. During this period, a migrant could fly from San Juan to New York City for as low as $35 (Mills, Senior, & Goldsen, 1967). Today, transportation from the island is more convenient and still inexpensive. Whereas the flight from San Juan to New York City took eight bumpy hours in the 1940s, the trip could be made as quickly as three hours and for as low as $365 in 2001. Convenient and inexpensive transportation has not only stimulated migration from the island to the mainland but has also helped make Puerto Ricans transients between the island and the United States. Many Puerto Ricans in New York return to the island to visit relatives, to vacation, or to take care of business for short periods.

The "Americanization" of Puerto Rico since 1898 and economic factors have played major roles in motivating Puerto Ricans to migrate to the United States. Since Puerto Rico became an American colony, U.S. culture and institutions have greatly influenced Puerto Rican culture and lifestyles. Americans forced the teaching of English in Puerto Rican schools for years and introduced textbooks that venerated George Washington and Abraham Lincoln rather than Puerto Rican leaders (Negron de Montilla, 1975). These books also described the United States as the neighbor to the North in which "democracy and freedom" flourished. American stores such as J.C. Penney and Sears dot the streets in San Juan as they do in Chicago.

During the period of high migration to the U.S. mainland in the 1950s, many Puerto Ricans who returned to the island told their relatives and friends about the "great" new life in New York City. The availability of jobs in New York City during periods of intensive migration and the higher pay Puerto Ricans could earn in New York, compared to San Juan, lured many Puerto Ricans from the island to the mainland.

Since the great period of migration to the U.S. mainland from Puerto Rico between 1946 and 1964, migration to and from the U.S. mainland has followed economic trends. When economic times are good on the mainland, the number of migrants from Puerto Rico increases. However, migrants tend to return to the island during economic hard times on the mainland. In 1953, migration from Puerto Rico to the mainland peaked at 74,000. Since the mid-1960s, migration from Puerto Rico to the mainland has been fluctuating. A deep drop occurred around 1976 (see Figure 11.1).

The population increase in the Puerto Rican mainland community today results primarily from new births rather than from migration, although migration still occurs. However, much of it consists of unemployed individuals who circulate from the island to the mainland and back again. These migrants often cannot find jobs on the island or the mainland.

Although the migration of Puerto Ricans from the island to the mainland is similar in many ways to other movements of peoples to the United States, it is unique in several ways. As Fitzpatrick notes, it was the first "airborne migration" in U.S. history (Fitzpatrick, 1987, p. 20). Puerto Ricans, unlike many of the earlier immigrants, are also U.S. citizens when they arrive in the United States. Puerto Ricans bring attitudes toward race that are different from and more complex than those in the United States. They also started migrating to the United States at a time when automation had eliminated most of the jobs requiring unskilled laborers. Most of these factors, along with the racism and discrimination they experience in the United States, have increased rather than mitigated their problems in the United States.

The Family

The family, which is important in traditional Puerto Rican culture, is experiencing tremendous changes on the island. Cultures are not static in modernized societies; they are dynamic and changing. As Puerto Rico becomes increasingly urbanized, many of its traditional rural values—including those related to the family—are changing. While the Puerto Rican family and its values are changing on the island, the family faces even more conflicts and problems when it moves to the U.S. mainland. It becomes part of a U.S. mainstream culture that is often unaware of and unsympathetic to traditional Puerto Rican values related to family and community. The racism and discrimination that the Puerto Rican family experiences in the United States also create adjustment problems.

The serious economic problems that faced the Puerto Rican community by the mid-1990s affected the family. In 1993, about 32.5% of Puerto Rican families were living below the official government poverty level (U.S. Bureau of the Census, 1994). This percentage was greater than that of all other Hispanics and also greater than that of African Americans and Whites. A deep sense of family remains within the Puerto Rican community despite the economic problems it faces.

A number of values are still strongly held within Puerto Rican families, including respect for the elderly and for parents, and extremely strong bonds within the family, particularly with the mother (Sanchez-Ayendez, 1988). The family, rather than the individual, tends to be the primary focus of identifica tion. The extended family is important, and all family members tend to feel obligated to care for and be responsible for one another. The protection of children, especially girls, is very important to the family. This protection is often viewed as overprotection by people outside the culture. These traditional values of Puerto Rican families are being challenged by modernization, by urbanization, and by the levels of assimilation occurring among the current generation of Puerto Ricans in the United States. However, they still have a great deal of tenacity in the Puerto Rican community.

Despite the problems that they face in the United States, many Puerto Rican migrants remain in the United States. A few return to the island for many different reasons, including the lack of a job, alienation, discrimination, and longing for their homeland, family, and friends. Most Puerto Ricans who remain in the United States retain important aspects of their culture but re-create and change their culture in ways that reflect their participation within U.S. society. How Puerto Ricans use language illustrates this process of cultural adaptation and change. While learning English, most Puerto Ricans also continue to speak Spanish. In 1990, about 41.4% of Puerto Ricans reported that they "speak Spanish, do not speak English very well"; 58.6% reported that they "speak Spanish, speak English very well" (U.S. Bureau of the Census, 1993, p. 7).

The Issue of Race and Racism among Puerto Ricans

Although racism exists in both Puerto Rico and the U.S. mainland, race is highly complex in Puerto Rico, and *social race* has different meanings in the two cultures. Scholars such as Zenon Cruz (1975) and Betances (1972) believe that social scientists have exaggerated the differences between racism in the United States and in Puerto Rico. These two researchers believe that most social scientists have underestimated the extent to which Blacks are victimized by racism in Puerto Rico. They believe that racism is an important part of Puerto Rican society. Although Zenon and Betances provide a needed perspective on race relations in Puerto Rico, social-class status in Puerto Rico interacts with race in complex ways. Upper-class Whites tend to exclude both poor Whites and poor Blacks from their social gatherings. However, poor Whites and poor Blacks tend to mix more freely in Puerto Rico than in the United States. Even though Whites tend to marry other Whites in Puerto Rico, racial intermarriage occurs more often in Puerto Rico than in the United States.

The primary identity for most Puerto Ricans is culture rather than race, whereas race has primacy in the United States. Most Puerto Ricans tend to think of themselves first as Puerto Rican and secondarily as *blanco, negro, trigueño,* or *indio.* Writes Rodriguez (1991): "Perhaps the primary point of contrast was that, in Puerto Rico, racial identification was subordinate to cultural identification, while in the United States, racial identification, to a large extent, determined cultural identification" (p. 52).

Puerto Ricans on the U.S. mainland are forced to fit into one of two racial categories: Black or White, categories that are often less meaningful in the Puerto Rican community. Puerto Ricans, both on the island and on the mainland, recognize and use a number of different racial categories, such as *blanco* (Whites), *prieto* (dark-skinned), *negro* (Blacks), and *trigueño* (tan) (Wagenheim, 1975). Other words they use to make color distinctions among themselves are *indio, grifo,* and *de color* (Padilla, 1958). When determining an individual's color, Puerto Ricans consider hair color and texture as well as skin color. Also, an individual's color classification is determined primarily by his or her physical traits rather than by the color of parents or relatives. Within one family there can be individuals who are considered *blanco, negro,* and *trigueño.* Also, the social status of individuals can be important factors in their racial classifications. In general, the higher an individual's social status, the less likely he or she will be considered *negro.*

The different ways in which color is recognized and treated on the mainland cause problems for the Puerto Rican migrant, especially for those who are intermediate in skin color. In their community, they are neither Black nor White; but they are often considered Black by outsiders. This causes the intermediate individual to feel alienated from both the White and Black communities in the United States. A study by Mills, Senior, and Goldsen (1967) indicated that Puerto Rican migrants who were intermediate in color experienced more adjustment problems in the United States than did individuals who were clearly identified as either Black or White.

The Puerto Rican Mainland Community

When they first started migrating to the United States, most Puerto Ricans settled in New York City. However, the percentage of Puerto Rican migrants settling in New York City has steadily decreased in recent decades; while the percentage settling in other mainland cities and states has increased. In 1940, 88% of the Puerto Rican population in the United States lived in New York City. By 1960, that number had declined to 69%. In 1990, 52% of Puerto Ricans lived outside New York state.

While 60% of Puerto Ricans in the United States lived in the states of New York, New Jersey, Pennsylvania, Massachusetts, and Connecticut in 2000, many lived in other parts of the nation. A considerable number of Puerto Ricans (27%) lived in Florida, Illinois, California, Texas, and Ohio. In 2000, most Puerto Ricans (86.7%) were concentrated in these ten states: New York, Florida, New Jersey, Pennsylvania, Massachusetts, Connecticut, Illinois, California, Texas, and Ohio. Pockets of them also lived in many other states, including Georgia (35, 532), Wisconsin (30,267), and Washington state (16,140) (see Table 11.1).

Pockets of Puerto Ricans in U.S. cities constitute ethnic neighborhoods. The Puerto Rican community is usually a poor community, with the characteristics of people who are poor. In 1994, Puerto Ricans had the lowest median family income of the major Hispanic groups and the largest percentage of persons below the poverty level (U.S. Bureau of the Census, 1994). The median family income was $20,301 for Puerto Ricans, compared to $23,714 for Mexicans, and $31,015 for Cuban Americans. In 1993, about 35.5% of Puerto Ricans lived below the poverty level, compared to 29.3% of Mexican Americans, 18.1% of Cubans, 33.2% of African Americans, and 11.6% of Whites.

TABLE 11.1   Puerto Rican Population in Selected States (2000)

State	Population	Percentage of Total State Population
New York	1,050,293	5.5
Florida	482,027	3.0
New Jersey	366,788	4.4
Pennsylvania	228,557	1.9
Massachusetts	199,207	3.1
Connecticut	194,443	5.7
Illinois	157,851	1.3
California	140,570	0.4
Texas	69,504	0.3
Ohio	66,269	0.6
Virginia	41,131	0.6
Georgia	35,532	0.4
North Carolina	31,117	0.4
Wisconsin	30,267	0.6
Hawaii	30,005	2.5
Michigan	26,941	0.3
Maryland	25,570	0.5
Rhode Island	25,422	2.4
Indiana	19,678	0.3
Arizona	17,587	0.3
Washington	16,140	0.3
Delaware	14,005	1.8
Colorado	12,993	0.3
South Carolina	12,211	0.3
Nevada	10,420	0.5

Source: U.S. Census Bureau (2001). *The Hispanic Population: Census 2000 Brief.* [On-line]. Available at Web site: http://www.census.gov/

The sound of Spanish, *bodegas,* travel agencies, and Pentecostal storefront churches are familiar sounds and sights in most Puerto Rican mainland neighborhoods. Although Puerto Rican mainland culture is decidedly different from Puerto Rican island culture, certain parts of the old culture are retained on the mainland. Hispanos, as many Puerto Ricans call themselves, usually speak Spanish at home and English when talking with outsiders. To obtain the foods to prepare favorite ethnic dishes, such as rice and beans, fried plaintains, or dried codfish, the family may shop at the *bodega,* the little corner grocery store usually run by Puerto Ricans. Increasingly, however, supermarkets are carrying Puerto Rican foods and other goods. Herbs and plants needed to cure illnesses or to fight the "evil" can be bought at the *botanicas.* Tickets for an air trip back home can be bought at the local travel agency, perhaps on easy terms. The Pentecostal Church, a fast-growing institution in the Puerto Rican mainland community, serves the spiritual needs of the migrants. The Puerto Rican community, with its *bodegas, botanicas,* and Pentecostal churches, helps to ease the cultural shock for the migrants and helps them to develop roots in their new land.

The Future

On most major indices, such as occupational status, education, and income, Puerto Ricans fall far behind the general U.S. population and most other Hispanic groups. Yet, the future of the Puerto Rican community can be shaped by educational, political, and social action. Puerto Ricans in the United States are a young and growing population: they had the second youngest median age, 27.3, of U.S. Hispanic groups in 2000 (U.S. Census Bureau, 2001). Mexican Americans were the youngest group, with a median age of 24.2. There are signs that the Puerto Rican community is becoming more politically and legally active than it has been in the past. At the beginning of the new century, the New York Puerto Rican community was playing an increasingly important role in local, state, and national elections.

A number of Puerto Rican educational and civic organizations are working to strengthen the Puerto Rican community. One of the most important is The ASPIRA Association, an organization founded in 1961 to promote educational achievement and leadership development among youths. Today, it is an important, active, and effective organization within the Puerto Rican community (ASPIRA Association, Inc., n.d.). Other important Puerto Rican organizations include the National Puerto Rican Coalition, which coordinates a group of organizations and works to improve the social and economic conditions of Puerto Ricans in the United States; and the Puerto Rican Legal Defense and Educational Fund, which litigates for Hispanics who live in the Northeast. The National Congress for Puerto Rican Rights (NCPRR) works to obtain "civil and human rights for Puerto Ricans."

The future of Puerto Ricans in the United States will be heavily influenced by political, economic, and social developments on the island. These two communities are integrally bound. Many Puerto Ricans see Puerto Ricans on the island and those on the mainland as one divided nation. Consequently, the status question that haunts the island cogently influences the ideologies, debates, and visions of mainland Puerto Ricans.

Teaching Strategies

To illustrate how content related to the Puerto Rican experience can be incorporated into a conceptual curriculum, I have identified three key concepts related to the Puerto Rican experience and sample strategies for teaching them. Strategies are presented for teaching *cultural conflict, racial categories,* and *colonialism* in the primary, intermediate and upper, and high school grades, respectively.

Primary Grades

CONCEPT

Cultural Conflict
Generalization: The Puerto Rican migrant family in the United States experiences many conflicts and problems because it encounters new norms, values, and roles on the mainland that conflict with those in Puerto Rico.

1. Read the following case study to the students and ask the questions that follow. During the discussion of the story, help the children to state the generalization in their own words.

The Ramos Family

Mr. and Mrs. Ramos and their two children, Maria, age three, and Carlos, age seven, live in New York City in an area called El Barrio. The Ramos family moved to New York two years ago from San Juan, Puerto Rico. When the family lived in San Juan, Mr. Ramos worked in a factory. Mrs. Ramos stayed at home and took care of the children and house.

Both Mr. and Mrs. Ramos were happy living in San Juan until some of their relatives moved from San Juan to New York City. First, Mrs. Ramos's two sisters, whom she liked very much, moved to New York. Later, Mr. Ramos's brother moved to New York. They missed their relatives very much. They wanted to be able to see them more often. Mr. and Mrs. Ramos decided to go to New York to pay their relatives a visit.

When Mr. and Mrs. Ramos arrived in New York to visit, their relatives were very glad to see them. Mrs. Ramos kissed her two sisters. She told them about all the news back home. Her sisters told her about New York City. They liked it very much. Mrs. Ramos became very excited about New York City as she listened to her sisters talk about it. Mr. Ramos and his brother were also glad to see each other. Mr. Ramos told his brother how the family was doing in San Juan. Mr. Ramos's brother told him about how good things were in New York. He told Mr. Ramos that he could make twice as much money in New York as he made in San Juan! Mr. and Mrs. Ramos enjoyed New York City for two weeks. When they left, they had decided that they would move to New York City as soon as they got back home.

When the Ramos family got to New York again, things were not as nice as they thought they would be. The family was not as happy as it had been in San Juan. They had to live with Mr. Ramos's brother for two months because they could not find a nice apartment right away. When they did find one, it cost much more than they had paid for rent in San Juan. Mr. Ramos looked a long time before he could find a job. To help the family pay its bills, Mrs. Ramos got a job in a garment factory. Mrs. Ramos was the only person in the family working. She began to make more and more decisions for everyone in the family.

Mr. Ramos spent most of each day looking for a job. He spoke good Spanish but many companies would not hire him because he spoke little English. Since Mrs. Ramos was working and Mr. Ramos was job hunting, Carlos and Maria had to spend a lot of time without either parent. Sometimes they would get into trouble with the neighborhood children.

Carlos became sad when he started to school. He was a top student in Puerto Rico. However, he did poorly in school in New York. He could not read English well. He fell further and further behind in school each week. The teacher called him "Charlie" instead of "Carlos." The children teased him because he spoke "funny." Carlos tried hard to speak English, even at home. His parents wanted him to speak Spanish at home so that they could understand him.

After looking for three months, Mr. Ramos found a job in a hotel. The family then moved into their own apartment. Things got better then. Mr. Ramos wanted Mrs. Ramos to quit her job and stay at home with the children. Mrs. Ramos wanted to keep working because she felt that it took more money to live in New York than in San Juan. Sometimes the family wished that they had stayed in San Juan.

The Ramos family has now been in New York City for two years. They are much happier now, but they still miss their friends and relatives in San Juan. Mr. Ramos understands why Mrs. Ramos wants to work. Carlos is speaking better English and getting better grades in school. The family is planning to visit Puerto Rico during the Christmas season. Carlos is counting the days until Christmas!

Questions
1. Why did the Ramos family move from San Juan to New York City?
2. Was New York City like the family expected it to be? Why or why not?
3. What problems did each of the family members have in New York City that he or she did not have in San Juan?
4. Which family member faced the greatest problems in New York? Why?

5. Which family member faced the fewest problems in New York? Why?
6. What problems do you think the family faced in New York City that are not brought out in the story? Why?
7. How do you think the family will feel about New York a year from now? Do you think that the family will move back to Puerto Rico? Why or why not?

Intermediate and Upper Grades

CONCEPT

Racial Categories
Generalization: Racial categories differ in Puerto Rico and on the U.S. mainland. These differing racial categories make the experience of Puerto Rican migrants to the mainland more difficult.

1. Find old copies of magazines such as *Ebony, Hispanic, Essence, Black Enterprise,* and *Life.* Locate pictures of people who look (a) obviously European American, (b) obviously African American, and (c) like fair-skinned African Americans. Mount these pictures on cardboard.
2. Show the students three of the pictures, one that will fit into each of the categories described above. Ask the students to name the "race" of the person in each picture. They will most likely say that one of the pictured persons is "White," and that the other two are "Black" or "African American." Ask: "Why do we use only two categories to classify the people in these pictures?" With the use of careful questions, explain that in the United States any person, regardless of his or her physical appearance, is considered "Black" or "African American" if he or she has any *known* African ancestry.
3. Show the class mounted pictures of (a) a fair-skinned African American male adult, (b) a fair-skinned African American female adult, (c) a dark-skinned African American male child, (d) a female child who looks Caucasian.
4. Ask the students to name the "race" of each of the pictured persons. After discussing their responses, tell the class that the pictures represent a Puerto Rican family that recently moved from San Juan to New York City. In the pictures are mom, dad, brother, and sister. Point out that, even though we may call the parents and the son "Black," Puerto Ricans have words to describe each color. Introduce these words. They would call the parents *trigueño,* the son *Negro* or *de color,* and the daughter *blanca.* Tell the students that in Puerto Rico "color" has a special meaning that is different from its meaning in the United States. Ask the students what race the different family members would belong to in the United States and why. Through questioning, bring out that all of them would be considered "Black" or "African American" and why.
5. Ask: "Now that the family is in New York City, what kinds of racial problems might they encounter?" "Why?" Through questioning, reveal that mother and father will be considered "Black" on the mainland even though they were intermediates (*trigueños*) in Puerto Rico. Discuss with the class the kinds of

identity and social problems that the couple will face on the mainland and how they might cope with them. Ask the class the following questions:

a. How do you think mother and father will feel when mainland Whites call them "Black" or "African American"?

b. How do you think they will feel when African Americans call them "Black"? Do you think they will identify with the Black struggle for civil rights? Why or why not?

c. Do you think they will want to be called "White" or "Black"? Why? What problems might they encounter when seeking to obtain their preferred racial identification? Why? How might they go about solving them?

6. With these and other questions, bring out the generalization that Puerto Rican migrants to the mainland who are intermediate in color have serious racial and adjustment problems because they are neither White nor Black in Puerto Rico but are forced to be "Black" on the mainland. Ask the class these valuing questions: Do you think that it is right to consider intermediates on the mainland "Blacks"? Why or why not? Do you think they should be considered "White"? Why or why not? If you were an intermediate Puerto Rican on the mainland, would you want to be considered "White" or "Black"? Why? When asking such valuing questions, accept all responses and maintain an open classroom atmosphere. Ask the class these questions:

a. What special identity and racial problems might the son have in his family? In school? In the community? Why? How might he deal with them?

b. What special racial and identity problems might the daughter have in the family? In school? In the community? Why? How might she deal with them?

Read the following case study to the class and ask the questions that follow.

Mr. Diaz and Mr. Seda on the Mainland

Mr. Diaz looks Caucasian. In Puerto Rico he and Mr. Seda, who is *de color,* were close friends. They both now live in New York City. When they first came to New York City, they would visit each other often, as they had done in Puerto Rico. Eventually Mr. Diaz started visiting Mr. Seda less and less and would often act unfriendly when Mr. Seda came to visit him, especially when his White friends were over. Mr. Diaz's White friends would always give Mr. Seda strange looks when he came over. Mr. Diaz began to understand that in New York City he was expected to mix socially with Whites only. Now, Mr. Diaz never visits Mr. Seda, and Mr. Seda goes to Mr. Diaz's house very seldom. When he does, he stays only a short time. The last time that Mr. Seda visited Mr. Diaz's home, Mr. Diaz left in the middle of the visit with a White American friend. He told Mr. Seda that he and his White American friend had to go out and take care of some important business.

Questions
1. What is the main problem in this case study?
2. What kind of relationship did Mr. Diaz and Mr. Seda have in Puerto Rico?

3. Why did their relationship change when they moved to the mainland?
4. If you were Mr. Diaz, would you act as he acted when he moved to the mainland? Why or why not?
5. If you were Mr. Seda, would you act as he acted when he moved to New York City? Why or why not?

VALUING ACTIVITY

Ask the students independently to complete these open-ended sentences. After they have completed them, discuss their responses and summarize the lesson by highlighting the generalization about the racial problems Puerto Rican migrants experience on the U.S. mainland.

1. Mr. Diaz should _____

2. Mr. Seda should _____

3. Mr. Diaz values _____ more than _____

4. Mr. Diaz values _____ more than _____

5. If I were Mr. Diaz, I would _____

6. If I were Mr. Seda, I would _____

High School Grades

CONCEPT

Colonialism
Generalizations: Since the late fifteenth century, Puerto Rico has been controlled by foreign powers. This has caused rebellions, political ambiguity, and instability on the island.

1. Give the students a copy of the questions below and ask them to read a selection about the Taino Indians prior to 1493. One source is Irving Rouse (1992), *The Tainos: Rise and Decline of the People Who Greeted Columbus.* Tell them to be able to respond to these questions when they have finished their reading. After the students have completed the reading assignment, discuss the questions.
   a. How did the Tainos obtain food?
   b. What kind of political system did they have?
   c. What kind of religion did they have?
   d. What was a typical day like for (1) a Taino adult female, (2) a Taino adult male, (3) Taino children?
   e. What kinds of relationships did the Tainos have with other American Indian groups?
   f. What kinds of weapons did the Tainos use when they were at war with other Indian tribes?

2. Divide the class into research groups and ask them to prepare and give short reports on each of the following topics. They should be encouraged to present their reports to the class in the form of debates, simulations, and role-play situations, using visual aids such as charts and graphs.
   a. Columbus's trip to North America and his relationship with the native populations
   b. The establishment of Spanish domination in Puerto Rico in the 1500s
   c. The *encomienda* system of forced labor that the Spanish established in Puerto Rico during the early years of domination
   d. Ways in which the Tainos resisted Spanish colonization by rebelling and running away
   e. Spanish domination in Puerto Rico in the 1600s, 1700s, and 1800s
   f. *Grito de Lares* of 1868
   g. The political, economic, and social status of Puerto Rico in 1898
   h. The Spanish-American War (causes and effects)
   i. The American takeover of Puerto Rico in 1898
   j. The Treaty of Paris, 1898

   After the students have a basic understanding of Puerto Rican history up to 1898, they can then become involved in activities like those below to gain a better understanding of the island's political and economic status today.

3. Ask the students to pretend that they are members of the U.S. Congress in 1898. Spain has just ceded Puerto Rico to the United States. Their job is to decide on specific political and economic policies for their new territory. They must develop a plan for governing the island and have it approved by majority vote. After this exercise is completed, ask the students to compare their plan with the plan the United States used to govern Puerto Rico during the first two years of U.S. rule and with the plan delineated in the Foraker Act of 1900. Ask the students to discuss the similarities and differences in the three plans and possible reasons for them.

4. Ask the students to research the positions advocated by the following political parties regarding the political status of Puerto Rico:
   a. The Independence party (Independence)
   b. The New Progressive party (Statehood)
   c. The Popular party (Commonwealth)

   After this research, ask three students to role-play an advocate of each status position. The advocate of each position should argue his or her position in front of the class. The three speakers will debate the status question and answer questions posed by the class. After the debate and discussion, each class member will vote for one of the three following positions: (1) the Commonwealth, (2) statehood, or (3) independence. After the voting, conduct a class discussion in which the class will compare their choice with the choice made by the citizens of Puerto Rico in a plebiscite held in 1993. (See the chronology at the beginning of this chapter.) The students should discuss the reasons for the similarities and differences in their choice and the choice made by Puerto Rican citizens.

5. Ask a group of students to role-play a discussion between the individuals named below about what should be the future of Puerto Rico. Conduct a class discussion about the role-play situation when it ends.
   a. Pedro Albizu Campos
   b. Luis Muñoz Marin
   c. Luis A. Ferré
   d. Rafael Hernandez Colon
   e. A U.S. businessperson who is president of a company that owns several factories in Puerto Rico
   f. A southern U.S. senator
   g. A U.S. congressional representative from the Midwest
6. Since the Spanish colonized Puerto Rico in the sixteenth century, there have been uprisings and rebellions against oppression on the island. Ask the students to prepare a short research paper on forms of resistance to oppression in Puerto Rico since the sixteenth century. Make sure that they note resistance as exemplified by (a) the Taino Indians, (b) the Lares Rebellion of 1868, (c) the Nationalist party, (d) the university student uprisings in Puerto Rico in the 1960s, (e) the protests over the Navy exercises and the death of a security guard on Vieques Island in Puerto Rico that occurred in 1999 and continued into 2001.
7. After the students have completed and discussed their papers, ask them to write and present a dramatization about "The Struggle for Home Rule in Puerto Rico." They can invite another class or their parents and friends to attend the presentation.

REFERENCES

The ASPIRA Association, Inc. (n.d.). *The ASPIRA Story, 1961–1991.* Washington, DC: Author.

Babin, M. T. (1971). *The Puerto Ricans' Spirit.* (B. Luby, Trans.). New York: Collier Books.

Betances, S. (1972, Winter;1973, Spring). The Prejudice of Having No Prejudice in Puerto Rico. Part 1, *The Rican,* 41–52; Part II, *The Rican,* 22–37.

Chenault, L. R. (1938). *The Puerto Rican Migrant in New York City.* New York: Columbia University Press.

Fitzpatrick, J. P. (1987). *Puerto Rican Americans: The Meaning of Migration to the Mainland* (2nd ed.). Englewood Cliffs, NJ: Prentice-Hall.

Grayson, G. W. (2001, October 12). A Call to Patriotism: Keep Vieques Open. *Wall Street Journal,* p. A15.

Mills, C. W., Senior, C., & Goldsen, R. K. (1967). *The Puerto Rican Journey: New York's Newest Migrants.* New York: Russel and Russel.

Negron de Montilla, A. (1975). *Americanization in Puerto Rico and the Public School System 1901–1920.* Rio Piedras: University of Puerto Rico Press.

Nieto, S. (1995). Unpublished review of J. A. Banks, *Teaching Strategies for Ethnic Studies* (5th ed.). Boston: Allyn and Bacon, 1991.

Padilla, E. (1958). *Up from Puerto Rico.* New York: Columbia University Press.

Population Reference Bureau. (2001, May). *2001 World Population Data Sheet of the Population Reference Bureau* (Book Ed.). Washington, DC: Author.

Rodriguez, C. E. (1991). *Puerto Ricans Born in the U.S.A.* Boulder, CO: Westview.

Rouse, I. (1992). *The Tainos: Rise and Decline of the People Who Greeted Columbus.* New Haven: Yale University Press.

Sanchez-Ayendez, M. (1988). The Puerto Rican American Family. In C. H. Mindel, R. W. Haberstein, & R. Wright, Jr. (Eds.), *Ethnic Families in America: Patterns and Variations* (3rd ed.; pp.173–195). New York: Elsevier.

Trías Monge, J. (1997). *Puerto Rico: The Trials of the Oldest Colony in the World.* New Haven: Yale University Press.

U.S. Bureau of the Census. (1990). *Current Population Reports, Population Characteristics, P23–183.* Washington, DC: U.S. Government Printing Office.

U.S. Bureau of the Census. (1993). *We, the American Hispanics.* Washington, DC: U.S. Government Printing Office.

U.S. Bureau of the Census. (1994). *Statistical Abstract of the United States: 1994* (114th ed.). Washington, DC: U.S. Government Printing Office.

U.S. Census Bureau (2000). *Poverty Rate Lowest in 20 Years, Household Income at Record High, Census Bureau Report.* [On-line] Available: *http://www.census.gov/Press-Release/www/2000/cb00–158.html*

U.S. Census Bureau (2001). *The Hispanic Population: Census 2000 Brief.* [On-line]. Available: *http://www.census.gov/*

Wagenheim, K. (1975). *Puerto Rico: A Profile* (2nd ed.). New York: Praeger.

Zenon Cruz, I. (1975). *Narcisco Descubre Su Trasero.* Homacao, PR: Editorial Furidi.

ANNOTATED BIBLIOGRAPHY

Books for Teachers

Especially Recommended

Acosta-Belén, E., Cruz, J. E., Santiago, C. E., Rodriguez, C. E., Gonzalez-Rodriguez, Y., Benitez, M., Santiago-Rivera, A., & Sjostrom, B. R. (Eds.). (2000). *Adiós, Borinquen querida: The Puerto Rican Diaspora: Its History, and Contributions.* Albany: University of Albany Press.

This book offers an overview of the historical, cultural, and political development of Puerto Rican immigrant communities within and outside of the United States (Cuba, the Dominican Republic, Mexico, and St. Croix). The contributors are distinguished scholars and writers in the field of Puerto Rican Studies.

Bigler, E. (1999). *American Conversations: Puerto Ricans, White Ethnics, and Multicultural Education.* Philadelphia: Temple University Press.

This study explores, through conversations with students, teachers, parents, and community leaders, how the introduction of multicultural and bilingual education to a school in upstate New York divided the town's community.

De Wagenheim, O. J. (1998). *Puerto Rico: An Interpretive History from Pre-Colombian Times to 1900.* Princeton: Markus Wiener.

An informative and well-crafted interpretive history of Puerto Rico.

De Wagenheim, O. J., & Wagenheim, K. (2001). *The Puerto Ricans: A Documentary History.* New York: Markus Wiener.

This book is a documentary and analysis of Puerto Rico's history from the beginning of the Island's settlement by the Spanish to the mass migration to the United States after WW II.

Flores, L. (2000). *From Bomba to Hip-Hop: Puerto Rican Culture and Latino Identity.* New York: Columbia University Press.

This book explores how Puerto Ricans in New York have created a unique identity for themselves. The author describes architecture, literary traditions, musical styles, and cul-

tural movements and compares them to those of the city's other ethnic and racial minority groups.

Nieto, S. (Ed.). (2000). *Puerto Rican Students in U.S. Schools.* Mahwah, NJ: Lawrence Erlbaum.

This is a collection of reflective essays, research studies, and poems about the education and schooling of Puerto Rican students in the United States. The authors address issues of identity, culture, ethnicity, language, gender, social activism, community involvement, and policy implications.

Sanchez-Korrol, V. (1999). *Teaching U.S. Puerto Rican History.* Washington, DC: American Historical Association.

This text offers a comprehensive historical overview of the Puerto Rican experience in the United States. Special attention is given to pedagogical strategies for teaching Puerto Rican American history.

Trías Monge, J. (1997). *Puerto Rico: The Trials of the Oldest Colony in the World.* New Haven: Yale University Press.

An informative and readable history that argues that Puerto Rico is the oldest colony in the world.

Other Books

Barreto, A. A. (2001). *The Politics of Language in Puerto Rico.* Gainesville, FL: University Press of Florida.

This book is directed toward Puerto Rican language policies and examines the connections between language, cultural identity, and politics.

Cepeda, O. (1999). *Baby Bull: From Hardball to Hard Time and Back.* Navasota, TX: Taylor.

In this autobiography one of the first Puerto Rican baseball stars describes his career as well as the hardships of his post-career life.

Colón, J., Padilla Aponte, E. K., & Padilla, E. (Eds.). (2001). *Lo Que el Pueblo Me Dice: Cronicas de la Colonia Puertoriquena en Nueva York.* Houston: Arté Publico Press.

This is the first collection of Spanish-language journalistic chronicles of everyday life representing three decades of the development of the Hispanic community in the city. The chronicles are edited by Edwin Padilla, who provides an analytic, social, and historical framework in the introduction.

Cruz, J. E. (1998). *Identity and Power: Puerto Rican Politics and the Challenge of Ethnicity.* Philadelphia: Temple University Press.

A critical analysis of the role of ethnicity in political processes as well as an advocacy for an identity politics that is sensitive about history and historical processes of oppression.

Dávila, A. M. (1997). *Sponsored Identities: Cultural Politics in Puerto Rico.* Philadelphia: Temple University Press.

This book explores how views and representations of national identities are constructed and challenged by party ideologies, corporate economic goals, and cultural grassroot movements in Puerto Rico.

Fitzpatrick, J. P. (1997). *The Stranger Is Our Own: Reflections on the Journey of Puerto Rican Migrants.* Ashland, OH: Sheed & Ward.

A personal memoir about the life of a Puerto Rican immigrant.

Glasser, R. (1997). *The Stranger Is My Flag: Puerto Rican Musicians and Their New York Communities, 1917–1940.* Berkeley: University of California Press.

This books describes the social history and forms of cultural expressions of Puerto Ricans. It provides an understanding of how the complexities of cultural nationalism and cultural authenticity become important representatives for the national consciousness of Puerto Ricans on both sides of the Atlantic.

Glasser, R. (1998). *Aquí Me Quedo: Puerto Ricans in Connecticut.* Connecticut: Department of Education.

A collection of oral history narratives of Puerto Ricans who migrated to or were born in Connecticut.

Guerra, L. (1998). *Popular Expression and National Identity in Puerto Rico: The Struggle for Self, Community, and Nation.* Gainesville, FL: University Press of Florida.

This book presents the social and political history of Puerto Rico from 1940 to 1989. In drawing on unstudied folktales, songs, and riddles—as well as the literary movement—the author provides a new reading of Puerto Rican culture and identity by analyzing it through the lenses of gender, class, and race.

Hernandez, C. D. (1997). *Puerto Rican Voices in English.* New York: Praeger.

This book presents a collection of interviews with fourteen of the most prominent Puerto Rican writers living in the United States. The writers portray how they were affected by their early displacement of national culture and how the perceived racial, cultural, and linguistic bias in both the United States as well as Puerto Rico can turn into violence and hate or the wish to excel and to communicate.

Maldonado, A. W. (1997). *Teodoro Moscoso and Puerto Rico's Operation Bootstrap.* Gainesville, FL: University Press of Florida.

This book examines Puerto Rico's rise from poverty to economic success under the guidance of Teodoro Moscoso. The author combines biographical information, history, economics, and politics to offer an explanation for Puerto Rico's economic transformation and success.

Matos-Rodríguez, F. V. (1999). *Women and Urban Change in San Juan, Puerto Rico, 1820–1868.* Gainesville, FL: University Press of Florida.

This book presents a unique contribution to the history of urban women in nineteenth-century Puerto Rico. The author examines how economic and social changes affected the women of San Juan and how they reacted in return.

Matos-Rodríguez, F. V., & Hernández, P. J. (2001). *Pioneros: Puerto Ricans in New York City 1896–1948.* New York: Arcadia Press.

This book is the first photographic portrayal of the history of Puerto Rican immigration to New York.

Munoz, V. I. (1996). *Where "Something Catches": Work, Love, and Identity in Youth.* New York: State University of New York Press.

This book presents the results of a qualitative study with 56 Puerto Rican youth and how they deal with questions of work, love, community, alternatives, and the support structure around them. Through this examination the author explores the identity development of Puerto Rican youth.

Ortiz, A. (1996). *Puerto Rican Women and Work: Bridges in Transnational Labor.* Philadelphia: Temple University Press.

In a collection of interdisciplinary essays the author traces the connections between women, work, and the different stages of capitalism in the history of Puerto Rico.

Perez y Gonzalez, M. E. (2000). *Puerto Ricans in the United States.* Westport, CT: Greenwood.

This book examines the experiences of Puerto Rican immigrants in the United States and the development of Puerto Rican urban culture in America.

Sánchez-González, L. (2001). *Boricua Literature: A Literary History of the Puerto Rican Diaspora.* New York: New York University Press.

This book offers a historical analysis and overview of Puerto Rican or Boricua literature.

Santiago-Valles, K. A. (1994). *"Subject People" and Colonial Discourses: Economic Transformation and Social Disorder in Puerto Rico, 1899–1947.* New York: State University of New York Press.

This book offers a provocative sociological analysis of the social and political processes that reshaped Puerto Rican society in the first half of the twentieth century.

Soto, L. D. (1996). *Language, Culture, and Power: Bilingual Families and the Struggle for Quality Education.* New York: State University of New York.

This book presents a case study of the Puerto Rican American community in an industrial city in Pennsylvania. Through the lens of this community the author examines the political dimensions of bilingualism, bilingual schooling, and empowering education. The book includes a foreword by Christine Sleeter.

Thomas, P. (1997). *Down These Mean Streets.* London: Vintage Books.

A classic memoir about growing up in Spanish Harlem as a dark-skinned Puerto Rican child in a family that refused to acknowledge its African heritage.

Torres, A., Velazquez, J. E., & Pantojos-Garcia, E. (Eds.). (1998). *The Puerto Rican Movement: Voices from the Diaspora.* Philadelphia: Temple University Press.

This anthology discusses the history of organizations and social movements of the 1960s and 1970s that emerged to promote Puerto Rican independence from the United States.

Weiler, J. D. (2000). *Codes and Contradictions: Race, Gender, Identity, and Schooling.* New York: State University of New York Press.

This book examines how school processes influence the identities and the identity development of young working-class women of African American, Latina, Puerto Rican, and White European descent.

Whalen, C. (2001). *From Puerto Rico to Philadelphia: Puerto Rican Workers and Postwar Economies.* Philadelphia: Temple University Press.

This book describes the experiences of Puerto Rican immigrants to Philadelphia and analyzes the contract labor programs, state policies, changes in regional and local economies, social networks, and individual decisions that structure the lives of the immigrants.

Books for Students

Aliotta, J. J. (1995). *The Puerto Ricans* (2nd ed.). Series: *The Immigrant Experience.* New York: Chelsea House.

An informational series book that offers an overview of life and culture on the island, the history of migration to the U.S. mainland, and the lives of Puerto Ricans living on the mainland. (Middle School)

Belpré, P. (1996). *Firefly Summer.* Series: *Recovering the U.S. Hispanic Literary Heritage.* Houston, TX: Piñata Books.

A recently discovered novel written by the pioneering librarian (the first Puerto Rican librarian in New York City), who died in 1982. The story depicts an upper-class Puerto Rican teenager who comes home from boarding school to spend the summer on her parents' farm early in the twentieth century. (Middle School/High School)

Bernier-Grand, C. T. (1995). *Poet of Puerto Rico: Don Luis Muñoz Marin*. Chicago: Orchard Books.

An illustrated book about the famous Puerto Rican leader. (Primary)

Bernier-Grand, C. T. (1999). *In the Shade of the Níspero Tree*. New York: Orchard.

A Puerto Rican preteen learns unpleasant truths about race and class when her darker-skinned best friend and later she too are excluded from the island's elite social circles. (Middle School)

Colón-Villá, L. (1998). *Salsa*. Illustrated by R. Collier-Morales. Houston, TX: Piñata Books.

This bilingual book offers an introduction to salsa music through the eyes of a young Puerto Rican girl. (Primary)

Delacre, L. (1993). *Vejigante/Masquerader*. New York: Scholastic.

A bilingual book that tells the story of a boy who makes a costume for the carnival celebration in Ponce. (Primary)

Fradin, D. B., & Fradin, J. B. (1995). *Puerto Rico*. Danbury, CT: Children's Press.

A short illustrated book that describes Puerto Rico. (Intermediate)

Johnson, J. (1995). *Puerto Rico*. Minneapolis: Lerner.

A history of Puerto Rico that is illustrated with interesting photographs. Available in both English and Spanish editions. (Intermediate)

London, J. (1998). *Hurricane!* Illustrated by H. Sorenson. New York: Lothrop.

A young boy living near the beach in Puerto Rico witnesses the awesome power of a hurricane. (Primary)

Mohr, N. (1986). *Going Home*. New York: Dial.

This sequel to Felita focuses on the dilemmas faced by a Nuyorican girl who returns to Puerto Rico. (Middle School). Other books by Nicholasa Mohr include Nilda *(1973),* El Bronx Remembered *(1975),* Felita *(1979), and* In Nueva York *(1977).*

Mohr, N. (1996). *Old Letivia and the Mountain of Sorrow*. Illustrated by R. Gutierrez. New York: Viking.

The well-known author of books for older children offers a folktale-based original picture book story about a curandera who embarks with her animal friend on a dangerous mission to save the island from hurricanes. (Primary)

Mohr, N., & Martorell, A. (1995). *The Song of el Coquí and Other Tales of Puerto Rico*. New York: Viking.

This collection of stories reveals the rich ancestral traditions of Puerto Rican culture. (All levels)

Ortíz Cofer, J. (1995). *An Island Like You: Stories of the Barrio*. New York: Orchard.

Twelve interconnected stories depict the lives of Puerto Rican and other Latino teenagers who reside in the same building in a Paterson, New Jersey, neighborhood. (Middle School/ High School)

Ortíz Cofer, J. (1998). *The Year of Our Revolution*. Houston: Arte Público.

Entertaining and revealing poems and short stories describe the author's experience of growing up in the Puerto Rican barrio of Paterson, New Jersey, in the turbulent 1960s. This book begins approximately where Ortíz Cofer's acclaimed memoir of her life on the island, Silent Dancing: A Partial Remembrance of a Puerto Rican Childhood *(Arte Público, 1990), ends. (Middle School/High School)*

Padilla, F. (2000a). *Mami Amor's Little Stories.* Illustrated by E. S. Padilla. Long Beach, NY: LI-BROS; Encouraging Cultural Literacy.

A Puerto Rican boy tells of his ancestor, Mami Amor, who came from her beautiful but impoverished island to Chicago in the 1940s and her job as a needleworker in a textile factory. (Primary)

Padilla, F. (2000b). *My Two Lights.* Illustrated by E. S. Padilla. Long Beach, NY: LIBROS; Encouraging Cultural Literacy.

Through his music teacher, a Puerto Rican boy living on the mainland learns about his homeland, the beauty of his Spanish language, and the power of music. (Primary)

Press, P. (1995). *Puerto Rican Americans.* Series: *Cultures in America.* Tarrytown, NY: Marshall Cavendish/Benchmark Books.

An informational book with color photographs, of interest to students at the elementary level. (Intermediate)

Santiago, E. (1998). *Almost a Woman.* Reading, MA: Perseus Books.

The author of When I Was Puerto Rican *(Perseus, 1993) continues her story, beginning when she arrived in Brooklyn from the island at the age of thirteen. She describes her many roles in her family, her parents' tight supervision, and her extraordinary efforts to succeed as a student and as an actress and dancer. (High School)*

Santiago, R, (ed.). (1995). *Boricuas: Influential Puerto Rican Writers—An Anthology.* New York: One World/Ballantine.

Fifty selections—essays, poems, short stories, and plays—present writings of prominent, often controversial, Puerto Rican authors from the nineteenth century to the present. (High School)

Wakefield, C. C. (1999). *Navidad Latinoamericana/Latin American Christmas.* Illustrated by F. Reinoso. Lancaster, PA: Latin American Creations.

Christmas in 25 Latin American countries is presented through prayers, folktales, songs, and stunning color illustrations. Though its coverage is broad, this book has a definite Caribbean flavor. (Intermediate and Up)

Wallner, A. (2000). *Sergio and the Hurricane.* Illustrated by the author. New York: Henry Holt.

In San Juan, Puerto Rico, Sergio is excited about a coming hurricane until he helps his family prepare and learns about the destructive power of nature. (Primary)

12 Cuban Americans

Concepts, Strategies, and Materials

*If in things concerning my country I should be given a
choice above all others...this would be the good I would
choose: I should want the cornerstone of our Republic to
be the devotion of Cubans to the dignity of humankind.*

—José Marti

This chapter discusses the background and experience of a small but significant group of Hispanics in the United States. Cubans have lived in small communities in New York, Tampa, and Key West, Florida since the latter part of
the nineteenth century. Large numbers did not immigrate to the United States
until after Fidel Castro assumed power in the revolution that occurred in
1959.

To fully comprehend Cuban Americans in the United States today, one
must understand the circumstances that led them to emigrate. While levels of
intensity may differ, there is a near-universal dislike among Cuban Americans
of the communist government of Cuba. However, as time passes and there are
more Cuban Americans who are born in the United States, those with more
moderate perspectives increase in number. This chapter illustrates how Cuban
immigrants have sought the American dream while simultaneously maintaining a passion for their homeland.

This chapter was contributed by **Carlos F. Diaz**, Professor of Education, Florida Atlantic University, Boca Raton, Florida. Professor Diaz is the editor of *Multicultural Education in the 21st Century* (Longman, 2001) and co-author of *Global Perspectives for Educators* (Allyn and Bacon,
1999).

CUBAN AMERICANS: HISTORICAL PERSPECTIVE

Important Dates	Events
1959	Fidel Castro took over the reins of power in Cuba from the government of dictator Fulgencio Batista.
1961	Diplomatic relations between the United States and Cuba were severed. The Cuban exile brigade 2500 landed at the Bay of Pigs on the southern coast of Cuba, in an ill-fated attempt to overthrow the Castro regime.
1962	Commercial air flights between the United States and Cuba were ended. Immigration to the United States became strictly clandestine. The Cuban missile crisis prompted President Kennedy to blockade Cuba. The Soviet Union eventually withdrew the missiles from Cuban soil.
1965	Beginning of the Cuban Refugee Airlift program. Flights from Cuba to Miami, Florida, were sponsored by the U.S. government.
1973	Termination of the Cuban Refugee Airlift program. Immigration to the United States returned to a clandestine status or took place through a third country, such as Spain or Mexico.
1977	Diplomatic interest sections were established by the U.S. and Cuban governments in embassies of third countries. Cuba used the Czechoslovakian embassy in Washington and the United States used the Swiss embassy in Havana. This move was strongly opposed by most Cuban Americans. Fidel Castro allowed U.S. citizens and their Cuban dependents living in Cuba who wished to leave to depart Cuba.
1980	125,000 Cubans arrived in the United States via a boatlift from Mariel. Reaction in the United States ranged from welcome to open hostility.
1984	The Immigration and Naturalization Service ruled that Cubans who entered the United States via Mariel with the classification of "entrant" would be permitted to apply for permanent resident status under the Cuban Refugee Readjustment Act of 1966.
1985	In response to Radio Martí broadcasts beamed at Cuba, Fidel Castro stopped familial visits of Cuban Americans and abrogated the agreement with the United States to repatriate Mariel Cubans who were being held in American jails. Xavier Suarez was elected mayor of Miami, Florida. He was the first Cuban American to be elected to that office.

Important Dates	Events
1987	Mariel refugee inmates imprisoned in Atlanta, Georgia, and Oakdale, Louisiana, rioted and took hostages on learning they might be deported. Riots ended after the U.S. government set up a review process for anyone facing deportation.
1988	The Cuban American National Foundation began a program with the U.S. Immigration's approval to reunite Cubans in third countries with relatives in the United States. The foundation paid all travel and relocation costs.
1989	Rep. Ileana Ros-Lehtinen became the first Cuban-born member of the U.S. Congress in a special election to replace the late Rep. Claude Pepper. Florida followed the precedent set in California, Illinois, and other states and voted 84% to 16% to amend the state constitution declaring English the state's official language. Cuban Americans largely opposed this measure.
1994	Fidel Castro announced that he would not stop Cubans attempting to flee the island. A massive rafting exodus followed, with the U.S. Coast Guard interdicting Cubans and sending them to camps at the Guantanamo naval base.
1995	Cuba and the United States negotiated an agreement that would slowly bring refugees from Guantanamo and Panama to the U.S. Future entry visas for Cubans were set at 20,000 per year.
1998	Pope John Paul II visits Cuba.
2000	The case of Elian Gonzalez riveted national attention for several months. Ultimately, courts ruled that Elian be returned to his father to live in Cuba.

Cuban Immigrants to the United States

Since the 1960s, Cubans have been one of the largest groups immigrating to the United States. Of the foreign nationals entering the United States from Spanish-speaking nations, they have been the second largest immigrant group, surpassed only by Mexicans. The number of Cubans immigrating to the United States between 1971 and 1980 (276,800) was 28% larger than the number that settled in the United States between 1951 and 1960 (78,300) (U.S. Immigration and Naturalization Service, 1998). After the 125,000 entrants from the Mariel boatlift in 1980, Cuban immigration declined during the remainder of the decade. Immigration from Cuba has been a sporadic process since 1959. In 1994, the Castro government temporarily suspended enforcement of Cuban law forbidding Cuban citizens from leaving national territory by "illegal means." This temporary window of opportunity resulted in tens of thousands of *balseros* (rafters) openly launching their rafts in an effort to reach Florida or at least a U.S. Coast Guard cutter. This window was closed after negotiations between the Clinton administration and the Castro government established that Cuba would again enforce its law forbidding illegal exit and the United States would fill all or most of its allotment of 20,000 visas for legal Cuban entrants.

Cuban Americans are a group with low visibility because their relocation has occurred almost exclusively in a few large urban areas. In 2001, they numbered around 1.3 million, or about 4% of the Hispanic population of the United States. The largest Cuban American community is in the greater Miami, Florida area and includes more than 500,000 people. Other large concentrations are found in the New York City metropolitan area and in the greater Los Angeles area (see Table 12.1).

The Cubans' brief history on U.S. soil shares some common elements with older and more established immigrant groups. Yet, many unique differences distinguish their exodus. Most Cubans have migrated to the United States since the Castro revolution of 1959. Those who came did so primarily because they felt threatened by the political situation they experienced in Cuba. This contrasts with most other American immigrants who came to the United States searching mainly for economic improvement for themselves and their families.

Another characteristic of the Cuban influx is that those who left the island in search of a political haven are not a representative sample of the Cuban population at large. A demographic study by Fagen, Brody, and O'Leary (1968) indicated that "a disproportionate number of refugees come from the middle and upper strata of pre-revolutionary society" (p. 16). People in the

TABLE 12.1 Cuban American Population in Selected States (2000)

State	Population	State	Population
Florida	850,841	Illinois	11,344
New Jersey	79,443	Louisiana	10,684
New York	69,262	Maryland	9,507
California	64,262	North Carolina	9,292
Texas	22,464	United States	1,232,736
Nevada	14,878		

Source: Based on estimated data from the U.S. Census Bureau, 2000. *(http://www.census.gov/)*

lower socioeconomic strata who opposed the revolution had fewer resources at their disposal to turn their dissatisfaction into some viable action.

The middle and upper strata of Cuban society were most heavily represented in the first wave of immigration during the early 1960s. As time progressed, Cuban immigrants became a more representative sample of the Cuban population. However, the total number of Cuban immigrants in the United States still contains a higher proportion of business and professional people than are present in the Cuban population.

This overrepresentation of the Cuban upper class among immigrants can be partly explained by the fact the people in this class felt particularly threatened by governmental changes that eroded their economic position. Most Cuban Americans were never part of the elite in their homeland so their departure cannot be attributed to a loss of great wealth. They left their native land primarily because of their genuine opposition to the political system and for reasons of family reunification.

Another group that is overrepresented in the Cuban American population is older people. Barriers to their exit from the island have been considerably fewer than those faced by younger Cubans. Another factor contributing to this demographic trend is that many Cuban families sent for their parents or grandparents after they had gained an economic foothold in the United States.

The ethnic composition of Cuban Americans is also disproportionate to the Cuban population. According to Pérez (1980), "Black Cubans were probably less likely to emigrate because of their perception that race relations in the United States are less satisfactory than they are in socialist Cuba" (p. 257). Even though Black Cubans are underrepresented among immigrants, their numbers increased significantly after the Mariel influx in 1980. Caucasian and Chinese Cubans are found in greater proportions among Cubans in the United States than in the Cuban population. In prerevolutionary Cuba, Caucasian and Chinese Cubans were more prevalent in the middle and upper economic strata of society. Conversely, Black Cubans were more likely to be present in the lower economic class. Most Cuban Americans, regardless of racial and ethnic background, share an opposition to the Castro regime in Cuba. Among those who immigrated as adults, it is difficult to describe the depth and emotional nature of their sentiments. The desire for political as well as economic stability has shaped the Cuban migration to the United States.

The Cuban immigrant has generally accepted and lived by the predominant American ethos that hard work will ultimately be rewarded. Considering the deprived economic conditions that most started with, the results have been notable. Their accomplishments have caused some observers to tout them as a "model minority," much like their Japanese American counterparts. Yet the success of Cubans should not be construed so as to obscure the general plight of Spanish-speaking Americans. For most, this success has not occurred without hardship. Their accomplishments do not mean that Cuban Americans do not have problems. Their median income still lags behind the national average. To attain their median income, a disproportionate number of working wives are found in Cuban American households. Also, the cohesive nature of the Cuban family has sometimes suffered because of economic pressures.

The assimilation of Cubans has occurred at different levels among people living in various locations in the United States. Like other immigrant groups, assimilation has been less for the older segment of the population and for Cubans living in cities with large Cuban communities. The continuum of assimilation ranges from the almost perfectly integrated to some who have failed to accept the permanence of their U.S. surroundings.

Life in Cuba

On January 1, 1959, the city of Havana, Cuba rocked with the effects of a drastic change. The regime of dictator Fulgencio Batista had been deposed by *la Revolucion*, led by a bearded young rebel named Fidel Castro. His triumphal entry into the capital city was seen by nearly everyone as the coming of a new messiah. His popularity was more than that of a political figure; he had all the markings of a charismatic leader.

Promises of economic prosperity and of uniting the Cuban people were among the many Fidel Castro made. The synthesis of the Cuban revolution took place in a slow, deliberate series of steps, to the delight of some and the disillusionment of others. The Agrarian Reform confiscated large holdings of land in private hands. This land became government property and farmers became government employees.

As the course of the revolution drifted politically left, a marked polarization of Cuban society began to occur. A person either supported the revolution or was thought of as a *gusano* (worm), a parasite to progress without whom the revolution was better off. True to the Cuban sense of humor, the expression *abrir los ojos* (see the light) marked a person who took exception to revolutionary policies. These political divisions permeated the family unit and caused bitter disagreements among relatives who advocated the revolution and those who opposed it. Many of these rifts remain today. The Cuban revolution affected everyone, regardless of his or her place in society. Fundamental changes reached the economic, political, social, and religious sectors of Cuban life.

The educational system in Cuba was affected fundamentally by the revolution. The number of schools in rural areas was increased in a campaign to end *analfabetismo* (illiteracy), and new high schools were located primarily in rural areas as well. Many urban students had to board at school in order to obtain a secondary education. In the public schools, instruction in the humanities and the natural and physical sciences was fraught with political socialization, which placed a premium on loyalty to the revolution. Along with expanding education in the rural areas, the Cuban government increased the number of health facilities. Clinics are more readily available to farmers than in prerevolutionary times.

The Cuban economy today deemphasizes consumer goods in favor of products for export. As a result of this emphasis, as well as of production lags, rationing is fairly common. The following ration limits were obtained by interviewing an exile and were in effect in 2001 (author's interview with a person who visited Cuba in 2001):

Rice	5 pounds per month
Beans	6 ounces per month
Coffee	1 ounce per person per week
Meat	Not available through the rationing process
Eggs	5 eggs per month
Sugar	2 pounds per month
Bread	¼ pound per day
Soap	½ bar available every 3–4 months (if available)

For Children

0–7 years of age	1 liter of milk per day

Clandestine Market

1 pound of rice	5 pesos
1 pound of pork	18 pesos
1 liter of milk	3 pesos
1 liter of gasoline	25 pesos
1 egg	2 pesos

The official exchange rate in 2001 was 22 pesos to one dollar.

Since the collapse of the Soviet empire, most of the favorable trading or bartering agreements Cuba had with former communist nations have collapsed. New goods must be purchased with hard currency, which the Cuban peso is not. Daily life in Cuba, particularly the procurement of sufficient food, has become increasingly difficult when compared to circumstances on the island prior to 1992. Salaries in 2001 ranged from 550 pesos ($25.00) per month for a physician to 180 pesos ($8.00) per month for an office worker. Pensioners typically receive under 100 pesos ($5.00) per month. The imbalance between legal wages and the prices of necessities has forced many Cubans to turn to the clandestine market or to barter.

Some fortunate individuals receive dollars or other foreign currencies from relatives abroad. These may be used in "dollar stores" where the Cuban peso is not accepted. In these stores one can purchase soap, toiletries, and many other goods that are not available in the regular stores.

In addition to the rationing, Cubans must plan on spending a fair amount of time waiting to buy their food items. It is not uncommon for a shopper to spend two hours or more per day making food purchases. Whenever something extra can be obtained, people do so for friends or relatives. Any outing from the home is a potential shopping trip. Because the availability of products is often sporadic, the shopping bag (*jaba*) is a constant companion.

Socioeconomic mobility in Cuba is accomplished by a mixture of individual talent, effort, and loyalty. The last of these factors creates some wrenching psychological dilemmas for certain individuals. To hold most of the managerial and many professional positions, the person must be a card-carrying *militante* (militant). Some people hold this status out of conviction for communist or revolutionary beliefs and others because the card is an asset for upward mobility in society. These people must be particularly careful of their associations.

A constant dilemma for the militants of convenience is whether their activities or associations will help or hinder their image as militants. It is also assumed that people with militant status will be prepared to serve on any international mission that may be assigned. This is also true for people studying any one of the professions, particularly those in the health fields. These missions may last two or three years, and some couples have been separated for that long.

Other adaptations to revolutionary society include having most salaries in the nation specified by the government. Money derived from working is not sufficient to purchase most foodstuffs or consumer goods. It must be accompanied by a ration coupon permitting the purchase of specific items.

Salary laws require workers to meet a production quota either of goods or services. If this quota is not reached, the worker's salary is reduced by a proportional amount. In addition to a worker's obligatory job, there is volunteer labor available on Sundays or holidays. This volunteer work may consist of cleaning details, construction projects, or harvesting sugarcane, as well as many other tasks. Workers who want to purchase a major item, such as a refrigerator, often accumulate many hours of volunteer labor.

Leaving the country entails many sacrifices. Invariably, relatives are left behind. This point is particularly significant when one realizes the close-knit nature of the Cuban extended family, which makes it difficult for members to break from the family unit.

Forfeiture of all possessions is another factor to consider. Everything a person has worked for in a lifetime finds its way into government hands. Also, there is the prospect of starting over in a strange environment. For most immigrants, this happens without command of the English language. Despite all these difficulties, however, more than a million Cubans have felt compelled to leave their homeland.

Opinions about the Castro regime vary within Cuba. Supporters point out that the Cuban government has vastly expanded health care and education. Cubans on the island who are strong supporters of the Castro government and its philosophy cite wide gaps in living standards between the elite and common people in other Latin American nations. These issues, however valid, are not salient with the Cuban American population. For most of them, the ills perpetrated by the Castro government outweigh any of its positive measures.

In the early 1960s, the United States accepted as a political refugee any Cuban who could reach its shores. In 1966, the Cuban Readjustment Act gave Cuban refugees the status of parolees and allowed a change to permanent resident status after two years in the United States. This law also gave Cubans special immigration status so their number would not be limited or counted against the limits allowed for other nations in the Americas.

This remained U.S. policy until the Refugee Act of 1980 removed special immigration status for Cuban immigrants. In order to accommodate the influx of Cubans in 1980, President Carter created a special immigration category of entrants. People who held this entrant status remained as temporary residents of the United States until late 1984, when the Immigration and Naturalization Service decided to allow them to apply for permanent residency status. Today, Cubans no longer hold officially favored immigration status.

Departure

Prohias and Casal (1973) have identified three stages in the migration of Cubans to the United States:

> They are as follows: A first stage, between January 1959 and October 1962, when commercial flights between Cuba and the United States were available; (b) a second stage, between October 1962 and December 1965, with a corresponding slowdown of the migration rate as Cubans had to resort to unconventional means (small boats, rafts, etc.) or flights through third countries to come to the United States; a third stage, with daily airflights between Varadero and Miami throughout most of the period (p. 257).

The third stage, known as the Cuban Refugee Airlift, was terminated in January 1973. From 1973 to 1980, Cubans reverted to the unconventional means of the second stage. In 1980, a temporary policy change by the Cuban government produced a fourth stage, resulting in a wave of 125,000 Cubans coming by sea from Mariel to Key West, Florida. At the conclusion of this boatlift in May 1980, Cubans reverted to stage two methods.

In 1988, the Cuban American National Foundation received permission from the U.S. Immigration and Naturalization Service to sponsor Cubans living outside of Cuba. This effort was to reunify them with relatives living in the United States. The visas granted to these individuals stipulated that their relocation would occur at no cost to the national, state, or local government.

The trauma of leaving Cuba varied greatly with the particular experience. Leaving by commercial airline in 1960 was fairly conventional. However, escaping in a small boat meant jeopardizing one's life. Also, the date of departure determined how much difficulty an exile would encounter in leaving the island. In general, the longer a family waited before making the decision to leave, the more obstacles it would have to face before it could secure permission to exit. In the early 1960s, many families sent their children out of Cuba via Catholic or other religious relief agencies in the hope that the parents could follow later. This effort was called Operation Peter Pan. Most of these families have been reunited; others are still waiting.

Many Americans have heard of Cubans reaching U.S. shores in small boats or rafts, but little publicity is given to the fact that many never made it after encountering a patrol boat or drifting away in the Gulf Stream current.

The Mariel Immigrants of 1980

In April 1980, more than 10,000 Cubans sought political asylum in the Peruvian embassy in Havana. The Cuban government's initial response was to allow them permission to leave Cuba via Peru or other willing Latin American nations, such as Costa Rica. Within days, that policy was changed to allow the exit of those people, as well as others who had sought to immigrate, directly to the United States. The Cuban American community in the United States saw this temporary respite in Cuban immigration policy as an opportunity to reunite themselves with relatives whom they had been trying to join for years.

A small port city on the northern coast of Cuba, Mariel, became the staging area for people waiting for transportation to the United States. On May 5, 1980, President Carter stated that the United States would receive the refugees "with an open heart and open arms." Nine days later, a presidential order forbade boats going to Cuba to pick up refugees. By then, hundreds of boats were on their way to or waiting in Mariel. Many Cuban American families spent their savings or pooled their earnings to pay for passage on a boat for relatives in Cuba.

The hundreds of boats that had crossed the Straits of Florida found a chaotic situation at the port of Mariel. Most boats had to anchor and wait, sometimes for weeks, until the government indicated that a group of people was ready for loading. Boat captains brought lists of people they came to transport, but often the lists were ignored or only one or two people on the list would be permitted to leave.

Meanwhile, food and supplies began to run low on board these vessels. Provisions had to be purchased from the Cuban government at three to six times their price in the United States. As time passed, tempers began to flare in the Mariel harbor.

People who had declared a willingness to leave via Mariel were gathered from all parts of Cuba. In some instances, people departing were publicly humiliated by zealous supporters of the revolution. Some people who declared a desire to leave through Mariel were not able to do so for logistical or other reasons. Their declaration caused them to lose their jobs, and many could not find other jobs.

The return crossing of the Straits of Florida was often a perilous ordeal. As a rule, boats were loaded beyond their capacity. Some captains objected to this, as well as to carrying people for whom they had not come. When the Cuban authorities insisted on both points, boat captains faced the dilemma of violating these directives or violating U.S. directives to stop the boatlift when they returned to Florida. More than fifty people died during these crossings. Some drowned when boats capsized in heavy seas, and others succumbed to carbon monoxide fumes in the holds of overloaded vessels. A frequently repeated ritual was of Cuban refugees kissing the ground after arriving in Key West, Florida.

As the flood of refugees continued, they were housed in a variety of temporary holding centers, including the Orange Bowl in Miami, Florida. People with immediate relatives were the most likely to be released quickly. Others without relatives waited patiently for relocation in other parts of the United States. As the numbers of refugees increased, a backlash of public opinion began. A Gallup poll conducted nationally in late May 1980 found that 59% of respondents felt that Cuban emigration was bad for the United States (Alpen, 1980). In the Miami area, a similar survey conducted by the *Miami Herald* in May 1980 found that 68% of the non-Latin White population and 57% of the African American population surveyed felt that the new wave of Cuban refugees would have a negative influence on the local community (Morin, 1980, p. 1).

The Cuban community in Miami raised more than $2 million in cash and other assistance to help accommodate the new arrivals. Nevertheless, the size of the influx made it necessary to relocate many Cubans in holding centers outside southern Florida. As Cuban refugees were relocated on military bases in predominantly rural areas of Arkansas, Pennsylvania, Wisconsin, and Florida, residents of those areas vehemently protested the Cuban presence.

The characteristics of the Cubans who emigrated via the Mariel boatlift showed that there was a higher proportion of Black Cubans, single males, and blue-collar workers than among previous groups of Cuban immigrants. Much has been written about the undesirable or criminal element that came to the United States during the boatlift. The Cuban government seized the opportunity to rid itself of people who had committed serious crimes or suffered mental or physical problems; but people in these categories constituted fewer than 5% of the 125,000 entrants. Also, the fact that a person had spent time in a Cuban jail could be due either to criminal or political activity. Consequently, not all criminals would have had that label if they had been living in the United States. Most of the Mariel Cubans originally detained were eventually released. In 1992 about 1,200 Mariel Cubans had remained in jail since their arrival in the United States (Barberis, 1982). The bulk of these prisoners have been detained at the Atlanta Federal Penitentiary.

Most Cubans who came via the 1980 boatlift were of humbler origins than their predecessors but just as determined to improve themselves. A few gave the term *Marielito* a pejorative connotation. Unfortunately, that connotation has sometimes tainted the majority of Mariel Cubans who have worked hard and respected the law. Today, more than a decade after their arrival, the evidence indicates that Mariel Cubans have generally adjusted well to U.S. society.

The Cuban Rafters of 1994

While Cubans have been risking their lives trying to cross the Straits of Florida in makeshift rafts for decades, some unusual events occurred in the summer of 1994. The sequence began with a small Cuban vessel that was hijacked by a group of Cubans seeking to come to Florida. In the process, a Cuban military officer was killed. The vessel eventually made its way to Florida.

The Castro government protested that the United States was harboring hijackers and should return the group to Cuba. When the United States refused to do so, Fidel Castro retaliated by refusing to stop any Cubans who tried to leave the nation by sea. Tens of thousands of Cubans took to the ocean, mostly in makeshift rafts. The United States Coast Guard was rescuing thousands every day at the peak of this exodus.

President Clinton issued a proclamation that Cubans leaving in rafts would no longer be granted entrant status to the United States. The last vestiges of the Cuban Refugee Readjustment Act of 1966 had been nullified. Cuban rafters were confined in a camp at the military base in Guantanamo, Cuba. Some Cubans were transferred to a camp in Panama.

After negotiations between Cuban and U.S. authorities in New York, the Cuban government agreed to enforce Cuban law prohibiting exit from the country without documentation. The United States agreed to give all or nearly all of the 28,000 yearly visas to Cubans promised under an earlier accord negotiated in 1984. (An average of 2,000 to 3,000 visas per year had been granted from 1984 to 1994.) The fate of those Cubans detained in Guantanamo and Panama was resolved by an accord reached in 1995 between the United States and Cuba. Cubans in the Guantanamo and Panama camps would be slowly resettled in the United States, beginning with children and those who had close family relationships in the United States. Cubans in Cuba were to apply for U.S. entry visas. The United States promised to issue at least 20,000 per year.

The Case of Elian Gonzalez

On Thanksgiving Day of 1999, two men fishing off the coast of Fort Lauder-
dale, Florida, found five-year-old Elian Gonzalez clinging to an inner tube.
Two other adult survivors from the same boat that brought Elian were rescued
off the coast of Miami. Elian's mother and nine other Cuban refugees perished
in an effort to reach the shores of Florida. Thus began a protracted family and
diplomatic struggle over the future of a five year-old boy that was chronicled
throughout the world.

Elian was turned over to his great uncle, Lazaro Gonzalez and his family,
who resided in Miami. Shortly afterward, Elian's biological father, Juan
Miguel Gonzalez, requested that Elian be returned to live with him in Cuba.
The family of Lazaro Gonzalez refused the request and an international custody battle ensued.

Many observers who heard about this case on the news found the controversy perplexing. After all, when viewed strictly as a child custody issue between a father and a great uncle, wouldn't the law always support granting
custody to the natural father providing he is a fit parent?

If Juan Miguel Gonzalez had resided in the United States, there would
have been no controversy. However, because he was a citizen of Cuba, it was
understood by all parties that, if his father were granted custody, Elian would
definitely return to Cuba. Elian's return to Cuba was very problematic for
many Cuban Americans who felt that if this occurred, Elian's mother would
have died in vain and her desires ignored. They also felt that Elian's future
would be far more promising if he were allowed to remain in the United States.

Ultimately, this issue was resolved in the courts. Over a period of months
and through various hearings and appeals, the attorneys representing Juan
Miguel Gonzalez were prevailing. Meanwhile, Lazaro Gonzalez and his family
had received temporary custody of Elian from the Immigration and Naturalization Service (INS).

The Justice Department plan was to have a voluntary transfer of Elian to
INS custody and transport him to Washington, D.C., where he would reside
with his father until a final determination was made by the courts.

While this scenario was playing out in the United States, many demonstrations were held in Cuba involving hundreds of thousands of Cubans demanding that the United States "free Elian" and "return Cuba's son." Elian was
frequently featured in the Cuban media with commentary that his continued
stay in the United States amounted to an "international kidnapping."

In March of 2000, U.S. District Judge Michael Moore threw out a political asylum lawsuit that cleared the way for Elian Gonzalez to be returned to
his father in Cuba. Elian's Miami family attorneys appealed Judge Moore's decision to the 11th U.S. Circuit Court of Appeals in Atlanta.

While all parties waited for this decision, the Immigration and Naturalization Service revoked Lazaro Gonzalez's custody of Elian, but Lazaro did not

voluntarily turn Elian over to INS custody. After protracted discussions between the Miami family's lawyers and the Justice Department, Attorney General Janet Reno gave permission for Elian to be removed from Lazaro Gonzalez's home in the early morning of April 22, 2000. The dramatic raid caused consternation in many circles, but particularly among Cuban Americans in Miami, some of whom demonstrated in the streets.

On June 1, 2000, a three-judge panel of the Circuit Court of Appeals upheld Judge Moore's original ruling and the way was cleared for Juan Miguel Gonzalez to return to Cuba with Elian. He did so on June 28, 2000.

Adaptation to Life in the United States

Most immigrants to the United States have come with the unwavering conviction of making this country their permanent home. In contrast, many Cubans arrived here with the thought of returning to their homeland as soon as the political climate changed. Although grateful to the United States for their asylum, their ultimate plans were not to remain in the U.S. Thus, they did not feel the immediate need to assimilate into the mainstream culture. With the passing of time, only the most optimistic clung exclusively to this viewpoint. Because the Castro regime showed strong signs of longevity, exiles tried to adapt to their new environment.

The adaptation of Cubans to American life has often been difficult. This process has been more extensive in areas where the Cuban population is small. In a city like Miami, with its large Cuban community, it is possible to live without crossing the boundaries of the ethnic neighborhood, and assimilation is not imperative. One major change has been to forsake the more leisurely mood of the Cuban lifestyle. According to the *New York Times* (1971), "Conversion to the pace of American life has threatened to disrupt the traditional Cuban way of life. The initial cultural shock was compounded by the dizzying social changes underway in this country that perplexed most Americans" (p. 4).

The high percentage of Cuban American working wives has had a significant social, as well as economic, impact on the Cuban community. Richmond (1980) found that, "Resources of the wife, particularly as they compared favorably to the resources possessed by her husband, were found to be an additional influence in the absorption of a more egalitarian ideology" (p. 115). The traditional dominant role of the husband in the Cuban household has undergone some modification, particularly in locations where families live in a largely non-Cuban community.

One problem encountered by Cuban parents was having their children adhere to Cuban values, norms, and customs. These permitted less freedom than their American peers enjoyed. This gap was felt more acutely by daughters in Cuban families than sons, because traditionally girls have been more closely supervised by parents.

Where Cubans resettled in large numbers, they were received in a variety of ways. A former Cuban lawyer related his impression in the following manner: "There are many people in Miami who still resent the Cubans settling here," he said, "but for the most part, since we have been the most successful immigrants in American history, Americans find it hard to look down their noses at us because we arrived here loaded with American characteristics. We are just too outgoing and enterprising and hard-working for them to stay mad at us" (*New York Times*, 1971, p. 4).

The reactions experienced by Cuban immigrants depended on the time and location of their immigration. People who were relocated to cities and towns with low Hispanic populations experienced little negative reaction. The influx of a few families is probably noticed little in most communities. Among Cubans who settled in areas like Miami, Florida, initial opposition to their arrival came from people in unskilled and blue-collar jobs. These new arrivals were perceived as an economic threat. People with higher socioeconomic positions were relatively unconcerned and often praised the hardworking émigrés.

With time and command of English, Cubans began to climb the socioeconomic ladder and to assert themselves economically and, to a lesser extent, politically. In 1969, Dade County (Miami) had 3,449 Hispanic businesses. By 1977, that figure had become 8,248, and in 1985 it had grown to 15,000. The Hispanic (mostly Cuban) population of Dade County had an annual income in 1985 of $6.7 billion (Oppenheimer, 1985). In 2001, the economic output of the Dade County Hispanic business community exceeded that of Hispanic businesses in Los Angeles, which has more than double the Hispanic population of Miami.

When Cubans started to become a potent economic force in Miami, and in other cities where their numbers were significant, they encountered difficulties from segments of the community that traditionally held most of the economic and political influence and wanted no change. Many of these people had been relatively unconcerned a decade or two before. Today, they realize that Cuban Americans are a viable economic entity and a competitive force. Competition is not always welcomed.

Like many immigrant groups, Cuban Americans have formed their own organizations to promote common interests. Groups such as the Latin American Chamber of Commerce were formed in Miami and claim the greatest membership among Cuban American businesspeople. While a time may come when members of this association may join the Greater Miami Chamber of Commerce in large numbers, the Latin chamber is expected to continue in the foreseeable future.

In 2000, the median income of Cuban Americans ($38,312) was higher than that of Puerto Ricans ($30,129) and Mexican Americans ($31,123), but was slightly below the median income ($40,816) for the entire nation (U.S. Census Bureau, 2000). The higher Cuban median income (compared to Puerto Ricans and Mexican Americans) was partly explained by an unusually high percentage of Cuban American women in the workforce and the higher average age of the Cuban American population.

In 1980, the entrance of thousands of Mariel Cubans into the U.S. workforce in predominantly low-skill jobs temporarily decreased Cuban American median income. However, their economic status increased sharply within ten years. According to Olson and Olson (1995), Mariel Cubans "were proving to be as successful in learning English, finding jobs and building businesses as the earlier generation of Cuban immigrations after only 10 years in the United States" (p. 91).

When they tried to pursue their former occupations in the United States, many Cubans ran into difficulties. The main obstacle to white-collar employment was mastery of the English language, which most did not have. In the professional fields, degrees earned in Cuba were often not recognized, and individuals frequently returned to college if they wanted to obtain work related to their former professions in Cuba. Even though many Cubans have regained their former occupational status and some have even surpassed it, a slight loss of occupational status remains.

The typical newly-arrived exile family in the 1960s received some assistance from the Cuban Refugee program while it existed. Afterwards, Cubans took whatever employment was immediately available, anticipating that their preferred work could be obtained later. When the concentration of Cubans in the Miami area became substantial, the government started a resettlement program. This program offered jobs and one month's free rent to immigrants who agreed to move outside Florida. In recent years, some Cubans who had been relocated trickled back into the South Florida area after they had achieved a financial foothold.

Many Cubans arriving via the 1980 boatlift had a more difficult time, especially single males with no family in the United States. Many waited months behind camp fences looking for an organization or person to sponsor their release. As time passed, frustration grew and even erupted into hostility at some camps. Even after being released in the care of a sponsor, some Mariel Cubans found it difficult to adjust to a competitive capitalist society with opportunities but few guarantees. After decades of working in a socialist economic system, some were unaccustomed to or unsure of work patterns and habits in the United States. Others adapted quickly and easily.

A rift sometimes developed between the older, established Cuban immigrant and the Mariel émigré. The former sometimes felt that the latter were insufficiently driven to succeed or grateful for the assistance received. This situation is similar to the relationship that had developed in the latter part of the nineteenth century between the established German American Jews and the new arrivals from Eastern Europe.

Mariel refugees have had a more difficult time adjusting to U.S. life than their predecessors for a variety of reasons. They arrived in the midst of a recessionary economic cycle, which made obtaining the first jobs more difficult. On average, they possessed fewer marketable skills than did their predecessors. A year after their arrival, 45,000 Mariel entrants were living below the official poverty line and committing suicide at a rate seven times the U.S. average (Kelly, 1981). Despite difficult economic conditions and homesickness at first, both rates diminished significantly in the years that followed.

The children who entered via Mariel also had to make major adjustments, as did the school systems that were to receive them. Writes Silva (1985): "In absolute numbers, the Dade County Public Schools faced integrating a school population larger than 95% of the school districts in the United States" (p. 23). The Dade County schools enrolled more than 11,500 Cuban refugee children in the 1980–1981 school year. Students were divided between two entrant facilities established exclusively for Mariel students, and the remaining students attended special programs in schools designated as entrant centers, as well as neighborhood schools.

Mariel Cubans often cite a lack of closeness and spirituality about life in the United States. Many centered their lives in Cuba around these qualities, which helped them endure hardships and privations. They see themselves as distinct from the older émigrés, some of whom they view as living in a frozen Cuban culture. This frozen culture is based solely on Cuban values, beliefs, and attitudes and all aspects of contemporary life are compared to this Cuban cultural baseline. These people exist as a subculture within a subculture. It will be interesting to see the degree to which Mariel Cubans will exhibit some of the characteristics of the older Cuban immigrants as time passes.

The process of assimilation has been most difficult for the elderly Cuban population. They represent an unusually high percentage of the exile population because older people faced fewer restrictions in trying to leave the island. This elderly population faced the usual problems of the aged, compounded by an environment to which many cannot adapt. For those whose families have strayed from traditional Cuban customs regarding the aged, they miss being the center of the family. Elderly persons living alone are found in larger-than-expected numbers in the Cuban American community. Many of the Cuban elderly who live in an extended family household provide the crucial day-care function that allows many Cuban women to join the labor force.

As might be expected, the Cuban American elderly are the least culturally assimilated segment of the Cuban community in the United States. Most speak minimal or no English and are thus limited from taking part in many facets of American life. Their children and grandchildren are often their link to the non-Cuban community. Some, though not most, of these people belong to what has been described as the "frozen culture."

News from relatives in Cuba keeps Cuban Americans of all ages aware of life in their former country. They feel deeply the difficulties and privations that loved ones may be experiencing, and they do whatever they can to help ameliorate the circumstances. In 1979, the Cuban government began to allow familial visits. Tens of thousands of Cubans in the United States returned to the island with suitcases bulging with clothes, food, and gifts for relatives. These visitors were described by the Cuban population as belonging to "the community." The stories of their lives in the United States were sometimes exaggerated, representing more affluence than truly existed, but it became evident to Cubans in Cuba that most visitors were not suffering the way the Cuban government had claimed. These visits brought badly-needed foreign exchange to Cuba; therefore, they were allowed to continue for quite some time.

Politically, Cuban Americans have been generally more conservative than most recently arrived immigrants. However, this conservatism should not be equated unequivocally with American conservatism. Cuban Americans are conservative on foreign policy issues, especially if those issues concern Cuba or communism. They tend to be considerably more moderate on domestic social issues.

In the Miami metropolitan area, Cubans are becoming an increasing portion of the electorate through naturalization. In the fall of 1981, Raul Martinez was elected mayor of Hialeah, Florida, thus becoming the first Cuban American mayor of a large U.S. city. Until 1982, no Cuban American had been elected to the state legislature of Florida, even though Cuban Americans comprised approximately one half of Miami's Dade County. In 1982, Florida changed from multimember to single-member legislative districts, and a number of Cuban Americans were elected to serve in the state house of representatives. The mid- and late 1980s saw Xavier Suarez elected mayor of Miami, followed by Joe Corollo; Cuban Americans were also elected to the Florida state senate. In 1989, Ileana Ros-Lehtinen was elected to the U.S. House of Representatives, becoming the first Cuban American member of Congress. She was joined by two fellow Cuban Americans, Lincoln Diaz-Balart of Miami and Robert Menendez of Union City, New Jersey, who were elected in 1991 and 1993 respectively. As more Cuban Americans become naturalized citizens and turn their attention to U.S. politics, their political participation and influence should grow proportionately.

The Second Generation

The Cuban American community now has a significant population that immigrated to the United States when they were young children or were born in the United States. This second generation represents a unique group of English-dominant bilingual persons who function well in both the Cuban American community and within mainstream society. They range approximately from age twenty to fifty and are found in nearly every walk of life.

They are sometimes referred to as YUCAS (young upwardly mobile Cuban Americans). The term has a double meaning because the yucca is a starchy root that Cubans frequently eat. The perspectives of this second generation are neither those of their parents nor of their American peers. One American-born young woman in her early twenties commented, "The Cubans consider me an American and the Americans consider me a Cuban." Another American-born young man observed, "I didn't realize how Cuban I was until I left South Florida for Boston to attend college." Many of these young people understand the anachronisms in Cuban American culture but are respectful of the persons who hold them.

Cuba is not a personal experience or memory for most of these people. They know of Cuba only from their parents' accounts, which typically grow fonder with each telling. It is thus understandable that most do not hold as strong an attachment for a place and a way of life that appears mythical.

Most of this second generation is fundamentally pragmatic. They are generally less politicized and conservative than their parents, but they still see themselves as culturally distinct. Their identity as Cuban Americans often does not include thinking of themselves as minority group members. They sometimes are surprised when they interact with other young Hispanics who identify with minority group status.

As a rule, the YUCAs see the perpetuation of the Spanish language through their own children as a desirable goal even if some of their own command of Spanish grammar is rudimentary. A study by Garcia and Diaz (1992) of language use among Hispanic (mostly Cuban American) high school seniors in Miami confirmed that most of the youth spoke English in formal and informal settings; Spanish predominated in familial settings. The one exception to this pattern was that English was used more than Spanish as the preferred language among siblings. The continued use of English among siblings suggests that the family setting is no longer the sole province of the Spanish language. Time will tell whether this generation of Cuban Americans will be able to pass on significant knowledge of Spanish to its children.

This group understands and respects the sacrifices and hardships that their parents faced as a consequence of immigration. However, they are generally not preoccupied with nostalgia. They seek the best in both cultures in order to carve out their own unique identity in U.S. society.

Cuban Americans Today

Cuban Americans represent an ethnic group that, while making economic, social, and cultural contributions to the United States, also seeks to maintain their cultural identity. In general, Cubans have adapted relatively well to American life.

Cuban Americans have had a relatively low degree of social disorganization and the amount of cultural assimilation has exceeded the degree of structural assimilation. Where large Cuban settlements occur, a great deal of the social and civic life still revolves around the ethnic community. In Miami, theaters show films in Spanish; the city has Hispanic civic clubs and a Latin Chamber of Commerce. Miami has become a de facto bilingual city.

This Latinization of Miami, while a boon to economic development with Latin America, has created a discernible backlash among a significant portion of the non-Latino community. In 1980, voters in Dade County (Miami) approved a local "anti-bilingual ordinance" barring the expenditure of county taxes to use or promote any language other than English. The same community owes much, if not most, of its economic viability to Latin American tourists and trade.

In 1989, Florida voters amended the state constitution to make English the state's official language. This amendment was overwhelmingly approved by an 84% vote of the electorate. Cuban Americans usually agree with other Hispanic groups that these efforts are lightly veiled attempts to limit the viability and options of Hispanic Americans. Cuban Americans, like their Mexican American and Puerto Rican counterparts, believe that it is imperative that people who choose to live in the United States should learn to speak English. It would be almost impossible to find an individual in the Cuban community who does not want his or her children taught English. However, many Cuban Americans regard English-only legislation as emblematic of coerced assimilation. Some feel that any pressure to assimilate implies they are not acceptable as they are.

Another language-related issue with significant support among Cuban Americans is bilingual education. Most feel that bilingual education is a necessary bridge for limited and non-English-speaking students to succeed in U.S. classrooms. Elimination of these programs would not find support among most Hispanics in this nation, including Cuban Americans. Concluded Baratz-Snowden, Rock, Pollack, and Wilder (1988), "Cuban Americans see learning of the non-English language as one of the three most important things that a child should learn at school" (p. 47).

The average Cuban immigrant has gone through a great psychological transition, the severity of which is strongly related to age at the time of leaving. Much trauma was involved. Many former professional men in Cuba had to begin in middle age as unskilled workers. This change required some mature adjustment in order to cope.

It would be conjecture to estimate how many Cubans would return to their native land if the Castro regime were replaced by a government more acceptable to them. Many have established roots in the United States that cannot be severed. Others would find the lure of a free Cuba irresistible, even though they might be well established in the United States.

Even though most Cuban Americans are opposed to any thaw in relations between the governments of Cuba and the United States, a growing number favor accommodation, particularly if it can help bring families together. The intellectual and academic Cuban American community tends to be more favorable to a less rigid policy toward Cuba than do blue-collar Cubans.

Today, Cuban Americans are the third largest Spanish-speaking group in the United States; Mexican Americans and Puerto Ricans rank first and second. The Cuban experience in the United States has been a complex one. However, Cuban Americans represent a largely beneficial addition to American society.

Teaching Strategies

CONCEPT

Immigration

Generalization: Many Cuban immigrants found themselves unable and/or unwilling to live with the Castro government and chose to leave their homeland instead.

1. Divide your class into small groups and instruct them as follows: Your family is forced to move to a country in which the language and customs are alien. Each of you is allowed to take only a small amount of clothes. All of your possessions are left behind and forfeited, because you cannot return. Describe what your life might be like where you are going. What clothing would you take with you? Why? How well do you think your family would fare? What adjustments would all of you have to make? The students' reactions can be taped or written. The taping would provide more spontaneous responses. Afterwards, compare and discuss reactions among groups.
2. After sufficient background information is presented, ask each student to write an essay titled, "If I Had Been a Cuban in 1959, What Would I Have Done?"
3. Organize a debate in which one side takes the position that deposing the Castro regime is feasible and the other feels it is impossible.
4. Read the following story to the class and ask the questions that follow.

The Pina Family

Ernesto Pina was a fisherman who lived in Cardenas, on the north coast of Cuba. He and his wife, Iliana, had never been wealthy, but fishing had always provided for the necessities of life. Ernesto always seemed to be able to return with fish of one type or another.

They had been happy to see the tyrant Batista deposed by the Castro revolution. Ernesto felt that Fidel Castro had the interests of the "little man" like himself at heart. One day when he returned to the fishery to sell his catch, Ernesto was informed that part of it would go to the government. Officials said that his fish would be exported and goods received in return would help the revolution. Ernesto did not want to be considered greedy, but he needed his entire catch to support his family. At the risk of being caught, he would hide some fish and sell them privately to his friends.

The family's only son, Jose, was sixteen and had been forced to join the militia. Neither parent liked this, but it could not be helped.

One night Ernesto and Iliana were talking and she suggested going to the United States. Yet, both knew that they could not depart legally, because Jose was of military age. Obviously, they could not leave their only son behind. So the three decided to try to escape in the fishing boat one night. They knew they would be shot in the water if discovered, but decided to take the risk anyway.

The eventful night came, and the Pina family slipped away from the harbor. Ernesto was sailing the craft because he did not want the noise of the engine to be heard. He had been quite careful to wait for the proper tide and a moonless night. After a short time, they heard an engine; the sound kept coming closer. It was the shore patrol! He lowered the sail quickly and they hid in the bottom of the boat. The patrol boat passed within fifty yards but had not spotted them. They had been saved by the darkness!

When morning came, Ernesto started his small engine because the breeze had faded. He hoped for the best because he did not have much gasoline. After two days at sea he was beginning to worry. His family was sunburned, he was out of gasoline, and he had not yet spotted the Florida coast. Yet, they kept their faith. They were lucky to be seen by a U.S. Coast Guard cutter, which towed them into port. As the three stepped off the boat onto American soil, they each said a prayer for having been so fortunate.

Questions

1. If you had been one of the Pina family and found yourself in their circumstances, would you have taken the risk they did? Why or why not?
2. What problems did Mr. Pina encounter that made him decide to leave Cuba?
3. Why didn't the Pina family attempt to leave Cuba by legal means?
4. What kind of future do you foresee for the Pina family in the United States?
5. Have each student (either in writing or orally) describe the circumstances of a political situation in the United States that would cause him or her to escape to a foreign nation, which would involve risking his or her life.

CONCEPT

Intergenerational Conflict

Generalization: The second generation of any immigrant group is going to absorb from the larger society values, beliefs, and priorities that are sometimes at odds with their parents' beliefs.

Read the following story to the class and ask the questions that follow.

The Rodriguez Family

Carlos Rodriguez is a young, successful professional person working in the Miami branch of a major American corporation. His wife, Maria, teaches in the public schools; their daughters, Gloria and Cecilia, are ages three and four.

Both Carlos and Maria's parents live within a twenty-minute drive. Maria's parents provide the much-needed day care for their granddaughters, and Carlos's parents are happy to substitute if needed. Most other family members who left Cuba are also living in the greater Miami area; family gatherings are frequent and well attended.

One day Carlos tells his wife of a possible promotion, which would involve moving to Minneapolis. Carlos can choose to accept the promotion or can stay in his current job.

Carlos and Maria informed their parents before deciding. As expected, both sets of parents were opposed to the family's moving. They pointed out that Carlos's and Maria's combined income enabled them to live comfortably and that in Minneapolis, the girls would be cared for by strangers and their contact with their grandparents would be limited. Maria's father also remarked that some things are more important than higher positions and more money, such as family.

Questions

1. What is the value system that is prompting the objections from the Rodriguez's grandparents?
2. How do the grandparents' values compare with the predominant values in U.S. society regarding advancement and mobility?
3. When you think of the term *family*, do you think of it as a nuclear or an extended family?
4. If you think Carlos and Maria should remain in Miami, give at least three reasons.
5. If you think the Rodriguez family should move to Minneapolis, give at least three reasons.

CONCEPT

Nativism
Generalization: A new group of immigrants arriving in the United States is likely to encounter rejection from some segments of the population.

The following is an example of letters to the editor that appeared in South Florida newspapers in response to the 1980 Mariel boatlift. Read the sample letter to the students and ask the questions that follow.

South Florida Saturated
As a citizen of South Florida for the past ten years, I strongly object to the masses of Cuban refugees being dumped on our shores. I am also distressed at the lack of response by national and state elected officials to stop this alien infusion.

We are having sluggish economic times and adequate housing is scarce for American citizens. How can we continue to be "nice guys" and accept more Cubans and Haitians. We already have enough!

We, the tax paying public of Florida, are being forced to subsidize these unwanted refugees that should either stay in their own country or go elsewhere. Included among these refugees are Castro's gifts of criminals, insane, and other undesirables.

I also understand that Cubans are training military groups on Florida soil. Why can't we prosecute these people? Meanwhile, many of our own Americans around the country need the assistance being given to these people we don't want.

Why can't we take care of our own first and forget about the headaches of other nations?

Name withheld by request

Questions

1. What facts does the letter's author use to substantiate his or her positions?
2. Compare the positions in the letter with the idea that the United States is the land of immigrants.
3. Do you agree or disagree with the author's positions? Which ones? Explain the reasons for your responses.
4. As a comparative exercise where library facilities permit, ask students to look for letters to the editor in major newspapers concerning immigration around 1910. Afterward, ask the students to compare reactions to immigration in 1910 to the letter above.

REFERENCES

Alpen, D. (1980, May 26). Carter and the Cuban influx. *Newsweek*, p. 25.

Baratz-Snowden, J., Rock, D., Pollack, J., & Wilder, G. (1988). *Parent Preference Study.* Princeton, NJ: Educational Testing Service.

Barberis, M. (1982). Hispanic America. (Editorial Research Reports), *Congressional Quarterly.* Washington, DC: U.S. Government Printing Office.

Diaz, W. (1984). *Hispanics: Challenges and Opportunities.* New York: Ford Foundation.

Fagen, R. R., Brody, R. A., & O'Leary, T. J. (1968). *Cubans in Exile.* Stanford, CA.: Stanford University Press.

Garcia, R. L., & Diaz, C. F. (1992). The Status and Use of Spanish and English among Hispanic Youth in Dade County (Miami), Florida. *Language and Education* 6,(1), 13–22.

Kelly, J. (1981, May 18). Closing the Golden Door. *Time*, p. 27.

Morin, R. (1980, May 11). Dade Fears Refugee Wave, Poll Shows. *Miami Herald*, p. 1.

New York Times. (1971, April 16), p. 4.

Olson, J. S., & Olson, J. E. (1995). *Cuban Americans: From Trauma to Triumph.* New York: Twayne.

Oppenheimer, A. (1985, August 25). Dade's Latins Feel a Separate Economy. *Miami Herald*, p. 1.

Pérez, L. (1980). Cubans. In S. Thernstrom, A. Orlov, & O. Handlin (Eds.), *Harvard Encyclopedia of American Ethnic Groups* (pp. 256–261). Cambridge: Harvard University Press.

Prohias, R. J., & Casal, L. (1973). *The Cuban Minority in the U.S. Cuban Minority Planning Study.* Boca Raton: Florida Atlantic University.

Richmond, M. L. (1980). *Immigrant Adaptation and Family Structure among Cubans in Miami, Florida.* New York: Arno Press.

Silva, H. (1985). *The Children of Mariel: Cuban Refugee Children in South Florida Schools.* Washington, DC: The Cuban American National Foundation.

U.S. Census Bureau. (2000). *Statistical Abstract of the United States, 2000.* Washington, DC: U.S. Government Printing Office.

U.S. Department of Commerce. (1993). *We, the American Hispanics,* Washington, DC: U.S. Government Printing Office.

U.S. Immigration and Naturalization Service (2000). *Statistical Yearbook of the Immigration and Naturalization Service, 1998.* Washington, DC: U.S. Government Printing Office.

A N N O T A T E D   B I B L I O G R A P H Y

Books for Teachers

Especially Recommended

Boswell, T. D., & Curtis, J. R. (1984). *The Cuban-American Experience: Culture, Images and Perspectives.* Totowa, NJ: Rowman and Allanheld.

This is a useful source for understanding the cultural adjustments Cuban immigrants have made in the United States.

García, M. C. (1994). Cuban women in the United States. In A. Jiménez (Ed.), *Handbook of Hispanic Cultures in the United States* (pp. 203–217). Houston: Arte Público Press.

An informative and comprehensive overview of the experiences of Cuban American women.

Garcia, M. C. (1996). *Havana USA: Cuban Exiles and Cuban Americans in South Florida, 1959–1994.* Berkeley: University of California Press.

An excellent and well-documented source about the major trends in the Cuban American community of Miami, Florida.

Olson, J. S., & Olson, J. E. (1995). *Cuban Americans: From Trauma to Triumph.* New York: Twayne.

This book provides a comprehensive discussion of Cuba and the migration and settlement of Cuban Americans in the United States. It includes chapters on the Mariel Cubans and on the status of Cuban Americans in 1995.

O'Reilly Herrera, A. (2001). *Remembering Cuba: Legacy of a Diaspora.* Austin: University of Texas Press.

This collection of short essays is organized around a series of themes such as "Crossing the Generational Divide" and "the Culture Wars." The authenticity of these essays provides an excellent snapshot of the Cuban immigrant experience.

Poyo, G. E., & Díaz-Miranda, M. (1994). Cubans in the United States. In A. Jiménez (Ed.), *Handbook of Hispanic Cultures in the United States* (pp. 301–320). Houston: Arte Público Press.

Cuban immigration, Cuban communities in the United States, and Cuban women and Cubans of color are among the topics in this informative historical overview of the Cuban American saga. Includes a helpful bibliography.

Other References

Alpern, D., et al. (1980, May 26). Carter and the Cuban Influx. *Newsweek,* pp. 22–31.

This article describes immigration policy during the 1980 Mariel boatlift.

Cortés, C. E. (Ed.). (1980). *Cuban Exiles in the United States.* New York: Arno Press.

A series of articles written in the early 1970s that discuss mostly the occupational adaptation of Cubans in the United States.

Fagan, R. R., Brody, R. A., & O'Leary, T. J. (1968). *Cubans in Exile*. Stanford, CA: Stanford University Press.

This is a major published source on Cubans in Miami, Florida, and their reasons for leaving Cuba. It is complete with demographic information on the Cuban exodus.

Fox, G. E. (1979). *Working-Class Émigrés from Cuba*. Palo Alto, CA: R. E. Research Associates.

This sociological study examines the attitudes toward many aspects of life in Cuba of recently arrived blue-collar Cubans in the Chicago area.

Grillo, E. (2000). *Black Cuban, Black American*. Houston, TX: Arte Público Press.

Grillo's memoir discusses his life in Ybor City (Tampa), Florida, in the 1920s, '30s, and '40s, and navigating the cultural norms of the Cuban, African American, and White communities.

Hernandez, A. (Ed.). (1980). *The Cuban Minority in the U.S.* (Vol. 2). New York: Arno Press.

This is a continuation of the 1973 Prohias study concentrating on educational and occupational mobility and the needs and problems of Cuban American youth and the elderly population.

Jaffe, A. J., Cullen, R., & Boswell, T. (1980). *The Changing Demography of Spanish Americans*. New York: Academic Press.

This source covers all Hispanic groups in the United States. It contains an excellent chapter on the education, demographics, and other variables of the Cuban American population.

Kelly, J. (1981, May 18). Closing the Golden Door. *Time*, pp. 4–27.

This article discusses efforts to stem the tide of immigration. It contains an interesting excerpt on Cubans who have been imprisoned since they arrived on the Mariel boatlift in 1980.

Linehan, E. J. (1973, July). Cuba's Exiles Bring New Life to Miami. *National Geographic, 144,* 68–95.

This is an excellent article with many photographs and a good source for students to peruse.

Mackey, W. R., & Beebe, V. N. (1977). *Bilingual Schools for a Bicultural Community*. Rowley, MA: Newburg House.

This work examines a variety of models used in bilingual education in Miami to accommodate students arriving from Cuba.

Masud-Piloto, R. (1988). *With Open Arms: Cuban Migration to the United States*. Totowa, NJ: Rowman and Littlefield.

This book focuses on the Cuban migration from 1959 to 1980. The author suggests that humanitarian concerns of either the United States or Cuba had little to do with migration. Rather, refugees became the prime weapon in the political war between the two nations.

Mindel, C. H., Habenstein, R. W., & Wright, R., Jr. (Eds.). (1988). *Ethnic Families in America: Patterns and Variations* (3rd ed.). New York: Elsevier.

The chapter on the Cuban American family contributed by Jose Szapocznik and Roberto Hernandez contains an insightful section explaining the West African and Iberian influences on the Cuban character and family life.

Oppenheimer, A. (1985, August 25). Dade's Latins Feel a Separate Economy. *Miami Herald*, p. 1.

This newspaper article provides valuable statistics to document the size and importance of the Latin (mostly Cuban) component of the economy in Miami, Florida.

Pérez Firmat, G. (1995). *Next Year in Cuba*. New York: Anchor Books/Doubleday.

This book was authored by someone who came to the United States as a child. He grew up in Little Havana and left South Florida to become an academic. This book chronicles that journey.

Poyo, G. E. (1989). *With All and for the Good of All: The Emergence of Popular Nationalism in the Cuban Communities of the United States, 1848–1898*. Durham, NC: Duke University Press.

> *An excellent source for teachers interested in examining the long-established Cuban communities in the United States. The author examines the connection between these communities and the struggle for independence in Cuba.*

Richmond, M. L. (1980). *Immigrant Adaptation and Family Structure among Cubans in Miami, Florida*. New York: Arno Press.

> *This reprint of a 1974 doctoral dissertation provides the reader with considerable information on how the immigration experience affected the Cuban family.*

Silva, H. (1985). *The Children of Mariel: Cuban Refugee Children in South Florida Schools*. Washington, DC: The Cuban American National Foundation.

> *This report examines the programs established by the Miami (Dade County) school system to cope with an immediate influx of more than 15,000 non-English-speaking students. Statistics abound to document funding and the nature of the academic programs offered through 1982.*

Szapocznik, J., Cohen, R., & Hernandez, R. (Eds.). (1985). *Coping with Adolescent Refugees: The Mariel Boatlift*. New York: Praeger.

> *This source emphasizes the psychological adaptation of young Mariel refugees, particularly in the internment camps. A mental health perspective is taken in this work.*

Valdivieso, R., & Davis, C. (1988). *U.S. Hispanics: Challenging Issues for the 1990s*. Washington, DC: Population Reference Bureau.

> *This source analyzes trends affecting the Hispanic community now and in the future. Cuban Americans are contrasted with other Hispanic groups in such areas as education, income, political trends, and use of the Spanish language.*

Weyr, T. (1988). *Hispanic U.S.A.* New York: Harper and Row.

> *This source contains information about Cuban American immigration, education, politics, and economic position interwoven with similar data concerning other Hispanic groups.*

Books for Students

Ada, A. F. (1998). *Under the Royal Palms: A Childhood in Cuba*. New York: Atheneum.

> *The Cuban-born author describes her childhood in Cuba in the 1940s by means of the many colorful individuals who passed through her life. Winner of the 2000 Pura Belpré award for writing. (Intermediate/Middle School)*

Bernardo, A. (1996). *Fitting In*. Houston, TX: Piñata Books.

> *Five short stories portray issues of identity, assimilation, family relationships, and friendships among Cuban American teenagers living in Miami. (Middle School)*

Boza, M. (1998) *Scattering the Ashes*. Tempe, AZ: Bilingual Review Press.

> *For mature readers, this memoir describes the isolation and homesickness that led Boza's father, an influential Cuban journalist before the Revolution and a popular exile writer in Miami afterward, to take his own life in 1989. (High School)*

Caseley, J. (2000). *Praying to A. L.* New York: HarperCollins.

> *The culturally diverse relatives of a girl of mixed Cuban American and Jewish American background help her to cope with the long illness and death of her father. (Middle School)*

Condé, Y. (1999). *Operation Pedro Pan: The Untold Exodus of 14,048 Cuban Children.* New York: Routledge.

A powerfully presented history of the evacuation of thousands of children to the United States after Castro's victory, written by one of those who experienced firsthand the separation from her parents and the dislocations of a new language and culture. (High School)

Figueredo, D. H. (1999). *When This World Was New.* Illustrated by E. O. Sanchez. New York: Lee & Low.

A boy immigrates with his parents from his warm green island in the Caribbean to a wintry northern city where he sees snow for the first time. Based on the Cuban American author's own experiences as an immigrant in the 1960s. (Primary)

García, P. (1997). *From Amigos to Friends.* Houston, TX: Piñata Books.

Three friends from diverse class backgrounds in Cuba are separated by the Revolution; two end up in Miami but follow separate paths. (Middle School/High School)

Hoobler, D., & Hoobler, T. (1995). *The Cuban American Family Album.* New York: Oxford University Press.

This informative, interesting, and well-illustrated book includes photographs and other primary resources. (Intermediate and Up)

Méndez, A. (1994). *Cubans in America.* Minneapolis: Lerner.

This informative book describes the historical background of Cuban Americans in Cuba as well as their experiences in the United States. It is well illustrated with black-and-white photographs. (Intermediate and Up)

Muñoz, E. M. (1998). *Brand New Memory.* Houston, TX: Arte Público.

An assimilated Cuban American teenager learns about family, heritage, love, and loss when her grandmother comes from Cuba for a visit. (High School)

Rivera, B. (1997). *Midnight Sandwiches on the Mariposa Express.* Houston, TX: Arte Público.

Older teens will enjoy this entertaining tale of life and politics in a small New Jersey city dominated by recent Cuban American immigrants. (High School)

Suárez, V. (1997). *Spared Angola: Memories from a Cuban-American Childhood.* Houston, TX: Arte Público.

The acclaimed novelist describes growing up in Cuba in a family opposed to the Revolution, his years in exile in Spain, and his arrival in Los Angeles as a young teenager unable to speak English or to fit into the tough barrio culture. (High School)

PART FIVE

Asian Americans and Arab Americans

Concepts and Strategies

This part consists of content, concepts, teaching strategies and materials for teaching about Asian Americans and Arab Americans. Although different in many ways, these groups also share similarities. First, each term—*Asian American* and *Arab American*—describes diverse groups that differ in many significant ways. The Japanese are very different from the Hmong, just as the Iranians and the Lebanese differ in important ways. Second, Edward Said (1978) describes how the Europeans constructed the idea of *Orientalism* to refer to peoples in Asia as well as in the Middle East. Writes Said:

> Taking the late eighteenth century as a very roughly defined starting point Orientalism can be discussed and analyzed as the corporate institution for dealing with the Orient—dealing with it by making statements about it, authorizing views of it, describing it, by teaching it, settling it, ruling over it: in short, Orientalism as a Western style for dominating, restructuring, and having authority over the Orient (p. 3).

He continues: "In brief, because of Orientalism the Orient was not (and is not) a free subject of thought and action" (p. 3).

When teaching about Asian Americans and Arab Americans, teachers can use Said's concept of Orientalism to help students examine the ways in which this concept was used historically and is being used today to construct ideas of the Japanese, the Chinese, the Iranians, and the Lebanese as "different." By having students examine and deconstruct images of Asian Americans and Arab Americans that are widespread within the popular media and the wider society, teachers can help students understand the ways in which the concept of Orientalism still functions in Western societies and why its destructive power needs to be questioned and replaced with transformative, multicultural knowledge.

R E F E R E N C E

Said, E. (1978). *Orientalism.* New York: Vintage Books.

13 Asian Americans

Concepts, Strategies, and Materials

In America, Asian immigrants and their offspring have been actors in history.... Their dreams and hopes unfurled here before the wind, all of them—from the first Chinese miners sailing through the Golden Gate to the last Vietnamese boat people flying into Los Angeles International Airport—have been making history in America.

—Ronald Takaki

This chapter consists of content, concepts, teaching strategies, and materials for teaching about three of the oldest Asian groups in the United States, the Chinese Americans, Japanese Americans, and Filipino Americans.

Asian Americans, one of the most diverse and interesting ethnic groups in the United States, are rarely studied in the elementary and high school grades. When discussed in textbooks and in the popular media, they are often used to illustrate how an ethnic group of color can succeed in the United States. Because of their tremendous educational, occupational, and economic success, Asian Americans are often called the *model minority* in the popular media. It is true that some Asian American groups are better educated, have a higher occupational status, and earn more money than other Americans, including White Americans. However, the model minority concept is problematic for several reasons.

Problems with the Model Minority Concept

A focus on the economic success of Asian Americans results in several problems. It obscures the tremendous economic diversity within Asian American communities and the problems Asians have. When we look only at the group characteristics of Chinese Americans, for example, the serious economic problems of the new immigrants are overlooked. In 1990, about 42% of the Chinese immigrants had menial service, low-skilled, and blue-collar jobs. About 52% had managerial and technical jobs (U.S. Bureau of the Census, 1993a). Takaki (1998) has called the unskilled Chinese immigrant workers "a colonized labor force" (1989, p. 425). Many Chinese immigrant women work as seamstresses in San Francisco and in New York for long hours at very low wages. The model minority concept also obscures the stories of successful members of other ethnic groups, such as upwardly mobile African Americans and Hispanics. Finally, when overly emphasized, the model minority argument can divert attention from the racism that Asian Americans and other people of color in the United States still experience (Takaki, 1998). Daniels (1988) states that diverting attention from racism was one intent of William Petersen (1966), the writer who first used the concept of *the model minority* in a *New York Times Magazine* article.

Rapid Increases in the Asian American Population

Asian Americans increased 41% between 1990 and 2000, from 7.2 million to 10.2 million, compared to a 58% increase for Hispanics, 16% for African Americans and 11.6% for the total U.S. population (U.S. Census Bureau, 2001). The number of Asians immigrating to the United States has increased substantially since the Immigration Reform Act became effective in 1968. Five Asian nations—China, India, the Philippines, Vietnam, and Korea—were among the top twelve nations from which immigrants came to the United States in 1998 (U.S. Census Bureau, 2000). Table 13.1 shows the number of immigrants to the United States from 1981 to 1998 from selected Asian nations.

The United States now has a sizable population of Vietnamese Americans (1,122,528), which increased by 45% between 1990 and 2000. After U.S. participation in the Vietnam War ended (1973) and Communists took control of that nation (1975), thousands of Vietnamese refugees rushed to the United States. Only 226 Vietnamese immigrated to the United States in 1965, but more than 87,000 came to the United States in 1978. Between 1981 and 1998, 775,300 Vietnamese immigrants settled in the United States (see Table 13.1).

The number of Chinese immigrants settling in the United States from China and Hong Kong has also increased substantially since 1965. In 1965, for example, 4,769 immigrants from China settled in the United States. Between 1981 and 1998, however, 735,500 immigrants entered the United States from China and 126,800 from Hong Kong (see Table 13.1) (U.S. Census Bureau, 2000).

TABLE 13.1   Asian Immigrants to the United States from
Selected Nations: 1981–1998

Country of Birth	Total	Percentage of Asian Immigration
Philippines	927,400	17.7
Vietnam	775,300	14.8
China*	735,500	14.0
India	573,000	10.9
Korea	481,400	9.2
Iran	251,700	4.8
Laos	186,900	3.6
Pakistan	157,900	3.0
Cambodia	131,500	2.5
Hong Kong	126,800	2.4
Thailand	106,700	2.0
Japan	93,300	1.8
Taiwan**	90,600	1.7

*Data for Taiwan included with China for 1981–90.
** Immigration for the years 1991–1998.

Source: U.S. Census Bureau (2000). Statistical Abstract of the United States (120th ed.). Washington, DC: U.S. Government Printing Office.

The Chinese—with a population of 2.4 million in 2000—remained the largest Asian American population. However, Asian Indians outgrew all of the other Asian populations; they increased 51% between 1990 and 2000, from 815,000 to 1, 678,765. The demand for highly-skilled workers in the United States and the lack of ample high-tech jobs in India were major reasons for the rapid increase in the Asian Indian population.

Korean Americans

The number of Koreans and Asian Indian immigrants to the United States has also increased tremendously since the Immigration Act of 1965 became effective in 1968. The Korean American population increased from 10,000 in 1960 to about one-half million in 1985 (Takaki, 1998). The first Koreans who came to the United States arrived in 1885. Later, between 1890 and 1905, 64 Korean students came to study in the United States (Kim, 1980). A significant number of Koreans were recruited to work in the sugar plantations in Hawaii in the early 1900s. However, few Korean immigrants settled in the United States until the 1970s. Only 6,231 Koreans immigrated to the United States between 1951 and 1960 and 34,526 between 1961 and 1970 (U.S. Immigration and Naturalization Service, 1985). However, 481,400 immigrated to the United States between 1981 and 1998.

Koreans are one of the largest immigrant groups settling in the United States. Like the new immigrants from the Philippines, many of the new Korean immigrants are college-educated professionals. In 1990, immigrants from Korea had one of the highest percentages of a population holding a bachelor's degree or higher, 34.4%, compared to 23.1% for immigrants from the United Kingdom, 19.1% for immigrants from Germany, and 43% for immigrants from the Philippines (U.S. Bureau of the Census, 1993a).

Asian Indian and Pakistani Immigrants

Only a small number of immigrants from India settled in the United States prior to 1965. A total of about 130,000 came during the period between 1820 and 1976 (Takaki, 1998). Most of the immigrants who came during the nineteenth century were professionals, adventurers, merchants, and monks (Jensen, 1980). A few thousand agricultural workers came to California between 1904 and 1923. Only 1,973 immigrants from India came to the United States between 1951 and 1960; 31,200 immigrated to the United States between 1961 and 1979 (U.S. Immigration and Naturalization Service, 1985).

Since 1971, immigrants from India have been entering the United States in substantial numbers. About 573,000 Indian immigrants settled in the United States between 1981 and 1998. A significant number of immigrants from Pakistan have also entered the United States since 1960. About 157,900 Pakistani immigrants settled in the United States between 1981 and 1998.

The U.S. Census indicates that 1.7 million Asian Indians were living in the United States in 2000. In 1990, large numbers were concentrated in northeastern states, including New Hampshire (79,440) and Massachusetts (23,845). However, they were spread throughout the United States: for example, 159,973 lived in California, and 20,848 lived in Ohio (U.S. Bureau of the Census, 1993b). Asian Indians are English speaking and are a highly educated group. Among the immigrants are a large number of engineers, scientists, physicians, dentists, and other professionals. Like the new Filipino immigrants, they are settling in the United States primarily because of the paucity of professional job opportunities in their native land and the need for highly skilled workers in the United States.

Southeast Asian Americans

The Southeast Asians who have settled in the United States have come from three contiguous nations, Vietnam, Kampuchea (Cambodia), and Laos. The Europeans referred to this area as *Indochina* because it had been historically influenced by India and China. The Southeast Asian Americans consist of Vietnamese, Laotian, Cambodian (Kumpucheans), Hmong, and ethnic Chinese refugees who fled to the United States in the aftermath of the Vietnamese War. In the decade before 1975, only about 20,000 Vietnamese immigrated to the United States (Wright, 1989). It is not known how many immigrants came from Laos and Kampuchea (Cambodia) during this period. The first refugees from Southeast Asia fled to the United States in 1975. Their journey to the United States was directly related to the ending of the Vietnam War and the resulting communist governments in Vietnam, Laos, and Kampuchea.

The Southeast Asians, like the Cuban refugees from 1959 to 1962, sought refuge in the United States when communist governments came to power in their homelands. A large number of Southeast Asian refugees were resettled in the United States between mid-May 1975 and December 31, 1978. This was one of the largest emergency resettlement programs in the nation's history.

The number of Vietnamese, Laotians, and Kampucheans in the United States grew significantly between 1981 and 1998. Vietnam was one of the ten nations that sent the most legal immigrants to the United States during this period. More than one million (1,093,700) immigrants from Vietnam, Laos, and Kampuchea settled in the United States between 1981 and 1998 (see Table 13.1). Most of these immigrants (71%) came from Vietnam.

The Vietnamese population in the United States is one of the nation's fasting growing populations. There were about 615,000 Vietnamese living in the United States in 1990 and 1,122,528 in 2000, a 45% increase within this ten-year period. A number of developments have contributed to the rapid growth in the Indochinese population in the United States. Indochinese refugees continued to come to the United States from refugee camps in Southeast Asia between 1981 and 1989. Many Vietnamese, including Amerasian children (children of American fathers and Vietnamese mothers) and their close relatives have been permitted to immigrate to the United States by federal policies designed to facilitate family reunification. About 10,000 Amerasian children were scheduled for resettlement in the United States in 1989.

The Southeast Asians came to the United States for many different reasons. Singular political, economic, or personal concerns motivated some of the refugees to leave their homeland. Others were motivated by many factors. Many of the Southeast Asian refugees had been directly touched by the trauma of the Vietnam War (1954–1975) or its aftermath. The Southeast Asians left their nations as refugees and are now in the process of becoming Americans.

Asian Americans: A Diverse Group

Asian Americans are one of the most highly diversified ethnic groups in the United States. They vary greatly in both cultural and physical characteristics. The attitudes, values, and ethnic institutions often differ within Japanese

American, Chinese American, Filipino American, and Asian Indian communities. However, the first waves of Chinese, Japanese, and Filipino immigrants had some parallel experiences in the United States. For example, their immigration began when there was a need for cheap labor, but they were harassed and demeaned, and eventually immigration laws were passed to exclude them. After the Chinese Exclusion Act was passed in 1882, there was still a desire for cheap laborers in Hawaii and California. Consequently, Japanese immigrants began arriving in California in significant numbers in the 1890s. When the Gentlemen's Agreement of 1908 and the Immigration Act of 1924 halted Japanese immigration, California farmers imported Filipinos from Hawaii and the Philippines to work in the fields. Anti-Filipino forces emerged on the West Coast and culminated in 1934, when Congress limited Filipino immigration to fifty people per year. This quota constituted, in effect, the virtual exclusion of Filipino immigrants.

Because of their tremendous diversity, similarities, and unique experiences in the United States, the study of Asian Americans can help students increase their ethnic literacy and develop a respect for cultural differences. Table 13.2 shows the percentage distribution of the Asian American population for selected groups in 2000.

The Chinese, Japanese, and Filipino Americans: Overview

This section of this chapter discusses content, concepts, strategies, and materials for teaching about the three Asian American groups that have lived in the United

TABLE 13.2   Resident Population of Asian Americans: 2000

Country of Birth	Population	Percentage of Asian Population
Chinese	2,432,585	23.7
Filipino	1,850,314	18.1
Asian Indian	1,678,765	16.4
Other Asian*	1,285,234	12.5
Vietnamese	1,122,528	11.0
Korean	1,076,872	10.5
Japanese	796,700	7.8

*Other Asian alone, or two or more Asian categories.

Source: U.S. Census Bureau (2000). *Statistical Abstract of the United States* (120th ed.). Washington, DC: U.S. Government Printing Office.

States the longest: the Chinese Americans, Japanese Americans, and Filipino Americans. These groups have important similarities as well as differences. Each group that came to the United States sought the American dream, satisfied important labor needs, and became victims of an anti-Asian movement designed to prevent their further immigration to the United States. Chinese Americans, Japanese Americans, and Filipino Americans have also experienced tremendous economic, educational, and social mobility and success in U.S. society.

The number of Chinese, Japanese, and Filipino immigrants that settled in the United States between 1951 and 1960 was small compared to the numbers from Europe. However, the number of immigrants to the United States from China and the Philippines has increased enormously since the Immigration Reform Act of 1965 became effective in 1968. The number of Japanese immigrating to the United States since 1968 has remained moderate. Between 1951 and 1960, 19,300 immigrants from the Philippines and 25,200 from China and Hong Kong settled in the United States. Between 1981 and 1998 the numbers were 927,400 from the Philippines, 126,800 from Hong Kong, and 735,500 from China (see Table 13.1).

As a result of the increasing number of immigrants from China, Hong Kong, and the Philippines, as well as from other Asian nations, the Japanese are becoming an increasingly smaller percentage of the Asian American population. In 1970, Japanese Americans were the largest Asian American group, followed by the Chinese and the Filipinos. By 2000, however, the Japanese were one of the smallest Asian American group, exceeded in size by the Chinese, Filipinos, Asian Indians, Vietnamese, and Koreans. The Japanese were the only one of these groups with a population of less than one million (see Table 13.2).

The story of the Chinese, Japanese, and Filipinos in the United States has been largely one of success, if we measure success by the educational, income, and occupational levels these groups have attained. They have achieved tremendous educational, income, and occupational success even though they have historically been the victims of racism and discrimination and are still often the victims of subtle discrimination. The stories of the Chinese, Japanese, and Filipinos in the United States can help students understand how the American dream can be pursued and attained. However, when these groups are studied, the problems that Asian Americans still face in U.S. society, such as cultural conflict, identity, and attaining a balance between their ethnic cultures and the mainstream culture, should not be glossed over. The poverty that exists in many Asian American communities, especially in urban ethnic communities, where newly arrived immigrants settle in large numbers, should also be studied.

When studying about Asians in the United States, students should examine and analyze the new wave of racism that has been directed against Asian Americans and Arab Americans. This new wave of racism, which emerged in the 1980s, has been expressed in a number of ways, including ugly racial incidents on college campuses. The rising number of Asian students at some of the nation's most prestigious colleges and universities has evoked comments that some Asians have interpreted as a call for restrictive quotas. In 2001, Asian Americans made up 24% of the undergraduate and 13% of the graduate students at Stanford, 30% of the total student body at the University of California at Berkeley, and 12% of the total student body at Harvard.

Many Americans, particularly unemployed auto workers, blame Japan for the stiff competition from Japanese car manufacturers. This hostility has sometimes been directed at Japanese Americans because some Americans do not distinguish Japanese nationals and Japanese Americans. This hostility has taken diverse forms, including bumper stickers that read, "Unemployment—Made in Japan" and statements such as "Auto unemployment is an economic Pearl Harbor" (Daniels, 1988, p. 342). An odious incident occurred on June 19, 1982: an unemployed auto worker, Ronald Ebens, and his stepson beat Vincent Chin to death in a Detroit suburb. Ebens thought Chin was a Japanese American. Despite their success—and sometimes because of it—Asian Americans are still victims of racism and discrimination. Some Americans still consider Asian Americans "strangers from a different shore" (Takaki, 1998).

Chinese Americans

The Immigration

When the news reached the Guandong Province in southeast China that there was a "Golden Mountain" across the Pacific, a number of young men violated both Chinese law and tradition and headed for the promised land. The decision to leave China for a foreign land was a serious one because it was illegal to immigrate and violators could be severely punished. Also, Confucian doctrine, an integral part of Chinese life during this period, taught that a young man should value his family above all else and, thus, should not leave it. However, both the promises of the land of the Mountain of Gold and the severe living conditions in the Toishan district in Guandong, from which most of the first Chinese immigrants hailed, helped push the young immigrants across the Pacific.

Political upheaval, famine, local warfare, excessive taxes, a severely depressed economy, and a rugged terrain in Toishan inimical to farming motivated young Chinese males to seek better opportunities in an unknown land where, according to a pervasive myth, one could easily strike gold and return to China a rich man. Most of the Chinese who headed for California were young married men. They were self-proclaimed "sojourners" who intended to earn their fortunes in the United States and return to their families in China. Because of tradition and the rough voyage across the Pacific, their families were left behind.

The journey across the Pacific was rugged and hazardous. On their arrival in California, the Chinese immigrants experienced a rude awakening. Although

CHINESE AMERICANS: HISTORICAL PERSPECTIVE

Important Dates	Events
1850	The U.S. Census showed 450 Chinese immigrants in the United States. This number increased to 34,933 in 1860. The California legislature passed a discriminatory Foreign Miner's Tax, which forced Chinese immigrants to pay a highly disproportionate share of the state taxes.
1859	Authorities in the Guangdong Province legalized the recruitment of Chinese laborers.
1882	The Chinese Exclusion Act was enacted by Congress. It stopped the immigration of Chinese laborers for ten years.
1974	The U.S. Supreme Court ruled in *Lau* v. *Nichols* that the San Francisco Unified School District was denying Chinese American students who did not speak English "a meaningful opportunity to participate in the public educational program." This ruling by the high court established a legal basis for bilingual educational programs. Such programs were later established in various parts of the nation.
1980	The U.S. Census indicated that the Chinese were one of the largest groups that immigrated to the United States between 1970 and 1980. The percentage of Chinese in the United States increased 88% between 1970 and 1980, compared to 11% for the total population and 6% for Whites.
1982	Vincent Chin was beaten to death in a Detroit suburb by an unemployed auto worker and his stepson. Ronald Ebens, the unemployed auto worker, thought Chin was of Japanese descent.
1992	More than 49,000 immigrants from China and Hong Kong entered the United States, which made the Chinese the second largest Asian group immigrating to the United States. The Filipinos were the largest immigrating Asian group.
2000	The 2000 Census indicated that Chinese Americans were the largest group of Asian Americans, with a population of 2,432,585.

White Americans expressed little overt hostility toward the Chinese when they first started immigrating to the West Coast in substantial numbers in the 1850s, they considered them exotic, strange people. Whites thought that the Chinese were strange because of their traditional Chinese clothing, language, queue hairstyle (which Whites called pigtails), and skin color. Almost from the beginning, the Chinese were the victims of curiosity and racism. Writes Melendy (1972): "From almost the first moment the Chinese landed in San Francisco in the 1850s, they were subjected to harsh treatment. The aim was to exclude them from the United States because of basically *racist* fears and beliefs" (p. 20; emphasis added).

Labor.   In addition to receiving a curious and strange welcome from Californians, the Chinese immigrants found that the mines in which they had to dig for gold had already been thoroughly gone over by White gold diggers. They had to dig for the scraps. However, some Chinese immigrants managed to secure respectable sums of money by remining White claims.

When Congress decided to build a railroad linking the Missouri River to the Pacific Coast in 1862, the Central Pacific issued a call for men to build the western portion of the railroad. Because of the back-breaking work involved in building a railroad over the rugged Western terrain, few Whites would take the work. But the Chinese took up the challenge and almost single-handedly built the Pacific portion of the transcontinental railroad. While the nation celebrated the completion of the railroad on May 10, 1869, 25,000 laborers, most of them Chinese, lost their jobs.

It was not easy for the Chinese immigrants to save money because of the large debts they had incurred when they arranged to come to California. Most of them came to the United States through a credit-ticket system, which was similar to the indenture system used to bring many European immigrants to North America. In this system, a moneyless Chinese man could borrow money from a relative or fellow villager to pay for his passage to California. Chinese organizations, such as the Hui Kuan or Landsmanner, collected the money from the immigrant and sent it to the individuals from whom it was borrowed.

The leaders of the Hui Kuan also provided the immigrants with a place to eat and sleep on their arrival in San Francisco and sent groups of them to work in the mines. Before the worker received his wages, the amount he owed for his passage was deducted. Because of the credit-ticket system, some immigrants ended up worse off financially than they had been before they came to California. Some found that their return to China was indefinitely delayed. What at first promised to be a nation of gold turned out, for many, to be a land of disillusionment and shattered dreams. Writes Melendy (1972): "The Chinese existed at a poverty level, receiving low wages for their work. Even so, they gained materially a bit more than they had in China. The dream of coming to the Golden Mountain to make a fortune and return home still seemed possible to most. For many, however, this was the impossible dream" (p. 20).

Despite the difficulties the Chinese immigrants experienced, many were able to find enough work in a wide range of occupations that most Whites found unpalatable, such as domestic work, work on railroads, and intensive farming, to save enough money to return to China to visit their families and to father children, hopefully sons. The immigrants who returned to China usually told about the promises of California but said little about its difficulties. Also, the home folks were impressed with what seemed like sizable sums of money the sojourners brought back to China. As the news about the Mountain of Gold spread, and immigrants returned home with money or sent money home to their families, the number of Chinese immigrating to California rose tremendously.

Anti-Chinese Agitation

According to the 1860 census, there were 34,933 Chinese in the United States. By 1880, that number had risen to 105,465. Although the increase was sizable, there were still few Chinese immigrating to the United States compared to the number of European immigrants. Between 1820 and 1930, 38 million immigrants entered the United States, mostly from Europe. However, many Whites became alarmed at the number of Chinese entering the United States, and a vicious movement developed to keep them out. Although leaders of the anti-Chinese movement claimed that the Chinese could not be assimilated and that they competed unfairly with Whites on the labor market, racism was one of the main forces behind the anti-Chinese movement. As Saxton (cited in Melendy, 1972) has pointed out, "The Chinese inherited the long-standing hostility of Whites against people of color, particularly Blacks. White Californians, conditioned to the notion that Blacks were inferior persons and servile workers, easily transferred these perceptions to the Chinese" (p. 18).

Led by Dennis Kearney and the California Workingmen's party, "The Chinese Must Go" became the rallying cry of the anti-Chinese movement. Leaders of all types joined in the movement to push the Chinese out of the West. Labor leaders were among the most staunch anti-Chinese advocates. Politicians jumped on the bandwagon in order to gain votes. As the hostility against the Chinese mounted, they became increasingly defenseless. Unlike the Japanese, they did not have a strong nation that could threaten the balance of world power when its citizens in the United States were ill treated.

The anti-Chinese movement spread as the Chinese moved to such states as Washington, Oregon, Colorado, and Wyoming. Anti-Chinese activities took the form of racist newspaper stories; violent attacks against defenseless men, women, and children; and highly discriminatory laws aimed particularly at the Chinese, such as the Queues Ordinance, the Laundry Ordinance, and the 1876 Cubic Air Law. One of the most blatantly discriminatory laws was the Foreign Miner's Tax passed by the California legislature in 1850. Applied most effectively against the Chinese, it forced them to pay a highly disproportionate share of the taxes collected under the law. Taxes paid by the Chinese largely financed the California state and county governments during this period (Chun-Hoon, 1973). The movement to ban the immigration of Chinese culminated with the passage of the Immigration Act of 1882. This bill stopped the immigration of Chinese laborers for a period of ten years. A victory for the anti-Chinese leaders, it was followed by a series of similar bills that drastically reduced Chinese immigration for decades. The number of Chinese entering the United States dwindled from 39,579 in 1882 to 472 in 1893.

Violence and Riots.   Violence directed against the Chinese was widespread in the late 1880s. An anti-Chinese riot occurred in San Francisco as early as 1869. A White mob in Los Angeles attacked a Chinese community in 1871. When the conflict ended, nineteen Chinese Americans had been killed and their community was in shambles. Another anti-Chinese riot exploded in Denver, Colorado, in 1880. One Chinese was killed and most of the homes in the Chinese community were wrecked during the riot. A serious anti-Chinese riot occurred in Rock Springs, Wyoming, in 1885. Twenty-eight Chinese were killed, fifteen were wounded, and many were driven from their homes. The property destroyed was estimated at $150,000. Most of the White aggressors in these riots went unpunished, partly because testimony against a White person by a Chinese was inadmissible in the courts.

Chinatowns

The Chinese responded to this violence by moving farther eastward, to the Northeast (where they also became the victims of violence), and by retreating into ethnic communities in urban areas. Writes Lyman (1970): "By the end of the nineteenth century, the California Chinese had, for the most part, died off, returned to China, moved eastward or settled into the ghettos of American cities referred to as 'Chinatowns'" (p. 14).

Despite its outer glitter, life in Chinatown was and is tough and depressing. Because most of the male immigrants did not bring their wives to California and were unable to marry Caucasians because of miscegenation laws, Chinatown was made up primarily of desperate and lonely men who sought their recreation in the form of prostitution, gambling, and opium smoking. Because of the high population of lonely and virile men, and the scarcity of females, prostitution loomed large in Chinatown in the 1800s. It was controlled by the Chinese secret societies that paid off police officials so that they could "safely" practice their business. Competition between the various Chinese societies for power, women, and money was keen, and violence between them often erupted. These conflicts were sensationalized by the White press and were popularized as "tong wars." Such stories made good copy and were eagerly sought by many journalists. These news stories played into the hands of the anti-Chinese racists and were fully exploited.

Prostitution, tong wars, gambling, and opium smoking are largely things of the past in Chinatown. However, powerful antiquated Chinese organizations that care little about the masses still exercise considerable power. Poverty, squalor, and disease are rampant in some Chinese urban communities. San Francisco's Chinatown has one of the highest population densities in the nation. Many women in San Francisco's Chinatown work in the garment industry for very low wages. Housing and education in San Francisco's Chinatown are among the worst in the nation. The power elite in Chinatown, which profits from the misery of the masses, has helped obscure its outrageous conditions and publicized its glitter. Chinatown has been described as a "gilded ghetto whose tinseled streets and brightly lit shops barely camouflage a pocket of poverty in the metropolis" (Lyman, 1970, p. 8).

Chinese Americans Today

Chinatown served as a port of entry for most of the earlier immigrants; it provided them with a sense of security, ties with the old world culture, and a partial escape from discrimination. Many Chinese Americans who are descendants of these earlier immigrants have experienced upward social and economic mobility and are leaving Chinatown. They have joined the exodus to the suburbs (Horton, 1995). However, the American Chinatowns are still viable and important communities. The newly upwardly mobile Chinese Americans who are moving to suburban communities are being replaced in Chinatown by new waves of immigrants from China and Hong Kong. In 1990, 69.3% of the Chinese Americans were foreign-born, compared to 32.4% of the Japanese (U.S. Bureau of the Census, 1993a). In his anthropological study of New York's Chinatown, Wong (1982) identifies four groups that live there: (1) old overseas Chinese, (2) American-born Chinese and naturalized Chinese Americans, (3) jump-ship sailors and refugees, and (4) disenchanted/disenfranchised youths. The refugees from Southeast Asia face tremendous economic hardships and work long hours each day, sometimes from eighteen to twenty hours.

The new immigrants who have entered the United States since the Immigration Reform Act of 1965 have been bipolar in their social-class backgrounds. In 1990, about 42% of Chinese Americans were menial service, low-skilled, and blue-collar workers. About 52% were managerial and technical workers (U.S. Bureau of the Census, 1993b). Even though the economic and educational levels of the total Chinese population are high, a large group of the new immigrants have low-paying jobs that are highly concentrated in restaurants and textile work. The bipolar nature of the Chinese community is also reflected in where they live. Many of the lower-level workers live in Chinatown, whereas many of the professional and upper-status workers live in suburban communities. Monterey Park, California, a suburban community of

Los Angeles that had a population of 61,000 in 1988, had 50% Chinese residents. It had become "America's first suburban Chinatown" (Horton, 1995; Takaki, 1998, p. 425).

The social, educational, and economic characteristics of the total population of Chinese Americans in 1990 were impressive. Most Chinese Americans (about 73.6%) who were twenty-five years or older were high school graduates, compared to 79.8% for Whites, and 75.2% for all persons (U.S. Bureau of the Census, 1993b). The median family income of Chinese Americans in 1990 was $41,316, compared to $35,225 for all persons. Chinese Americans were also highly concentrated in managerial, professional, and technical jobs in 1990: 35.8% of them held managerial and professional specialty jobs, compared to 26.4% for all persons. In addition, 31.2% of them held technical, sales, and administrative support occupations in 1990, compared to 31.7% for all persons. On most leading indicators of success in 1990, the Chinese in the United States exceeded the general population (U.S. Bureau of the Census, 1993b).

Because of the educational, occupational, and economic success of Chinese Americans, many of them have moved out of Chinatown to other areas within the city, but they are still primarily urban and metropolitan dwellers. Most lived in metropolitan areas in 1990. Almost all poor Chinese, aged bachelors, and most recent immigrants live in Chinatown. Other groups, however, also live there. Although many Chinese Americans have joined the larger society, the Chinatowns of the nation are still viable communities that satisfy important human and cultural needs. Even the highly assimilated Chinese American occasionally returns to Chinatown on the weekend for a good ethnic meal or to buy certain Chinese products unavailable in predominantly White communities.

The Chinese community has experienced an influx of immigrants since the passage of the Immigration Act of 1965, which gave a liberal quota of 170,000 to people who lived in Eastern Hemisphere nations. A chain migration has developed. Once they are in the United States and have become citizens, many Chinese send for relatives under the provisions of the immigrant act that allow families to join other family members. The process multiplies. Between 1970 and 1980, the Chinese population in the United States increased 88%, while the White population increased 6%. In 1965, only 4,769 Chinese immigrants entered the United States, whereas 49,300 individuals born in China (Mainland and Taiwan) and Hong Kong immigrated to the United States in 1998. The Chinese American population in 2000 was 2.4 million, which made them the largest Asian American group. They made up 23.7% of the Asian American population (see Figure 13.1).

Despite the tremendous increase in the Chinese American population since 1965, Asians comprised only a small percentage of the U.S. population in 2000. The 10.2 million Asians made up 3.6% of the U.S. population of 281 million in 2000. The Chinese population in the United States grew 32% between 1990 and 2000, compared to 57.9% for Hispanics and 11.7% for the

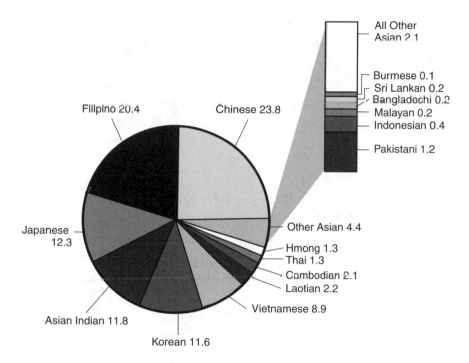

FIGURE 13.1 Asian American Population for Selected Groups: 1990 (percent distribution)

Source: U.S. Bureau of the Census (1993). *We, the American Asians.* Washington, D.C.: U.S. Government Printing Office.

total U.S. population. The rapid growth of the Chinese population in the United States is likely to have a number of important consequences. One possible consequence is that U.S. foreign policy will focus more on Asia. Although Asian Americans make up only a small percentage of the total U.S. population, they are highly concentrated in Hawaii and the West Coast states.

Japanese Americans

The Immigration

Because of overpopulation, depressed farming conditions, and political turmoil in Japan in the late 1800s, its citizens began immigrating to Hawaii and the U.S. mainland in search of better economic opportunities. The arrival of 148 Japanese contract laborers in Hawaii in 1868 to work on the plantations violated Japanese law. Japanese immigrants did not arrive in the United States

JAPANESE AMERICANS: HISTORICAL PERSPECTIVE

Important Dates	Events
1868	One hundred forty-eight Japanese contract laborers arrived in Hawaii.
1869	The unsuccessful Wakamatsu Colony, made up of Japanese immigrants, was established in California.
1906	The San Francisco Board of Education ordered all Asian children to attend a segregated Oriental school.
1907–08	The United States and Japan made the Gentlemen's Agreement, which was designed to reduce the number of Japanese immigrants entering the United States.
1913	The California legislature passed a land bill making it difficult for Japanese immigrants to lease land.
1924	An immigration bill was passed by Congress that stopped Asian immigration to the United States.
1930	The Japanese American Citizenship League was founded.
1941	Japan attacked Pearl Harbor on December 7.
1942	On February 19, President Franklin D. Roosevelt issued Executive Order 9066, which authorized the internment of Japanese Americans who lived on the West Coast.
1946	The last internment camp was closed.
1948	The Japanese American Evacuation Claims Act, signed by President Harry S. Truman, authorized some compensation for the financial losses incurred by Japanese Americans during the internment. The U.S. government eventually compensated the Japanese Americans for property loss at the rate of about 10¢ per dollar.
1952	The McCarran-Walter Immigration Act was passed by Congress. It ended the total exclusion of Asian immigrants, which had begun with the passage of the Immigration Act of 1924. Asian Americans were granted naturalization rights.
1972	Statistics indicated that 47% of the Japanese Americans living in Los Angeles were married to non-Japanese spouses.
1986	A U.S. Court of Appeals reinstated the claim that the U.S. Government illegally took property from a group of Japanese interned during World War II. This case made it possible for claims by survivors to be heard in court.

Important Dates	Events
1988	The American Civil Liberties bill was passed by Congress and signed by President Reagan. It provided an apology for the internment of Japanese Americans during World War II and a $20,000 payment for each survivor of the internment.
2000	The U.S. 2000 Census indicated that the Japanese American population decreased between 1990 and 2000 by 51,300. This was caused by the low birthrate among Japanese Americans and their low rate of immigration.

and Hawaii in significant numbers until the Japanese government, because of internal problems, legalized immigration in 1886. There were 55 people of Japanese ancestry in the United States in 1870; 2,039 in 1890; and 111,010 in 1920 (Lyman, 1970). The largest number of Japanese immigrants arrived in the United States between 1891 and 1924; about 200,000 came during this period (Kitano, 1976).

After the anti-Chinese forces had successfully stopped Chinese immigration, epitomized by the Chinese Exclusion Act of 1882, there was still a need for seasonal farm laborers in the developing West. The Japanese immigrants filled the labor void in agriculture and in other areas that had been created by the cessation of Chinese immigration. Why Whites on the West Coast halted the immigration of one group of Asians and then encouraged the coming of another is a curious and complex historical event. However, it was only a matter of time before the anti-Asian forces, already mobilized, began to attack aggressively the Japanese Americans as they had earlier attacked the Chinese.

Most of the first Japanese immigrants were young men, some of whom were married. They hoped to earn a small fortune in the United States and return to Japan. Like the Chinese, however, most of them remained in North America. There were many similarities in the experiences of Japanese and Chinese immigrants to the United States. However, there were some significant differences that profoundly influenced the development of the Chinese American and Japanese American communities. Organizations emerged within the Little Tokyos of America, as in early Chinatown, to help the new immigrants secure lodging, food, and jobs.

There were also few women among the first Japanese immigrants. Like the Chinese, the men had to share the women who were available. However, the man–woman ratio never became as imbalanced within the Japanese American community as it became in the Chinese community because the Japanese immigrants were able to marry Japanese women, despite the exclusion laws directed against Japanese immigrants. Although the men were in the United States and the women in Japan, marriages were arranged with photographs. The wives would later join their husbands, whom they had never seen, in the United States. These women became known as "picture brides."

The picture-bride custom was similar in some ways to the "tobacco bride" custom that was practiced in the Jamestown colony. The Virginia Company sent 90 European women to Virginia in the spring of 1620. Each man who married one of the women had to pay 120 pounds of the best tobacco to help pay for his bride's transportation costs from Europe. In later years, the company continued to send more "maids" to Virginia to marry the lonely male colonists.

Although the picture-bride marriage practice was opposed vigorously by anti-Japanese groups, it was consistent with Japanese custom and continued until outlawed in Japan in 1920. Many parents of second-generation Japanese Americans (*Nisei*) were married in a "picture" ceremony. (Japanese Americans use specific terms to designate each generation: *Issei, Nisei, Sansei,* and *Yonsei* refer to the first, second, third, and fourth generations, respectively.) These marriages worked amazingly well, partly because traditionally romantic love had not been a major factor in Japanese marriages, which were more the joining of two families rather than two individuals. This Japanese adage expresses cogently this attitude toward marriage: "Those who come together in passion stay together in tears."

Although most of the Issei men were much older than their picture brides, the fact that they were able to marry helped the Japanese to establish strong families in the United States. Some writers consider the Japanese family the most significant factor in the social and economic mobility of Japanese Americans. Strong families developed early in the Japanese American community, partly because of the picture-bride custom, and a large and assertive second generation of Japanese Americans emerged. Such a generation did not develop among the Chinese for several decades because of their lack of family life. There were few Chinese women available and Chinese men were unable to marry Whites. Because of exclusion laws that prohibited the immigration of Chinese females, family life in the Chinese American community developed slowly. As a result, the Chinese community was made up primarily of destitute, lonely, aging, and exploited men for several decades.

When they arrived on the West Coast, the Japanese immigrants worked in a variety of fields, including agriculture, the railroads, domestic work, gardening, small businesses, and industry. Because of job discrimination, they worked mainly in self-employment types of occupations. Consequently, they made their greatest impact in such fields as agriculture, gardening, and small business. Of all these areas, their accomplishments in agriculture, and especially truck farming, were the most impressive. Much of the land they were able to farm was considered unarable and largely useless by most White farmers. With a great deal of ingenuity and the use of intensive farming techniques, the Japanese began to dominate certain areas of California truck farming. They produced 90% of the state's peppers, strawberries, celery, and snap beans in 1941. In the same year, they raised a large percentage of California's cucumbers, tomatoes, cabbage, carrots, lettuce, and onions (Melendy, 1972).

The Japanese immigrants were often praised for their industry and eagerness when they first arrived in California. However, their tremendous success in agriculture eventually alarmed and frightened Anglo American farmers, who no longer saw the Japanese merely as ambitious workers and servants, but rather as tough competitors in the marketplace. To halt their success and to drive them out of California, White farmers and labor leaders inflamed anti-Asian feelings and warned of a new "Yellow Peril."

Some familiar faces and organizations, such as Dennis Kearney and the California newspapers, renewed their anti-Asian tactics. Anti-Japanese attitudes were pervasive on the West Coast, and almost every institution was affected. In 1906, the San Francisco Board of Education ordered all Asian American children, including the Japanese, to attend the segregated Oriental school. Japan was upset by this order and considered it a gross insult. Because of Japan's growing military strength, President Theodore Roosevelt thought the order might cause a serious conflict with Japan. Consequently, he intervened and persuaded the school board to rescind it.

To help mitigate the pervasive anti-Japanese feelings on the West Coast, the United States and Japan worked out an agreement designed to reduce drastically the immigration of Japanese laborers to the United States. This agreement, which became known as the Gentlemen's Agreement, was completed in 1908. Japan agreed to halt the immigration of laborers to the United States and the United States agreed to end discrimination against the Japanese. After this agreement, the number of Japanese entering the United States was reduced drastically. However, the anti-Japanese movements continued unabated. The most extremist groups wanted nothing less than total exclusion of the Japanese.

"The Japs Must Go!" became the rallying cry of the anti-Japanese movements. Racist headlines in the press, attacks on Japanese businesses, and other forms of violence occurred. The anti-Japanese forces won a major victory when the California legislature passed the Alien Land Bill in 1913. Japanese immigrants were considered "aliens ineligible for citizenship." This bill, designed to drive the Japanese out of farming, prohibited the Issei from leasing land for more than three years. Although the Japanese found this law devastating, they were able, to some extent, to circumvent it. Consequently, it did not have the impact its architects had hoped. Many Issei used their children's names to secure land or obtained land with the help of White friends. In 1920, the California legislature passed a more severe law, which was destined to have the effects the legislators had hoped the 1913 law would have. This law prevented the Issei from leasing land and prohibited them from using their children's names to lease land they could not legally lease themselves. This law served as the prototype for laws later passed in such states as Arizona, New Mexico, Oregon, Utah, and Wyoming.

Even though the Alien Land Law of 1920 successfully reduced the number of Japanese Americans in agriculture, the anti-Japanese movement continued in full force. The groups comprising this movement wanted a total victory, which they viewed as a complete halt of Japanese immigration to the United States and the removal of the Japanese from California. They claimed that, despite the Gentlemen's Agreement, the picture brides were swelling the Japanese population in the United States and that the Japanese were having an alarming number of children. The phobia of these groups was totally unfounded. The proportion of Japanese immigrants in the United States has always been small. From 1915 to 1924, when the movement to exclude Japanese immigrants was intense, 85,197 Japanese immigrants entered the United States, which comprised only 2.16% of all immigrants during this period (Petersen, 1971). A total of 45,533,116 immigrants came to the United States between 1820 and 1971 but only 370,033 of these were Japanese. In 1920, there were only 111,010 Japanese immigrants in the United States. Thus, the "problem" was clearly fiction—politics, economic competition, and racism—not the number of Japanese immigrants—caused alarm about the "swelling" Japanese population in the United States.

The anti-Japanese forces experienced a long-awaited victory when the Immigration Act of 1924 was passed. This act fixed quotas for European countries on the basis of the percentages of their immigrants living in the United States and prohibited the immigration of aliens ineligible for citizenship. The act, in effect, stopped Asian immigration. Writes Kitano (1976): "The 1924 immigration act was a major victory for racists, nativists, and exclusionists, and there is little doubt that it was resented by an insulted and bewildered Japan, which having understood that she was to become an important member of the family of nations, did not now understand this slap in the face" (p. 28).

The Internment

On December 7, 1941, Japan attacked Pearl Harbor. Hysteria emerged on the West Coast as the anti-Japanese groups spread rumors about the so-called fifth column and espionage activities among the Japanese (Daniels, 1971). Some Whites argued that all Japanese Americans were still loyal to their mother country; others claimed that it was impossible to tell a "good Jap" from a "bad Jap." Rumors, which spread like wildfire, suggested that the United States was in danger of being attacked by a fleet of Japanese soldiers and that Japanese Americans were helping to plan the attack. A tremendous fear of what came to be known as the Yellow Peril haunted the Pacific Coast. Daniels notes that the fear of conquest by Japan was irrational and racist (Daniels, 1971, p. 29). The press reinforced and perpetuated the fear by printing highly fictionalized and sensationalized news stories about the Japanese "threat."

It is significant to note that White California farmers and politicians played key roles in creating and perpetuating myths about the Yellow Peril. The farmers had long wanted to drive the Japanese out of California; politicians used the issue to gain votes and to divert attention from real political and social issues. It is also worth noting that we know of no sabotage activities in which Japanese Americans were involved during the war. In his perceptive study of the internment, Daniels (1971) argues that the decision to remove the Japanese from the West Coast was a political rather than military decision. Military officials knew during the war that the Japanese on the West Coast were not a security risk. However, because anti-Japanese groups in California urged the removal of the Japanese, it was politically expedient to intern them.

The uproar on the West Coast and the fear that spread throughout other parts of the nation resulted in the issuance of Executive Order No. 9066 by President Franklin D. Roosevelt on February 19, 1942. This order authorized the secretary of war to declare military areas "from which any or all persons may be excluded, and with respect to which, the right of any person to enter, remain in, or leave shall be subject to whatever restrictions the Secretary of War...may impose in his discretion." Although mention of the Japanese Americans by name is notably absent from the document, the order was clearly aimed at them. It authorized the secretary of war to remove Japanese Americans from the West Coast (declared a "military area") and to set up federal concentration camps to which they would be forcibly removed.

The Japanese were first sent to assembly centers, which served as temporary living quarters. Later, a total of 110,000 Japanese Americans (two thirds of whom were citizens of the United States) were located in these ten concentration camps: Tule Lake and Manzanar in interior California, Minidoka in Idaho, Topaz in Utah, Poston and Gila River in Arizona, Heart Mountain in Wyoming, Granada in Colorado, and Rohwer and Jerome in Arkansas. Most of the camps were located in desolate and barren areas that had hot weather in the summer and cold weather in the winter. They were fenced in with barbed wire and guarded by soldiers.

The internment had some adverse effects on the culture and life of the Japanese Americans. Because of the wide differences in the cultures of Japan and the United States, the Issei and Nisei had been less able to understand each other than most other immigrants and their children. The camp experience increased their alienation. The position of the Issei was further undermined in the camps because often their children, who were U.S. citizens, were able to obtain responsible jobs for which the Issei did not qualify. This was a severe blow to the self-image and confidence of the Issei male, because for centuries the oldest Japanese male had been the undisputed head of the household.

Other events undermined the strength and cogency of the Japanese family, which traditionally had been the pivotal force within the Japanese community. The female often made as much money as the male, and the family had to eat in a communal dining room. The father was unable to exercise his usual authority because of such situations. Consequently, family solidarity was lessened in the camps.

Widespread conflict developed within the camps over the question of loyalty. The Nisei often questioned the loyalty of the Issei. Japanese nationals accused the leaders of the Japanese American Citizenship League, who cooperated with the War Relocation Authority, of participating in the oppression of the Japanese. In their eagerness to prove their loyalty to the U.S. government, some Japanese helped federal authorities to conduct witch hunts for "suspected" Japanese. The internment showed how a dehumanizing experience could demoralize a group, which had traditionally had high group solidarity and trust, and cause mistrust and suspicion within it.

Japanese Americans Today

The U.S. Japanese population has never been very large. Japanese immigration was halted by the Immigration Act of 1924 and did not resume until the ban on Asian immigration was lifted when the McCarran-Walter Act was passed in 1952. Although this act set a quota of only 185 Japanese immigrants per year, Asian immigrants were no longer totally excluded.

Compared to the other Asian immigrant groups, few Japanese have immigrated to the United States since the passage of the Immigration Reform Act of 1965. This is because of the highly developed nature of the economy of Japan and its ability to provide jobs for large numbers of technical and professional workers. Most of the immigrants who come to the United States from nations such as the Philippines, Korea, and India—and many of those from China and Hong Kong—are professional workers who are unable to find jobs consistent with their educations in their native lands. This is not the case in Japan. Between 1981 and 1998, 93,300 immigrants came to the United States from Japan, compared to 927,400 from the Philippines, 735,500 from China, and 573,000 from India (see Table 13.1).

As a result of its small immigrating population and low birthrate, Japanese Americans are one of the smallest of the Asian American groups and have one of the smallest foreign-born populations. In 1990, most Japanese Americans (about 67.6%) were U.S.-born citizens (U.S. Bureau of the Census, 1993a).

The Japanese American population was 796,700 in 2000, a decrease of 51,300 since 1990. Because they have a relatively low immigration rate, Japanese Americans had the lowest level of foreign-born among its population than any other group of Asian Americans in 1990 (32.4%). Japanese Americans are highly culturally assimilated. This is indicated by their high rate of out-marriage with other groups (Kitano & Daniels, 1995). In 1989, the out-marriage rate for Japanese Americans living in Los Angeles County was 51.9%. It was 58.3% for women and 41.7% for men.

The Japanese Americans have been termed the so-called model American ethnic minority because of their success in education, social-class mobility, and low levels of crime, mental illness, and other social deviances. In 1990, the Japanese median family income was $51,500 compared to $35,225 for all Americans (U.S. Bureau of the Census, 1993b). The Japanese also had high educational achievement in 1990; 87.5% of Japanese twenty-five years or older were high school graduates or higher, compared to 75.2% for all persons in the United States. The Japanese were also highly concentrated in managerial, professional, and technical occupations in 1990 (employed persons age sixteen and older); 37% of the Japanese had managerial and professional specialty occupations, compared to 26.4% for all persons. In addition, 34.4% of the Japanese had technical, sales, and administrative support occupations, compared to 31.7% for all persons (U.S. Bureau of the Census, 1993b).

Writes Petersen (1971): "By almost any criterion of good citizenship that we choose, not only are Japanese Americans better than any other segment of American society, including native Whites of native parents, but they have realized this remarkable progress by their own almost unaided effort.... Every attempt to hamper the progress of Japanese Americans, in short, has resulted in enhancing their determination to succeed" (pp. 4–5).

Breaking Silence and the Future of the Japanese in U.S. Society

The silence that many Japanese Americans had kept about their internment during World War II was broken during the hearings before the Commission on Wartime Relocation and Internment of Civilians (CWRIC). Congress created the Commission "to determine whether a wrong was committed against those American citizens and permanent residents relocated and/or interned as a result of Executive Order Numbered 9066 and other associated acts of the Federal Government, and to recommend appropriate remedies." The Commission held twenty days of hearings and took testimony from more than 750 witnesses between July and December 1981. Many people who spoke before the Commission were Japanese Americans who had been interned. They told about their experiences in poignant and moving language.

In December 1982 the Commission issued its report, *Personal Justice Denied* (Report of the Commission on Wartime Relocation and Internment of Civilians, 1982). The report condemned the internment and in June 1983 recommended that Congress allow $1.5 billion to provide personal redress to the Japanese who were interned during the war years. The Commission stated in its report:

> The promulgation of Executive Order 9066 was not justified by military necessity and the decisions which followed from it—detention, ending detention and ending exclusion—were not driven by analysis of military conditions. The broad historical causes which shaped these decisions were race prejudice, war hysteria and a failure of political leadership. Widespread ignorance of Japanese Americans contributed to a policy conceived in haste and executed in an atmosphere of fear and anger at

Japan. A grave injustice was done to American citizens and resident aliens of Japanese ancestry who, without individual review or any probative evidence against them, were excluded, removed and detained by the United States during World War II (p. 18).

It was a long road of debate and controversy, both within and outside of Congress, between the Commission's recommendation of redress for internees in June 1983 and the enactment of the American Civil Liberties bill by Congress in August 1988. The bill offered the Japanese Americans an apology for their internment and provided a payment of $20,000 for each internee. The payments, which were scheduled to begin in 1990, were to be made over a ten-year period, were to go to older persons first, and could be made to survivors' descendants in the event of the survivor's death. Because the payments were to be made over a ten-year period, many internees would die before the total payment was made. President Ronald Reagan praised the Japanese who served in World War II when he signed the bill and said that the nation was gravely wrong when it interned the Japanese Americans.

The success of the Japanese in U.S. society is indisputable. However, the future of Japanese culture, values, and behaviors in the United States is uncertain. Their success is probably a result largely of traditional Japanese values, attitudes, and beliefs. With a high out-marriage rate and a relatively low rate of immigration, cultural and structural assimilation into the mainstream society may erode the most important values that have taken the Japanese down the road to success. However, a more hopeful possibility is that, as they become structurally integrated into the mainstream society, they will enrich it with traditional Japanese values and remain to some extent culturally Japanese as they become full participants in U.S. society.

Filipino Americans

Early Filipino Settlement in the United States and Hawaii

Filipinos came to Hawaii and the United States in the first decades of the twentieth century seeking work and better opportunities. An early community of Filipinos in Louisiana has been documented by Espina (1988). Espina's research cites October 18, 1587 as the earliest known date when Filipino sailors aboard a Spanish galleon landed in what is known today as Morro Bay, San Luis Obispo County, California. Eventually, these sailors—"Manilamen"—jumped ship to escape Spanish domination and, around 1763, founded the first permanent Filipino settlement in the bayous of Louisiana. These men developed a dried shrimp industry in their Louisiana settlement.

Significant numbers of Filipinos did not settle in the United States and Hawaii until the turn of the century. Most Filipino immigrants were categorized

FILIPINO AMERICANS: HISTORICAL PERSPECTIVE

Important Dates	Events
1587	Filipino sailors landed in Morro Bay, San Luis Obispo County, California. They were among the first Asians to cross the Pacific Ocean for the North American continent because of the Manila galleon trade between Mexico and the Philippines.
1763	The first permanent Asian settlements in the continental United States were Filipino villages in the bayous of Louisiana. Filipino sailors escaped from Spanish colonizers.
1898	Filipinos fought Spanish rule, established the Malolos Congress, and elected Emilio Aguinaldo as the first Philippine president.
	The United States refuted Philippine claims to independence and purchased the islands for $20 million under the terms of the Treaty of Paris that ended the Spanish-American War.
1899– 1901	Filipinos fought for independence from the United States in the Filipino-American War.
1902	The Organic Act of July 1902 recognized the Philippines as an unincorporated territory of the United States.
1906	More than 200 Filipino contract laborers, *Sakadas*, were brought to Hawaii by the Hawaiian Sugar Planters Association.
1911	The Filipino Federation of Labor was founded in Hawaii.
1929	An anti-Filipino riot occurred in Exeter, California, in which more than 200 Filipinos were assaulted.
1930	Fermin Tobera, who later became a Filipino martyr, was killed in an anti-Filipino riot in Watsonville, California.
1934	Congress passed the Tydings-McDuffie Act. This act promised the Philippines independence in 10 years and limited Filipino immigration to the United States to 50 per year.
1935	President Franklin D. Roosevelt signed the Repatriation Act on July 11. This act offered free transportation to Filipinos who would return to the Philippines. The 2,190 who took advantage were unable to return to the United States except under the quota system.

Important Dates	Events
1940	Under the terms of the Nationality Act of 1940, Filipino immigrants to the United States could become citizens through naturalization. U.S. citizenship was extended to other categories of Filipino Americans on July 2, 1946.
1941	Japan attacked the Philippines.
1946	On July 4, 1946, the Philippines becomes independent.
1965	Larry Itliong organized Filipino farm laborers.
1965	The Immigration Reform Act of 1965 opened the door for an influx of Philippine professionals to the United States. More than 32,000 Filipinos immigrated to the United States in 1974.
1990	The Immigration Act of 1990, Section 405, gave Filipino servicemen who were trained in the Philippines and who fought for the United States during World War II between 1939 and 1946 the opportunity to apply for U.S. citizenship.
1992	More than 61,000 Filipino immigrants entered the United States, making them the largest national group to enter the United States that year except the Mexicans.
2000	The 2000 U.S. Census indicated that Filipinos were the second largest Asian group and was the largest immigrating Asian group between 1981 and 1998.

as *pensionados* or *sakadas*, although some were neither. *Pensionados* were government-sponsored students who returned to the Philippines to apply the knowledge they acquired in the United States. *Sakadas* were contracted laborers who were recruited to work in the sugar fields of Hawaii for three years and either returned to the Philippines, remained in Hawaii, or ventured to the mainland. *Sakadas* were cheap and exploited field hands lured by the promise of a better life in America.

The Philippine revolution against Spanish domination began in 1896. By 1898, Spain and the United States were fighting the Spanish-American War. With the bulk of Spain's military forces concentrated in the Caribbean, its weakened position in the Philippines led the United States to seek control of the Philippines. The refusal of the United States to accept the Filipinos' claim to independence in 1898 launched the Filipino-American War. By 1902, the

United States assumed guardianship over the Philippines, thus establishing Filipinos as nationals.

The Immigration

The magnet that pulled Filipinos to Hawaii and the United States came primarily from without rather than from within. Immigration from the Philippines during the 333 years that the islands were ruled by Spain was virtually nil. However, when the United States acquired the Philippines after the Spanish-American War in 1898, it was only a matter of time before farmers in Hawaii and the United States would successfully lure Filipinos away from the islands to work as cheap and exploited field hands. Recruiting and transportation agents lured Filipinos away from their homeland with high-pressure propaganda about the promises of Hawaii and the United States. Because of chronic unemployment and widespread poverty in the islands, thousands of Filipinos left their native land in search of the dream.

Because Chinese immigration had come to an abrupt end in 1882, Japanese immigrants had been the main source of cheap labor for plantation owners in Hawaii and big farmers on the U.S. West Coast. However, the Gentlemen's Agreement of 1907–1908 substantially reduced Japanese immigration, and the Immigration Act of 1924 virtually stopped it. When Japanese immigration ended, a new source of cheap labor was desired by farmers in Hawaii and in the United States. The United States had recently annexed both Puerto Rico and the Philippines. Each nation was regarded as a promising source of cheap labor. However, the attempt to start large-scale immigration from Puerto Rico failed, and the farmers turned to the Philippines, where they had considerable success. The powerful Hawaiian Sugar Planters Association became so alarmed when the Gentlemen's Agreement restricted Japanese immigration in 1907–1908 that it brought more than 200 Filipino workers to Hawaii that year. The association wanted to make sure that, when Japanese immigration stopped, there would be a new source of labor just as abundant and cheap.

Filipino immigration to Hawaii continued and escalated after 1907. However, until the 1920s, most of the Filipino immigrants remained in Hawaii and did not come to the U.S. mainland. In 1920, there were only 5,603 Filipinos in the United States. However, from 1923, when Filipino immigration to the United States gained momentum, until it reached its peak in 1929, large-scale immigration to the mainland occurred. In 1929 alone 5,795 Filipinos entered California. Between 1907 and 1910, about 150,000 immigrants left the Philippines and headed for Hawaii or the United States. Although the highly glorified and exaggerated tales spread by recruiting and transportation agents were the magnet that pulled hundreds of Filipinos from their homeland, the letters and money sent back home by immigrants, as well as the desire to get rich quickly, helped to motivate them to leave the poverty-stricken islands.

Filipino immigrants in the United States had some unique group character-istics that were destined to make their lives on the West Coast harsh. As the third wave of Asian immigrants, they were victims of the accumulated anti-Asian racism. They were also a young group. According to McWilliams (1943), they were the youngest group of immigrants in U.S. history. They ranged in age from about sixteen to thirty; most, 84.3%, were under thirty. Also, most of the immigrants were sojourners who hoped to return to the Philippines after attain-ing the riches of America. Like the other Asian sojourners, the longer they stayed in the United States, the more their hope waned that they would ever be able to return home.

The immigrants were predominantly male. The sex ratio was imbalanced, as it was in early Chinese American communities, because few Filipino women immigrated because female immigration violated tradition.In 1930, there was 1 woman for every 143 men. The Filipinos immigrated from a country that was a U.S. colony in which the American myth of "all men are created equal" was taught in the schools. Thus, unlike the other Asian groups, they came to the United States expecting to be treated like equals. Their acceptance of this myth made their adjustment in the United States more difficult.

Work.   Like other Asian immigrants, the Filipinos came to Hawaii and the United States to do work the Whites disdained and refused to do. They were hired, usually under a contract system, to pick asparagus and lettuce and to do other kinds of "stoop" field work. In addition to farming, the Filipinos, espe-cially after World War II, worked as domestics. They cooked, washed dishes, and worked as house servants. Some worked in the fishing industry and in canneries.

The Filipino Community.   Unlike the Japanese and Chinese, the Filipinos were unable to develop tightly knit ethnic communities. The Little Manila dis-tricts in cities such as Los Angeles and San Francisco were primarily entertain-ment centers and stopping places for the field hands between seasons. The Filipinos could not establish highly cohesive communities because their jobs kept them moving and because, like the Chinese immigrants, they were unable to have much of a family life because of the small number of Filipino females.

The types of entertainment and recreation that emerged within Filipino American communities reflected the sociological makeup of young, unmarried males searching for meaning in life in a hostile and racist atmosphere. Prostitu-tion, cockfighting, and gambling were favorite pastimes for the lonely, alien-ated men. The Filipino-owned dance halls, in which White girls danced and sold or gave other favors to the immigrants, were popular and a source of widespread tension between Filipinos and White men. Whites passed laws pro-hibiting Filipinos from marrying White women. However, these laws had little effect on biological drives and mutual attraction between White women and

Filipino men. Stockton, California, was dubbed the Manila of the United States because so many Filipinos settled there. It was the site of much conflict and tension between Filipinos and Whites. Although there were few tightly organized Filipino communities, a strong sense of group solidarity and sense of peoplehood emerged among Filipinos. Strong nationalism, as the gifted Filipino American writer Carlos Bulosan epitomized (San Juan, 1972), was widespread among Filipinos in the United States.

Anti-Filipino Agitation. As the third wave of Asian immigrants to the West Coast, Filipinos inherited all of the anti-Asian prejudice and racism that had accumulated since the Chinese started immigrating to the United States in the 1850s. When Filipino immigration reached significant levels in the 1920s, familiar anti-Asian screams about the Yellow Peril were again heard. These anti-Asian movements were, again, led by organized labor and patriotic organizations such as the American Federation of Labor and the Native Sons of the Golden West. The arguments were identical to those that had been made against the Chinese and Japanese; the victims were different but the victimizers were the same. Labor groups claimed that Filipinos were "unfair competition"; patriotic groups argued that they were unassimilable and would pollute the "pure" White race. One exclusionist warned (cited in Divine, 1957, p. 70), "This mongrel stream is small, but when it is considered how rapidly it multiplies and grows it is clear that the tide must be stemmed before it gets beyond control."

Labor and nativistic groups had succeeded in halting Chinese and Japanese immigration by urging Congress to pass exclusion laws. However, the Filipinos presented a different problem. They could not be excluded as "aliens" under the provisions of the Immigration Act of 1924 because of their peculiar and ambiguous legal status. Because the United States had annexed the Philippines in 1898, its citizens were not aliens. However, unlike Puerto Ricans, they were not citizens of the United States either. Filipinos were "nationals" or "wards" of the United States. Consequently, they could not be excluded with the immigration laws that applied to foreign nations. Representative Richard Welch of California nevertheless fought hard to get an outright exclusion act through Congress in 1928. The attempt failed, but Welch succeeded in rallying widespread support for the anti-Filipino cause.

The failure of the Welch bill convinced the leaders of the exclusion movement that they had to try another strategy. The desire for independence within the Philippines had become intense by the late 1920s. The Philippines' independence movement gave the exclusionists new hope for a cause that had become an obsession: to exclude and deport Filipinos. They jumped on the independence bandwagon. If the Philippines became independent, they correctly reasoned, its citizens could be excluded under the provisions of existing immigration laws. The passage of the Tydings-McDuffie Act on March 24, 1934, was a significant victory for the exclusionists.

In addition to promising the Philippines independence, the Tydings-McDuffie Act limited Filipino immigration to the United States to 50 people per year. This act, as was the intention of its architects, virtually excluded Filipino immigration to the United States. Even this bill did not totally satisfy the exclusionists. They not only wanted Filipino immigration stopped, but they also wanted Filipinos deported. They pushed the so-called Repatriation Act through Congress. President Franklin D. Roosevelt signed the act on July 11, 1935. Under the terms of the act, any Filipino could obtain free transportation back to the Philippines. However, there was an insidious catch to this inducement. Once they returned, they could not reenter the United States. Few Filipinos were seduced by this act. Only about 2,000 returned to the Philippines under its provisions.

Riots and Anti-Filipino Violence.   Both before and after the Filipino exclusion and deportation acts, anti-Filipino Whites carried out a vicious and active campaign of violence against Filipinos in the western states. One of the first anti-Filipino riots broke out in Yakima, Washington, on September 19, 1928. Some of the most serious riots occurred in California, where most Filipino immigrants first settled. On October 24, 1929, Whites attacked and assaulted more than 200 Filipinos and did considerable property damage in Exeter, California. Fermin Tobera, a lettuce picker, was killed in a riot that occurred in Watsonville, California, in January 1930. Tobera's murder greatly disturbed people in his native homeland, and a National Humiliation Day was declared in Manila. Some Filipinos felt that Tobera had been ruthlessly slain by a "mob of blood-thirsty Americans" (Wallovits, 1966, p. 124). Three people were shot in a riot that occurred near Salinas, California, in August 1934. An anti-Filipino riot occurred as late as June 1939 in Lake County, California. Writes McWilliams (1943): "No reparations or indemnities were ever made for these repeated outrages; nor were the culprits ever punished" (p. 240).

Filipino Americans Today

Between 1981 and 1998, Filipinos were the second largest group immigrating to the United States, exceeded only by immigrants from Mexico. The number of Filipinos entering the United States increased from 3,130 in 1965 to 34,500 in 1998. The Filipino population in the United States increased 23.9% in the decade between 1990 and 2000, while the total U.S. population, in contrast, increased by 11.7%. In 2000, there were about 1,850,314 Filipinos living in the United States. Significant percentages lived in California and Hawaii; most lived in urban areas.

Most Filipinos who came to the United States in the 1920s were unskilled laborers. The Immigration Act of 1965 not only significantly increased the number of Filipino immigrants to the United States but also changed the characteristics of the immigrants. The majority of the immigrants now entering the United States from the Philippines are professional, technical, and kindred workers. These immigrants come to the United States to seek jobs that are more consistent with their training than those they can obtain in the Philippines. A significant number of them are specialists in the health professions. Professional and technical workers from the Philippines have encountered some difficulties obtaining licenses to practice their crafts in the United States and have experienced language problems and discrimination. Sometimes doctors, dentists, and pharmacists must take lower-level jobs out of their fields until they can obtain the licenses needed to practice their professions in the United States. Many Filipinos who eventually practice their professions in the United States have obtained additional training in U.S. schools.

The significant number of professionally trained Filipinos who have immigrated to the United States since the Immigration Act of 1965 was enacted has changed substantially the social and demographic characteristics of the Filipino Americans. In 1990, 66.4% of Filipinos in the United States were foreign-born. In terms of numbers, there were more foreign-born Americans of Filipino origin than of any other group other than Mexicans. There were 913,000 foreign-born Filipinos and 4,298,000 Mexicans. However, the Filipinos did not have the highest percentage of foreign-born persons among the Asian Americans; 79.9% percent of the Vietnamese were foreign-born and 79.4% of the Laotians were foreign-born (U.S. Bureau of the Census, 1993a).

Before 1970, Filipinos were heavily concentrated in the lower strata of the population on most indices, such as education, income, and job status. However, data from both the 1980 and 1990 U.S. censuses indicate that the group characteristics of Filipino Americans—based on several criteria related to education, income, and job status—do not differ significantly from the Japanese, Chinese, and other Asian groups in the United States (see Table 13.1). Like the Chinese and Japanese, Filipinos are ahead of the general population on most of these indices. In 1990, the median family income for Filipinos was $46,698, compared to $35,225 for all persons in the United States. The percentage of Filipino high school graduates, twenty-five years or older, was 82.6%, compared to 75.2% for all persons in the United States (U.S. Bureau of the Census, 1993b).

Kim's (1978) study of Filipinos in Chicago indicates why the median family income of Asian families might be higher than that of White families. In many Asian families, both parents are highly trained and have professional jobs. Kim describes the typical Filipino in her study as follows:

> In broad terms, the Chicago Pilipino [sic] respondent can be categorized as young, well-educated, and fairly well-off financially: he [or she] is in his early thirties, has finished college, and may have a graduate or professional degree. Unlike most of the other groups in the study, it does not matter in this area whether the Pilipino respondent is male or female. In either case, the educational level and job level—skilled, white-collar, or professional—will probably be about the same. The Pilipino

female will also be just about as likely as her male counterpart to have a full-time job, or to hold more than one job (p. 172).

A study of the Chinese, Japanese, and Filipinos in the United States will help students to understand how these groups resisted racism and discrimination and attained success in U.S. society. However, their success was attained and is maintained by hard work, tenacity, and the will to overcome. Despite their success in U.S. society, Asians are still the victims of racism and discrimination, both subtle and blatant. Violent incidents against Asian Americans received national attention in 1985. A *New York Times* article, for example was entitled "Violent Incidents against Asian-Americans Seen as Part of Racist Pattern" (Butterfield, 1985). Part of the violence may have its roots in the U.S. response to competition from the Japanese; some Americans blur the distinction between Japanese Americans and foreign Japanese. The violence may be partly a response to the significant number of Asian immigrants now entering the United States. Regardless of the cause of this new wave of anti-Asian violence, it reminds us that racism is an integral part of U.S. society that can victimize any racial or ethnic group, no matter how successful.

Teaching Strategies

Concepts such as *immigration, discrimination,* and *cultural diversity* are highlighted in the historical overviews. This part of the chapter illustrates strategies for teaching three concepts, *similarities and differences, immigration,* and *discrimination.* An infinite variety of strategies can be used to teach each of these concepts. However, these activities are illustrative and can serve as a guide to teacher planning. Although each concept can and should be taught at all grade levels, we discuss strategies for teaching *similarities and differences* in the primary grades, *immigration* in intermediate and upper grades, and *discrimination* in the high school grades.

Primary Grades

CONCEPT

Names (similarities and differences)
Generalization: We all have names. However, our different names often give other people clues about our different origins, cultures, and experiences.

Introduction
Similarities and *differences* are two concepts that can be effectively taught in the primary grades. These concepts can be understood by young children when they are taught with concrete examples. A unit on names can help primary grade children learn that even though we all have names (a similarity), our names often give

other people clues about our different origins, experiences, and cultural backgrounds. It is appropriate to help children better understand the nature and origins of names when they are studying Asian Americans because teachers and students often find some Asian names, such as Vietnamese names, difficult to pronounce and understand.

1. Begin this unit by telling the class that the people who live in our nation, the United States (point it out to the children on a primary globe), came from many different nations and lands. Ask the students: "Can you name some of the nations from which the people in the United States came?" Record accurate responses on the board or butcher paper.

   Using a primary globe, show the students some of the nations and continents from which immigrants to the United States came. Ask the students if any of them have ever traveled to any of these nations and continents. If any of them have, ask them to tell briefly about their trips.

   Say to the class: "The ancestors of American Indians came to what is now the United States thousands of years ago. The ancestors of many Jews and Italians came to the United States almost 100 years ago. Other Americans, such as many Cubans and Vietnamese, have lived in the United States for fewer than 50 years. People from different parts of the world have many different ways of living, often believe different things, eat different kinds of food, and have different religions. Often people from various nations keep some of their differences after they have lived in the United States for many years. People in various nations often have different kinds of names. Many Americans, whose ancestors came from many different nations or who came from different nations themselves, have names that sound and look different from the names of other groups. These different kinds of names give us clues about the homelands of their ancestors or about their homelands, and about their ways of life and beliefs."

   Write the following names on the board or butcher paper:

   Susan Schmidt
   Juan Rivera Sanchez
   Jennifer Kim
   Patrick O'Shea
   Ito Matsuda
   Wing Chu
   Katherine Ann Shilenski
   Hoang Hy Vinh

   Say to the class: "Here are the names of eight of the children in Mrs. Gonzales's third-grade class in a school in Los Angeles. Do their names give us any clues about where their ancestors came from, about what foods they might eat, and about which holidays they might celebrate?"

   After giving the students an opportunity to state their ideas about what the children's names reveal about them, tell them a little about each of the eight students in Mrs. Gonzales's class. A brief description of each student follows.

Susan Schmidt. Susan's ancestors came to the United States from Germany in the 1820s. However, Susan says she is a *complete* American. She has no German characteristics that she knows about.

Ask the class: "Why do you think Susan has an American, rather than a German, given name? Why does she consider herself completely American rather than part German? Do any of you have German names? If so, do you feel totally American or part German? Why?"

Juan Rivera Sanchez. Juan was born in Mexico and moved to Los Angeles last year. Unlike Susan's name, Juan's name includes both his father's surname (Rivera), and his mother's maiden surname (Sanchez). This is a common practice in Spanish-speaking nations. In Mexico, it is correct to call Juan "Mr. Rivera."

Ask the class: "Why do you think that in Spanish-speaking nations children's names often include both their father's surname and their mother's surname before marriage? If your name included both of your parents' surnames (and not just your father's), how would your name be written? If you don't know your mother's surname before she married, ask a parent tonight and be prepared to share your name written with your father's surname and your mother's surname before she married." (Note: Some of the children's mothers might use their maiden surnames, rather than the surnames of their spouses. Some of them may also be single parents who have never used any other surname.)

Jennifer Kim. Jennifer's grandparents came to the United States during the Korean War in 1952. Jennifer does not speak Korean but enjoys Korean foods. She also likes to visit her relatives who speak Korean and talk about what life was like in Korea.

Ask the class: "Why do you think Jennifer has an American, rather than a Korean, given name? Do you think Jennifer feels like a total American, or part Korean and part American? Why do you think she feels this way?"

Patrick O'Shea. Patrick's great-grandparents came to the United States from Ireland. He thinks of himself as both Irish and American—as an "Irish American."

Ask the class: "Why do you think Patrick feels more Irish than Susan feels German?"

Ito Matsuda. Ito was born in Japan and came to the United States when he was two years old. Ito speaks Japanese and English. He feels that he is both Japanese and American. At home, the Matsuda family usually eats Japanese, rather than American, food. Most of the time the Matsudas speak Japanese, rather than English, when talking to each other.

Ask the class: "Why do you think Ito is more Japanese than Jennifer is Korean?"

Wing Chu. Wing's family moved from China to the United States last year. Wing is still learning to speak English. Most of his family's friends are Chinese. He lives in a Chinese neighborhood.

Ask the class: "Do you think Wing feels Chinese and American, or Chinese? Why do you think he feels this way?"

Katherine Ann Shilenski. Katherine's grandparents came to the United States from Poland before her parents were born. Katherine does not speak Polish and knows only a little about the Polish culture. She has often heard her parents talk about the problems of the people in Poland. Katherine is interested in learning more about the culture and language of her ancestors. She hopes to visit Poland someday.

Ask the class: "Why do you think Katherine feels more Polish than Susan feels German?"

Hoang Hy Vinh. Vinh came to the United States with his parents from Vietnam three years ago. Vinh's name is different in one important way from the names of his classmates. His surname (Hoang) is written first, his middle name (Hy) next, and his first or given name last (Vinh). Because of respect for him and his ancestors, the people in Vietnam would not address Vinh by his surname (Binh, 1975). Rather, they would call him "Vinh" or "Mr. Vinh." Point out to the class how Susan's, Jennifer's, Juan's, and Patrick's names, and most of their names, are written differently from Vinh's. Ask the students to write their names in the Vietnamese way and read them aloud.

Ask the class: "What problems do you think Vinh's teachers and classmates might have with his name? How do you think these problems make Vinh feel? If you moved to Vietnam and went to school, what do you think the teachers and students would call you? Why? How do you think this would make you feel?"

2. Tell the students to ask their parents to tell them the national origins of their surnames. End this unit by making a chart on butcher paper (or on the board) that shows each student's surname and the nation from which it came. Ask the children to tell as much as they can about the nations from which their surnames came, and whether their families eat foods, celebrate holidays, or have customs related to those nations. Second- and third-grade students can do research on these nations using a source such as *Britannica Junior.*

   Note: Some children in your class might not be able to find out the nations from which their surnames came. It is difficult, for example, for many African Americans to find out the national origins of their surnames. In these cases, label their names *American* on the class chart and ask these students to tell what *American* customs their families practice.

Intermediate and Upper Grades

CONCEPT

Immigration
Generalization: The first groups of Asians to immigrate to the United States came to improve their economic conditions and to fulfill labor needs in Hawaii and in the continental United States.

1. Read to the class accounts that describe the early immigrations of Chinese, Japanese, and Filipinos to the United States (see the bibliography at the end of this chapter for appropriate references).

Students should be able to answer the following questions when they have finished the readings:

   a. What economic, social, and political problems did the Chinese, Japanese, and Filipinos have in China, Japan, and the Philippines?
   b. What were the labor needs on the West Coast of the United States?
   c. Why did the immigrants leave China, Japan, and the Philippines?
   d. Was the United States what they expected? Why or why not?

2. Carefully study the historical summary on Filipino Americans in this chapter and read Chapter 9, "Dollar a Day, Dime a Dance: The Forgotten Filipinos," in Ronald Takaki (1998), *Strangers from a Different Shore: A History of Asian Americans*. Prepare a two-page summary of the economic, social, and political conditions of the early Filipino immigrants who went to Hawaii and the United States. Assign this summary to the students as a third reading.

3. After the students have read and discussed each of the three readings, have them complete Table 13.3.

4. When the students have completed the chart, have them summarize and generalize about why many Chinese, Japanese, and Filipinos immigrated to Hawaii and the United States, and about the labor needs they satisfied there.

5. Have the students role-play the situation below, which involves a representative of the Hawaiian Farmers Association trying to persuade a Filipino worker to go to Hawaii to work on a sugar plantation in 1910. After the role-play situation, ask the students the questions that follow. The role descriptions follow.

Mr. Howard Smith, the Hawaiian Sugar Planters Association Representative
Mr. Smith has been hired to recruit workers for the association. He realizes that his job depends on his success in recruiting workers. He also realizes that if he

TABLE 13.3   Data-Retrieval Chart on Asian American Immigrants

	Chinese Immigrants	Japanese Immigrants	Filipino Immigrants
Economic situation in homeland when immigration began			
Political situation in homeland when immigration began			
Social conditions in homeland when immigration began			
Labor needs on U.S. mainland when immigration began			
Labor needs in Hawaii when immigration began			

truthfully explains the situation in Hawaii, he will obtain few workers. He therefore decides to paint a rosy picture of the work on the sugar plantation in Hawaii. He explains to Mr. Ilanos that the contract is for three years and that the association will pay his transportation from the Philippines to Hawaii.

Mr. Jose Ilanos, a Filipino Who Lives in the Philippines
Mr. Ilanos is a young man with a wife and two children. He is a hard worker. However, in the last few years he has not been able to make enough money to support his family. He has heard about Mr. Smith and is interested in talking to him. However, his wife does not want him to leave the Philippines. Moreover, he has heard from friends that the work in Hawaii is hard and that the pay is rather low.

Questions
1. Did Mr. Smith succeed in persuading Mr. Ilanos to go to Hawaii to work? Why or why not?
2. If Mr. Ilanos decides to go to Hawaii, do you think that Mrs. Ilanos would go with him? Why or why not?
3. If Mr. Ilanos decides to go to Hawaii, what do you think will happen to him? Why? Do you think he might eventually immigrate to the United States? Why or why not?
4. If Mr. Ilanos decides to remain in the Philippines, what do you think will happen to him? Why?
5. Were there any other options open to Mr. Ilanos besides keeping his same job or going to Hawaii to work on the sugar plantations? If there were, what were they? If there were not, why?
6. If you were Mr. Ilanos, would you have accepted a contract from Mr. Smith? Why or why not?

VALUING ACTIVITY

Read the following story to the class and ask the questions that follow.

Father and Son

Mr. Robert Morimoto is a second-generation Japanese American who lives in an upper-middle-class, predominantly White suburban community near Los Angeles. He is a successful businessman. Mr. Morimoto is proud to be an American and believes that, even though our country has problems, any person, regardless of his or her race, can make it in the United States if he or she really tries. Mr. Morimoto does not like to talk about the years that he spent in the Heart Mountain federal concentration camp in Wyoming during World War II. The internment, he feels, is a thing of the past. Japanese Americans should not dwell on it too much today. Mr. Morimoto is impatient with those Sansei who talk about the internment all of the time. He feels that they have had it easy and do not have much right to criticize their country the way that they do.

Mr. Morimoto and his son have many fights because of their different beliefs. Henry is a student at a local university and is president of the Asian American Student Association on campus. Henry believes that the United States is a racist nation that oppresses all people of color, including the Japanese Americans. He often talks about the internment and harshly criticizes Japanese Americans like his father who try to "sweep it under the rug." Henry believes that all Third World people (by which he means all non-Whites) should join together to fight oppression and racism in America. When they had their last verbal fight, Henry told his father that, even though he was successful in business, he had no political power in America, and was Yellow on the outside but was White on the inside. Mr. Morimoto became very upset with Henry. He told Henry that he would either have to start treating him with respect or move out of his house.

Questions
1. Why do you think Mr. Morimoto feels the way he does?
2. Why do you think Henry feels the way he does?
3. Do you think that Henry is treating Mr. Morimoto fairly?
4. Do you think that Mr. Morimoto is treating Henry fairly?
5. If you were Henry, what would you do? Why?
6. If you were Mr. Morimoto, what would you do? Why?

High School Grades

CONCEPT

Discrimination

Generalization: Asian Americans have been the victims of widespread prejudice and highly discriminatory immigration and migration laws.

Initiate this unit by showing the students a videotape about the internment such as *Rabbit in the Moon* (see Appendix C for details about this videotape). This powerful and informative videotape describes the powerful human effects that the internment had on Japanese American communities. After viewing the videotape, ask the students to write one-sentence reactions to it. Divide the class into groups of three to five to discuss their written reactions to the videotape. Each group should be asked to develop a written reaction to be shared later with the entire class.

1. Ask individual students or small groups of students to prepare short research reports on the following topics and present them to the class:
   a. the California Foreign Miner's Tax of 1850
   b. anti-Chinese riots that occurred in the 1800s
   c. the Chinese Exclusion Act of 1882
   d. anti-Asian groups that developed on the West Coast in the late 1800s and continued through the 1930s, such as the Native Sons of the Golden West
   e. the California Alien Land Laws that prohibited Japanese immigrants from owning or leasing land
   f. the internment of Japanese Americans
   g. the Immigration Act of 1924

    h. anti-Filipino riots that occurred in the 1920s and 1930s
    i. the Tydings-McDuffie Act of 1934
    j. the Repatriation Act of July 11, 1935

2. When students share their reports, have them list on a master chart (a) ways in which all of the laws and actions were similar, (b) ways in which they were different, and (c) ways in which they discriminated against Asian Americans. Through the use of higher-level questions, help the students derive the key generalization stated previously.

3. Have your students role-play a session of Congress in which the Chinese Exclusion Act of 1882 is debated. The entire class can participate. However, assign several specific students to lead the debates. For example, ask one student to play the role of a California senator who is anxious to be reelected, and thus is strongly in favor of the act. Ask another student to argue against the act. Before the role-playing begins, read and discuss the act with the class. It is reprinted in Alexander Yamato, Soo-Young Chin, Wendy L. Ng, and Joel Franks (Eds.). (1993). *Asian Americans in the United States* (Vol. 1). Dubuque, Iowa: Kendall/Hunt, pp. 235–240.

    When the main speakers start debating, the other class members can participate both by asking them questions and by arguing on the floor. When the discussion of the act is complete, the students should then vote on it. After the voting, the role-playing should be discussed, as well as the actual historical events. The students should discuss why their voting results were similar to or different from that of Congress in 1882 and why. In this activity, try to help the students create the political and social atmosphere of the late 1800s. One way this can be done is to ask each student to pretend that he or she is a senator from a specific state with a particular mandate from his or her constituency.

4. Ask a group of students to do research and complete Table 13.4. After the students have completed the table, ask them to (a) write a generalization about the percentage of Asian immigrants that came to the United States between 1861 and 1960 and the total number of immigrants that came to the United States during this period; and (b) discuss, using the completed chart, whether White Americans on the West Coast had valid reasons to fear what was called the Yellow Peril. Ask them to discuss their answers to this question: "If Whites on the West Coast had no valid reasons to fear a Yellow Peril, why do you think that Asian Americans were the victims of so much hostility and harassment?"

5. Ask the students to read a book on the internment. Some recommended books follow:
   - Yoshiko Uchida. (1984). *Desert Exile: The Uprooting of a Japanese-American Family.* Seattle: University of Washington Press.
   - Charles Kikuchi. (1993). *The Kikuchi Diary: Chronicle from an American Concentration Camp.* Edited by John Modell. Urbana: University of Illinois Press.
   - Deborah Gesensway and Mindy Roseman. (1987). *Beyond Words: Images from America's Concentration Camps.* Ithaca, NY: Cornell University Press. (This book contains powerful art by artists who were interned.)

6. After they have read a book on the subject, ask them to do the following:
       a. compare the interpretation of the internment in the book read with the interpretation in a high school American history textbook or some other source;

TABLE 13.4 Asian Immigrants in the United States

Period	Number	Percentage of all Immigrants
1861–1880		
1881–1900		
1900–1914		
1914–1925		
1925–1940		
1940–1960		
1960–1970		
1970–1980		
1980–1990		
1990–2000		

b. discuss why they think the internment occurred;

c. discuss the role of the Japanese American Citizenship League during the internment;

d. discuss the roles of the following men in the internment:
   (1) President Franklin D. Roosevelt
   (2) Secretary of War Henry L. Stimson
   (3) Lieutenant General John L. DeWitt
   (4) Assistant Secretary of War John J. McCloy
   (5) Colonel Karl R. Bendetsen
   (6) Major General Allen W. Gullion

7. Role-play a meeting of the men listed in 6.d. discussing whether the Japanese should be interned during World War II.

8. Discuss the moral implications of the internment, that is: Should the internment have occurred? Why or why not? Who was responsible for the internment? What does the internment teach us about our society? Do you believe that an ethnic minority group could be interned today? Why or why not? Why were the Japanese interned and not the Germans?

9. Ask the students to review the hearing and testimony made before the Commission on Wartime Relocation and Internment of Civilians and to identify the factors that resulted in the passage of the American Civil Liberties bill in 1988. The hearing and testimony are summarized in Report of the Commis-

sion on Wartime Relocation and Internment of Civilians (1982), *Personal Justice Denied.*

10. To summarize this activity, ask the students to write an essay on "The Meaning of the Internment—Then and Now."

11. Asian American authors, like other American writers, often express their reactions to and experiences with prejudice and discrimination in their writings. Literary works by Asian Americans can provide students with insights that cannot be gained from factual sources. To help your students understand better the reactions of Asian Americans to discrimination, have the class read and discuss selections from the following books:

   a. John Okada, *No-No Boy,* a powerful and well-crafted novel about a Japanese American who refused to fight in World War II

   b. Carlos Bulosan, *America Is in the Heart,* a poignant, beautiful, and revealing book that can serve as an excellent springboard for a discussion about anti-Filipino discrimination in the United States

   c. Frank Chin et al. (Eds.), *Aiiieeeee: An Anthology of Asian-American Writers,* which includes stories, poetry, and excerpts from novels

   d. Asian Women of California, *Making Waves: An Anthology of Writings by and about Asian Women.* (Part 6 of this excellent anthology is called "Thunderstorms: Injustice." The readings provide first-hand accounts of the injustice experienced by Asian American women.)

   e. Mine Okubo, *Citizen 1366,* an individual who was interned describes her experiences.

REFERENCES

Binh, D. T. (1975). *A Handbook for Teachers of Vietnamese Students: Hints for Dealing with Cultural Differences in Schools.* Arlington, VA: Center for Applied Linguistics.

Butterfield, F. (1985, August 31). Violent Incidents against Asian-Americans Seen as Part of Racist Pattern. *New York Times,* I, p. 8.

Chun-Hoon, L. K. Y. (1973). Teaching the Asian American Experience. In J. A. Banks, (Ed.), *Teaching Ethnic Studies: Concepts and Strategies* (pp. 119–147). Washington, DC: National Council for the Social Studies.

Daniels, R. (1971). *Concentration Camps USA: Japanese Americans and World War II.* New York: Holt.

Daniels, R. (1988). *Asian America: Chinese and Japanese in the United States since 1850.* Seattle: University of Washington Press.

Divine, R. A. (1957). *American Immigration Policy, 1924–1952.* New Haven, CT: Yale University Press.

Espina, E. (1988). *Filipinos in Louisiana.* New Orleans: A. F. Laborde & Sons.

Horton, J. (1995). *The Politics of Diversity: Immigration, Resistance, and Change in Monterey Park, California.* Philadelphia: Temple University Press.

Jensen, R. (1980). East Indians. In S. Thernstrom, A. Orlov, & O. Handlin (Eds.), *Harvard Encyclopedia of American Ethnic Groups* (pp. 296–301). Cambridge: Harvard University Press.

Kim, B. C. (1978). *The Asian Americans: Changing Patterns, Changing Needs.* Montclair, NJ: Association of Korean Christian Scholars in North America. [AKCS]

Kim, H. (1980). Koreans. In S. Thernstrom, A. Orlov, & O. Handlin (Eds.), *Harvard Encyclopedia of American Ethnic Groups* (pp. 601–606). Cambridge: Harvard University Press.

Kitano, H. H. L. (1976). *Japanese Americans: The Evolution of a Subculture* (2nd ed.). Englewood Cliffs, NJ: Prentice-Hall.

Kitano, H. H. L., & Daniels, R. (1995). *Asian Americans: Emerging Minorities* (2nd ed.). Englewood Cliffs, NJ: Prentice-Hall.

Lyman, S. M. (1970). *The Asian in the West.* Reno: Desert Research Institute.

McWilliams, C. (1943). *Brothers under the Skin.* Boston: Little, Brown.

Melendy, H. B. (1972). *The Oriental Americans.* New York: Hippocrene Books.

Petersen, W. (1966, January 6). Success Story, Japanese Style. *New York Times Magazine,* pp. 20 ff.

Petersen, W. (1971). *Japanese Americans.* New York: Random House.

Report of the Commission on Wartime Relocation and Internment of Civilians. (1982, December). *Personal Justice Denied.* Washington, DC: U.S. Government Printing Office.

San Juan, E., Jr. (1972). *Carlos Bulosan and the Imagination of the Class Struggle.* Quezon City: Philippines Press.

Takaki, R. (1998). *Strangers from a Different Shore: A History of Asian Americans* (Rev. ed.). Boston: Little, Brown.

U.S. Bureau of the Census. (1993a). *We, the American Foreign Born.* Washington, DC: U.S. Government Printing Office.

U.S. Bureau of the Census. (1993b). *We, the American Asians.* Washington, DC: U.S. Government Printing Office.

U.S. Bureau of the Census. (1994). *Statistical Abstract of the United States 1994* (114th ed.). Washington, DC: U.S. Government Printing Office.

U.S. Census Bureau (2000). *Statistical Abstract of the United States* (120th ed.). Washington, DC: U. S. Government Printing Office.

U.S. Census Bureau (2001). [On-line]. Available: *http://www.census.gov/*

U.S. Immigration and Naturalization Service. (1985). *Statistical Yearbook of the Immigration and Naturalization Service, 1984.* Washington, DC: U.S. Government Printing Office.

U.S. Immigration and Naturalization Service. (1993). *Statistical Yearbook of the Immigration and Naturalization Service, 1992.* Washington, DC: U.S. Government Printing Office.

Wallovits, S. E. (1966). *The Filipinos in California.* Unpublished master's thesis, University of Southern California.

Wong, B. P. (1982). *Chinatown: Economic Adaptation and Ethnic Identity in Chinatown.* New York: Holt.

Wright, J. W. (Ed.). (1989). *The Universal Almanac 1990.* Kansas City: Andrews and McMeel.

A N N O T A T E D   B I B L I O G R A P H Y

Books for Teachers

Multiethnic

Amerasia Journal. Published by the Asian American Studies Center, 3232 Campbell Hall, University of California, Los Angeles, CA 90024.

> *Amerasia is a scholarly journal that publishes papers that deal with historical and contemporary Asian American experiences in the United States.*

Ancheta, A. (1998). *Race, Rights and the Asian American Experience.* New Brunswick, NJ: Rutgers University Press.

> *This book focuses on the distinctive experience of racial discrimination faced by Asian Americans and how the American legal system fails to recognize that discrimination can differ among racial and ethnic groups.*

Bow, L. (Ed.). (2000). *Betrayal and Other Acts of Subversion.* Princeton, NJ: Princeton University Press.

Asian American women writers negotiate agency among contradictory identity positions and discourses. Recommended for teachers of literature, Asian American studies, and feminist studies.

Chin, J. L. (Ed.). (2000). *Relationships Among Asian American Women.* Washington, DC: American Psychological Association.

Voices of women scholars address issues of cultural and gender role identity and stereotypes as they influence and are influenced by relationships with family, community, and the law.

Fong, T. (1998). *The Contemporary Asian American Experience: Beyond the Model Minority.* Upper Saddle River, NJ: Prentice-Hall.

Written in the style of journalistic sociology, this book provides an insightful analysis of Asian American experiences. Historical and contemporary perspectives are included.

Ghymn, E. (Ed.). (2000). *Asian American Studies: Identity, Images, Issues: Past and Present.* New York: Peter Lang.

A collection of essays that focuses on identity, images, and current issues of Asian Americans and their American-born children. The essays, written by Asian American scholars from different disciplines, discuss intergenerational conflicts within the Americanization process and the identity formation process by combining American culture and the culture of origin.

Kitano, H. H. L., and Daniels, R. (2001). *Asian Americans: Emerging Minorities.* Upper Saddle River, NJ: Prentice-Hall.

A readable book that provides important historical and contemporary insights on the experiences of Asian Americans.

Kumar, A. (2000). *Passport Photos.* Berkeley, CA: University of California Press.

The author combines theory, poetry, cultural criticism, and photography to describe the current immigrant conditions for Asian Americans.

Lim, S. G., and Chua, C. L. (Eds.). (2000). *Tilting the Continent: Southeast Asian American Writing.* Minneapolis, MN: New Rivers Press.

A must read for educators. One of the first anthologies of Southeast Asian writers that contain selections from recent immigrants as well as fourth-generation authors. This collection contains diverse insiders' views about the lives of Southeast Asian Americans.

Lott, J. T. (1998). *Asian Americans: From Racial Category to Multiple Identities.* Walnut Creek, CA: Alta Mira Press.

Taking a historical perspective, Lott discusses the complexity of Asian American identities and issues of deconstructing minority/majority classifications and the changing meanings of these labels.

Manalansan, M. F. (Ed.). (2001). *Cultural Compass: Ethnographic Explorations of Asian America.* Philadelphia, PA: Temple University Press.

A collection of essays by a diverse group of Asian American scholars, this book builds on current contemporary perspectives of Asian American identities within geography and the complexities of emotional and physical space.

Min, P. G. (Ed.). (2002). *The Second Generation: Ethnic Identity among Asian Americans.* Lanham, MD: Alta Mira Press.

This collection of essays describes the contemporary identity issues of second-generation ethnic Asian Americans, mainly Chinese, Filipino, Japanese, Korean, Indian, and Vietnamese.

Min, P. G., & Kim, J. H. (Eds.). (2001). *Religions in Asian America: Building Faith Communities*. Lanham, MD: Alta Mira Press.

This book provides a comprehensive overview of the religious practices of Asian Americans and how these religions differ from European models. It describes how religious communities work through the issues of gender, race, transnationalism, economics, and social services, and the passage of an ethnic identity to future generations.

Min, P. G., & Kim, R. (Eds.). (1999). *Struggle for Ethnic Identity: Narratives by Asian American Professionals*. Walnut Creek, CA: Alta Mira Press.

Through a collection of personal narratives written by young Asian American professionals who have achieved a moderate degree of professional success, this book examines ethnic attachment and ethnic identity among first- and second-generation Asian Americans.

Nam, V. (Ed.). (2001). *Yell-Oh Girls!* New York: HarperCollins.

Voices of young Asian American female writers present the unique challenges of Asian American females in the United States. The contributors engage in a dynamic conversation about contemporary issues affecting the conceptualization of Asian American girls.

Okihiro, G. Y. (2001). *Common Ground: Reimaging American History*. Princeton, NJ: Princeton University Press.

The author presents a different perspective on diaspora and transnationalism, and their effects on the formation of Asian Americans in American history.

Pang, V. O., & Cheng, L. L. (Eds.). (1998). *Struggling to Be Heard: The Unmet Needs of Asian Pacific American Children*. Albany, NY: State University of New York Press.

In this book, Asian American scholars offer diverse theoretical frameworks integrating curriculum, instruction, mental health issues, language issues, policy, disabilities, delinquency, and culture. The contributors discuss insiders' perspectives on the issues of invisibility as a model minority and the unmet needs of students.

Park, C. C., & Chi, M. M. (Eds.). (1999). *Asian-American Education: Prospects and Challenges*. Westport, CT: Bergin and Garvey.

This book is a comprehensive survey that describes the linguistic and sociocultural aspects of seven Asian American groups: Cambodian, Chinese, Filipino, Hmong, Japanese, Korean, and Vietnamese. The contributors, who wrote intimately about their respective ethnic groups, share insights about educational issues, needs, and challenges faced by each group.

Prashard, V. (2000). *The Karma of Brown Folk*. Minneapolis, MN: University of Minnesota Press.

This book describes the plights of South Asian immigrants in the United States.

Shankar, L. D., & Srikanth, R. (Eds.). (1998). *A Part, Yet Apart: South Asian in Asian America*. Philadelphia: Temple University Press.

An informative and thoughtful collection of papers that examines a range of issues related to the experiences of South Asians in the United States.

Takaki, R. (1998). *Strangers from a Different Shore: A History of Asian Americans* (Rev. ed.). Boston, MA: Little, Brown.

A classic Asian American history by the noted scholar of Asian American studies, Takaki provides a comprehensive account and analysis of the narratives and documents the major historical events describing the struggles and identity transformations of Asian Americans in the United States.

Tuan, M. (1998). *Forever Foreigners or Honorary Whites? The Asian Ethnic Experience Today*. New Brunswick, NJ: Rutgers University Press.

In this book, the author examines the racial conceptualization of Asian Americans by undertaking an in-depth analysis of belonging through assimilation and identity formation issues.

Williams-Leon, T., & Nakashina, C. (Eds.). (2001). *The Sum of Our Parts: Mixed Heritage Asian American*. Philadelphia. Temple University Press.

This collection of essays by a diverse group of scholars presents their thoughts on multiracial and multiethnic Asian America.

Wu, J. Y., & Song, M. (Eds.). (2000*). Asian American Studies: A Reader*. New Brunswick, NJ: Rutgers University Press.

This informative anthology provides diverse and informative perspectives on the experiences of Asian Americans.

Yu, H. (2001). *Thinking Orientals: Migration, Contact, and Exoticism in Modern America*. New York: Oxford University Press.

This intellectual history of Asian Americans provides a history of race in the United States.

Zhou, M., & Gatewood, J. V. (Eds.). (2000). *Contemporary Asian America: A Multidisciplinary Reader*. New York: New York University Press.

A valuable resource, this comprehensive collection of theoretically grounded accounts of Asian American experiences provides insights into contemporary issues of assimilation and transformation.

Zia, H. (2000). *Asian American Dreams: The Emergence of an American People*. Gordonsville, VA: Farrar, Straus and Giroux.

Zia incorporates a personal account of her struggles and that of a diverse Asian American group into this thoughtfully written story of human struggles and transformations. The transformation from "aliens" into Americans provides insight into the question: What does it take to become fully American?

Chinese Americans

Cassel, S. L. (Ed.). (2002). *The Chinese in America: A History from Gold Mountain to the New Millennium*. Lanham, MD: Alta Mira Press.

Chinese Americans have been called "model workers" but have also been perceived as perpetual foreigners in America. Contributors to this book describe labor immigration history and policies that define the Chinese American experience.

Chang, L. (2000). *Beyond the Narrow Gate: The Journey of Four Chinese Women from Middle Kingdom to Middle America*. New York: Plume.

The author describes biographical narratives of four women and their experiences as Chinese immigrants and Chinese Americans in the United States.

Chen, Y. (2000). *Chinese San Francisco 1850–1943: A Transpacific Community*. Stanford, CA: Stanford University Press.

This comprehensive book describes the social and cultural history of Chinatown in San Francisco. It outlines Chinatown's creation and community development up to the 1940s.

Chin, K. (1999). *Smuggled Chinese: Clandestine Immigration to the United States*. Philadelphia, PA: Temple University Press.

An important work that describes issues related to clandestine Chinese immigrants to the United States. Chin argues that human smuggling will continue as long as many nationality groups do not have fundamental human rights and economic security in their homelands.

Chin, T. P. (2000). *Chinese American History 1930–1970*. Philadelphia, PA: Temple University Press.

A well-written and comprehensive historical account of the life and history of Chinese Americans from 1930 to the 1970s.

Choy, W. (1999). *Paper Shadows: A Memoir of a Past Lost and Found.* New York: St. Martin's Press.

In this narrative biography, the author presents an account of life in the Chinese diaspora.

Freedman, A. L. (2000). *Political Participation and Ethnic Minorities: Chinese Overseas in Malaysia, Indonesia, and the United States.* New York: Routledge.

This empirical study compares the political activity of three distinct groups of overseas Chinese. It describes the politicizing of Chinese ethnicity in three different nations, including the United States.

Ho, W. (1998). *In Her Mother's House: The Politics of Asian American Mother–Daughter Writing.* Walnut Creek, CA: Alta Mira Press.

In this book on Chinese American feminism, Ho describes the tensions of contemporary Chinese American women's identity formation.

Kwong, P. (2001). *Chinatown, New York: Labor and Politics 1930–1950* (Rev. ed.). New York: New Press.

This book presents an in-depth history of Chinese labor and a provocative critique of the response of the United States and the union movement struggles with immigrant workers.

Larson, L. L. (2001). *Sweet Bamboo: A Memoir of a Chinese American Family.* Berkeley, CA: University of California Press.

This book provides an invaluable history of a Chinese American family in Los Angeles before the twentieth century. The author sheds light on the Americanization process of this family.

Lee, A. W. (2001). *Picturing Chinatown: Art and Orientalism in San Francisco.* Berkeley, CA: University of California Press.

An informative and significant book on art and orientation in San Francisco's Chinatown.

Lin, J. (1998). *Reconstructing Chinatown: Ethnic Enclave, Global Changes.* Minneapolis, MN: University of Minnesota Press.

New York City's Chinatown is examined in a global context through the conflicts and interaction of labor and capital, the community, and the state.

Pan, L. (Ed.). (1999). *The Encyclopedia of Chinese Overseas.* Cambridge, MA: Harvard University Press.

This encyclopedia is a historical description of the overseas Chinese. The chapter on the United States provides an historical overview of migration and heritage.

Prager, E. (2001). *Wu Hu Diary: On Taking My Adopted Daughter to Her Hometown in China.* New York: Random House.

The search for a Chinese child's identity creates a deeper emotional bond between a Caucasian mother and her adopted Chinese daughter.

Tung, M. P. (2000). *Chinese Americans and Their Immigrant Parents: Conflict, Identity and Values.* New York: Haworth Press.

Insiders "and outsiders" perspectives are revealed in this book that describes and analyzes Chinese American immigration and cultural experiences.

Wong, W. (2001). *Yellow Journalist: Dispatches from Asian America.* Philadelphia, PA: Temple University Press.

The author maps a different reality of Chinese and Asian American communities and conscience. Through anecdotes about his family and community, the author provides a picture of important social, cultural, and political moments of the Chinese and Asian American community.

Japanese Americans

Fiset, L. (1998). *Imprisoned Apart: The World War II Correspondence of an Issei Couple*. Seattle, WA: University of Washington Press.

A powerful story of a young Japanese teacher and his bride who came to Seattle to study English language and literature and made Seattle their home until the internment and the couple's separation. Emotional and political struggles to clear their name and reunite unfold in their correspondence.

Higashidi, J. (2000). *Adios to Tears: The Memoirs of a Japanese Peruvian Internee in a U.S. Concentration Camp* (2nd ed.). Seattle, WA: University of Washington Press.

A true story of a Japanese Peruvian who was deported from Peru to the United States. It is a moving personal account of the author's life in three countries.

Hosokawa, B. (1998). *Out of the Frying Pan: Reflections of a Japanese American*. Niwot, CO: University of Colorado Press.

A leading Japanese American journalist documents bittersweet personal memories and diverse voices about the unconstitutional incarceration of Japanese Americans in World War II.

Inada, L. F. (Ed.). (2000). *Only What We Could Carry: The Japanese American Internment Experience*. Berkeley, CA: Heyday Books.

This book contains a collection of documents from writers who share their voices through diverse literary forms, including narratives, letters, stories, and graphic arts. The writers reveal the victims' powerful emotions and struggles during wartime hysteria.

Niiya, B. (Ed.). (2001). *Encyclopedia of Japanese American History*. New York: Facts on File.

An A-to-Z reference from 1868 to the present. This is a rich and excellent resource for teachers, with an introductory essay by Gary Okihiro.

Okihiro, G. Y. (1999). *Storied Lives: Japanese American Students and World War II*. Seattle, WA: University of Washington Press.

The author describes race relations between Japanese American college students and volunteers of the National Student Relocation Council on a university campus.

Shimabukuro, R. S. (2001). *Born in Seattle: The Campaign for Japanese American Redress*. Seattle, WA: University of Washington Press.

Using interviews and documents from the internment, the author provides a narrative explaining the campaign and redress movement from the 1960s to the 1990s.

Takami, D. A. (1998). *Divided Destiny: A History of Japanese Americans in Seattle*. Seattle, WA: University of Washington Press.

This book provides a vivid and concise history of Japanese Americans in Seattle, before and after World War II.

Tateishi, J. (1999). *And Justice for All: An Oral History of the Japanese American Detention Camps* (2nd ed.). Seattle, WA: University of Washington Press.

This book captures the personal feelings and experiences of thirty Japanese Americans through oral history.

Uchida, Y. (1997). *Picture Bride*. Seattle, WA: University of Washington Press.

Uchida's novel brings to life the stories of the picture brides and their new life in America before and during the turmoil of World War II.

Weglyn, M. N. (1995). *Years of Infamy: The Untold Story of America's Concentrations Camps* (2nd ed.). Seattle, WA: University of Washington Press.

In this important book, Weglyn details the untold accounts of the American concentration camps in which Japanese Americans were interned during World War II.

Filipino Americans

Bonus, R. (2000). *Locating Filipino Americans: Ethnicity and the Cultural Politics of Space.* Philadelphia, PA: Temple University Press.

This is one of the few ethnographic books that provides a grounded approach to the study of Filipino American ethnicity and identity formation. It effectively and eloquently captures the narratives of the author's subjects.

Bulosan, C. (1973). *America Is in the Heart.* Seattle, WA: University of Washington Press.

This classic book describes the inner thoughts and personal journey of a Filipino laborer's struggle to become American. Bulosan, a Filipino American laborer who lived during the colonialization and postcolonialization era, was a self-taught and talented writer.

Cordova, F. (1999). *Filipinos: Forgotten Asian Americans, A Pictorial Essay/1763-circa-1963* (3rd ed.). Seattle: Demonstration Project for Asian Americans.

This book provides a description of Filipino migration and community transformation from 1763 to 1963. Pictures, essays, and excerpted interviews record the journey and transformation of Filipino Americans from labor migration to pensionados.

Filipinas Magazine. Published by Filipinas Publishing, Inc., 655 Sutter St., Suite 333, San Francisco, CA 94102.

A current events magazine, Filipinas describes Filipino Americans' contemporary social, cultural, economic and political issues.

Francia, L. H., & Gamalinda, E. (Eds.). (1998). *Flippin': Filipinos on America.* Philadelphia, PA: Temple University Press.

Filipino and Filipino American writers describe their lives in their own words through stories, poetry, and prose.

Guillermo, E. (1999). *Amok: Essays from an Asian-American Perspective.* San Francisco, CA: Asian Week Books.

Amok is a collection of witty and unsettling essays written by journalist and commentator Guillermo. Guillermo's insights demolish many assumptions about Asian Americans.

Okamura, J. Y. (1998). *Imagining the Filipino American Diaspora: Transnational Relations, Identities, and Communities.* New York: Garland.

After eighteen years of research on Filipino Americans, Okamura reconceptualizes the Filipino American population as a transnational diaspora rather than as an immigrant or ethnic minority. This book presents a refreshing perspective and analysis of Filipino Americans as a marginalized minority within a global diaspora.

Posadas, B. M. (1999). *The New Americans: The Filipino Americans.* Westport, CT: Greenwood Press.

This book provides a general and basic historical overview of Filipino American immigration history from the 1700s to post-1965.

Root, M. P. (Ed.). (1997). *Filipino Americans: Transformation and Identity.* Thousand Oaks, CA: Sage.

Through a collection of essays and scholarly contributions, this book addresses the historical impact of colonialism on ethnic identity formation, race and human relations, and contemporary issues that affect the identity and definition of Filipino Americans.

San Juan, E., Jr. (2000). *After Postcolonialism: Remapping Philippines—United States Confrontations.* Lanham, MD: Rowman and Littlefield.

An intellectual analysis of Philippines—United States relations that discusses diaspora and identity conflicts after postcolonialism.

San Juan, E., Jr. (Ed.). (1995). *On Becoming Filipino: Selected Writings of Carlos Bulosan.* Philadelphia, PA: Temple University Press.

A classic, this book is the first extensive collection of Bulosan's writings, which describe his mission to redefine Filipino Americans from the 1930s up to the 1950s.

San Juan, E., Jr. (Ed.). (1995). *The Cry and the Dedication: Carlos Bulosan.* Philadelphia, PA: Temple University Press.

Bulosan captures the pain and desire for independence and democracy among Filipinos in their struggle against Spanish and later American colonization in the Philippines. Editor San Juan provides an introduction to Bulosan and his works.

Stroebel, L. (2001). *Coming Full Circle.* Thousand Oaks, CA: Sage.

This book provides descriptions and reflections on being Filipino American.

Books for Students

Multiethnic

Chiu, C. (1996). *Lives of Notable Asian Americans: Literature and Education.* Series: *The Asian American Experience.* New York: Chelsea House.

This collection of brief biographies is illustrated with photographs of the subjects. (Intermediate and Up)

Hong, M. (Ed.). (1993). *Growing Up Asian American.* New York: William Morrow.

Thirty-two classic stories by new and established writers. (High School)

Lee, J. F. J. (1991). *Asian Americans: Oral Histories of First to Fourth Generation Americans from China, the Philippines, Japan, India, the Pacific Islands, Vietnam and Cambodia.* New York: New Press.

These oral histories are a rich and informative source. (High School)

Yamanaka, L-A. (1999). *Name Me Nobody.* New York: Hyperion.

The gritty lives of Hawaii's multiethnic teens are detailed in frank language and pidgin dialect in this and other novels by the acclaimed author, including Heads by Harry *(Farrar, Straus & Giroux, 1999) and* Blu's Hanging *(Farrar, Straus & Giroux, 1997). (High School)*

Chinese Americans

Chang, A. (2000). *Grandfather Counts.* Illustrated by A. Zhang. New York: Lee & Low.

Helen, or Yin Hua, as she is known in Chinese, is upset and confused when her grandfather leaves China to live with her family in the United States. (Primary)

Chiu, E. (1997). *The Lobster and the Sea.* Illustrated by M. Takahashi. Chicago, IL: Polychrome.

A Chinese American girl cannot understand why her beloved grandfather wants to return to China. (Primary)

Hoobler, D., & Hoobler, T. (1994). *The Chinese American Family Album.* New York: Oxford University Press.

An excellent, involving, and well-illustrated book. (Middle School/High School)

Krach, M. S. (1997). *D Is for Doufu: An Alphabet Book of Chinese Culture.* Illustrated by H. Zhang. Auburn, CA: Shen's Books.

This beautifully illustrated alphabet book depicts aspects of Chinese culture throughout history as well as valued cultural attributes. (All Ages)

Lee, M. (1997). *Nim and the War Effort.* Illustrated by Y. Choi. New York: Farrar, Straus & Giroux.

> *Nim, a young immigrant to the United States from China, confronts prejudice during World War II but wins the respect of her peers when she and her grandfather take part in a contest to collect newspapers for the war effort. (Primary)*

Look, L. (1999). *Love as Strong as Ginger.* Illustrated by S. T. Johnson. New York: Atheneum.

> *A Chinese American girl visits the crab factory where her immigrant grandmother works. (Primary)*

Mah, A. Y. (1999). *Chinese Cinderella: The True Story of an Unwanted Daughter.* New York: Delacorte.

> *Born in China just before World War II, the author, her family's fifth daughter, is rejected by her parents because they want a son. Her relationships with her grandfather and aunt and her success in school give her the courage to leave China and to earn a medical degree in England. (Middle School/High School)*

Namioka, L. (2000). *Yang the Eldest and His Odd Jobs.* Illustrated by K. de Kiefte. New York: Little, Brown.

> *In this recent book in Namioka's series about the Yang siblings, the oldest finds a job to pay for a new violin but almost becomes more interested in making money than in pursuing his music. An accident at work makes him realize what is most important. (Intermediate)*

Russell, C. Y. (1997). *Moon Festival.* Illustrated by C. Z-Y. Zhang. New York: Honesdale, PA: Boyds Mills.

> *The Moon Festival, China's beloved harvest festival, is described through simple text and attractive illustrations. The story centers on a Chinese girl who lives with her grandfather in a small village and misses her parents most at this time of the year. (Primary).*

Tong, B. (2000). *The Chinese Americans.* Series: *The New Americans.* Westport, CT: Greenwood.

> *This series title highlights successive waves of migration, the Chinese Americans' response to exclusion and discrimination, political mobilization, economic and social life today, ethnic identity of various generations, and notable Chinese Americans. (High School)*

Yang, D. J. (2000). *The Secret Voice of Gina Zhang.* Middleton, WI: Pleasant.

> *In this contemporary story, Jinna, a recent immigrant from China, must find her voice in a new school despite her shyness and not knowing the language. (Middle School)*

Ye, T. (1999). *Share the Sky.* Illustrated by S. Langlois. Toronto: Annick/Firefly.

> *A Chinese girl worries about the day she will journey to North America to rejoin her parents, and, once there, her correspondence with her grandparents in China helps to allay her anxieties in a strange new world. (Primary)*

Yep, L. (2000). *The Journal of Wong Ming-Chung: A Chinese Miner.* Series: *My Name Is America.* New York: Scholastic.

> *A 10-year-old Chinese boy comes to California to help his uncle during the Gold Rush. (Intermediate)*

Yep, L. (2000). *The Magic Paintbrush.* Illustrated by S. Wang. New York: HarperCollins.

> *Eight-year-old Steve, living in San Francisco's Chinatown, turns to art to cope with the death of his parents and the destruction of his home in a fire. (Intermediate)*

Japanese Americans

Bunting, E. (1998). *So Far from the Sea.* Illustrated by C. K. Soentpiet. New York: Clarion.

> *A Japanese American family remembers a deceased grandfather and visits the World War II internment camp where he spent his sad and lonely last months. (Primary)*

Hobbler, D., & Hoobler, T. (1995). *The Japanese American Family Album.* New York: Oxford University Press.

> *A well-illustrated, informative, and captivating book. (Middle School/High School)*

Hoobler, D., & Hoobler, T. (1999). *The Ghost in the Tokaido Inn.* New York: Philomel.

> *A teenage boy who dreams of becoming a samurai saves the day when he discovers the thief of a priceless jewel while traveling with his merchant father in nineteenth-century Japan. This book shows the rigid class structures and interfamilial intrigues in Japan during this period. (Middle School)*

Krasno, R. (2000). *Floating Lanterns and Golden Shrines: Celebrating Japanese Festivals.* Illustrated by T. Sugita. Berkeley, CA: Pacific View Press.

> *This attractive introduction to Japanese festivals features legends and folktales, craft activities, recipes, and lively color illustrations. (Primary/Intermediate)*

McCoy, K. K. (1999) *Bon Odori Dancer.* Illustrated by C. Yeo. Chicago: Polychrome.

> *Keiko, a modern Japanese girl, continues the tradition of dancing in the Obon festival. This festival, which predates the introduction of Buddhism to Japan, unites "the living and the dead." (Primary)*

Uchida, Y. (1982). *Desert Exile: The Uprooting of a Japanese American Family.* Seattle: University of Washington Press.

> *A well-known writer tells the personal story of the internment of her family during World War II in this moving and powerful book. Other books by Uchida include* The Best Bad Thing *(Atheneum, 1983);* A Jar of Dreams *(Atheneum, 1982);* The Happiest Ending *(Atheneum, 1985); and* Journey to Topaz *(Atheneum, 1985). (Middle School/High School)*

Walters, E. (2001). *Caged Eagles.* Victoria, BC: Orca Books.

> *Tadashi, a Japanese Canadian boy, is relocated to an internment camp during World War II. He and his younger sisters reveal the confusion, turmoil, and harsh conditions of the camp. Tadashi's friendship with a Native American boy on the eve of the war is detailed in* War of the Eagles *(Orca, 1998). (Middle School)*

Filipino Americans

Arcellana, F. (1999). *The Mats.* Illustrated by H. Alagra. La Jolla, CA: Kane/Miller.

> *Marcelina's father, an inspector for telegraph lines in the Philippines, sends a letter to his family telling them he is bringing them new sleeping mats. Distinctive, colorful illustrations enhance this book from the Philippines. (Primary)*

Bacho, P. (1998). *Dark Blue Suit.* Seattle: University of Washington Press.

> *Twelve interconnected stories portray a Filipino American youth growing up in Seattle in the 1950s and 1960s and the interesting and diverse collection of people he encounters. (High School)*

Bautista, V. (1998). *The Filipino American from 1763 to the Present: Their History, Culture, and Traditions.* Farmington Hills, MI: Bookhaus.

> *This comprehensive narrative of Filipino American history also profiles 150 prominent individuals in a variety of endeavors. (High School)*

Brainard, C. M., & Litton, E. F. (Eds.). (2000). *Journey of 100 Years: Reflections on the Centennial of Philippine Independence.* Santa Monica, CA: Philippine American Literary House.

> *A collection of 17 essays by Filipino American scholars, folklorists, journalists, and literary figures explores aspects of Philippine history and the lives of Filipino Americans. While some of the essays are quite academic in style, most are accessible to readers high*

school age and up. Brainerd also edited Fiction by Filipinos in America *(New Day Publishers, 1993), a collection of stories by 23 Filipino American authors. (High School)*

Espiritu, Y. L. (1995). *Filipino American Lives.* Philadelphia: Temple University Press.

An informative collection of first-person narratives. Pre- and post-1965 immigrants share their sojourns in the United States. (High School)

Gilles, A. A. (2001). *Willie Wins.* Illustrated by C. Angel. New York: Lee & Low.

Willie hears his father's stories of growing up in the Philippines and receives for a school contest an alkansiya, a bank made from a coconut shell. Other children make fun of Willie's bank, but the alkansiya contains a special treasure. (Primary)

Kinkade, S. (1996). *Children of the Philippines.* Illustrated with photos by E. Little. Series: *The World's Children.* Minneapolis: Carolrhoda.

Attractive photos and accompanying text describe the lives of a variety of Filipino children, rich and poor, urban and rural, Catholic and Muslim. (Intermediate)

Krasno, R. (1997). *Kneeling Carabao and Dancing Giants: Celebrating Filipino Festivals.* Illustrated by I. C. Lee. Berkeley, CA: Pacific View Press.

Key Filipino festivals are arranged chronologically in an attractively illustrated book that features historical information on the Philippines, legends and folktales, craft activities, recipes, and lively color illustrations. (Primary/Intermediate)

Posadas, B. (1989). *The Filipino Americans.* Series: *The New Americans.* Westport, CT: Greenwood.

This series title offers a brief history of the Philippines, then details the history of immigration to the United States, the transformation of Filipino American culture and politics, challenges facing Filipino Americans, and famous Americans of Filipino descent. (High School)

Villanueva, M. (1993). *Nene and the Horrible Math Monster.* Illustrated by R. Unson. Chicago: Polychrome Books.

A Filipino American girl struggles with math and with the stereotype that all Asian American children are good at math. (Primary)

Korean Americans

Balgassi, H. (1996). *Peacebound Trains.* Illustrated by C. K. Soentpiet. New York: Clarion.

A Korean girl waiting for her mother to return home from the army hears her grandmother's stories of deprivation, loss, and survival during the Korean War. Older readers will enjoy Balgassi's Tae's Sonata *(Clarion, 1997), the story of a Korean American middle schooler who clashes with her more traditional mother and wonders where she fits in. (Intermediate)*

Bercaw, E. C. (2000). *Halmoni's Day.* Illustrated by R. Hunt. New York: Dial.

Jennifer is worried that her Korean grandmother will not fit in with the other grandparents at her school on Grandparents' Day. (Primary)

Choi, S. N. (1997). *Yunmi and Halmoni's Trip.* Illustrated by K. Dugan. Boston: Houghton Mifflin.

Yunmi joins her grandmother on a trip back to Korea, but she worries that her grandmother is having too good a time and will not want to return to New York. (Primary)

Na, A. (2001). *A Step from Heaven.* Asheville NC: Front Street Books.

A Korean girl, Young Ju, immigrates with her family to California as a toddler and in the next 14 years confronts homesickness, language barriers, friendship issues, questions of identity, and the disapproval of her father who fears she has become too Americanized. Winner of the 2002 Michael L. Printz Award for Outstanding Young Adult Literature.

Pak, S. (1999). *Dear Juno.* Illustrated by S. K. Hartung. New York: Viking.

A young Korean American boy exchanges pictures with his grandfather, who lives in Seoul. (Primary)

Park, F., & Park, G. (2000). *The Royal Bee.* Illustrated by C. Z-Y. Zhang. Honesdale, PA: Boyds Mills.

This folktale of a boy who longs to attend school despite his family's poverty reveals the traditional values and social hierarchies of Korea before the twentieth century. (Primary)

Wong, J. S. (2000) *The Trip Back Home.* Illustrated by B. Jia. San Diego: Harcourt.

A Korean American girl travels with her mother to visit her grandparents, who live in the Korean countryside. (Primary)

South Asian Americans

English, K. (1999). *Nadia's Hands.* Illustrated by J. Weiner. Honesdale, PA: Boyds Mills.

A Pakistani American girl is worried that the dye applied to her hands for a wedding will not come off in time for school on Monday. (Primary)

Gilmore, R. (1994). *Lights for Gita.* Illustrated by the author. Gardiner, ME: Tilbury House.

It is Gita's first winter in North America, and Divali, the Hindu festival of light, doesn't seem the same in the cold, dark winter. But during an ice storm, Gita's celebration takes on a new beauty. (Primary)

Krishnaswami, U. (1999). *Shower of Gold: Girls and Women in the Stories of India.* North Haven, CT: Linnet Books.

Eighteen traditional stories, accompanied by detailed source notes, present a range of women who have played a role in India's history, mythology, and lore. Also by the same author is The Broken Tusk: Stories of the Hindu God Ganesha *(Linnet Books, 1996). (Middle School)*

Kuklin, S. (1998). *Iqbal Masih and the Crusaders against Child Slavery.* New York: Henry Holt.

Compelling photos and text recount the life of the young antislavery activist in Pakistan who was assassinated at the age of twelve. (Middle School/High School)

Leonard, K. I. (1997). *South Asian Americans.* Series: *The New Americans.* Westport, CT: Greenwood.

A detailed overview of the history, cultures, and lives of Americans who trace their heritage to India, Pakistan, Bangladesh, Afghanistan, Nepal, Bhutan, and Sri Lanka. (High School)

Lewin, T. (1995). *Sacred River.* Illustrated by the author. New York: Clarion.

Stunning watercolor illustrations describe the Ganges River and its spiritual significance for the Hindu majority of India. (Primary)

Rahaman, V. (1997). *A Little Salmon for Witness.* Illustrated by S. Speidel. New York: Lodestar.

Rajiv, a boy of South Asian heritage living in Trinidad, longs for a treat for his grandmother's birthday, but the family has no money for extras. This warm picture book depicts one of the many South Asian families who make their home in the West Indies. (Primary)

Severance, J. B. (1997). *Gandhi: Great Soul.* New York: Clarion.

An accessible biography of the Father of India that discusses his strategy of nonviolent resistance. (Middle School)

Sreenivasan, J. (1997). *Aruna's Journeys*. St. Louis, MO: Smooth Stone Press.

Eleven-year-old Aruna thinks she has a hard time fitting in at her White middle-class school, but when she travels to India to visit relatives, she gets caught up in conflicts over her Indian identity and the roles of girls and women in the country of her heritage. (Intermediate/Middle School)

Takaki, R. (1995). *India in the West: South Asians in America*. Series: *The Asian American Experience*. Philadelphia, PA: Chelsea House.

A well-written series book that traces the successive waves of South Asian immigration to America, with a focus on immigrants from India. (Middle School/High School)

Southeast Asian Americans

Coburn, J. R. (1998). *Angkat: The Cambodian Cinderella*. Illustrated by E. Flotte. Auburn, CA: Shen's Books.

A retelling of the classic tale, found in variants in over 80 cultures throughout the world. (Primary)

Do, H. D. (1999). *The Vietnamese Americans*. Series: *The New Americans*. Westport, CT: Greenwood.

A scholar and former refugee from Vietnam offers a history of immigration to the United States from Vietnam from the 1970s to the present. The book also explores prejudice against Vietnamese immigrants, challenges faced by the new immigrants, and the ways in which Vietnamese Americans have shared their food and culture. (High School)

Garland, S. (1998). *My Father's Boat*. Illustrated by T. Rand. New York: Scholastic.

A boy and his father, Vietnamese immigrants who fish on a boat in the Gulf of Mexico, reflect on their new home and lives. (Primary)

McKay, L. (1998). *Journey Home*. Illustrated by D. and K. Lee. New York: Lee & Low.

Mai accompanies her mother, who was adopted as a child from Vietnam, on a journey to the country of her birth. (Primary)

Murphy, N. (1997). *A Hmong Family*. Illustrated with photos by P. Ford. Series: *Journey between Two Worlds*. Minneapolis: Lerner.

This series title features an eleven-year-old Hmong American boy who came to Minneapolis with his family at the age of three. (Intermediate)

Shepard, A. (1998). *The Crystal Heart: A Vietnamese Legend*. Illustrated by J. D. Fiedler. New York: Atheneum.

This tale recounts the unfortunate result of a meeting between a rich young woman and a poor fisherman. (Primary)

Tran, N-D. *To Swim in Our Own Pond: A Book of Vietnamese Proverbs*. Illustrated by X-Q. Dang. Auburn, CA. Shen's Books.

This bilingual picture book presents 22 popular Vietnamese proverbs along with their English equivalents. (Primary)

Yin, C. (1997). *In My Heart I Am a Dancer*. Ilustrated with photos by R. Márquez. Philadelphia, PA: Philadelphia Folklore Project.

Yin, a dancer, offers a memoir of growing up in the turmoil of Cambodia in the 1970s, escaping to Thailand, and journeying to the United States, all the while maintaining his life's dream. A moving account of hope and persistence in the face of extreme hardship. (All Ages)

14 Arab Americans

Concepts, Strategies, and Materials

> *The more I answered to Arab, the more I puzzled over the discrepancy between what most people believed about Arabs and what I knew of Arab Americans. The stereotypes just didn't fit. Terrorist, oil sheik, master of the seraglio—it was impossible to connect these terms with my uncle who baked blueberry muffins for his wife's breakfast and washed out her [clothes] by hand, or with my other uncle who belonged to the Rotary Club, voted Republican, and was a deacon in the Baptist church.*
>
> —Evelyn Shakir (1997), p. 1

Arabs have been becoming Americans for well over a century. Yet, for most of that time, both in popular literature and in the national conversations on ethnicity, they have been invisible as an American ethnic group. Within the last four decades, their invisibility has been transformed to a public image in large part defined by the stereotypes mainstream America has come to associate with Arabs. Their contributions to American social and public life, the development of their institutional life, and their extraordinarily strong family values have been "the best kept ethnic secret in America" (Hatab, n.d.).

This chapter was contributed by **Paula Hajar**, Ed.D., an educator and long-time activist and researcher in the Arab American community. Dr. Hajar received her undergraduate degree from Radcliffe College, and graduate degrees from Antioch University and Harvard University Graduate School of Education. She is a former faculty member of Teachers College, Columbia University.

The achievements of Arabs, their reasons for coming to America, and their struggles are like those of other immigrant groups. However, Arabs continue to be victims of widespread stereotypes long after the defamation of other ethnic groups has faded from public discourse. This chapter, in addition to describing their progress and problems in the United States, describes how Arab Americans are rising to the challenge of combating stereotypes and defining themselves.

Who Is an Arab?

Language defines the Arab: an *Arab* is a person whose mother tongue is Arabic or who descends from such a person. Though spoken in local dialects, the Arabic language is unified by a standard (classical) written form, which is also used orally in formal situations, including on television and radio. There are over twenty countries in which Arabic is the official language. These countries stretch from the Arabian Peninsula in southwest Asia across North Africa to the Atlantic. Figure 14.1 shows the nations that make up the Arab world.

Muslim is a religious descriptor. Muslims are followers of Islam, the religion that claims that there is only one God and that Mohammed is his prophet. While the vast majority of Arabs are Muslim (95%), Arabs account for no more than 20% of the total number of Muslims in the world (about 1.1 billion).

Included among Arabs worldwide are millions of Arab Christians, as well as prominent communities of Arab Jews. Both of these groups have made important contributions to Arabic culture and history. When Arabs first began to immigrate to the United States, over 90% were Christians. In recent years, more Arab Muslims than Christians have immigrated to the United States, but Christians still comprise the majority of Arab Americans. Some scholars estimate a ratio of two to one; others suggest a three to one ratio (El-Badry, 1994).

There has always been a discrepancy between the number of people who report Arab ancestry of any kind on the U.S. Census and scholarly estimates of the size of the Arab community. This discrepancy exists for many reasons; fear of discrimination is an important one. While the official count was close to 1.5 million Arab Americans in the 2000 U.S. Census, Arab American scholars estimated the population as four million. Of these, about 45% had Lebanese backgrounds, 14% were from Syria, 9% from Egypt, 2.5% from Iraq, and 2% from Jordan.

There was also a growing population of Palestinians, though they often identified as *Arab* and, for that reason, could be anywhere from 5% to 19% of the total. In certain parts of the United States there were also visible communities of Moroccans and Yemenis (Zogby, 1995). Arab countries that have not contributed substantial numbers of immigrants to the United States include Mauritania, Algeria, Tunisia, Libya, Sudan, Somalia, and Djibouti, in North

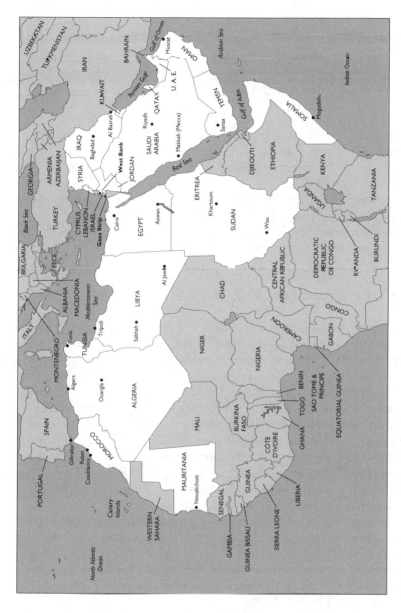

FIGURE 14.1 Map of Arab Nations The Gaza Strip and parts of the West Bank are currently under Palestinian control. The final status of the borders, the final status of Jerusalem, and the future of Palestinian refugees are still under Palestinian-Israeli negotiation.

Source: Anan Ameri & Dawn Ramey, *Arab American Encyclopedia.* Farmington Hills, MI: Gale Group. Reprinted with permission of the Gale Group.

Africa, and Saudi Arabia, Kuwait, Bahrain, Qatar, United Arab Emirates, and Oman, in southwest Asia.

Arabs in History: Their Links to the West

Western civilization has inherited a great deal from the Arabs. Much of Western science, medicine, architecture, music, and mathematics is built on what originated or was developed in the medieval Arab world, in particular during the 800 years when Arabs dominated the Mediterranean, especially southern Spain (ca. AD 700 to 1500) (Hayes, 1983; Macron, 1992; Shabbas, 1998; Tschanz, 1997). Westerners' ignorance of what they have inherited from Arabs and other Muslims during this period deprives them of knowledge of a rich heritage that could not only be a source of enrichment, but could illuminate periods of European history such as the European Renaissance.

Early Arab Immigration to the United States

Although the first Arabs came to North America in the sixteenth century, they didn't begin immigrating to the United States in significant numbers until the late 1870s. Ninety to 95% in the first wave, which lasted until the early 1920s, were Christians. They came from what was, until the end of World War I, the Ottoman province of Syria, an area that included what is now Syria, Lebanon, Jordan, and Palestine/Israel. With the demise of the Ottoman Empire in 1917, this area came under French and British League of Nations mandates. Lebanon and Syria didn't achieve independence from France until 1943 and 1946, respectively. Jordan gained independence from Britain in 1961, and Palestine was subsumed under Jordanian and Israeli rule when Israel was established in 1948. Well into the 1950s, the immigrants from all these areas and their descendants were referred to and referred to themselves as Syrian.

Immigration from Syria was spurred by a number of pull-and-push factors. Among them were the experience of Arabs in three American world's fairs: Philadelphia, in 1876, Chicago, in 1893, and St. Louis, in 1904. Arabs brought to these fairs elaborate recreations of scenes from Arab life; they took back to their hometowns tales of the economic opportunities that awaited the adventurous in America (Younis, 1995).

American missionaries also caused Syrians to become interested in the United States. Early in the nineteenth century Christian missionaries had begun traveling to Lebanon, Syria, and Palestine to convert Muslims (as well as Eastern-rite Christians) to Protestantism. In addition to proselytizing, they established hospitals, clinics, and schools. In 1866, they established the Syrian Protestant College, later known as the American University of Beirut. Their accounts of the

ARAB AMERICAN: HISTORICAL PERSPECTIVE

Important Dates	Events
1868	The first calls were sounded for Arab independence from the Ottoman Turks in a meeting of the secret and seditious Syrian Scientific Society.
1876	The Centennial Exposition in Philadelphia was the first of three world fairs to bring to the United States merchants from the Arab world, many of whom stayed, becoming peddlers, importers, and, later, U.S. citizens.
1878	The first Arab American family, the Arbeelys, immigrates to the United States.
1886–91	Immigration from Turkey begins to pick up steam, leaping in a single year from 15 (1886) to 208 (1887); by 1891, the year's total is 2,448.
1907	Universal military conscription was declared by the Ottoman Turkish government, ending Syrian Christians' exemption from conscription, and further encouraging Syrian emigration.
1908	The Syrian Business Directory was published, listing Syrian-owned businesses in every state in the United States. It contained 3,000, demonstrating the entrepreneurial spirit of the Syrian immigrants.
1909	A case challenging Syrian immigrants' rights to American naturalization on racial grounds, because they were from Asia, was brought in a South Carolina court. It was not settled until 1915.
1914–18	World War I left Lebanon devastated by famine, further encouraging immigration.
1920	France and England divided areas of the former Ottoman Empire after their victory in World War I, creating new semi-colonies, known as mandates: Syria, Lebanon, Transjordan, and Palestine.
1920	"Ar-Rabitah Al-Qalamiyah" (The Pen League) was formed in New York City by Kahlil Gibran. This emigre literary society had an unparalleled impact on the course of Arabic literature, especially poetry.
1923	*The Prophet* by Kahlil Gibran was published by Alfred A. Knopf in New York City.

Important Dates	Events
1924	The Johnson-Reed Act drastically curtailed immigration from outside northwestern Europe, including from the Arab world.
1947–48	The British withdrew forces and government apparatus from Mandate Palestine without resolving territorial disputes between Palestinian Arabs and Zionist Jews. War broke out. The Jewish population seized Palestinian lands far in excess of those specified in the 1947 UN General Assembly partition solution. Hundreds of thousands of Palestinians became refugees. The state of Israel was declared. Some Palestinians emigrated to North America.
1953	The National Federation of Syrian-Lebanese American Clubs was formed.
1960	St. Jude's Hospital was founded in Memphis, Tennessee, by Lebanese-American entertainer Danny Thomas with the help of the Syrian-Lebanese and general Arab-American community.
1967	War between Israel and the Arab states broke out in June. This event caused further Palestinian immigration to the United States.
1967	The Association of Arab-American University Graduates (AAUG) was established to enlarge the discourse with regard to the troubles in the Middle East.
1972	"Operation Boulder" was instituted by the Nixon Administration to combat "terrorism" in the United States. This operation resulted in the surveillance and harassment of many "ethnic Arabs."
1972	The National Association of Arab Americans (NAAA) was founded as a political lobby in Washington, D.C.
1973	As a result of the October Arab-Israeli war, the Organization of Petroleum Exporting Countries (OPEC) shut off oil from the American market. American oil companies sharply increased prices, creating a bogus oil shortage, and Arabs were blamed for the high prices. Stereotyping of Arabs intensified in the news and entertainment media.
1974	James Abourezk was elected the country's first Arab-American Senator.
1980	The American-Arab Anti-Discrimination Committee (ADC) was founded in Washington, DC.

Important Dates	Events
1983	In the U.S. presidential elections, Arabs participated significantly in the Rainbow Coalition, the first time they were a critical mass at a national political convention.
1984	The Arab American Institute (AAI) was formed in Washington D.C. to encourage Arab Americans to participate in the electoral process and to promote access to the political parties.
1986	August 2: Iraq invaded Kuwait. U.S. began a military buildup in the Persian Gulf; public hostility against Arabs and Arab Americans rose.
1989	The Arab-American contingent of the Jesse Jackson delegates to the Democratic National Convention put the Palestinian homeland issue on the agenda.
1993	The World Trade Center in New York City was bombed; the perpetrators convicted in court were Arabs or non-Arab Muslims.
1995	On April 19, the bombing of the Alfred P. Murrah federal building in Oklahoma initially stirred up anger and violence directed at Arab and Muslim communities. Congress opened a discussion of a broad anti-terrorism bill that would unconstitutionally restrict the civil liberties of some Arab Americans and Arabs residing in the United States.
1995	Congress passes the Antiterrorism and Effective Death Penalty Act. This bill gives the FBI expanded surveillance powers over the legal and peaceful activities of immigrant communities and organizations. It allows for the deportation of noncitizens if they are suspected of links to organizations abroad that the U.S. government has designated as terrorist. It states that U.S. citizens can be given a ten-year prison sentence for donating funds to humanitarian programs linked to such organizations. Congress passes an Immigration Bill that allows for the use of secret evidence against immigrants and foreign visitors in order to deport them. Over a dozen Arabs are held on secret evidence for up to four years.
2000	The Second Intifada (uprising) by Palestinians under Israeli occupation and the Israeli response to it resulted in hundreds of Palestinian civilian deaths and generated anti-Arab reporting in the American media. It also mobilized new political activism among Arab Americans across the United States.

economic opportunities in the United States and of U.S. democratic values made Syrians eager to seek their fortunes in America.

There were push factors as well. These included factional conflicts; fear (after 1908) of Ottoman conscription; the land squeeze that resulted from improved health conditions on Mount Lebanon; and the famine that devastated Lebanon during World War I. Some scholars have concluded that, in a society in which so much emphasis was placed on family status, the most compelling reason to emigrate was to be able to send money home to secure the economic well-being of the immigrant's family. According to Tannous (1943), "By 1925, practically every household in every village in the Lebanon Mountains had at least one of its members living as a permanent emigrant somewhere in the Americas" (p. 265). In 1907 the U.S. Immigration Committee reported to the Senate that Syrian immigrants were sending home more money per capita than the immigrants of any other nationality (Hitti, 1924). Though the earliest Syrian immigrants were primarily single men who came to the United States for a brief economic adventure, by the early 1900s whole families were coming to start new lives.

Among the early Syrian American communities, New York was the first and for sixty years the largest and most influential. Boston was second in size and strength, and there were other enclaves in New England and upstate New York.

Many, if not most, of the earliest Syrian immigrants began work in America as peddlers. Some eventually settled and opened businesses. By 1908 the Syrian Businessman's Directory could list 3,000 Syrian-owned businesses scattered throughout every state (Mokarzel & Okash, 1908). The Syrian-Lebanese penchant for business, particularly the family business, continued to characterize the group until the end of the twentieth century.

Their organizational life defined the identity of these early immigrants. Religion, for example, was a strong focal point of the early Syrian identity, and churches were among the first Syrian American institutions. Most of the early immigrants belonged to one of three Eastern Christian rites: Antiochian Orthodox, Melkite Catholic, and Maronite Catholic. The first two trace their roots to the earliest Christian traditions (and, in fact, until 1724 were one and the same); the Maronites became recognized as a separate rite in the eighth century. The liturgies of the Antiochian Orthodox and Melkite churches are in Arabic, and the Maronite liturgy is in Aramaic, the language spoken by Jesus. As Ottoman subjects who were ruled according to their religious sects, the non-Muslim Syrian immigrants identified strongly with these sects.

The Arabic language press also played a significant role in helping Syrians to maintain their Arab identity. Nineteen hundred to 1930 marks the Golden Age of the Arabic-language press. Between 1890 and 1930 about 75 Arabic language periodicals came and went out of existence in the United States (Hatab, 1974). Many were organs of the various religious sects, but most worked to keep the culture alive while helping the immigrant community assimilate. The community's leading intellectuals edited and wrote for these journals. In 1920 they organized themselves into the New York-based *Ar-Rabitah al-Qalamiyya,* or The Pen League. One of the leaders was Kahlil Gibran, best known for his book *The Prophet,* still widely read today. Though Gibran was closely identified with Boston, to which he had immigrated from Lebanon with his family in 1895 at age twelve, from 1911 until his death in 1931 he lived and worked much of the year in New York City, mingling with the American art community there as well as with Arab émigré writers.

Gibran and the other *mahjar* (émigré) poets were greatly influenced by the work of Walt Whitman. In their experimentation with free verse, the *mahjar* poets liberated Arabic poetry from its traditional constrictions of form. Their work revolutionized Arabic writing in the Arab world, and today the *mahjar* poets are studied in high schools and colleges throughout the Middle East. Ironically, with the obvious exception of Gibran, these poets are virtually unknown among U.S.-educated Arab Americans (Orfalea, 1984).

Many of the earliest Syrian organizations were based on village or town of origin, e.g., Aleppian Clubs and Homsian clubs. Later Syrians added American models, e.g., a Syrian Girl Scout troop in Boston, a Syrian Junior League chapter in Brooklyn. Among the most enduring Syrian organizations were women's clubs (Shakir, 1987). Both New York and Boston had Syrian Ladies Aid Societies, established in 1907 and 1917, respectively. In the 1950s, the National Federation of Syrian Lebanese Clubs was formed. This was the Syrian community's earliest effort to organize on a national scale. The Federation led the way in presenting to the public and elected officials the Arab community's concerns about conditions in the Middle East and the influence of United States policies there (Hagopian, 1969).

Assimilation and the Effects of Immigration: Restrictions on the Arab American Community

The smooth assimilation of Syrians in the United States was marred by a series of court cases that began in 1909 and lasted until 1915. The cases challenged the right of Syrians to become U.S. citizens because they were viewed as Asians. These cases were tried mainly in the circuit courts of southern states. The issue culminated in the Dow Case (1915), in which it was reasoned that as Semites, Syrians were, like Jews, White, and therefore eligible for naturalization (Naff, 1985; Younis, 1995.)

The Johnson-Reed Act (1924) drastically curtailed the flow of immigrants from countries outside of northern and western Europe. This had the effect of cutting Syrians off from the constant cultural rejuvenation that aids in cultural maintenance, and accelerated their assimilation. In fact, most of the early immigrants had been eager to assimilate. With the exception of the naturalization cases, there had been little systematic or overt discrimination against Arabs; yet, in a general climate of nativism, Syrians were encouraged in many ways to "Americanize," and they seem to have complied, at least outwardly (Hitti, 1924).

By the 1940s, the Arabic press had lost much of its readership. By the 1950s and 1960s, for newer generations of American-born Arabs, even the spoken Arabic language had become "the language of old people." In fact, its forms and expressions were the ones that the immigrant generation had brought with them a half century before. Although the Arabic churches were streamlining their liturgies and replacing Arabic with English, many second-generation Syrians were finding Protestant and Roman Catholic churches more accessible. By the 1960s, out-marriage had become four times more common than marrying within the group (Kayal & Kayal, 1975). To be Syrian, at that point, meant little more than eating Syrian food and dancing the *debkeh* at Syrian weddings. Arabic culture in the United States was disappearing.

The Post-1965 Immigrants

What saved the Arab American community from cultural extinction was a confluence of factors. First, there was the coming of age of the third generation of Arab Americans who—like a number of grandchildren of immigrants who were influenced by the civil rights and the ethnic revitalization movements—were seeking a "return" to their roots. Second, and more important, there was the lifting of immigration restrictions in 1965, after which Arab immigration numbers began to climb.

Most of the new immigrants came to the United States searching for economic, professional, and educational opportunities. The continuing civil strife and outbreaks of wars between Israel and nations in the Arab world—and between Israel and the Palestinians—from 1967 to 2001 had increased the pressure to emigrate. By the end of the century, there were large Arab American communities in San Francisco and southern California, New York City and vicinity, northern New Jersey, Dearborn and Detroit, Chicago, Boston, Houston, Cleveland, Toledo, Columbus, Cincinnati, and Akron. About 40% of Arab Americans were immigrants when the new century began (Zogby, 1995).

The immigrants who settled in the United States after 1965—both Muslim and Christian—were, on the whole, much more educated than the Syrians who came in the early 1900s. They were also more cosmopolitan, politically astute, and critical of U.S. policies than many of the descendants of the early wave. Some were less willing than earlier immigrants to give up their Arab values and perspectives. In contrast to the third- and fourth-generation descendants of the earliest immigrants, who were now mostly middle class (Kayal & Kayal, 1975; Naff, 1985; Zogby, 1990), there was more economic diversity among the new immigrants, i.e., both more visible prosperity and more poverty.

Because the new immigrants were coming from sovereign Arab countries, they were more secure in their Arab identities than the earliest immigrants had been. Muslim and Christian in roughly equal numbers, they established mosques and increased the rolls of the Arabic churches, in many cases making Arabic once again the main language of their liturgies. Their presence—as well as the reaction of Arabs born in the United States to the anti-Arab sentiments that emerged in the United States during the 1967 Arab-Israeli war—caused many of the American-born Syrians and Lebanese to re-identify with their Arab heritage.

In 2001, Americans of Lebanese descent still comprised a plurality of the Arab American community. However, many more Arab countries were now represented. Egyptians, Yemenis, Iraqis and Moroccans had growing populations. Palestinians were becoming stronger both in numbers and in political and cultural influence and were particularly active within new Arab American organizations and in bringing Arab issues to the attention of non-Arab Americans.

Muslims in America

Due to the recent immigration of Arab Muslims and Muslims from other countries—as well as American conversions—Islam is one of the fastest growing religions in the United States and the second largest (after Christianity) (Eck, 2001). The data reported by the Council on American-Islamic Relations (2001) indicate that Muslims in the United States are growing significantly. According to the Council, 75% of mosques have experienced an increase in the number of participants in the last five years, 30% of whom are converts. The Council's data also indicate that 30% of all U.S. mosques were founded in the 1990s.

New Muslim immigrants have taken the lead in reviving Arabic culture in the United States. They are establishing Islamic institutions and building schools in which their children can learn Arabic, something rarely done by first-wave Syrian Christians. By 2001, there were over 1,200 mosques in the United States, an increase of 50% over the previous seven years (Council on American-Islamic Relations, 2001). The number of U.S. chapters of the Muslim Student Association had almost doubled, from 240 to 473. Islamic educational advisory councils were more active than ever in 2001. They were working to increase the accuracy of the portrayal of Islam in textbooks, the media, and in American political discourse.

Largely because they believed it would be difficult to practice their faith in a secular society, Arab Muslims did not participate in large numbers in the earliest immigration movement to the United States. Even today, many Muslims fear that the materialistic and individualistic American lifestyle contradicts the more spiritual and family-centered orientation of Islam. The practices of prayer (five times a day) and fasting (one full month each year during daylight hours) are often hard to maintain in a society that does not support these practices. Muslim norms of modesty contrast with the freer dress and behavior of the secular American mainstream. Muslim parents worry that their children will find American freedoms appealing and will abandon their own traditions.

The are many contrasts between Arab culture and mainstream American culture. First, like many other traditional cultures, Arabs tend to stress the needs of the family over the needs of the individual. Much more social engineering by elders is tolerated—and even expected—than is the norm in mainstream American society. Decisions in Arab families are often made by parents or other older relatives. Arranged marriages are largely a practice of the past for most Arab Americans. However, many traditional Arab immigrant families still arrange them. Even among Arabs born in the United States, parental desires are rarely discounted, and marriage is still considered by many Arab Americans to be as much a union of two families as of two individuals.

A traditional differentiation of parental roles exists in most Arab American families. Although it is now common for Arab American women to work outside the home, the father is usually seen as the family's principal breadwinner and its public representative. The mother controls the domestic sphere. There is also a tradition among many Arab families of supporting and being supported by the extended family. Large Arab families traditionally have felt it their duty to support each other in many different ways. This support includes providing start-up finances for new businesses, covering tuition expenses for education, providing relatives with employment, supporting the aged, and helping to arrange marital matches.

Modesty is prized among Arabs, and "immodest" behavior by a woman in particular can seriously jeopardize not only her name but also her family's social status. How immodesty is defined differs from one family to another, but the "talk of people" is a serious social constraint in Arab society. An important source of tension for Arab Americans is the freedom Americans have versus the constraints in the Arab family culture.

It is important to point out here that, while most Americans see Arab women as oppressed, most women in Arab society are neither powerless nor retiring. Precisely because of the constraints under which they live, their social skills and intuitions are highly developed, and they are articulate, assertive, and resourceful in finding ways to shape their own fates and direct the fortunes of their families (Shakir, 1997). In addition, their highly valued and specified roles and responsibilities as mothers and wives and economic partners to their husbands relieve them of many confusions and discontents that mainstream U.S. women have experienced since the sexual revolution of the 1960s, though for many the proximity of such a different culture causes discontent (Hajar, 1993).

Hospitality is another bedrock Arab value, and is one way Arabs have traditionally demonstrated their sense of self-worth. Elaborate Arab hospitality is legendary; for some Arabs it is the essence of "being Arab." Hosting guests for unlimited stays, having weddings that last for several days, and taking time from work to escort visiting friends and relatives around town are common practices in Arab countries. However, they are usually out of the question in the competitive work- and self-oriented climate of the United States (Hajar, 1993).

Changing Patterns of Assimilation

The challenges many post-1965 Arab immigrants have had to face as they adjust to American society have led to the establishment of Arab family centers in many cities. The most well known is the Arab Community Center for Economic and Social Services (ACCESS) in Dearborn, Michigan, a suburb of Detroit. Since 1971, ACCESS has been providing Arab families with such services as emergency food programs, counseling, tutoring, language classes, help with entitlements, job referrals and training, as well as workshops on health, American culture, and assimilation. Similar centers have been established in Chicago, New York, Washington, D.C., Toledo, and San Francisco.

Some immigrants resist counseling that is offered outside the context of family, church, and mosque. They see the American style of counseling, with its intrinsic promotion of individualism, as weakening the family (Aswad, 1988; personal communication with Emira Habiby-Brown, director of New York's Arab Family Center, 1997). Indeed, while many new immigrants are interested in participating fully in the American political and economic systems, they have no intention of assimilating completely, if that means that their own values will be undermined.

Anti-Arab Stereotyping

Negative stereotyping is one of the most troubling problems for Arab Americans. Throughout history, Europeans have portrayed Arabs as "the other," a phenomenon Palestinian American scholar Edward Said has called "orientalism" (Said, 1978). Centuries ago Europeans viewed Arabs as a threat because of their overwhelming cultural and economic power during their eight centuries in Spain and the Mediterranean region. During the Crusades (supposedly about religion but which, like most wars, had economic roots) Europeans portrayed Muslims as practitioners of a "false religion," and referred to Muhammad, its prophet, as the anti-Christ.

One modern-day trigger for negative Arab stereotypes was the 1973 Arab-Israeli War and the ensuing oil embargo. Although at the time the United

States was only importing 6% of its oil from Arab countries, oil companies used the opportunity to raise oil prices. Through their advertising they generated the idea that the Arabs were the cause of the long gas lines.

Negative stereotyping has increased since the late 1960s and 1970s. The image of "the Arab" now serves a multitude of cultural, political, and economic purposes, as it did during the Crusades. Americans, like the Europeans before them, use the Arab as a way of defining who they (Americans) are not; they have created in the media (political cartoons, movies, fiction) a matrix of descriptors of Arabs (craven, backward, dirty, devious, sexually predatory) that are supposed to stand in opposition to the qualities (bravery, intelligence, cleanliness, principled discretion, and honesty) that White Americans use to define themselves.

News reporting, by omission and/or selectivity or sticking to stock story frames, has been complicit in perpetuating the stereotypes. These images, which are pervasive in American culture and political discourse, largely went unchallenged until a new generation of Arab American organizations—whose membership was drawn increasingly from the post-1965 immigrants and their children—set about to challenge them. By 2001, as a result of their efforts, there has been some increase in sensitivity to the harm of the negative images, yet there have been few countervailing positive images of Arabs as normal people with complicated lives.

In works of fiction, the movies, television, and in advertising, Arabs are still invariably typed as the villain (Michalak, 1988; Sabbagh, 1990; Shaheen, 1988, 1997, 2001; Stockton, 1994). It is with this media bombardment as text and backdrop that anti-Arab attitudes are enacted in daily life (Shrag & Javidi, 1995). Stereotypes permeate the language surrounding anti-Arab hate crimes, cases of defamation, and incidents of job discrimination.

The producers of children's programs have perpetuated some of the most negative images of Arab Americans. Cartoons and cartoon movies, particularly those made by the Disney company, have been particularly offensive (Shaheen, 1980, 1988, 2001). Several Disney movies released in the 1990s included gratuitous "bad Arab" characters (including *The Father of the Bride II* and Disney's *Aladdin*). These and others were the focus of protest efforts. The negative Arab stereotypes that are common in children's programming is particularly significant. Any story seen or heard in the early years of a child's life constitutes a "first story," a narrative structure against which all later narratives are judged. When individuals are taught that Arabs are evil by these narratives, they internalize the images as norms and carry them their entire lives (Shrag & Javidi, 1995).

Arabs as terrorists and other negative stereotypes have become standard fare in adult movies. By the 1980s the Islamic militant was the stock character of many B-movies (*Delta Force, Wanted Dead or Alive, Iron Eagle*), but by the nineties it was high-profile blockbusters such as *True Lies, The Mummy, The Siege,* and *Rules of Engagement* that were perpetuating the anti-Arab messages. In *The Siege,* Arab Americans were portrayed as real threats to the very life of New York City (real news footage was interwoven with the story to convey a semblance of truth), and the very practices of Islam (washing before prayer) were linked to terrorist acts. In *Rules of Engagement,* the Arab country of Yemen and all its citizens were portrayed as united in their mindless hatred of and complicity against the United States and Americans. The movie includes the bombing of the American Embassy in Yemen as an integral part of the plot. In fact, there is no history of tension between Yemen and the United States and the plot is totally fictitious. Movies have become the modern-day texts for many Americans, and this movie will be as much "information" on Yemen as many Americans will ever get.

Many teachers have worked to present accurate information on Arabs and the Arab world. However, most social studies and history texts used in the United States, either by omitting treatment of the Arab world altogether, or by treating Arabs in a superficial or pejorative way, have actually contributed to the stereotyping and the misinformation. One common distortion found in textbooks is the emphasis on nomadic life. Though Bedouin nomads account for no more than two percent of Arab society today (and in fact, many Bedouins now use pick-up trucks and other motorized vehicles) traditional Bedouin lifestyle is commonly treated as if it were representative of all Arabs (Shabbas, 1998). Another distortion is to omit the Palestinian perspective in textbook treatments of the Arab-Israeli wars and to treat the issue solely from the Israeli perspective. A distortion exists in texts when they do not discuss the close links between Islam, Judaism, and Christianity (Barlow, 1994). These three faiths are quite similar in terms of beliefs and texts.

Anti-Arab Hate Crimes

Since 1979, when Americans were taken hostage by Iranian students (whom Americans mistakenly believed to be Arab), there has been a precipitous rise in violence against Middle Easterners in the United States. Since then, whenever there is an incident involving Americans and Middle Easterners anywhere, there is often a domestic reaction against Arabs and Arab Americans in the United States. Across the country, on radio talk shows and in political speeches, anti-Arab and anti-Muslim stereotypes and rhetoric surface and various forms of hate crimes against Arabs increase. The violence against Arabs has included bombings, shootings, arson attacks, beatings, death threats, harassment, and intimidation (ADC Special Report, 1995; ADC Special Report, 2001; Ekin & Gorchev, 1991). Even when Arabs have nothing to do with an incident, there is an anti-Arab reaction. For example, there was a dramatic increase in anti-Arab hate crimes in the immediate aftermath of the Oklahoma City bombing (ADC, 1995).

Fallout from the ongoing Arab-Israeli dispute generates another source of hate crimes. The most significant example of this type occurred in the fall of 1985 when Alex Odeh, western regional director of the American-Arab Anti-Discrimination Committee in Santa Ana, California, was killed by a bomb trip-wired to his office door. The FBI claimed the case was a top priority but for ten years no progress was made in solving it. The FBI has offered a reward of one million dollars for information leading to the arrest of the perpetrators (ADC Times, 1996).

Like other minorities, Arab Americans have, from time to time, suffered the abridgment of their civil rights. For example, in times of crisis or tension they have had to endure FBI surveillance. This happened during the Nixon years (Abraham, 1994) and during the Gulf War (ADC, 1995).

Since the late 1990s, new policies have been implemented by government agencies that seem to target Arab Americans. Because of their looks, names, or their travel histories, many Arab Americans have been singled out at airports for extensive questioning and humiliating searches (ADC Special Report, 2001; Lewis, 1997). Even more serious has been the use, since 1996, of secret evidence to detain individuals who are considered a threat to U.S. security. Over twenty men, all Arabs and/or Muslims, were held without formal charges for up to four years. The U.S. government has failed to win a single case involving secret evidence because the courts have found secret evidence to be a violation of due process. Arab American organizations have played a major role in bringing attention to these issues and working for legal redress.

New Arab American Activism: The Maturing of an Ethnic Community

In 1967, in the wake of the Arab-Israeli war, the Association of Arab-American University Graduates (AAUG) was formed in order to enlarge the discourse around the ongoing strife in the Middle East. Its highly educated membership, strengthened by new immigrants, held conferences and symposia and published books and monographs about the community and the issue of Palestine. Several of the earliest modern studies of the Arab community in the United States were sponsored by this organization.

The second in this new generation of Arab American organizations was the National Association of Arab Americans, or "N-Triple A" (NAAA). The NAAA was established in 1972 to lobby the U.S. government on its Middle East policies. Both organizations use the word "Arab" as a self-identifier by Arabic-speaking Americans, including people who had previously called themselves Syrian or Lebanese or Syrian-Lebanese. This name change reflects both the presence of many new Arab Americans who are not necessarily Syrian or Lebanese, and the recognition that there is strength in identification with a larger group.

James Abourezk, the first Arab American to be elected to the U.S. Senate, formed the third organization, the American-Arab Anti-Discrimination Committee (ADC) in 1980. The need for an organization such as ADC had become clear by 1979 after the FBI initiated a sting operation called ABSCAM, in which FBI officials posing as rich Arab sheiks attempted to bribe American elected officials. Dismayed by the stereotypes implicit in such an operation, the outgoing Senator Abourezk created ADC to combat racism, discrimination, and the stereotyping of Arabs in government as well as in entertainment, the news media, and in education.

The work of ABSCAM, the continuing crises in the Middle East, the presence of a critical mass of new and educated Arab-American activists, and the populism and pluralism spawned by the civil rights movement of the 1960s produced significant growth in the ADC. Within three years it had grown into the nation's largest Arab American organization. By 2001, it had 80 active chapters and between 21,000 and 25,000 members. Members wrote letters, organized protests, and met with politicians and the CEOs of companies with offensive ad campaigns. Though ADC has raised public consciousness about the offensiveness of stereotyping Arabs, the stereotyping continues.

Arab Americans experienced exclusion from the political process for many years. Sometimes individual Arab Americans had their campaign contributions spurned because candidates "feared being associated with 'Arab interests'" (Abourezk, 1989). At other times candidates were criticized if they met with Arab groups; and "Arab money" was viewed as tainted (ADC, 2001). To remedy this political exclusion, and stimulated by the receptivity of Jesse Jackson's Rainbow Coalition to Arab American participation in 1984, a third national Arab American organization, the Arab American Institute (AAI), was established in 1985. Its goals were to organize Arab Americans to participate effectively in all aspects of the political process, i.e., as issue advocates, as voters who rally for targeted candidates, and as political candidates themselves. AAI's successes are reflected in the fact that several dozen new Arab American political clubs across the United States have been able to send over fifty Arab American delegates to each national convention since 1988.

The 1988 presidential campaign was a watershed event in Arab Americans' struggle for full political participation and visibility. After several years of intensive organizing by AAI, Arab American Democrats won local races to the Democratic National Convention as Jackson delegates. The Jackson campaign's Arab American delegation was second in size only to that of the African American delegation. In the platform debate, the Arab American delegates helped to place on the agenda a discussion of the right to self-determination for Palestinians. The plank was not submitted to a vote, but the fifteen-minute debate was considered a political first, demonstrating the difficulties Arab Americans had faced around any discussion of U.S. policies in the Middle East (Samhan, 1989).

In the 2000 campaign, as had been the case since 1988, several dozen Arab American political clubs sent over 50 delegates to each national convention. That year, for the first time, Arab Americans were a sought-after political constituency. Four major presidential candidates addressed high-profile gatherings of Arab Americans. In one presidential debate George W. Bush even raised the two issues that are particularly problematic for the Arab-American community: airport profiling and the use of secret evidence. He recognized Arab Americans as a group, which had not been done on national television at election time since Jessie Jackson's 1984 Democratic Convention speech. A significant number of foreign-born Arab Americans ran for local elections in Michigan, Ohio, Illinois, and California in 2000, an important political development for Arab Americans.

In other states, cities, and towns, the political exclusion of Arab Americans continued. Several high-profile elections in Michigan, New York, and New Jersey were clouded by race baiting, and candidates who accepted support from Arab American and/or Muslim groups were accused by their opponents of being terrorist sympathizers. What is different and a source of hope is that the community, through its organizations, has become better able to respond effectively to these smear campaigns.

The Contributions of Arab Americans to American Life

Philip Hitti, an eminent historian of the Middle East, called the early Syrian American immigrants "ready made Yankees" (1924). Largely middle class or aspiring to it, they were devoted to the work ethic. Though the majority operated businesses that started with peddling, others worked in factories such as the Detroit auto plants and the textile mills on the East Coast. Arabs helped build the U.S. labor movement. Perhaps their chief distinction was their deep devotion to family life; most were low-profile solid citizens of their communities.

When Arab Americans have been more high profile they have often been pioneers and mavericks, and they have made contributions to every aspect of American life. Besides poet Kahlil Gibran, such pioneers include consumer advocate Ralph Nader; Senator James Abourezk, known during his term as the most radical Senator in the Senate; heart surgeon Dr. Michael DeBakey (who pioneered the heart bypass operation); Michael Shadid, who founded the first cooperative hospital; Candy Lightner, who founded Mothers Against Drunk Driving; and Christa McAuliffe, first teacher in space, who died on the ill-fated *Challenger*.

Other famous Arab Americans include radio personality Casey Kasem; CEO of Ford Motor Company, Jacques Nasser; fashion designers Joseph Abboud and Norma Kamali; opera singer Rosalind Elias; pop singers Paul Anka, Gloria Estefan, and Paula Abdul; actors F. Murray Abraham, Kathy

Najimi, and Tony Shalhoub; and poet Naomi Shihab Nye. A significant and lasting contribution was made by entertainer Danny Thomas when he founded St. Jude's Children's Research Hospital in Memphis, Tennessee in 1962. The acronym of its fundraising arm is ALSAC, which stands both for Aiding Leukemia Stricken American Children, and for Association of Lebanese-Syrian American Charities. St. Jude's is one of the most important institutions in the world in the battle against childhood leukemia and treats its young patients at no expense to their families. School children may know about this hospital through the annual national St. Jude's Math-a-thon.

Arab Americans Today

Arab Americans today are prospering both as individuals and as a community. In 1989 the average household income of Arab Americans was $39,580, compared with the U.S. average of $35,225. While about 20.3 % of all Americans had graduated from college and received higher degrees, among Arabs the figure was almost twice as high (36.3%) (Zogby, 1995). Arab Americans are also making gains politically. Since the 1970s, four U.S. Senators and eight U.S. Representatives have claimed Arab heritage. Since the 1980s, four Arab Americans have held Cabinet-level positions: Reagan's Chief of Staff, John Sununu; Clinton's Secretary of Health and Human Services, Donna Shalala; George W. Bush's Secretary of Management and Budget, Mitch Daniels, and his Secretary of Energy, Spencer Abraham. Arab Americans are represented on the national councils of both major political parties.

Arab Americans have experienced no ceiling in terms of economics, education, or occupations. What has complicated their assimilation process has been the stereotyping and misinformation that is deeply embedded in American culture, nurtured by the often problematic relationships between the United States and some Arab countries and further complicated by domestic politics. These factors have impeded public discourse on issues having to do with the Arab world, and, at times, have threatened Arab Americans' civil rights at home.

Regardless of whether their ties to their countries of origin are strong, even third- and fourth-generation Arab Americans who have long identified as Americans find themselves questioning the use of their tax dollars to purchase weapons that are used against people in their families' countries of origin. They question, as well, sanctions that have cost the lives of thousands of Iraqi children. The problem is especially intense for Palestinian Americans, as the long-standing commitment of the United States to Israel has resulted in its continuous financial and military support of what Palestinians consider to be an occupation of their land.

Because of the issues described above, a growing number of Arab Americans are becoming involved in human rights and political action activities.

Their goal is to bring to the attention of other Americans and elected officials an Arab American perspective on events in the Middle East. These activities—including protest demonstrations and teach-ins—reached a high point when Israel occupied Lebanon in 1982. They peaked again in 1991 when the Gulf War occurred, and in 2000 when the second *intifada* began in Jerusalem.

Arab Americans have also turned their energies toward learning about and supporting all forms of new and traditional Arabic culture, both for its own sake and as a way to work for old issues. In the 1990s and into the new millennium, Arab festivals, lasting from one evening to one month, were spreading across the United States. These festivals have included traditional performance arts such as music and dance, storytelling and poetry reciting, and Arabic films. Arabic food, a cuisine that has been winning over the palates of non-Arab Americans for at least a generation, is usually a major attraction at these events. Museums and theaters are now willing to offer space to Arab cultural events. This willingness heralds a new era for Arab Americans.

After generations of keeping their ethnicity quiet, more and more Arab Americans are publicly expressing pride in their heritage. In the last few decades, Arab American parents, activists, and educators have presented their concerns to school boards, curriculum committees, and publishers. They have asked to be included in multicultural events and committees and to be depicted accurately in teaching materials. There are now teacher workshops that help teachers identify unwarranted assumptions and distorting language about Islam and the Arab world. Arab Americans are writing about their lives, and, in so doing, creating new and more nuanced images of themselves in the minds of other Americans.

Teaching Strategies

To illustrate how content related to Arab Americans can be used to integrate the curriculum, exemplary strategies are identified for teaching these concepts at the grade levels indicated: *adaptation and resourcefulness* (primary grades), *contributions* (intermediate and upper grades), and *stereotyping* (high school grades).

Primary Grades

CONCEPT

Adaptation and Resourcefulness

Generalization: Arabs who came to the United States were willing to overcome major obstacles to realize their American dreams.

Background: Early Arab immigrants arrived with a determination to achieve the American dream despite the hard work involved. Finding factory work too confining, most started as peddlers. They developed regular routes and clientele, and, despite their humble appearance, were soon earning more annually, on average, than the American farm, factory, or mine worker (Naff, 1985). Their success depended on their resourcefulness and quick-wittedness, goodwill, cooperation with each other, and willingness to endure hardships and even danger.

1. Read to the students chapters from Naff's *The Arab Americans* and Harik's *The Lebanese Americans* that deal with the early immigrant peddlers. Students who have high reading skills should read "On the Road" (Chapter 5) in Naff's *Becoming American* (pp. 161–200). You can summarize or retell the funniest anecdotes from this book to younger students.

2. As you share these readings, list with the class the kinds of difficulties the Syrian peddlers encountered on the road, and the ways they dealt with them. Have the students use notes from this list to write and act out various peddling scenarios, making props and costumes and taking the roles of the peddlers and their American customers. Make sure there are no good guys and bad guys, because the difficulties were usually humorous and arose from language gaps on all sides.

3. Have a discussion about the period of adjustment migrants and immigrants experience when they first arrive in a new place. Talk about the jobs many immigrants or people new to an area take when they first arrive and how they are often willing to do almost any kind of work to get started. Have students go home and investigate what the immigrants or other ancestors in their families did to earn their first dollar.

4. While it is common to picture the wife in a family as taking care of the house and the children, the Syrian wife was usually behind the cash register, taking care of the customers and the books. Discuss with the students family cooperation, including in business ventures. Ask them to share examples of relatives who helped each other build businesses or to overcome economic hard times. This will be a good opportunity for the students to interview family members and report their findings to the class.

Intermediate and Upper Grades

CONCEPT

Contributions
Generalization: Arab Americans have made many contributions to world civilization and to American life.

1. Using Naff's *The Arab Americans* as the main text, have students choose a topic and do individual or group research projects on various contributions of the Arabs to world civilization. Topics could include Arab architecture, art, science, medicine, mathematics, and astronomy. The *Arab World Notebook* and AWAIR (Arab World and Islamic Resources), its distributor, have many suggestions for materials for this lesson.

2. Have students report to the class or build exhibits that present their findings. Have a fair on "What the Western World Learned from the Arab East."

3. Have the students read "Meeting the Challenge" (the final chapter in Naff's *The Arab Americans*, "Some Lebanese Americans of Note," the chapter on Arab Americans in the *Arab World Notebook*, or the September/October 1986 issue of *Aramco World Magazine*. Ask each student to choose one individual to research. Encourage the students to be ingenious about sources (e.g., beyond looking at already published materials, they might create a list of questions to put in a letter to send to the subject, if still alive, or to his or her family or someone in the same field, if deceased). Possibilities: heart surgeon Michael DeBakey; consumer advocate Ralph Nader; Top 40 disk jockey Casey Kasem; Academy Award–winning actor F. Murray Abraham; Heisman Trophy winner Doug Flutie; singers Paula Abdul, Tiffany and Gloria Estefan; actors Kathy Najimy and Tony Shalhoub; the biographers of Kahlil Gibran, Jean and Kahlil Gibran; Marlo Thomas on her late father, the comedian and actor Danny Thomas, founder of the St. Jude's Research Hospital.

VALUING ACTIVITY

Background for teachers: essay on Arabs and Lebanese families by Abudabbeh and Simon in McGoldrick's *Ethnic Families*, or sections on the Arab (or Syrian) family in Naff's *Becoming American*. Arab family relations are extremely close. Interdependence, rather than independence, is promoted in many ways. Ask the students to research Arab family values by reading about Arab families in Harik's *The Lebanese in America*, Macron's "Celebrations of Life: Arab-Americans in Cleveland," in Naff's *The Arab Americans*, or by watching *Tales from Arab Detroit*, a videotape produced by Joan Mandell. Ask the students to make a list of practices they have read about that seem unusual. Then divide the class into small groups. Ask each group to compare an Arab practice with an American behavior or custom, discuss it, and list the advantages and disadvantages of each. Ask the students to share their results in a whole-class discussion.

Possible topics:

- the chaperoning of girls
- arranged or approved marriages
- living at home until marriage
- living at home after marriage
- helping relatives start businesses
- taking responsibility for educating relatives' children
- working in the family business rather than starting one's own career
- putting relatives up who need a place to stay
- parents supervising children's attire
- parents supervising children's friendships

Using this material, ask the students to write a "Dear Amal" column (Amal instead of Ann, as in Ann Landers). Ask them to write letters from parents and children who are experiencing the cultural clash over various issues (most having to do with freedom and limits, freedom corresponding to individualism, limits corresponding to the constraints imposed by the interests of an extended family).

High School Grades

CONCEPT

Stereotyping
Generalization: Many Americans view Arabs through the negative clichés and stereotypes that are institutionalized in the media.

1. Have students research and discuss in groups that seem appropriate and meaningful to them—racial, ethnic, or gender—the stereotypes about them or their group. Discuss the ways that stereotypes oversimplify the complexity of groups and individuals. Ask the students to describe ways in which individuals within a group differ from the stereotypes about it. Ask the students to summarize their discussion.

2. Have students read at least one of Jack Shaheen's essays on the Arab's image in the media (e.g., *The TV Arab, The Influence of the Arab Stereotype on American Children*, a chapter in *Arab and Muslim Stereotyping in American Popular Culture*, or the introduction to *Reel Arabs: How Hollywood Vilifies a People*), or "Cruel and Unusual" by Lawrence Michalak.

3. Ask the students to look for images of Arabs in the following: political cartoons, political commentary, movies, television shows, textbooks, advertisements, news reports, and political discourse. (They can also look in the same venues for images or mention of Islam and Muslims.) Ask the students to keep a scrapbook of these images for a period of time (e.g., one month), noting positive, negative, and neutral language. Analyze and report to the class. You might also want to rent from a video store several of the movies mentioned by Shaheen, Michalak, or the American-Arab Anti-Discrimination Committee (ADC) and ask students to look for stereotypes in them.

4. Contact the American-Arab Anti-Discrimination Committee for news on their current anti-defamation campaigns (4201 Connecticut Avenue, NW, Suite 300, Washington, D.C. 20008; Tel: (202) 244-2990; Fax: (202) 244-3196; E-mail: *adc@adc.org*; Web: *http://www.adc.org*). Ask the students to discuss the merits of the case and decide whether to take the action ADC recommends, e.g., write a letter to the CEO of the offending companies. Track responses.

REFERENCES

Abourezk, J. (1989). *Advise and Dissent: Memoirs of South Dakota and the U.S. Senate.* Chicago: Lawrence Hill.

Abraham, N. (1994). Anti-Arab Racism and Violence in the United States. In E. McCarus (Ed.), *The Development of Arab American Identity* (pp. 155–214). Ann Arbor: University of Michigan Press.

ADC Special Report: Anti-Arab Racism in the United States—1995. (1995). Washington, DC: ADC (American-Arab Anti-Discrimination Committee).

ADC Times. (August–September, 1996). Justice Department Offers $1 Million Reward for Arrest of Odeh Assassins. (n.a.)

Aswad, B. (1988). *Social Needs Assessment of Immigrant Women from Lebanon and Yemen.* Dearborn, MI: Arab Community Center for Economic and Social Services (ACCESS).

Barlow, B. (Ed.). (1994). *Evaluation of Secondary-Level Textbooks for Coverage of the Middle East and North Africa*. Ann Arbor, MI: Middle East Studies Association and the Middle East Outreach Council.

Council on American Islamic Relations. (2001). [On-line]. Available: *http://www.cair-net.org*

Eck, D. (2001). *A New Religious America: How a "Christian Country" Has Become the World's Most Religiously Diverse Nation*. New York: HarperSanFrancisco.

Ekin, L., & Gorchev, L. (Eds.). (1991). *ADC Special Report: 1991 Report on Anti-Arab Hate Crimes: Political and Hate Violence against Arab Americans during the Gulf War*. Washington, DC: ADC (American-Arab Anti-Discrimination Committee) Research Institute.

El-Badry, S. (1994, January). The Arab-American Market. *American Demographics* (pp. 22–30).

Gibran, G. K. (1923). *The Prophet*. New York: Alfred A. Knopf.

Hagopian, E. (1969). The Institutional Development of the Arab-American Community of Boston: A Sketch. In E. Hagopian & A. Paden (Eds.), *The Arab-Americans: Studies in Assimilation* (pp. 67–83). Wilmette, IL: Medina University Press International.

Hajar, P. (1993). Arab Immigrant Parents and American School People: An Ethnography of a Cross-Cultural Relationship. Cambridge: Harvard Graduate School of Education. Unpublished doctoral dissertation.

Harik, E. M. (1982). *The Lebanese in America*. Minneapolis: Lerner.

Hatab, H. (n.d.). Arabs in the U.S.: No Longer the Best Kept Secret in Ethnic America. (pamphlet). Washington, DC: American-Arab Anti-Discrimination Committee (ADC).

Hatab, H. (1974). Syrian-American Ethnicity: Structure and Ideology in Transition. Unpublished master's thesis. American University of Beirut, Beirut, Lebanon.

Hayes, J. R. (Ed.) (1983). *The Genius of Arab Civilization: Source of the Renaissance*. Cambridge, MA: MIT Press.

Hitti, P. (1924). *The Syrians in America*. New York: George H. Doran.

Horner, N. (1989). *A Guide to Christian Churches in the Middle East*. Elkhart, IN: Mission Focus Press.

Kayal, P., & Kayal, J. (1975). *The Syrian-Lebanese in America: A Study in Religion and Assimilation*. Boston: Twayne.

Lewis, N. (1997, August 11). Arab-Americans Protest 'Profiling' at Airports. *New York Times*, p. A12.

Macron, M. (1992). Arab Contributions to Civilization. Washington, DC: American-Arab Anti-Discrimination Committee (ADC) Issue Paper #6.

Macron, M. (1992) A Celebration of Life: Memories of an Arab-American in Cleveland. Washington, DC: American-Arab Anti-Discrimination Committee (ADC) Issues Paper #7.

Michalak, L. (1988). Cruel and Unusual: Negative Images of Arabs in Popular Culture. Washington, DC: American-Arab Anti-Discrimination Committee (ADC) Occasional Paper #15.

Mokarzel, S., & Okash, H. F. (1908). *The Syrian Business Directory: 1908–1909*. New York: Al-Hoda.

Naff, A. (1985). *Becoming American: The Early Arab Immigrant Experience*. Carbondale: Southern Illinois University Press.

Orfalea, G. (1984). *U.S.-Arab Relations: The Literary Dimension*. Occasional Paper Series: Number Two. Washington, DC: National Council on U.S. Arab Relations and Arab American Cultural Foundation.

Sabbagh, S. (1990). *Sex, Lies, and Stereotypes: The Image of Arabs in American Popular Fiction*. Washington, DC: ADC Issues Paper #23.

Said, E. (1978). *Orientalism*. New York: Random House.

Samhan, H. H. (1989). Arab Americans and the Elections of 1988: A Constituency Come of Age. In B. Abu-Laban & M. Suleiman (Eds.), *Arab Studies Quarterly*, Special Issue: Arab Americans: Continuity & Change. Belmont, MA: Association of Arab-American University Graduate and Institute of Arab Studies.

Shabbas, A. (Ed.). (1998). *Arab World Studies Notebook.* Berkeley: AWAIR (Arab World and Islamic Resources and School Services), and Washington, DC: Middle East Policy Council.

Shaheen, J. (1980). The Influence of the Arab Stereotype on American Children. Washington, DC: ADC Issue Paper #2.

Shaheen, J. (1884). *The TV Arab.* Bowling Green, OH: Bowling Green State University Popular Press.

Shaheen, J. (1988). ABSCAM: Arabiaphobia in America. Washington, DC: ADC Issue Paper #1.

Shaheen, J. (1997). *Arab and Muslim Stereotyping in American Popular Culture.* Washington, DC: Center for Muslim-Christian Understanding: History and International Affairs. Edmund A. Walsh School of Foreign Service, Georgetown University.

Shakir, E. (1987). Good Works, Good Times. In E. Hooglund (Ed.), *Crossing the Waters* (pp. 133–143). Washington, DC: Smithsonian Institution Press.

Shakir, E. (1997). *Bint Arab: Arab and Arab-American Women in the United States.* Westport, CT: Praeger.

Shrag, R. L, & Javidi, M. N. (1995). Through a Glass Darkly: American Media Images of Middle Eastern Cultures and Their Potential Impact on Young Children. In Y. R. Kamalipour (Ed.), *The U.S. Media and the Middle East: Image and Perception* (pp. 212–221). Westport, CT: Praeger.

Stockton, R. (1994). Ethnic Archetypes and the Arab Image. In E. McCarus (Ed.), *The Development of Arab-American Identity* (pp. 119 53). Ann Arbor: University of Michigan.

Tannous, A. (June, 1943). Acculturation of an Arab-Syrian Community in the Deep South. *American Sociological Review,* 8(3), 264–271.

Tschanz, D. (1997, May/June). The Arab Roots of European Medicine. *Aramco World Magazine,* 20–31.

Younis, A. (1995). *The Coming of the Arabic-Speaking Peoples to the United States.* New York: Center for Migration Studies.

Zogby, J. (1990). *Arab America Today.* Washington, DC: AAI (Arab American Institute).

Zogby, J. (1995). *Arab American Demographics.* Utica: Zogby International.

ANNOTATED BIBLIOGRAPHY

Books for Teachers

Especially Recommended

Haddad, Y. Y. (1986). A Century of Islam in America. The Muslim World Today Occasional Paper No. 4. Washington, DC: Islamic Affairs Programs, The Middle East Institute.

This is a comprehensive overview by a noted scholar.

Hooglund, E. J. (Ed.). (1985). *Taking Root/Bearing Fruit* (Vol. 2). Washington, DC: ADC.

The second of two volumes of community studies sponsored by ADC. It has stories about Vicksburg, Mississippi; Shaw, Mississippi; New Castle, Pennsylvania; Providence, Rhode Island; and Ross, North Dakota (home of the first mosque built in North America). These are real stories, quirky and beautifully written.

Hooglund, E. J. (Ed.). (1987). *Crossing the Waters: Arabic-Speaking Immigrants to the United States before 1940.* Washington, DC: Smithsonian Institution Press.

Eleven original essays and case studies on Arab Americans in such diverse communities as El Paso, Boston, Waterville (Maine), and Birmingham (Alabama). Not the usual overviews, these delightful essays are about specific immigrants, or aspects of immigrant life, and are wonderfully written.

Kamalipour, Y. R. (Ed.). (1995). *The U.S. Media and the Middle East: Image and Perception.* Westport, CT: Praeger.

This collection of essays and reports is one of the most creative in print on many aspects of this topic. It probes the sources of the negative images of Arabs in U.S. culture and offers fascinating history as well as theories about the reasons for these images.

McCarus, E. (Ed.). (1994). *The Development of Arab-American Identity.* Ann Arbor: University of Michigan Press.

The essays in this authoritative and up-to-date collection on Arab American life are well researched, comprehensive, and well written. The book includes probing articles on the development of the Arab stereotype and the progression of anti-Arab violence, as well as essays on politics, art, religion, identity, and assimilation.

Michalak, L. (1988). *Cruel and Unusual: Negative Images of Arabs in Popular Culture.* Washington, DC: ADC Occasional Paper #15.

This essay covers songs, television shows, political cartoons, and movies. It includes a chart that shows the trend toward increasing negativity in movies over time (1921–1970) and discusses causes.

Naff, A. (1987). *Becoming American: The Early Arab Immigrant Experience.* Carbondale: Southern Illinois University Press.

This book is another classic. One of the few that is not an anthology, it focuses on Arabs who came to the United States in the pre-1950 period. Naff is an authority in this field; her account weaves in 125 interviews with the early immigrants.

Shaheen, J. (1997). *Arab and Muslim Stereotyping in American Popular Culture.* Georgetown: Center for Muslim-Christian Understanding, History and International Affairs. Edmund A. Walsh School of Foreign Service, Georgetown University.

Shaheen is one of the noted experts in the field of the Arab image in the media. His works are quite readable and the substance is informative and illuminating.

Shaikh, M., & Mansuri, S. (Eds.). (1995). *Teaching about Islam & Muslims in the Public School Classroom.* Fountain Valley, CA: Council on Islamic Education.

This handbook is essential for anyone intending to teach about Islam or who has Muslim students. It has clear information as well as a useful glossary and an excellent and extensive list of resources for teachers as well as for students of all ages.

Shakir, E. (1987). Good Works, Good Times. In E. Hooglund (Ed.), *Crossing the Waters* (pp. 133–143). Washington, DC: Smithsonian Institution Press.

This lyrical essay on the early years of the Syrian Ladies Aid Society of Boston describes the strength and resilience of the early Syrian immigrant women.

Shakir, E. (1997). *Bint Arab: Arab and Arab-American Women in the United States.* Westport, CT: Praeger.

This beautifully written book interweaves a memoir and portrait of the author's mother with a well-told general history of Arab America. The book contains interviews with about thirty Arab American women.

Zogby, J. (Ed.). (1984). *Taking Root/Bearing Fruit: The Arab-American Experience.* (Vol. 1). Washington, DC: ADC.

The first volume of essays on the community published by ADC, it reports on Allentown, Pennsylvania; Boston; Brooklyn; Detroit; Houston; Portland, Maine; San Francisco; Utica, New York; and Worcester, Massachusetts. It also provides regional surveys and includes a collection of famous essays (some of them from the early mahjar period) on or by members of the community.

Other Resources

Abinader, E. (1991). *Children of the Roojme: A Family's Journey.* New York: W. W. Norton.

   This three-generation saga covers the author's family's life in Lebanon, the immigrant experience, and their life in the United States. It is based on diaries, letters, and interviews.

Abourezk, J. (1989). *Advise and Dissent: Memoirs of South Dakota and the U.S. Senate.* Chicago: Lawrence Hill.

   This autobiography of the first Arab American Senator and founder of the American-Arab Anti-Discrimination Committee is both entertaining and informative. It gives insight into the political experiences that shaped a key perspective.

Abraham, N., & Shryock, A. (Eds.). (2000). *Arab Detroit: From Margin to Mainstream.* Detroit: Wayne State University Press.

   This anthology of essays creates a richly detailed portrait of Arab Americans in Detroit. Food, music, religion, and identity politics are among the topics; analysis, memory, poetry, and biography are among the approaches taken.

Abraham, S. Y., & Abraham, N. (Eds.). (1983). *Arabs in the New World: Studies on Arab-American Communities.* Detroit: Wayne State University, Center for Urban Studies.

   This classic source contains essays on the history, emigration experience, and religion of the immigrants, with five case studies on Lebanese, Yemenis, and Iraqi Chaldeans of Detroit and Dearborn.

Abu-Laban, B., & Suleiman, M. (Eds.). (1989). Arab Americans: Continuity and Change. *Arab Studies Quarterly, 11* (2 & 3).

   This volume contains essays on identity, adaptation, art, and politics as well as personal stories of young people growing up Arab in America. It also contains critical studies of the Arab world.

ADC Special Report: Anti-Arab Racism in the United States—1995. (1995). Washington, DC: Author.

   This report chronicles and analyzes hate crimes against Arabs after the Oklahoma City bombing.

ADC Research Institute. (1997). *Teachers Guide to Resources on the Arab World.* Washington, DC: ADC Research Institute.

   This guide provides a useful list of organizations, periodicals, book distributors, audiovisual sources, and university Middle East study centers with resources for teachers.

Antonius, G. (1965). *The Arab Awakening.* New York: Capricorn.

   This is the fascinating and brilliantly told story of the late nineteenth-century Arab National Movement that eventually led to the first great immigration movement from Syria. It starts with the Turkish conquest and ends just after World War I. The detail is astonishing and the book reads like a novel.

Gibran, J., & Gibran, K. (1974). *Kahlil Gibran: His Life and World.* Boston: New York Graphic Society.

   This is the definitive work by the subject's cousin and namesake and the cousin's wife. The authors' access to Gibran's extensive correspondence makes this an intimate portrait.

Haddad, Y. (1994). Maintaining the Faith of the Fathers: Dilemmas of Religious Identity in the Christian and Muslim Arab-American Communities. In E. McCarus (Ed.), *The Development of Arab-American Identity* (pp. 61–84). Ann Arbor: University of Michigan Press.

   This is an overview of the religions of Arab Americans.

Haiek, J. (Ed.). (2001). *Arab American Almanac.* Glendale, CA: News Circle.

This excellent reference includes essays on the history of the Arab American community, and has directories, by subject and by state, of various types of Arab American institutions.

McGoldrick, M., Giordano, J., & Pearce, J. (Eds.). (1996). *Ethnicity and Family Therapy* (2nd ed.). New York: Guilford.

This wonderful resource on the family dynamics of various ethnic groups contains a chapter on Arabs by N. Abudabbeh, and a separate one on the Lebanese by J. Simon.

Nye, N. S. (1995). *Words under the Words.* Portland, OR: Eighth Mountain Press.

This is a collection of poems from three previous collections. Nye is well known as a Palestinian and as an American poet. Some of her poems include themes from her ethnic and family experience.

Orfalea, G. (Ed.). (1982). *Wrapping the Grapeleaves: A Sheaf of Contemporary Arab-American Poets.* Washington, DC: American-Arab Anti-Discrimination Committee.

This chapbook contains eleven poems by Arab Americans—eight of them about family relationships. This is an excellent classroom resource.

Orfalea, G. (1988). *Before the Flames: A Quest for the History of Arab Americans.* Austin: University of Texas Press.

This personal account of the author's quest to find out what it means to be Arab American in these times blends historical background with family stories and quotes from the author's interviews with the famous and not quite famous, including actor F. Murray Abraham and late entertainer Danny Thomas.

Orfalea, G., & Elmusa, S. (Eds.). (1999). *Grapeleaves: A Century of Arab American Poetry.* Northampton, MA: Interlink.

This poetry anthology introduces some of the major poets, living and dead, of Arab America. It contains biographical and autobiographical commentary. Poets who write from the Arab American experience include Naomi Shihab Nye, D. H. Milhem, Sam Hazo, and Lawrence Joseph. All of these have also published their own volumes.

Saudi Aramco World Magazine (formerly *Aramco World*). Address: Saudi Aramco World, Post Office Box 2106, Houston, TX 77252-2106.

Educators are encouraged to subscribe to this glossy bimonthly. It has wonderful photographs and subscriptions are free. Articles are about aspects of the Arab world and occasionally cover Arab Americans and their accomplishments.

Shabbas, A. (Ed.). (1998). *Arab World Notebook.* Berkeley: AWAIR; and Washington, DC: Middle East Policy Council.

This is a wonderful collection of essays and teaching resources on the Arab world, past and present. It has many ideas for lesson plans and includes a section on Arab Americans.

Shaheen, J. G. (2001). *Reel Bad Arabs: How Hollywood Vilifies a People.* New York & Northhampton: Olive Branch Press.

An engaging 500-page compendium of original reviews of over 900 films, showing how the vast majority of them dehumanize Arabs. It also includes Best and Worst Lists, as well as a list of films Shaheen recommends.

Suleiman, M. (Ed.). (1999). *Arabs in America: Building a New Future.* Philadelphia: Temple University Press.

This book has sections on Arabs and the American legal system, Arab American youth and family, the Palestinian community in Chicago, the Arab Shiite community in the

United States, Arab American health and welfare issues and political activism, and several pieces on Arab American identity.

Younis, Adele L. (1995). *The Coming of the Arabic-Speaking People to the United States.* New York: Center for Migration Studies.

Though not published until 1995, this book contains information that many researchers on the Arab American community relied on when it was still a dissertation. Younis did much of the original work on the early Arab American experience. This book also contains Philip Kayal's most up-to-date Arab American bibliography.

Books for Students

Ameri, A., & Ramey, D. (Eds.). (2000). *Arab American Encyclopedia.* Detroit: ACCESS/The Gale Group.

Articles cover every aspect of Arab American life and include essays on history, immigration, language, religion, work, education, family, holidays, health, civil rights, organizations and political activism, music, literature, arts, media, and community portraits. (Primarily for middle school, but could be used both for upper elementary and high school)

Ashabranner, B. K. (1991). *An Ancient Heritage: The Arab American Minority.* New York: HarperCollins.

This book tells the story of the Arab Americans through their own words and the memories of the author growing up with them in Oklahoma. It also shows the connection they still have with their homelands. It contains many photographs. (Intermediate)

Geha, J. (1990). *Through and Through: Toledo Stories.* St. Paul: Graywolf Press.

This amusing book contains eight short stories depicting life in the Syrian Lebanese community in Toledo, Ohio, from the 1930s to the present, and themes ranging from the domestic to the criminal. (High School)

Harik, E. M. (1987). *The Lebanese in America.* Minneapolis: Lerner.

Similar in richness to the Naff book (1988), this one focuses on the Lebanese as a separate community. (Intermediate and Middle)

Naff, A. (1988). *The Arab Americans.* New York: Chelsea House.

Part of the Peoples of America *series, this is an excellent, rich, and comprehensive overview of the Arab American story by one of the leading chroniclers of this ethnic group. It does not shy away from presenting or interpreting complicated issues. It is an excellent book for the teacher new to the topic. It also contains good pictures. (Middle and High School)*

Nye, N. S. (1994). *Sitti's Secrets.* New York: Four Winds Press.

This is a poetic story of a little girl who visits her grandmother in her village on the West Bank and blends in with the lives of her relatives there. The writing and the pictures are extraordinary. (Primary)

Nye, N. S. (1997). *Habibi.* New York: Simon & Schuster.

This is the semi-autobiographical story of a young Arab American teenager who returns for a year with her American family to live in her father's hometown near Jerusalem. It shows her difficulties in adjusting to attitudes different from the ones she grew up with in America. It is a pleasure to read. (Intermediate and Middle)

Peduzzi, K. (1990). *Ralph Nader: Crusader for Safe Consumer Products and Lawyers for the Public Interest.* Milwaukee, WI: Gareth Stephens Books.

One of the People Who Have Helped the World *series, this book explores the ways that Arab American consumer advocate Ralph Nader and those he has inspired take on the wealthiest and most powerful organizations in America to defend the safety, health, and consumer rights of all Americans. (Upper Elementary and Middle)*

Contact Information for Resource Organizations

ACCESS (Arab Community Center for Economic and Social Service)
2651 Saulino Court, Dearborn, MI 48120
Tel: (313) 842-7010; Fax: (313) 842-5150
E-mail: *access-com@worldnet.att.net*

American-Arab Anti-Discrimination Committee (ADC)
4201 Connecticut Avenue, NW, Suite 300, Washington, DC 20008
Tel: (202) 244-2990; Fax: (202) 244-3196;
Web site: *http://www.adc.org.*

Americans for Middle East Understanding (AMEU)
475 Riverside Drive, New York, NY 10015-0241
Tel: (212) 870-2053; Fax: (212) 870-2050
E-mail: *ameu@aol.com*   Web site: *http://members.aol.com/ameulink*

Amideast
1730 M Street NW, Suite 1100, Washington, DC 20036
Tel: (202) 776-9600; Fax: (202) 776-7000
E-mail: *inquiries@amideast.org*   Web site: *http://www.amideast.org*

Arab American Institute (AAI)
1600 K Street NW, Suite 601, Washington, DC 20006
Tel: (202) 429-9210; Fax: (202) 429-9214
Web site: *www.aaiusa.org*

AWAIR (Arab World and Islamic Resources and School Services)
2137 Rose Street, Berkeley, CA 94709
Fax (510) 704-0517
E-mail: *awair@igc.apc.org*   Web site: *http://www.telegraphave.com/gui/awairproductinfo.html*

Council on American Islamic Relations (CAIR)
453 New Jersey Avenue, SE
Washington, DC 20008
Tel: (202) 488-8787; Fax: (202) 488-0833
E-mail: *cair@ix.netcom.com*   Web site: *http://www.cair-net.org*

Council on Islamic Education
P.O. Box 20186, Fountain Valley, CA 92728-0816
Tel: (714) 839-2929; Fax: (714) 839-2714
E-mail: *info@cie.org*   Web site: *http://www.cie.org*

Linda Adams, Editor
Middle East Outreach Council Newsletter
c/o University of Utah Middle East Center
260 S. Campus Dr., Rm. 153
Salt Lake City, UT 84112-9157

APPENDIX A

Ethnic Groups in U.S. History
A Chronology of Key Events

Date	Event
1513	Juan Ponce de León landed on the Florida peninsula while en route from Puerto Rico. The relationship between Europeans and Indians north of Mexico began.
1519	Hernán Cortéz, the Spanish conquistador, and a group of Spaniards arrived in the region that is now Mexico.
1565	The Spaniards established the St. Augustine colony in Florida, the first settlement organized by Europeans in present-day United States.
1619	The first Africans arrived in the English North American colonies.
1620	The Pilgrims came to America from England on the *Mayflower* and established a settlement at Plymouth, Massachusetts.
1637	More than 500 American Indians were killed by the colonists in a massacre known as the Pequot War.
1654	The first Jewish immigrants to North America settled in New Amsterdam to escape persecution in Brazil.
1683	German immigrants settled in Pennsylvania.
1718	The Scots-Irish began immigrating to North America in large numbers.
1754–63	The French and Indian War occurred.
1798	A Federalist-dominated Congress enacted the Alien and Sedition Acts to crush the Republican party and to harass aliens.
1812	The War of 1812, a war between the United States and Britain, caused deep factions among the Indian tribes because of their different allegiances.

Date	Event
1815	The first mass immigrations from Europe to North America began.
1830	Congress passed a Removal Act, which authorized the removal of Indians from east to west of the Mississippi.
1831	Nat Turner led a slave revolt in which nearly 60 Whites were killed.
1836	Mexico's President Santa Anna and his troops defeated the Texans at the Alamo. Six weeks later Santa Anna was defeated by Sam Houston and his Texan troops at San Jacinto.
1845	The United States annexed Texas, which had declared itself independent from Mexico in 1836. This was one key event that led to the Mexican-American War.
1846–48	A series of potato blights in Ireland caused thousands of its citizens to immigrate to the United States.
1846	On May 13, 1846, the United States declared war on Mexico and the Mexican-American War began.
1848	The United States and Mexico signed the Treaty of Guadalupe Hidalgo that ended the Mexican-American War. Mexico lost nearly one-third of its territory, and the United States acquired most of the territory that comprises its southwestern states.
1850	The California legislature passed a discriminatory Foreign Miner's Tax that forced Chinese immigrants to pay a highly disproportionate share of the state taxes.
1855	Castle Garden, an immigration station, opened in New York City. The antiforeign Know-Nothing Movement reached its zenith and had a number of political successes in the 1855 elections. The movement rapidly declined after 1855.
1859	Juan N. Cortina, who became a U.S. citizen under the provisions of the Treaty of Guadalupe Hidalgo, led a series of rebellions against Anglo-Americans in the Southwest.
1863	On January 1, 1863, President Abraham Lincoln issued the Emancipation Proclamation, which freed slaves in those states still fighting the Union.
1864	Nearly 300 Cheyennes were killed in a surprise attack at Sand Creek, Colorado. This event is known as the Sand Creek Massacre.

Date	Event
1869	The transcontinental railroad, linking the U.S. west to the east, was completed. Chinese laborers did most of the work on the Pacific portion of the railroad.
	The unsuccessful Wakamatsu Colony, made up of Japanese immigrants, was established in California.
1871	A White mob in Los Angeles attacked a Chinese community. When the conflict ended, 19 Chinese were killed and their community was in shambles.
1876	In the disputed Hayes-Tilden election, the Democrats and Republicans made a political bargain that symbolized the extent to which northern Whites had abandoned southern Blacks.
	Sioux tribes, under the leadership of Sitting Bull, wiped out Custer's Seventh Cavalry at Little Big Horn. This was one of the last victories for American Indian tribes.
*1882	The Chinese Exclusion Act was enacted by Congress. Another congressional immigration act established a head tax of fifty cents and excluded lunatics, convicts, idiots, and those likely to become public charges.
1885	A serious anti-Chinese riot occurred in Rock Springs, Wyoming. Twenty-eight Chinese were killed, and many others were wounded and driven from their homes.
1886	The Apache warrior Geronimo surrendered to U.S. forces in September 1886. His surrender marked the defeat of the Southwest tribes.
	The Haymarket Affair in Chicago increased the fear of foreign "radicals" and stimulated the growth of nativistic sentiments in the United States.
	The Statue of Liberty was dedicated as nativism soared in the United States.
1887	Congress passed the Dawes Severalty Act, which was designed to terminate partially the American Indians' special relationship with the U.S. government.
1888	The Scott Act prohibited the immigration of Chinese laborers and permitted only officials, teachers, students, merchants, and travelers from China to enter the United States.
1890	Three hundred Sioux were killed in a conflict at Wounded Knee Creek in South Dakota.

Date	Event
1891	Eleven Italian Americans were lynched in New Orleans during the height of American nativism, after being accused of murdering a police superintendent.
1892	Ellis Island opened and replaced Castle Garden as the main port of entry for European immigrants.
1893	Queen Liliuokalani of Hawaii was overthrown in a bloodless revolution led by American planters.
	The Republic of Hawaii was established, with Stanford B. Dole as president.
1896	In a historic decision, *Plessy* v. *Ferguson*, the Supreme Court ruled that "separate but equal" facilities were constitutional.
1898	Hawaii was annexed to the United States.
	Under the terms of the Treaty of Paris, the treaty that ended the Spanish-American War, the United States acquired Puerto Rico, Guam, and the Philippines. Cuba became independent of Spain but was placed under U.S. tutelage.
1900	With the Foraker Act, the United States established a government in Puerto Rico to which the president of the United States appointed the governor and the Executive Council.
1901–10	Almost 9 million immigrants entered the United States, most of whom came from southern and eastern Europe.
1908	The United States and Japan made the Gentlemen's Agreement, which was designed to reduce the number of Japanese immigrants entering the United States.
1910	The National Association for the Advancement of Colored People (NAACP) was organized.
	A Mexican revolution caused many Mexican peasants to immigrate to the United States looking for jobs. Other immigrants came to escape political turmoil and persecution.
1913	The California legislature passed a land bill that made it difficult for Japanese immigrants to lease land.
*1917	Thirty-nine African Americans were killed in a bloody riot in East St. Louis, Missouri.
	A comprehensive immigration bill was enacted that established a literacy test for entering immigrants.
	The Jones Act was passed by the U.S. Congress, making Puerto Ricans U.S. citizens and subject to the draft.

Date	Event
1920	The Hawaiian Homes Commission was started to benefit the native Hawaiians, but little of the land involved was used for its stated purpose. The number of people born in Puerto Rico and living in the United States was 11,811. That number increased to 58,200 in the year 1935.
*1924	The Johnson-Reed Act established extreme quotas on immigration and blatantly discriminated against southern and eastern European and non-White nations.
1925	A large number of Filipinos began to immigrate to Hawaii and the U.S. mainland to work as field laborers.
1927	The Filipino Federation of Labor was organized in Los Angeles.
1928	The League of United Latin American Citizens was formed in Harlingen, Texas.
1929	An anti-Filipino riot occurred in Exeter, California, in which more than 200 Filipinos were assaulted.
1930	The Japanese American Citizenship League was organized.
*1934	Congress passed the Tydings-McDuffie Act, which promised the Philippines independence and limited Filipino immigration to the United States to 50 per year.
1935	President Franklin D. Roosevelt signed the Repatriation Act. The act offered free transportation to Filipinos who would return to the Philippines. Those who left were unable to return to the United States except under a severe quota system.
1942	On February 19, 1942, President Franklin D. Roosevelt issued Executive Order 9066, which authorized the internment of Japanese Americans who lived on the West Coast.
	The United States and Mexico made an agreement that authorized Mexican immigrants to work temporarily in the United States. This project is known as the *bracero* program.
1943	White violence directed at African Americans led to a serious riot in Detroit, in which 34 people were killed. The anti-Mexican zoot suit riots occurred in Los Angeles during the summer.
1946	On July 4, 1946, the Philippines became independent.
*1952	The McCarran-Walter Immigration and Nationality Act was passed by Congress. It eliminated race as a factor in immigration. However, the national origins quota system remained but was liberalized.

Date	Event
1954	The Refugee Relief Act permitted 5,000 Hungarian refugees to enter the United States.
	In a landmark decision, *Brown v. Board of Education*, the Supreme Court ruled that school segregation was inherently unequal.
	The U.S. Immigration and Naturalization Service began Operation Wetback, a massive program to deport illegal Mexican immigrants.
1959	Fidel Castro took over the reins of power in Cuba from the government of Fulgencio Batista. After this revolution, many Cuban refugees entered the United States.
	Hawaii became the fiftieth state of the United States.
1960	On February 1, 1960, the sit-in movement, which desegregated public accommodation facilities throughout the South, began in Greensboro, North Carolina.
1961	The National Indian Youth Council was organized.
1962	Commercial air flights between the United States and Cuba ended. Immigration from Cuba to the United States became strictly clandestine.
1963	More than 200,000 people participated in a "March on Washington for Freedom and Jobs."
1964	The Civil Rights Act of 1964, the most comprehensive civil rights bill in American history, was enacted by Congress and signed by President Lyndon B. Johnson.
1965	With the passage of the Civil Rights Act of 1965, Puerto Ricans were no longer required to pass an English literacy test to vote in New York state.
	*The Immigration Reform Act of 1965 was passed by Congress. This act, which became effective in 1968, abolished the national origins quota system and liberalized American immigration policy. Immigration from Asia and Latin America increased after this act was passed.
	A grape strike led by César Chávez and the National Farm Workers Association began in Delano, California, a town in the San Joaquin Valley.
	Rodolfo "Corkey" Gonzales formed the Crusade for Justice in Denver. This important civil rights organization epitomized the Chicano movement that emerged in the 1960s.

Date	Event
1965	The Cuban Refugee Airlift program began. Flights from Cuba to Miami, Florida, were sponsored by the U.S. government. The program was terminated in 1973.
1965–68	A series of riots occurred in U.S. cities in which African Americans expressed their frustrations and discontent.
1966	Stokely Carmichael issued a call for Black Power during a civil rights demonstration in Greenwood, Mississippi.
1970	Herman Badillo was elected to the U.S. House of Representatives, the first Puerto Rican elected to Congress.
1973	African Americans were elected mayors in Detroit, Atlanta, Los Angeles, and other cities.
1974	The U.S. Supreme Court ruled in the *Lau* v. *Nichols* case that schools should provide students with instruction in their native language. This ruling gave bilingual-bicultural education in the United States a tremendous boost.
1975	U.S. participation in the Vietnam War had ended (1973), and Communist governments took control of Vietnam and Cambodia (Kampuchea). Many Indochinese refugees settled in the United States. Between 1971 and 1978, 110,200 Vietnamese refugees immigrated to the United States.
1978	In the case of *Regents of the University of California* v. *Bakke,* the Supreme Court of the United States upheld the idea of affirmative action but ruled against strict racial quotas. The Court concluded that the affirmative action program at the Medical School of the University of California at Davis was unconstitutional.
1980	The 1980 U.S. Census indicated that the population of some ethnic groups in the United States increased dramatically in the decade between 1970 and 1980. Mexicans, Koreans, and Chinese were among the groups whose population increased the most. While the White population increased only 6% between 1970 and 1980, the population of Asian and Pacific Islanders more than doubled (from 1.5 million to 3.5 million), and the Hispanic population increased more than 60%. The Refugee Relief Act of 1980 was enacted. It enabled more refugees to enter the United States.

Date	Event
*1986	The Immigration Reform and Control Act of 1986 was passed by Congress and became law. The act imposed severe penalties on employers who knowingly hired illegal immigrants, and it gave amnesty to many illegal immigrants who had been living in the United States since January 1, 1982.
1988	The Civil Liberties Act of 1988 was passed by Congress and signed by President Ronald Reagan. The act provided compensation for the Japanese Americans and the Aleuts of the Pribilof Islands and the Aleutian Islands for the losses they incurred for being forcibly relocated during World War II.
*1990	The Immigration Act of 1990 made some significant changes in immigration law. It set immigration at 675,000 annually (beginning in 1995) to consist of 480,000 family-sponsored, 140,000 employment-based, and 55,000 "diversity immigrants." It revised political and ideological grounds for exclusion and deportation.
1994	Nativistic sentiments throughout the nation were epitomized by the passage of Proposition 197 in California. This proposition denied undocumented workers and their children schooling and nonemergency medical care.
2000	The 2000 U.S. Census indicated that ethnic groups of color made up about 29.4% of the United States population.
2001	After the September 11th tragedy in which almost 3,000 people were killed by terrorists believed to be Arabs, a number of Arab Americans were victims of racist attacks in the United States. President George W. Bush spoke out against these attacks and appealed to Americans to treat fellow citizens fairly.

APPENDIX B

Internet Resources for Teaching about Ethnic and Cultural Diversity

Notice: Between the time Web site information is gathered and then published it is not unusual for some sites to have closed. Also the transcription of URLs can result in unintended typographical errors. The publisher would appreciate notification where these occur so that they may be corrected in subsequent printings and editions. Thank you.

General Multicultural

Applied Research Center

www.arc.org

ARC is a public policy, educational and research center that focuses on issues of race and social change. ARC produces a magazine called *Colorlines,* available on-line along with numerous other articles and perspectives by staff members. Additionally, ARC has several projects designed to foster worldwide and national awareness and action.

The Balch Institute for Ethnic Studies

www.balchinstitute.org/

The Balch Institute is a multicultural library, archive, and educational center. Its mission is "to promote greater intergroup understanding by documenting and presenting American ethnic and racial experiences."

Center for Multicultural Education, University of Washington, Seattle

depts.washington.edu/centerme/home.htm

Based at the University of Washington, the Center for Multicultural Education focuses on research projects related to equity issues, intergroup relations, and

499

the achievement of students of color. The Center's site lists its publications, research projects, upcoming and past events, conferences, lectures, degree programs, courses, and faculty. The Center's publications include the *Handbook of Research on Multicultural Education* (Jossey-Bass/Wiley, 2001) and *Diversity within Unity: Essential Principles for Teaching and Learning in a Multicultural Society*. The latter publication can be downloaded from the Center's Web site as a pdf file. James A. Banks is the director of the Center.

Clearinghouse for Multicultural and Bilingual Education

www.weber.edu/MBE/HTMLs/MBE.html

The Clearinghouse is a database designed to provide educators from preschool to higher education with commercial and noncommercial sources for multicultural and bilingual information, materials, and resources.

Educational Justice

www.edjustice.org/

This program's mission is to "promote access to quality education for students from all racial and cultural groups." Sharing resources plays a large part in its goal and this page provides massive amounts of resources. Included are topic-specific resources as well as a curriculum page for all subjects and groups or cultures.

Ellis Island Records

www.ellisislandsrecords.org

Ellis Island Records is an informational database site where individuals can research their ancestors and personal heritage. Among the services provided are a passenger search, purchase of passenger documents, and creation of family scrapbooks.

Facing History and Ourselves

www.facinghistory.org/facing/fhao2.nsf

Facing History and Ourselves encourages teachers and students to examine history and legacies of prejudice and discrimination. This site contains a massive resource section including study guides to go with films and lectures, books, and multimedia. This site, which has excellent resources on teaching about the Holocaust, helps teachers and students to understand the Holocaust in the context of prejudice and discrimination in U.S. society today. It also has a teacher in-service component.

Immigration History Research Center

www1.umn.edu/ihrc

Based at the University of Minnesota, the Immigration History Research Center makes available to the public its archival and published materials related to immigration and ethnicity. This site is particularly useful for eastern, central, and southern European groups.

The National Association for Multicultural Education (NAME)

www.nameorg.org

NAME is a national professional organization that provides resources and support that help educators implement "a philosophy of inclusion and promote cultural and ethnic diversity as a national strength." NAME organizes an annual conference that deals with issues of diversity and multicultural education. It also has a number of regional organizations that sponsor conferences.

National Clearinghouse for Bilingual Education

www.ncbe.gwu.edu/

The U.S. Department of Education's Office of Minority Language Affairs funds this organization. Its goal is to provide information relating to "the effective education of linguistically and culturally diverse learners in the U.S." The site includes links such as the on-line library, database, language and educational links, and classroom materials.

National Women's History Project

www.nwhp.org

In an attempt to provide teachers with information and materials regarding women's perspectives and contributions to society, the National Women's History Project offers much more than an on-line catalog. It also offers a learning page where teachers can discover resources and teacher support, student-specific links, and current events such as National Women's History Month. A significant part of the project's materials deal with women of color.

The Population Reference Bureau

www.prb.org

The Population Reference Bureau provides basic population and demographic data for the United States and the world. Many of its reports focus on U.S. ethnic groups. Recent reports include *Immigration to the United States,*

America's Diversity and Growth: Signposts for the 21st Century, and *First Glimpses from the U.S. Census.* The site also includes specialized lesson plans and educational articles on different topics.

REACH Center

www.reachctr.org

The Reach Center provides training and learning experiences in multicultural education and ethnic history for school districts, schools, and individuals. The cross-cultural training REACH offers helps participants gain knowledge and understanding of different cultural groups. The goal of REACH is to help all people function well in a diverse society. Gary Howard, the director of REACH Center, is the author of *We Can't Teach What We Don't Know: White Teachers, Multiracial Schools* (Teachers College Press, 1999).

Rethinking Schools

www.rethinkingschools.org

Rethinking Schools is devoted to reforming urban schools and addressing issues involving race. Rethinking Schools is "committed to equity and to the vision that public education is central to the creation of a humane, caring, multiracial democracy." The site includes a searchable index of all articles that have appeared in its periodic publication, *Rethinking Schools. Rethinking Schools* was founded by and is run by classroom teachers.

Social Studies School Service

www.socialstudies.com

The Social Studies School Service is a distributor of social studies teaching materials. It publishes a multicultural catalog that covers immigration, ethnic studies, diversity, and human relations. The on-line catalog provides searches and links by region. Other topics include religions and specific American histories such as women's history and Native American history.

Teaching for Change

www.teachingforchange.org

Teaching for Change is part of the Network of Educators on the Americas. The site provides teachers with resources to help integrate diverse cultures and experiences into the curriculum and updated material and resources on specific topics and current events. The site contains an on-line catalog.

Teaching Tolerance

www.teachingtolerance.org

The goal of this site is to fight hate and promote tolerance. Specific pages for teachers, parents, and students provide materials and information to foster equity within schools and society. This site is excellent for providing relevant current events and plans of action to help foster classroom discussion and exploration.

United States Census Bureau: Minority Links

www.census.gov/pubinfo/www/hotlinks.html

Minority Links provides easily accessible data on minority populations in the United States. In addition to basic census data, the site includes social characteristics, economic characteristics, profiles, news releases, and other related topics.

American Indians

The Alaska Native Knowledge Network

www.ankn.uaf.edu

The Alaska Native Knowledge Network is designed to serve as a resource for collecting and exchanging information related to Alaska Native knowledge systems and ways of understanding. It has been established to assist Native people, government agencies, educators, and the general public in learning about and understanding Alaska Native people.

The Cradleboard Teaching Project

www.cradleboard.org

This teaching project is based on linking Indian and non-Indian children through the learning process. The Cradleboard curriculum and lessons are designed to be interactive multimedia Native studies lessons in which partner classes are linked through technology and learn together. In addition, Cradleboard offers numerous links to tribal Web pages, a question-and-answer forum, and five core curriculum samples from a Native American perspective from elementary to high school level.

National Congress of American Indians

www.ncai.org

The National Congress of American Indians (NCAI) serves as a forum for policy development among its 250 tribal governments members. NCAI informs the public and the federal government about tribal self-government, treaty rights, and a wide range of federal policy issues affecting tribal governments.

The National Museum of the American Indian, Smithsonian Institution National Museum

www.nmai.si.edu

The National Museum of the American Indian presents in-depth, activity-based educational programs. It has an on-line Resource Center that provides a bibliography of suggested books and links to other sites relating to Native Americans.

Native Village

www.nativevillage.org/

Native Village was created as an educational and current events resource for Native youth, teens, families, educators, and friends. The writers of this site publish two weekly news editions: *Native Village Drum* and *Native Village Youth and Education News.* Each issue shares Indian news from all parts of the Americas.

Native Web

www.nativeweb.org

Native Web is an educational organization dedicated to using technology to disseminate information from and about indigenous cultures throughout the world. This site is complete with a comprehensive resource center including Web links, books, music, a nations index, and a geographical region index.

Virtual Library on Native Americans

http://www.hanksville.org/NAresources/

This Virtual Library on Native Americans provides a comprehensive index of Native American teaching resources on the Internet. The links provided allow teachers and students to explore the multitude of resources available on the Web.

Native Hawaiians

Hawaiian Culture Online

www.hookele.com/visitmaui/

Hawaiian Culture Online is a comprehensive site. Among the information provided are Web directories, information on cultural stories, music, plants, and language links.

Hawaiian Home Page

www.geocities.com/~olelo/home.html

The Hawaiian Home Page contains links to culture, language, current events, organizations, and music. This site is a good place to start becoming familiar with Hawaiian culture

Hawaiian Independence

www.hawaii-nation.org/index.html

This site is dedicated to issues revolving around Hawaii as an independent and a sovereign state. The historical and archived information is excellent, as well as the list of links and cultural information.

Native Hawaiians

www.nativehawaiians.com

This site answers the question "Who are native Hawaiians?" and provides an historical time line, the latest news, articles, lesson plans, and a press kit. There are links to a few other sites, including the Office of Hawaiian Affairs.

African Americans

African Americans in History

www.uga.edu/~iaas/History.html

This site provides brief biographical sketches of several key figures in African American history.

African Americans in the Humanities, 20th Century

www.ithaca.edu/staff/jhenderson/humafro.html

This site primarily provides links to sites that contain biographical information about important African American personalities of the twentieth century. It also contains links to Asian, Hispanic, and Native American personalities.

The Black World Today

www.tbwt.com

TBWT's mission is to use the Internet to empower Black people in the United States and internationally. The news and features presented on the site are general news of value and interest to African Americans. Numerous commentaries are featured that reveal varying opinions about current events as well as African and Caribbean issues. TBWT also provides links to help build the African American community.

The Faces of Science: African Americans in the Sciences

www.princeton.edu/~mcbrown/display/faces.html

This site profiles African American men and women who have contributed to the advancement of science and engineering. The site includes African American chemists, biologists, inventors, engineers, and mathematicians.

European American Ethnic Groups

American Institute of Polish Culture

www.ampolinstitute.org/links.html

The American Institute of Polish Culture maintains a good Web site of their own but their list of links to other pages about Polish culture is an excellent resource for any subject.

Center for Migration Studies

www.cmsny.org

CMS is committed to studying all aspects of human migration including historical, economic, political, and sociodemographic. This site includes a documentation center with a comprehensive library as well as numerous links to related European Web sites and others in the Federation of Centers for Migration Studies.

Center for the Study of White American Culture

www.euroamerican.org

The Center for the Study of White American Culture is a multiracial organization that examines different racial and cultural groups of White Americans. The Center promotes the idea that "Knowledge of one's own racial background and culture is essential when learning how to relate to people of other racial and cultural groups." This site has a great list of links including one about European American heritage where people can learn about ethnic heritages. Additionally, there is a White studies library that can be searched by subject.

One Stop Italian American Culture and Heritage

www.osia.org/public/culture.htm

This site offers a good variety of resources from literature to current events. There is even an Italian American magazine available to read.

Slovak-American International Culture Foundation

www.slovakculture.org/

This foundation is designed to provide information about Slovak-American and Slovak contributions to society. The site provides good cultural background information.

Jewish Americans

Jewish Americans: History and Bibliography for Children and Young Adults

http://falcon.jmu.edu/~ramseyil/muljew.htm

This is primarily a site with links to other sources for children's books, bibliographies, and publishers. Some of the specific categories listed are biographies, Jewish holidays, the Holocaust, professional resources, and history.

Multicultural Research: Jewish American/ Judaic Research

www.union.edu/PUBLIC/LIBRARY/guide/mcjewish.html

This site has been put together by the Multicultural Resource Center of the Schaffer Library Union College for the purpose of providing sources and tools for academic research. It is primarily a site with numerous links to other sources for Jewish culture and history such as private centers, societies and organizations, communication networks with worldwide news updates, and an on-line book catalog.

National Museum of American Jewish History

http://nmajh.org/exhibitions/

The National Museum of American Jewish History site offers virtual tours of online exhibitions.

Mexican Americans

AEL: Mexican American Education

www.ael.org/eric/mexicans.htm

AEL is a nonprofit institution whose mission is to link educational research and knowledge gained from practice to improve teaching and learning. This site is linked to the ERIC database and includes other good links such as books related to Mexican American education.

Hispanic American History and Literature for K–12

falcon.jmu.edu/~ramseyil/hispan.htm

This site offers a comprehensive list of resources for teachers of all grade levels. The list contains categories such as biography, periodicals, Hispanic heritage, history, and Mexican Americans.

Mexican American Studies and Research Center (MASRC)

w3fp.arizona.edu/masrc/

MASRC is committed to public policy on Mexican Americans and addresses issues of concern to this group. The Center achieves these goals through its comprehensive curriculum, research agenda, and publications.

The Mexican Museum

thecity.sfsu.edu/users/Mex/Welcome.html

The Mexican Museum Web page allows you to browse their current and permanent collections of Mexican American and Chicano contemporary art. The museum also offers curriculum and materials for teachers.

Park Net: A History of Mexican Americans in California

www.cr.nps.gov/history/books/index.htm

This is a site of the National Park Service describing A History of Mexican Americans in California. Although this site is specific to California, it describes in detail various time periods including the Mexican War, post-conquest, 1900–1940, WWII, the Chicano Movement, and the future. The site also includes a good list of specific links to historical sites.

Puerto Ricans in the United States

Black and Puerto Rican Studies Resource Page

www.hunter.cuny.edu/blpr/resources.html

This page provides an excellent overview of Puerto Rican history and culture as well as good bibliographies on Puerto Rican literature and art. In addition, there is a good biographical source list of important Puerto Rican historical figures.

Puerto Rico and the American Dream

prdream.com/index.html

Puerto Rico and the American Dream is an extremely thoughtful site on the history, culture, and politics of Puerto Rico. The site includes a film section, an online gallery, discussion boards, historical time lines, oral histories, and announcements and current event postings.

Selected Reference Sources on Puerto Rico and Puerto Ricans in the W. E. B. Du Bois Library

http://www.library.umass.edu/instruction/handouts/prbiblio.html

This site includes almanacs and bibliographies. Other resources provide information on topics such as culture, economics, education, health, and race relations.

Yale-New Haven Teachers Institute

http://www.yale.edu/ynhti/curriculum/units/1991/2/91.02.06.x.html

The content of this site is a curriculum called "The Heritage and Culture of Puerto Ricans" by the Yale-New Haven Teachers Institute. It was designed to supplement social studies in grades three and four, but may be adapted for all levels.

Cuban Americans

Latin American and Caribbean Center

http://lacc.fiu.edu/

The Latin American and Caribbean Center (LACC) is part of Florida International University. This site describes the Center, public education and outreach efforts (including teacher training workshops, faculty development in foreign language education, and distance learning), publications and resources, grants and research, and news and events. The Cuban Research Institute is within the LACC and offers degree programs, symposiums, and information on current events.

Simon Fraser University Library

http://edocs.lib.sfu.ca/projects/Cuba/

This site provides an annotated bibliography of novels written in English about Cuba/Cubans/Cuban Americans from 1851–2000, compiled by the Simon Fraser University Library. It is a good resource for secondary teachers but it excludes children's and young adult fiction.

University of Miami Libraries: Cuba and Cuban Americans on the Internet

www.library.miami.edu/netguides/cubanet.html#top

This site is quite possibly the most comprehensive place to visit if you are looking for links relating to Cuban Americans. You can view links in such categories as archives, culture and history, databases, newspapers, and directories. The site even provides links to the Institute for Cuban and Cuban American Studies.

Asian Americans

The Asian American Curriculum Project (AACP)

AsianAmericanBooks.com/

The mission of the AACP is to educate the public about the Asian American experience by offering materials for all age groups, all levels of education, and all Asian ethnic groups. The AACP publishes an excellent and comprehensive catalog of materials for teaching about Asian Americans. This is an excellent nonprofit organization that has been engaged in its important work since 1970. Florence M. Hongo is the general manager of AACP.

Asian American Studies Center, UCLA

www.sscnet.ucla.edu/aasc/

This center is on the UCLA campus and contains much more than just class listings. This excellent research center provides updates on important events and functions.

Asian Virtual Library

www.ss.uno.edu/ss/Ahist/libraryhp.html

The University of New Orleans maintains this site, and it is complete and extensive. The layout of the site allows one to search by specific country in the general categories of East Asia, South Asia, Southeast Asia, and West Asia. In addition to the vast amount of information contained in these links, there are several links that provide help and resources for teaching about Asia by region, theme, and age group. Lesson plans and advice are provided.

Chinese Historical and Cultural Project

www.chcp.org/index.html

Based in Santa Clara, this organization's goal is to promote and preserve Chinese American and Chinese history. It has numerous ongoing projects such as the Golden Legacy Curriculum and Seminar Series, educational grants, and a virtual museum and library.

East and Southeast Asia: An Annotated Directory of Internet Resources

http://newton.uor.edu/Departments&Programs/AsianStudiesDept/asianam.html

This site includes links to a vast amount of information of interest and pertaining to many Asian groups. These links are divided into categories such as multiculturalism, general information, political and social issues, media, communities, culture and arts, immigrations, and academic resources.

Filipino American National Historical Society (FANHS)

www.fanhs-national.org

FANHS provides information about many aspects of Filipino issues today. Some of the beneficial information on this site includes ongoing research, public forums, exhibits, journals, film and book reviews, and bibliographies of resources.

Institute for Korean American Culture (IKAC)

www.ikac.org/

IKAC sponsors events to promote Korean American culture such as dance and drumming festivals. Its Web site provides book lists for categories such as art and literature, culture, and mental health.

Vietnamese American Council

www.viet-nam.org

The mission of this organization is to promote the advancement of Vietnamese Americans in American society while maintaining their Vietnamese cultural heritage. This site contains a great page of links, culture, history, and current events.

Wing Luke Asian Museum, Seattle, Washington

www.wingluke.org/index.htm

This Seattle museum home page has access to a research center that contains links to information in categories such as Asian Pacific American, Chinese American, Filipino American, and Japanese American.

Arab Americans

Arabs in America

www.arabia.com/english/

Arabs in America provides many links to cultural sites, religious information, film, current events, and chat rooms. The site also provides a search engine that allows one to search for specific topics on all Arab sites.

Arab American Institute

www.aaiusa.org/

This site includes news and views and general information regarding Arab Americans. Additionally, the site includes a bibliography for further research.

Book Links: The Arab World and Arab Americans

www.ala.org/BookLinks/v09/arab.html

Book Links is designed to connect the library to the classroom. This site offers a bibliography of books designed to help teachers learn about and teach Arab Americans.

Detroit Free Press: 100 Questions and Answers about Arab Americans

http://www.freep.com/jobspage/arabs/

The Detroit Free Press developed this site in the city with the United States' most concentrated Arab American population. Its format is 100 Questions and Answers about Arab Americans: A Journalist's Guide.

Publishers of Multicultural Books and Materials

Anti-Defamation League Resources

www.adl.org

The Anti-Defamation League offers a resources catalog of materials that help teachers and parents teach about communication and respect among diverse groups. These resources are designed to confront prejudice, hatred, bigotry, and discrimination while teaching the value of diversity and tolerance.

Children's Book Press

http://www.cbookpress.org

This is a nonprofit publisher that specializes in bilingual and multicultural literature, publishing stories that reflect "the traditions and cultures of the emerging majority in the U.S." Additionally, the teaching and learning page provides examples of workshops given by the authors and on-line resources created by teachers to accompany the books.

Intercultural Press

interculturalpress.com/shop/index.html

The Intercultural Press provides books, simulations, videos, and training material about crossing cultures designed for a variety of audiences. The Education and Theory section is of particular interest.

Lee and Low Books

www.leeandlow.com

Lee and Low is an independent children's book publisher specializing in multicultural themes with which children of color, as well as all children, can identify. The search engine allows you to search by title, author, illustrator, or subject. There is also a teacher resource center and a book talk link.

The New Press

www.thenewpress.com/

The New Press is a nonprofit company created as an alternative to large commercial publishers. It is committed to publishing works of educational, cultural, and community value. Its site includes a "tools for teachers" section complete with free teacher guides.

Northland Publishing

www.northlandpub.com

Based in Arizona, Northland Publishing specializes in themes of the West and Native American material. There is a specific section for children's literature, which includes tools for teachers.

South End Press

www.southendpress.org/

This nonprofit publisher works to provide material to readers who are interested in social change. The goal of South End Press is to print books that encourage critical thinking and constructive action. This site also provides links to magazines, radio shows, and organizations that share the goals of South End Press.

Temple University Press

www.temple.edu/tempress/

Temple University Press publishes books in the social sciences and humanities that address social justice issues and produces a specific catalog for ethnic studies. Its Web site provides links to award winners, bestsellers, and series. Many of the books the Press publishes are interdisciplinary and can fit into several categories.

Publishers Not on the Internet

Arte Público Press

1-800-633-2783

Arte Público specializes in publishing contemporary and recovered literature by Hispanic authors in the United States. It offers general catalogs as well as specific catalogs for categories such as women's/feminist titles, drama, poetry, reference, piñata books for children and young adults, and recovering the U.S. Hispanic literary heritage.

APPENDIX C

Videotapes and CD-ROMs on Multicultural Education and U.S. Ethnic Groups

For Teachers and Teacher Education

A Class Divided. Producer/Distributor: Arlington, VA: PBS Video. *(www.pbs.org)*

An innovative teacher who discriminated against her class on the basic of eye color to teach them about the pain of prejudice is united with them after twenty years in this powerful presentation. This videotape shows how this teacher, Jane Elliott, made a difference, an inspiration to us all.

Culture, Difference and Power (Multimedia CD-ROM for Windows and Macintosh). Author: Christine Sleeter. Publisher: Teachers College Press, New York, 2001. *(www.teacherscollege press.com)*

This innovative and interactive electronic book, designed for future and practicing teachers, contains 45 original readings by the author, an instructor's manual, and 80 videoclips that feature 5 classrooms, 7 teachers, 1 school leadership team, 5 noted theorists, and 2 artists.

Good Morning Miss Toliver. Producer/Distributor: Foundation for Advancements in Science and Education (FASE), 4801 Wilshire Boulevard, Suite 215, Los Angeles, CA 90010. *(www.fastenet.org/)*

In this half-hour videotape, viewers visit the classroom of Kay Toliver, a creative and perceptive teacher in New York City's East Harlem Tech/P.S.72. She teaches engaging math lessons by creating math problems that relate to the East Harlem community.

In Whose Honor: American Indian Mascots in Sports. Producer: Jay Rosenstein. Distributor: Hohokus, NJ: New Day Films. *(www.newday.com)*

This videotape chronicles the struggle of Charlene Teters, a Native American student, to end the use of a Native American chief as a football team mascot at the University of Illinois, Champaign-Urbana. The videotape describes the social action taken by Teters to end the tradition, as well as the strong opposition by the board of trustees and alumni who want to maintain a tradition that is deeply beloved by vocal and influential alumni and board members.

Off Track: Classroom Privilege for All. Authors: Michelle Fine, Bernadette Anand, Markie Hancock, Carlton Jordan, & Dana Sherman. Publisher: Teachers College Press, NY. *(www.teacherscollegepress.com)*

Viewers witness students learning in an untracked world literature course in which use of a critical pedagogy of groupwork, collaboration, and serious individualized attention create an innovative classroom in which all students learn at high levels.

Rabbit in the Moon: A Documentary Memoir. Produced by Emiko Omori and Chizuko Omori. Distributor: Honokus, NJ: New Day Films. *(www.newday.com/)*

> *A powerful presentation of the internment of Japanese Americans that blends a rewriting of history with a description of the erosive effects of the internment on the Japanese American community. The legacy of these effects remains.*

Status Treatments for the Classroom. Producer and author: Elizabeth Cohen. Distributor: New York: Teachers College Press. *(www.teacherscollegepress.com)*

> *This videotape is based on the book* Designing Groupwork: Strategies for the Heterogeneous Classroom *(2nd ed.), by Elizabeth Cohen (Published by Teachers College Press). This excellent videotape demonstrates how teachers can create equal status among students in the classroom and consequently enhance the academic achievement of students of color. Both the videotape and the book are highly recommended for staff development.*

For Students

Act of War: The Overthrow of the Hawaiian Nation. Distributor: San Francisco: CrossCurrent Media. *(www.naatanet.org/)*

> *The struggle of Native Hawaiians to reclaim their land and the historical events that led to their current situation are described in this one-hour program.*

The American Story. Producer/Distributor: New York: Anti-Defamation League. *(www.adl.org/)*

> *The lives of twelve families from different ethnic groups are profiled in this series. Titles in the series include families from these U.S. ethnic groups: Puerto Rican, Japanese, Polish, Mexican, Native American, Jewish, Greek, and Italian. This series is excellent for involving students in discussion. The range of ethnic groups covered in the series is another strong characteristic. Each video presentation is 23 minutes, which makes the set excellent for teaching purposes.*

The Americans: The Latin American and Caribbean Presence in the U.S. Producer: WGBH, Boston; Distributor: Annenberg/CPB Collection. *(www.learner.org/)*

> *This 60-minute videotape examines the Hispanic experience in the United States by focusing on three groups: Cubans in Miami, Puerto Ricans in New York City, and Mexican Americans in Southern California.*

Arab Americans. Distributor: AWAIR, 2137 Rose Street, Suite 4, Berkeley, California 94709; Fax: (510) 704-0517; E-mail: *awair@ige.ape.org (www.telegraphave.com/guiawairproductinfo. html)*

> *Based on the Chelsea House series "People of North America," this 30-minute video, primarily geared to upper elementary and secondary school students, examines Arab American immigration against the larger backdrop of the entire American immigration story.*

Autobiography of Malcolm X. Distributor: Princeton, NJ: Films for the Humanities & Sciences. *(www.films.com)*

> *This video presentation on the life of Malcolm X includes dramatizations as well as interviews with scholars.*

Becoming Americans. Producer: Ken and Ivory Waterworth Levine. Distributor: Honokus, NJ: New Day Films. *(www.newday.com/)*

> *This documentary film focuses on the Hmong refugees from Laos. It is a powerful presentation that is excellent for stimulating discussion. Available in both 30-minute and 60-minutes versions.*

Before Columbus: Native Americans Tell Their Own Story. Producer/Distributor: Princeton, NJ: Films for the Humanities & Sciences. *(www.films.com)*

> Each of the five parts of this program consists of 28 minutes. Titles in the series are Invasion; The Right to Their Own Land; Temples into Churches; Teaching Indians to Be White; Rebellion; *and* The Indian Experience in the 20th Century.

Benaat Chicago (Daughters of Chicago): Growing Up Arab and Female in Chicago (1996). Distributor: American Friends Service Committee, 637 S. Dearborn, Chicago, IL 60605. Tel: (312) 427-2533; Fax: (312) 427-4171; E-mail: *jbing-canar@afsc.org (www.afsc.org/)*

> Produced by Jennifer Bing and Mary Zerkel of the Chicago Office of the American Friends Service Committee and the Arab-American Community Center of Chicago, this 30-minute video documents the lives of Arab American teenagers growing up on Chicago's southwest side. It depicts the source of pride of Arab American young women and addresses issues of stereotypes and racism against Arabs.

Chicana. Distributor: New York: Women Make Movies. *(www.wmm.com/)*

> The important roles and contributions of Mexican American women are described in this 23-minute videotape.

Collecting Stories from Exile: Chicago Palestinians Remember 1948. (1999). Distributor: American Friends Service Committee, 637 S. Dearborn, Chicago, IL 60605. Tel: (312) 427-2533; Fax: (312) 427-4171; E-mail: *jbing-canar@afsc.org (www.afsc.org/)*

> Produced by the Chicago Office of the American Friends Service Committee and the Arab-American Action Network of Chicago, this 28-minute oral history project documents the lives of Chicago Palestinians who survived the 1948 Arab-Israeli War.

Different and the Same. Producer/Distributor: Pittsburgh, PA: Family Communications. *(www.misterrogers.org/)*

> This series of videotapes is designed to teach children in grades 1 through 3 about racial and ethnic differences and to develop respect for differences. The nine program segments are contained within three videotapes. Puppets are central characters in these effective and useful videotapes for use with young children. Program segment titles include Sticks and Stones, Proud to Be Me, *and* I Am American, Too.

Dollar a Day, Ten Cents a Dance: A Historic Portrait of Filipino Farmworkers in America. Distributor: San Francisco: CrossCurrent Media. *(www.naatanet.org/)*

> This 30-minute program describes the Filipino immigrants who settled in the United States in the 1920 and 1930s. Their community consisted primarily of men.

Eyes on the Prize: America's Civil Rights Years. Series I and II. Producer: PBS Video; Distributor: Culver City, CA: Social Studies School Service. *(www.socialstudies.com)*

> This is an outstanding series of 57-minute color videotapes that cover the civil rights movement in depth from 1954 through the mid-1980s. Part I (six videotapes) covers the period from 1954 to 1965. Part II (eight videotapes) covers the period from 1965 through the mid-1980s. Every school system, as well as college and university media centers, should purchase this outstanding series.

Hidden Heritage: The Roots of Black American Painting. Distributor: Falls Church, VA: Landmark Films. *(www.landmarktheatres.com/Films/FilmIndex_frameset.htm)*

> African American art from the American Revolution to World War II is described in this 52-minute videotape.

Ida B. Wells. Distributor: New York: William Greaves Productions. *(www.williamgreaves.com/)*

> The life of the crusader against lynching is described in this 53-minute program.

In Black and White: Conversations with African American Writers. San Francisco: California Newsreel. *(www.newsreel.org/)*

This set of six videotapes (151 minutes) features six African American authors: Charles Johnson, Gloria Naylor, Toni Morrison, Alice Walker, August Wilson, and John Wideman.

In No One's Shadow: Filipinos in America. Distributor: San Francisco: CrossCurrent Media. *(www.naatanet.org/)*

This 28-minute videotape describes the historical saga of Filipinos in the United States, with emphasis on the twentieth century.

In the White Man's Image. Distributor: Arlington, VA: PBS Video. *(www.pbs.org)*

The Carlisle School for Indian Students founded in the early part of this century is profiled in this 58-minute videotape.

Japanese American Women: A Sense of Place. Distributor: New York: Women Make Movies. *(www.wmm.com/)*

Japanese American women describe the conflict of cultures and identity they experience in America (27-minute videotape).

The Latino Family. Distributor: Princeton, NJ: Films for the Humanities & Sciences. *(www.films.com)*

Changes in the traditional Mexican American family are revealed by depicting three generations of one family.

The Life and Legend of Sojourner Truth. Distributor: Princeton, NJ: Films for the Humanities & Sciences. *(www.films.com)*

Readings from Sojourner Truth's speeches and interviews with scholars make up an important part of this videotape about the life of a significant abolitionist and women's rights advocate.

Malcolm X: Make It Plain. Arlington, VA: PBS Video. *(www.pbs.org)*

The life of the civil rights leader is the subject of this 60-minute videotape.

More Than Bows and Arrows. Producer/Distributor: Seattle, WA: Camera One. *(www.camera-one.com/)*

The contributions that Native Americans have made to American culture are highlighted in this 53-minute program.

Multicultural Peoples of North America. Producer: Library Video. Distributor: Culver City, CA: Social Studies School Service. *(www.socialstudies.com)*

This series of fifteen 30-minute videotapes is based on the Chelsea House series of books, The Peoples of North America. Titles are African Americans; The Amish; Arab Americans; Central Americans; Chinese Americans; German Americans; Greek Americans; Irish Americans; Italian Americans; Japanese Americans; Jewish Americans; Korean Americans; Mexican Americans; Polish Americans; and Puerto Ricans. Each videotape is 30 minutes long.

Power, Politics and Latinos. Distributor: Los Angeles: Producer: National Latin Communication Center. Distributor: Alexandria, VA: PBS Video. *(www.pbs.org)*

The political participation of Latinos is the subject of this 56-minute program, with emphasis on the 1992 election.

Preserving the Past to Ensure the Future. Distributor: New York: Anti-Defamation League. *(www.adl.org/)*

This powerful 15-minute video deals with the one and a half million children who were victims of the Holocaust.

The Road to Freedom. Distributor: San Francisco: California Newsreel. *(www.newsreel.org/)*

> *In this 58-minute videotape, the historical events that culminated in the landmark Brown vs. Board of Education Supreme Court decision are described.*

Roll of Thunder, Hear My Cry. Distributor: New York: Macmillan/McGraw-Hill School Publishing. *(www.mmhschool.com/)*

> *A 46-minute dramatization of the powerful novel by Mildred Taylor. The novel chronicles events in the life of the Logan family, a family that lived in Mississippi in the 1930s.*

Sacred Spirit: The Lakota Sioux, Past and Present. Distributor: Princeton, NJ: Films for the Humanities & Sciences. *(www.films.com/)*

> *Oglala Lakota Sioux living on and off the Pine Ridge reservation share their perspectives on the history and present-day realities of their people.*

The Shadow of Hate: A History of Intolerance in America. Producer/Distributor: Montgomery, AL: Teaching Tolerance. *(www.tolerance.org/index.jsp)*

> *This 40-minute program uses historical footage, photographs, and voices of individuals who participated in historical events to depict the intolerance directed against various ethnic, cultural, and minority groups in American society. This teaching package consists of the video, a 128-page text, Us and Them, and a teacher's guide.*

Slaying the Dragon. San Francisco: CrossCurent Media. *(www.naatanet.org/)*

> *The Hollywood and television images of Asian American women are described in this 60-minute videotape.*

Tales from Arab Detroit. (1995). Produced by Joan Mandell. Distributor: Hohokus, NJ: New Day Films. *(www.newday.com/)*

> *In the context of a visit to Detroit of a famous old Egyptian singer and storyteller, this 45-minute video asks three generations of Arab Americans, both immigrants and their American-born children, the question: What does it mean to be Arab in America in these times? The video shows clearly the importance of the family in the lives and consciousness of Arab Americans.*

Teens Talk Race Relations. Distributor: New York: Anti-Defamation League. *(www.adl.org/)*

> *Several aspects of race relations are presented through dramatic situationsin this 25-minute videotape.*

A Time for Justice: America's Civil Rights Movement. Producer/Distributor: Montgomery, AL: Teaching Tolerance. *(www.tolerance.org/index.jsp)*

> *This 38-minute program describes the civil rights movement with the use of actual historical footage and the voices of people who participated in it. This teaching package consists of the videotape, a book, Free At Last, and a teacher's guide.*

Unfinished Business: The Japanese Internment Cases. Distributor: San Francisco: CrossCurrent Media. *(www.naatanet.org/)*

> *The stories of three Japanese American men who resisted the military orders to be interned are told in this 60-minute videotape.*

Voices in Exile: The L.A. Eight. (1989). Distributor: New Day Films, 22D Hollywood Aveue, Hohokus, NJ 07423. Toll-free phone: (888) 367-9154. Fax: (201) 652-1973. E-mail: tncndy@aol.com *(www.newday.com/)*

> *In this 30-minute video, Joan Mandell and Laura Hayes chronicle the first year of the court case known as the L.A. Eight. It includes interviews with the FBI and Immigration and Naturalization Service officials as well as with the eight accused and their counsel. The voice-over is by Casey Kasem, the radio disc jockey.*

A Weave of Time: The Story of a Navajo Family, 1838–1986. Distributor: Los Angeles: Direct Cinema. *(www.directcinema.com/)*

This 60-minute documentary describes four generations of a Navajo family.

APPENDIX D

The Carter G. Woodson
Award Books

The Carter G. Woodson Award is presented each year by the National Council for the Social Studies in honor of the distinguished African American historian and educator who wrote books for adults and young people, founded and edited the *Journal of Negro History,* and contributed in many significant ways to interracial understanding. The Award is designed to "encourage the writing, publishing, and dissemination of outstanding social science books for young readers that treat topics related to ethnic minorities and race relations sensitively and accurately."

A complete list of the Carter G. Woodson Book Award winners for the years 1974 to 2001 is available on-line at *www.socialstudies.org/awards/woodsonlist.html* In this Appendix, we include the recipients of the Woodson Award for 1999, 2000, and 2001.

1999

Elementary

Story Painter: The Life of Jacob Lawrence by John Duggleby (Chronicle Books)

Elementary Honor Books

Celebrating the Chinese New Year by Diane Hoyt-Goldsmith (Holiday House)
The Riches of Oseola McCarthy by Evelyn Coleman (Albert Whitman and Company)

Secondary

Edmonia Lewis: Wildfire in Marble by Rinna Evelyn Wolfe (Dillon Press)

Secondary Honor Books

Life in a Japanese American Internment Camp, by Diane Yancey (Lucent Books)
Women of Hope: African Americans Who Made a Difference by Joyce Hansen (Scholastic Press)

2000

Elementary

Through My Eyes, by Ruby Bridges (Scholastic Press)

Elementary Honor Books

Magic Windows/Ventanas mágicas, written and illustrated by Carmen Lomas Garza (Children's Book Press)

Children of the Tlingit, written and photographed by Frank Staub (Carolrhoda Books)

Secondary

Princess Ka'iulani: Hope of a Nation, Heart of a People, by Sharon Linnéa (Eerdmans Books for Young Readers)

Secondary Honor Books

The Rise and Fall of Jim Crow: The African-American Struggle Against Discrimination, 1865–1954, by Richard Wormser (Franklin Watts)

Black Hands, White Sails: The Story of African-American Whalers, by Patricia C. McKissack and Fredrick L. McKissack (Scholastic Press)

2001

Elementary

The Sound That Jazz Makes, by Carole Boston Weaterford, illustrated by Eric Velasquez (Walter and Company)

Elementary Honor Book

Children of the Relocation Camps, by Catherine A. Welch (Carolrhoda Books)

Middle Level

Let It Shine: Stories of Black Women Freedom Fighters, by Andrea Davis Pinkney, illustrated by Stephen Alcorn (Gulliver Books, Harcourt, Inc.)

Middle Level Honor Book

Carter G. Woodson: The Man Who Put "Black" in American History, by Jim Haskins and Kathleen Benson, illustrated by Melanie Reim (The Millbrook Press)

Secondary

Tatan'ka Iyota'ke: Sitting Bull and His World, by Albert Marrin (Dutton Children's Books)

Secondary Honor Book

Issues in Racism, by Mary E. Williams (Lucent Books)

APPENDIX E

Twenty Classic and Landmark Books in Ethnic Literature

Adamic, L. (1932). *Laughing in the Jungle: The Autobiography of an Immigrant in America*. New York: Harper and Brothers. (Slavic American)

Anaya, R. A. (1972). *Bless Me, Ultima*. Berkeley, CA: Tonatiuh International. (Mexican American)

Banks, J. A., & Banks, C. A. M. (Eds.). (2001). *Handbook of Research on Multicultural Education*. San Francisco: Jossey-Bass/Wiley.

Bulosan, C. (1973). *America Is in the Heart*. Seattle: University of Washington Press. (Filipino American)

Ellison, R. (1952). *Invisible Man*. New York: New American Library. (African American)

Galarza, E. (1971). *Barrio Boy*. Notre Dame, IN: University of Notre Dame Press. (Mexican American)

Haley, A. (1976). *Roots: The Saga of an American Family*. Garden City, NY: Doubleday. (African American)

Handlin, O. (1951). *The Uprooted: The Epic Story of the Great Migrations That Made the American People*. New York: Grosset and Dunlap. (European American)

Howe, I. (1976). *World of Our Fathers: The Journey of the Jews to America and the Life They Found and Made*. New York: Simon & Schuster. (Jewish American)

Kingston, M. H. (1976). *The Woman Warrior: Memories of a Girlhood among Ghosts*. New York: Vintage. (Chinese American)

Momaday, N. S. (1966). *House Made of Dawn*. New York: Signet. (American Indian)

Morrison, T. (1987). *Beloved: A Novel*. New York: Knopf. (African American)

Novak, M. (1973). *The Rise of the Unmeltable Ethnics*. New York: Macmillan. (European American)

Okada, J. (1976). *No-No Boy*. San Francisco: Combined Asian American Resources Project. (Japanese American)

Rolvaag, O. E. (1927). *Giants in the Earth: A Saga of the Prairie*. New York: Harper and Row. (Norwegian American)

Takaki, R. (1989). *Strangers from a Different Shore: A History of Asian Americans*. Boston: Little, Brown. (Asian American)

Takaki, R. (1993). *A Different Mirror: A History of Multicultural America*. Boston: Little, Brown.

Walker, A. (1982). *The Color Purple*. New York: Harcourt Brace. (African American)

Wong, J. S. (1945). *Fifth Chinese Daughter*. New York: Harper and Row. (Chinese American)

Wright, R. (1966). *Black Boy: A Record of Childhood and Youth*. New York: Harper and Row. (African American)

INDEX